THE FIRST CENTURY OF THE REPUBLIC.

THE FIRST CENTURY

OF

THE REPUBLIC:

A REVIEW OF AMERICAN PROGRESS.

BY

THE REV. THEODORE D. WOOLSEY, D.D., LL.D.; F. A. P. BARNARD, LL.D.; HON. DAVID A. WELLS; HON. FRANCIS A. WALKER; PROF. T. STERRY HUNT; PROF. WILLIAM G. SUMNER; EDWARD ATKINSON; PROF. THEODORE GILL; EDWIN P. WHIPPLE; PROF. W. H. BREWER; EUGENE LAWRENCE; THE REV. JOHN F. HURST, D.D.; BENJAMIN VAUGHAN ABBOTT; AUSTIN A. FLINT, M.D.; S. S. CONANT; EDWARD H. KNIGHT; AND CHARLES L. BRACE.

NEW YORK:

HARPER & BROTHERS, PUBLISHERS,

FRANKLIN SQUARE.

1876.

PUBLISHERS' ADVERTISEMENT.

History, as it is usually written, touches only the state. The grandeur of state affairs and the magnitude of national vicissitudes, on the one hand, and, on the other, the ambition of political leaders and the antagonism of parties—transferred, it may be, in some mighty crisis, from the peaceful senate to the martial camp—afford the material and the personages of a drama so exciting, and of so popular a character, that the writer who most skillfully embodies these elements becomes the peer of the statesmen and military heroes whom he has glorified. But this social form or structure which we call the state, while it enfolds all other social forms, and sets its imposing seal upon the modest undertakings in industry, art, and learning, which constitute the life of the people, yet does it receive from this popular life all of its vitality, dignity, and meaning. Especially is this true of the republican form of polity, because that form more immediately and perfectly represents the people.

The thoughtful publicist, therefore, who, from a retrospect of the past century should seek to estimate our present condition as a nation, or our outlook for the future, would direct his attention not to our political annals, but to the industrial, æsthetic, intellectual, and moral development of our people. He would not refer to state papers, to the congressional record, to the history of the great parties that have upon various issues divided the nation, nor to our military capabilities as manifested in three great wars. His inquiries would relate rather to the part taken by the American people in the remarkable material progress of the last hundred years,—to their inventions, their manufactures, their development of the resources of the soil,—agricultural and mineral,—their commercial activity, their increase in population, their educational institutions, their advancement in science and art, their literature, their humane enterprises, and their moral and religious culture; while in such a review he could not ignore the important political experiment undertaken by this people in the formation and maintenance of the union of states under a federal constitution.

The work here submitted to the reader is precisely such a review as we have above indicated, of our progress during the first century of our national life—the result of inquiries undertaken not by one, but by a score of publicists, each one of whom is, in the field occupied by him, a specialist of the highest authority. Such a work, considered as the production of a single writer, would be impossible, since in nearly every department the review is the condensation of the results of life-long research and special study. A perusal of the table of contents, including the subjects of inquiry and the names of the authors, will discover the value and importance of the work as a comprehensive literary exposition of the century. The grand exhibition at Philadelphia is international, and not entirely American; it is limited to the display of the material symbols of progress; and it is confined almost entirely to the results of present activity in the various fields included in its representation. The exposition attempted in this work is an indispensable supplement to that exhibition. It connects the present with the past, showing the beginnings of great enterprises, tracing through consecutive stages their development, and associating with them the individual thought and labor by which they have been brought to perfection. It connects with the outward fact its formative idea. It is, moreover, in the main American; though, in certain fields, it was found impossible to wholly separate American from European enterprise without violent dislocation.

Nearly all of the papers here published were originally contributed to *Harper's Magazine;* the scheme of the entire series, and the plan, to some extent, of each paper having been determined upon before a single word was written. These papers during their serial publication have elicited the approbation of intelligent readers throughout the country. The successful execution of a project of such magnitude, and involving so important contributions from so many of the most eminent writers of America, has been generally accepted not only as adequate to the great anniversary occasion that suggested it, but also as an unprecedented event in the annals of periodical literature. Occasional articles in a magazine are usually of merely temporary importance; but these papers, containing information never hitherto collected and organized into one historical body, are a valuable contribution to the permanent history of our country. An unusually large amount of space was given to the department of *Mechanical Progress*, but not disproportionate, when it is considered how characteristic of the century has been the advance in this field, and how largely other progress has depended upon it. The same consideration justifies the elaborate and extended treatise on *Scientific Progress.* In the department of *American Literature*, too, it was impossible to present a satisfactory review, or, indeed, any thing beyond mere generalization, within the limits allotted to most of the papers. Each of these longer treatises, including also those on *Population* and *Monetary Development*, is in itself a volume of valuable information.

The scheme of the work is as novel as it is comprehensive, no similar undertaking having ever been attempted. While it is not overweighted with cyclopedic details, it traces, in every field of industrial and mental activity, the larger outlines of progress.

The results of this retrospect of a century's growth, in those fields which suggest a comparison between our own and the contemporaneous development of other countries, are such as to awaken a feeling of just pride in every American citizen. And the reflections naturally deduced from these results, as to the characteristic features of our people, contradict those which are drawn from a superficial review of the social and political abuses of the day, and are re-assuring as to the hopeful future of the Republic.

A carefully prepared analytical Index renders the contents of the volume available for reference, and gives it its full value as a comprehensive review of American progress.

Franklin Square, New York, July 20, 1876.

CONTENTS.

I.

INTRODUCTION: COLONIAL PROGRESS.

By EUGENE LAWRENCE.

II.

MECHANICAL PROGRESS.

By EDWARD H. KNIGHT.

VII.

GROWTH AND DISTRIBUTION OF POPULATION.

By the Hon. FRANCIS A. WALKER.

VIII.

MONETARY DEVELOPMENT.

By Professor WILLIAM G. SUMNER.

IX.

THE EXPERIMENT OF THE UNION, WITH ITS PREPARATIONS.

By T. D. WOOLSEY, D.D., LL.D.

X.

EDUCATIONAL PROGRESS.

By EUGENE LAWRENCE.

XI.

SCIENTIFIC PROGRESS.

I. *THE EXACT SCIENCES.*

By F. A. P. BARNARD, D.D., LL.D.

II. *NATURAL SCIENCE.*

By Professor THEODORE GILL.

XII.

A CENTURY OF AMERICAN LITERATURE.

By EDWIN P. WHIPPLE.

XIII.

PROGRESS OF THE FINE ARTS.

BY S. S. CONANT.

XIV.

MEDICAL AND SANITARY PROGRESS.

BY AUSTIN FLINT, M.D.

XV.

AMERICAN JURISPRUDENCE.

BY BENJAMIN VAUGHAN ABBOTT.

XVI.

HUMANITARIAN PROGRESS.

BY CHARLES L. BRACE.

XVII.

RELIGIOUS DEVELOPMENT.

BY THE REV. JOHN F. HURST, D.D.

THE FIRST CENTURY OF THE REPUBLIC.

I.

INTRODUCTION.—COLONIAL PROGRESS.

FIFTY-ONE doubtful and divided men, of infinite variety in opinions, education, and character, met in the hot days of July, 1776, in that plain room at Philadelphia where was decided the chief event of modern history, to found a republic. They were about to reverse all the inculcations of recent experience, and to enter at once upon a new era of uncertainty. From all the models of the past they could borrow little, and they overleaped barriers that had affrighted all former legislators. Not Cromwell and Hampden, not the plebeians of Rome and the Demos of Athens, not the republicans of Venice nor the Calvinists of Holland and Geneva, had ventured upon that tremendous stride in human progress that would alone satisfy the reformers of America. Educated in the strict conceptions of rank and caste which even Massachusetts had cultivated and Virginia carried to a ludicrous extreme, they threw aside the artificial distinction forever, and declared all men equal. One sad exception they made, but only by implication. Rousseau had said that men born to be free were every where enslaved; but Adams and Jefferson demanded for all mankind freedom and perfect self-control. Yet still the same dark shade rested upon their conception of independence. But in all other matters they were uniformly consistent. In all other lands, in all other ages, the church had been united to the state. The American reformers claimed a perfect freedom for every creed. Men trained in the rigid prelatical rule of Virginia and the rigorous Calvinism of Massachusetts joined in discarding from their new republic every trace of sectarianism. Religion and the state were severed for the first time since Constantine. Of the many important and radical changes that must take place in human affairs from the prevalence of the principles they enunciated a large part of the assembly were probably unconscious. Yet upon one point in their new political creed all seemed to be unanimous. The people were in future to be the only sovereigns. The most heterodox of all theories to European reasoners, the plainest contradiction to all the experience of human history, they set forth distinctly, and never wavered in its defense. The English Commons had been content to derive all their privileges from the condescension of the crown. The people of France were the abject slaves of a corrupt despotism. Two or three democratic cantons in Switzerland alone relieved the prevalence of a rigid aristocracy. All over Germany, Italy, and Scandinavia the people were so contemned, derided, and oppressed as scarcely to deserve the notice of the ruling classes. The few ruled over the many, and slavery was the common lot of man. Nor when the reformers of America proclaimed the sovereignty of the despised people, torn and dismembered by the tyranny of ages, could they hope to escape the reproach of wild enthusiasm, or to be looked upon as more than idle dreamers.

Yet the chiefs of the republican party were men so resolute, pure, sagacious, as to deserve the esteem of the most eminent of the Europeans. Touched by a secret pang of admiration for an integrity which he did not share, the historian Gibbon, in the midst of a stately review of the miseries and the joys of all mankind, confessed the sentiment while he clung to his salary and his place.

Robertson and Hume, bound to the scheme of royalty by pensions, honors, and official station, dropped a sigh for that independence which they were never to know. Adam Smith lent the Americans a full and generous sympathy. Fox, Burke, and Barré, Wilkes, and even Chatham, joined the brilliant but narrow circle of the friends of America. On the Continent philosophers and poets, princes and statesmen, watched with a singular attention the revolt of the New World against the traditions of the Old. Voltaire from his Swiss retreat, or in the assemblies of Paris, rejoiced over "Franklin's republic." Vergennes was amazed at the blindness of the English ministry, and the folly of their king. And when the story of Bunker Hill and of the rising fame of Washington came like a sudden illumination over the Atlantic, all Europe began to study with critical interest the characters and the histories of the men who had already shown a consciousness of their natural rights and a power to defend them. The congress of deputies at Philadelphia was no longer an obscure and isolated assemblage; it was plainly laboring upon a grand political problem under the scrutiny of all mankind.

In the following sketch of the progress of the colonies up to the period of freedom I shall endeavor to describe the country as it appeared to Adams and Jefferson, Chatham and Burke, its poor resources, its savage territory, its isolated and divided people. Nothing, indeed, gives us a clearer view of the mental vigor of our ancestors than that they should have foreseen and secured the union of so many distant settlements into one grand nation,[1] and should have predicted with John Adams that the day of independence was the opening of a new era of hope for millions yet to come. A notion had prevailed among Europeans that America could only be the parent of degenerate and feeble races. Buffon had suggested and Raynal confirmed the theory. No man of intellectual ability, no poet, philosopher, or statesman, Raynal said, has yet appeared in the New World. Franklin, Washington, the two Adamses, Jefferson, rose up before mankind almost while he spoke. Yet whoever surveyed the slow advance of civilization in the wilderness under the restraints and discouragements of the English control might scarcely wonder at the doubts of the French philosophers, or hardly see in the long chain of feeble settlements the future homes of civilization.

At the founding of the republic the colonists were accustomed to boast that their territory extended fifteen hundred miles in length, and was already the seat of a powerful nation. But of this vast expanse the larger part even along the sea-coast was still an uninhabited wilderness.[1] Although more than a century and a half had passed since the first settlements in Massachusetts and Virginia, only a thin line of insignificant towns and villages reached from Maine to Georgia. In the century since the Declaration of Independence a whole continent has been seamed with railroads and filled with people, but the slow growth of the preceding century had scarcely disturbed the reign of the savage on his native plains. On the coast the province of Maine possessed only a few towns, and an almost unbroken solitude spread from Portland to the St. Lawrence. A few hardy settlers were just founding a State among the Green Mountains destined to be the home of a spotless freedom. In New York, still inferior to several of its fellow-colonies in population, the cultivated portions were confined to the bay and shores of the Hudson. The rich fields of the Genesee Valley and the Mohawk were famous already, but the savages had checked the course of settlement. It was not until many years after the war of independence that the fairest part of New York was despoiled of its wealth by a careless agriculture. Schenectady was a frontier town, noted for a mournful doom, and even Albany and Kingston were not wholly secure from the stealthy invasions of the Indian. Pennsylvania, a frontier State, comparatively populous and wealthy, protected New Jersey and Delaware from their assaults; but Pittsburg was still only a mili-

[1] "A voluntary association or coalition of the colonies, at least a permanent one, is almost as difficult to be supposed; for fire and water are not more heterogeneous than the different colonies," says Burnaby, Pinkert., vol. xiii. p. 751. Yet in 1742 Kalm saw the coldness of the people toward England. Pinkert., vol. xiii. p. 461. He was even told that in thirty or forty years they would form a separate, independent state.

[1] Holmes, Annals. Bancroft. Gordon. Ramsay.

tary post, and the larger part of the population of the colony was gathered in the neighborhood of the capital.[1] Woods, mountains, and morasses filled up that fair region where now the immense wealth of coal and iron has produced the Birmingham of America.[2]

The southern colonies had grown with more rapidity in population and wealth than New York and Pennsylvania. Virginia and the Carolinas had extended their settlements westward far into the interior. Some emigrants had even wandered to Western Tennessee. Daniel Boone had led the way to Kentucky. A few English or Americans had colonized Natchez, on the Mississippi. But the settlers in Kentucky and Tennessee lived with rifle in hand, seldom safe from the attacks of the natives, and were to form in the war of independence that admirable corps of riflemen and sharp-shooters who were noted for their courage and skill from the siege of Boston to the fall of Cornwallis. The Virginians were settled in the Tennessee mountains long before the people of New York had ventured to build a village on the shores of Lake Erie or the Pennsylvanians crossed the Alleghanies. But still even Virginia is represented to us about this period as in great part a wilderness.[3] Its own lands were yet uncultivated, and its territory nearly clothed in forests. And in general we may conclude that the true boundary of the well-settled portions of the allied colonies did not in any degree approach the interior of the continent. In the North the line of cultivated country must be drawn along the shores of the Hudson River, omitting the dispersed settlements in two or three inland districts. The Delaware and a distance of perhaps fifty miles to the westward included all the wealth and population of Pennsylvania. The Alleghanies infolded the civilized portions of Virginia, and North and South Carolina can not be said to have reached beyond their mountains. So slowly had the people of North America made their way from the sea-coast.

But little was known[4] of the nature of the country spreading from the borders of Pennsylvania and Virginia to the Mississippi. It was called the Wilderness. It was usually painted in the fairest colors by those who had explored it. The table-land near the Ohio was supposed to be one of the fairest and most fertile portions of the world;[1] the rich plains of Kentucky might support a nation; and the forests, the meadows, and the valleys lay waiting to be possessed. But the fear of the savage still guarded the tempting region. The dark and bloody ground had no charm for the pacific settler; the wilderness was pathless, and it was a journey of twelve days in wagons from Baltimore to Pittsburg. But of the immense and impenetrable regions beyond the Mississippi our ancestors had scarcely formed a conception.[2] It was a land of fable, where countless hosts of savages were believed to rule over endless plains, and to engage in ceaseless battles. Long afterward it was thought that the vast tide of the Missouri might in some way mingle with the waters of the Pacific.[3] The great Northwest, now the granary of the world, the peaks of the Rocky Mountains, and the rivers of Columbia were all unknown; nor could the most acute observer, shut up in the narrow limits of the Hudson and the Delaware, suppose that within a hundred years the Atlantic would be joined to the Pacific by frequent highways, or that the frightful solitude beyond the great river would be the centre of a throng of vigorous republics.

Within the cultivated districts a population usually, but probably erroneously, estimated at three millions were thinly scattered over a narrow strip of land. The number can scarcely be maintained. The New England colonies could have had not more than 800,000 inhabitants; the middle colonies as many more; the southern a little over a million. New York had a population of

[1] Before 1795 there were few settlements north of the Ohio. Cincinnati had then only ninety-four cabins, and five hundred inhabitants.

[2] Hist. Col. Penn., Day, p. 59.

[3] Winterbotham, U. S., i. Great part of Virginia is a wilderness, says Burnaby, Pinkert., xiii. p. 716.

[4] Holmes. Bancroft. The French Jesuits had explored the country, and hoped to rule it. Parkman, Pioneers.

[1] "The Ohio," says Winterbotham, i. 189—twenty years later—"is the most beautiful river on earth;" but as late as 1819 Michigan was thought to be a worthless waste, and Cass first explored its rich fields. Life of Cass, p. 79.

[2] St. Louis was settled in 1763, but was still a small frontier town, scarcely known to the colonists.

[3] New York Hist. Magazine, August, 1871. "The Missouri has been navigated for 2500 miles; there appears a probability of a communication by this channel with the western ocean." This was said in 1803.

248,000, and was surpassed by Virginia, Pennsylvania, Massachusetts, Maryland, and was at least equaled if not exceeded by North Carolina. Its growth had been singularly slow. The small population of the union was composed of different races and of almost hostile communities. There was a lasting feud between the Dutch at Albany and the people of New England, for it was believed that the former had held a correspondence with the Indians during the recent war, and purchased the spoil taken from the New England villages. The Germans settled in Pennsylvania retained their national customs and language, and were almost an alien race. Huguenot colonies existed in several portions of the country. The north of Ireland had poured forth a stream of emigrants. Swedish settlements attracted the notice of Kalm along the Delaware. In North Carolina a clan of Highlanders had brought to the New World an intense loyalty and an extreme ignorance. The divisions of race and language offered a strong obstacle to any perfect union of the different colonies. But a still more striking opposition existed in the political institutions of the various sections. In the South royalty, aristocracy, and the worst form of human slavery had grown up together. In no part of the world were the distinctions of rank more closely observed, or mechanical and agricultural industry more perfectly contemned. In New England the institutions were democratic, and honest labor was thought no shame. In the South episcopacy was rigorously established by law; in New England a tolerant Puritanism had succeeded the persecuting spirit of Cotton Mather and Winthrop.

In the period before the Revolution it was the custom to look upon the southern colonies as the land of wealth and material splendor. Their soil produced the chief exports of the New World; their system of agriculture, however abhorrent to the feelings of the more cultivated Northerner, was attended by a remarkable success; their population grew rapidly; they held a ruling position among the colonies in the eyes of all strangers. Virginia had so far surpassed all the other colonies as to seem almost the mother and mistress of the whole. Her own people had named her the "ancient dominion," and her progress was so rapid as to suffer no hope that New York or Massachusetts could ever rival her wealth and power. The population of Virginia alone was half a million—more than twice that of New York.[1] Her exports of tobacco, corn, and other productions reached a value of nearly three millions of dollars. Her ample territory was penetrated by navigable rivers, and it was supposed that the James and the Potomac must at some time form the outlets for the commerce of the West—a hope from which the Hudson seemed forever cut off by the difficulties of transport from Albany to the lakes.[2] But, with all its advantages, Virginia was weighed down by influences that careful observers saw must lead to a speedy decay. No colony, indeed, was apparently less likely to become the founder of a republic and the patron of human equality. Through all its earlier history Virginia had been noted for its intense loyalty to the Stuarts and its hatred of every element of reform. The planters of Virginia ruled over their abject commonalty with a severity that the English aristocracy had never for many generations equaled. All those feudal restrictions and abuses which the Massachusetts colonists had come to the New World to avoid had been brought over to Virginia by its earlier settlers, and fostered into more than European strength. The church establishment was supported by the colony, and all religious toleration was unknown, at least to the constitution. Nowhere had ecclesiastical tyranny been so fostered by the government. The industrial classes of Virginia had been kept by law in stolid ignorance, when Connecticut had enforced the education of all its citizens. Governor Berkeley had boasted, in 1671, that the colony had neither printing-presses, colleges, nor schools, and had prayed there might be none there for at least a hundred years. His wish had nearly been fulfilled. In 1771 the commonalty of Virginia were noted for their ignorance and brutality; the gentry alone con-

[1] Holmes, 1732, Annals and Note. The population of Virginia was estimated very differently by different observers; but Holmes inclines to the largest number. The census of 1790 seems conclusive. It gives Virginia 876,000, while New York had but 340,120, Pennsylvania 434,373. See Ramsay.

[2] Winterbotham discusses the question, and decides in favor of the Potomac.

trolled the politics and managed the finances of the colony. Virginia, too, had been the first of all the colonies to import slaves,[1] and had set an example that had been too eagerly followed. She had practiced both white and colored slavery. The English government had early made her borders a convict colony, and the records bear frequent accounts of highway robbers who had been reprieved that they might go to Virginia; and on one occasion London sends "one hundred of its worst disposed children, of whom it was desirous of being disburdened," to be apprenticed in the colony.[2]

The ruling class in Virginia were the planters. They were often cultivated and intelligent men, who had been educated in English universities or in the best schools of their native land. Their possessions were immense, and had usually come to them from their ancestors. Entails prevented any division of the family property, and it was a common complaint at the time that all the land of Virginia was held by a few hands. Mechanical, agricultural, or commercial pursuits were forbidden by custom to the planting class. It was thought beneath a member of the great families to engage in trade, and Scotch emigrants and foreign adventurers pursued a gainful traffic, engrossing the wealth of the country, while the land-owner slumbered in indolence and fell into poverty on his ancestral estate. The towns of Virginia were small and wretched, fever-stricken and neglected. The wealth of the ruling families was wasted in building immense mansions in the solitude of their plantations, where they emulated the splendors of the English country-seats, and exercised a liberal hospitality. One of the wealthiest of the landed proprietors was Lord Fairfax, the early patron of Washington. In his youth he had cultivated letters, and it was even rumored that he had written for the *Spectator*. His estate in Virginia contained more than five millions of acres.[3] The fine mansion, Belvoir, seated among the fairest scenery of the Potomac, where he lived with his brother, and Greenway Court, which he built in the Shenandoah Valley, where he died, in 1782, were scenes of frequent festivity. But the accomplished lord was ardently loyal; his property, valued at £98,000, was confiscated at his death, and the land he had selfishly withheld was divided among the people. The fair widow whom Washington had wooed and won with stately assiduity was also a large landed proprietor. But the Revolution broke up the system of entails, and gave a new impulse to the prosperity of the colony.

Notwithstanding the establishment of episcopacy, the growth of dissent had been rapid in Virginia, and at the opening of the colonial struggle the Dissenters were more numerous than Churchmen. That valuable race, the Scotch-Irish, had settled in large numbers within its borders. Education, too, had made some progress. William and Mary's College, sluggish as had been its advance, had sent out many cultivated men. Liberal principles and a love of freedom had never been wanting to the people. Eminent Virginians had already become shocked at the fatal results of slavery, and there were no stronger advocates of abolition than Jefferson and Lee. Throughout the whole colony there was a plain desire for enlarged political progress, and, happily for Massachusetts, her wrongs were felt nowhere more deeply than among the Virginia reformers. Nor was the project of independence any where more favorably received than by that large class of the population who had felt in their own lives the evils of a tyrannical government. Her immense territory, which reached, at least in theory, over the mountains to the Mississippi, and through the whole valley of the Ohio, her wealth and commerce, her population, greater than that of any other colony, and, above all, the rare abilities and patriotism of her citizens, made Virginia the centre of reform, and perhaps the most effective instrument in binding the whole country into a perfect union. Happy had she followed the teachings of Jefferson[1] and the example of Carter, and destroyed slavery when she cast aside feudalism.

[1] Gordon, i. 56. Mr. Bancroft has traced with his usual accuracy and force the course of this infamous traffic. Hildreth, i. 565.

[2] Calendar, State Papers, English, 1618, 1623, p. 10, 118, 552.

[3] Sabine, Am. Royalists. Fairfax and Sparks. Life of Washington.

[1] Jefferson proposed the abolition of slavery in Virginia, but found it expedient to withdraw his project.

Less corrupted by European traditions than Virginia—a land where the English and the German, the Swiss, the Scotch-Irish, Quakers, the children of Skye, and the sad hosts of Africa were mingled strangely together—North Carolina had early shown a wider liberality of thought than her powerful neighbor. Caste and rank had less prevalence; her people were industrious, and her prosperity great. North Carolina was already the fifth colony in importance; the population reached nearly two hundred and fifty thousand.[1] South Carolina, less populous, but with nearly twice as many slaves as whites, was noted for the haughty manners of its planters, the ignorance of its people, the high education of some of its leading men, their open dislike for slavery. No South Carolinian of any intelligence at this period but lamented that so dark a stain rested upon his native colony. Maryland, too, possessed a weight in the country in 1775 that must seem strange to the modern politician. It possessed a larger population than either New York or the Carolinas. Its Roman Catholic planters were sometimes intelligent and liberal. Maryland still belonged to the heir of the Calvert family, but its people cared little for a degenerate race whose early excellence had faded away. A colony of Scots from the north of Ireland had settled at Baltimore, and were probably of greater value to the rising State than most of its planters and all its proprietors. But slavery, an established church,[2] a proprietary government, a rigid division of rank and caste, had apparently linked Maryland so closely to Virginia and the South in politics as to give little room for the progress of freedom. It was, indeed, the first colony to express a wish to withdraw the declaration of independence when sudden reverses fell upon the republican armies.

The four New England colonies, separated from the South by an immense distance, and a journey of many days, and sometimes weeks, by sea or land, were altogether different from their neighbors in politics.[3] Two of them, Connecticut and Rhode Island, were free from all internal control from England, elected their own governors, and practiced a democratic republicanism.[1] In Connecticut, at least, all men were already equal, all were educated, and slavery was abolished practically. In Massachusetts the governor was appointed by the English king, but his salary was regulated by the province; yet the Massachusetts people had been rapidly advancing in political knowledge; mental cultivation had always marked their chief men. Their Puritan clergy had produced many of the early authors of America; they were usually wise, austere, and patriotic. Liberty, even in that imperfect form in which it existed under a colonial rule, had shown its fairest results in New England. The people were prosperous, the government well administered, the courts pure, the clergy respected, the general morality above that of any other community. The sentiment of human equality had already prevailed over the influence of English caste and Puritan theocracy; a bold, free nation had arisen, not quite so numerous as the Dutch, who had defied the arms of Philip II., or the Swiss, who had overthrown the Hapsburgs, yet capable even alone of founding a republic that not all the powers of the Old World could overthrow. Its population was purely English, its manners republican and plain, its people accustomed to labor and to reflect.

The middle colonies were less democratic than New England. New York, like Virginia, had been weighed down by a system of entails and by immense landed estates that limited immigration. It is stated that the German colonists were so badly treated by its land-owners that they imbibed a lasting hostility for its people, moved away in large bodies to Pennsylvania, and prevailed upon all their countrymen to follow them. They hoped to make Pennsylvania a new Germany.[2] A kind of colonial aristocracy had grown up in New York. Its Dutch

[1] I have usually adopted Ramsay's numbers, which seem confirmed by the first census, i. 146.

[2] Episcopacy was rigorously established in Maryland after 1688.

[3] Dwight, New England, paints some years later the virtues of his countrymen. In Connecticut, he says, "there is a school-house sufficiently near every man's door," i. 178. See Hildreth, i. 508.

[1] Palfrey, New England, ii. 567, 568, notices the unexampled liberality of the two charters.

[2] Large numbers of Scotch-Irish also came to Pennsylvania about 1773. Holmes, Ann., ii. 187. They came from Belfast, Galway, Newry, Cork, 3500, with no love for England.

population were, however, attached to freedom, and the presence of a royal governor and council had not tended to increase the respect for English institutions. Strong religious differences had already agitated the people. The Episcopal Church was opposed to the Presbyterian, and Calvinism led on the way to independence. In Pennsylvania the proprietary government was conservative, and opposed to violent measures. New Jersey, rich, highly cultivated, and prosperous, was strongly affected by its Presbyterian college at Princeton, and was naturally opposed to prelatical England. It is indeed curious to notice how largely the religious element entered into the dispute between the king and the colonies.[1] The English revolution of 1688 was re-enacted in America, and King George dethroned because it was feared that he meant to assail the consciences of the people. Men felt that should the king succeed in conquering them, he would have a prelate in every colony, and a rigid rule against progressive dissent. In the middle colonies the Presbyterians led the way to freedom; in the southern the liberal Churchmen, Huguenots, and Scotch Presbyterians. Thomas Paine, in his famous argument for separation, relied much upon the fact that the people of America were in no sense English, but rather a union of different races met for a common purpose in the New World, and resolute chiefly to be free. It was this common aim that produced that harmony which was so seldom interrupted between the various inhabitants of the different colonies, and which formed them at last into one nation.

In the course of a century within their narrow fringe of country the colonists had transformed the wilderness into a fertile and productive territory.[2] Agriculture was their favorite pursuit. Travelers from Europe were struck with the skill with which they cultivated the rich and abundant soil, the fine farm-houses that filled the landscape, the barns overflowing with harvests, the cattle, the sheep. The northern and middle colonies were famous for wheat and corn.[1] Pennsylvania was the granary of the nation. In New Jersey the fine farms that spread from Trenton to Elizabethtown excited the admiration of the scientific Kalm.[2] Long Island was the garden of America, and all along the valleys opening upon the Hudson the Dutch and Huguenot colonists had acquired ease and opulence by a careful agriculture. The farm-houses, usually built of stone, with tall roofs and narrow windows, were scenes of intelligent industry. While the young men labored in the fields, the mothers and daughters spun wool and flax, and prepared a large part of the clothing of the family. The farm-house was a manufactory for all the articles of daily use. Even nails were hammered out in the winter, and the farmer was his own mechanic. A school and a church were provided for almost every village. Few children were left untaught by the Dutch dominie, who was sometimes paid in wampum, or the New England student, who lived among his patrons, and was not always fed upon the daintiest fare. On Sunday labor ceased, the church-bell tolled in the distance, a happy calm settled upon the rural region, and the farmer and his family, in their neatest dress, rode or walked to the village church. The farming class, usually intelligent and rational, formed in the northern colonies the sure reliance of freedom, and when the invasion came the Hessians were driven out of New Jersey by the general rising of its laboring farmers, and Burgoyne was captured by the resolution of the people rather than by the timid generalship of Gates.

The progress of agriculture at the South was even more rapid and remarkable than at the North. The wilderness was swiftly converted into a productive region. The coast, from St. Mary's to the Delaware, with its inland country, became within a century the most valuable portion of the earth. Its products were eagerly sought for in all the capitals of Europe, and one noxious plant of Virginia had supplied mankind with a new vice and a new pleasure. It would be

[1] J. Adams to Morse, December 2, 1815; and see Gordon, i. 143. Mr. Whitefield tells the colonists in 1764 their danger.

[2] Burnaby, Pinkert., xiii. 731, notices the flourishing condition of Pennsylvania, and observes that its courteous people are "great republicans."

[1] Burnaby, p. 734. "The country I passed through," he says of New Jersey, "is exceedingly rich and beautiful."

[2] Kalm, Pinkert., vol. xiii. p. 448, notices the rich farms near Trenton.

useless to relate again the story of the growth of the tobacco trade. Its cultivation in Virginia was an epoch in the history of man. Tobacco was to Virginia the life of trade and intercourse; prices were estimated in it; the salaries of the clergy were fixed at so many pounds of tobacco. All other products of the soil were neglected in order to raise the savage plant. Ships from England came over annually to gather in the great crops of the large planters, and Washington, one of the most successful of the Virginia land-owners and agriculturists, was accustomed to watch keenly over the vessels and their captains who sailed up the Potomac to his very dock.[1] The English traders seem to have been often anxious to depreciate his cargoes and lower his prices. Virginia grew enormously rich from the sudden rise of an artificial taste. From 1624, when the production of tobacco was first made a royal monopoly, until the close of the colonial period the production and the consumption rose with equal rapidity, and in 1775, 85,000 hogsheads were exported annually, and the sale of tobacco brought in nearly $4,000,000 to the southern colonies.[2] This was equal to about one-third of the whole export of the colonies. Happily since that period the proportion has rapidly decreased, and more useful articles have formed the larger part of the export from the New World to the Old.

One of these was rice. A Governor of South Carolina, it is related, had been in Madagascar, and seen the plant cultivated in its hot swamps.[3] He lived in Charleston, on the bay, and it struck him that a marshy spot in his garden might well serve for a plantation of rice. Just then (1694) a vessel put in from Madagascar in distress, whose commander the Governor had formerly known. Her wants were liberally relieved. In gratitude for the kindness he received the master gave the Governor a bag of rice. It was sown, and produced abundantly. The soil proved singularly favorable for its culture. The marshes of Georgia and South Carolina were soon covered with rice plantations. A large part of the crop was exported to England. In 1724, 100,000 barrels were sent out from South Carolina alone. In 1761, the value of its rice crop was more than $1,500,000. Its white population could not then have been more than 45,000, and it is easy to conceive the tide of wealth that was distributed annually among its small band of planters. They built costly mansions on the coasts and bays, lived in fatal luxury, were noted for their wild excesses, and often fell speedy victims to the fevers of the malarious soil. Indigo, sugar, molasses, tar, pitch, and a great variety of valuable productions added to the wealth of the South. But cotton, which has grown through many vicissitudes to be the chief staple of British and American trade, was, at this period, only cultivated in small quantities for the use of the farmers. It was spun into coarse cloths. But it was not until Whitney's invention, in 1793, that it could be readily prepared for commerce, and to the inventive genius of Connecticut the Southern States owe the larger part of their wealth and political importance.

Extensive as had been the results of the labors of the American farmer at this period, he had achieved the conquest of the wilderness in the face of dangers and obstacles that seemed almost overwhelming. None of the appliances of modern agriculture lay at his command. His tools were rude yet costly, his plow a heavy mass of iron, his cattle expensive, and at first scarcely to be obtained. The fevers and malaria of the new climate, the sharp frosts, the unknown changes, even the not infrequent earthquakes and celestial phenomena, must have covered him with alarm. Before him lay the dark and pathless wilderness, behind him the raging seas. A whole ocean separated him from his kind. In front the savage hovered over the advancing settlements, and not seldom filled the thin line of cultivated country from Albany to Savannah with the tidings of fearful massacres. Often the frontier families came flying from their blazing homes, scarred and decimated, to seek shelter from the unsparing foe. Yet more cruel or more unfriendly than the terrors of the wilderness, the climate, or even the savage, seemed to the colonists the conduct of their royal government in England. Instead of aiding the struggling settlers in

[1] Washington to his factors.

[2] Pitkin, Commerce U. S. Doyle, American Colonies, 1869, has gathered together many useful details.

[3] The legend is told by Pitkin, 101, and Ramsay.

their contest for life, it had treated them as objects of suspicion and dislike. A fear that they might plan at some future time a separation from the mother country governed all the English legislation.[1] Hence laws were early imposed upon them that might well have checked the whole progress of their agriculture. They were forced to purchase all their supplies from England. They were scarcely permitted to have any commercial intercourse with any foreign country, or even with each other.[2] They were obliged to send all their tobacco, sugar, indigo, rice, furs, ores, pitch, and tar directly to England, and there accept the price the English traders were willing to give. It was forbidden them even to send their produce to Ireland. These jealous restrictions must have kept many an acre from being planted, and prevented that rapid progress which free trade could alone incite. Franklin showed clearly that in this way the colonies had always paid a heavy tax to England, of far greater value than any stamp act could ever give, and that the English merchants and traders had already grown rich by the onerous burdens they had laid on America.[3] Had the colonial ports been opened to foreign traffic, every article must have risen in price, or the demand for it increased beyond conception. But the English had always treated the colonists with a severity like that which Spain once practiced in South America, and which she now exercises over the creoles of Cuba. Corrupt and worthless Englishmen were sent out as governors, councilors, judges, and even clergymen. They looked with disdain on the colonists they plundered, and hastened back to England to defame the reputation of the abject race. It is plain that most Englishmen looked upon the Americans as serfs. They had no rights that Parliament could not abrogate, and no security even for their own earnings. England plundered the American farmer almost at will, and robbed of his just profits the sturdy laborer in the valleys of Vermont, and the wealthy rice planter in the swamps of South Carolina.

[1] England now treats her colonies with the gentleness advised by Burke and Franklin, and her authors condemn the old tyranny as strongly as Americans. Mr. Doyle, of Oxford, has produced a careful essay on the progress of the colonies, 1869.

[2] Ships might sail for wines to Madeira and some Spanish ports, under certain restrictions.

[3] Franklin to Shirley, December, 1754.

The commerce of the colonies flourished equally with their agriculture. It was chiefly in the northern colonies that ships were built, and that hardy race of sailors formed whose courage became renowned in every sea. But the English navigation laws weighed heavily upon American trade. Its ships were, with a few exceptions, only allowed to sail to the ports of Great Britain. No foreign ship was suffered to enter the American harbors. The people of England were resolved to prevent all foreign interference in the trade of the colonies, and the American ports were rigidly shut out from the commerce of the world. Isolated from the great centres of traffic, and even from exchanging many articles with each other, bound by a most oppressive monopoly, restrained by a selfish policy, the colonists yet contrived to build large numbers of ships, and even to sell yearly more than a hundred of them in England. The ship-yards of New England were already renowned. Boston, New York, and Philadelphia were seats of an important trade. On the island of Nantucket the whale-fishery had been established that was to prove for a brief period the source of great profit, and a school of accomplished seamen. The spermaceti-whale was still seen along the American coast, but the New England whaler had already penetrated Hudson Bay, and even pierced the antarctic. The Revolutionary War broke up the trade, and the English captured two hundred of its ships, besides burning the oil stored on the island.[1] In consequence of the rigid navigation laws, smuggling prevailed along all the American coast, and swift vessels and daring sailors made their way to the ports of France and Spain to bring back valuable cargoes of wine and silks. Boston was the chief seat of ship-building, and its fast-sailing vessels were sent to the West Indies to be exchanged for rum and sugar. In 1743[2] it was estimated that New England employed one thousand ships in its trade, besides its fishing barks. But when the laws were more strictly enforced, the shipping trade of Boston de-

[1] Pitkin. Mrs. Farrar's Recollections, p. 2, whose father was a chief sufferer. [2] Holmes, Annals, 1743.

clined. British war vessels watched the colonial ports, and cut off that large source of wealth which the colonists had found in an illicit commerce with Spain and the West India Islands, and it was with no kindly feeling that New England and New York saw the gainful traffic destroyed which had brought them in a stream of French and Spanish gold.[1] The rude English officials not seldom made illegal seizures. Every custom-house officer was turned into an informer, and no cargo seemed altogether secure. There was no redress except in an appeal to England. Yet the American commerce still flourished, even within the narrow limit to which it was confined, and the colonists bore with admirable patience the exactions and restrictions to which they were subjected in order that New York and Boston might not compete with London and Bristol. In fact, the navigation laws had prevented altogether that natural and healthy growth which might have made the colonial sea-ports even in 1775 considerable cities. But twenty-four thousand tons of shipping were built in the colonies in 1771, and the whole exports were in 1770 three millions of pounds sterling, and the imports about two and a half millions. It was noticed that the value of the tobacco exported was one-fourth larger than that of the wheat and rye.[2] The rise of American commerce had seemed wonderful to Burke, Barré, and all those Englishmen who were capable of looking beyond the politics of their own narrow island; but no sooner had America become free than its trade doubled, trebled, and soon rose to what in 1775 would have seemed incredible proportions. New York, Boston, and Philadelphia became at once large cities, and England was enriched by American freedom.

One gainful source of traffic to the colonial and British merchants had been the slave-trade. Immense numbers of these unwilling emigrants were forced upon the colonial markets, chiefly by the inhuman policy of England. A strong feeling of disapprobation for this species of merchandise had early grown up in the minds of the Americans, and Pennsylvania, New England, and even South Carolina were anxious to discourage it by imposing a heavy tax on slaves. But

[1] Gordon, i. 153. [2] M'Pherson. Pitkin, p. 11.

the English Parliament abrogated all their humane legislation. No sentiment of Christian mercy seems to have moved the bishops, lords, and accomplished statesmen who held the control of the American trade. The English merchants insisted upon their monstrous traffic. In one year six thousand slaves were brought to South Carolina; fifteen thousand were forced upon all the colonies. It is at least an indication of the higher degree of civilization to which the inhabitants of the New World had attained that they were the first to exclaim against the horrors of slavery, and that they taught the English intellect one of the most striking principles of modern progress. If in any particular men have risen beyond the cruel selfishness of the earlier ages, it is in the recognition of the principle that human slavery shall no more be tolerated. The Pennsylvanians as early as 1713 protested against the barbarous traffic.[1] One of the chief grievances of New England was that the English were resolute to force slaves upon them; and when the colonies became free, they proceeded at once to indicate a period after which no more Africans should be imported into America. They were the first to fix the ban of civilization upon an infamous traffic, which had been sanctioned by the usages of all ages. If they did not abolish slavery itself, it was because the cruel legislation of English statesmen had implanted the evil so deeply in the midst of the new nation that nothing but a fearful civil convulsion could eliminate and destroy it.

In manufactures the colonists can be said to have made but little progress. The English government had rigorously forbidden them to attempt to make their own wares. A keen watch had been kept over them, and it was resolved that they should never be suffered to compete with the artisans of England. The governors of the different colonies were directed to make a careful report to the home government of the condition of the colonial manufactures, in order that they might be effectually destroyed.[2] From their authentic but perhaps not always accurate survey it is possible to form a general con-

[1] Memoirs Hist. Soc. Penn., vol. i. part i. p. 362. George Fox had always disapproved of slavery.

[2] Report of Board of Trade.

ception of the slow advance of this branch of labor. South of Connecticut, we are told, there were scarcely any manufactures. The people imported every thing that they required from Great Britain. Kalm, indeed, found leather made at Bethlehem, in Pennsylvania, as good as the English, and much cheaper. He praises the American mechanics; but, in general, we may accept the report of the governors that all manufactured articles employed in the family or in trade were made abroad. Linens and fine cloths, silks, implements of iron and steel, furniture, arms, powder, were purchased of the London merchants. But this was not always the case in busy New England. Here the jealous London traders discovered that iron foundries and even slitting-mills were already in operation; that fur hats were manufactured for exportation in Connecticut and Boston; that the people were beginning to supply their own wants, and even to threaten the factories of England with a dangerous rivalry. The English traders petitioned the government for relief from this colonial insubordination, and Parliament hastened to suppress the poor slitting-mills and hat manufactories of our ancestors by an express law.[1] The hatters, who seem to have especially excited the jealousy of their London brethren, were forbidden to export hats even to the next colony, and were allowed to take only two apprentices at a time. Iron and steel works were also prohibited. Wool and flax manufactures were suppressed by stringent provisions. American factories were declared "nuisances." No wool or manufacture of wool could be carried from one colony to another; and, what was a more extraordinary instance of oppression, no Bible was suffered to be printed in America.[2]

Under this rigid tyranny American manufactures had sunk into neglect. Massachusetts had ventured to offer a bounty on paper-making, and some Scottish-Irish had introduced the manufacture of linen; iron furnaces had been erected in various parts of the country, and its immense mineral wealth was not altogether unknown. But it is safe to conclude that from Maine to Georgia no species of artistic manufactures existed within the colonial limits. The farm-house and the spinning-wheel were the only centres of a native industry which the British Parliament could not suppress. Of those two great sources of American progress, coal and iron, the latter had assumed some importance. Pennsylvania, New Jersey, and Virginia had begun to produce pig-iron in an imperfect state. The ore might be exported to England, and even Ireland, and it was already known that the colonies could produce such large quantities of the metal as would supply their own wants, and perhaps those of Europe.[1] As they were not suffered to manufacture even a nail or a pin, a wheel or a plow, England made immense profits by returning the raw iron to America in various articles of trade. Coal was known to exist within the colonies, and was mined in Virginia.[2] Speculative observers foresaw the day when furnaces and factories might spring up along the banks of the Delaware and the Potomac, and the mineral wealth of the country be made to contribute to the prosperity of the colonies. But of that immense and inexhaustible store-house of the finest coal the world possesses which lies in the Lehigh Valley and upon Mauch Chunk Mountain our ancestors could have had no conception. No one supposed that beneath the rude and pathless forest, on lands that seemed destined to perpetual sterility, covered with savages, and terrible even to the hunter, there lay mines richer than Golconda, and stores of wealth beyond that of Ormuz and the Ind. Or had any statesman of 1775 ventured to predict that on the site of Fort Pitt, in the heart of a terrible wilderness, at the junction of two impetuous streams, was to spring up, within a century, a city where coal and iron, lying together in its midst, should be the source of a boundless opulence, he would have lost forever all reputation for discretion. The journey from the Delaware to Pittsburg was long the terror of the Western settler.

It was long after the Revolution that a hunter who had been out all day on Mauch

[1] Pitkin, 7. [2] Bancroft, v. 266.

[1] Kalm, Pinkert., xiii. p. 473. Pennsylvania, he thought, could supply all the globe with iron, so easily was it procured. "But coals have not yet been found in Pennsylvania [p. 405], though people pretend to have seen them higher up," he says.

[2] M'Farlane, Coal Regions. The mines near Richmond were worked long before the anthracite bed of Pennsylvania was discovered, p. 514.

Chunk Mountain, and had found no game, and who was returning weary and disheartened to his cabin, with no means to purchase food for his family, struck with his foot as he passed along a black crystal. He stooped and examined it.[1] The first specimen of that priceless mineral which has transformed the wilderness into a populous nation, and contributed to the comfort of millions, lay before him. The rain fell fast. The hunter was tired and hungry. Yet he took up the apparently worthless stone and carried it with him to his cabin. Mauch Chunk then lay bare and bleak, the haunt of wild beasts and savage men, and had not the hunter preserved his shining mineral, might still have hidden its secret stores for another decade. He showed the specimen to a friend; it was taken to Philadelphia. The mountain was explored, and a company formed to work the mine. But it was at first unsuccessful, and many years elapsed before Pennsylvania became conscious of its hidden treasures, and discovered that it possessed mines richer than those of the Incas and perennial fountains of industrial progress. The unlucky discoverer, it seems, reaped little profit from his good fortune. His land was taken from him by a prior claim. He died in poverty. Great companies, possessed of enormous capital, and spanning with their combined railroads half the continent, now encircle the Mauch Chunk Mountain with their avenues of trade. Coal has been found heaped upon the sides of the hills, and compressed in huge masses in the valleys. The richest and almost the only bed of anthracite in the world has been discovered beneath the path of the solitary hunter.

The wild men of the woods and marshes were to our ancestors objects of interest as well as terror.[2] In the earlier period of the colonial history their numbers had been exaggerated, and it was believed that a hundred thousand painted savages might at some moment throw themselves on the white settlements. But it was found at length that one nation was alone formidable, and that an Indian empire had risen beneath the shadows of the forest that resembled in its extent, its cruelty, and its love of glory the most renowned of European sovereignties and conquerors. In the seventeenth century the Six Nations had their seat in that fair and fertile portion of New York that reaches from Albany to Lake Erie. Onondaga was their capital. A single sachem ruled with undisputed authority over the obedient league.[1] A passion for conquest and a love of martial fame had led this singular confederacy to exploits of daring that seem almost incredible. They held in a kind of subjection all the territory from Connecticut to the Mississippi. The wild tribes of Long Island obeyed the commands of Onondaga; and even the feeble Canarsie, on its distant shore, trembled at the name of the Mohawk. Under the shade of the endless forests, over the trackless mountains, and across rapid rivers, the war parties of the Six Nations had pressed on to the conquest of Pennsylvania and New Jersey, and all Virginia yielded to their arms.[2] They fought with the Cherokees on the dark and bloody ground of Kentucky. The Illinois fled before them on the fair prairies, now the granary of the continent. The savages seem to have resembled the extinct races whose bones are found in the prehistoric caves of Kent and Dordogne. They were cruel, and rejoiced in the tortures of their captives. Their wigwams were filthy and smeared with smoke, adorned with scalps, and hung with weapons of war. Cunning and deceit formed a large part of their tactics. They rejoiced to fall upon their enemies by night and massacre the flying inhabitants of the blazing wigwams. Yet in their rude society the savages manifested the elements of all those impulses and passions that mark the civilization of Europe.[3] They were fond of fine dress, and their women produced rich leather robes, glittering with decorations in colored grasses and beads, head coverings, adorned with feathers, and moccasins of singular beauty. They danced, they sang, with a skill, vigor, and precision that Taglioni might have envied or a Patti approved. The Iroquois boast-

1 Mem. Penn. Hist. Soc., i. part ii. p. 317.

2 The Indians had the vanity of all feeble intellects, and thought themselves the superiors of all mankind. Colden, i. 3.

1 Schoolcraft, Notes on the Iroquois, p. 88. Onondaga was the seat of government from the earliest period.

2 Morgan, League of the Iroquois, p. 13. They penetrated to Virginia in 1607; in 1660–1700 the French assailed them.

3 Schoolcraft, 135–139. Morgan, 384.

ed that they had themselves invented twenty-six different dances. They exchanged visits from wigwam to wigwam, and practiced a courtesy that might have instructed Paris. They had their orators, who polished their sentences with the accuracy of Cicero. With a simple faith they worshiped the Supreme Spirit; and yearly, in February, when the germs of life were opening, met to return thanks to their Maker that he had preserved their lives for another year. A white dog was sacrificed, prayers were offered, hymns of thanksgiving sung,[1] and on the wild shores of the Seneca or Cayuga lake a natural worship hallowed the savage scene.

Of the numbers of the Indian tribes it is of course impossible to form any exact estimate. But it is believed that in the height of their power the Six Nations never possessed more than seventeen thousand warriors, and that in the year 1774 they had scarcely two thousand. Their whole number was then estimated at ten thousand souls.[2] Their wars with the French and with the native races had rapidly reduced their strength. It was stated by Tryon at this time that the wilderness from Lake Erie to the Mississippi could furnish twenty-five thousand warriors, and was inhabited by one hundred and thirty thousand Indians. In the South the Cherokees were the ruling race, and might, with their allies, produce several thousand men. It was with these fierce and relentless warriors that the English hoped to devastate the long line of frontier settlements from Lake Ontario to the Savannah. Twenty thousand Indians, it was thought, would fall upon the unprotected colonists, and with the scalping knife and the musket force them to submit to the British king. Nothing more incited the colonies to independence than this unheard-of barbarity. It was when all the distant settlements were threatened by an Indian invasion that they resolved upon perfect freedom; and even the patient Washington when he heard the news could not restrain his malediction upon the cruel tyrant, and urged an instant separation.[1] In periods of peace the Indians had afforded the colonies an important branch of trade. Furs and skins were exported in large quantities to Europe, and the most successful trappers were the Six Nations, who brought their wares to Albany, and the less warlike tribes who dealt with the merchants of Fort Pitt. Gold and silver were of no value to the savages. They would only receive their payment in wampum or strings of shells[2]—a currency that passed freely over all the continent—or in powder, shot, and muskets, rum, and sometimes articles of dress. A fine uniform or a glittering coat was sometimes exchanged for large tracts of land. A string of periwinkle shells, purple or white, was valued at a dollar; and the first church in New Jersey, it is related, was built and paid for from contributions in wampum.[3] New York and Albany in the early Dutch period had almost adopted the currency of the savage. There are, indeed, marked traces of the influence of Indian customs and superstitions among the whites. Their omens, dreams, and intense belief in witchcraft, their incantations and spells, seem to have convinced Cotton Mather and the New England divines of their close connection with the spirit of evil,[4] and helped to increase the sense of a present Satan in the neighboring forests. To the wild hunters of the border the savages taught their keen study of nature, their caution, and their impassiveness. The frontiers-men borrowed their moccasins, hunting shirts of leather, and caps, their patience of cold and hunger, and rivaled them at last in the pursuit of game. At the close of the Revolution the power of the Six Nations was broken forever. They had taken the side of the English, except only the friendly Oneidas, and the last of the Mohawks found a refuge in Canada.[5] The other tribes sold their possessions, and nearly all moved away. Canandaigua, Cayuga, Oneida, Onondaga, gave names to flourishing white colonies from New England, and with the destruction of

[1] Morgan, 39. They even confessed their sins of the past year, we are told. Their belief in witchcraft, omens, dreams, is told by Schoolcraft, p. 141. They had a vampire, he thinks.

[2] Campbell, Tryon County, p. 24 and note.

[1] Washington to Reed. Reed, Original Letter, p. 66. He denounces "the tyrant and his diabolical ministry."

[2] Schoolcraft, p. 358.

[3] Colden, i. 11, notices that they had no slaves. They adopted the captives they saved alive.

[4] Satan was believed to haunt the New England woods in the form of a "little black man." Cotton Mather.

[5] Morgan, p. 30.

the Indian rule New York rose rapidly to the first place in population and power among its sister States.

Next to the Indians, along that wide fringe of border land that skirted the banks of the Hudson, the declivities of the Alleghanies, and the western counties of the Carolinas on the brink of the Wilderness, lived the hardy race of the pioneers. The home of the woodsman was usually a log-cabin; his chief wealth his musket and a family of healthy children. Far away from the centres of civilization, more familiar with the manners of the wigwam than of the city, generous, fanciful, fond of nature, and of the trees and rivers, mountains and plains, around him, always ready for change and new adventure, the pioneer lived in ceaseless excitement, and sank at last to rest under the green sod of some untried land. His life was, indeed, never secure from the treacherous assaults of the wild men of the woods. The Indians were as fickle as they were mobile and active. The pioneers, trained in constant watchfulness, produced some of the most noted and possibly the most eminent of the men of the Revolution. Washington himself was in his early youth educated in the arts of frontier life. Poor, self-instructed, accurate,[1] truthful, at nineteen he had as a surveyor studied the wilderness west of the Alleghanies, and learned the life of the woods. At a later period he traveled on foot with a pack on his shoulders from Winchester to the Ohio, through the heart of the forest. Later still he led the provincial troops through the woods and mountains, and became famous as a commander; and when the fate of freedom rested on him alone, his experience in the forest and the wilderness guided him to the victories of Trenton and Princeton. Daniel Boone, the founder of a State, was a more accurate example of this wayward class. From his cottage on the Yadkin, where, surrounded by wife, children, and comparative ease, he might well have lived content, an irresistible desire to explore the mysterious wilderness drew him away. He climbed the tall Cumberland Mountains, and saw with a kind of rapture, he relates, the lovely plains of Kentucky, the buffaloes cropping the rich meadows, the flowers blooming in the waste.[1] He descended into the paradise, was captured by some Indians, who came upon him and his companion from a cane-brake, escaped, was found by his brother in the wilderness, to his unspeakable joy; and when his brother left him, built a hut, and lived alone, he declares, in inexpressible happiness. From the summit of some commanding hill he delighted to trace the windings of the Kentucky through its ample plains, or hunted for his daily food through the teeming woods. "Through an uninterrupted scene of sylvan pleasures," he writes, "I spent my time."[2] He resolved to return to North Carolina for his family, and found a settlement in the smiling waste. He sold his farm. With wife and children and a small band of settlers, he climbed again the wild Cumberland Mountains. The Indians attacked the small party, his son fell in battle, but the ardent pioneer persisted in his vision, and founded Boonesborough, on the banks of the Kentucky, in the wilderness he loved so well. A small stockade was built. It was attacked by the Indians. Boone was taken prisoner in a warlike expedition, but instead of torturing him, the Shawanese adopted him into their tribe and treated him as a brother. Again he escaped, and in his wooden fort at Boonesborough sustained a siege that had nearly proved successful. The savages were repulsed, peace and liberty came together, and the bold pioneer died in the scene he had looked upon with rapture, the founder of a new nation, and surrounded by a grateful people.[3]

Such were the men who led the way to the frontier settlements, who first crossed the Alleghanies, who penetrated beneath the shadow of Lookout Mountain, or ventured into Cherry Valley, when the Six Nations still ruled over Western New York. They formed a long line of isolated colonies, and disputed with the savages the possession of the wilderness. Behind them, protected by their necessary vigilance, the more peaceful settlers cultivated their ample farms and lived in prosperous ease. Yet the border

[1] The careful drawings of the self-taught Washington show the methodical nature of his mind. See Sparks, Life.

[1] Filson's Kentucky. Boone's Narrative.

[2] Narrative, p. 36.

[3] Filson, p. 49. "He lived at last," it is said, "in peace, delighted by the love and gratitude of his countrymen."

land was never safe from a hostile invasion. When the English first incited the savage tribes to a general rising the whole frontier was penetrated by a series of murderous attacks. The settlers on the outskirts of North and South Carolina fled from their blazing homes or perished in an unsparing massacre. The Indians who followed Burgoyne filled New York with slaughter. Vermont and New Hampshire trembled before their threats. Cherry Valley armed in its defense.[1] The fate of Wyoming has been told in immortal song. The shores of the Hudson were no longer safe. Brandt and his band of savages penetrated into Orange County, and the massacre of Minisink alarmed the Huguenot farmers in the rich valleys of the Shawangunk and the Dutch in the hill country around Goshen. As the savages pressed on into Orange County they came to a school-house which was yet filled with its children. They took the school-master into the woods and killed him. They clove the skulls of several of the boys with their tomahawks; but the little girls, who stood looking on horror-struck and waiting for an instant death, were spared. A tall savage—it was Brandt—dashed a mark of black paint upon their aprons, and when the other savages saw it they left them unharmed. Swift as an inspiration the little girls resolved to save their brothers.[2] They flung over them their aprons, and when the next Indians passed by they were spared for the mark they bore. The school-master's wife hid in a ditch and escaped. It was amidst such dangers that our ancestors founded their new republic, and forced on the course of progress.

Within the more cultivated portions of the country the most influential person in every town was usually the clergyman. In New England the authority of the ministers was no longer what it had been in the days of Cotton and the Mathers. A revolt had taken place against the spiritual hierarchy which had opened the way for intellectual freedom. But the New England pastor was distinguished always for virtues and attainments that gave him a lasting prominence. In his youth he had passed through a spiritual exercise which had fixed him in the path of virtue. He examined his own nature with the accuracy of a Pythagorean. He had laid down rules to himself that formed the guiding principles of his life. Sloth he abhorred; he resolved to lose no moment of time; to do nothing that he should be afraid to do in his last hour; to consecrate himself to the service of his Maker.[1] The image of ideal virtue had dawned upon him in its surpassing loveliness, and he wandered away into the still woods and pleasant fields filled with sweet visions of the divine Messiah. Yet he knew that the world was full of trouble and vexation, and that it would never be another kind of a world. It was thus that Jonathan Edwards meditated in the dawn of his intellectual youth, and many another ardent follower of Calvin. The New England minister was fond of scholastic theology. He keenly pursued the delicate and refined distinctions of election and grace, of free-will and predestination, but seldom wandered far from the decisions of the Geneva school. Yet he had learned self-control, and was well fitted to direct the conduct of others. Elected by the voice of the people to the ministry of a town or city congregation, his scholarship and his decision gave him a political and personal influence that he was not afraid to use.[2] The clerical families were often connected by the closest ties of relationship, and the pastorate descended from generation to generation. The Cottons and Mathers ruled over Boston for nearly sixty years. Edwards was the grandson of a clergyman, succeeded to his charge, married a clergyman's daughter, and married his own daughter to the Rev. Aaron Burr. Yet the people of Northampton, where he was settled, with the largest salary in New England, rebelled against his authority. He removed to Stockbridge, and became at last president of the College of New Jersey on the death of his son-in-law, Burr.

These cultivated men were usually ardent

[1] Campbell, Tryon County, is full of the trials of frontier life.

[2] Eager, Orange County, p. 391. It was July, 1779.

[1] Edwards, Diary and Life.

[2] The minister was sometimes obliged to rule his people with no tender hand, and violent controversy often arose, which sometimes "came to hard blows." Life of Edwards, i. 464. The people of Northampton were of "a difficult and turbulent temper," etc.

patriots. But their patriotism was no doubt stimulated by the dread of a religious rather than political tyranny. A fear prevailed in all New England that Parliament and the king were resolved to impose bishops upon each of the colonies, and to enforce by law the ritual of the Church of England. Whitefield had warned the colonies of a coming woe. The imprudent conversation of young Episcopal ministers in Connecticut and Boston added to the apprehension. Archbishop Secker had suggested the idea of an American episcopate,[1] and the project was already entertained in England of reducing New England to a subjection to the national Church by lavish bribes to its independent clergy, and by the reform or suppression of all the colonial charters. Cambridge had even been suggested as the seat of a colonial bishop, and an Episcopal church had already sprung up beneath the shadow of Harvard College under the auspices of the Society for Propagating the Gospel in America. Then Mayhew of Boston began a series of publications that sounded an alarm throughout the country. He felt the danger; he saw the unscrupulous nature of the men who ruled in England. The "overbearing spirit of the Episcopalians"[2] he brooded over, until he almost felt once more the clerical tyranny from which the gentle Robinson had fled, and which had impelled the *Mayflower* over the stormy sea. "Will they never let us rest in peace," he cried, "except where all the weary are at rest?[3] Is it not enough that they persecuted us out of the Old World?" Yet Mayhew was still sufficiently loyal to hope that King George was "too good and noble" to suffer it. When the controversy with England began, Mayhew was ever ready to support the liberties of his country, and his pulpit resounded with patriotic exhortations. Almost every Congregational minister was equally faithful. Like the Huguenot and the Covenanter, they even fought in the ranks, and sometimes led their townsmen to battle, and fell among the first.

The clergy of the middle and southern colonies were persons less distinctly the leaders of the people than in New England. The Episcopalian ministers were often mild and amiable men who cared nothing for politics. They were inclined to the English rule, but were not unwilling to share the fortunes of a new nation. Some, however, were bitter and relentless in their Toryism; their violence helped to bring discredit on their cause, and their religious intolerance led them to their ruin. In New York the Dutch and Presbyterian clergy were often eminent for their virtues and their scholarship; their churches in the city were to the eyes of our ancestors splendid, their salaries high, their congregations numerous and attentive. The Presbyterian church in Wall Street, the new Dutch church, and even the old, were scarcely surpassed by Trinity and St. Paul's. Meantime a new religious influence had been impressed upon the nation by the preaching of Whitefield, and in 1742 a revival had swept over the country that never lost its effect. Villages and cities had been stirred by the impulse of reform. Many strange and some not attractive scenes had followed it. Children held their meetings for prayer apart.[1] Women had been roused to unreflecting fanaticism, and imposture and hypocrisy had flourished in the general excitement. Yet it was acknowledged that every where morality had received a real impulse at the hands of faith. The clergy themselves profited by the general movement, and became better fitted to guide the people. The Roman Catholic clergy at this period had lost much of their early intolerance. The Society of the Jesuits had been abolished, a series of moderate and reputable popes had ruled at Rome, and reform seemed about to invade the councils of the Vatican. The fanatical reaction of the nineteenth century had not yet begun.

In the towns and villages the lawyers shared with the clergy the intellectual influence of the time. Many of them were well-read and accomplished men, who joined to their technical knowledge a considerable acquaintance with letters, or were noted for their natural eloquence. John Adams had prepared himself by a careful study of his profession to defend with legal accuracy the rights of his countrymen. William Smith,

[1] Gordon, i. 143, gives the general apprehension and the plan. [2] Mayhew, Second Defense, p. 64.
[3] Observations, p. 156.

[1] Edwards, Life.

of New York, was known as a faithful historian as well as jurist, and formed the intellect of John Jay. Colden wrote well. In Virginia Patrick Henry had won his first renown by an impassioned appeal against the avarice and the ambition of the Established Church. Jefferson had trained himself by practice in the courts before he essayed to condense in a brief memorial the rights of man. Nothing indeed is more remarkable at this period than the nicety and clearness with which the various points in dispute between the colonies and England were discussed in every part of the country, and the superiority in argument which the legal writers of America showed over their opponents in London when they treated of the professional elements of the controversy. Otis and Adams reasoned with calmness and force, while Johnson raved and Mansfield blundered. In the grand argument which the American lawyers addressed to the suffrages of the civilized world there was a depth of reflection and a wide acquaintance with the principles of the common and international law that proved to acute observers their just claim to freedom. No one could think such men unworthy to found a state.

The chief cities of our ancestors were all scattered along the sea-coast. There were no large towns in the interior. Albany was still a small village, Schenectady a cluster of houses. To those vast inland capitals which have sprung up on the lakes and great rivers of the West our country offered no parallel. Chicago and St. Louis, the centres of enormous wealth and unlimited commerce, had yet no predecessors. Pleasant villages had sprung up in New England, New Jersey, and on the banks of the Hudson, but they could pretend to no rivalry with those flourishing cities which lined the sea-coast or its estuaries, and seemed to our ancestors the abodes of luxury and splendor. Yet even New York, Philadelphia, and Boston,[1] extensive as they appeared to the colonists, were insignificant towns compared to the European capitals, and gave no promise of ever approaching that grandeur which seemed to be reserved especially for London and Paris. In 1774 the population of New York was perhaps 20,000; that of London 600,000. The latter was thirty times larger than the former, and in wealth and political importance was so infinitely its superior that a comparison between them would have been absurd. Boston, which has crowned Beacon Hill, pressed over the Neck, and even covered with a magnificent quarter a large surface that was once the bed of the Charles River, was in 1774 a town of 15,000 or 18,000 inhabitants, closely confined to the neighborhood of the bay. The Long Wharf may still be seen on the ancient maps; the Common was used as a public resort;[1] the Hancock House was illuminated at the repeal of the Stamp Act, and the Sons of Liberty raised on the Common a pyramid of lamps, from the top of which fire-works lighted up the neighboring fields. But Beacon Hill was still used by its owner as a gravel-pit, and it was feared by the citizens that he might level it altogether. The Boston of 1774, which proclaimed freedom and defied the power of England, would scarcely rank to-day among the more important country towns. New York was more populous, but it was still confined to the narrow point of land below the Park. The thickly built part of the town lay in the neighborhood of Whitehall. Some fine houses lined Broadway and Broad Street,[2] but to the west of Broadway green lawns stretched down from Trinity and St. Paul's to the water. Trees were planted thickly before the houses; on the roofs railings or balconies were placed,[3] and in the summer evenings the people gathered on the house-top to catch the cool air. Lamps had already been placed on the streets.[4] Fair villas covered the environs, and even the Baroness Riedesel, who had visited in the royal palaces of Europe, was charmed with the scenery and homes of the citizens. Extravagance had already corrupted the plainer habits of the earlier period. The examples of London and Paris had already affected the American cities. The people of New York drank fiery Madeira,

[1] Burnaby describes Boston as the most cultivated of the American cities. Dwight thinks New York "magnificent" at a later period.

[1] Drake, Boston, 685.

[2] Riedesel, Mem., iii. 170, etc.

[3] Kalm. Riedesel, Mem., iii. 170. Watson, Annals New York, p. 227. A stage ran to Philadelphia in 1776.

[4] New York, Miss Mary L. Booth. Gordon, i. 138, notices the heavy taxes of Boston—higher than those of London.

and were noted for their luxury. Broadway was thought the most splendid of avenues, although it ended at Chambers Street. And twenty years later, when the City Hall was built, it was called by Dwight (a good scholar) the finest building in America.[1] The streets of New York and Boston were usually crooked and narrow, but the foresight of Penn had made Philadelphia a model of regularity. Market and Broad streets were ample and stately. The city was as populous as New York, and perhaps the possessor of more wealth. It was the first city on the continent, and the fame of Franklin had already given it a European renown.[2] Yet Philadelphia when it rebelled against George III. was only an insignificant town, clinging to the banks of the river; and New York invited the attack of the chief naval power of the world with its harbor undefended and its whole population exposed to the guns of the enemy's ships. The southern cities were yet of little importance. Baltimore was a small town. Virginia had no large city. Charleston had a few thousand inhabitants. Along that immense line of sea-coast now covered with populous cities the smallest of which would have made the New York and Boston of our ancestors seem insignificant, only these few and isolated centres of commerce had sprung up. The wilderness still covered the shores of Long Island, New Jersey, Delaware, and the Carolinas almost as in the days of Raleigh.

To pass from one city to another along this desolate shore was, in 1775, a long and difficult journey. Roads had been early built in most of the colonies. In Massachusetts they were good, except where they passed over the hills. In New York a good road ran through Orange and Ulster counties to Albany. That between New York and Philadelphia was probably tolerable. In the southern colonies but little attention was paid to road-building, and even those in the neighborhood of Philadelphia were often almost impassable. A stage-coach ran in two days from New York to Philadelphia, but the passengers were requested to cross over the evening before to Powle's Hook, that they might set out early in the morning.[1] Sloops sailed to Albany in seven or eight days.[2] From Boston to New York was a tedious journey. In fair weather the roads of the time were tolerable; but in winter and spring they became little better than quagmires. There was therefore but little intercourse between the people of the distant colonies, and in winter all communication by land and water must have been nearly cut off. Had it been told to our ancestors that within a century men would ride from New York to Philadelphia within three hours, or pass from the Atlantic to the Pacific in seven days, that the passage from Boston to Charleston would be made within three days, or from Liverpool to New York within ten, they would have placed no more confidence in the prediction than in the speculations of Laputa. Nor did they dream that Franklin's discoveries had made the closer union of the human race still more certain. The northern cities were usually built of brick or of stone, and many of the farm-houses were of the latter material.[3] The former had been imported from Holland for the first New York buildings; and even Schenectady, a frontier town, was so purely Dutch as to have been early decorated with Holland brick. In the country stone was easily gathered from the abundant quarries on the Hudson or along the New England hills. Many large, low, stone houses, with lofty roofs and massive windows, may still be seen in the rich valleys opening upon the Hudson, almost in the same condition in which they were left by their Huguenot or Dutch builders, and apparently capable of enduring the storms of another century.[4] Brick-making was soon introduced into the colonies, and the abundant forests supplied all the materials for the mechanic. Fortunately no palaces were built, no royal parks required, no Versailles nor Marly indispensable to our ancestors, no monasteries, no cathedrals. A general equality in condition was nearly reached. Not five men, we are

[1] Dwight, Travels, iii. 329, notices the magnificent style of living, etc.

[2] Watson, Philadelphia.

[1] Advertisement, The Flying Post. Watson, Ann. Phil., p. 257, notices the bad roads.

[2] Trumbull, Mem., p. 26.

[3] Kalm. Burnaby. Mr. Stone's valuable edition of the Riedesel memoirs throws much light upon the condition of the colonies.

[4] Early New York (1669) "was built chiefly of brick and stone, and covered with red tiles." Brodhead, New York, ii. 153.

told, in New York and Philadelphia expended ten thousand dollars a year on their families. The manners of the people were simple; their expenses moderate. Yet nowhere was labor so well rewarded nor poverty so rare. Franklin, who had seen the terrible destitution of England and of France, pronounced his own country the most prosperous part of the globe, and was only anxious to protect it from that tyranny which had reduced Europe to starvation, and snatched their honest earnings from the hands of the working classes. He saw that those who labored were the best fitted to govern. The wages of the farm laborer in the northern colonies was probably three times that of the English peasant, and the general abundance of food rendered his condition easier. Fuel, however, before the discovery of coal, seems to have been sometimes scarce and dear. Kalm notices that complaints of its dearness were frequent in Philadelphia—now the seat of the chief coal market of the world.[1] Wines and liquors were freely consumed by our ancestors, and even New England had as yet no high repute for temperance. Rum was taken as a common restorative. The liquor shops of New York had long been a public annoyance. In the farther southern colonies, we are told, the planter began his day with a strong glass of spirits, and closed it by carousing, gambling, or talking politics in the village tavern. Our ancestors were extraordinarily fond of money, if we may trust the judgment of Washington, who seems to have found too many of them willing to improve their fortunes from the resources of the impoverished community.[2] But in general it must be inferred that the standard of public morals was not low. In comparison with the corrupt statesmen of England and France, or with the members of the English Parliament, who were nearly all willing to accept and to give bribes, the American politicians seemed to the European thinkers the most admirable of men. Washington rose above his species, and Franklin, Samuel and John Adams, Jefferson, Gadsden, and Lee were wise and prudent beyond example. Our generals and soldiers, when compared to those England sent over to conquer them, were evidently of a higher and purer race. Burgoyne,[1] Howe, and the greater part of their associates shocked the rising refinement of colonial society by their gross vices and shameless profligacy as much as by their inhumanity. Gates, Arnold, and Lee, who imitated them, were exceptions to the general purity of the American officers, and of these two were English-born and one a traitor.

The desire for a higher and purer life was indeed the finest trait of American politics and society. The Declaration of Independence embodied the real feeling of the people. They were anxious to promote human equality, to enforce the common brotherhood of man, to cultivate refinement, to escape from the gross vices of mediæval barbarism which still covered all Europe. They had learned the necessity of religious and political toleration by the slow course of experience. In the opening of their history religious toleration had been unknown. New England had persecuted Episcopalians, Quakers, Dissenters. Stuyvesant, in New York, had sent Quakers in chains to Holland, and been reproved by his superiors at the Hague. Virginia was bitterly intolerant, and by the boasted constitution of Maryland in 1649 the Socinian was deemed worthy of death, and whoever reproached the Virgin Mary was fined, imprisoned, or banished.[2] But these harsh laws were gradually swept away, and in 1775 a practical toleration prevailed in all the colonies. No one of any intelligence any longer desired to propagate his faith by penal laws. An equal progress had been made in politics. Virginia was willing to abandon its entails and its oligarchy; Massachusetts to assert a democratic equality; New York to break down its colonial aristocracy forever. All the colonies united in throwing aside the restrictions of European prejudice, and by a remarkable revolution provided for the creation of a re-

1 Pinkert., xiii. 407.

2 Washington to Reed, Reed's Original Letters, p. 63.

1 Riedesel, Mem., iii. p. 125. Lord Auckland was constantly intoxicated. Burgoyne and his mistress spent half the night drinking Champagne while his troops were starving. Such were the morals England taught to the colonies.

2 Bozman, Maryland. Lord Baltimore probably hoped to make Maryland a purely Roman Catholic colony, but in 1649 England would not permit it, i. p. 351; ii. p. 662.

public, in which the people should be the only rulers.

I shall conclude this imperfect sketch by a brief review of the intellectual condition of America. It had produced no Shakspeare nor Milton, it possessed no poets and historians; but it is quite probable that the Northern States of America were better educated in the ideas of Milton and Shakspeare than even England or France. Of the people of New England the larger proportion could read and write, while of the two centres of European civilization the great majority of the population were sunk in hopeless ignorance. From the dawn of its history New England had insisted that its people should all be educated; and New York and Pennsylvania had not lingered far behind it.[1] Connecticut imposed a heavy fine upon every father of a family who had neglected to teach his household the elements of knowledge,[2] Massachusetts had enforced a similar provision, and even South Carolina had directed a school to be planted in every township. It was the aim of the New World to open the minds of all its people to the light of literature, and to cultivate the whole community. It sought mental as well as political equality. But in France and England the royal governments found no leisure and had little inclination to teach their people. It was only in Protestant Holland and Germany that men were yet allowed to learn the "sweet influences" of a rule of letters.

In their eager and resolute desire to make knowledge free to all, our ancestors at once planted in the wilderness the printing-press. Three years had not passed after the landing of the first colony in Pennsylvania when the clank of the machine that had reformed Europe and discovered America resounded under the shade of the primeval forest.[3] It was with knowledge rather than arms that the followers of Penn hoped to found their state; and nearly fifty years earlier Massachusetts had erected its first printing-press at Cambridge, and had consecrated New England to literature and thought. Our ancestors were plainly resolved that the New World should be a land of printers. Pamphlets, sermons, political pieces, resounded through the wilderness, and at an early period Cotton Mather alone had printed in England and America three hundred and eighty-two of his own productions. In the opening of the eighteenth century (1704) a weekly paper, *The News Letter*, was published at Boston.[1] It was then the only newspaper printed in British America. It was a foolscap half sheet, and was thought sufficient to contain all the news of the day. In 1725 William Bradford issued at New York the New York *Gazette*, a foolscap sheet. The two Franklins, James and Benjamin, edited at Boston the *New England Courant;* and suits for libel, imprisonment, and fines were the reward of several of the early editors. James Franklin was in jail for four weeks; Zenger, of the New York *Courant* (1733), was also soon in the grasp of the law. But through all its early trials the printing-press passed successfully. The newspaper became as necessary to the colonists as their daily food. In 1775 four were printed in New York, and as many each in Philadelphia and Boston. The free school proved the best ally of the printer, and popular education laid the foundation of a nation of readers. The power of the press was soon manifested. Reform and revolution followed in its path. Yet the rude machine at which Franklin and Bradford labored seemed to lag behind the wants of even an early age; to print a few hundred copies of a small sheet required incessant toil; and Faust himself must have looked with amazement and awe upon one of those giant printing-presses that in our day consume their miles of paper, pour forth ten thousand huge sheets of accurate typography every hour, and relate the story of mankind.[2]

Various colleges or schools for the higher education of the people had already been planted in America. Harvard had long held a high renown even in Europe, and had been

---

[1] Ramsay, i. 26. Palfrey, ii. 45.

[2] Ramsay, i. 78. In Connecticut the parent neglecting education was fined twenty shillings. Baroness Riedesel noticed that all the women of New England could read. The Virginians of the back country she finds ignorant and "inert." They sometimes exchange wives, are cruel to their slaves; but she was no friendly judge.

[3] Thomas, Printing, and Bancroft.

[1] Mr. Hudson, in his interesting account of American journalism, notices a previous newspaper, in 1690, which had the unusual fate of lasting only one day, p. 44.

[2] The invention of Hoe's rotary press has made the cheap newspaper possible, and cultivated the minds of millions.

fostered by liberal donations from English Dissenters. In its earlier history it had been unlucky in its principals: one had proved to be a Jesuit, another a Baptist.[1] To preside over Harvard was a favorite aim of Cotton Mather that was never gratified. Many of the eminent men of the colony had been cultivated in its careful course of study. Samuel and John Adams were its graduates, and it had long been the school of Massachusetts and of Boston. Classical learning still formed the foundation of all mental training, and no one was thought capable of professional excellence who was not learned in the languages of Greece and Rome. Yet it is worthy of notice that Washington had never construed a line of Virgil, and was wholly self-educated, and that Franklin learned his pure style and strong passion for letters and science in the composing-room.

Dartmouth College had been recently founded to teach the Indians, which it failed to do. Yale was more flourishing. Columbia College, in New York, founded in 1756, had but two professors and twenty-five students; but among them were to be numbered John Jay and Alexander Hamilton. In New Jersey Princeton College, under the presidency of Dr. Witherspoon, a cultivated Scotchman, flourished, though with a poor endowment;[2] it had sixty students and fine buildings. In Virginia William and Mary's College had been founded with an ample liberality by the two sovereigns whose names it bore; it was endowed with a large income, and was designed to make Virginia a scene of wide intelligence. But the region of slavery could not be made favorable to mental progress. The college languished;[3] its students were few; it is chiefly memorable as having furnished Jefferson with some facilities for study.

In all the American colleges it is doubtful if three hundred students were educated annually. More scholars are now gathered at a single university than in the year 1775 were found in all the famous seats of learning of the country. Yet the colleges, however imperfect, were still of real value to the people. They spread an acquaintance with the chief masters in science and letters, and helped to supply the press with literature, and diffuse knowledge. Yet of the earlier American authors who attained fame, the chief had never passed through a regular course of study. Irving had gathered the charms of his perfect style from nature and practice in the newspapers. Cooper, Halleck, Drake, were self-educated and refined. Pure literature, in fact, is seldom taught in colleges, which have usually been little more than professional schools. The chief aim of education must always be to excite inquiry and awaken the slumbering faculties. A just conception of its purpose our ancestors had formed. They saw that there should be no limit to the spread of knowledge, and hoped that a system of instruction would grow up among the people that would prove a lasting bond of union. Their extravagant vision has been in part fulfilled. The common-school system has flowed from the germs which the Puritans, Huguenots, and Dutch planted in the wilderness, and the college is gradually assuming a more popular character.[1] In the period of the Revolution, with one or perhaps two exceptions, the colleges were firmly on the side of progress. Harvard gave its brightest geniuses to the cause of freedom, its transatlantic Hampden to fall at Bunker Hill, its Adams to found a nation. Yale was rigidly patriotic. Princeton College, under Witherspoon, formed a bulwark of independence. Yet the influence of the colleges was only a faint impulse compared to that of the general intelligence of our educated people, and that strong passion for liberty which had grown up from the simpler school-house and the modest library.

Books, which had discovered America and first disturbed the wilderness, were not wanting to our ancestors. The booksellers sold freely the new works of Johnson, Burke, or the famous Dr. Goldsmith, and one Boston house numbered ten thousand volumes on

---

1 Winthrop.

2 Burnaby, Pinkert., xiii. 733. Princeton College had only "two professors besides the provost."

3 Ramsay, i. 263, notices its decay. Burnaby, Pinkert., xiii. p. 714.

1 In cities, it is said, colleges seldom flourish, yet the eagerness with which students avail themselves of the advantages of the Boston Latin School or the New York Free College, a school of mines or a popular law school, shows that utility must be one trait of the college course.

its shelves. Several public and private libraries already existed. Kalm mentions the collection of excellent works, chiefly English, in the public library founded by Franklin in 1742 at Philadelphia. The wealthier people of the town paid forty shillings currency in the beginning, besides ten shillings annually. Several smaller libraries were also founded near it. Boston showed a "more general turn for music, painting, and the fine arts" than either of the more southern towns.[1] But literature still hesitated to flourish in the New World. Mather, Edwards, sermons, pamphlets, newspapers, were the chief sources of the mental progress of our ancestors. It was idle to look for a Homer or Shakspeare in so wild a land;[2] nor is it likely that a fourth epic will be sung for many a cycle. But reading was a characteristic trait of the whole people, and curiosity and inquiry the chief impulses of their civilization. In military affairs the colonists had shown courage and capacity. New England troops had grown famous at the conquest of Louisbourg, the siege of Havana, and the fall of Quebec. While the English ministry were denouncing them as a feeble, abject race, more intelligent observers in England knew that the colonists were only cowards in cruel and inhuman deeds. Virginia's troops had fought bravely in the wilderness, and Washington was the most renowned of the colonial commanders. In military stores, guns, powder, arms, the country was deficient; nor did its people suppose that they would ever be drawn into another great war.

Around the thin line of settlements occupied by our ancestors a circle of various and almost hostile races hemmed in their progress. Between the austere and Puritanic New Englander and the loose, profligate,[1] yet often courageous clergy and people of Quebec there could be no friendship. Canada refused to join in the cause of independence. Its French population turned with aversion from an alliance with heretics and Saxons. To the westward the Canadian and clerical influence governed all the Indian tribes. The Mississippi was held by the Spaniards and by a few English planters who steadfastly refused to join the colonists.[2] New Orleans, recently transferred to Spain, was at first unwilling to sell arms and powder to the boats that had sailed down the great river from Pittsburg. The English in West Florida were hostile to the colonies; Spanish Florida was still undecided. It was with no confidence in any exterior aid that the colonists looked out upon their beleaguered territory in the hot days of July, 1776. On every side around them they saw the impending horrors of a war of extirpation. Canada teemed with military preparations; the savages were aroused through all the wilderness; the cities on the coast were threatened with sudden ruin; Howe was already landing on Staten Island; disunion tore the ranks of the reformers. Yet on the 2d of July, 1776, a bell rang cheerfully over Philadelphia that spoke the liberation of America. Samuel Adams had won his cause.[3] The 2d of July seemed to John Adams the grandest day of all the ages.

---

[1] Burnaby, Pinkert., xiii. 747.

[2] Ramsay, i. 275. Its earliest poems were in Latin.

[1] Riedesel, Mem., iii. p. 87. Macgregor, Progress of Commerce, i. 141, notices the immorality of the Canadians. One minister of state stole £400,000.

[2] Gayarré, Louisiana, Spanish Dominion, p. 109. Finally the Spaniards attack the English.

[3] Samuel Adams, to his disciple and kinsman John, was the "wedge of steel" that split the bond between England and America. J. Adams to William Tudor, June 5, 1817. So Jefferson looked to Samuel Adams as his guide and teacher.

II.

MECHANICAL PROGRESS.

UNITED STATES PATENT-OFFICE, WASHINGTON, D. C.

IT is no common century. Compared with its predecessors, it appears rather as a contrast than a development. It is not easy to state its relation to the past in terms of progression, since it may be said to have leaped into existence, and an adequate statement describes radical changes rather than evolution.

The search for the "lost arts" is an agreeable literary and scientific ramble, with nooks containing treasures which well reward the explorer; but one's eyes must be sadly out of focus if the distant, laborious ingenuities of remote ages are more distinct in the field of vision than the majestic works of the present. A locomotive is a more pregnant fact than a pyramid or a sculptured cavern. The subject is one to which it is not possible to do full justice, even in a volume, either by a general sketch or by particular instances. We purpose to take a rapid preliminary survey of the field of mechanical activity, and then to devote the principal portion of our space to details respecting a few prominent subjects, thereby enabling the reader to form a judgment from the sum of the parts, instead of a superficial estimate from a cursory glance at the multitudinous whole.

The inquiry, whether it proceed by a general survey or by investigation of detached portions, will reveal the following facts:

1. No nation has had exclusive concern in the production of any one class of inventions, and yet we need not go beyond the area of the English-speaking nations to make a thorough exhibit of the mechanical progress of the period under review.

2. Nations allied by ties of blood and similarities of tone, temper, taste, and opportunity develop in parallel lines which continually inosculate. This is well illustrated in the tools and methods of the machine-shop. England and America are rich in coal and iron, have the same incentives to industry, and the machines of each are largely the growth of successive improvements from the respective nations, in each of which a host of inventors are laboring at the solution of the same problems.[1]

3. Peculiar conditions of peoples, even of the same race, elicit distinct varieties of tools and methods. This diversity is exemplified in the appliances used in America for subduing the wilderness and cultivating lately cleared land, as compared with the husbandry implements of Britain.

Our people in the colonial period were generally engaged in husbandry, lumbering, trading, hunting, and fishing. The exports were grain, meat, naval stores, tobacco, and pelts. But few mechanic arts were carried on systematically, except ship-building. Car-

[1] It is our purpose in this series to treat of *American* progress in the various fields of activity. But in this field of Mechanical Progress, as in some others, it is plainly impossible to exclude what has been accomplished by other nations.—Ed.

pentry, blacksmithing, and tanning were regular trades. In the cities other industries engaged attention, but in the country the clothes, hats, and shoes of the people and the harness of the horses were made by the people at their houses in the winter or in seasons of inclement weather.

There were some other industries in a few favored localities—some paper mills in Massachusetts and Pennsylvania, some cloth mills at Boston and Germantown, Pennsylvania. Beaver hats were made in a few places; linen, at a settlement near Boston; glass was manufactured in Massachusetts and New Hampshire; the hand card, the spinning-wheel, and the loom constituted almost always a part of the furnishing of country houses.

The roads were bad, the equipages clumsy, as they were, indeed, in England at that time. Twenty-four gentlemen's carriages were owned in Philadelphia in 1761. Country squires and patricians rode in their coaches and four, or even six, when the journey was long or the season unpropitious. Postilions and outriders were the acme of style. Judge Reed, of Pennsylvania, imported a skillful "whip" for his four-in-hand. The country wagons and the agricultural implements were rude and ineffective. Carts, plows, and hoes were made by the country mechanic of such material as he could procure, little metal being used in either. Strips of iron made by hammering out old horseshoes were the facings of the wooden mould-boards of plows. The laws of England had rigorously maintained the dependence of the provinces, forbidding all important works in iron, and the war found the people unprepared to supply their sudden needs. The war was to a large degree fought by men in homespun and hunting shirts, armed with the frontiers-man's trusty rifle.

When peace rendered possible commercial and mechanical enterprise, a new era dawned. Many things which the colonists had cheerfully imported from the mother country began to be made at home, and many industries which had been repressed by law to keep the colonies subordinate and dependent began to be developed. In 1787 the first cotton mill in America was built at Beverly, Massachusetts. In 1789 Samuel Slater introduced the Arkwright system of mill spinning. The exportation of machinery from England was successfully prevented, and Slater was obliged to make the carding, drawing, roving, and spinning mechanism from memory. In 1783 Oliver Evans had introduced his improvements in grain mills, and a few years afterward his steam-engine—the first double-acting high-pressure steam-engine on record. In 1785 Rumsey, and in 1788 Fitch, had their boats on the Potomac and Delaware respectively. In 1787 Jacob Perkins had his nail-cutting machines and dies for coin. In 1794 Whitney's cotton-gin, and in 1797 Whittemore's card-sticking machine, came to the help of the cotton interest. Other inventions followed in rapid succession.

The progress above noted occurred within fifteen years after the treaty of peace. It is doubtful whether on the 4th of July, 1776, there were more than two steam-engines in the thirteen colonies, one at Passaic, New Jersey, the other in Philadelphia. The Newcomen engine was as yet only partially supplanted by the Watt, and offered but moderate inducements for any purpose except pumping water from copper and lead mines, whose rich ores paid for the wasteful use of wood or coal.

The great advance in machinery, and especially our own active part in it, is very recent. Persons yet alive remember the first crossing of the Atlantic by a steamboat, the *Savannah.* Those yet in the prime of life recollect the opening of the first railway to passenger traffic. Horatio Allen drove the first locomotive which was imported. Thus the century under consideration, from a mechanical point of view, is most readily segregated from its predecessors. It is not saying too much to assert that at its commencement the coal of England was scarcely valued except for household uses. As to the coal of America, its extent and its utility were not even suspected. Machinery as yet was not. The steam-engine of Newcomen was pumping in some few mines in England. This engine condensed its steam in the cylinder beneath the piston, cooling the cylinder at each stroke, and using the condensation of the steam as a means of producing a partial vacuum, in order to obtain the value of the atmospheric pressure above the piston. The *duty* or valuable ef-

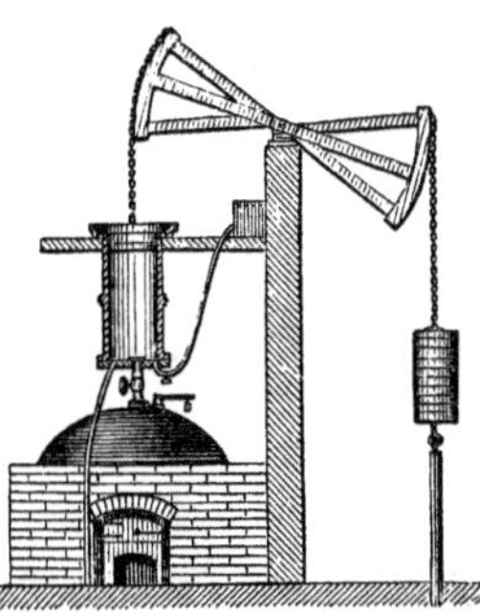
NEWCOMEN'S STEAM-ENGINE.

fect of the Newcomen engine in 1769 was 5,500,000 pounds of water raised one foot high by one bushel of Welsh coal. Watt's inventions were made between the years 1769 and 1784, and before the year 1800 the duty of the Cornish engine was quadrupled; by 1840 it was again quadrupled. Watt added to the steam-engine the *separate condenser* and the *air-pump*. By the former he avoided the cooling of the cylinder before each effective stroke of the piston; by the latter he made the vacuum more perfect. He subsequently made the additions of the *parallel motion*, of the *steam-jacket* to the cylinder, and of the *cylinder cover*, and made the steam act positively against the piston, instead of merely using it to produce a vacuum. Afterward he made the engine *double acting*, that is, used pressure of steam on the sides of the piston alternately; then he increased the strength of the parts, the rapidity of the stroke, and the pressure of the steam. Coal, the black slave, had been chained below from time immemorial, and Watt contrived a way of setting him to work. Up to this period there had been scarcely any progress; after it hosts of inventions crowd upon the scene and clamor for notice. The Watt period inaugurates the century whose progress in the mechanic arts is under consideration.

The utilization of coal in the production of steam for driving machinery is the turning-point in the history of mechanical development, and made possible improvements in various other directions.

If there had been no Watt, Smeaton, Arkwright, Hargreaves, Cartwright, Cort, Murdoch, Whitney, Trevethick, and Stephenson, the victory of Colonel Clive at Plassey might not have proved the precursor of the occupation of the whole of Hindostan. But for the machinery which by gradual accretions gave to England an increased power of production more than equivalent to the addition of a population equal to that of China to her industrial forces, the farther works of Clive, the victories of Hastings, Cornwallis, Wellesley, Napier, Hardinge, and Gough, would not have occurred, and in their places would have been mere raids or desultory expeditions, half commercial and half military, after the first burst of conquest and spoliation.

This accession of labor was in a shape more tense and patient than even the enduring Chinaman, for its muscles were of iron, its food could be dug from the earth, and when at last worn out, it could be worked over again, and had not to be boxed, labeled, and sent back to be deposited near the tablets of its ancestors.

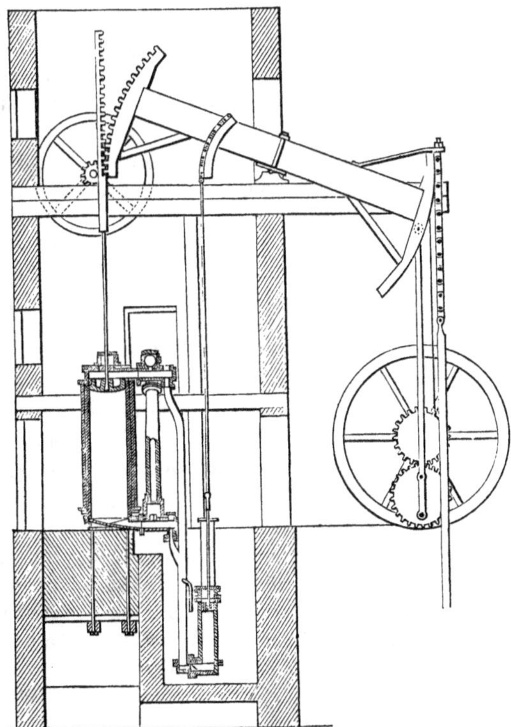
WATT'S DOUBLE-ACTING STEAM-ENGINE, 1769.

The capacity of the steam-engines of England may be otherwise stated. It is estimated that the great Pyramid of Ghizeh occupied the labor of 100,000 men for twenty years in the erection alone. The steam-engines of England, worked by 36,000 men, would raise the same quantity of material to the same height in eighteen hours. Thus reckoning ten hours to the day, and three hundred working days to the year, three thousand pyramids might be erected by the steam-power of England in the period occupied by the builders of that of Ghizeh.

The multiplication, in the course of years, by fiftyfold of the working power of England caused such an enormous increase of material that privy councils, armies, and fleets vied with each other in explorations by sea and land. The Northwest Passage, which has a literature and a history of its own—a history exultant and yet sad—only meant a short road to India around one end of that terribly long continent which barred Europe from sailing westward to Asia.

There is no more truthful accessible test of the comparative ingenuity of periods in a given country than the number of patents granted therein. Our national patent system has been in operation only since 1790, but that of England is much older. The following table gives the numbers of patents granted in decades for the two centuries.

Previous to 1790 patents were granted by individual States, as to Fulton, Fitch, Rumsey, Evans, and others.

Decade ending	England.	Decade ending	England.	United States.
1680	49	1780	297	....
1690	55	1790	512	....
1700	101	1800	675	306
1710	20	1810	936	1,086
1720	45	1820	1,125	1,748
1730	94	1830	1,533	2,986
1740	48	1840	2,710	5,488
1750	85	1850	4,666	5,942
1760	99	1860	25,201	23,140
1770	221	1870	35,079	79,612

The factory system is the growth of the century now closing. When Richard Arkwright was traveling over the hills of Lancashire, buying the tresses of the country lasses to make wigs, and Hargreaves was working at the rudimentary carding-machine, the artisans of the country worked each in his little shop. The wool-stapler dealt out his lots of wool to the carders and spinners, who took it home and returned the agreed-upon quality and weight of yarn; to another set of workmen the yarn was apportioned for weaving; other tradesmen finished the work. The same practice prevailed with the hardware makers and ironmongers; the nailers of Wolverhampton, the artificers of Birmingham, the cutlers of Sheffield, the carpet-weavers of Axminster—each received at his house a quota of material such as he or his family could make up in a few days, and returned the finished work to his employer. It is easy to imagine how this may have been managed, for it is only within a comparatively few years that the business of boot and shoe making has been aggregated into factories and performed by machinery.

In the factory the labor-saving machines which have superseded the laborious hand operations are employed in great numbers with comparatively few attendants. The steam-engine, fed by coal and water, or the water-wheel, provides the power required, and the duty of the attendant is to supply the constantly recurring need for fresh materials, to mend breaks, or repair faults. Instead of being a mere fashioner of a piece at a time, the workman becomes a supervisor of nearly automatic machinery, whose appetite for material he is required to anticipate and satisfy, and whose occasional eccentricities it is his duty to correct.

The development of the cotton manufacture furnishes the best and perhaps earliest example of the factory system. Arkwright appears to have worked at his cotton machinery for several years, and in company with several partners, who successively furnished means and then tired of the project, before he erected the mill at Nottingham, which was worked by horse-power. This mill was erected in 1770; another one was established in 1771, in which the machinery was driven by a water-wheel. So new was the idea of employing other than hand or foot labor that his spinning-machine was long known as the "water-frame," and the product as the "water-twist." His other improvements were patented in 1775, and thus the century starts with Mr. Arkwright fresh upon the track, leading in a race the success of which has changed the aspect of our commercial and social systems.

Arkwright, in spite of fraudulent trespassers and expensive lawsuits, lived to see the perfect triumph of his ingenuity and sedulous care. His suits developed the conditions and situations which taxed the wisdom of the judges, and elicited the decisions and maxims that have given shape to the patent system of England and the United States. Arkwright *v.* Nightingale, the King *v.* Arkwright, are cases that form the "hard pan" of the Patent Law.

We shall see how well the facts of the various branches of invention arrange themselves within the period we are considering—how the rank and file of inventions array themselves in battalions, brigades, divisions, on one side of the line chronological. Turn we to steam in its original form as a pumping engine, or to its subsequent duties as a transporting agent on water or on the land, or as a driver of machinery; or look we abroad to other lines of enterprise and industry—the manufacture of cotton and wool, the production and manufacture of iron, wood-working machinery, hydraulic engineering, the manufacture and applications of gas, electricity in its various forms and applications, the construction of instruments of measurement and precision, domestic machinery—we find that each group forms in regimental order within the bounds we have indicated.

This, though unexampled, was not fortuitous; the time was ripe. Yet there was but slight indication beforehand of the new departure. It was as if by a mysterious impulse all started at once, the utilization of the buried stores of coal by means of the Watt engine being the great fact of the new dispensation.

The field is too great to give even a brief account of each division, and a few must be selected as examples from which the general progress may be deduced.

AGRICULTURAL IMPLEMENTS.

There is no apology needed for beginning our review with farming implements. However disinclined a citizen may be to blister his hands by chopping fire-wood or mauling rails, he freely admits the respectability of the employment and its ancient fame. Admitting, then, the precedence of the husbandman, we will first look at the principal agricultural tool—the plow.

This tool has never outgrown its resemblance to the forked limb which was first used as a hoe and then as a plow. With such tools as they could muster, men shaped the tough limbs and crotches of trees into implements. The forked piece (A) was trimmed and became the hoe (B), a thong binding the handle and blade portions to prevent their splitting apart. We give pictures (C) of two ancient Egyptian hoes now in the Berlin Museum. A similar one may be seen in the Abbott Museum, New York. Two suitable sticks (D) were notched and lashed together. Two other resources of a people destitute of metal are shown (E, F), one, of the South Sea Islanders, the blade made of a scapula, the other made of a walrus tooth on a handle. It is shown (G, H, I) how men made plows from similar materials; one limb formed the share, the other the beam; or (as in I) one the beam and the other the handle and sole, with a point which forms the share.

The actual change in the plow for more than thirty centuries has been but local. The greater part of the world uses a plow much like those pictured on the palaces of Thebes. Those used in our colonial period were a very slight departure from that pattern. The plow was of wood; it was formed of pieces whose shape adapted them to become parts of the structure. The beam, standard, and handles—if the plow had two,

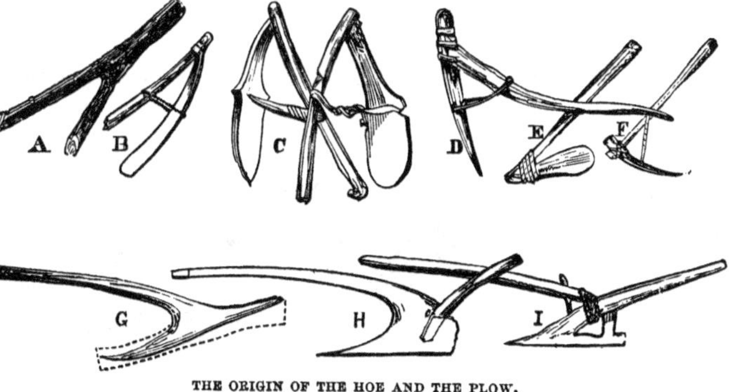

THE ORIGIN OF THE HOE AND THE PLOW.

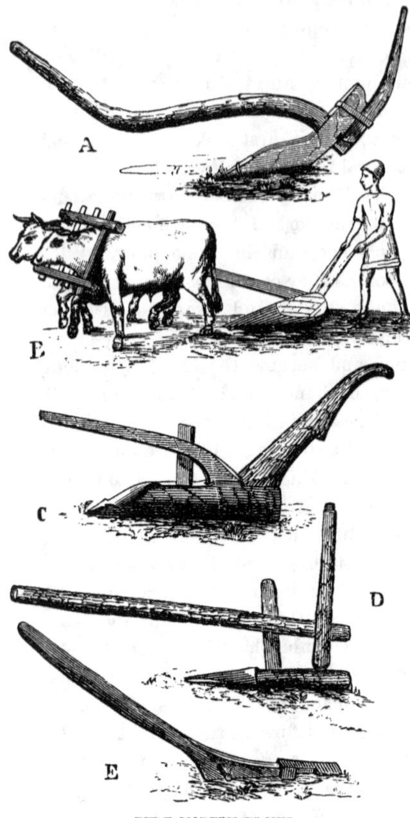

RUDE MODERN PLOWS.

A, an East Indian plow. B, a modern Egyptian plow. C, a Mexican plow. D, a Chinese plow. E, an ancient British implement, which yet survives in the western wilds of Scotland. The latter is pointed with iron, and may have been the origin of the *bull-tongue* plow, more familiar to men of '76 than to the farmer of the present day.

which was not always the case—were of seasoned stuff; the mould-board was a block of wood which had a winding grain approximating the curve required.

The accompanying figures show a number of plows yet used in some foreign countries. These differ in no essential respect from plows shown on the tombs of Egypt, the vases of Etruria, the bass-reliefs of Greece, and the medals of Rome. The plows of the south of France, of Spain, of Calabria, Greece, Turkey, and Syria are very similar.

The plow of the past is now utterly abandoned by us, and we have a new tool of a different material, still, however, preserving the peculiar family feature; it will never get over the resemblance to that primordial limb.

The plow of 1776 was all of wood except the wrought iron share and some bolts and nuts whereby the parts were fastened together. The standard rose nearly vertically, having attached to it the beam and the sole-piece. On the nose of the beam hung the clevis; the mould-board and share were attached to a frame braced between the beam and the sole. The wooden mould-board was sometimes plated with sheet-iron or by strips made by hammering out old horseshoes. A clump of iron shaped like a half spear formed the point. It was known as a "bull plow," "bull-tongue," or "bar-share" plow. Two pins in the standard formed the handles, and it required the strength of a man to manage it. The work was slowly and ill performed by cattle.

The shovel plow, which until lately was the principal plow of the South, and is yet largely used in furrowing out ground for hoed crops, such as corn, cane, and potatoes, and in tending the same, is clearly a derivative from the old crotched stick.

The order of improvement is about as follows: Some time in the last century a certain plow was imported into England, probably from Flanders, which had been long far in advance of England in gardening and horticulture. Queen Elizabeth used to get salads from Flanders as a change from the interminable beef and beer. This implement was known as the *Rotherham* plow; but whether the name was a corruption of Rotterdam no one knows. It was a very tidy implement in shape, but was all of wood, with the exception of a sheet-iron covering to the working parts. This required frequent renewal. James Small, of Berwickshire, Scotland, introduced the

AMERICAN PLOW OF 1776.

plow (*a*) with a cast iron mould-board and a wrought iron share. His was the first cast iron plow. He made the shares also of cast iron in 1785.

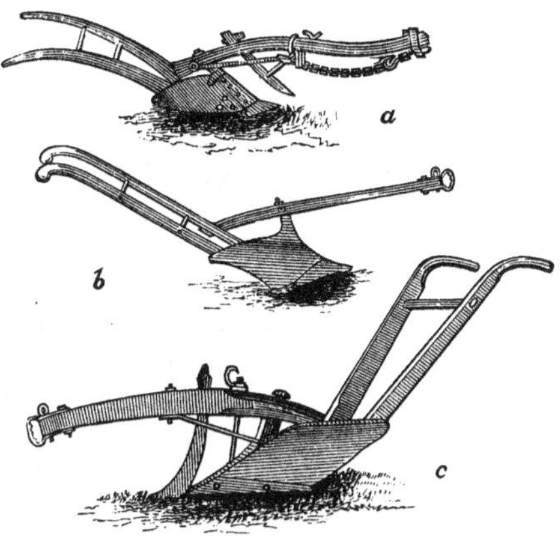

PLOWS: 1785–1874.

a, Small's. *b*, Wood's. *c*, Gibbs's.

Thomas Jefferson from 1788 to 1793 studied and experimented to determine the proper shape of the mould-board to do the work effectively and offer the least resistance, treating it as consisting of a lifting wedge and an upsetting wedge, with an easy connecting curve.

Newbold, of Burlington, New Jersey, in 1797 patented a plow with a mould-board, share, and land-side all cast together.

Peacock in his patent of 1807 cast his plow in three pieces, the point of the colter entering a notch in the breast of the share.

Ransome, of Ipswich, England, in 1803 chilled the cast shares on the under side, so that they might keep sharp by wear.

Jethro Wood, of Scipio, Cayuga County, New York, patented improvements in 1819. He made the best and most popular plow (*b*) of its day, and was entitled to much credit for skill and enterprise, but lost his fortune in developing his invention and defending his rights. He, however, overestimated the extent of novelty in his invention. He seems to have thought it the first iron plow. Its peculiar merit consisted in the mode of securing the cast iron portions together by lugs and locking pieces, doing away with screw-bolts and much weight, complexity, and expense. Wood did more than any other person to drive out of use the cumbrous contrivances common throughout the country, giving a lighter, cheaper, and more effective implement. It was the first plow in which the parts most exposed to wear could be renewed in the field by the substitution of cast pieces.

In 1820 Timothy Pickering, of Salem, Massachusetts, first recognized the importance of straight transverse lines on the mould-board. The shape was such that it might be cut from a conical frustum.

In 1854 the Gibbs plow (*c*) had its straight transverse lines horizontal, the surface from which it might be cut being a cylinder with its axis horizontal.

The Howard plow shows the favorite style of plow in England. The long stilts give great power to the plowman. The wheels determine the depth accurately, except in short and sudden rises and hollows.

It is impossible here to describe the minor improvements of this implement, great as is the sum of their importance—the rolling colter, the wheel which takes the place of the sliding sole, adaptations for setting the plow for *depth* and for *land*, to prevent clogging, etc.

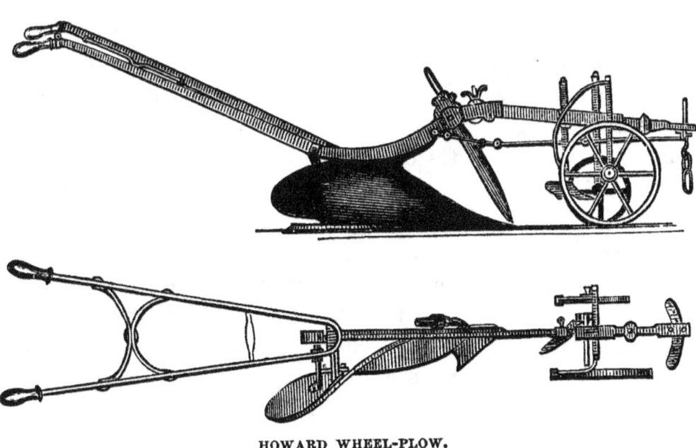

HOWARD WHEEL-PLOW.

Aaron Smith, of England, first made that form of double plow which has a small advance share and mould-board to turn over the sod, followed by the usual share and mould-board to invert the furrow-slice, and thus completely bury the surface soil. It is

FOWLER'S STEAM-PLOW.

now much used in England, and is especially made by Ransome. In the West it is called the double Michigan plow.

Substitutes for the plow are found in spading machines, which aim to do the work more in the order of hand spading, which is confessedly better than plowing. They are not likely to supersede plows. Other forms of substitutes are the various cultivators, known by the local names of *grubbers*, *scarifiers*, *horse-hoes*, etc., their action being to drag teeth or small shares through the ground to loosen and aerate it, giving it a tilth suitable for sowing or planting. They are also used for stirring the ground in the balks between rows of growing plants, known as *hoed* crops, such as corn, cane, or potatoes, but the more a man sticks to his cultivator, and the less he bothers with the hoe, the better will be the result, if the amount of the planting be large.

The steam-plow has proved a success under favorable circumstances. Few are at work in the United States; many hundreds in England. A large number were sent to Egypt, where the Khedive is determined to be a second Pharaoh on the old order announced by Joseph, who bought the personal property, then the land, then the people, and then rented the land to them for a fifth of the produce—the same share as Solomon received for his vineyard.

Steam-plows are constructed on several principles:

1. A traction engine dragging plows: this is not a success as yet.

2. A pair of engines on trucks on the sides of the field, and dragging gangs of plows back and forth, the engines moving a piece ahead between each pull. The cut shows a modified form with a single engine, endless rope, and a traveling truck on the opposite side of the field to carry the pulley over which the rope runs and returns.

3. A single engine, and ropes so arranged around the field on bearers, known as *porters*, as to drag the plow-gang in any required direction by suitably changing the position of the porters which determine the direction of motion of the rope.

The improvements in seeding machines and grain drills have effected a saving of seed, more careful planting or sowing, and greater economy in labor.

One hundred years ago our fathers toiled in the harvest field with the sickle. In Flanders they had a kind of cradle known as the Hainault scythe, but it was unknown to English-speaking peoples. The bent back, the gathering left arm, and the sweeping sickle painfully reaped the bunches of grain, which were thrown into heaps large enough to form gavels for binding. The cradle was a great improvement upon the sickle, the long and deep-reaching blade of the grain scythe, aided by the fingers of the cradle, making a progress in the harvest field which left the sickle and reaping-hook far in the rear.

The American War of Independence was not long over before attempts were made to construct machines which would bring into use horse labor as a substitute for the severe hand-work.

The reaping machine has attained its present degree of completeness after seventy-five years of persistent effort. General attention had been but little directed to the subject until the year 1851, when at the World's Fair in London the American machines created much excitement, and caused the forgotten experiments of half a century to be withdrawn from their limboes and exhibited to cool the enthusiasm of "those foreigners." Experiments in reaping machines had been pursued to a much greater extent in Britain than in the United States until within a then comparatively recent period; but the essential features which secured success were American.

The first reaping machine on record is that described by Pliny about A.D. 60, and by Palladius some centuries later. It is stated by these authors to have been used in Gaul; the former writer says in the extensive plains in that part known as Rhætia. It consisted of a cart pushed by an ox, and having a comb-like bar in front which stripped off the ears of the wheat and allowed them to fall into the box, while the straw remained on the ground. It was used in level places, and where the straw was not wanted for winter fodder. The implement has been re-invented after the lapse of fourteen centuries, and is now used as a "header" for gathering clover seed.

After this Gallic implement there is a long gap, and the first machine, or rather suggestion, of the moderns is that of Pitt, in 1786, which had a cylinder with rows of combs or "ripples," which tore off the ears and discharged them into the box of the machine.

It is a part of our purpose to show the cumulative character of invention, and also to illustrate the fact that nearly the whole aim seems to be fixed in a particular direction for a long course of years; then the germ of the eventual success enters unexpectedly, and remains unnoticed for a period, after which the interest is transferred to the previously overlooked type, which in its immature form gave little prospect of success.

For about twoscore years attention was principally directed to revolving cutters or systems of revolving blades. The motion of the cutting apparatus being derived from the rotary motion of the wheels supporting the implement, it naturally occurred to connect the axle or wheels with a rotary cutter, and later with an oscillating one, which had its analogues in the swing of the scythe and the reach of the sickle. The first reciprocating knife was in 1822.

As to the mode of attaching the horses, it was almost universally deemed necessary to hitch them behind the implement, which they pushed before them. Up to 1823 but four inventors hitched the team in front of the implement. As soon as this idea did occur to inventors, they made the horse walk alongside the swath cut by the knives, constituting what is known as the *side cut.*

In 1806 Gladstone, of England, patented his *front-draft side-cut* revolving-knife machine. A segment *bar* with *fingers* gathered the grain and held the straw while the knife

REAPING IN GAUL, FIRST TO FOURTH CENTURY A.D.

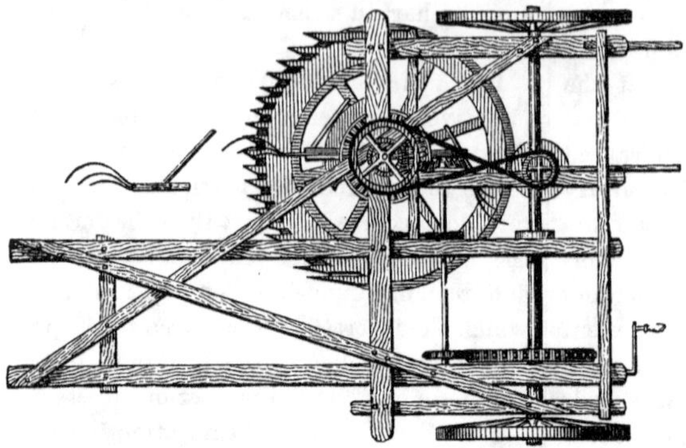

GLADSTONE'S REAPING MACHINE, ENGLAND, 1806.

the grain, which was laid over to the cutter by a revolving reel. A *divider* was used on each end of the platform. The driver and raker had seats on the machine.

In 1849 Haines, of Illinois, suspended the frame carrying the conveyer, reel, and cutter to the axles of the bearing-wheels, and hinged the frame to the tongue, so that it was capable of turning upon its bearings by means of a lever to elevate and depress the cutter.

cut it, the fingers having the function of shear blades. The forward draft was also adopted by Mann in 1820, and by Ogle, of England, in 1822, who shows the first *reciprocating knife bar*. It is the type of the successful machines, but was constructed so poorly that its merits never became apparent. It was drawn by horses *in advance;* the cutter bar *projected* at the *side*, and it had a *reel* to gather the grain to the cutter. The machine had a *grain platform*, which was tilted to drop the gavel. This was the *first dropper*. In 1826 Bell made a working machine. It was pushed before the horse; the grain was cut by *knives vibrating* on *pivots*. It had a grain reel; the grain fell upon an *inclined traveling apron*, which carried it off and delivered it at the side.

In 1828 Samuel Lane, of Maine, combined the reaper and the thresher.

In 1833 Hussey, of Maryland, made the first valuable harvester. It had open fingers, with the knife reciprocating in the space. The open-topped slotted finger was patented by Hussey in 1847. The cutter bar was on a hinged frame.

In 1834 M'Cormick, of Virginia, patented his reaper, which, with various improvements in 1845 and 1847, received a Council medal at the London World's Fair in 1851. This machine had a sickle-edged sectional knife reciprocated by crank and pitman by gear connection to the drive-wheel on which the frame rested; spear-shaped fingers gathered

BELL'S REAPING MACHINE, ENGLAND, 1826.

Since 1851 nearly 3000 patents have been granted in the United States for harvesters and attachments therefor.

In the summer of 1855, at a competitive trial of reapers, about forty miles from Paris, France, three machines were exhibited from America, England, and Algiers. The following was the result in a field of oats: the American machine cut an acre in twenty-two minutes; the English machine cut an acre in sixty-six minutes; the Algerian machine cut an acre in seventy-two minutes.

Some of the subsequent improvements may be enumerated as follows: The Sylla and Adams patent (1853), having a cutter bar hinged to a frame, which is in turn hinged to the main frame. This is the principal feature of the "Aultman and Miller," or "Buckeye," harvester. The combined rake and reel of the "Dorsey" machine (1856), sweeping in a general horizontal direction across the quadrantal platform. The "Henderson" rake, on what is known as the "Wood" machine (1860), having a chain below the platform, which carries the rake in a curved path. The Sieberling "dropper" (1861), which is a slatted platform vibrating to discharge the gavel. The Whiteley pat-

THE AMERICAN SELF-RAKING REAPING MACHINE ("CHAMPION" PATTERN).

ents, which constitute the "Champion" machine of Springfield, Ohio.

The threshing machine first saw the light in 1786. It was invented by Andrew Meikle, of Tyningham, East Lothian, Scotland. It is true that attempts had been made by Menzies in 1732 and Stirling in 1758, but they proceeded on a wrong principle, and were abandoned. Menzies's had a series of revolving flails, and Stirling's had a cylinder with arms upon a vertical shaft running at high velocity. Meikle invented the drum

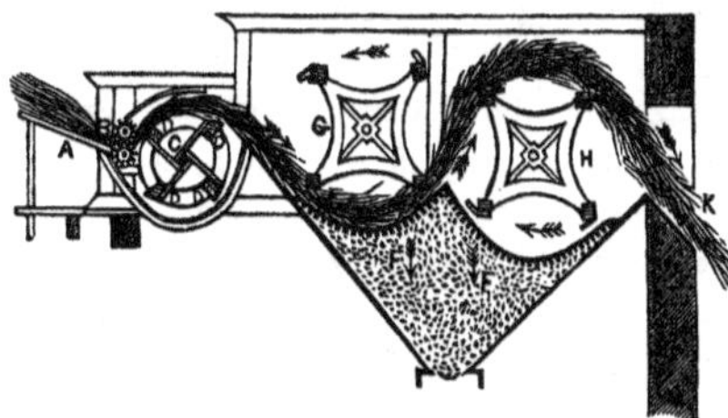

MEIKLE'S THRESHING MACHINE, 1786—INTERIOR VIEW.

with beaters acting upon the grain in the sheaf, which was fed between rollers. The English improvement was to make the beating drum work in a concave known as the *breasting*, the grain and straw being scutched and rubbed between the two and carried to the shaker, which removed the straw from the grain and chaff, a large amount of grain also falling through the bars of the concave.

The American improvement upon this consists mainly—besides numerous details which secure speed, lightness, and effectiveness—in having upon the drum, spikes or teeth which pass between fixed spikes on the concave; the grain in the straw being subjected to a severe beating and rubbing action as it passes in a zigzag course between the two, being carried by the teeth of the drum. The latter is now usually a skeleton cylinder of iron bars with sword-shaped spikes secured by threaded tangs and nuts. The front edges of the spikes are rounded and smooth to prevent breaking of the grain; the spikes of the concave have smooth edges presented toward the coming grain for a similar reason. The English still adhere to the flat beaters, like narrow wings or slats, placed longitudinally, and with edges projecting outwardly from the drum. The Americans adhere to the spiked cylinder. A fair trial between the two was had on the farm of Mr. Mechi, Tiptree Hall, Kelvedon, England, in 1853. The American machine was operated by the two persons who had shipped it from the United States; one of them was the present writer. The trial was conclusive. The American machine was driven by a portable engine of six horse-power, and averaged sixty-four bushels of wheat per

THE AMERICAN THRESHING MACHINE.

ENGLISH THRESHING MACHINE.

hour; 448 bushels of barley were threshed in six hours, nearly treble the work of the English competing machines, and the grain in much cleaner condition.

The editor of the London *Times*, Mr. Mowbray Morris, himself witnessed the operation, and wrote as follows in an editorial of the following day, November 1, 1853:

"The machine, which is portable, weighs only fourteen hundred-weight, threshes easily, and without waste, at the rate of one bushel in forty seconds, and turns out the grain perfectly clean and ready for market. It is therefore about twice as light in draught as the lightest of our machines of the same description; does as much if not more work than the best of them, and, with much less power, dresses the grain, which they do not, and can be profitably disposed of at less money than our implement-makers charge.....We build threshing-machines strong and dear enough and tremendously heavy either to work or to draw. The American farmer demands and gets a machine which does not ruin him to buy or his horse to pull about, which runs on coach and not wagon wheels, and which, without breaking the heart of the power that drives it, yields the largest and most satisfactory results. Nothing, therefore, can better illustrate the difference in mechanical genius in the two countries than this grain separator as compared with its British rivals."

It may be mentioned that the apparent perversity with which the British retain flat beaters instead of the teeth is that in many parts of Britain there is a profitable market for trussed straw; the straw is less broken by the beaters than by the teeth, is in more unbroken lengths, and trusses more readily and handsomely.

The saving in the operations of husbandry by the use of modern implements and methods is equal to one-half the former cost of working. By the improved plow, labor equivalent to that of one horse in three is saved. By means of drills two bushels of seed will go as far as three bushels scattered broadcast. The plants come up in rows, and may be tended by horse-hoes; being in the bottoms of little furrows, the ground crumbles down against the plant, which is not so readily *heaved out* by the winter's frost. The reaping machine is a saving of more than one-third the labor when it cuts and rakes, and will eventually save fully three-fourths when it is made to bind automatically, as it shortly will be. The threshing machine is a saving of two-thirds on the old hand-flail mode. The root-cutters for stock in England, and in some places in the Northern States and Canada, much reduce the labor of winter feeding. The saving in the labor of handling hay in the field and barn by means of horse-rakes and horse hay-forks is equal to one-half. With the exception of the grain drill, which had a precarious existence previous to 1776, all these improvements have been commenced and brought to the present relative perfection within the century now closing.

THE STEAM-ENGINE AND ITS APPLICATIONS.

We have no space for the repetition of the history of the steam-engine—to recite the toys and experiments of Hero, Da Vinci, De Garay, Porta, the mythical De Caus, the water-raising apparatus, not engines, of Worcester and Savary, and the engine of Papin, in which steam was first used against a piston in a cylinder.

Our century opens with the engine of Newcomen in action, as shown on page 41. This engine had a vertical open-topped cylinder above the boiler. It had two valves, which were operated by hand; one admitted steam below the piston, which was raised by the weight of the pump-rod. The steam having filled the space below the piston, was then shut off, and the valve of the water-injection pipe was opened. The jet of water condensed the steam in the cylinder, and produced a partial vacuum therein; the weight of the atmosphere pressed down the piston, and raised the pump-rod. This was really quite excellent in its way, and the atmospheric engine is yet a very useful pumping engine. It was as great an advance on Captain John Savary's water elevator as James Watt's subsequent improvement was upon itself. To recite its faults and inefficiencies—for it had both—is but to recite the inventions of Watt.

Watt's first patent was taken out in 1769, in conjunction with a Mr. Roebuck, who afterward retired from the partnership, and Watt found an excellent successor to him in Matthew Boulton, of Soho, near Birmingham.

The fame of the steam-engine traveled to the English colonies even before the date of the invention of Watt, but, for such mills as the colonists erected, the water-powers on the streams were yet abundantly sufficient. It is doubtful whether there were more than

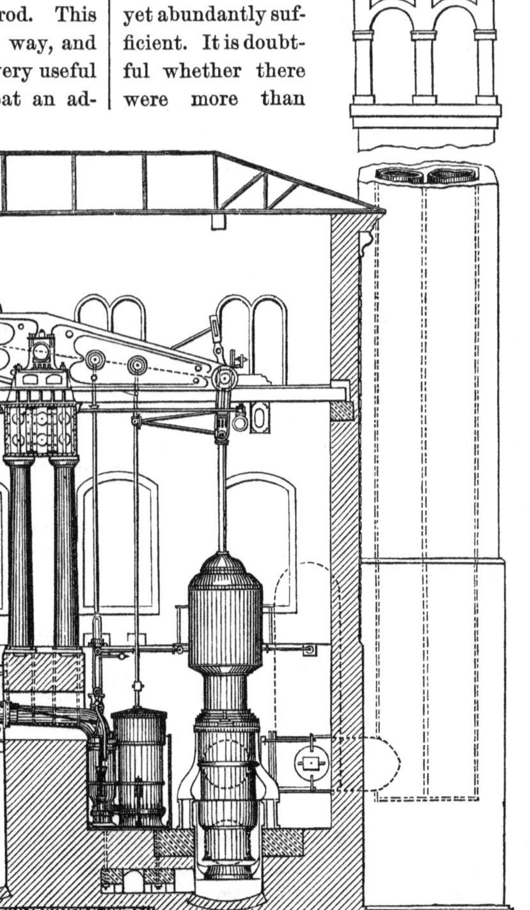

SINGLE-ACTING CORNISH PUMPING ENGINE.

two steam-engines in the colonies. They were both of the Newcomen kind. One was imported in 1736 for the Schuyler copper mines at Passaic, New Jersey; the other was built in 1772 by Christopher Coles, of Philadelphia, for use in a distillery.

The principal use, for a long time, of the steam-engine in England continued to be in pumps for draining mines and for supplying water to cities. London for this latter purpose had a Boulton and Watt engine in the vicinity of London Bridge. This type of engine has permanently received its name from the locality of its first triumphs, and is known as the Cornish. It is the largest, heaviest, most expensive, and most economically driven engine known to the engineer —a valuable stationary engine when parties are capable of spending a large sum to secure a machine which may be run at a small outlay. It is a large investment of capital for the sake of an economic administration. The one shown in the illustration on the previous page is a single-acting Cornish engine. The cylinder is 100 inches in diameter; working stroke, 11 feet; the plunger is 50 inches in diameter, 11 feet stroke. When working full stroke it pumps 150 gallons per second to a height of 140 feet.

The Louisville pumping engine is of this character. The new engines at Brooklyn and Cincinnati are direct, the pump being below the cylinder. Spring Garden, Philadelphia, and Belleville, New Jersey, have the Cornish; Cambridge, Massachusetts, and Newark, New Jersey, the Worthington Duplex. Of the 115,000,000 of gallons forming the daily supply of London, 79,000,000 gallons are pumped by the class of engine shown in the illustration.

The improvement in the Cornish engine is capable of being more definitely stated than that of any other form, for it has been closely observed and tabulated for many years. The figures express what is called the *duty*. This term was adopted by Watt to express the actual amount of water lifted one foot by the bushel of coal. The *duty*, therefore, is the test of comparative merit of engines, and the figures following clearly indicate the improvement in the Cornish pumping engine:

Year.	Pounds, 1 foot high.
1769, the Newcomen engine	5,500,000
1772, Newcomen engine, improved by Smeaton	9,500,000
1778 to 1815, Watt engine	20,000,000
1820, improved Cornish, average duty of a large number of engines	28,000,000
1826, improved Cornish, average duty	30,000,000
1830, improved Cornish, average duty	43,350,000
1839, improved Cornish, average duty	54,000,000
1850, improved Cornish, average duty	60,000,000

There are some brilliant instances above these averages, as of the

"Consolidated" mines, highest duty, 1827	67,000,000
"Fowey Consols" mines, highest duty, 1842	97,000,000

The *duty* of the best American pumping engines runs well up with these figures.

Steam was first applied to drive cotton machinery by Richard Arkwright, in England, in 1785, and to grind plaster and saw stone by Oliver Evans, in Philadelphia, about the same time. It was many years before the steam-engine was applied in the United States to factory use, but that application of the engine rapidly increased in England. It was Watt's engine in substantial respects, though other persons increased and harmonized the proportions, giving it a power and completeness far beyond what its admirable inventor lived personally to witness.

STEAM NAVIGATION.

The steam-engine was used for transportation on the water before it was adapted to land carriages. This was owing to its having started as an atmospheric engine, where the force was derived from the pressure of air upon the piston when a partial vacuum was produced by the condensation of steam in the cylinder. The engine was relatively large and heavy, and in its proportions was better suited to a boat than to a wagon. The use of high-pressure steam was an afterthought. Though Watt, with his singular sagacity, added to his specification the idea of adapting high-pressure steam to the purposes of river and land locomotion, it was but as a caveat, for he built none.

The origin of the steamboat has been a vexed question for nearly a century. As the parties who first worked at the problem with success could not apportion among themselves the exact measure of credit to which each was entitled, so by carefully fanning the flames of national vanity the subject has been kept afloat, and of three nations each has its advocates, who feel bound to depreciate the claims of all others. The truth is, the engine was Newcomen's, and then Watt's, and the boat was any body's; and persons went to work here and there, with varying degrees of success, depending upon political influence, social standing, moneyed resources, or friends thus provided, and last, not least, mechanical talent for harnessing the engine to the paddle or propeller used to push against the water.

In this struggle great pertinacity was exhibited in Scotland and America. To deal out the exact proportion of credit due to each man is not easy; one measure is to be awarded to skill in mechanical adaptation, another to skill in fitting and proportioning.

In 1780 was patented the present arrangement of connecting-rod, crank, and fly-wheel. The Marquis de Jouffroy in that year successfully worked a steamboat 140 feet long on the Saône. Joseph Bramah (1785) patented a rotatory engine on a propeller shaft. Here occurs the term "screw-propeller," since so common. In 1787 Patrick Miller, of Dalswinton, published a specification of a triple boat, with paddles in the intervals, and a deck over the three boats. The same year a double boat was steamed on the Frith of Forth. John Fitch, of Philadelphia, the next year obtained a patent for the application of steam to navigation in Pennsylvania, New York, New Jersey, and Delaware. The boat had vertical reciprocating paddles, and made eighty miles per day. It proceeded upon an entirely wrong principle.

In 1802 Symington ran the *Charlotte Dundas* on the Forth and Clyde Canal. She had a double-acting Watt engine, working by a connecting-rod to a crank on the paddle-wheel shaft. This is the first instance of these parts being thus combined.

SYMINGTON'S STEAMBOAT, "CHARLOTTE DUNDAS."

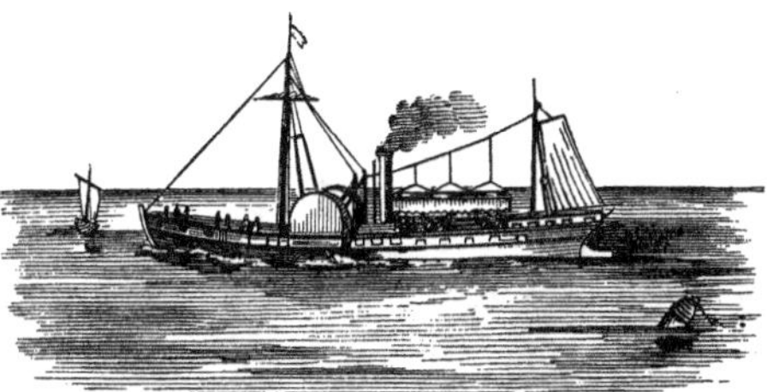

FULTON'S STEAMBOAT, "CLERMONT," 1807.

The idea of canal use alone engaged the inventor, and the boat was rejected because the canal banks were likely to be damaged.

In 1804 John Cox Stevens, of New Jersey, constructed a boat on the Hudson, driven by a Watt engine, with a tubular boiler of his own invention. It had a bladed screw-propeller. The same year Oliver Evans had a stern-paddle-wheel boat on the Delaware and Schuylkill rivers. It was driven by a double-acting high-pressure steam-engine, which was the first of its kind, and was geared to rotate the wheels by which the boat was moved on land, and driven in the water when the power was transferred to the paddle-wheel at the stern.

In 1807 Robert Fulton, of New York, went from that city to Albany in the *Clermont*, a boat of 160 tons burden, with side paddle-wheels, driven by an engine which he purchased when in England of Boulton and Watt. She ran during the remainder of the year as a passenger boat. She was the first that ran for practical purposes, and proved of value. The outside bearing of the paddle-wheel shaft and the guard were invented by Fulton. The boat may be considered to have been about the sixteenth steamboat; nevertheless the popular verdict is a just and righteous one. To Fulton much more than to any other one man is due the credit of the introduction of steam navigation. His enterprise opened the way, and he was the first to apportion the strength and sizes of parts to the respective strains and duties. He had previously seen Symington's boat, and had launched an experimental one, 66 feet long, on the Seine. The former may have directed his attention to the matter, and the latter was a useful apprenticeship. Mr. Charles Brown had built for Mr. Fulton, between 1806 and 1812, six steamboats of lengths varying from 78

BELL'S STEAMBOAT, "COMET," 1812.

to 175 feet, and tonnage 120 to 337, prior to the practical working of any steamboat in Europe.

The first steamboat in the Mississippi Valley was the *Orleans*, of 100 tons, built at Pittsburg by Fulton and Livingston in 1811. She had a stern wheel, and went from Pittsburg to New Orleans in fourteen days. The next was the *Comet*, of 25 tons, in 1814. She made three or four trips, was taken to pieces, and the engine was set up in a cotton factory. The *Vesuvius*, in 1814, was the next. She made a number of trips, but eventually exploded.

Henry Bell, of Scotland, in 1812 built the *Comet*, of 30 tons, with side paddle-wheels, which plied between Glasgow and Greenock on the Clyde, and the next year around the coasts of the British Isles.

In 1818 the *Walk-in-the-Water*, of 360 tons, was built at Black Rock, Niagara River, by Noah Brown, of New York, for traffic on the lakes. Her Boulton and Watt engine was made in New York and transported by boat to Albany and by teams to Black Rock. The boilers were prepared in New York and sent piecemeal to the lake. The vessel was lost in a gale in 1821.

In 1819 the *Savannah*, 380 tons burden, crossed the Atlantic from America, visited Liverpool, St. Petersburg, and Copenhagen, and returned. Six years later the *Enterprise* rounded the Cape of Good Hope and went to India.

In 1838 the *Great Western* (1340 tons) and the *Sirius* steamed across the Atlantic from England. Two years afterward the Cunard line was started, and was followed by the Collins line in 1850. The *Great Eastern* was built in 1858, the French iron-clad *La Gloire* in 1859, the English iron-clad *Warrior* in 1860, and the Ericsson *Monitor* in 1862.

Feathering paddle-wheels, such as Morgan's, were largely used in the British navy. Manly's are somewhat noted here. Holland's oblique paddle float, and many others, might be noted were there room for detail.

The steamboats of our American rivers and lakes have no equals in the world, nor are there such waters elsewhere to afford a theatre for such boats.

The paddle-wheel has to a large extent given place to the screw-propeller. There is perhaps but one paddle-wheel steamer in the United States navy, the *Powhatan*.

The screw-propeller was invented by numerous people, if we are to assume that each person who put forward a claim or who patented it supposed himself to be an original inventor. Several notices of it occur, but it came more distinctly into notice when brought forward by Ericsson in 1836.

PACIFIC MAIL STEAM-SHIP COMPANY'S SCREW STEAM-SHIP "CITY OF PEKING."

The supernaturally wise old sea-dogs and landsmen of the British Admiralty sneered at the innovation, but Captain Robert F. Stockton and Francis B. Ogden, of New Jersey, appreciated it. The former introduced it to the United States Navy Department, and the war steamer *Princeton* was launched upon the Delaware. The *Robert F. Stockton*, an iron vessel fitted with a screw-propeller, was launched upon the Mersey in 1838, and crossed to the United States the next year. Her name was changed to *New Jersey*, and she was the first screw-propeller vessel practically used in America, as Ericsson's *Francis B. Ogden* was the first in Europe. Ericsson accomplished for the screw-propeller in England and America what Fulton did for the paddle-wheel in America and Bell in England.

Other improvements have been added, including Woodcroft's increasing pitch screw and Fowler's and Hunter's vertical submerged paddle-wheels.

THE LOCOMOTIVE.

It is not easy from the stand-point of the present to realize the original difficulty in adapting the steam-engine to the propulsion of carriages. There was a fixed belief in regard to steam, derived from the mode of using it in the atmospheric engine of Newcomen and from the cautious habit of Watt, that the safest method was merely to obtain a vacuum by its condensation, so as to bring the unbalanced atmospheric pressure upon one side of the piston. This involved a great weight and bulk of machinery, and long prevented the adaptation of the engine to land transportation. The steamboat engine used by Miller, of Dalswinton, in 1787 differed from Watt's in the saving of weight by the abolition of the air-pump, and depended upon abundant injection of water to produce a vacuum. Watt was afraid of high-pressure steam, and we can fancy, had he lived to be on board one of our Western river boats, and heard the energetic cough of the escaping steam, he would have wished himself safely back again with Brother Boulton, and among the models and drawing-boards of his sanctum at the "Soho Works." He had no faith in an engine without a condenser, and, as the event proved, no steam-carriage could succeed till the weight of the engine was reduced by the removal of the condenser, air-pump, and their cumbrous appendages, even at the expense of greater cost of fuel in working.

This situation continued until 1802, when two Cornish engineers, Trevethick and Vivian, obtained a patent for a steam-carriage adapted for common roads, or, by an adaptation of the tires of the wheels, for railways. The engine was built, and was tried and modified till 1805, when it became a useful locomotive on the Merthyr-Tydvil Railway, in South Wales, in drawing coal cars. It is the most remarkable engine in the history of the locomotive. It had a horizontal cylinder inclosed in the boiler, the piston and rod operating a crank axle, which communicated power through gear wheels to the axle of the driving-wheels.

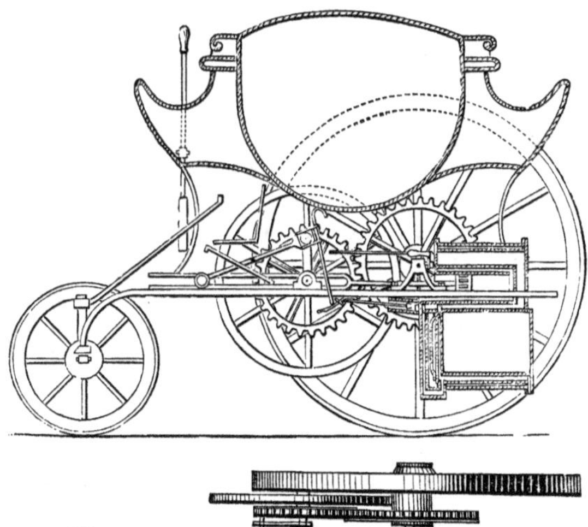

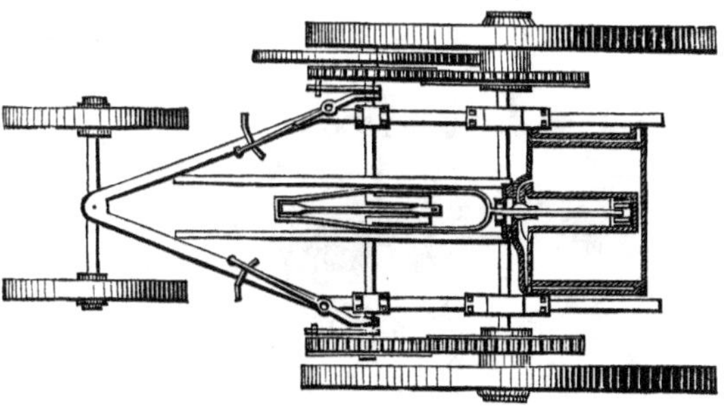

TREVETHICK AND VIVIAN'S LOCOMOTIVE, MERTHYR-TYDVIL, 1805.

EVANS'S LOCOMOTIVE.

It was high-pressure, non-condensing, and exhausted into the chimney. (The latter is not shown in their official drawing.) It was the first locomotive to run on tram-ways or on rails. The steam-cocks were operated from the crank axle, as were also the feed-pump and the bellows for urging the fire. The body of the carriage followed the old English stage shape. It was not alone that these men devised several features that experience has retained, but they were the first to disregard the prejudice against high steam, and to make a compact engine which would neither overtax the wheels nor take up all the room, to the exclusion of passengers and goods.

Oliver Evans, of Philadelphia, labored for a number of years to obtain help to construct his high-pressure engine, which was built in 1802 for running a marble saw and plaster mill, and in 1804 was adapted to a scow for dredging in the Delaware River.

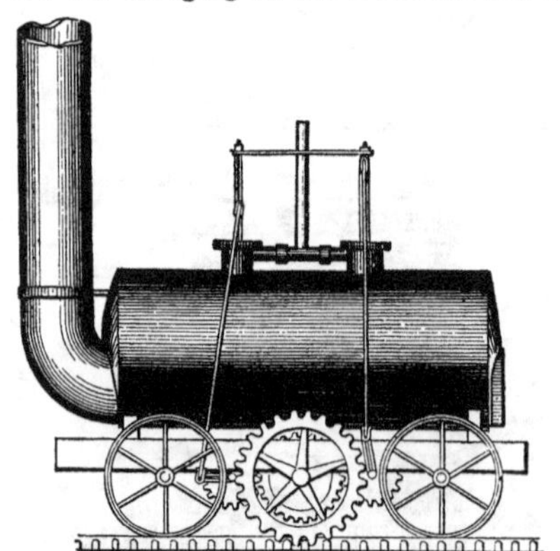

BLENKINSOP'S LOCOMOTIVE, "LORD WELLINGTON," 1811.

By an ingenious band connection to wheels, or to a stern-wheel paddle shaft, he made his scow travel on land or water, as the case might be. It was an ungainly affair, with vertical cylinder, working-beam, and fly-wheel—useless for land locomotion. Mention may also be made of M. Cugnot's carriage, in 1769, with two single-acting vertical engines acting alternately upon the two front wheels. It is yet preserved in Paris. Symington, in 1786, had also a steam-carriage with a Watt condensing engine. These engines lacked in several respects the conditions of success, but deserve mention.

It was among the coal mines that tram-ways with tracks of flag-stones for the wheels of coal wagons first came into use; it was also in the collieries that iron rails were first laid, and the wheels of cars made with grooves, and afterward with flanges, to enable them to keep on the track. It was twenty-five years after the use of the locomotive in South Wales before the railway was used except for transporting coal.

The next locomotive after that of Trevethick and Vivian was one made by Blenkinsop in 1811 for working at the Hunslet-Moor Colliery, near Leeds.[1] The flat-faced wheels ran upon a tram-way, and a cog-wheel, driven by pinions and connecting rods from the pair of vertical cylinders, drove the engine by meshing into a rack on one side of the track. The idea prevailed at the time that

[1] A large number of the illustrations for this paper have been borrowed from *Knight's Mechanical Dictionary*, published by J. B. Ford aud Co., New York.

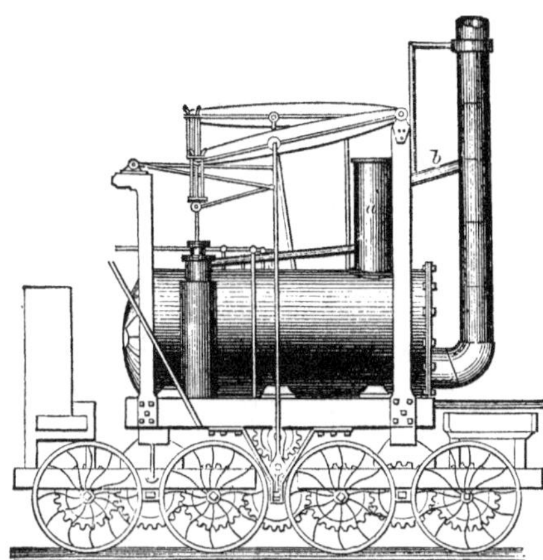

HEDLEY'S LOCOMOTIVE, "PUFFING BILLY," 1813.

the tractional adherence of the driving-wheels to the rail was not sufficient, but that the wheels would slip. The fire was built in a large tube passing through the boiler; the tube was bent to form a chimney. It drew trains of thirty tons weight three and three-quarter miles per hour.

In the spring of 1813 William Hedley built a locomotive with four smooth driving-wheels to run on a smooth rail. The machine failed to accomplish much on account of its small boiler. Hedley thereupon in the same year built another engine, shown above, having a return flue boiler, and mounted on eight driving-wheels, which were coupled together by intermediate gear wheels on the axles, and all propelled by a gear in the centre, driven by a pitman from the working-beam.

Hedley's locomotive was objected to by residents of Newcastle on account of the smoke. He therefore passed the smoke into a large receiver (*a*), and turned the exhaust steam upon it. From the receiver the steam and smoke were conveyed by a pipe (*b*) to the chimney, which device soon developed into the steam blast.

"Puffing Billy" was at work more or less until 1862, when it was laid up as a memorial in the British Patent-office Museum. Hedley died in 1842.

In 1815 Dodd and Stephenson patented an engine with vertical cylinders. The adherence to this form was on account of its supposed value in pressing the wheels down upon the track. Stephenson, in 1825, made an engine for the Killingworth Railway, and his engines were employed on iron tracks by the Stockton and Darlington Railway, and at the Newcastle collieries. His first locomotive on this railway had two vertical cylinders, and the driving-shaft had cranks at an angle of ninety degrees. The axles of the wheels were coupled by an endless chain passing around both axles.

In 1829 the Liverpool and Manchester Railway, then the most extensive and finished work of the kind ever undertaken, and the first passenger railway, was completed, and the directors offered a reward of £500 for the best locomotive which should fulfill certain imposed conditions. Among these were that it was to consume its own smoke, draw three times its own weight at a rate of not less than ten miles an hour, and the boiler pressure was not to exceed fifty pounds per square inch. The weight was not to exceed six tons, nor the cost £550.

Three engines competed—the "Rocket," constructed by George Stephenson; the "Sanspareil," by Timothy Hackworth; the "Novelty," by Messrs. Brathwaite and Ericsson.

The "Rocket" weighed 4 tons 5 hundred-weight, and its tender, with water and coke,

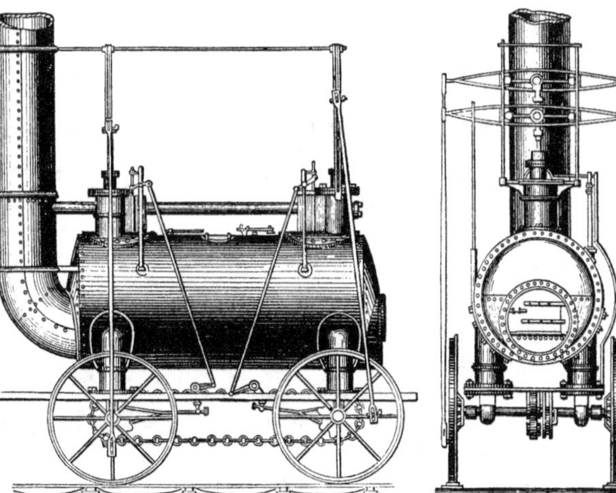

DODD'S AND STEPHENSON'S LOCOMOTIVE, 1815.

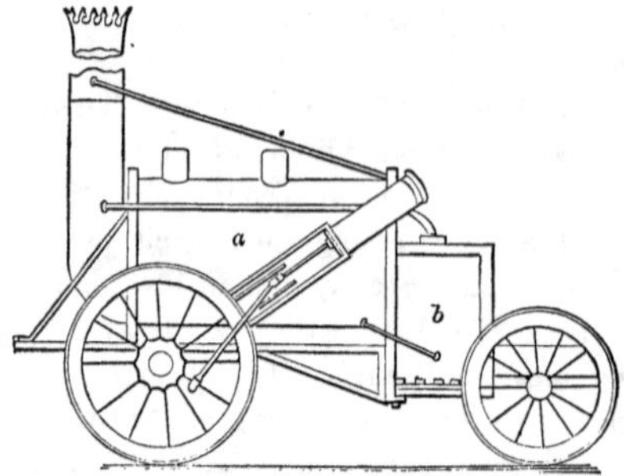

STEPHENSON'S LOCOMOTIVE, "ROCKET," 1829.

3 tons 4 hundred-weight. It had two loaded carriages attached, weighing a little over 9 tons 10 hundred-weight. The greatest velocity attained was $24\frac{1}{6}$ miles per hour, and the average consumption of coke per hour 217 pounds.

The "Sanspareil" attained a speed of $22\frac{2}{3}$ miles per hour, but with an expenditure of fuel per hour of 692 pounds.

The "Novelty" carried its own water and fuel. In consequence of successive accidents to the working arrangements, this engine was withdrawn from competition. A fourth engine, the "Perseverance," by Burstall, not being adapted to the track, was withdrawn.

The opening of the Liverpool and Manchester Railway, September 15, 1829, was an era in civilization, and one of the first victims of the iron horse was slain on that day —Mr. Huskisson, Home Secretary in the British cabinet. Eight locomotives were used on that day, and while the engines were watering at the Parkside station, some of the guests descended to the road. While Mr. Huskisson was talking to the Duke of Wellington the famous "Rocket" came by, knocked down Mr. Huskisson, and the wheels passed over his left leg. He was placed on board the "Northumbrian," driven by George Stephenson, who conveyed him fifteen miles in twenty-five minutes, at the rate of thirty-six miles an hour—the most marvelous achievement yet. Mr. Huskisson died the same night at Eccles.

The "Rocket" engine was superseded in 1837, as too light for the work, and was condemned for life to the collieries. Here it proved itself capable of a rate of sixty miles an hour; but being again convicted of levity while on duty, it was cashiered, and its place filled by heavier machines of twelve tons. After a few years of inglorious retirement, some one, not totally oblivious of how it would look in history, recalled the old soldier from his limbo, and he now enjoys the company of his elder brother, Hedley's "Puffing Billy," in the English Patent-office Museum.

The boiler (*a*) of the "Rocket" was a cylinder six feet long, and had twenty-five tubes. The fire-box (*b*) had two tubes communicating with the boiler below and above, and was surrounded by an exterior casing, into which the water from the boiler flowed, and was maintained at the same level as that in the boiler.

In the accompanying engraving (B) is shown a longitudinal vertical section of a modern English locomotive. The boiler is surrounded by two casings, one within the other, united by stays. The tubes (*a*) are of brass, 124 in number, and the boiler has longitudinal stays connecting the ends. Into the smoke-box (*b*) the blast-pipe (*c*) discharges. The steam from the upper part of the boiler enters the steam-dome (*d*), the amount being governed by a regulator controlled by a winch. This serves to obviate in a great degree the effects of priming.

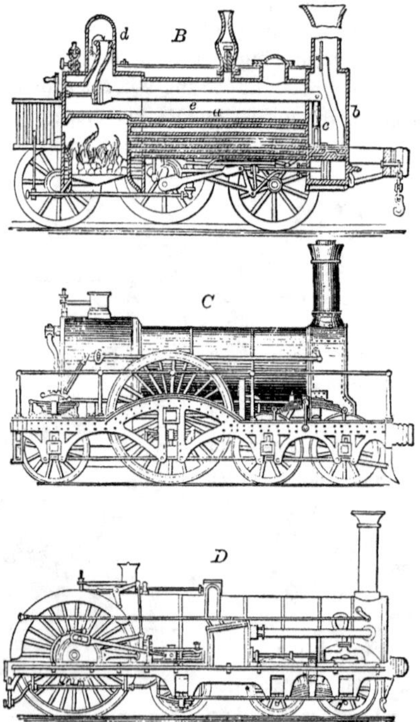

ENGLISH LOCOMOTIVES.

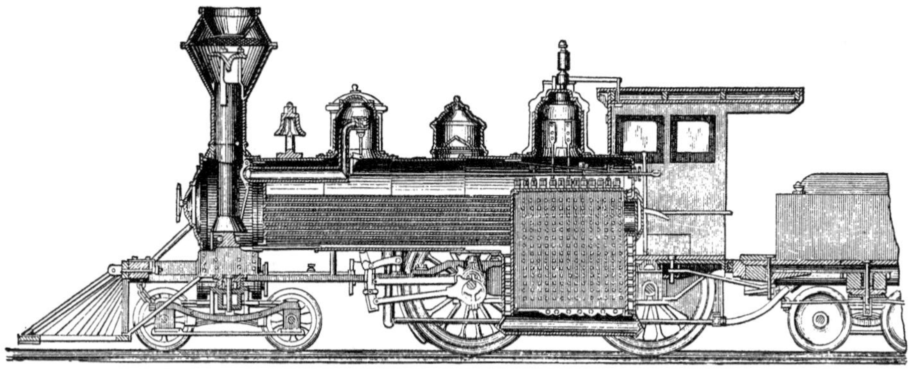

AMERICAN LOCOMOTIVE—CENTRAL LONGITUDINAL SECTION.

The engine has four drivers, 60¾ inches in diameter, and a four-wheeled swing-bolster truck, and weighs, with water and fuel, about 65,000 pounds. The flues, 144 in number, are 2 inches in diameter, and 11 feet 5 inches in length. The fire-box, of cast steel, is 66 inches long, 34½ inches wide, and 63 inches deep. Water space, 3 inches sides and back, 4 inches front. Grates, cast iron. The cylinders are horizontal. Valve motion graduated to cut off equally at all points of the stroke. The tires are of cast steel, and the wheel centres of cast iron with hollow spokes and rims; the wrist pins of cast steel, the connecting rods of hammered iron. The truck wheels are 28 inches in diameter. All the principal parts of these engines are interchangeable.

The steam-pipe (*e*) has two branches, each entering one of the boxes containing the valves by which the flow of steam to the cylinders is controlled.

In the same engraving is shown an express engine (C) designed by Gooch for the Great Western Railway, where an unusual rate of speed is maintained. The boiler has 305 tubes, two inches in diameter. The cylinders are eighteen inches in diameter, and twenty-four stroke, the driving-wheels eight feet in diameter, the heating surface of the fire-box 153 square feet. There is also an illustration (D) of an express engine designed by Crampton for the narrow gauge.

The first locomotive run on rails outside of England was the "Stourbridge Lion," made by Stephenson, and brought from England for the Delaware and Hudson Canal and Railroad Company by Horatio Allen. This was in August, 1829. It was soon found that English locomotives, adapted for gentle curves, were ill suited for the exigencies of American railroads, where curves of as small a radius as 200 feet were sometimes employed. Mr. Peter Cooper devised an engine which solved the difficulty. This was also in 1829.

The first railway in the United States was one of two miles long, from Milton to Quincy, Massachusetts, in 1826. The cars were drawn by horses. The Baltimore and Ohio was the first passenger railway in America, fifteen miles being opened in 1830, the cars being drawn by horses till the next year, when a locomotive was put on the track, built by Davis, of York, Pennsylvania. It had an upright boiler and cylinder. The Mohawk and Hudson, sixteen miles, from Albany to Schenectady, was the next line opened, and the cars were drawn by horses till the delivery of the locomotive "De Witt Clinton," which was built at the West Point Foundry, New York. This was the second locomotive built in the United States; the first was made at the same shop for the South Carolina Railway.

The above engraving represents a central longitudinal section of an approved form of American locomotive engine as made at the Baldwin Locomotive Works, Philadelphia.

The ordinary speed attained on English railways is greater than that usual in this country. The Great Western Express, from London to Exeter, travels at the rate of forty-three miles an hour, including stoppages, or fifty-one miles an hour while actually running. Midway between some of the stations a speed of sixty miles an hour is attained, and on

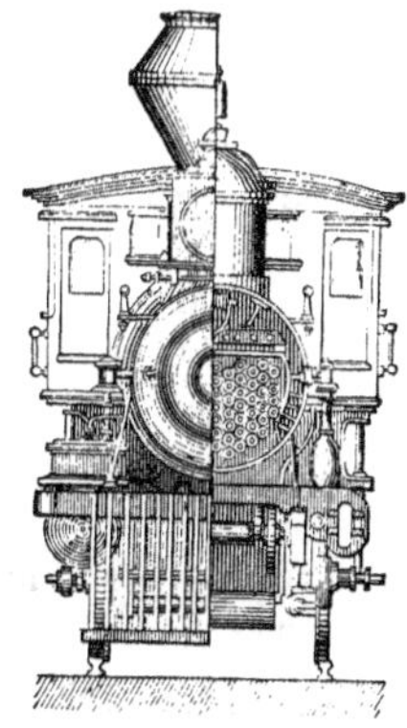

AMERICAN LOCOMOTIVE—END ELEVATION AND TRANSVERSE SECTION.

experimental trips seventy miles an hour has been reached, or nearly thirty-three yards per second.

Very high speed has been attained on special occasions on American roads, probably fully equal to any time ever made in England. For instance, it is stated that a train conveying some officials of the New York Central Railroad made the distance from Rochester to Syracuse, eighty-one miles, in sixty-one minutes—said to be the fastest time ever made in America.

The life of a locomotive engine is stated in a paper read before the British Association at thirty years. Some of the small parts require renewal every six months. The boiler tubes last five years, and the crank axles six years; tires, boilers, and fire-boxes, seven to ten years; the side frames, axles, and other parts, thirty years. During this period the total cost of repairs is estimated at $24,450 in American money, the original cost of the engine being $8490. It therefore requires for repairs in eleven years a sum equal to its original cost. In this time it is estimated that an engine in average use has run 220,000 miles.

COTTON MANUFACTURE.

Cotton was known to the ancients as *tree-wool*, being mentioned by Herodotus, Pliny, and many others. It was introduced into Spain by the Arabs, and flourished as long as religious toleration existed in the peninsula, and from this land it reached the less civilized parts of Europe. When the best part of the inhabitants was expelled, when the University of Cordova became a thing forgotten in the peninsula, when the memory of Alhazen was lost, and the era of the Pedros and Philips commenced, then the cotton-plant too faded away, and all the industries growing out of this beautiful staple expired.

Cotton was, however, known to the Mexicans when discovered by Cortez. This man without a conscience sent of his stolen goods to Charles V. "cotton mantles, some all white, others mixed with white and black, or red, green, yellow, and blue; waistcoats, counterpanes, tapestries, and carpets of cotton; and the colors of the cotton were extremely fine."[1]

[1] Clavigero's *Conquest of Mexico.*

Although there are several native American varieties of cotton, our plant is a native of India, and it has formed the staple material of garments there from time immemorial.

Cotton goods were made in Manchester in 1641, of "cotton-wool brought from Smyrna and Cyprus." Cotton seed was brought to England from the Levant, taken thence to the Bahamas, and thence to Georgia in 1786. The first cotton mill in America was at Beverly, Massachusetts, 1787. Slater's mill was erected at Pawtucket in 1789. Slater was an apprentice of Strutt and Arkwright, and introduced into the United States the Arkwright system of associated and combined machines, being the founder of the New England factory practice. The success of these mills is referred to in the report of Alexander Hamilton, Secretary of the Treasury, 1791, who proposed to remove the duty on cotton, as it was "not a production of the country," and to "extend the duty of seven and a half per cent. to all imported cotton goods."

The beauty and softness of the goods made of this material, which was new to the people of Europe, recommended it to persons of means and taste, and the importation from India assumed large proportions. The names of *calico* and *muslin*, from Calicut and Moussoul, indicate clearly enough whence the market was supplied at an early day. The English manufacturers struggled against many difficulties, three of which may be named—the lack of suitable machinery; the opposition of the wool trade, which induced the authorities even to hang criminals in cotton garments to render the goods unpopular; and the lack of supply of cotton.

The cotton from the boll yields only from one-quarter to one-third ginned fibre, and the labor of removing the seed by hand seemed at this critical moment to set a limit to the production, or at least render it so expensive that the goods could not come into general use among the masses of the people, who were used to being tolerably well fed and housed, and could not live on twopence a day and support their families, like the Hindoos. It is true that in India a sort of roller-gin had been in use from time immemorial—one which pinched the fibre and carried it away from the seed, whose size prevented it from passing between the rollers; but this was comparatively slow, and does not appear to have been known in America, where the hand-picking was in vogue. Besides, it is only suitable for certain staples of cotton. The great need of the producer and the manufacturer was a machine to remove the cotton from the seed with rapidity and economy.

At this juncture appears Eli Whitney, of Massachusetts, who in 1794 patented the *cotton-gin*. The name *gin* is short for *engine*, and is a frequent curt expression for a handy machine. Whitney's *saw-gin* (A) comprises two cylinders of different diameters mounted in a wooden frame, and turned by a handle or belt and pulley so as to rotate in opposite directions, the brush cylinder the faster. The smaller cylinder carries on its circumference from sixty to eighty circular saws, and the larger cylinder a series of brushes. The teeth of the saws pass in between a number of bars, forming a grating. The cotton, as picked from the pods, is thrown into the hopper; the saws strip the fibre from the seeds, which fall through the bottom of the hopper, while the wool is cleansed from the teeth of the saws, and delivered by a sloping table into a receptacle below. A more modern and complete form of the machine (B) is shown in our engraving.

The crop of cotton increased from 189,316 pounds in 1791 to 2,000,000,000 pounds in 1859. Whitney and his partner received $50,000 from the State of South Carolina, and a tariff of so much per saw per annum from the States of North Carolina and Georgia for a short term of years.

After the gin come the *opener* and *scutcher*, which separate the locks of cotton, remove the dirt, and convert the tangled fibre into a light and flocculent *bat* or *lap*. The machines of this stage of the process have a number of names, the marks of the rough humor of the Lancashire men among whom they originated. They were known as *willowers*, from the practice of beating with willow wands, or as *devils* and *wolves*, from their toothed drums, which tore the locks apart, the fibre passing from one to another, and the dust and dirt being carried off by a suction blast, or falling through the meshes of wire-cloth into a box beneath the machine.

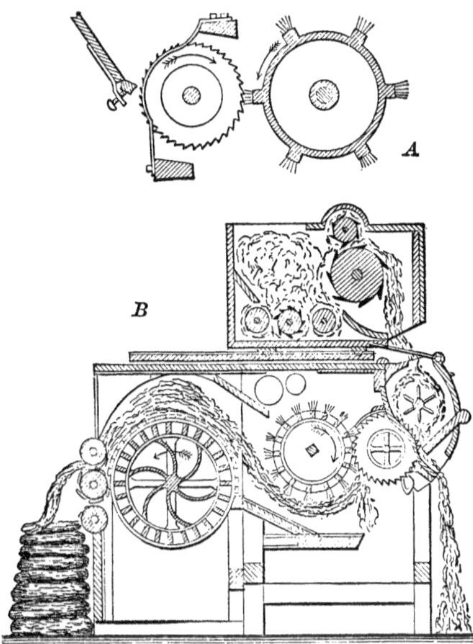

WHITNEY'S COTTON-GIN.

The *carding-machine* reduces the mass of cotton to a fleece or sliver, the fibres laid parallel, so that they may be drawn and twisted into a yarn. Hand cards were not superseded by machine cards until about 1770, although attempts had been made at carding-machines by Lewis Paul in 1748, and by Hargreaves in 1760. To the latter, to Arkwright, and to Mr. Peele, the father of the first Sir Robert and the grandfather of the statesman, the invention is ascribed. It was hardly possible that this necessary link in the chain of machines should long lack a discoverer.

Lewis Paul in his patent of 1748 had a number of parallel cards on a bed, or on a cylinder, with intervening spaces. It was used in connection with an upper card or a concave, and when the strips were full they were taken off, and the roving removed from each. Peele in 1779 introduced the cylinder. His machine had strips of card around the drum to give separate *slivers* or *cardings*, and a can, which rotated on its base, to give a slight twist to the rovings. This was perhaps the first *roving can*. The *card-sticking* machine was invented by Amos Whittemore, of Massachusetts, and patented by him in 1797.

Next in order of operation, though the first to feel the rising tide of invention, was the *spinning machine*. In ancient Egypt,

SPINNING-WHEEL.

Phœnicia, Arabia, India, Greece, and Rome the *distaff* and *spindle* were the means of spinning. The *spinning-wheel* may have originated among our cousins of Hindostan, as it was certainly known there at a somewhat distant period; it appears in our illuminated missals of the fourteenth century, but only among the lady population, being used by spinsters and matrons of rank. The great bulk of the spinning was by the distaff, which indeed is still used in many parts of the continent of Europe. Among English-speaking peoples it survived latest in the *flax-wheel*, in which a continuous thread was spun from a tussock of combed flax held upon a distaff at one end of the machine.

So far as we are concerned, the commencement of our century finds the spinning of cotton and wool in the condition of many previous ages and centuries; it was done upon hand spinning-wheels. This was true as to work done for the household and that which was done in the way of business, being distributed by the spinning masters of a neighborhood to the operatives, who did the work at their own houses. When Hargreaves invented the spinning-jenny in 1768 cotton and woolen mills were unknown.

The wool being carded into rolls in which the fibres were arranged in one direction, the spinner attached the end of one to the spindle, which was then revolved by whirling the large wheel, a band passing over the periphery of the latter and over a little pulley on the spindle. The left hand of the operator drew out the roll as it was twisted, the degree of its elongation and the hardness of the twist depending upon the distance it was pulled out and the number of revolutions. In practice, the spinner steps back a distance after setting the wheel a-whirling, and, when the twist is satisfactory, by shifting the yarn from the point to the shaft of the spindle, and then setting the spindle again in motion, the yarn is wound upon the spindle, excepting the end of the yarn, which is left projecting from the point for the attachment of another roll. Another feature must also be noticed, as it has a very close bearing upon what was followed in the most perfect known spinning machine, the *mule*, of which more presently. The spinner, after drawing out the roll, giving the wheel a whirl, and walking backward from it, dropped the roving, and then, advancing to the spindle, took the roving between the finger and thumb; then, giving a rapid revolution to the wheel, she walked backward away, allowing the roving to slip through the grip with just such friction as would secure the required tightness of twist. This done, the yarn was wound upon the spindle, and the double process repeated with another carded roll.

This was the way with wool, and subsequently with cotton; but it was not until the rising demand for cotton yarn occurred that machinery was invented to supplement the individual exertions of the spinner. Machinery was first applied to silk, but the material was expensive, the demand limited, and the process essentially different. Lewis Paul led off in this line of invention in his patent of 1738, in which he introduced the idea of successive pairs of *drawing rollers* for elongating the roving, the speed of the consecutive pairs increasing so that each pulled upon the roving between it and the preceding pair, the eventual extension depending upon the relative rates of the increase of speed of the successive pairs. He also gave to one or more of the pairs of rollers a revolution in a plane at right angles to that of their individual rotation, so as to give a twist to the yarn. This invention is said to have originated with Wyatt, Paul being only a promoter; however that may have been, it was not successful, owing, doubtless, partly to want of skill in the making, and also to intrinsic difficulties, for the same invention, in a modified form, was patented in 1848, and had a fair trial on a large scale in Rhode Island before it was finally abandoned.

In 1758 Lewis Paul tried again to adapt machinery to the work. This invention was the precursor of the *bobbin-and-fly frame.* He seems to have been unfortunate in his combinations.

The cardings being attached endwise, are fed between rollers which deliver the long sliver to a bobbin, which takes it up faster as to length than it is delivered by the rollers, and so stretches it according to the quality required. There is an indistinct intimation of a *flyer* in the drawing of this machine in the stretch between the feed rollers and the bobbins. Had he put the *drawing rollers* of his former patent to the *feed rollers* and *bobbin* of his new one, he might, perhaps, have forestalled Arkwright.

Hargreaves's *spinning-jenny* was the direct outgrowth of the spinning-wheel, unlike the Paul *drawing head,* which had a radically different construction. Something had to be done to meet the increased demand for cotton yarn. James Hargreaves was the man for the occasion. It is said that the first suggestion in the right direction was caused by the upsetting of a spinning-wheel by one of his children. *It continued to run when the spindle was vertical.* Here was the solution. He had frequently tried to spin several yarns at once on as many spindles, but the latter being horizontal, the yarns interfered. He made a machine in 1764 with eight vertical spindles in a row, fed by eight rovings, which were held by a fluted wooden clasp of two parallel slats. The ends of the rovings being attached to the spindles, the wheel was revolved by the right hand, rotating the spindles, and the clasp which lightly clipped the rovings was drawn away from the spindles, paying out the roving, which was twisted by the rotation of the spindles, and stretched by the retraction of the clasp and the amount taken up by the twist. When the clasp reached the back of the machine the yarn was wound on the spindles, the clasp resumed its place near them, fresh rovings were pieced on to the ends of the former ones, and the work was repeated.

The clasp was, as it were, a long finger and thumb to hold a row of rovings, and the machine was eventually made to contain as many as eighty spindles. Hargreaves spun in secret so much yarn that the jealous workmen broke into his house and destroyed the machine. He deviated a little from his first design in drafting the specification for his patent of 1770. He there had a series of bobbins holding *slubs*—soft rovings having but little twist—which pass from thence to a row of spindles, all rotated from a common driving-wheel. Between the two, with divisions for the slubs, was a clasp, which was managed by the left hand, to bring such a pressure upon the roving as the required twist might warrant. A *presser-wire* regulated the winding of the yarn on the spindles in the intervals of spinning.

It being proved that he had sold several of his machines before his application for a patent, the latter was set aside, and he never was reasonably remunerated.

When the machine of Arkwright, which is next in order of date, came into use, the *spinning-jenny* of Hargreaves still held its superiority in yarn, the product being used for the *weft,* while the *water-twist* of the Arkwright *roller-machine* was used for the *warp.* Subsequently the principal features of the jenny were embodied with others selected

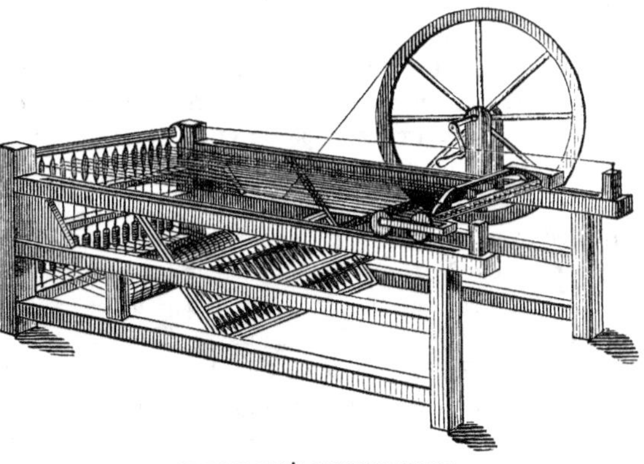

HARGREAVES'S SPINNING-JENNY.

ARKWRIGHT'S SPINNING MACHINE (FROM THE ORIGINAL DRAWING).

from the Arkwright *drawing frame* to form what was playfully termed the *mule*, by which name it is universally known up to date. It was said also that until the invention of the Arkwright machine cotton yarn was seldom used for warp, owing to its softness and weakness, the jenny not giving a sufficiently hard twist to bear the strain of the loom. Goods were therefore usually made, at the period referred to, with a *linen warp* and *cotton woof*.

Arkwright's invention for "making of weft or yarn from cotton, flax, and wool," patented 1769, was the most brilliant of its time and class. It was designed to be driven by horse-power, a band from a drum on the master-wheel shaft giving motion to the various parts. It was much improved in later years, and was driven by water-power after its success justified larger operations. This soon followed, and in 1785 steam-power was first applied to cotton spinning. The cotton rovings were wound upon large bobbins at the back upper part of the machine, and were drawn from them by four pairs of *drawing rollers*, which, moving with a graduated accelerated speed, elongated the rovings, and passed them to the flyers and spindles on the lower part of the machine. The four essential parts of this apparatus have not been dispensed with in ordinary spinning, and constitute the *bobbin-and-fly frame*, or *roving-frame*, which bids fair to hold its ground for spinning ordinary numbers to the end of time.

The drawing rollers were suggested by the Lewis Paul machine of 1738; but the *flyers* and the general combination are of the highest order of merit, and are to be attributed to Arkwright.

Reference has been made in the introductory remarks to the factory system initiated by Arkwright in his cotton mills, 1768–1785. Arkwright was the first man to associate consecutively the various processes in cotton manufacture under the same roof. This series of machines for carding, drawing, and roving was patented in 1785, and from Arkwright's period we date the origin of the factory system. This was the year after the ratification by Congress of the definitive treaty of peace signed at Paris, and four years before Washington became President.

Thenceforward the system had but to grow and extend; to grow, in bringing other departments of the cotton manufacture, and eventually those of wool, flax, and hemp, into the same method; to extend, in respect of its boundaries, geographical and economical—the latter by the inauguration of parallel practices in other interests, such as the working of metal, leather, and wood.

The invention of cotton machinery was no exception to the general rule: Arkwright did best what had been attempted before. Arkwright had his Lewis Paul, just as Fulton had his Symington and Rumsey, and as Stephenson had his Trevethick and Hedley.

Many other improvements might be cited, such as Jenks's ring-and-traveler spinner, if we had the space. The list of spinning machines closes with the *mule*, and at present there is nothing better to offer. The perfected mule has been called the "iron man" from the wondrous skill with which it operates. Apparently instinct with life and feeling, it performs its allotted course as implicitly as a mere water-wheel, but the exquisite provisions for timing—what may be called the opportuneness of its movements—give it an air of volition and prevision. These features belong to the *automatic mule*, or the *self-acting mule*, as it also called. It was not thus in the original mule of Crompton. In this the main features were present, but were brought into and continued in action by the care and judgment of the operator.

Samuel Crompton was a young weaver when he applied his mind to the solution of the problem how to make a machine which should avoid certain faults present in the Hargreaves and the Arkwright machines. This he succeeded in doing in 1779. He placed his spindles on a traveling carriage, which backed away from the roving bobbins to stretch and twist a length of the rovings, and then ran back to wind the yarn upon the spindles. The immediate object was to deliver the roving with the required degree of attenuation, and twist it as delivered. The work of this machine was finer than any heretofore produced, and the improved self-acting mule still maintains its superior character. Even at the first it was called the "muslin wheel," as its yarns rivaled in softness the finer kinds from India. Crompton took no patent for it, but was rewarded with a Parliamentary grant of £5000 thirty-three years afterward. He died in 1827.

Previous to the invention of the mule few spinners could make yarns of 200 hanks to the pound, the hank being always 840 yards. The natives of India were at the same time making yarns of numbers varying from 300 to 400. By the best constructed mules yarn has been made in Manchester of number 700, which was woven in France. The illustration will give an idea of the machine, though

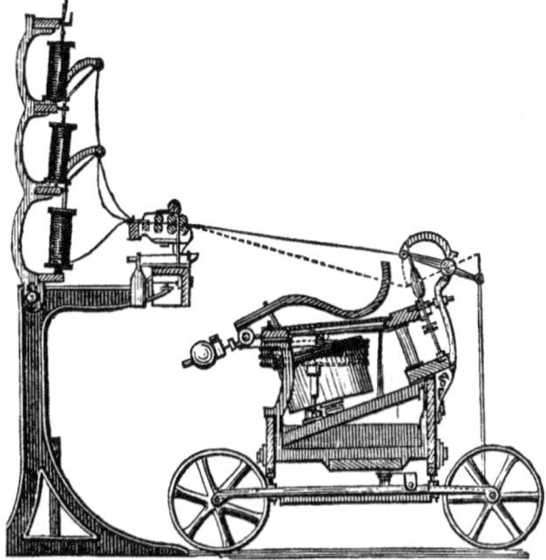

MULE SPINNER.

it has not the complicated parts of the self-acting mule.

The mule of Crompton had only twenty to thirty spindles, and the distance traveled by the carriage was five feet. The distance traveled is now much greater, and some mules carry 1200 spindles.

The drawing and stretching action of the mule spinner makes the yarn finer and of a more uniform tenuity than the mere drawing and twisting action of the *throstle*. As delivered by the rollers, the thread is thicker in some parts than in others; these thicker parts, not being so effectually twisted as the smaller parts, are softer, and yield more readily to the stretching power of the mule; by this means the twist becomes more equable throughout the yarn.

The mule carriage carrying the spindles recedes from the rollers with a velocity somewhat greater than the rate of delivery of the reduced roving, the rapid revolution of the spindles giving a twist to the yarn, which stretches it still farther. When the rollers cease giving out the rovings, the mule spinner still continues to recede, its spindles still revolving, and thus the stretching is effected.

When the *drawing*, *stretching*, and *twisting* of the yarn are thus accomplished, the mule disengages itself from the parts of the carriage by which it has been driven, and the carriage is returned to the rollers, the thread being wound in a *cop* upon the spindle as the carriage returns.

The specific difference between the action of the throstle and the mule is, that the former has a continuous action upon the roving, *drawing*, *twisting*, and *winding* it upon the *spindle*, while the mule *draws* and *twists* at one operation as the carriage runs out, and then *winds* all the lengths upon the spindles as the carriage runs in. The automatic disengagement is the invention of Roberts, in 1830, and of Mason.

The jenny and the drawing frame being fairly at work, the cry was now, "What is to become of the yarn? there will not be hands enough to weave it." The Rev. Edmund Cartwright set himself to the solution of the problem, and took out a patent for a power-loom in 1785, and a second in 1787. He was at great expense, and worked under the disadvantage of being a poor mechanic, having very little judgment in the proportion of parts or the convenient modes for the transmission of motion. One of the great difficulties in his way was in the fluffy and spongy character of the warp, and in the necessity for stopping the loom to dress a length of warp. This was avoided by the invention of the sizing and dressing machine of Radcliffe, of Stockport, in 1802, which took the yarns from the warping machine, carried them between two rollers, one of which revolved in a reservoir of thin paste, then between brushes, which rid the yarns of superfluous and uneven paste, then over a heated copper box, which dried them, and then wound them on the yarn-beam of the loom. The power-loom was only extensively adopted about 1801—the year of expiration of Cartwright's principal patent. He received £10,000 from Parliament. The justness of Cartwright's claim to the power-loom may be appreciated when it is stated that his loom, patented in 1787, has automatic mechanical devices to operate all parts. It was a memorable success for a man of letters, whose first attempt at a power-loom was made in 1784, before he had ever seen a loom. Eventually, by the exertions of Horrocks, of Stockport, in 1803, and the adaptation of the steam-engine to the work, the power-loom became fixed in use. Jacquard, of Lyons, France, Roberts, of Manchester, England, and more lately Bigelow, Crompton, and Lyall, of this country, have brought the machine to a degree of perfection which is a marvel to the uninitiated, and an object of respect to those who happen to be a little better informed in technical matters.

It may be mentioned that the mill at Waltham, Massachusetts, erected in 1813, was the first in the world in which were combined machines for all the processes which convert the raw cotton into cloth. The mills of Arkwright, at Cromford, in Derbyshire, erected 1771–75, and that of Slater, at Pawtucket, Rhode Island, 1790, had no power-looms.

Crompton is a name twice famous in the history of the manufacture of fibre. His loom, represented in the accompanying cut, is not a loom for cotton, but a more complicated structure for figure-weaving, as in carpet-making.

The Jacquard loom is the most distinct-

CROMPTON'S FANCY LOOM.

ively curious in the list of looms. Jacquard, of Lyons, is reported to have conceived the idea in 1790, and in 1801 he received from the National Exposition a bronze medal for his invention of a machine for figure-weaving, which he patented.

The appendage to the loom which constitutes the Jacquard attachment is to elevate or depress the warp threads for the reception of the shuttle, the action being produced by cards with punched holes, which admit the passage of needles which govern the warp threads. The holes in a card represent the warps to be raised for a certain passage of the shuttle, and the needles, dropping into the holes, govern the formation of the shed so that the required threads of warp come to the surface. The next card governs the next motion of the warps; and so on, the required color being brought up or kept up, as the case may be. For figured stuff, from the finest silk to the most solid carpet, figured velvets and Wilton carpets, we are indebted to the genius of Jacquard, who made it possible to do by machinery what was before an expensive operation requiring skillful hands.

While the art of the dyer is as old as Tyre, and the colors of antiquity are not, perhaps, excelled in lustre and stability, the variety has increased, and the modes have become more numerous and cheap. Dye baths and mordants were well understood in India two thousand years ago, as were also one or more styles of calico-printing, including chintz patterns and the resist process, which helped to make the fortunes of the Peele family.

Pliny refers to the skill of the Egyptians as "wonderful" in imparting to white robes a number of colors by steeping "with dye-absorbing drugs" (mordants), after which the goods take on several tints when boiled in a dye bath of one color. Cortez was met in Mexico by people who wore cotton dresses with Dolly Varden patterns in black, blue, red, yellow, and green.

These instances, which are but a tithe of what offers, show that calico-printing is old enough, and, indeed, it was practiced as a profession at Augsburg at the latter part of the seventeenth century, about which time it was introduced into England. Hand processes, however, were all that were known. Their nature it is not so easy to determine, but Robert Peele, a farmer of Blackburn, invented the method of *printing by blocks*, each cut out to correspond with its part of the pattern, and laid in apposition by means of *register pins*. This may have been about 1776, a year or two before his invention of the *mangle* and the *cylinder carding-machine*, the roller principle of which seems to have suggested the *calico-printing machine* (1785), which has its pattern engraved on the face of a cylinder, and which, with various improvements in detail, remains in use to the present day. The object he chose for his first attempt at hand-printing was a parsley leaf. The women of his family ironed the goods, and he was long called, without intentional disparagement, "Parsley-leaf Peele."

In this machine the pattern for each color is engraved on a cylinder which revolves so as to dip its lower surface in a trough of color; the face of each cylinder is scraped clean by a blade called a *doctor*, leaving the color only in the engraved lines; the cloth passes against the cylinders in turn, and receives a portion of its pattern from each. By an American improvement the number of cylinders which may be applied to each web is increased to twelve. The mode of engraving the cylinders has undergone a complete change since the invention by Jacob Perkins, of Massachusetts, of the roller-die and transfer process, in which a design on an engraved and subsequently hardened steel die is impressed into the copper cylinder in repetition to any required extent.

Robert Peele was also fortunate in securing two very valuable processes, known as the *discharge* and *resist* styles. The latter he is said to have bought of a commercial traveler for £5, and to have made £250,000 by it. The *discharge* style is a process in which the cloth is printed with a material which prevents the mordant from becoming fast, so that when the dye is applied and the cloth washed, the dye is not fast at those places. The *resist* style is one in which the cloth has a pattern printed in paste, and is then dyed in indigo. The paste resists the coloring matter, and these parts are white on a blue ground when the cloth is washed.

The name of Peele, the self-taught dyer and mechanic, and his son and grandson, the two Sir Roberts, the latter being the statesman who was killed by a fall from his horse in 1850, are indissolubly associated with the cotton manufacture, and more specifically with the carding and the calico-printing.

IRON.

Early memorials point to the use of stone and flint, of copper and bronze, before the era of iron commenced, though the extraction of iron from its ore and its forging into shape antedate the historic period. Moses and the Hebrew chroniclers, 1450–700 B.C., Job, Homer, Ezekiel, Hesiod, Aristotle, Thucydides, Xenophon, Diodorus, and Pliny refer to the metal. It has been found by Belzoni, Vyce, Abbott, and Mariette in positions which indicate its use at the building of the Pyramids and the erection of the Sphinxes, and by Layard at Nimroud. The production of iron in large quantities is, however, quite recent, and the casting of it was an unexpected result incident to the enlargement of the furnace, the increased power of blast, and perhaps in part to the working of certain ores which were not so tractable under rude methods.

Pure iron is almost infusible, and the ancient processes succeeded in reducing the metal to a spongy condition, the impurities being removed by fluxes in the form of a slag, and by subsequent hammering and reheating. The product was a steel, and was produced in one process from the ore. In many parts of the world very widely separated the same methods were used. In small cold-blast furnaces rich ore is heated in contact with incandescent charcoal, the viscid mass being hammered to remove earthy impurities. This plan is yet practiced in India, Africa, Malaya, Madagascar, and formed the

"Mass of iron, shapeless from the forge,"

offered by Achilles as a prize at the funeral games of Patroclus, recorded in Homer's Iliad.

Dr. Livingstone refers to the iron-smelting furnaces of the tribes encountered in his *Expedition to the Zambesi.* The articles produced by these peoples are hammers, tongs, hoes, adzes, fish-hooks, needles, and spear-heads. The *assagais* of the Caffres are made of iron similarly procured, and of excellent quality. The *wootz* of India is still produced in the manner partially described by Aristotle when speaking of India, and by Diodorus Siculus, referring to the iron ores of the island of Ethalia.

IRON FURNACE OF THE KOLS, HINDOSTAN.

Our illustration represents a blast-furnace of the Kols, a tribe of iron smelters in Lower Bengal and Orissa. The men are nomads, going from place to place, as the abundance of ore and wood may prompt them. The charcoal in the furnace being well ignited, ore is fed in alternately with charcoal, the fuel resting on the inclined tray, so as to be readily raked in. As the metal sinks to the bottom, slag runs off at an aperture above the basin, which is occupied by a viscid mass of iron. The blowers are two boxes with skin covers, which are alternately depressed by the feet and raised by the spring poles. Each skin cover has a hole in the middle, which is stopped by the heel as the weight of the person is thrown upon it, and is left open by withdrawal of the foot as the cover is raised.

Variously modified in detail and increased in size, these simple furnaces are to be found in several parts of Europe, the Catalan and Swedish furnaces resembling in all probability those of the Chalybes, so famous in Marathon (490 B.C.), and those of the *fabrica* or military forge established in England by Hadrian (A.D. 120) at Bath, in the vicinity of iron ore and wood. The brave islanders met their Roman invaders with scythes, swords, and spears of iron, and the export of that metal from thence shortly afterward is mentioned by Strabo.

During the Roman occupation of England some of the richest beds of iron ore were worked, and the *débris* and cinders yet exist to testify to two facts—one, that the amount of material treated was immense; the other, that the plans adopted were wasteful, as it has since been found profitable to work the cinders over again.

During the Saxon occupation the furnaces were still in blast, especially in Gloucestershire.

The early Norman sovereigns were so intent upon skinning the Jews and Saxons that it became dangerous to succeed in any business, success inviting the barons to plunder. Accordingly we find in the time of King John that iron and steel were imported from Germany.

The business lumbered along for some centuries, the government tinkering at it now and again, the exportation being prohibited in the fourteenth century, and the importation of iron in the fifteenth century.

The direct method of obtaining wrought iron from the ore prevailed until the commencement of the fifteenth century, and then gradually gave way to a less direct process, but one more convenient in the handling of large quantities. Furnaces, operating by the aid of a strong blast, to *melt* the iron and obtain *cast iron*, which is carbureted in the process, were in use in the neighborhood of the Rhine about 1500. A second process in a *forge* hearth was used to eliminate the carbon and other impurities, and the result was *wrought iron*.

The statement is shortly made, but it took several centuries to accomplish it with wood, and several other centuries to devise means for substituting pit-coal for charcoal.

In the reign of Elizabeth blast-furnaces were of sufficient size to produce from two to three tons of pig-iron per day by the use of charcoal. In the small works the iron was made malleable before being withdrawn from the blast-furnace, and in larger works was treated by the refinery furnace.

Wood becoming scarce, and a number of furnaces having gone out of blast, in 1612 Simon Sturtevant was granted a patent for thirty-one years for the use of pit-coal in smelting iron. Failing in his proposed plans, he rendered up his patent in the following year. Successive persons applied for a patent for the same, the government continuing desirous of encouraging the development of home resources. Dudley in 1619 succeeded in producing three tons of iron per week in a small blast-furnace by the use of coke from pit-coal. The parties who yet possessed plenty of wood, and with whom the production of iron was fast becoming a monopoly, urged the charcoal burners to destroy the works of Dudley, which was done. Dudley's patent was granted for thirty-one years, which would bring it to 1650, the time of the Protectorate, when England had a ruler fit to succeed Queen Bess. The celebrated statute of King James, limiting the duration of patents to fourteen years, was passed in 1624. Dudley's petition for an extension was refused.

Iron of poor quality continued to be made in districts where wood was scarce, and of good quality from charcoal in places where forests yet remained. The demand for iron continuing to grow—a natural effect of advancing civilization — iron was imported from Sweden and Russia in large quantities and of excellent quality. The forests of these countries gave them a natural advantage over England, whose forests had by this time become thinned out, so that the use of wood for iron smelting had been forbidden by act of Parliament in 1581 within twenty-two miles of the metropolis or fourteen miles of the Thames, and eventually was prohibited altogether.

The art of making iron with pit-coal and of casting articles of iron was revived by Abraham Darby, of Colebrookdale, about 1713, and was perseveringly followed, although it was but little noised abroad. In the *Philosophical Transactions* for 1747 it is referred to as a curiosity.

The extension of the iron manufacture dates from the introduction of the steam-engine, which increased the power of the blast, and the blowing engines, driven by manual, horse, or ox power, were henceforth operated by steam-engines. The dimension of the blast apparatus was increased from time to time, and about 1760 coke was commonly used in smelting. In 1760 Smeaton erected at the Carron Works the first large

MODERN BLAST-FURNACE.

blowing cylinders, and shortly after Boulton and Watt supplied the steam-engines by which the blowers were driven. Neilson, of Glasgow, introduced the hot blast in 1828. Aubulos, in France, in 1811, and Budd, in England, in 1845, heated the blast by the escaping hot gases of the blast-furnace. In the smelting of iron four tons weight of gaseous products are thrown off into the air for each ton of iron produced.

As a means of estimating by comparison the value of the hot blast, some facts may be mentioned. Mushet states that at the Clyde Iron-works, before the introduction of the hot blast, the quantity of materials necessary for the production of one ton of pig-iron was,

Calcined ore	1¾ tons.
Coke	3 "
Limestone	½ ton.

In 1831, when the system was coming into use, the blast being *warm*,

Calcined ore	2 tons.
Coke	2 "
Limestone	½ ton.

In 1839, with a hot blast,

Calcined ore	1¾ tons.
Coke	1¾ "
Limestone	½ ton.

The saving in fuel being nearly one-half.

In addition may be mentioned the fact that anthracite coal and black band ore are intractable under the cold blast, but the former yields an intense heat and the latter a rich percentage of good iron with the hot blast.

The Calder Works in 1831 demonstrated the needlessness of coking when the hot blast is employed.

Experiments in smelting with anthracite coal were tried at Mauch Chunk in 1820, in France in 1827, and in Wales successfully by the aid of Neilson's hot-blast ovens in 1837. The experiment at Mauch Chunk was repeated, with the addition of the hot blast, in 1838–39, and succeeded in producing about two tons per day. The Pioneer furnace at Pottsville was blown-in July, 1839.

The first iron-works in America were established near Jamestown, Virginia, in 1619. In 1622, however, the works were destroyed and the workmen with their families massacred by the Indians. The next attempt was at Lynn, Massachusetts, on the banks of the Saugus, in 1648. The ore used was the bog ore, still plentiful in that locality. At these works Joseph Jenks, a native of Hammersmith, England, in 1652, by order of the Province of Massachusetts Bay, coined silver shillings, sixpences, and threepences known as the "pine-tree coinage," from the device of a pine-tree on one face. The coinage of these pieces by Massachusetts excited the ire of the king, who, as Junius said to the Duke of Grafton, "left no distressing examples of virtue even to [his] legitimate posterity." The king indignantly declared to Sir Thomas Temple that they had invaded his prerogative by coining money. Sir Thomas, who was a real friend to the colonies, took a piece out of his pocket and presented it to the king. "One side was a pine-tree of that kind which is thick and bushy at the top. Charles asked what that was. 'The royal oak, Sir, which preserved your

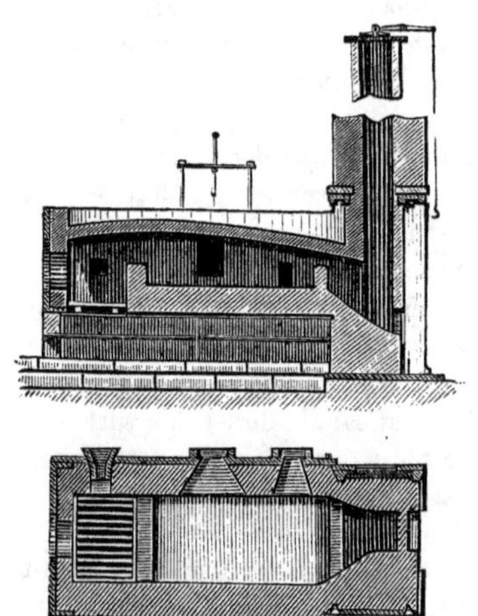

PUDDLING FURNACE.

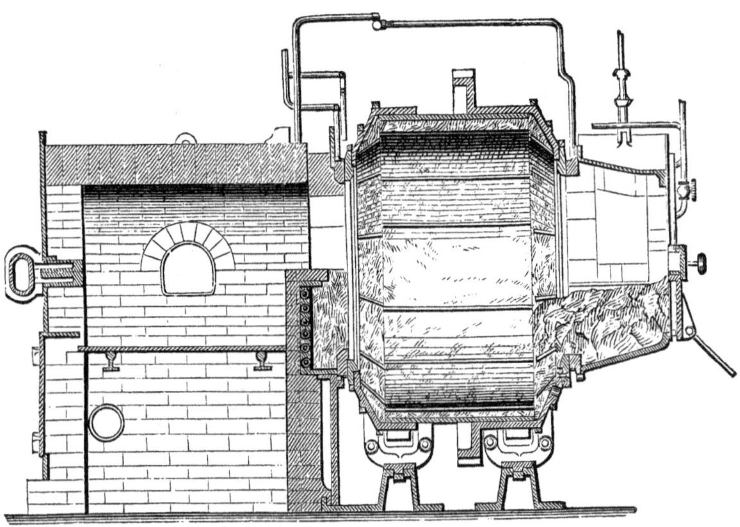

DANKS'S MECHANICAL PUDDLER.

majesty's life!' The king resumed his good humor, calling the colonists a 'parcel of honest dogs.'"

By dint of successive efforts, cast iron was produced in something like sufficient quantities to meet the demand, the furnaces enlarging as the blowing engines increased in power.

The next step was to simplify and expedite the processes by which the cast iron was made malleable. In 1780, two years before the conclusion of the peace between Great Britain and the Federal government, Henry Cort invented the puddling furnace, which he patented in 1784, and which revolutionized the business of making malleable iron. The charge of iron, say 540 pounds, is placed on a hearth in a reverberatory chamber whose bottom and sides are lined with refractory slags rich in oxide of iron. When the iron is melted, the slags rise through it and float on the top. The oxygen in the silicates combines with the carbon in the iron, decarbonizing it, the puddler stirring it vigorously to bring the carbon and other impurities of the iron in contact with the oxidizing flame. The iron granulates and throws off carbonic oxide, and eventually agglutinates, or, as the puddler says, "comes to nature." A deoxidizing flame is then used to protect the iron while it is being made into balls, which are shingled or squeezed to remove slag and compact it for rolling. The bed of Cort's furnace was of sand. Rogers, some years afterward, made the bottom of iron, and lined it with cinder.

The operation of puddling is a great tax upon the strength and endurance of the men, both on account of the violent labor and of the exposure to the intense heat of the furnace.

Mechanical puddlers have been substituted for hand labor with some success. The rotating hearth of Danks, of Cincinnati, has attained more celebrity in this country and in England than any other furnace for that purpose. The barrel-shaped chamber lined with refractory material is

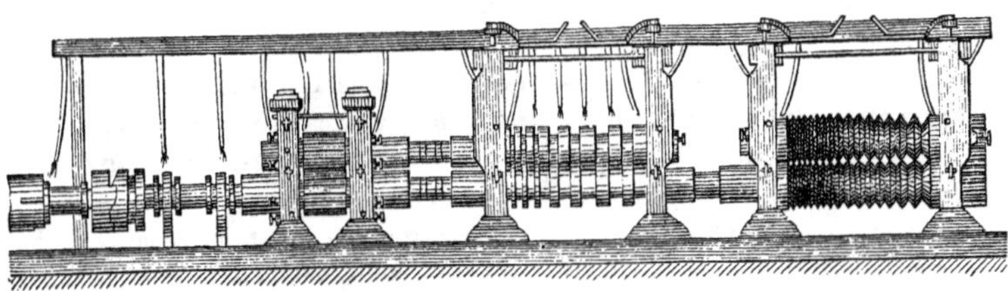

ROLLING-MILL FOR IRON BARS.

placed between the furnace and the chimney, and the iron, after it has become melted, is rolled round and round as the chamber revolves, and thereby all parts are in turn exposed to the action of the flame.

The *ball* from the puddling furnace is dragged or rolled to the steam or trip hammer or the squeezer, where it is compacted and has the dross driven out of it, making a *bloom*. In this condition it is shipped from some iron-works, while others carry it a step farther before putting it upon the market.

Here occurred the next great necessity. Was the bar-iron always to be brought to shape by the hammer alone? Again Cort came to the rescue with the invention of the mill with grooved rollers, which he patented in 1783. The yearly value of this improvement in England and the United States amounts to hundreds of millions of dollars.

Years after the death of the unrewarded Cort the rolling-mill was made to form plates for armor of ships of war. In 1842 the late R. L. Stevens, of Hoboken, New Jersey, commenced the construction of an iron-clad war vessel under an agreement with the government, which has not yet been completed. In 1855 some armor-clad floating batteries were used by the French in the Black Sea. The *La Gloire*, launched in 1859, was plated with rolled iron of 4½ inches thickness, and was the first large iron-clad. The first English armored vessel, the *Warrior*, had the same thickness of armor. The thickness has since been much increased: the *Bellerophon* has 6 inches, the *Hercules* 9, *Peter the Great* (Russian) 12 to 14. The plating of the *Monitor* turret was 9 inches, the *Weehawken* 11, laid on in several thicknesses. Armor plating has been rolled in England of 15 inches thickness, carried by the *Glatton* turret. The turret of the *Peter the Great* is 16 inches—one thickness of 14 and one of 2 inches.

While the capacity of the rolling-mill has seemed adequate to all calls, the business of the forge has also had its grand achievements, resulting from the use of the steam-hammer. This was invented by Nasmyth about 1838, and patented in 1842. It is true that there existed a description of Devereau's hammer in 1806 which recited the main features, but it seems to have excited no attention, and to have been followed by no hammer. To Nasmyth we are indebted for it; even he had to work against prejudice, which prevented its being used in England until after it had been tried in France by some more appreciative persons, whose attention had been in some way directed to it.

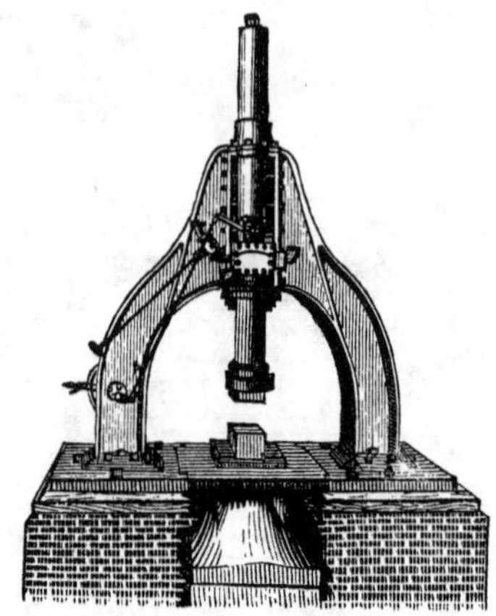

NASMYTH'S DOUBLE-FRAME STEAM-HAMMER.

The helve of the steam-hammer is the piston-rod of an overhead steam-engine, by which it is lifted. To drop it, the steam which lifted it is allowed to escape from below the piston, and the force of the blow is, in some hammers, increased by admitting the steam above the piston, which adds the force of the steam to that due to the weight and fall of the hammer. The sizes vary, having a very wide range, the weight of the hammer varying from 50 pounds to 80,000 pounds, the stroke from six inches to six feet. They are single or double acting, have single or double frame, according to size, and all have a capacity for giving a blow of any required fraction of their full power, and using any part of their range of stroke. The anvils are made as heavy as 250 tons weight.

The series of operations is here complete down to the point of shaping the metal while hot by rolling or by forging; but a great and hitherto unrealized improvement was sought by which the metal might be purified by chemical means. Inventors in Europe and America attacked the problem, but it was reserved for Bessemer to give it form, substance, and success.

The process consists in placing a charge, say five tons, of molten iron in a vessel placed on trunnions, and known as a *convert-*

or, the bottom of the vessel having channels to admit in divided streams a blast of air which passes through the melted metal, its oxygen entering into combination with the silicon, carbon, phosphorus, sulphur, etc., forming gaseous compounds, which are liberated and driven up the chimney. The iron is melted in cupolas and tapped into the convertor, which is a pear-shaped vessel about fifteen feet high and nine feet diameter, hung upon trunnions, to one of which the apparatus is attached which rotates the vessel in a vertical plane; through the other trunnion passes an air-pipe which is continued down the outside of the vessel and opens into a chamber at the bottom which communicates with the main chamber through 120 holes, each three-eighths of an inch in diameter. These holes are in fire-bricks, and the vessel itself is lined with refractory material.

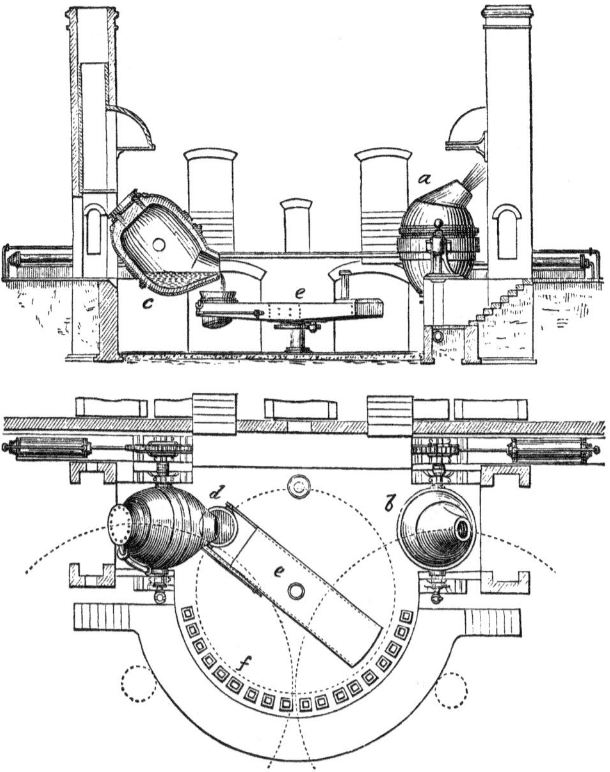

BESSEMER PLANT.

The vessel is turned partly down, the mouth being presented upwardly to take its charge from a ladle suspended from a crane and sweeping in the arc of a circle between the cupola and the convertor. The blast is then turned on, the vessel righted, the air pressure preventing the iron entering the blast holes, and the spout being presented to a canopy which leads the evolved gases up the chimney: this is shown at *a b*. The silicon of the pig-iron oxidizes first without very intense flame, but as the carbon begins to burn the heat rises to 5000° Fahrenheit, and the light is so brilliant as to cast shadows across sunshine. In fifteen or twenty minutes the marvelous illumination ceases more suddenly than it began, and this change in the flame indicates the critical moment of the elimination of most of the carbon. The blast is stopped, the convertor turned on its side, and six hundred pounds of melted spiegeleisen are turned in. The reaction is instantaneous and violent. The manganese of the spiegeleisen combines with any sulphur that may remain in the bath, forming compounds which pass into the slag. It also decomposes in the slag silicates of iron taking the place of the iron and returning it to the bath. Finally, the carbon and manganese together reduce the oxide of iron formed during blowing, and which would affect the malleability of the iron. This done, the monster, as if weary of swallowing boiling iron and snorting fire, turns its mouth downward and disposes of its contents into a kettle upon a turn-table. This act is shown at *c d*. The ladle on its turntable *e* is then swung over the moulds *f*, ranged round the semicircular pit like a row of Ali Baba's wine jars, each capable of holding a bandit. The glowing metal is drawn into the moulds from a tap hole in the ladle, and as each mould is filled the molten metal is covered with a steel plate and a packing of sand. When the ingots have solidified they are tipped out of the moulds and carried away by tongs or traveling cranes to the shops, where they are hammered or rolled into the required forms of bars, rails, plates, and what not. The product is usually a grade of steel, though the quality may be varied by changes in the details of the process.

Like Arkwright, Bessemer has become very wealthy, and for every dollar he has made, his country has been enriched by hundreds. The actual working process in America has been materially improved by Mr. Holly, who is consulting engineer of the principal Bessemer works in this country.

This was a great improvement for most purposes over the old process of cooking the iron in the puddling furnace to deprive it of its silicon and carbon, tilt-hammering the ball to a bloom, rolling the bloom to a bar, cutting the bar in pieces, and building it with charcoal solidly into a cementation furnace, where it might absorb carbon to constitute it steel. This old process is still pursued for the finer qualities, the blister-steel produced from the cemented bar being several times worked before it becomes the best cast steel for our finest cutlery. The process of making cast steel was invented by Benjamin Huntsman, of Ottercliff, near Sheffield, England, in 1770, so that this great invention comes practically within the century. The blister-steel is broken into pieces, fused in crucibles of refractory clay or graphite, made into ingots in cast-iron moulds, and then rolled.

But the convenience of casting iron into shape, instead of laboriously forging it into the varied and sometimes difficult forms required, is so great that a process for making cast-iron articles malleable became a great necessity. This was invented in Sheffield by Samuel Lucas, and patented by him in 1804. The process is as follows: The castings are inclosed in iron boxes, and surrounded with pounded iron-stone or some of the metallic oxides, as scales from the forge, common lime, or other absorbents of carbon, used either together or separately. The boxes are placed in the furnace, subjected to a strong heat for about five days, and allowed to cool gradually within the furnace. The time and other circumstances determine the depth of the effect. Thin pieces become malleable entirely throughout, admit of being readily bent, and may be slightly forged; thicker pieces retain a central portion of cast iron, but in a softened state, and not so brittle as at first. On sawing them through, the exterior coat of soft metal is perfectly distinguishable from the remainder.

In the processes of hand forging, annealing, and tempering we have nothing to claim over the methods or the productions of former ages and other nations, such as the Arabs and Persians.

As with the processes involving the *production* and *refining* of iron, and the shaping of the heated metal by *casting, forging*, and *rolling*, so with the shaping of the cold metal by *turning* and *planing*—all the important improvements are within the century. The lathes and boring-machines of the time preceding Watt were rude and small affairs. The steam-cylinder invented by Papin about 1690, and first used successfully by Newcomen and Calley in 1711, was so ill bored that its piston required to be covered with water to prevent leakage of air downward, and hence the Newcomen engines were always vertical. Watt's first engine, with a cylinder eighteen inches in diameter, was built at Kinneal in 1770. In 1775 he entered on a partnership with Boulton, who took a two-thirds share in the patented engine, which worked with one-quarter the fuel used by the Newcomen engine performing similar work. Boulton was a man worthy of the occasion, and the works at Soho equal to the demand.

The mature conceptions of these great mechanicians required a far finer style of execution of work, and a set of workmen arose who introduced exactness and system into the shop. Ramsden, about 1770, invented the micrometer-screw dividing-engine for graduating astronomical and surveying instruments, and reduced the error in ascertaining longitude by the Hadley quadrant to one-fiftieth. Bramah, in 1784, produced his lock, which was in its day a marvel of skill and finish; also the hydraulic press and the numbering machine for bank-notes and pages of account-books. Boulton and Watt, in 1788, were celebrated for the perfection of their mint apparatus, coining the silver of the Sierra Leone Company, the copper of the East India Company, and sending two complete mints to the Emperor Paul I. of Russia. In Bramah's workshop Clement and perhaps Maudslay were trained, one the inventor of the planing-machine, the other a builder of marine engines, who gave them shape when as yet steam navigation was in its infancy. Roberts of Manchester gave his attention to the perfecting of machinery for working in fibre, Whitworth especially to machine-tools and instruments for measuring with mathematical accuracy. We shall have occasion to mention presently the perfecting of the modes of manufacture, and to show the part America took in the matter.

The first turning-lathe was vertical—the potter's wheel—and was employed upon plastic material. After many centuries of use in this way, the spindle was made horizontal, and it was employed on wood. Its use on metal is comparatively modern. The screw-lathe is still more recent. One is described in a French work of 1578, and another in an English work of 1694. They were, however, rather bench tools for watch-makers and jewelers than machines. The work of originating correct screws, and perfecting the screw-cutting lathe, was taken in hand by Plumier 1701, Ramsden 1770, Robinson of Soho 1790, Donkin, Allan, Roberts, Whitworth, and others. The new era of the lathe commenced when the *slide-rest* was added. This was the invention of General Sir Samuel Bentham, about 1791. His particular *forte* was in wood-working machinery, but the slide-rest once invented would be readily adapted to the metal lathe, and the *slide-lathe* soon followed.

The application of a *screw* to the *slide-lathe* so as to render it capable of both *sliding* and *screw-cutting* was the next important improvement, and a great amount of time, perseverance, and capital was expended in endeavoring to perfect this portion of the lathe.

After this the *surfacing motion* was introduced, and also the use of a shaft at the back of the lathe, in addition to the regular screw, for driving the sliding motion by rack and pinion, instead of both the motions of sliding and screw-cutting being worked by the screw alone.

Thus step by step improvements were gradually brought forward; the fore jaw and universal chucks and other important appliances were added so as to render the lathe applicable to a great variety of work, even cutting spiral grooves in shafts, scrolls in a face-plate, skew wheels, and also turning articles of oval, spherical, and other forms. Whitworth's duplex lathe, with one tool acting in front and the other behind the work, was invented for turning long shafts, cast-iron rollers, cylinders, and a great variety of work where a quantity of the same kind and dimensions has to be turned.

The planing-machine was an outgrowth of the slide-lathe. Instead of the object turning upon centres against a tool, it is dogged to a traversing-table and moves against the tool in a right line. This machine-tool has dispensed to a great extent with chipping and filing, and is at the bottom of all successful fitting of machinery. It is next in importance to the lathe. It was invented about 1820, several excellent mechanics having about the same time worked at and solved the problem—Clements, who was a workman in Bramah's shop, Fox of Derby, Roberts and Rennie of Manchester. Bramah had, as far back as 1811, employed the revolving cutter to plane iron, adapting to metal the form previously used on wood-planing machines; this is the milling-machine lately so much improved and so deservedly esteemed.

The first planing-machines were moved by a chain winding on a drum; the rack and pinion, and eventually the screw arrangement, were substituted. Clements's machine, described in his letter to the "Society of Arts" (vol. xlix., p. 157 *et seq.*), included the reciprocating bed, guided and moved horizontally and automatically with a greater or lesser stroke. It had two cutters capable of being directed backward and forward, and at different elevations, so as to cut at each motion of the bed. The cutters were fixed in a sliding head, and were shifted automatically at the end of each stroke, horizontally or vertically. The cutters could be canted to any angle to plane either side of the work. It was, in fact, the planing-machine of the present day.

The next great improvement in the machine was the "Jim Crow" planer of Joseph Whitworth, of Manchester, 1835. This has the self-reversing cutter, which "wheeled about and turned about and did just so," operating both backward and forward with one tool without waste of time.

Other adaptations known by special names can not be overlooked. The *jack*, a small machine, named from its quick, handy ways and compact form. The *slotting*-machine and the *key-grooving* machine, by Roberts of Manchester, have mortise chisels reciprocated vertically by an eccentric, while the wheel to be slotted is laid horizontally on the lathe and fed toward the cutter between each stroke. The *milling*-machine has been referred to. It is only of late that it has been esteemed as it deserves and made much use of. The *shaping*-machine is one in which the object is chucked on a mandrel, the tool traverses above the work in a line parallel with the axis of the mandrel; the latter being slightly rotated between each stroke constitutes the feed, and the result is a circular or curved shape attained by straight cuts.

The machine-tools of the present day are a marvel, and the work turned out by them excels in quality and quantity any thing conceivable by the worthies of the first part of the present century. Watt, for instance —to select the most prominent of the men who combined to revolutionize the world of industry while smaller men were making all the noise in the manufacture of "holy alliances" which hardly survived their framers —Watt would have been infinitely gratified and astonished at the development and perfection of the machine-tools of the present day. He would see in them the cause and the effect; the ponderous and yet delicate machines driven by the engines which they had created; the tools the makers and yet the agents; the engines the movers of the tools by which they came to exist; their growth parallel in fitness, proportion, and magnitude, which are the elements of beauty, grace, and majesty.

A word as to the constitution of the machines themselves, of the means by which they are fashioned and adapted to perform their specific duties with smoothness, directness, and economy of power.

The system of making the component parts of a machine or implement in distinct pieces of fixed shape and dimensions, so that corresponding parts are interchangeable, is known as *assembling*. The term is, however, more strictly applicable to their fitting together after being separately and accurately made according to fixed patterns, and constantly compared by gauges and templates which test the dimensions.

This system of interchangeability of parts was first introduced into the French artillery service by General Gribeauval, about 1765. He reduced the gun-carriages to classes, and so arranged many of the parts that they could be applied indiscriminately to any carriage of the class for which they were made. The system was afterward extended into several of the European services and into that of the United States.

The first fire-arm attempted to be made on this system was the breech-loader of John H. Hall, of North Yarmouth, Massachusetts, 1811, of which 10,000 were made for the United States, $10,000 being voted the inventor in 1836, being at the rate of one dollar per gun. Some of them were captured in Fort Donelson, February 16, 1862. They were probably the first breech-loading military arms ever issued to troops.

The extent to which the system of gauges was actually carried with the Hall arm is not accurately known, but it is doubtless true that the principle was first brought to a high state of system and accuracy by Colonel Colt, of Connecticut, in the manufacture of his pistols. Among the most important of the extensions of the principle has been the making of special machines to fashion particular parts, or even special portions of individual pieces, so that each separate part may be shaped by successive machines, and bored by others, issuing in the exact form required.

This plan requires large capital, and will not pay unless a great number of similar articles be required, but has been extensively introduced into this country, and from hence into England, and to some extent on to the continent of Europe. All the government breech-loading fire-arms are thus made. The greater number of the military arms of Europe and Egypt are thus made in the United States for the various countries.

The Snider gun, a modification of an American model, is made at the Enfield Arsenal, England, on special machines made for that purpose in duplicate at the Colt Works, Hartford, Connecticut. Pratt and Whitney, of Hartford, are just completing for Germany a full set of special machines and gauges for the manufacture of the Mäuser rifle, adopted by Prussia for the confederate German States.

The first watch made on this plan was the "American" watch of Waltham, Massachusetts, the system extending down to the almost microscopic screws and other small parts. All the prominent sewing-machines are so made; the same with Lamb's knitting-machine, and probably others. Many kinds of agricultural implements, including plows, harvesters, threshers, and wagons, are made of interchangeable parts. The system has been carried into locomotive building; about seven grades of engines, it is understood, are employed on the Pennsylvania Central Railroad, corresponding parts of a given grade being precisely similar, so as to fit any engine of the class. This is the American system of *assembling*.

While upon the subject of instruments of precision, one or two instances may be given where the result was a marked success and affected large interests.

The American system of bank-note engraving is the invention of Jacob Perkins, of Newburyport, Massachusetts, in 1837. Previous to his time the engraving, whether of ornament or lettering, had been simply cut by hand upon the plate, which was then printed in the copper-plate press. Perkins's system is to engrave the design on separate blocks of softened steel, which are subsequently hardened. Each block so engraved is used to make a raised impression on a softened steel roller, which is rocked upon it under very heavy pressure. The roller is then hardened, and is used as a roller die to impress the steel plate from which the notes are printed. Each part of the face and back of the note is upon one or another of the roller dies, whose separate impressions upon the plate combine to make up the whole design, roller after roller being used after adjustment to its proper place over the plate. The table is provided with complete adjustments of peculiar delicacy.

PERKINS'S TRANSFERRING PRESS AND ROLLER DIE.

The invention was introduced into England by Perkins, but did not become popular. In Ireland it fared better. In this country it is supreme.

Postal and revenue stamps are so made in all instances. England makes them for the varied and widely separated nations of her vast empire. America, which originated the system, makes them for other nations in all quarters of the globe. The postal stamp itself, though now a necessity, is an affair but of yesterday, as it were, and was an outgrowth of cheap postage, for which let us thank Divine Providence and Rowland Hill.

Another triumph of the century is the watch. The invention of the compensation-balance of John Harrison covered the period 1728–1761. He died in 1776. Arnold and Earnshaw brought it to something near perfection. Harrison's fourth chronometer was sent in a man-of-war to Jamaica, which it reached five seconds slow. On the return to Portsmouth, after a five-months' voyage, it was one minute and five seconds wrong, showing an error of sixteen miles of longitude, and within the limit of the act of Parliament of Queen Anne, passed in 1714. This amount of accuracy has since been very much exceeded. He received the grant of £20,000 in installments, the reward of forty years' diligence.

The American system of watch-making, by gathering all the operations under one roof, making the parts as largely as possible by machinery, each part being made in quantity by gauge and pattern, and the

THE GREAT EQUATORIAL—UNITED STATES NAVAL OBSERVATORY.

pieces afterward *assembled,* dates back to 1852, but was afterward perfected, and the number of parts reduced from 800 to 156. In the year mentioned A. L. Denison and three coadjutors started the business in Roxbury, Massachusetts, thence moved to Waltham, Massachusetts, where the business now occupies a large factory, employs 700 hands, and turns out 80,000 watches annually. This is the pioneer establishment. Others are in operation at Elgin, Illinois; Springfield, Massachusetts; Newark and Marion, New Jersey.

Achromatic lenses were first made by John Dollond, of London, 1758. The discovery rendered the telescope of high powers possible. Without going into the optical principles involved, it may be stated that with refracting telescopes before Dollond an instrument of quite moderate magnifying power was 100 feet long. The equatorial of the Washington Observatory is the largest refractor in the world. It was made by Alvan Clark and Sons, of Cambridgeport, Massachusetts, the glass being cast by Chance and Co., of Birmingham, England. It was mounted in November, 1873, is thirty-two feet long, and, last and most important of the statement, it has an objective of twenty-six inches diameter.

With two other instruments of precision we may close this part of the subject, both means for accurate measurement:

1. The *contact level* invented by Repsold, of Hamburg, in 1820, as improved by Würdemann, of Washington. It is an adaptation of the spirit-level, for the production of exact divisions of scales, and for the determination of very minute divisions of length. It consists of a delicate level pivoted at its middle and across its length with a small tilt-weight at one end, which tips always in one direction. From the centre of the level downward extends a short rigid arm, with a plain polished surface perpendicular to the chord of the level against which the contact is made. The carrier of this instrument is either fixed or mounted in a slide governed by a micrometer screw. If, now, the end of a rod terminating in a hardened steel point be advanced horizontally till it bears against the contact arm, the level will gradually assume the horizontal position, and the movement of the bubble, as indicated by the scale upon the glass, will depend upon the relation of the radius to which the level tube is ground and the length of the contact lever. If the latter

be half an inch long, and the radius of the glass tube be 400 feet (levels for astronomical purposes are ground to a sweep of 800 and 1000 feet radius), the relation between the lever and radius is as 1 to 9600, and as $\frac{1}{50}$ of an inch can be readily read from the lever scale, $\frac{1}{480000}$ of an inch (9600×50) will be the difference in length which each such division on a scale indicates.

2. Whitworth's micrometer gauge is capable of measuring to $\frac{1}{1000000}$ of an inch. The principle of its action may be readily understood by the micrometer screw D, which is a pocket instrument made to measure to $\frac{1}{1000}$ of an inch. The screw has fifty threads to an inch, the head having twenty divisions on its circumference; consequently a turn of the head through one division advances the screw $\frac{1}{50}\times\frac{1}{20}=\frac{1}{1000}$ of an inch.

The millionth measuring instrument, shown by three views, A, B, C, has two head-stocks with a V groove between them, in which the square bars *b c* are laid, as is also the standard of the bar *d*, of which the length is to be tested. The sides of the groove and of the bars are worked up to as true a plane as possible, and are kept at right angles to each other. The ends of the bars are also made square with their sides, and brought to true planes, the ends being canted to present circular instead of square faces. Through each head-stock runs an accurately pitched micrometer screw, by which *b* and *c* are driven along the groove. The screw on the side of *b* has exactly twenty threads to the inch, and is turned by the wheel *f*, the circumference of which is divided into 250 parts. Consequently, by turning the wheel forward one division the bar is moved $\frac{1}{5000}$ of an inch.

The other screw has a similar thread, is driven by a worm-wheel of 200 teeth, into which gears a tangent screw *h*, having fixed upon its stem the graduated wheel *g*. The circumference of this wheel being also divided into 250 parts, a movement of one division corresponds to a traverse of $\frac{1}{20}\times\frac{1}{200}\times\frac{1}{250}=\frac{1}{1000000}$ of an inch on the bar *c*. Fixed pointers enable the exact movement of wheels *f* or *g* to be read off, so that this extremely minute difference in the length of any bars may be detected, provided the micrometer screws exert an equal pressure in every case.

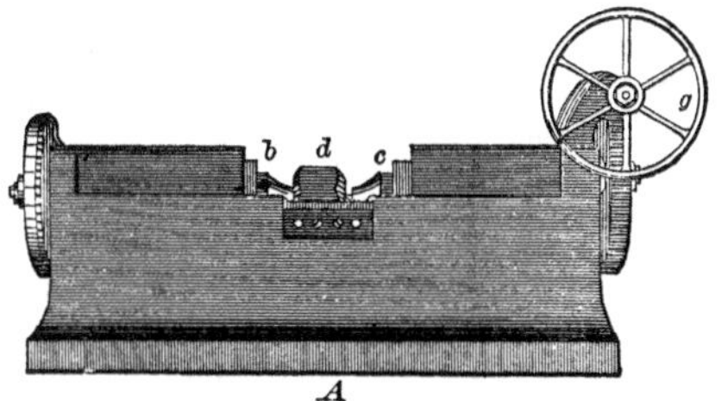

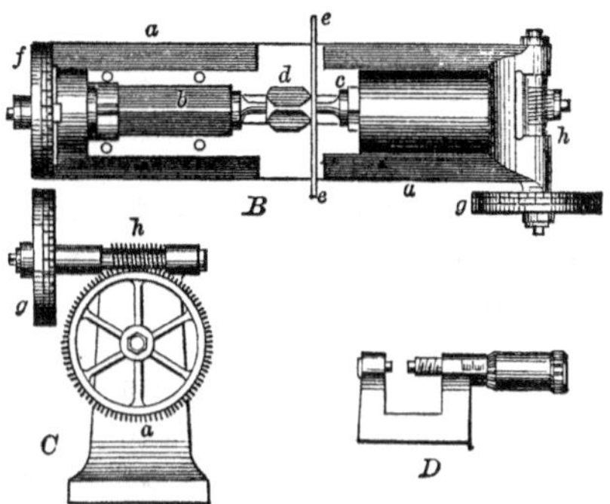

WHITWORTH'S MILLIONTH MEASURING GAUGE.

This equality of pressure is secured by a very simple and beautiful arrangement. Between one extremity of the steel bar under comparison and the sliding bar a small steel piece with true parallel sides is introduced. This piece is called the *feeler*, and its ends, *e e*, rest upon two supports on the sides of the bed. When little or no pressure is exerted on the bar *d*, the feeler falls back of its own weight if one of its ends is raised. A slight pressure prevents this falling back, and the friction between this piece and the ends of the bars becomes a very delicate measure of the pressure to which it is subjected.

ENGINEERING.

How shall we condense within the limits of the section of an article even a list of the engineering devices and expedients which distinguish the century nearly closed from any which has preceded it? The pyramids, temples, and obelisks of Egypt, the graceful architecture of Greece and of the Freemasons of the Middle Ages, the Roman roads and aqueducts, make the fame of the past. The present has a new set of devices, and its modes and structures are utterly beyond the conceptions of ancient times.

We will pass over the works which differ

in no essential respect from those of the past. Quays, sea-walls, and breakwaters were familiar to the Mediterranean nations, and our canals differ from those of the ancients only in having locks—not a small advance, by-the-way, and one for which we are indebted to the Italian engineers, the brothers Domenico. The canal of Sesostris—re-opened by Pharaoh Necho about 605 B.C., again by Ptolemy Philadelphus 300 B.C., once again by the Caliphs, and abandoned when Vasco da Gama circumnavigated the Cape of Good Hope—conducted the water of the Red Sea to the Nile near Belbeys, the Bubastis Agria of the Romans. It was ninety-six miles long. The track of the present Suez Canal only follows the former course to the Bitter Lakes, and then passes to Port Said on the Mediterranean. The sand and earth of the old canal were drearily excavated by fellahs who toiled with wooden shovels and baskets. The steam-dredges of M. De Lesseps were sixty in number, of two kinds, and deposited the 400,000,000 cubic yards of mud and sand on banks at a regulated distance from the canal.

The Pharos of Alexandria, said to have been 450 feet high, was a beacon to the roadstead of Alexandria. This city was built by what might have seemed the whim of a man who in the plenitude of his power came to Rhacotis, a place occupied by a little group of hovels, and spread his Macedonian cloak on the ground for the plan of a city to bear his name. He saw it rise in his mind's eye, and gave his directions for the avenues, the Serapæum, the Bruchion, and other public buildings, took up his line of march for the teeming East, and never saw Alexandria. Yet posterity approved his judgment, and his city has embalmed his name.

One of our contributions in the line of light-houses is the dovetailed block system introduced by Smeaton in 1760 at the Eddystone, copied by the Stephensons at Bell Rock, in the Frith of Forth, and at the Skerryvores, and still later at Wolf Island. Others are the screw-pile and the truss-frame systems, which are convenient in many places where the column of masonry is not suitable. Farther, the mode of lighting is much more eminently superior to the past than is the mere structure. When Smeaton had finished the Eddystone it was lighted by twenty-four tallow-candles stuck in a hoop. Even the Tour de Corduan, put up with so much expense in 1610 at the mouth of the Garonne, was for a long time lighted with burning logs in a large cresset. The catoptric system of lamps with parabolic reflectors was introduced into the Tour de Corduan soon after the invention of the circular-wick and centre-draught lamp by Argand, of Geneva, in 1784—a lamp which made the effective illumination of light-houses possible.

The dioptric system, by lenses, was attempted in England at the South Foreland light in 1752 and the Portland light in 1759, but failed for want of skill. It was revived and improved by Fresnel in 1810. It was adopted in the Lundy Island light in 1834, and is the best light, having several grades of size, according to importance of position.

In pile-driving we have better machinery than the Romans, who, however, made good work in bridges built on piles, and in constructing coffer-dams for building stone piers in river-beds. Elm piles driven by the Romans at London were in good order when removed to build the abutments of London Bridge in 1829. Cæsar threw a pile and trestle bridge across the Rhine in ten days. Trajan's bridge across the Danube was 4770 feet long, having twenty semicircular arches of 180 feet 5 inches span each. The piers were of stone, the superstructure wood. There were also many bridges in Rome.

For working beneath the surface of the water we, however, have several methods unknown to the ancients, and, indeed, only used to valuable purpose within the century. The first use of the diving-bell in engineering was by Smeaton in 1779. It had been used for a century or two as a curiosity or in reclaiming sunken treasures, and had been much improved by Halley and by Spalding in 1774, before it came into Smeaton's hands.

The *pneumatic caisson*, which now forms so important an aid in sinking piers to solid foundations beneath river-beds, is the invention of M. Triger, of France, where it was first used in sinking a shaft for a coal-pit through a stratum of quicksand, to reach the coal-measures in the vicinity of the river Loire, in France. It consisted of a tube made in sections, so as to be extended as the shaft deepened. The lower end was open, and divided by a floor with a tightly fitting trap-door from a middle chamber, the ceiling of which had a similar door. By means of an air-compressing pump the water was kept out of the lower chamber, where the men worked, and the buckets were handed up through the floors to the top, the middle chamber forming an air-lock, which was alternately in communication with the working-chamber below and with the air-chamber above it.

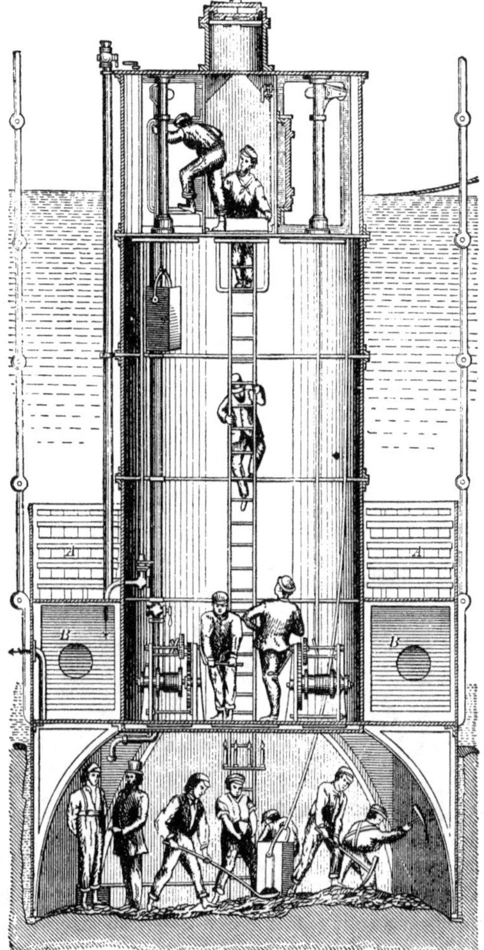

CAISSON AT COPENHAGEN.

The figure shows a caisson used some years afterward in building the piers of a bridge at Copenhagen, Denmark. A much improved and extended plan was adopted by Captain James B. Eads in building the river piers of the Illinois and St. Louis Railway Bridge across the Mississippi; and by Colonel W. A. Roebling for the piers of the suspension-bridge across the East River, New York. In each of the last-mentioned cases the caisson is a very heavy structure, designed when it reached the solid rock to remain there, be built up full of masonry or concrete, and then support the pier which was built upon it as it descended; the Triger caisson, after its function as a pneumatic excavating chamber was completed, formed a lining for the shaft in a treacherous soil; the Copenhagen caisson was lifted as the pier built at the bottom progressed upwardly.

The next illustration shows an East River caisson. The mode adopted for getting rid of the excavated material in the New York caisson is the invention of M. Fleur St. Denis,

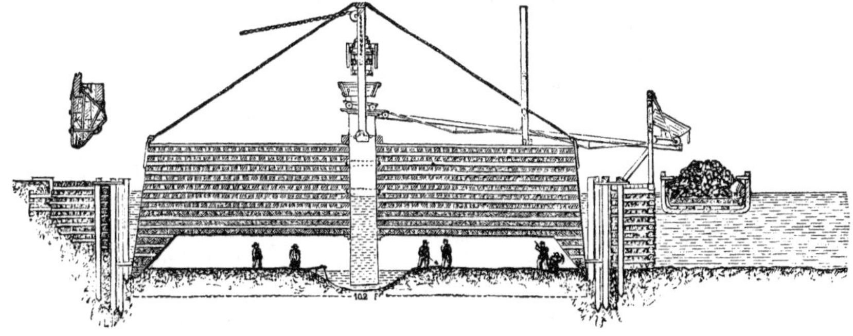
CAISSON OF THE EAST RIVER BRIDGE, NEW YORK.

FLOATING DERRICK, DEPARTMENT OF PUBLIC DOCKS, NEW YORK.

chief engineer des Chemins de Fer de l'Est, in France. It consists of a water-shaft whose lower end is submerged in water in a basin, and which is traversed by a dredging bucket or grapple, according as mud or rock has to be raised. The condensed air in the other part of the interior of the caisson keeps water excluded, and makes it habitable for the workmen.

In the St. Louis caisson the sand, mud, and stones as large as a hickory-nut were driven out of the collecting basin in the floor of the working chamber by means of a powerful jet of air which lifted a column of water in a tube, and with it the finer excavated material, the pipe discharging it over the side into a lighter.

The docks of some principal sea-ports are a marvelous feature both in character and in extent. London and Liverpool are celebrated for tidal docks. The first named had a particular object in grouping the merchantmen of special trades together in basins where the access between vessels and warehouses might be free, and within walls which were guarded by the custom-house authorities. It was also desirable to produce more wharf room. The high tides of the Mersey render the port of Liverpool very inconvenient for river and lighter work, and make tidal basins a necessity. The quays of Montreal are the best in America.

The large floating derrick of the New York Department of Public Docks picks up a block of 100 tons, is towed to the place of deposit, and then lowers the block into the position it is to occupy in the new river wall.

The dry-docks of the principal naval stations of the world are a great engineering success, and would have vastly astonished Archimedes, who had no resource but a bank of earth to embay his vessel, and then pump out the pond.

The floating dock *Bermuda* is an iron vessel of a rectangular shape, with a rounded bow and a strong caisson-gate at the stern. The vessel has a double skin, with a large intervening space. Into the inner basin a ship is floated while the dock is partially submerged; the caisson being closed, the water in the dock and space intervening between the two skins is pumped out so that the interior may be dry to allow work on the vessel, and the jacket may have sufficient flotative power to carry its load.

The *Bermuda* was built in England, and was towed to Bermuda by war vessels. This dock cost $1,250,000, and has the following dimensions: extreme length, 381 feet; width inside, 83 feet 9 inches; depth, 74 feet 5 inches. The weight is 8350 tons. The dock is U-shaped, and the section throughout is similar. It is built with two skins fore and aft at a distance of twenty feet apart. The space between the skins is divided by a water-tight bulk-head, running with the middle line the entire length of the dock, each half being divided into three

FLOATING DOCK "BERMUDA."

chambers by like bulk-heads. The three chambers are respectively named "load," "balance," and "air" compartments. The first-named chamber is pumped full in eight hours when a ship is about to be docked, and the dock is thus sunk below the level of the horizontal bulk-heads which divide the other two chambers. Water sufficient to sink the structure low enough to permit a vessel to enter is forced into the balance chambers by means of valves in the external skin. The vessel having floated in, the next operation is to place and secure the end caissons, which act as gates. When the water is ejected from the "load" chamber, the dock with the vessel in it rises, the water in the dock being allowed to decrease by opening the sluices in the caissons. The dock is trimmed by letting the water out of the "balance" chamber into the structure itself. The inside of the dock is cleared of water by valves in the skin, and it is left to dry. When it becomes necessary to undock the vessel the valves in the external skins of the "balance" chamber are opened in order to fill them, and the culverts in the caissons are also opened, and the dock sunk to a given depth. From keel to gunwale nine main water-tight ribs extend, further dividing the distance between the two skins into eight compartments; thus there are altogether forty-eight water-tight divisions. Frames made of strong plates and angle-iron strengthen the skins between the main ribs. Four steam engines and pumps on each side—each pump has two suctions, emptying a division of an "air" chamber—are fitted to the dock, and these also fill a division of the "load" chamber. When it becomes necessary to clean, paint, or repair the bottom of the dock, it is careened by the weight of water in the "load" chambers of one side, and the middle line is raised about five feet out of water. The *Royal Alfred*, bearing the flag of the admiral on the station, and weighing 6000 tons, was lifted by this dock, her keel resting on a central line of blocks arranged on the floor of the dock, the ship being shored up with timbers all around the top-sides.

Steam-pumps are important among the engineering devices of the day. The necessity of pumping water from mines, from ponds in draining, or from sunken vessels, coffer-dams, or wet excavations, has given great importance to that special application of the steam-engine.

The Cornish engine has already been referred to, but there is a host of machines for use on shipboard, for wrecking, at railway watering stations, and used by manufacturers who require water in large quantity.

Perronet was the greatest engineer of his

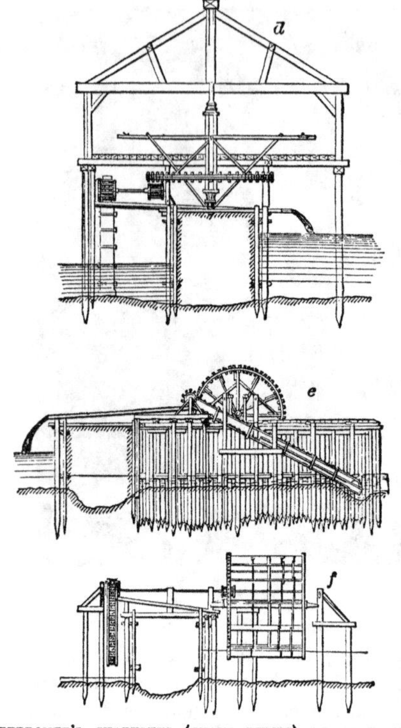

PERRONET'S CHAPELETS (CHAIN-PUMPS) AT ORLEANS, FRANCE.

time, the builder of the famous bridge of Neuilly, and many other structures in France, the finest of their day, some of which yet remain witnesses to his skill and perfect taste. It is understood that his masterpiece, the bridge of Neuilly, was partially destroyed by the French during the German invasion, to render it impassable to the enemy. This was the first *level* bridge. The Waterloo Bridge, by Rennie, is even a more magnificent example. This is mentioned to introduce the fact that the chief engineer of the *ponts et chaussées* in the reign of Louis XVI. had no better contrivance for pumping out his coffer-dams than a chain-pump —the old *noria*, the *na úra* of the Arabs, "the wheel broken at the cistern" of Eccles., xii. 6. Better made, it is true, but the same otherwise. Perronet's chapelets (*d*)—so called because the buckets were strung along on a band like the beads of a rosary—were worked by horse-power at Orleans, twelve at a time being employed, making 140 revolutions per hour. The pallets acted as buckets, and passed at the rate of 9600 per hour. *e* and *f* are views of another chapelet of Perronet, driven by a water-wheel in the stream outside the coffer-dam. The current water-wheels used for raising water for the city of London, 1731, were under the arches of London Bridge, and gave way to the Boulton and Watt engine.

For drainage purposes with moderate lifts we have much improved lately, and principally since 1840, about which time the centrifugal pump came into notice, the first form being an inversion of the turbine, the wheel being driven by steam to raise the water in the vertical chute.

In the fens of Lincolnshire for low lifts the scoop-wheel is much employed. At Haarlem Lake, Holland, are the largest pumping-engines in the world, perhaps. They are three in number, have annular cylinders of twelve feet diameter, with inner cylinders of seven feet diameter. One engine works eleven pumps, and the others eight each. Each engine lifts sixty-six tons of water per stroke to a height of ten feet; when pressed each lifts 109 tons per stroke to that height. Running economically, each lifts 75,000,000 pounds of water one foot high for ninety-four pounds of Welsh coal. The net effective force of each is 350 horses; the consumption of fuel is two and a quarter pounds per horse-power per hour. The surface drained by the three engines is 45,230 acres, an average lift of the water, depending on the state of the tides, being sixteen feet. All other drainage enterprises sink into insignificance

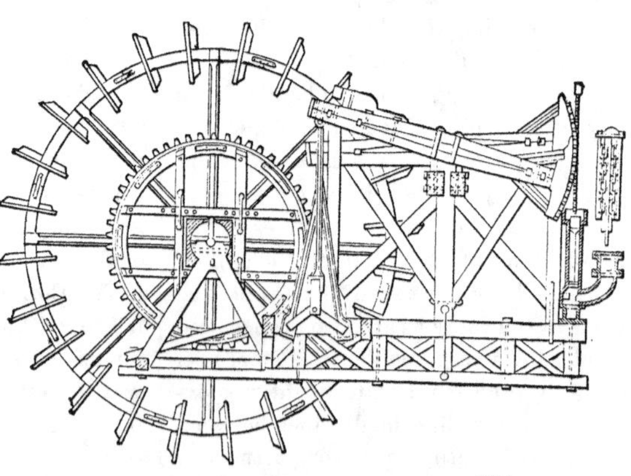

CURRENT WATER-WHEEL, LONDON BRIDGE, 1731.

beside those of Holland. They include an area of 223,062 acres drained by mechanical means.

Prominent among the engineering enterprises of the day are the tunneling of mountain chains and the removal, by drilling and blasting, of submarine obstructions.

It is just about 250 years since gunpowder was first used in blasting by the German miners in Hungary; now it seems strange that any great enterprise in rock should be attempted without it. The patient labor of the men who chiseled their way through a mile of rock near Vicovaro in making the second Roman aqueduct, the Anio Vetus, is rather sad than exhilarating when we consider the unpaid labor of the poor slaves who hewed out the tunnel.

Two vast jobs of tunneling ranges of mountains have lately been completed—the Mont Cenis and the Hoosac tunnels. Another, larger one is in progress—the St. Gothard. In each case the work was done, or is being done, by drills operated by compressed-air engines, the escaping air at the workings being an element of great value, as it provides fresh air at that point and establishes an outward current.

This whole business of exhausting air, compressing air, and using the comparative vacuum or the positive pressure, is very new. It is true, Otto Guericke had an air-pump in 1650, and Samuel Pepys says, February 15, 1665, of his visit to the Royal Society at Gresham College, "It is a most acceptable thing to hear their discourse and to see their experiments; which were this day on fire, and how it goes out in a place where the ayre is not free, and sooner out where the ayre is exhausted, which they showed by an engine on purpose."

These were but chamber experiments, and air used in an engine can not probably be traced back of Glazebrook's English patent of 1797, which had the principal features of the modern approved forms. Stirling's engine, 1827, was used at the Dundee Foundry, Scotland, for some years. Medhurst patented in 1799 the device of condensing air to be used at the workings into reservoirs at the bottom of the shaft by engines at the surface. Bompas had an air-driven carriage in 1828. The rock-drills at the Bardonneche end of the Mont Cenis tunnel were driven by air compressed by a curious apparatus devised by Sommeilleur, the volume of air compressed daily being 826,020 cubic feet, giving 137,670 feet at the drills under a pressure of six atmospheres. Air-pumps condensed the air at the French end of the tunnel.

Air, steam, and gunpowder are working hand in hand through the mountains and under the water. Now 18,500 pounds of gunpowder in three charges, simultaneously fired, tear at one crash 400,000 tons of chalk from the face of Round Down Cliff, near Dover; now twenty-three tons of powder in kegs heave the roof from the previously excavated cavern 50 by 140 feet beneath the Blossom Rock in the harbor of San Francisco. Jumper drills have long been pegging away at the works in the East River, where dangerous rocks and reefs are being removed to a safe depth, or cut away to improve the approaches or prevent dangerous currents and eddies. The works at Hallett's Point are among the most impor-

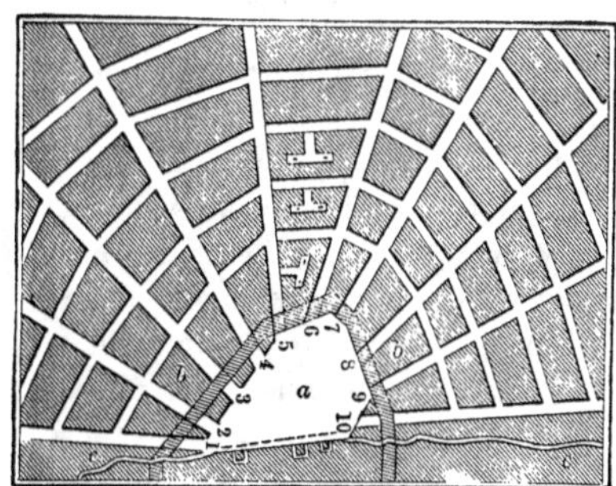

HEADING OF THE EXCAVATION, HALLETT'S POINT REEF, EAST RIVER, NEW YORK.

tant of these, and here the headings are driven radiating like the sticks of a fan, and are joined by cross galleries which leave square pillars to support the rock ceiling on which the sea beats. The galleries are numbered, and embouch into a common area (a), whence the excavated material is lifted by cranes; c is the shore line. The roof will come off some day with a bang, and the fragments will fall into the pit, and may be removed thence by grappling.

Closely allied to this work is that of boring Artesian and oil wells. These also seem to belong to us of "the latter days," although it has always been the case that wells dug in some strata become Artesian. If the source of supply be high enough, they

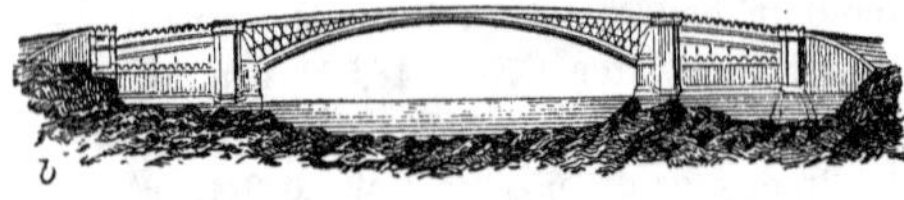

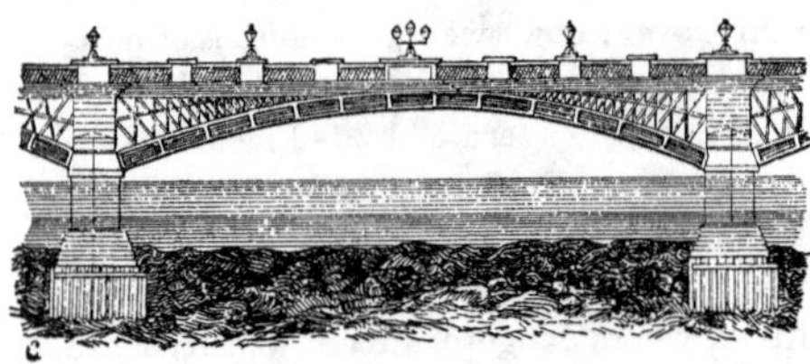

IRON ARCH BRIDGES.

a is a representation of the cast-iron arch bridge of 600 feet span projected by Telford for crossing the Thames. *b* was a bridge of cast-iron sections, 500 feet span, proposed by Telford for the Menai Straits in preference to the suspension-bridge of 570 feet span decided upon by the committee. *c*, the middle arch of Southwark Bridge, 240 feet span.

run over, as at Artois, from whence they are named.

If the Chinese of the province On-Tong-Kias did really bore the flowing wells to a depth of from 1500 to 1800 feet, we must admit that we have but few to exceed that depth. London's Trafalgar Square wells are only 393 feet; they soon reach water seams in the chalk. The well at Calais, France, is 1138 feet; Donchery, Ardennes, 1215 feet; Grenelle, 1802; Passy, 1913; brine well at Kissingen, 2000; Belcher's sugar refinery, St. Louis, 2197. The Columbus, Ohio, 2700 feet, and St. Louis County Farm, 3235 feet, are failures as Artesian wells.

Iron has entered largely into modern structures, and the time seems near at hand when important buildings will be made of brick, iron, and cement. Sir Joseph Paxton made a long step ahead in 1851, when he constructed of iron the building to which England invited the representatives of all nations. The constructors of iron houses in our cities must abandon the attempt to imitate in iron the shapes which are proper to such materials as brick and stone.

The great success, so far, is in roofs. Those of the Grand Central Railway Dépôt, Forty-second Street, New York, and the St. Pancras Station of the Midland Counties Railway, England, are eminent instances. The former was constructed by Buckhout, and is 652 feet long, 199 feet 2 inches between walls. It covers about three acres. The St. Pancras Station has a span of 240 feet, a length of 690 feet, covering five platforms, ten lines of rails, and a cab stand twenty-five feet wide.

The use of iron in structures marks the work of the century. Engineers have in their adaptation of the new material contrived a new set of forms and parts, and made an entirely new set of calculations. The genius and skill were not wanting before, we may say, but the previous century had not the iron in quantity.

Bridge-building affords a remarkable group of structures in iron. There are four forms, the *arch*, *truss*, *suspension*, *tubular*. The projects become more and more bold.

The first iron bridge was one of cast-iron sections across the Severn at Colebrookdale, in England, erected in 1779 by Darby and Wilkinson, unless we may mention a foot chain-bridge seventy feet long across the Tees in 1741, and credit the chain-bridge in a mountain pass at King-tong, in China. In 1796 Wilson erected an iron arch bridge 100 feet above the water over the Wear at Sunderland. In 1818–25 Telford spanned the Menai Straits by his so-called *chain*-bridge. Iron rods with coupling links form the catenary. Southwark Bridge (*c*) over the Thames is or was a structure of three arches of cast-iron voussoirs, and was erected in 1819.

The highest bridge in the world is the Verrugas Viaduct, on the Lima and Oroya Railway, in the Andes of Peru. It is 12,000 feet above the level of the sea, 575 feet long, and formed of three iron truss spans on iron piers.

The bridge lately built across the Mississippi at St. Louis has a compound system of steel tubular arches supporting the truss and road-beds. It has three spans of 497, 515, and 497 feet respectively. The middle arch has but one fellow in the world, that of Kuilinburg, in Holland. Its engineer is Captain Eads, and it has lately been opened amidst great rejoicing. It has a double-track railway upon the lower level, and a roadway thirty-four feet wide and two footways each eight feet wide upon the upper level. The Illinois roads which converge upon this viaduct have freight dépôts near the water, but the passenger trains pass through a tunnel 4800 feet in length beneath the river-side part of the city, and reach the up-town dépôt. Each span consists of four arches, having two members each, an upper and a lower one. Each member is of two parallel cast-steel tubes nine inches in exterior diameter set closely together, and each made in four segments, whose junctions form ribs. The upper and lower members are eight feet apart. The whole structure is stiffened by systems of diagonal, vertical, and horizontal braces.

The arch formed a very important member of many wooden bridges, and still does of some iron trusses.

Another tubular arch bridge is that of the Washington Aqueduct across Rock Creek, erected by General Meigs. It has a span of 200 feet and a rise of twenty feet, and consists of two ribs, each composed of seventeen cast-iron pipes, flanged and bolted together. The pipes are lined with staves to prevent freezing, and have a clear water way of three feet six inches. Through them passes the water for the supply of the city of Washington.

The Fairmount Bridge across the Schuylkill is 100 feet wide, was built by the Phœnixville Bridge Company, and is the finest example of an iron truss bridge in this country.

Those Chinese prevent many a broad and full statement by having anticipated the Western barbarians in so many things: gunpowder, the mariner's compass, movable-type printing, paper of rags, glazing of pottery, silk, and boring for gas and brine. Suspension-bridges also have been long used in China and Thibet. One noticed by Turner, near Tchin-Chien, was 140 feet long, on four catenary chains; one in Quito, observed by Humboldt, was of rope four inches in diameter, made of agave fibre; one in Aligpore, in Hindostan, is 130 feet in length, and made of cane with iron fastenings; Hooker notices several in Nepaul; Scamozzi refers to suspension-bridges in Europe in 1615.

The suspension-bridge was waiting for iron. The first iron suspension-bridge in Europe, possibly in the world, was a chain-bridge across the Tees in 1741. Telford threw one across the Menai Straits, 570 feet, in 1820; it is of rods with coupling links. The Fribourg Bridge, 880 feet, was erected in 1830. The Niagara Railway Bridge, 821 feet, was erected by Roebling, 1855. The Wheeling Bridge, across the Ohio, 1010 feet, erected by Ellet, was blown down. The Cincinnati Bridge, across the Ohio, was constructed by Roebling in 1866. It is 1057 feet between piers; each cable has 5180 wires, each laid with a given strain to bear its part of the load. This was a grand conception. The weight of wire is 1,050,183 pounds. The new Niagara Bridge, just below the basin of the falls, is 1264 feet span, 190 feet high, and was erected in 1869.

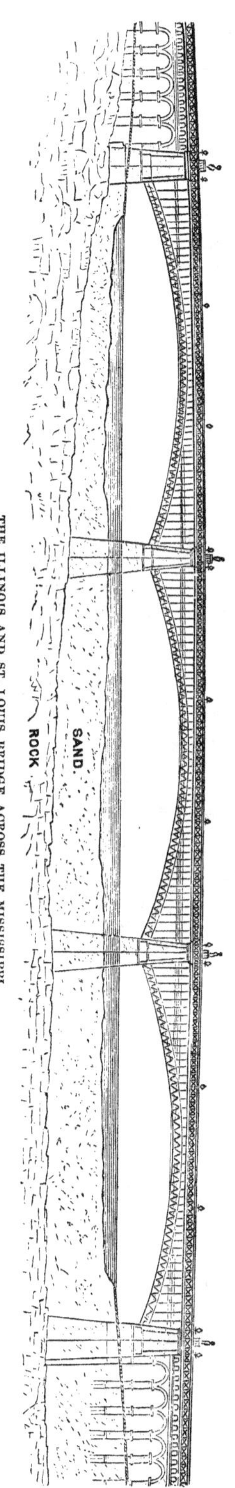

THE ILLINOIS AND ST. LOUIS BRIDGE ACROSS THE MISSISSIPPI.

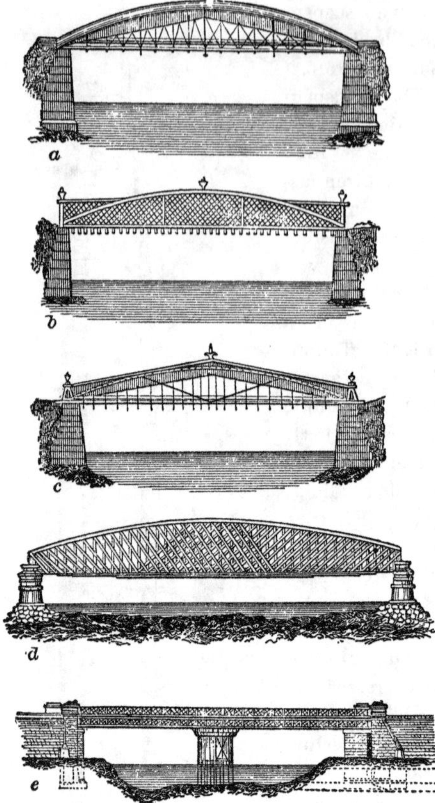

IRON TRUSS AND LATTICE BRIDGES.

a, b, c, are forms of trusses for moderate spans. *a*, rectanuglar-tube bridge. *b*, iron arch and lattice girder bridge. *c*, strut girder bridge. *d*, the principal span of the Kuilinburg Railway bridge over the Leck, a branch of the Rhine. It has nine spans; the one shown is 515 feet total length, 492 feet clear span. Its only rival in length is the middle span of Captain Eads's bridge across the Mississippi at St. Louis. *e* is a truss bridge over the Avon in England, the mid length resting on a cluster of screw piles.

We are now waiting for the completion of the New York and Brooklyn Bridge, 5862 feet between termini, 1600 feet between river piers, and 80 feet wide.

The tubular bridge erected at Conway, Wales, preceded that over the Menai Straits. Succeeding them is the Victoria Bridge across the St. Lawrence River at Montreal. The principle of all is the same: a tube of rectangular section forming a hollow girder. The material is cast and wrought iron, so disposed as to secure the valuable features of each kind. It was demanded that trains should be permitted to cross each way simultaneously at full speed on the two tracks; that it should be 100 feet above the water; that no centring should be used to temporarily obstruct navigation. Stephenson made the first estimates, and Fairbairn brought into use his great knowledge in the strength of materials and skill in the disposition of parts to bear strains to which different portions of a structure are subjected. The tubes are respectively 260, 472, 472, and 260 feet, the larger ones weighing about 4,032,000 pounds each. The tubes were built on floats, towed to their positions, raised by powerful hydrostatic jacks, the masonry being built beneath them as the lifting proceeded. The jacks rested on beams on the ledges of the towers. The lifting chains weighed 224,000 pounds each, and were of six-feet sections, which were taken out, a section at a time, after each lift was made, and the tube rested on the masonry beneath it while the piston of the jack descended ready for another lift. The pressure of the water beneath the ram was 2½ tons per square inch. The tubes were lifted 100 feet above tide-water, ascending in high perpendicular grooves in the faces of the towers, which were closed up by masonry as the lifting proceeded. It was opened for traffic in 1850.

The Victoria Bridge at Montreal had no such extremely heavy work. It is 176 feet less than two miles long, having twenty-five spans, the centre one 330 feet, the others each 240 feet long. The centre span is 60 feet above the summer level of the water, and has a slight descent toward each end. The cost was £1,250,000.

But one of the bridges mentioned above was standing when the old bell of the red brick house in Philadelphia rang out, "Proclaim liberty throughout the land and to all the inhabitants thereof!" The solitary exception was the chain-bridge across the Tees. This bridge has long since passed away, was but a solitary precursor of the coming age of iron bridges, and in mode of structure chains have given way to wire, first of iron, then of steel.

WOOD-WORKING.

In no department of mechanical progress has the advancement been more thorough than in the machinery for the working of

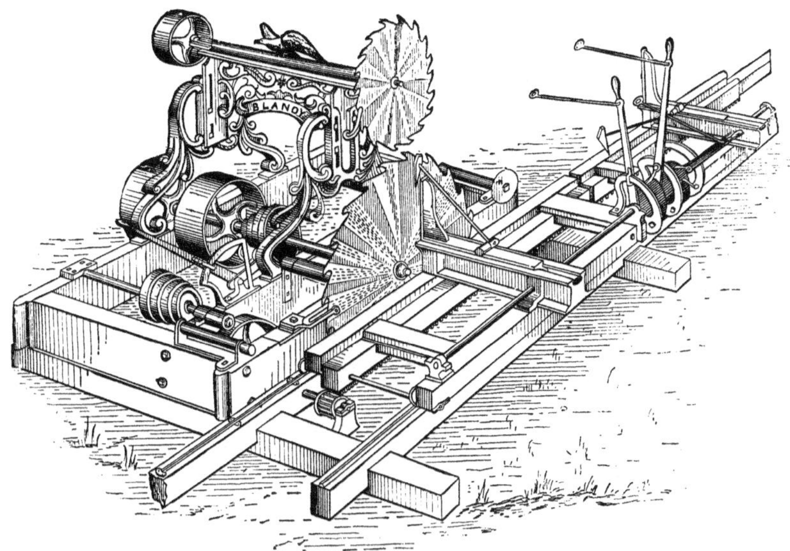

PORTABLE CIRCULAR SAW.

wood. Up to the beginning of the last quarter of the eighteenth century what were the tools and modes of the wood-worker? With the axe, adze, pit-saw, whip-saw, handsaw, chisel, and rasp excellent work was done; but it may be said that, with the exception of a few saw-mills, there was no machinery for wood-working. How infrequent were the saw-mills may be gathered from the fact that one established in England in 1663 by a Dutchman was abandoned from fear of personal violence on the part of the populace, and in 1767 one at Limehouse, in the eastern part of London, was destroyed by a mob of sawyers who considered their craft in danger.

The writer distinctly recollects when logs and tree trunks were habitually sawed from end to end, to work them into dimension stuff, by two sawyers, one standing on the log and the other in a pit beneath with a veil over his eyes to keep out the sawdust. And what a hard-working, sad, drunken set these sawyers were, and how the top-sawyer bossed the wretch in the hole, who pulled down, while he above, with shoulders like an Atlas, swung his weight upon the handles above! This lasted well into our century; but now we have a host of saw-mills of various kinds working on the most extensive scale at the great lumbering centres, and machines for special work in all cities where the stuff thus roughly "got out" into square stuff or merchantable lumber is sawed into plank, dimension lumber, slats, scale-boards, veneers, and what not.

The circular saw was introduced into England in 1790, but its inventor is not known. General Sir Samuel Bentham, the most renowned of all inventors of wood-working machinery, and to whom we shall have to refer several times, patented in 1793 the bench, slit, parallel guide, and sliding bevel guide. The machine has now attained an excellence and completeness which leave little to be desired.

In the stationary form of the machine the saws are either single or in gangs. The portable kind has an upper saw to complete the kerf made only partially through the larger logs by the lower saw. Such is known as a *double saw*. The log carriage travels on ways, the feed being by a pinion meshing into a rack beneath the carriage.

After the cut the head-blocks are simultaneously moved up, bringing the log a distance nearer to the saw equal to the thickness of the board desired, plus the width of the kerf made by the saw. Very rapid and handy are these saws, but the men of '76 never dreamed of such a thing. We had rude gate saws driven by flutter wheels, or geared up for motion from a larger wheel. There was then no premonition of the saw-mills which hum in all our ports and buzz in all the forests of the land.

The veneer saw, a peculiar adaptation of the circular saw, with thin segmental teeth on a thin hub of large diameter, was invented by Bramah.

Nor must we forget the scroll-saw, also named a jig saw from its rapid vertical motion. It has a narrow thin blade which eats its way in a wonderful manner through the stuff which is moved against it, sliding on the surface of a flat table through which the saw reciprocates. The band saw is for

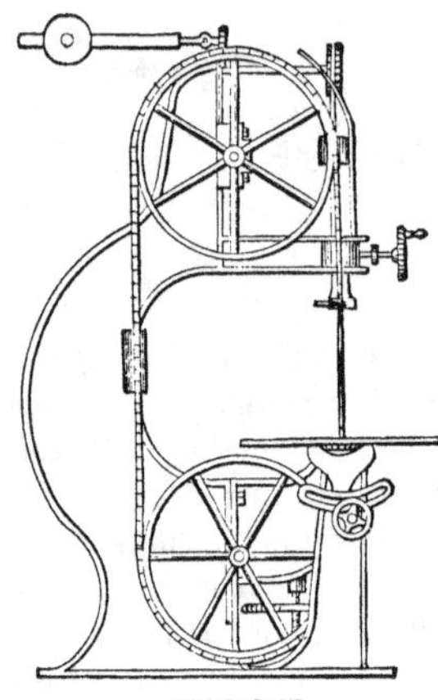

BAND SAW.

the same purpose, but is a steel ribbon with a serrated edge, and runs on two band wheels, one of which is driven by the steam-power.

The planing-machine for wood assumed three shapes before it settled into its present preferred form; indeed, there are yet two kinds. General Bentham's machine, patented in 1791, was like an immense plane pushed over the surface of the board. Bramah's machine, 1802, is what is called the *traverse planer*, the cutters being on the lower edge of a revolving disk, which revolves with its vertical arbor above the board, which passes beneath it. The more common and generally useful form of the planing-machine has revolving cutters on horizontal axes, which work the top of the board. By an extension of the principle another cutter may work the lower surface, and two others on vertical axes dress the edges, or square stuff may be dressed on all sides, or one or more of the cutters may have such conformation as to plane mouldings on the stuff.

This is the moulding-machine, whose usefulness it is hard to exaggerate, but the admirable Bentham and the equally useful and perhaps equally brilliant Bramah would gaze with keen zest upon the outgrowth of their genius and pains.

Another form of moulding-machine has a vertical shaft, with cutters of the conformation required protruding through a table, so as to work the edges of the stuff brought against them, directed by the hand or by a guide.

The joiner, or *general wood-worker*, is another of the late additions to the shop. The number of years it has been in use can almost be counted on the fingers of the two hands. Though the term may not have been so intended, yet it is well placed, for

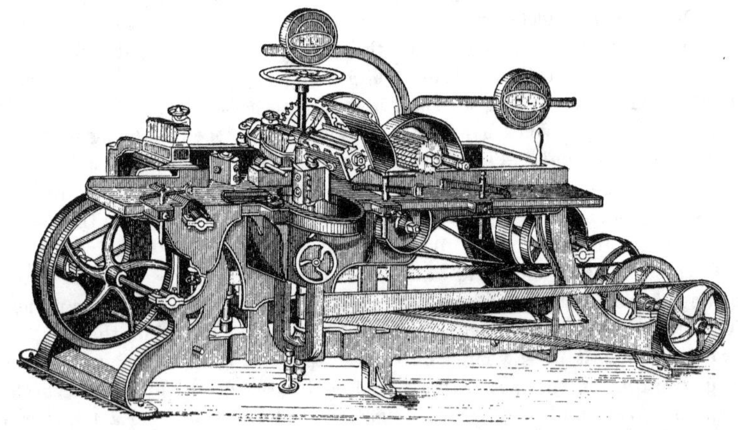

MOULDING-MACHINE.

it holds a very commanding rank. It planes flat, moulding, and beaded surfaces; it rips or crosscuts; it bores and counterbores; it mortises and tenons, executes squaring-up, grooving, tonguing, rabbeting, mitring, chamfering, and wedge-cutting; it is a jack-of-all-work, the handy man of the shop, with unflagging energy and singular versatility. It well represents the mature mind of the ages, being a *multum in parvo*, the combination of a set of separate machines, possessing the attributes of each, which it is ready to turn to account at any time, not always together, but in rapid succession at short notice.

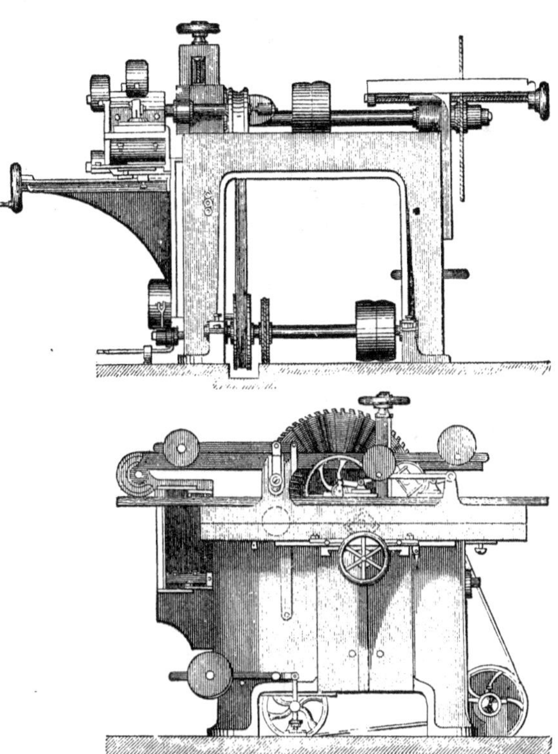

GENERAL WOOD-WORKER.

The mortising-machine may have had a precarious existence before General Sir Samuel Bentham, but we have no trace of it. Bentham describes the self-acting machine in his patent of 1793. His description includes the operation by which a hole previously bored is elongated by a chisel into a slot, and also the mode of making the mortise by a rotating cutter during the traverse of the work. He also had a pivoted table for oblique mortising, and a double or forked chisel for making narrow parallel mortises.

Brunel's machine for mortising the shells of ships' blocks was made for the British Admiralty in 1804. The block is chucked in a carriage, and has an automatic feed movement by means of a screw. The chisel (or chisels for blocks with more than one score) is in a vertically reciprocating slider in the frame above.

The latest improvements in mortising-machines have much increased their capacity and range of work, special machines being made for various duties. One principal feature is that for bringing the chisel into action and determining its depth of stroke by simply pressing upon a treadle, the chisel being quiescent as soon as the foot is lifted, and this without disconnection with the motor.

The tendency of the age is to rotary motion. The first machine in the world, perhaps, was the throwing wheel of the potter. In the oldest of the Egyptian paintings the creative spirit, Knep, is represented as turning man upon the potter's wheel. The Greek *tornos* does not appear to have been much superior to the *pole lathe* which was used by our ancestors, and is yet the useful machine of the Kabyles of Africa and the mountaineers of the Carpathians. In this the work is rotated in one direction by a treadle and a cord which winds on the mandrel, and in the other by the recoil of a spring pole. Our ancestors did not use turned work to any great extent; the hatchet and the drawing-knife fashioned the furniture of the rustic; a rather smoother mode of preparation fell to the lot of that made for the gentler born. Now the turning lathe is the machine of speed; broom handles are turned, and pails, clothes-pins, and the very commonest of articles.

The wood-turning lathe preceded that of metal many centuries, as that for clay long

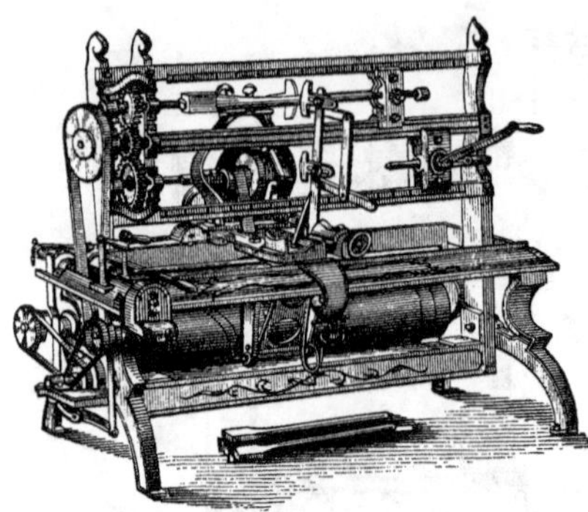

BLANCHARD'S SPOKE LATHE.

preceded the wood-lathe. We pass at once to the lathe for turning irregular forms, invented by Thomas Blanchard, of Boston, Massachusetts, in 1828, and since much improved by himself and others.

It is made for turning spokes, axe-handles, gun-stocks, and various other crooked and difficult shapes. The illustration shows it as adapted for turning spokes. These have very different shapes at different parts of their lengths, and spokes for different kinds of vehicles require very different shapes and proportions. Like the job of standing the egg on end, suggested by Christopher Colon to his curious friends, it is very easy to understand when explained; but it was a very ingenious contrivance and a great acquisition. The model is placed upon a slowly rotating mandrel at top; a tracer rests against each side of it, and governs the motions of the cutter frame, causing the revolving cutter to advance or recede to or from the stuff which is chucked between the centres of a mandrel below, and caused to rotate in correspondence with the model above. The cutter frame has a longitudinal motion along the frame, its cutter passing from end to end of the stick, and cutting more or less deeply in exact conformity with the model above. The piece to be cut is not shown in position, as it would hide the view of the cutter head.

It would not be fair to omit the statement that Condamine, De la Hire, and Plumier mention lathes in which the cutter is governed by a tracer passing over the irregular surface of a model; also that Brunel's machine for making the groove around ships' blocks for the ropes by which they are attached to the rigging has a revolving disk of brass with two cutters which receive their direction and depth from a shaper placed parallel thereto.

The first important collection of special wood-working tools was the machinery for making tackle blocks, invented by the elder Brunel, and made by Maudslay, 1802–08, for the British Admiralty. Fortunately General Bentham was at that time inspector of naval works, and so it only took twelve months to obtain the sanction of the commissioners to the adoption of the plans of the three excellent masters.

The machines are in three different sets, three in a set, for making different sizes, each set having a certain range of adjustability as to the sizes of blocks turned out. Altogether they make 214 sizes and kinds. With two additional machines for making dead-eyes, two for making iron pins, and one large boring machine, the number of machines is fifty. They were set up in 1808; cost $230,000. The saving over hand labor is variously estimated at from $83,000 to $150,000 per annum. Brunel, "the ingenious American mechanic," as Tomlinson calls him, received £1 per diem for superintendence, £1000 for the models, and £17,000 for his head-work.

The factory system is now in full vogue with wood-workers, and they can not desire a more honorable and thoroughly excellent triumvirate of leaders than Bentham, Brunel, Maudslay.

Our space will allow of scarcely more than a recapitulation of the remaining achievements which distinguish the present century.

ELEVATORS.

The *elevator*, as an ordinary apparatus in a hotel, business house, or building devoted to offices, is an American institution. The man-engine and the hoisting platform or cage have been for nearly a century the ordinary means of ascending mining shafts; the cage has more lately been introduced into factories to save the operators the labor of climbing, and now the winding apparatus has been much improved, the car luxuriously furnished and lighted, and safety devices introduced to prevent overwinding and to arrest descent if the rope breaks.

There are three principal forms: 1. That in which the winding drum is driven by a steam-engine, the rope passing over a pulley above the shaft, and thence downward to the suspended cage. 2. The hydraulic elevator, in which water from the city main acts upon a ram with great force, and *fleets*, as the sailor might say, the blocks of a compound tackle, drawing upon the rope which passes over the sheaves at a rate proportioned to the number of sheaves involved. 3. The direct hydraulic lift; in this the platform is supported by a piston working in a cylinder into which water is admitted from the city main. This requires a piston as long above the lowest floor as the height to be lifted, and a well or cylinder as great a depth below it. As the water runs into the cylinder it acts against the lower end of the piston, and when the platform is to be lowered, a faucet is opened, which allows the water to escape. It is safe, and is probably a French invention—the *Ascenseur Edoux*.

Besides these, there is a peculiarly American system of hoisting and storing grain, forming a prominent feature in the views of our sea-board and lake cities. An elevator-leg, as it is termed, reaches into the bin or well into which the wagons or cars have been discharged, or into the hold of the vessel. This leg is the extension device round which passes an endless belt with cups, each of which runs up full of grain and discharges into a hopper above, where the grain is weighed, and from whence it passes by spouts to the various bins. From these it is drawn, when reshipped, into cars or vessels.

In the American practice the grain is discharged into the hopper of a weighing machine gauged exactly for one hundred bushels; by opening a valve the contents are sent by a spout to the bin, the valve closed, and the elevating process resumed. Seven thousand bushels an hour are thus weighed. An elevator at Milwaukee is 280 feet long and 80 feet wide. The total length of the great driving-belt, urged by a 200 horse-power engine, is 280 feet, that is, the half, extending from cellar to comb, is 140 feet, and the down half is of course equal to it. This belt is 36 inches wide and three-quarters of an inch thick, and is made of six plies or thicknesses of canvas, with sheets of India rubber laid between them. It drives nine receiving elevators, or belts set with buckets, each of which lifts the grain 140 feet. The buckets are made of thick tin bound with hoop-iron, and are well riveted to the belt at intervals of fourteen inches. They are 6 inches across the mouth, 18 inches long, and when full each contains a peck. They do not usually go up quite full, but, allowing for this, there are 100 pecks (25 bushels) loaded on one side of the belt whenever it is at work. If all nine are running at once, as is often the case, the quantity of wheat lifted on these swift-running belts is 225 bushels. The established weight of a bushel of No. 2 Milwaukee spring wheat is 55 pounds. This would make the total lift of the receiving elevators during the time they are at work over 12,000 pounds.

The bins into which this wheat is poured are of great size, being 60 feet deep, 20 wide, and 10 across, containing 12,000 cubic feet. The total receiving and storing capacity of this building is 1,500,000 bushels. Of the crop of 1869 it received 7,000,000 bushels.

In discharging into the lake grain vessels, as soon as a ship is moored beside an elevator the hatches are removed, and great spouts extended over them from the bottom of one of the bins described. The gate is raised, and a torrent of wheat pours down. The loading power of these spouts is 12,000 bushels an hour. A vessel with a capacity for 18,000 bushels may be loaded in an hour and a half. The Oswego and Ogdensburg schooners, and vessels destined for the Welland Canal, usually take from 12,000 to 20,000 bushels. The Buffalo vessels are larger, often receiving 30,000, and in a few cases 45,000 bushels.

No other mode of handling grain has ever been devised which affords such facilities for unloading, weighing, storing, loading, moving from one bin to another for examination or for ventilation. A hundred years ago the shovel, sack, and the hoisting chain, or else the wheelbarrow, were the usual facilities of the grain merchant.

DOMESTIC MACHINERY.

Domestic machinery is not the least important of the features which characterize the present age.

The *sewing-machine* is an American invention of the last forty years. As was previously remarked of *reapers*, the European attempts at making machines to supersede the hand method served to exhibit the difficulty of the problem, but in no important degree to solve it. The shoe-sewing machine of Thomas Saint, patented in England in 1790, had a single thread, which was driven by a forked needle through a hole previously punched by an awl, and was then caught by a looper which held the loop so that it was entered by the needle and thread in their next descent, making a crochet stitch. The feed and the stitch-tightening movements were automatic.

The sewing-machine of Thimonnier, of Paris, was used in 1830 for making army clothing. Eighty of these machines, made of wood, were destroyed by a mob, which regarded them as an "invention of the enemy." They were afterward made of metal. Adams and Dodge, of Monkton, Vermont, in 1818, and more especially J. J. Greenough, of New York, in 1842, added improvements. Walter Hunt, 1832–35, made and sold lock-stitch sewing-machines, but neglected to pursue the business, which consequently attracted but little attention at the time. His extreme versatility prevented success; his inventions absorbed his time, and he seemingly had none left for securing the pecuniary results of his genius. He just missed, and by mere inattention, one of the grandest opportunities of the century. Elias Howe, with inferior inventive abilities, but with an adaptedness to follow out a single object persistently, and with business ability, reaped the field. The world, as we have had occasion to remark previously, thanks the man who gives an improvement into its hands. The name of Elias Howe is indissolubly associated with the success of the sewing-machine. This machine is no exception to the ordinary rule that an invention is a growth rather than an inspiration, and the discussion on the relative merits of inventors has been both voluminous and acrimonious. Examiners, commissioners, judges, each in their turn have found it a very knotty question how to apportion the respective credits. It is no small matter to conceive the need and apply one's mind to the intricacies of the problem. Then come the details. The original machine had a simple needle, and made a *running* stitch; next we see a machine which made a succession of loops, forming a *crochet* stitch; here the machine paused a while. A score of years was passed in devising modes of feeding, continuous or intermitting, by various arrangements of parts. The greatest advance up to that time was the *lock* stitch, invented by Hunt, and made by passing a shuttle containing a lower thread through the loop of an upper thread carried down through the cloth by an eye-pointed needle. This was also the feature of the "Howe" machine. Following this were many improvements, variations, and nice adjustments, such as A. B. Wilson's four-motion feed and rotating looping-hook, the latter of which draws down the needle thread, and drops through it the spool containing the lower thread. There is no room here even to recite the prominent improvements. Finally, the machine is much indebted to the skill and enterprise of the mechanics and tradesmen in whose hands it has grown to the wonderful proportions it now exhibits. Without impugning the genius of the earlier inventors, it may still be said that the present proximate perfection of the machine is due to the men who took up the work where Howe left it.

The original Howe machine had a curved eye-pointed needle attached to the end of a vibrating lever, and carrying the upper thread. The shuttle, carrying the lower thread between the needle and the upper thread, was driven in its race by means of two strikers carried on the ends of vibrating arms worked by two cams. The cloth was attached by pins on the edge of a thin steel rib called a baster-plate, which had holes engaged by the teeth of a small intermittingly moving pinion. This was the feed, and clumsy enough.

Space permits but one illustration, and the Singer is given as a representative machine. The well-known table and treadle are omitted, and the principal working parts only are shown. The motion derived from the treadle is imparted to the horizontal shaft, and communicated in two directions to the *needle bar* and to the *shuttle driver*. Various subsidiary movements occur which are tolerably familiar to our readers, and need not be explained at length.

About 2000 patents have been granted in

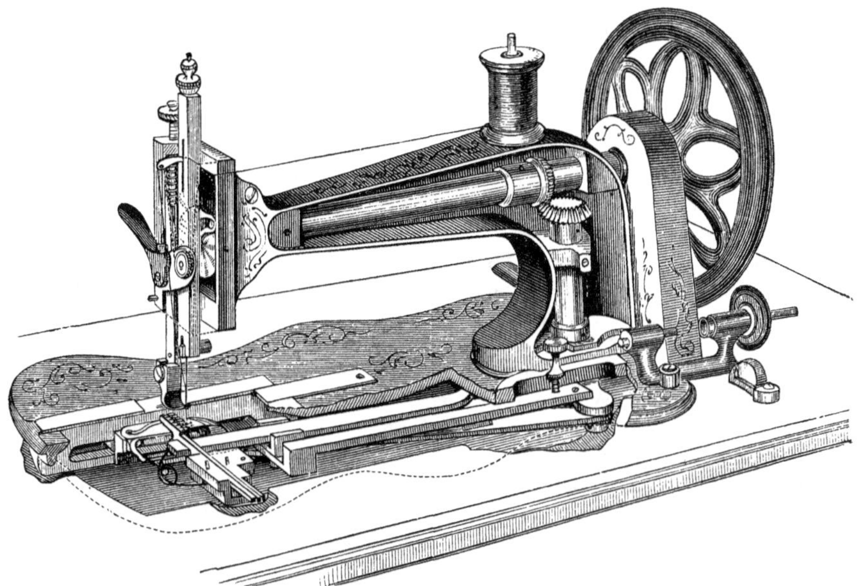

SINGER SEWING-MACHINE.

the United States for sewing-machines: one improvement after another, until there seems to be no end to the devices. Some have reference to special parts, others are adaptations of the machine to new uses and materials to which it had not before been accustomed.

If required to point out three mechanical contrivances upon which the most extraordinary versatility of invention has been expended, the writer would most unhesitatingly instance the *harvester*, the *breech-loading fire-arm*, and the *sewing-machine;* each of these has thousands of patents, and each of them is the growth of the last forty years.

Although each of these was on trial, and to some extent a success, previous to 1850, yet it may be said, in general terms, that their celebrity and usefulness date from about that time. The Hussey and M'Cormick reapers were largely introduced to our countrymen by their success at the London World's Fair in 1851; the breech-loaders were forced upon an unwilling Ordnance Bureau by the exigencies of the late war, the demand of the public, and the stern determination of some civilians who were in authority; the first valuable working sewing-machine was the "Singer," made in the fall of 1850. Last year (1873) about 600,000 sewing-machines were made and sold; 232,444 of these were of the "Singer."

The security of patents has encouraged men of talent, capital, and enterprise to engage in the sewing-machine business, and as much as $40,000,000 is now estimated to be employed in that manufacture. The retail prices of sewing-machines bear no proper relation to their cost, but the prices to the consumer result from the method of selling by means of a system of agencies and traveling canvassers, to the latter of whom so large a profit is allowed that they can afford to sell them on time, on trial, or on payment by installments. There are cheaper means, as with ordinary tools and articles of consumption and wear, of bringing the producer and consumer together; but in the sale of sewing-machines no substitute has been found for the personal solicitations of canvassers, who scour the country with their wagons, and receive for their pay one-half of the purchase price. The organization of the corps of agents by the general agent absorbs another fifteen per cent., so that the manufacturer receives only about thirty-five per cent. of the price. This system will not last longer than the necessity for personal effort at the homes of the people; and when it becomes an established *want* in every family, as it is now an actual *need*, the price may be expected to come down to what will afford but a usual profit upon the capital and skill employed. The principal patents have already expired, and the business will soon be open to competition, when the best devised and constructed machines will be sold merely on their own merits, without the adventitious aids of exclusive rights to sustain prices.

The business of boot and shoe making has received a fillip from the introduction of machinery, enriching the manufacturers and cheapening the product. Without occupying room by even naming the machines which furnish the shoe factory, it may be stated that the M'Kay sewing-machine was the result of three years' mental labor and hand-work, and involved an expenditure of $130,000 before a practical working machine was completed and put in operation in 1861. Since this time 225,000,000 pairs of boots and shoes have been made on these machines in the United States, besides many millions in England and on the continent of Europe. A very skillful operator has occasionally sewed as many as 900 pairs in a day of ten hours, and any good operator can easily sew from 500 to 600 pairs per day.

The *knitting-machine* is another form of iron-fingered curiosity, which will knit at an unexampled rate, and with admirable evenness of tension. It is singular, too, the variety of stitch that may be made on the machine by certain peculiar dispositions and combinations of the needles.

We must not forget the *apple-parer*, which was quoted some thirty years since in England as the last comical vagary of the funny and awkward American cousin. A paring bee may be had without apple-parers, but it takes much longer to empty the apple baskets and fill the kettle with the quarters, which are stewed in boiled cider to make apple-butter for the winter pies and "sass." It was no chance thought or mere whim that set our folks to work. American patents for apple-parers were granted in 1803, 1809, 1810, and since that time about eighty patents have been granted for other implements for the same purpose.

Besides this we have for the cook and kitchen-maid the almond-peeler, pea and bean shellers, peach and cherry stoners, raisin-seeders, bread and cheese cutters, butter-workers, sausage grinders and stuffers, coffee-mills, corn-poppers, cream-freezers, dish-washers, egg-boilers, flour-sifters, flat-irons, knife-sharpeners, and lemon-squeezers. Then we have for the dairy-maid the milking-machines, milk-coolers, churns, cheese-presses, and a number of other aids to leisure.

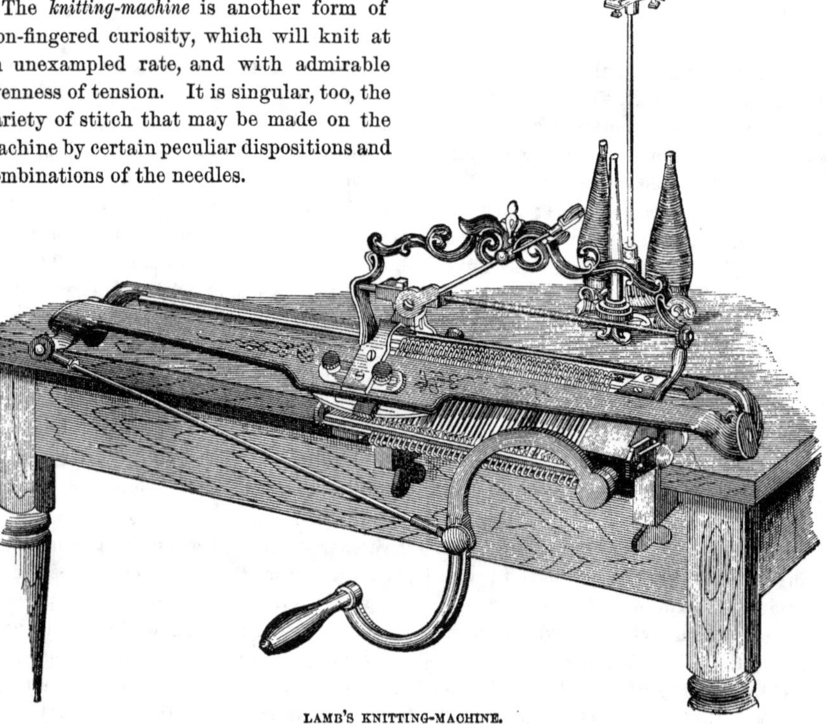

LAMB'S KNITTING-MACHINE.

We have, moreover, the baby-jumper and baby-walker for the nursery, and a wonderful variety of brooms, mops, carpet stretchers and fasteners, for the footman and housemaid.

Nor must the *washing-machine*, another strictly American notion, be disregarded. There are hundreds of patents. The typical forms are few; the variations on these forms are most amusingly numerous. The ins and the outs of invention have been wonderfully diversified. The typical forms are, agitators, rubbers (reciprocating and rotary), centrifugal, pressure-rollers, pounders, dashers, plunger and balls, and the circulatory system.

The wringer, consisting of a pair of rubber rollers, is a necessary laundry implement.

SAFES.

In former times strong rooms and iron-bound oaken boxes were used to hold the cash and the muniments of merchants and families. Such chests were fastened by letter locks, which are the predecessors of our permutation locks. These boxes were hardly burglar-proof, and no defense against fire, but were a security against peculation by dishonest servants.

About 1776 began the manufacture of sheet-iron safes, banded with hoop iron crossing on the outside at right angles. These were fastened by locks throwing several bolts, and also by a bar with hasp, staple, and padlock. Cast-iron chests were used in 1800.

Attempts were previously made to render strong rooms fire-proof by building the walls double and pouring in gypsum; but the first attempts at fire-proof portable safes were early in the nineteenth century, and consisted of wooden boxes covered with sheet iron and riveted bands, and an intervening thickness of gypsum.

After various experiments, in which the wooden box was saturated with potash lye or alum to render it incombustible, and was coated inside the sheet-iron casing with clay, lime, graphite, or mica, the boxes were made of iron inside and outside, with intervening non-combustible material, and known as "double chests." Such was the fire-proof safe patented in England in 1801. Asbestus was used in 1834. Chubb in 1835 attempted to make the safe burglar-proof by lining it with steel or case-hardened iron plates.

In 1843 Wilder made a safe of heavy plates of iron, with a filling of hydrated gypsum. Hydraulic cement, steatite, alum, and the neutralized and dried residuum of the so-called soda-water manufacture, were successively used.

Another idea was to connect the intervening space of the safe with the water main, to prevent a charring heat from reaching the contents when the outside became exposed to fire.

Lillie used slabs of chilled cast iron, and flowed cast iron over wrought-iron ribs. Herring made safes with boiler-iron exterior, hardened steel inner safe, and the interspace filled with a casting of franklinite over rods of soft steel.

The American safe of the best quality is really a first-class production, and is not equaled elsewhere. The locks are also wonderful specimens of ingenuity, worthy of an extended notice.

Safe-deposit companies in our principal cities have ranks of safes with curious unpickable locks inclosed in a room with grated doors, lighted by gas, and watched by attendants. These are rented to private parties.

Various plans have also been devised to give notice of tampering with the safe—electro-magnetic alarms, whistles sounded by setting free a body of compressed air imprisoned between the air-tight walls, generating asphyxiating gas in the chamber to choke the burglars. It is a race between the skilled mechanic and the equally skillful professional thief.

FIRE-ARMS AND ORDNANCE.

From the old wall piece or arquebuse with which the Swiss defeated Charles the Bold in 1476, to the Sharps, Remington, Winchester, or Maynard rifle, or the Parker shotgun, is a great step. So of the pieces used by the cavalry of 1554, and named from Pistoja, to the Colt or the Smith and Wesson revolver of our day. Equally great is the advance in ordnance from the cannon used at the siege of Cordova, 1280, and those with which Ferdinand captured Gibraltar from the Moors in 1308. The bore of the larger cannon down to the middle of the fifteenth century was as great as any modern pieces; but they carried large stones, had small powder chambers like a mortar, and could not possibly have withstood the modern charges of powder. The bronze gun *Tzar Pooschka*, cast A.D. 1586, had a bore of 36 inches; its projectile was said to weigh 2000 pounds, but its powder chamber had only 19 inches bore, only about 1 to 3.6 the area of the ball chamber. Its weight was 86,248 pounds. The bronze gun of Bejapoor, A.D. 1548, had a calibre of 28.5 inches, weight 89,600 pounds; that of Mohammed II., A.D. 1464, 25 inches, weight 41,888 pounds.

The modern guns are of scarcely equal calibre, seldom of greater weight, but are of very much greater strength, and the force of the projectile, due to its velocity, may be said to be out of comparison greater than that of those pieces of antiquity.

The Woolwich (England) 35-ton gun weighs 79,084 pounds; the large Armstrong (Big Will), 50,400; Krupp's 14-inch, 100,000; Rodman's smooth-bore 20-inch, 116,497. Every body is casting heavier and heavier guns, and these figures will not long represent the condition of things. The latest advance is in the guns for the British armor-clad *Inflexible*, which has armor 24 inches thick, and is to be furnished with four guns of 81 tons weight each (181,440 pounds). The total length of this gun, including the plug-screw at the breech end, is 27 feet; length of bore, 24 feet; calibre not determined, but either 14 or 16 inches. The ball of the piece, reckoned at 14 inches calibre, will be from 1000 to 1200 pounds, the charge of powder one-sixth of the weight of the ball. The 1000-pound shot, at an initial velocity of 1300 feet per second, will have a punching force of 11,715 foot-tons, the ball of 1200 pounds a penetrative force of 14,058 foot-tons. Eight years ago the English 7-ton gun was considered the limit of production. Entirely new sets of tools and plants have succeeded each other, as the 35-ton and 81-ton guns have been produced.

In getting gracefully back again from the great guns of the world to the military and sporting arms, we may pause a moment to regard a class of weapons which partake of the characteristics of each, known as machine guns, having a plurality of barrels, and mounted upon a carriage. The first hint of these was a piece upon a tripod, having a chambered breech revolving behind a single barrel. This was patented in England in 1718. The clumsy contrivance which Fieschi used in firing on Louis Philippe had a row of barrels fired simultaneously, and anticipated in the horizontal arrangement of its barrels the Requa battery in this country and the Abbertini mitrailleur of the continent of Europe. The mitrailleur of the French has a cluster of barrels, in whose rear is placed a chambered plate, each of whose chambers corresponds to one of the cluster of barrels, against whose rear it is locked before firing.

The most efficient weapons, all things considered, are the Gatling battery gun and the Taylor machine gun.

The Gatling gun, invented by Mr. J. R. Gatling, of Indianapolis, has now a regular place in the military equipment of the United States and of England. It has a revolving cluster of parallel barrels, in the rear of each of which, and rotating therewith, is its own loading, firing, and spent-capsule-retracting mechanism. The usual American ammunition with metallic capsule and the fulminate in the flange is used. The barrels and the mechanisms for loading and firing are rigidly secured upon an axial shaft, which is revolved by means of bevel gearing and a crank. The ammunition is fed in at a hopper. Each barrel receives its charge as it comes to the top in the course of its revolutions, and fires as it comes to its lowest position, the firing being thus consecutive, and with a rapidity depending upon the rate of rotation of the crank. The complement of the hopper, 400 cartridges, may be fired in one minute if desired. The gun is manufactured at the Colt Works, Hartford.

The Taylor gun is the invention of Mr. Taylor, of Knoxville, Tennessee, and has a cluster of stationary barrels, in the rear of which is a chamber to receive the cartridges; these are secured in a charging block, and forced into the barrels by a lateral movement of the vertical handle seen in the engraving. This handle is attached to an oscillating sleeve having internal studs, which work in spiral grooves in a sliding breech cylinder. The latter carries plungers, one for each barrel, containing central firing

TAYLOR'S MACHINE GUN.

pins, retracted by rotation of a crank shaft carrying suitable tappets, so that the barrels may be discharged in rapid succession. The piece is built at the Remington Works, Ilion, New York.

The military and sporting rifles and shot-guns of our country have no superiors. The trial at Creedmoor (1874) between the American and Irish teams did not prove the superiority of the breech-loader over the muzzle-loader, nor conversely; nor is there any difference worth mentioning between a string of 931 (Irish) and of 934 (American) in a possible 1080. It proved, however, the excellent character of the guns and the steadiness, sight, and skill of the men on both sides. The value of the breech-loading gun has been determined by other considerations than the actual shooting force, as rapidity of loading, the avoidance of shifting the gun end for end in loading, and also of assuming positions in handling which expose the marksman. The American style of fixed ammunition, carrying its fulminate in the base of the cartridge, has also a great convenience, and has riveted the former conclusion of the greater value of the breech-loader.

The cartridge was introduced by Gustavus Adolphus, who was killed at Lutzen in 1632. It at first only contained the powder, the bullets being carried in a bag. The idea of using sheet metal for cartridge cases originated with the French. In 1826 Cazalat patented a metallic cartridge case, drawn from a single piece of copper, and having an opening in the centre of the base for the communication of fire from the fulminate, which was covered with water-proof paper. Lefaucheux and Flobert, of Paris, improved and introduced the metallic cartridge, but it has received its final improvements in this country, being, in fact, a prominent feature in what is known as the *American system*.

The systems of breech-loading are three: the "movement of barrel," the "movement of breech block," and the "revolver." Of these genera there are thirteen species and twenty-six varieties. Of the different modes there are about 1050 patents in the United States Patent-office, beginning with the patent of J. H. Hall, of North Carolina, in 1811, for a rising breech block, which slipped from behind the bore to allow the cartridge to be inserted at the breech. Ten thousand of these arms were made for the United States government between 1811 and 1839, and some of them were captured at the taking of Fort Donelson.

While it is true that the use of breech-loaders dates back to the sixteenth century, that form of arm being almost as old as the muzzle-loader, the actual use of breech-loaders on a large scale in military service, or the habitual use of them by sportsmen, is quite modern. The Hall gun of 1811, mentioned above, was manufactured on a small scale, and appears to have been locked up in arsenals, where it was forgotten. The *needle-gun* was introduced into the Prussian service to a limited extent in 1846, and into the Danish and Norwegian soon afterward. The Schleswig-Holstein war was fought with needle-guns. The French Chassepôt is reputed to have been first used in the Italian struggle in the Garibaldi times.

Previous to our own war of 1861–65 our principal breech-loading arms were Sharps's, Burnside's, Maynard's, Merrill's, and Spencer's. The number of breech-loaders purchased by the United States government between January 1, 1861, and January 30, 1866, is stated to have been as follows, arms of which the purchases were below 10,000 being omitted:

Burnside	55,567	Remington	20,000
Gallagher	22,728	Sharps	80,512
Joslyn	11,261	Henry..............	30,062
Merrill	14,295	Spencer	94,156
Maynard	20,002	Starr	25,603

Some of the above have fallen out of public notice; the Sharps, Maynard, Remington and Winchester (known during the war as the Henry), Ward-Burton, Colt, and Springfield have taken front rank as military and sporting rifles, while the Parker, Maynard, and Remington are the prominent shot-guns. Reference has been made to the American system of assembling the parts, which are made interchangeable, and also to the development of the system by Colonel Colt, in the manufacture of his revolving-chambered pistol. The Smith and Wesson arm is made by the same process.

In 1866 Prussia with breech-loaders defeated Austria with muzzle-loaders. A few years afterward the Prussian *Zündnadelgewehr* and the French *Chassepôt* struggled for pre-eminence on the soil of France.

It may be added that, with a single exception, the main features of all the prominent military rifles originated in the United States. The exception is the European needle-gun, which is never likely to be used here. The English "Martini-Henry" gun is but a modification of the American "Peabody." Six hundred thousand of the Martini-Henry gun are now being made for the Turkish government. The "Winchester Repeating Arms Company," of New Haven, Connecticut, is making the ammunition for these guns. Four thousand tons of lead have been cast into bullets for the cartridges, and the boxing costs $100,000. These cartridges will freight eight vessels of 500 tons each. The first metallic cartridge used in a military arm was that of Dr. Edward Maynard. It was a cylindrical water-proof cartridge.

TELEGRAPH.

When the men of 1776 threw down the gage of battle, there were no means of signaling news other than by such semaphores as had existed in one form or another for 2500 years past, and are yet used by the Indians of the plains. Visible signals by swinging arms mounted on the tops of masts or of elevated buildings signaled the events even of Trafalgar and Waterloo along the Falmouth and Dover roads to London. In a less pretentious way, concerted fires and smokes by night or by day were made by the nations of antiquity, as recorded by Homer and Jeremiah; by the Highlanders, as recounted by Scott; and by the Indians of our Western plains, as lately described by General Custer.

The semaphoric system of Polybius was adapted to spell out messages letter by letter. Signaling by flags and lanterns is employed in military and railway practice.

The electric telegraph preceded the electro-magnetic by many decades. Gray, in 1729, noticed the conductivity of certain bodies; Nollet soon after passed a shock through 180 men of the French guards, and a line 100 toises in length; Watson observed that the transmission of the shock through 12,000 feet of wire was practically instantaneous, and signaled an observer by this means. Then came a number of experimenters, each of whom added something to the stock of knowledge on the subject. Le Sage, of Geneva (1774), had a wire for each letter, and pith-ball electroscopes for the excited agents. Lamond (1787) had a single wire and concerted movements of the pith ball. Cavallo, in 1795, proposed to transmit letters by combinations of dots and spaces. The next year Betancourt constructed a telegraph between Madrid and Aranjuez, a distance of twenty-seven miles. The messages were read by the divergence of pith balls.

Then came the discoveries of Volta, Galvani, Oersted, Ampère, Faraday, and Henry. The experiments of the first two mentioned are at the bottom of the discoveries in dynamic electricity. Oersted, in 1820, observed that the magnetic needle had a tendency to assume a direction at right angles to that of the excited wire. The farther experiments of Oersted and Ampère, and the discovery of Faraday that magnetism was induced in a bar of soft iron under the influence of a voltaic circuit, and that of Sturgeon, in 1825, that a soft iron bar surrounded by a helix of wire through which a voltaic current is passed is magnetized during the time such current continues, gave rise to the first really convenient and practical system of electro-telegraphy. One difficulty remained—the resistance of the transmitting wire to the comparatively feeble current engendered by the voltaic battery. This was overcome by Professor Henry, who, in 1831, invented the form of magnet now in use, and discovered the principle of *combination of circuits* constituting the *receiving magnet* and *relay*, or *local battery*, as they are familiarly known in connection with the Morse apparatus. The effect of a combination of circuits is to enable a weak or exhausted circuit to bring into action and substitute for itself a fresh and powerful one. This is an essential condition to obtaining useful mechanical results from electricity where a long circuit of conductors is used.

In 1832 Professor Morse began to devote his attention to the subject of telegraphy, and in that year, while on his passage home from Europe, he invented the form of telegraph since so well known as "Morse's."

A short line worked on his plan was set up in 1835, though it was not until June 20, 1840, that he obtained his first patent, and nearly four years elapsed before means could be procured, which were finally granted by the government of the United States, to test its practical working over a line of any length, though he had as early as 1837 endeavored to induce Congress to appropriate a sum of money sufficient to construct a line between Washington and Baltimore.

Morse's first idea was to employ chemical agencies for recording the signals, but he subsequently abandoned this for an apparatus which simply marked on strips of paper the dots and dashes composing his alphabet. The paper itself is now generally dispensed with, at least in this country, and the signals read by sound—a circumstance which conduces to accuracy in transmission, as the ear is found less liable to mistake the duration and succession of sounds than the eye to read a series of marks on paper.

Professor Morse deserves high honor for the ingenious manner in which he availed himself of scientific discoveries previously made by others, for many important discoveries of his own, and for the courage and perseverance which he manifested in endeavoring to render his system of practical utility to mankind by bringing it prominently to the notice of the public, and he lived to see it adopted in its essential features throughout the civilized world.

The attention of Wheatstone in England appears to have been drawn to the subject of telegraphy in 1834. His first telegraph comprised five pointing needles and as many line wires, requiring the deflection of two of the needles to indicate each letter. His first dial instrument was patented in 1840. Modifications were, however, subsequently made in it. The transmission of messages was effected by a wheel having fifteen teeth and as many interspaces, each representing a letter of the alphabet or a numeral, and thirty spokes corresponding to this, and forming part of the line. The circuit was closed by two diametrically opposite springs so arranged that when one was in contact with a tooth the other was opposite a space, when the transmitter was turned until opposite a particular letter and held there, a continuous current being produced, causing an index on the indicating-dial at the other end of the line, which had thirty divisions corresponding to those of the transmitter, to turn until it arrived opposite the letter to be indicated. The revolution of the index was effected by clock-work, the escapement of which was actuated by an electro-magnet at either end of a pivoted beam, the ends of which carried two soft iron armatures. One of the line wires, as well as one of the contact springs of the transmitter, and one of the electro magnets of the indicator, were afterward dispensed with.

A magneto-electric apparatus was subsequently substituted for the voltaic battery.

The single-needle telegraph of Cooke and Wheatstone is caused to indicate the letters and figures by means of the deflections to the right or left of a vertical pointer; for instance, the letter A is indicated by two deflections to the left, N by two deflections to the right, I by three consecutive deflections to the right and then one to the left,

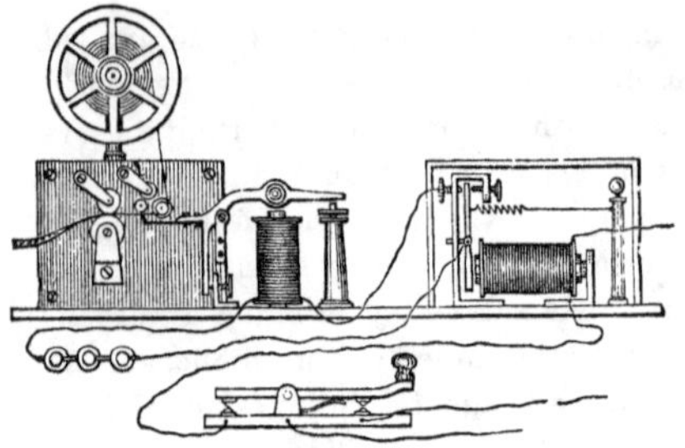

MORSE APPARATUS, CIRCUIT AND BATTERY.

MORSE KEY.

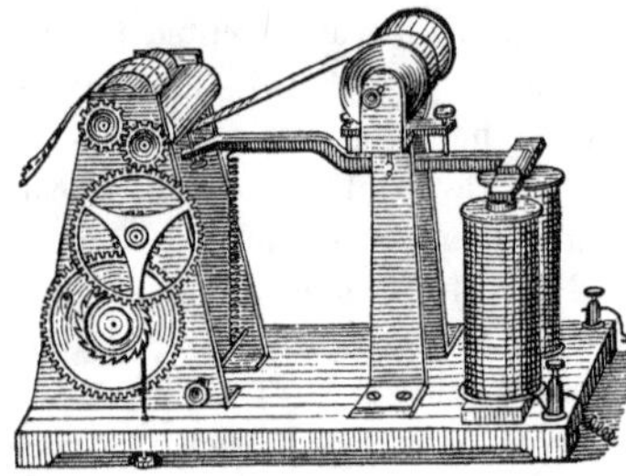

MORSE REGISTER.

and so on. This is extensively employed in Great Britain and India.

Bain, in 1846, patented the electro-chemical telegraph, which dispensed with the relay magnet at intermediate stations, and subsequently Gintl, in Austria, and Bonelli constructed telegraphs of this class varying in details from that of Bain.

The above diagram shows the system of indicator, relay, local battery, lines, and key.

The middle figure shows the *key*, which is worked by the sender of the message, and the lower figure the *register*, by which motions of the stylus under the excitement which renders it temporarily magnetic are recorded on the paper in dots or dashes, according to the length of time during which the circuit is maintained. This is the principal instrument in America and on the continent of Europe. Room fails to tell of the autographic systems of Caselli and Bonelli; the printing telegraphs of House and Hughes; the automatic telegraphs of Edison and others.

The *duplex telegraph*, by which messages are sent over the same wire in contrary directions at the same time, is so strange that

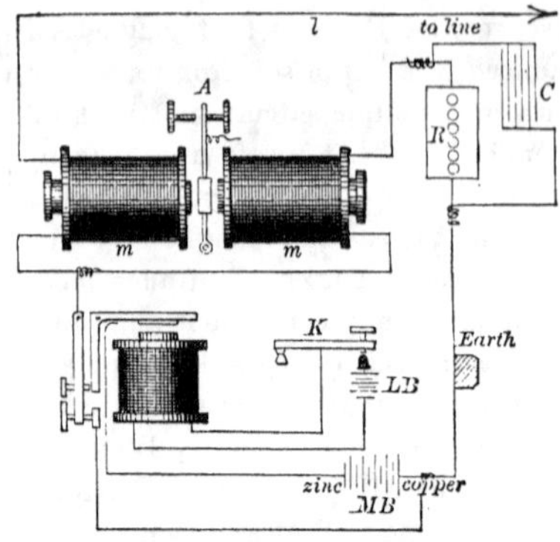

DUPLEX TELEGRAPH.

a diagram and short description will be given. Several plans of duplex telegraph have been proposed. The device selected for illustration is that of Stearns, of Boston, which is based upon the plan of Gintl, of Austria, 1853. The relay, or receiving instrument, is composed of two pairs of electro-magnets (*m m*) acting in opposite directions upon a common armature lever (*A*). The key is the armature of an electro-magnet which is in a local circuit controlled by a Morse key (*K*). *LB* is the local battery. The main battery (*MB*) current is equally divided between the relay magnets (*m m*), one-half passing through one set of magnets to the line *l*, and the other half passing through the other magnets and a rheostat (*R*), equal to the resistance of the main line, to earth. The relay magnets are thus equally excited, and their influence upon the armature neutralized, so that the outgoing current gives no signal at the sending station. A current received, however, traverses only one set of the electro-magnets, destroying the equilibrium, and causing a signal. The key is so constructed that it closes one circuit to the earth before breaking another, thus always preserving the continuity of the circuit, a condition essential in systems of this kind. A condenser (*C*) is placed in a shunt circuit to the magnets in the short or home circuit, in order to neutralize the effect of the extra current on the line magnets of the relay.

ELECTROPLATING.

Electroplating is an invention of the century. Volta himself experimented about 1800. Cruikshank noticed the corrosion in one wire and the precipitation of metallic

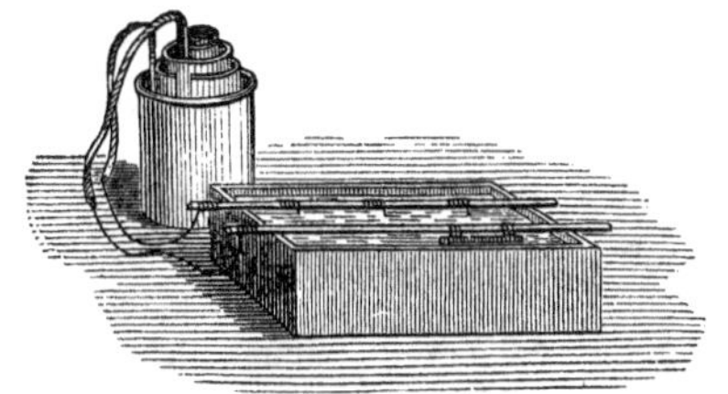

ELECTROPLATING.

silver on the other when passing the "galvanic influence" through the wires in a bath of nitrate of silver. Wollaston experimented in 1801. Spencer made casts from coins in 1838. Jacobi, of Dorpat, soon after gilded the iron dome of the Cathedral of St. Isaac, at St. Petersburg, with 274 pounds of ducat gold, deposited by battery. The art has grown into use, and now baser metals, in the shape of articles for household service, are cased with silver; electrotyped forms are used as printing surfaces; nickel is deposited on numerous articles which are exposed to damp, and on others to add to their beauty, as with movements of watches. It is impossible to enumerate the uses and applications, and not easy to exaggerate the value of the art.

ELECTRIC LIGHT.

The *electric light* is eminently the child of the century. In its production and its uses it touches nowhere upon the knowledge or the methods of the men of the previous periods. It is a pure gain of the present. The bright spark from the electrical machine had been observed by Wall in 1708, the Leyden-jar was invented by Cunœus in 1746, and the experiments of Dufay, Nollet, Gray, Franklin, and others soon gave valuable results. Another whole series of observations and inventions founded upon the discoveries of Volta and Galvani was necessary before the transient spark was succeeded by the intense and unremitting light developed between two pieces of carbon placed at the positive and negative ends of a voltaic circuit. The electricity may be developed either by a battery, or from magnets in connection with a series of helices arranged on a rotating wheel, the latter source being preferred for light-houses and in other situations where permanency is intended. The battery is the usual source for lectures in theatres having no regular laboratory.

The electric light was first brought into notice by Greener and Staite in 1846, in an arrangement by which small lumps of pure carbon nearly in contact, and inclosed in air-tight vessels, were rendered luminous by currents of galvanic electricity. The break in the continuity of the circuit at this point causes resistance, generating intense heat and the consumption of the carbon, which is accompanied by an extremely brilliant light. As the carbon burns away, one or both of the pieces require to be advanced, and the chief difficulty was found to be in maintaining the points at such a distance from each other as to render the light continuous. This is now effected by means of an electro-magnet and clock movement, the duty of the latter being to bring the points together as they are gradually consumed, while the magnet checks the clock action when not desired.

This light is very largely used in the lecture-room. It was introduced into Dunge-

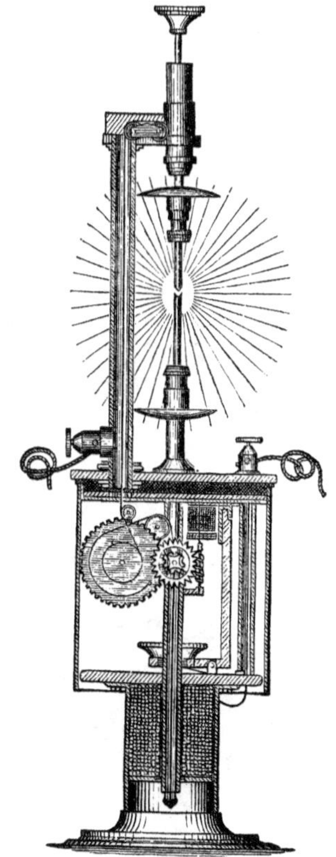

ELECTRIC LIGHT.

ness Light-house, on the southeast coast of England, in 1862; at La Hève, France, a year or two later. It was used in the excavating chamber in the base of the deep caissons of the St. Louis Bridge; during the excavation of the docks at Cherbourg; on various festal occasions in cities of America and Europe.

FIRE-ENGINES, ETC.

In *fire-engines* America has hardly a rival. When our century commenced a clumsy hand-engine was employed, a gradual improvement upon the mere syringe which was used from the time of Trajan down to the sixteenth century. At Augsburg, about 1518, force-pumps were mounted on wheels and worked by levers. At Nuremberg, in 1657, the town engine had a cistern and pump mounted on a sled; the brakes were worked by twenty-eight men, and threw a stream through an inch nozzle to a height of eighty feet. The Van der Heyden brothers about this time much improved the device. Newsham's engine, about the end of the seventeenth century, had the double-acting force-pump with air chamber. This was not superseded till about 1832, when our personal recollections commenced, and about that time improvements were rapidly made which culminated in the gorgeous hand-engines with which we ran, of which we boasted, and, lamentable to say, about which we fought.

Steam-power forcing-pumps for extinguishing fires were in use long before portable steam fire-engines. The first steam fire-engines were perhaps those mounted on barges on the river Thames, and which were moved or towed to fires occurring on the river front. Next was undoubtedly the portable steam-engine of Captain Ericsson. This was made in Manchester, England, about 1830, a little after he constructed the "Novelty" locomotive, which contended for the prize on that famous day in 1829 on the Liverpool and Manchester Railway. He also made a steam fire-engine in New York in 1842–43.

But, after all, the steam fire-engine as a fixed and valuable fact hails from Cincinnati, Ohio, where the talents of the brothers Latta and Mr. Shawk, inventors and builders, were seconded by the enterprise of

STEAM FIRE-ENGINE "WASHINGTON, NO. 1," BROOKLYN, NEW YORK.

Miles Greenwood. The "Citizens' Gift," one of the first successful engines, was built in 1853, and in 1866 was still among the most useful of her class. Since that time the principal cities of North America have been supplied with steam fire-engines; also many of the largest cities of England, and some few on the continent of Europe.

The American system of *fire-alarms* is likely to work its way gradually into the cities of Europe. It is one of those things which are difficult to introduce, and impossible to dispense with when once tried. We can not imagine such an impertinent and absurd proposition as to go back to the old times when the flames of a burning house were the signal to the watchman in the tower of the engine-house.

The fire-alarm telegraph first in use was merely a connection by Morse telegraph between fire-alarm stations. This was in use in New York and Berlin in 1851. The present system is founded upon the patented invention of Farmer and Channing, 1857. Mr. Channing wrote upon the subject in 1845, and in 1848 Mr. Farmer devised a means of ringing bells by electricity, and in an experimental trial that year the bell in the tower of Boston City Hall was rung by an operator in New York. The fire-alarm telegraph was first put up, in the year 1852, in Boston.

The primary requisites of a fire-alarm telegraph system are a telegraph line, a central receiving station, and a number of signal boxes suitably distributed for transmitting an alarm.

When there are a number of such boxes, as in most cities, they are not arranged upon the same circuit, but upon several circuits connected to some central station. The signal boxes generally used contain a spring or weight and gearing, rotating a circuit-breaking wheel and a fly for regulating the speed. The circuit wheel in one form is provided with projections, upon which a spring presses and closes the circuit, which is broken as the spring passes over the intervals between the cogs; in another form the surface of the wheel is smooth, an insulating material being let into the wheel so as to break the circuit. A train of gearing, upon one shaft of which is a cam or lug, operates the pivoted hammer. This gear is held in rest by the armature of a magnet acting as a detent; so every time a current passes, the armature allows the gearing to revolve, and the hammer strikes once. At the same time the smaller alarm gongs are struck in the engine-houses. In the houses the horses are kept ready harnessed. At the end of the halter strap (where halters are used) is a ring through which a bolt upon the manger passes, securing the horse; from the bolts a string or lever passes to a weight or spring kept inactive by the gong-hammer lever; the first stroke releases the weight, which, falling, pulls the string or lever, withdrawing all the bolts securing the halters, and loosing the horses. When halters are not used, but the horses are turned into box-stalls, the latter have sliding gates, which are raised by the same kind of devices.

In the strictly automatic system there is no operator at the central station, but a repeater of very complex organization, having connection with all the various circuits, so that, an alarm coming in on any one circuit, the repeater is prevented from receiving from any other circuit (to avoid interference of signals), and caused to repeat the alarm automatically upon all the circuits, including the various alarm devices. A register is also used with the repeater.

ATMOSPHERIC RAILWAY, ETC.

The *pneumatic tube* and *atmospheric railway* are other achievements of the century. It can not be said that they have come into extensive use for passengers, but for small parcels and letters they have been in successful use for fifteen years in London.

Dr. Papin, of Blois, in France, suggested the idea about the end of the seventeenth century, but, like some other children of his fertile brain, it never grew up. Medhurst in 1810 patented the idea of forcing a carriage on a pair of tracks along an air-tight tube by means of compression of air behind it.

Vallance in 1824 patented the other mode, exhausting the air in front of it. The idea was carried out at the Sydenham Palace, near London, where an ordinary railway carriage with a somewhat elastic piston traveled in an elliptical tunnel eight by nine feet in its minor and major diameters. The same idea is carried out in Beach's short tunnel under Broadway, New York, which has been visited by many of our readers.

Out of this grew the atmospheric railway, in which a piston traveling in a tube is connected to a carriage running upon rails outside, a long valve filling a slot in the top of the tube being displaced by a bar depending from the carriage, and falling into place again behind. This plan had many modifications, and was actually employed on two railways, but afterward abandoned—from 1844 to 1855 on the Kingstown and Dalkey, Ireland, 1¾ miles; from London to Croydon, England, 10 miles. Good speed was attained, heavy grades readily ascended, collision was impossible, but it was too liable to get out of order.

The *atmospheric brake* for railway cars is another recent feature, and has only attained its present excellence after many attempts. As many as twenty-four patents were granted from 1841 to 1865 for brakes actuated upon each car by a single impulse by the engineer, many of them employing air or steam as the means of applying the shoes to the car wheels.

The Westinghouse brake employs air as the means of transmitting power to the brakes. This is condensed to the required extent into a reservoir by a steam-pump upon the locomotive. From the reservoir it is conducted back beneath the cars of the train by pipes connected beneath the train by flexible tubes and valved couplings. Under each car is a cylinder to which the compressed air is admitted forward of a piston, the stem of which is connected to a bell-crank attached to the brake levers by rods, so that when air is admitted by the engineer to the pipes connected to the cylinders under each car, the brakes of each are simultaneously applied.

One test may be mentioned. September 18, 1869, a train of six cars descending the Horseshoe Bend of the Pennsylvania Central Railway, a grade of ninety-six feet to the mile, at the rate of thirty miles per hour, was brought to a stand-still in 420 feet—seven car lengths.

Blowers and *blowing engines* are but forms of air-compressing or air-exhausting pumps, but it is hard to overvalue them. They increase the draught in metallurgic furnaces; furnish vital air to close and fetid places, such as mines, cisterns, holds of ships; supply warmed, cooled, moistened, or medicated air to public buildings, schools, hospitals, etc.; furnish a drying atmosphere to lumber and grain kilns and powder mills; assist in evaporating liquids and removing the steam from the vicinity of the boiling solution; raise liquids on the principle of the Giffard injector, as in oil wells and subaqueous caissons; assist in the dispersion of liquids, as in atomizers and some forms of ice machines; remove dust and chips from saw-mills and planers, the fatal dust from the stones and glazers of cutlers; supply breath to organs.

The blower of three centuries since consisted of one open-ended box slipping into another; it was used for furnaces in that very remarkable city, Nuremberg, and was an improvement over the ordinary bellows. Later, about 1621, a bellows was used consisting of a valve oscillating in a sector chamber. The fan-blower dates from 1729. The water-bellows was invented by Hornblower.

The first powerful blast machines were probably those erected by Smeaton at the Carron Iron-works, 1760. The furnaces grew larger in size, and more powerful blowers were needed. Watt's engine came just in time to crown the whole affair with success and revolutionize the iron trade. Neilson invented the hot blast in 1828.

Power blowers are now used. The forms are piston; fan; vertical open-ended cylinder plunging in water; pair of wheels, with alternate vanes and packing surfaces, and rotating in concert.

BALLOONS.

Aerostation is almost all within the century. Since Icarus fell into the Ægean Sea very little advance has been made in flying machines, the flight of Dædalus from Crete to Sicily being altogether the most successful on record. Some presume to doubt *this*. *Ballooning* was rendered possible upon the discovery of hydrogen gas by Cavendish in 1766. It is true it had been produced before, but was not understood or used. Dr. Black the next year suggested its use for aerostation. The brothers Montgolfier ascended by a fire balloon in 1783; the ascensive power was obtained by heated air rising from a fire made in the open mouth of the balloon. Pilatre de Rozière and the Marquis d'Arlandes repeated the experiment the same year. MM. Charles and Robert inflated their balloon with hydrogen gas, and ascended 9700 feet and reached a distance of twenty-five miles in one hour and three-quarters. Ascensions after this became frequent. Pilatre and Romain tried to combine a hydrogen balloon with a fire balloon; the expanding gas reached the fire, the whole was consumed, and the aeronauts perished. Balloons of observation were used by the French army at Liege and Fleurus in 1794. This was repeated at Solferino in 1859, and with our Army of the Potomac. The most remarkable ascent for a long time was that of Gay-Lussac, in 1804, who reached the height of 23,040 feet. Glaisher, it is said, afterward ascended to a height of seven miles. Green, in 1820, introduced the plan of inflating with the ordinary illuminating gas of the streets.

The history of the balloon since this time embraces many names—Wise, King, Lowe, and Donaldson in this country; Gifford, Godard, and De Lorne in France. M. Godard conducted the balloon postal administration during the siege of Paris. Wise's trip from St. Louis is the longest on record, nearly 1200 miles.

WEIGHING MACHINES.

Probably no invention, if we except that of the locomotive, has to so great a degree expedited the transactions of commerce as the platform balance, invented by the Fairbanks Brothers about 1830. The business of making these weighing machines has grown to enormous proportions. From the Fairbanks manufactory at St. Johnsbury, Vermont, 50,000 scales are sent out annually to all parts of the world.

GAS.

Illuminating gas was unknown, except as a surface emanation or a laboratory production, in the year 1776. In China from time immemorial the natural flow of carbureted hydrogen has been used for lighting, and for boiling the brine yielded by salt wells. Similar convenient applications have been made at Fredonia, New York, Portland, on Lake Erie, Wigan, Scotland, in lighting, and at Kanawha, West Virginia, in evaporating brine. Gas emanating from a well 1200 feet deep is used at the "Siberian Works," Pittsburg, under the boilers and in the puddling furnaces. The fire-worshipers of Persia have regarded such emanations with high respect, and the holy fires of Baku, on the Caspian, have a great local fame, and are thus maintained.

Gas was first obtained by the distillation of coal in 1688 by Dr. Clayton; Boyle refers to it in that year. Watson, Bishop of Llandaff, 1756, Lord Dundonald, 1786, distilled coal and tar and burned the issuing gas. Murdock was the first to light a building

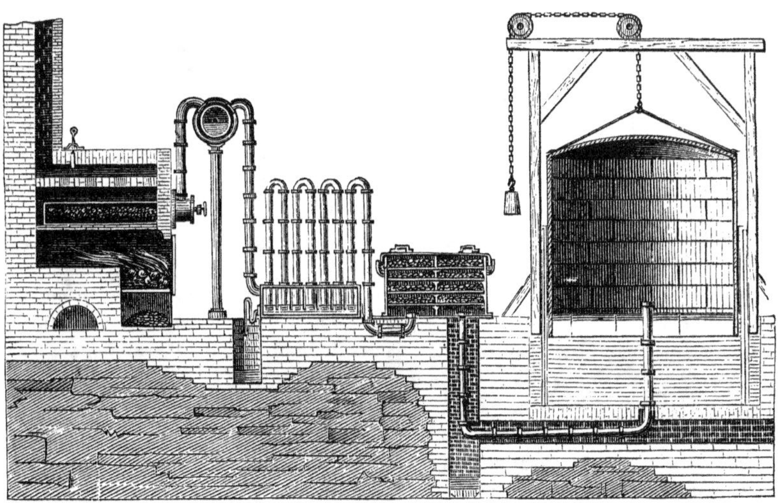

DIAGRAM OF GAS-WORKS.

with it. He thus lighted his house and offices at Redruth, Cornwall, in 1792. In 1798 he lighted with gas the works of Boulton and Watt at Soho. He illuminated these buildings in 1803 in the rejoicings for peace: Trafalgar, Austerlitz, and Jena, within four years afterward, are a curious commentary. Murdock's name stands at the head of the list as the man who reduced the idea to practice. In 1804–05 he lighted the cotton factory of Phillips and Lee, Manchester, with a brilliancy estimated to be equal to 3000 candles. This was a grand success.

In 1803 Winsor lighted the Lyceum Theatre, in London, and obtained a patent for lighting streets by gas. He established the first gas company. The first street lighted was one side of Pall Mall, in 1807; Westminster Bridge and the Houses of Parliament, in 1813; London streets commonly were lighted in 1815; Paris, the same year; Baltimore, 1816; Boston, 1822; New York, 1825.

This is all very recent, and yet how far into the past the dim period of street oil-lamps seems to have retreated! The mode of making illuminating gas is pretty generally understood. The coal is baked in retorts, and the gas flows therefrom in company with other vapors, which are removed by successive operations. It is conducted first to the convoluted pipes of the condenser, by which it is cooled and the tar precipitated. Thence it passes to the washer, where the ammonia is seized by the water, allowing the gas to pass on to the purifier, where it is deprived of its sulphur and carbonic acid by dry lime, or latterly by the hydrated sesquioxide of iron. Clegg invented the purifier and wet meter in 1807; Malam the dry meter in 1820.

SILVER.

The *silver processes* now adopted in our Western Territories are the result of long care and observation, with chemical analyses—the union of experimental test and scientific deduction.

Amalgamating pans and barrels are made in great variety; roasting furnaces and processes have been adapted to the varying characters of ore and the means at command for treating. One of the most satisfactory of the latter must stand as a representative of the whole family, as it is not possible to treat the matter either at length or in detail.

STETEFELDT'S ROASTING FURNACE.

The Stetefeldt roasting furnace for silver ores containing sulphur is what is technically known as a *shaft furnace;* the ground and stamped ore is dusted in a shower into a vertical shaft, up which the flame of a furnace is directed.

The ground ore is mixed with salt, and pulverized at the stamp battery. The pulp is carried by a conveyer to the feeder at the top of the shaft, and shaken through the sieve so as to fall in a shower through the flame of the gas entering at the side apertures low down in the shaft. The principal portion falls to the bottom, but the finer matter passing over is exposed to a flame arising from the mingled air and the carbonic oxide of a charcoal fire discharging into the downcast shaft leading to the series of chambers in which fine metallic dust is eventually deposited, and from which it is removed from time to time.

In the furnace shaft a double decomposition takes place, which converts the sulphide of silver into the chloride, in which latter condition it is brought, as one may say, within the grasp of the mercury. In the presence of sulphurous gases from the sulphide of silver the chloride of sodium is decomposed, and yields its chlorine to the silver, forming the chloride of silver, while the sulphurous gases uniting with the soda form sulphate of soda, which is washed out with the tailings. The material from the furnace is ready for the amalgamating pan.

ICE.

Ice is one thing in which Americans revel in the summer-time. No other nation lays in such a stock, or so peremptorily demands an abundant supply. American ice

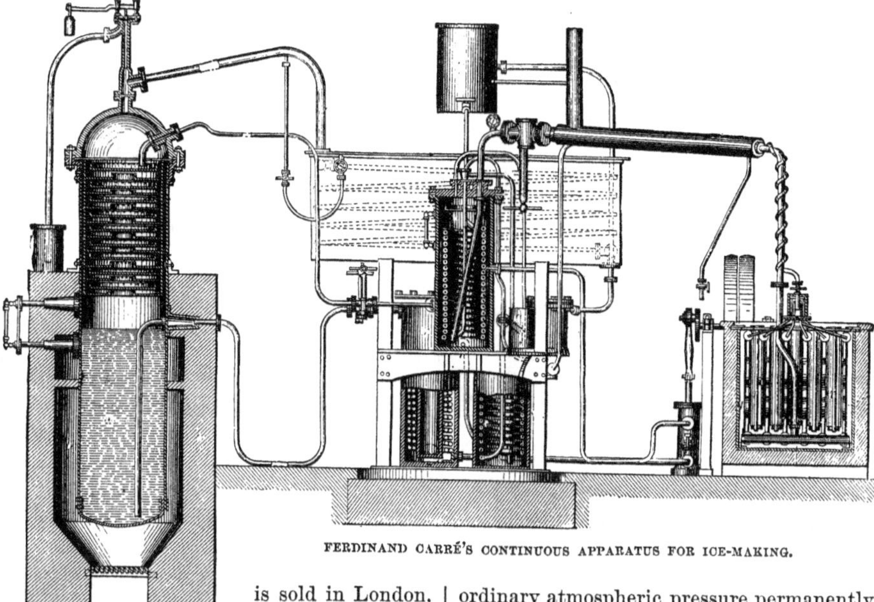

FERDINAND CARRÉ'S CONTINUOUS APPARATUS FOR ICE-MAKING.

is sold in London, Calcutta, and a hundred places between the two. Usually the ice is "harvested" on ponds or rivers in the North, and the business has created a whole set of peculiar contrivances for scraping off the surface and removing snow; sawing the sheet into blocks without quite detaching; splitting them off; floating them to the hoist; elevating them by endless chains; delivering them to the men who stow them in a solid mass occupying the whole interior of the barn.

More specially noticeable, however, are the machines for congealing water into ice, and which are commencing to work at a price below that at which the ice can be gathered and transported.

Speaking in short terms, there are four modes of making ice—vaporization, radiation, liquefaction, and sudden reduction of pressure.

Vaporization in a partial vacuum formed the basis of Dr. Cullen's attempts in 1755; in 1777 Nairne used sulphuric acid to absorb the vapor rising from water in an exhausted receiver. Edmond Carré's apparatus is on this principle, and is used to produce the *carafes frappées* so common in Parisian restaurants. In the continuous operation of Ferdinand Carré ammonia is employed as being more volatile than water, and under ordinary atmospheric pressure permanently gaseous. The apparatus is somewhat complicated, but effective. The water is in cans in a bath of uncongealable liquid, cooled by zigzag tubes, into which the liquid ammonia is conducted to expand, and thereby convert the sensible heat of the surrounding bath into latent, due to its assumption of the gaseous condition. There are many modifications of the vaporization principle, but no room to tell of them.

Liquefaction is another mode, and snow and ice are used in connection with salts. Combinations of salts are also used. Machines are also used in which air is exhausted by a steam-engine from a receiver, the expansion of liquid into a gaseous condition drawing heat from the water sufficient to congeal it.

SUGAR.

Sugar is mentioned by Dioscorides and Pliny as a kind of honey obtained from cane, and was introduced into Europe by the Arabs. The first mention of it in European annals is in the account of Nearchus, who commanded the fleet of Alexander. The Crusades added to the European knowledge of it, and in the twelfth century it was grown in Sicily. Thence it was taken to Madeira in 1420, and thence to the Canaries, to Brazil, and to San Domingo in 1506; to Barbadoes from Brazil in 1641. It is a native of the East Indies, and its name is from the

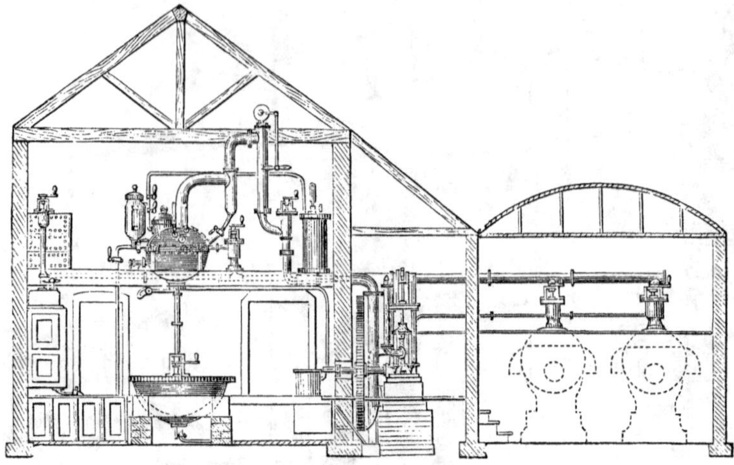

MODERN SUGAR PROCESS.

Sanskrit, *sarkara;* Persian, *schakar;* Hindostanee, *schukur;* Arabic, *sukkar.* *Kanda* (candy) is also Sanskrit.

It was used for many centuries as a vehicle in medicine before it became an article of food. For the refining processes we are indebted to the Venetians of the sixteenth century. As time passed, the clarification, defecation, and crystallization proceeded on a gradually improving scale, boiling, settling, filtering, white of egg, skimming, bone-black, etc., being used. Loaf-sugar was first made in Venice.

The vacuum-pan is the invention of Charles E. Howard, an English refiner, about 1813. In this a partial vacuum is obtained over the sirup, so that it will boil at a much lower temperature. This not merely saves fuel, but prevents charring and discoloration of the sugar. The modes of handling the sirup, so to speak, are also much simplified and assisted, the cane juice, by means of pumps or by gravity, flowing from the mill to the filters, to the defecators, to the filters again, to the vacuum-pan, and to the cooler.

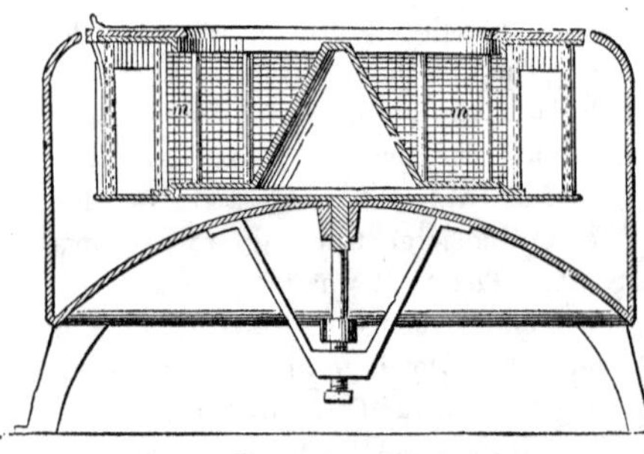

CENTRIFUGAL FILTER.

Another very important aid in sugar-making apparatus is the centrifugal filter, patented by Hurd, of Massachusetts, 1844. In this the magma is placed in a foraminous cylinder, and rotated with great rapidity, so that the liquid portion—the water and the uncrystallizable sugar—is expelled by centrifugal force, leaving the granulated sugar in the cylinder.

This really beautiful contrivance has since been adapted for many purposes as a drainer filter, and as a substitute for the clothes-wringer.

PORCELAIN.

Porcelain, although not finer in texture than the Chinese article of many ages back, nor of more graceful and agreeable shapes than the vases of Etruria and Greece, has, as far as we are concerned in the art, made almost all its progress within the century just passing away.

Wedgwood's improvements, 1759–70, date the commencement of a new era for us, although Böttcher was half a century earlier, and founded the works of Dresden. The establishment of the porcelain-works at Sèvres, in France, was somewhat later. In Prussia, Austria, Russia, Bavaria, and France the works are governmental. Staffordshire, the old home of Wedgwood, is the centre of the English works, which are all private ventures; the exports being largely to the United States.

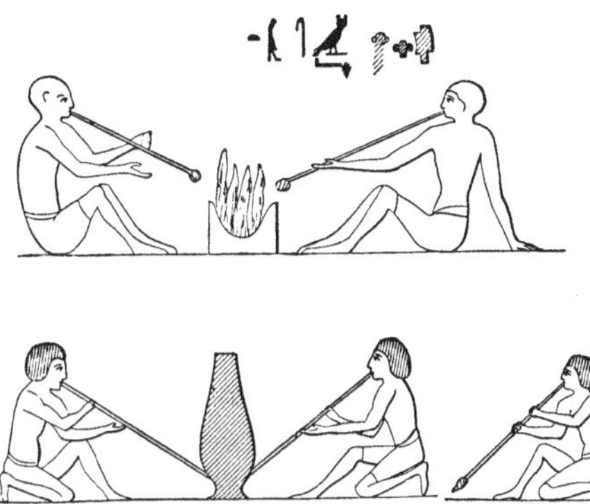

GLASS-MAKING IN EGYPT, 1500 B.C.

GLASS.

Glass was known in ancient Nineveh, and was skillfully worked by the ancient Egyptians, though it was mostly ornamental, and did not probably enter much into the common uses of life. Pliny describes the mode of making it, and it was used all down through the ages to our own time. It is only within the last three centuries that its use has become common. The manufacture of blown glass was introduced into England in 1559; plate-glass in 1673.

Cylinder glass was made for some scores of years before it was introduced into England in 1846, just in time for the great Exhibition building of 1851, which was designed by Sir Joseph Paxton, and roofed with cylinder glass made by Chance and Co., of Birmingham.

The process is as follows: The workman collects a mass of glass (*a*) around the end of his blowing tube, and then distends and rounds it by blowing and rolling it on the *marver*, or flat cast-iron table. The subsequent operations consist in reheating, blowing, and swinging, until the diameter and then the length of the cylinder required are attained, the glass successively assuming the forms *b c* represented in the figure. In the fourth stage, where it has assumed a conoidal form (*d*), the point is very thin, and the blower, having filled the shell with air at a pressure, places it in the furnace, when the expansion of the air by heat causes the conoid to burst at the apex (*e*). The edge of the hole is then trimmed with shears, and enlarged by the *pucellas*, a peculiar hand tool, which resembles a pair of spring sugar-tongs with flat jaws. The cylindrical form (*f*) being then perfected, the cylinder is ready to be removed from the blowing tube, a circular piece of glass coming away with the tube, so as to make an opening in the other end of the cylinder. This separation is effected by a red-hot bent iron, in which the cylinder is turned round a few times, so as to expand the glass at that point (*g*). A drop of water on the heated line makes an instant fracture. The cylinder is then split by a diamond, or by means similar to that which removed the disk from the end (*h*). *Flatting* and *annealing* finish the process.

These are accomplished in separate furnaces, or apartments heated by the same furnace. In the combined form the *flatting furnace* consists of consecutive chambers heated by a furnace beneath. The cylinder is placed on the heated floor of the flatting furnace, with the cracked side uppermost. The heat of the furnace causes it to soften and spread out, when all the curves and lumps are removed by a straight piece of wood fastened crosswise at the end of an iron handle, and wetted before applying. The flatting stone is made very smooth, as any inequalities are transferred to the glass. The sheet of glass is then pushed into the

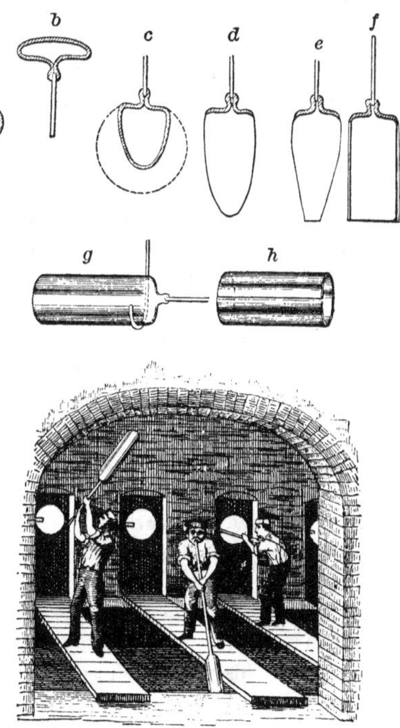

SUCCESSIVE STAGES OF CYLINDER GLASS.

annealing chamber, where it is set upon edge, and left to cool gradually.

The operations of making crown and cylinder glass are exceedingly interesting, and have some marked peculiarities. Wonderful is the command attained by skill over the plastic stuff, and in no other art except pottery is there such a growth beneath the hand of the operator.

The lower illustration shows the men, each one on his platform, one swinging his prolonged bulb above his head, another blowing and swinging it beneath his feet, while a third is observing the operation of heating the glass, which he keeps constantly turning round by means of the rod to which it is attached.

In articles of *bijouterie* and *virtu* we have nothing to claim of elegance or beauty over the Venetians of centuries back. In glass-cutting the most interesting of modern inventions is Tilghman's sand blast, by which a stream of sharp sand or emery is directed upon glass to drill it, as may be required, or to sink a pattern into it, or sink a panel around a raised pattern. It is also used for drilling stone, and even the hardest varieties, such as agate and porphyry.

PAPER.

As Pliny remarked in the first century of our era, "All the usages of civilized life depend in a remarkable degree upon the employment of paper; at all events, the remembrance of past events." This he said of the material obtained by splitting apart the successive folds of the papyrus stalk, a reed growing plentifully then in the marshy grounds of Egypt, but which is now somewhat rare.

Paper, as we understand it, was not then known to the Mediterranean nations, and perhaps not out of China. Paper made by the maceration of rags was introduced into Europe by the Spanish Saracens during the eighth century. It was, of course, made by hand, as it is in Asia at present.

All paper-making machinery is included within our century. By the hand process the rags, being sorted, washed, and bleached, are cut in pieces, and then ground or beaten to a pulp. This was done in mortars till the invention of the rag engine in Holland, about the middle of the seventeenth

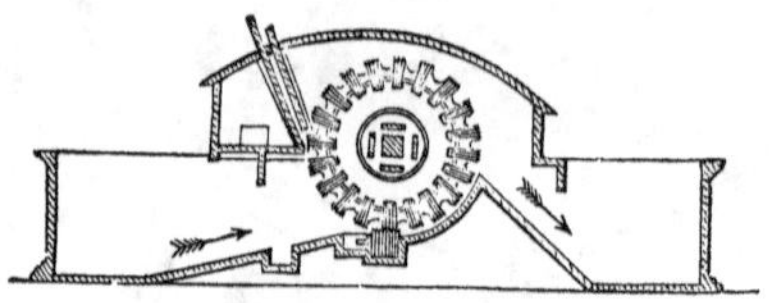

PULPING ENGINE.

century. As now practiced, the beater or pulping engine grinds the rags into pulp, which is transferred to a vat.

By the hand process, which is extinct in Europe and America, except for some grades of drawing and writing papers, the paper-maker dips into the vat a shallow triangular frame, known as the *mould*, having a closely woven wire-cloth, a sort of flat sieve with wire meshes. Lying upon this is an open rectangular frame like a slate frame, and known as a *deckle*, which forms a margin for the sheet of paper to be made. He dips the two into the pulp, and withdraws them in horizontal position, the mould being full. The water drips away as the man shakes the mould to felt the fibres, and he transfers the soft sheet to a sheet of felt, over which he lays another sheet of felt, on this a second sheet of moulded pulp, and so on, until the pile is high enough to be pressed. It is a second time piled, without the felt sheets, and again pressed, then sized, calendered, and made into reams.

Ten centuries passed and saw the civilized nations of the world making paper thus.

A few years after the commencement of our century, Robert, a Frenchman, devised a machine for making a web of paper from pulp. Before 1800 he had made it succeed in a degree, but it took a number of years and the brains of many co-workers before valuable results were attained. The scene of the effort was shifted from the paper mill of François Didot, of Essones, France, to the works of the wealthy brothers Fourdrinier, in England, who were assisted by Donkin in bringing the machine to perfection.

In the Fourdrinier or *flat web* machine the previously prepared pulp is introduced into a vat, where it is thinned with water previously expressed from the sheet during its formation, and agitated by means of a rotary stirrer. Passing through a peculiarly formed strainer, the invention of Ibbotson, by which it is freed from knots, the pulp, in a stream the thickness of which is regulated according to that of the paper to be made, falls upon an apron, which conducts it a short distance to an endless wire-gauze flat web, by which it is carried forward and over a box partially exhausted of air; this flattens the web of paper, and partially extracts the water. The width of the sheet is governed by traveling deckles or side straps, which prevent any portion of the pulp from passing away at the sides of the wire-gauze. The web is then conducted upon endless blankets between two sets of rollers, which express most of the remaining water, and partially obliterate the marks of the wire-gauze, and dried by passing between several pairs of hollow steam-heated rollers, being finally wound upon a roller at the farther end of the machine, or delivered on to another machine by which it is cut into lengths.

In 1809 Mr. Dickinson, an English paper manufacturer, invented the *cylinder* machine.

In this a hollow brass cylinder perforated with holes and covered with wire-gauze is substituted for the flat web of the Fourdrinier machine. The air is partially exhausted from the cylinder through its hollow journals, producing the same effect as the vacuum box over which the web passes in the Fourdrinier machine. The remaining part of the process of manufacture is very similar in each. Combinations of the two systems are found: a web of cylinder paper, which is strongest in one direction, and one of Fourdrinier paper being united; also a number of webs united before drying to form a heavy paper or card-board; or a fine web of pulp has fibres of silk strewed upon it to be imbedded in the paper to form a paper for fractional currency. The quality of paper depends mainly upon that of the material, though the making is responsible for the evenness of its thickness and the smoothness of its surface. The best quality made in this country is hardly so good as that made from the longer fibres of silk or *broussonetia* by the Chinese; but our best is from new—that is, unworn—linen stocks, the clippings of garment making. Cotton rags are not so good, and old, worn rags, partly rotten, are worse. After this we reach still commoner material for stout brown paper, such as hemp and old rope, and the cheapest of all is straw, for wrapping paper.

INDIA RUBBER.

What would the men before '76 have said to the India rubber manufacture? The substance was first brought to England from Brazil as a curiosity early in the eighteenth century, and about 1776 it seems that Priestley suggested that it was "excellently adapted for removing pencil marks from paper." It was dissolved in turpentine, and used by Peal in 1791 as water-proofing composition for fabrics. Hancock and Mackintosh, about 1823, were the first to apply the gum to the uses of water-proof clothing. The gum was placed between two thicknesses of fabric, and was a sticky affair at the best. The business never really prospered until the discovery of the *vulcanizing* process by Goodyear, the subject of his patent of June 15, 1844. He preferred the proportions of twenty-five caoutchouc, five sulphur, seven white lead; but these quantities and the nature of the substances employed were varied by Goodyear himself and by his successors. The same may be said of the heat employed in combining the substances, this being generally proportionate to the degree of hardness required in the vulcanite.

The history of invention does not furnish an instance of greater persistence under discouragement than is afforded by the struggles of Charles Goodyear. It was a purely tentative process. He first mixed the gum with half its weight of magnesia to dry it and remove the stickiness; but the compound softened. He then tried India rubber sap with magnesia, with better results. Next he tried surface treatment with nitric acid. This scheme, which seemed promising, was overthrown by the financial crisis of 1837. After a number of attempts, Goodyear shifted on to the line previously traveled by Hayward—the use of sulphur. Hayward had mixed and covered the rubber with sulphur, and exposed it to the sun's rays, producing a superficial hardening. While experimenting with some goods which had been thus made and returned as rotten, a piece of it was charred by contact with the stove, and the result was sufficient to indicate to the alert mind of Goodyear that what was needed was the baking of the rubber and sulphur together. He then devoted himself to details, the proper proportions for given qualities of goods, the materials to be added to give color and solidity, the uses to which this admirable compound may be put. The results of his genius, care, and persistence are all around us.

METEOROLOGICAL INSTRUMENTS.

The *meteorological instruments* of the present day derive much of their public interest from the tri-daily report of the numerous stations to the Signal-office in Washington, where the generalizations are made, and from whence conjectures for the following twenty-four hours are transmitted. The principal instruments are the *anemometer*, for direction and rate of the wind; the *barometer*, for the atmospheric pressure; the *thermometer*, for atmospheric temperature.

Weather-cocks for indicating the direction of the wind are as old as the sailing of boats, but an instrument for measuring its force can be hardly said to have existed before 1776, when Lind invented an anemometer, which has been long since superseded by those of Whewell, Ostler, Robinson, and others. The present anemometers are self-recording. The *barograph*, or registering barometer, used at the Chief Signal-office, War Department, Washington, is shown in the figure. The barometer is in a dark case, with the mercury column exposed at a slit through which the light of a lamp passes. At the farther end of the machine, shown at the left in the cut, is a cylinder wrapped with sensitized paper so as to blacken with light. This cylinder and its paper cover are moved by clock-work so as to rotate once in forty-eight hours. The image of that part of the slit above the mercurial column is thus caused to form a continuous dark band of irregular width on the paper, becoming narrower as the mercury rises and widening as it descends in the tube, the width of the band indicating not only the relative changes, but also the absolute height of the barometer. A shutter operated by the clock-work cuts off the light for four minutes at the end of each second hour, leaving a vertical white line on the paper.

By the expansion of a zinc rod on each side of the barometer tube, in connection with a glass rod and lever, the thermometric changes are made, and the true barometric indications, with corrections for temperature, are photographically recorded. The strip after remaining forty-eight hours is taken off, the unaltered nitrate washed out, and it is filed away, an enduring record of the condition of the barometer for two days.

The thermometers are read three times a

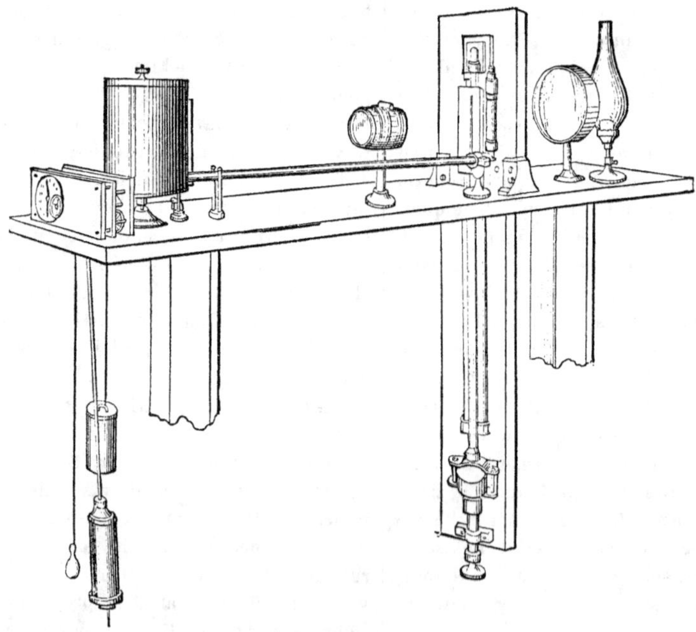

THE BAROGRAPH.

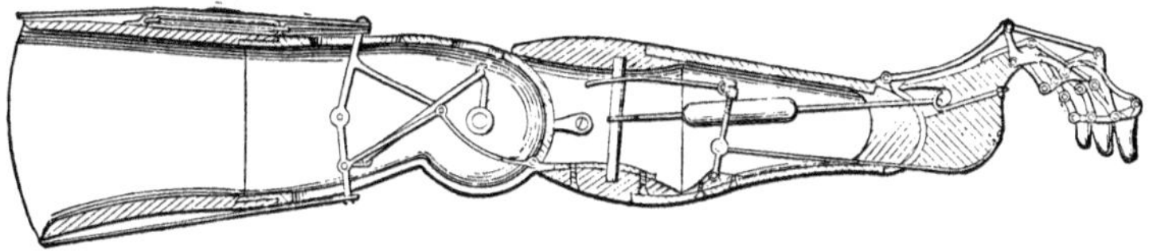

CONDELL'S ARTIFICIAL ARM.
(Longitudinal section of left arm.)

day, but may be made similarly self-recording. Maximum and minimum thermometers are a usual furnishing of observatories. The differential thermometer of Leslie is a hygrometrical instrument for ascertaining the degree of aqueous saturation of the atmosphere by means of the dew-point.

ANÆSTHETICS.

The use of *anæsthetics* has been brought to system, and new agents of ascertained strength and effect have been devised. Former ages used stupefying drugs and poisons which struck directly at the vital force. *Cannabis indica* was used in the Orient, *mandragora* by the Greeks and Romans. The modern anæsthetic agents are cold, deutoxide of nitrogen, chloroform, ether, hydrate of chloral, and some others of less note. From the times when Morelli, in 1674, at the siege of Besançon, invented the tourniquet, and Peré (1550) introduced the ligature and dispensed with actual cautery to arrest the bleeding of the stump, no such act has been accomplished for maimed humanity as the introduction of a safe anæsthetic. As Charles IX. said when he hid the Huguenot surgeon in his royal chamber to guard him from the assassins on the night of St. Bartholomew, "there is only one Peré." Palissy, another Huguenot, was similarly shielded by Catherine de Medicis, the queen-dowager, as there was "only one potter." Palissy died in prison eventually. Ether was known for many centuries before Drs. Morton and Jackson, of Boston, brought it into notice as an anæsthetic in 1846. Chloroform was discovered in 1831; first used as an anæsthetic by Dr. Simpson, of Edinburgh, in 1847.

ARTIFICIAL LIMBS.

Artificial limbs and other *prosthetic appliances* have advanced with the line—artificial hands and legs whose simulation of the natural is so close that a casual observer will not notice the difference.

The artificial arm illustrated has three motions derived from the stump, the arm being secured by bands to the body. The forward motion of the stump flexes the fore-arm, the phalanges are closed and opened by a sort of rotative motion which draws upon a cord, and the backward motion of the stump gives extension to the fore-arm. A man with only four inches of stump may with this arm take his handkerchief from his pocket, wipe his nose, pick up a marble from the table, and put it in his pocket. It does not take as long to learn the use of it as it does to become accustomed to the natural arm; but then the practice with the latter begins with very early life, and when the use is acquired it is much the better of the two.

Artificial arms, ears, eyes, feet, gums, hands, legs, noses, palates, pupils, and teeth are all to be purchased closely matching the remaining parts, or made to any shape desired in cases where no natural portion remains to protest against want of uniformity.

Mechanical dentistry is one of the triumphs of our time and country. Not only is excellence in the art a very recent achievement, but it is more thoroughly understood here than elsewhere. Pepys's diary records that his wife's "tooth was new done by La Roche, and was indeed pretty handsome," but it was probably a piece of ivory or walrus tooth.

AQUARIA.

Aquaria have been constructed on a scale sufficient to show aquatic animals and plants in their natural condition, and with a reasonable degree of freedom. The mode of aerating the water by a jet of air introduced into and ascending in bubbles through the water has much simplified that part of the matter. The proper understanding of the reciprocal duties and effects of the animal and vegetable tenants lies at the bottom of the success with an aquarium. The office of the flora is to abstract the excess of carbonic acid gas due to the breathing of the fauna, and restore the oxygen, as with the terrestrial flora. Then certain animals which feed on decaying vegetable matter are put in the miniature pond to act as scavengers to the community. The demonstration of these conditions is due to R. Warrington, 1850. N. B. Ward is also not to be forgotten. An aquarium 36 by 150 feet was constructed in 1860 in the Jardin d'Acclimation in Paris by Lloyd. The same person erected a large one at Hamburg. An aquarium at Manchester, England, has 750 feet frontage. The aquarium of the Paris Exposition was a large and effective one. That of Brighton is on a grander scale than any other. It occupies ground 100 by 715 feet, the general structure being a quadrangular series of tanks with plate-glass sides, and a central roofed apartment lighted through the tank sides so as to give the idea of being under water. The tanks have fresh or salt water to suit the tenants, and vary in size from 11 by 20 to 30 by 55 feet.

An aquarium car lately went from New England to San Francisco with young fish for stocking the Pacific rivers.

MATCHES.

The old-fashioned match was simply a wooden splint dipped in brimstone, and kindled from a piece of tinder set on fire by a spark from the flint and steel.

The tinder was sometimes ignited by an air-compressing pump. In other cases the matches were tipped with chlorate of potash, and set on fire by plunging in a vial containing asbestus saturated with sulphuric acid. Dobereiner's lamp, in which a hydrogen jet is brought in contact with platinum sponge, and a coil of platinum wire kept red-hot by alcohol, were also sometimes employed, rather, however, as curiosities than devices of general practical use.

Lucifer-matches have now superseded all other appliances for producing an instantaneous light, throughout the civilized world at least, and have become an article of manufacture employing an enormous capital. They are made by sawing or splitting blocks of soft wood into splints, which are dipped into a composition containing either phosphorus or chlorate of potash as a basis, and dried.

Round matches are made by forcing the splints through plates having circular apertures, which at once cut out and compress them; the machinery employed cuts as many as 30,000 splints per minute. These are sold by the hogshead to those who make a special business of applying the composition, which is also effected by machinery.

MUSICAL INSTRUMENTS.

Musical instruments should not be overlooked. They have advanced within the century equally with the other subjects stated.

The organ is as old as Ctesibus of Alexandria, who lived in the Ptolemaic period. The pressure of air was obtained by a sort of water-bellows, the pipes were but very few, and the compass of course quite limited. Down through the ages we find that it had a precarious existence. Haroun-al-Raschid and the excellent Gerbert of Rheims are two of the great names associated with its possession and use. The missals of the Middle Ages show a variety of clumsy contrivances for evoking sounds from pipes by machinery, but excellence was not attained much before the time of Father Smith (referred to by Pepys), who crossed the Channel to repair the damages occasioned in the English churches by the Parliamentary soldiers. Since this time the instrument has been much enlarged, its power, compass, and capacity increased, perhaps without increasing its sweetness. The great organ of Haarlem has sixty stops and 8000 pipes; one at Seville 5300 pipes. The organ of the "Albert Hall of Arts and Sciences," London, has 111 stops, 14 couplers, 32 combinations, and about 9000 pipes. The organs of the Boston Music-Hall, Baltimore Cathedral, and Plymouth Church, Brooklyn, are among the largest in this country.

The parlor organ is an outgrowth of the accordeon, which was introduced in Europe in 1821. The first metallic-reed musical instrument was the *Eolodicon*, by Eschenberg, of Bohemia, 1810. The rocking melodeon was a large accordeon on a stand. Carhart, in this country, has done more than any one else in the improvement of this instrument. He introduced the exhaust plan in 1846. Previous to this the air had been forced through the reed slits, and is still so in Europe. His first instrument had four octaves, but they were afterward increased. Mason and Hamlin in 1855 had instruments with seven octaves, four sets of reeds, and two manuals.

The piano is the successor of a whole series of stringed instruments, dating from the harp. It is a *prostrate harp*, whose strings are beaten by hammers actuated by keys. The citole, clavicymbalum, virginal, spinet, and harpsichord occupy the period from the fourteenth to the eighteenth century. The piano-forte was really invented by Christofori, of Florence, 1711, but it was near the end of the century before it had attained excellence enough to supersede the spinet and harpsichord, the strings of which were twanged by plectra. The grand point to be attained in the piano, or as it was early called, the *hammer harpsichord*, was for the hammer to fall back immediately after striking the string, so as to allow the latter free vibration.

The improvements in this instrument are marvelous, and our country is in the front rank of ingenuity and excellence. The names of Broadwood, Collard, Erard, Steinway, Chickering, Knabe, with many others we can not find space to name, go to an admiring posterity in company.

PRINTING.

The art of taking an impression from an inked stamp is of great antiquity, being found in the most ancient Egyptian and Assyrian remains. Of yore the rude king who smeared his hand with red ochre or the soot from a burning lamp, and then made the impression of his palm and digits beneath a grant of land, was a printer in his way in thus *putting his hand* to the document. Then came seals, engraved in *relief* or *intaglio*, and delivering an impression of the design upon bark, leaf, or skin, either white marks on a dark ground or dark on a light ground, according to the character of the engraving. Seals containing the pronomens of the Pharaohs, each in its cartouch, rewarded the early explorers in the valley of the Nile, and more lately the stamps and tablets of the recorders of the cities of Mesopotamia have been disinterred by thousands. The impressions, having been made in plastic clay, and then baked, have endured without injury a sepulture of twenty-five centuries. They exhibit the kindred arts of engraving and plastic moulding. It may be safely assumed that they were also used for giving printed impressions, but such memorials are, in the nature of the case, less permanent. Some of the ancient stamps in the British Museum are of bronze, and have reversed raised letters, evidently intended to print on bark, papyrus, linen, or parchment.

To this stage of progress various nations of the world had advanced, and yet it can hardly be said that printing, as we understand the word, had been thought of. This evidently originated in China, but it is not certain that Europe derived it from thence. The first notice that we find of printing is in the Chinese annals. Du Halde cites the following from the pen of the celebrated Emperor Van Vong, who flourished 1120 years before Christ. This was about the time of Samuel the prophet, and a little before Codrus, the last of the Athenian kings.

> "As the stone 'Me' [ink, in Chinese], which is used to blacken the engraved characters, can never become white, so a heart blackened by vice will ever retain its blackness."

Other Catholic missionaries concur with Du Halde in supposing printing from blocks to have been invented at least as early as 930 to 950 B.C. The plan adopted was to take a block of pear-tree wood, squared to the dimensions of two pages of the work. On the smooth surface of the block the written pages are inverted, and the paper rubbed off, leaving the ink on the block, which is then delivered to the engraver, who cuts away all the parts not inked. No press is used, but the surface being inked by one brush, the paper is laid upon the block and dabbed down by a dry brush; the sheet is lifted, carrying the ink with it, and is folded with the blank sides in, one side only being printed; the folded edge being outward, the Chinese or Japanese book looks like one with uncut leaves. The first four books of Kung-fu-tze (Confucius) were thus printed between 890 and 925 A.D., and

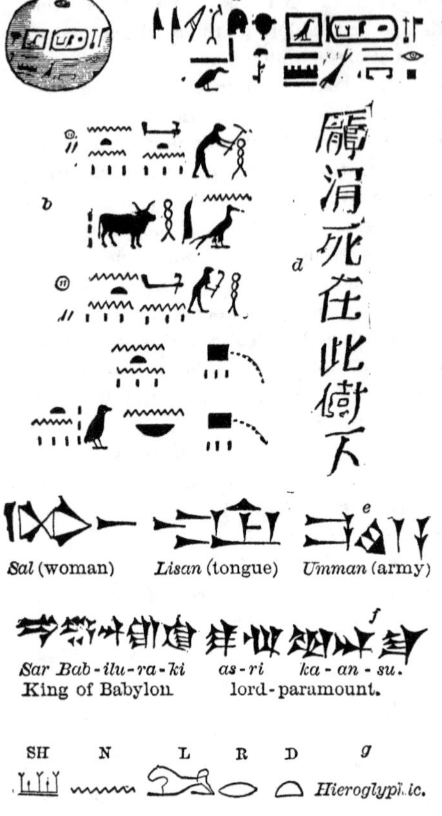

EGYPTIAN AND CUNEIFORM, IDEOGRAPHIC AND SYLLABIC.

the description equally applies to the mode yet practiced.

The same system was used in Europe in the thirteenth century for printing playing-cards and ornamenting fabrics; later, the works known as *block books*, each page being an engraved block like those of the Chinese. Such was the *Biblia Pauperum*, one of the earliest of European block books, compiled by Bonaventura, the chief of the Franciscans, in 1260. In manuscript form, as a book of forty or fifty pages of illustrated Bible scenes and passages, this Poor Man's Bible was a favorite for five centuries. It was printed as a block book about A.D. 1400. The *Speculum Humanæ Salvationis* of Koster, of Haarlem, to whom the credit of the invention of printing has been hence ascribed, was also a block book. Volumes by the score have been written on the rival claims of the cities of Mentz and Haarlem to the invention of printing. From a careful examination of the subject it would appear that Mentz has the prior right, and that the general verdict in favor of Gutenberg is correct.

About the year 1041, a period when Edward the Confessor was King of England, another forward step was made in China. A blacksmith named Pi-Ching invented a mode of printing from plates formed from movable types, each of which represented a word. The types were about the thickness of a half dollar, each had a word on its face, and they were arranged in order on a backing plate, to which they were attached by mastic.

The Chinese have never advanced beyond *ideographs*, or *word signs*, in which arbitrary symbols (*d*) are made to represent things, qualities, or actions. The language has no elasticity, and, like the Egyptian hieroglyphics (*a b*), is incapable of fulfilling modern requirements. In this respect it is like the ancient Scythic cuneiform (*e*); but the genius of the Mesopotamian nations could not be thus cramped, and the language gradually took on the syllabic form: the cuneiform of the second period (shown in *f*) is a transition form. The Persian cuneiform was substantially syllabic. Other languages of Asia early assumed the phonetic form, in which signs stood for sounds, though it was many ages before the vowels were written definitely. The Phœnician (*h*), which is the basis of all the principal alphabets of Europe, had its twenty-two letters 700 B.C., when the black basalt stone was used to celebrate the successes of the King of Moab. *i* is a portion of the inscription in hieroglyphic and demotic from the Rosetta Stone.

That which the Chinese were incapable of doing, from the nature of the case, was done by John Gutenberg, who was born in 1400, at Mentz. In company with Faust and others he printed several works with wooden types and wooden blocks: the *Alexandri Galli Doctrinale* and *Petri Hispani Tractatus* in 1442; and subsequently the *Tabula Alphabetica, Catholicon Donati Grammatica*, and the *Confessionalia*. In 1450 the Bible of 637 leaves was printed by Gutenberg and Faust with *cut* metallic types. Faust retired from partnership with Gutenberg in 1455 and became allied with Schoeffer, and they published in 1457 the *Codex Psalmorum* with cut metallic types; the *Durandi Rationale*, published by them in 1459, was the first work printed with cast metal types. Gutenberg took other partners, and published the *Catholicon Jo. de Janua* in 1460. He used none but wooden or cut metal types till the year 1462. Gutenberg died in high honor in the year 1468.

Peter Schoeffer, of Gernsheim, the partner of Faust and former workman of Gutenberg, was the inventor of *cast* types, the greatest invention of any of the series.

It may be mentioned that, in the early stages of the art, sheets were printed but on one side, and the backs of the pages pasted together. The pages were without running title, running folio, or direction word. The forms were usually folios, sometimes quartos. The character was a rude Gothic mixed with an engrossing character, and designed to imitate handwriting. Scarcely any division was made between words; the orthography was arbitrary and irregular; abbreviations, in imitation of cursive writing, were numerous; punctuation was confined to a double dot (:) or a single one (.), afterward a stroke (/), known as a *virgule*, was used for a slighter pause, and grew into a comma (,). Capitals were so sparingly employed that the beginning of sentences and proper names of men and places were not thus distinguished. This honor was reserved for paragraphs, and here the space was left vacant by the printer that the illuminated capitals might be put in by hand.

a

b

c

d

e

f

PHONETIC LANGUAGES OF ASIA.

a, Sanskrit. *b*, Hebrew. *c*, Samaritan. *d*, Syriac. *e*, Syrio-Chaldaic. *f*, Arabic.

h

i

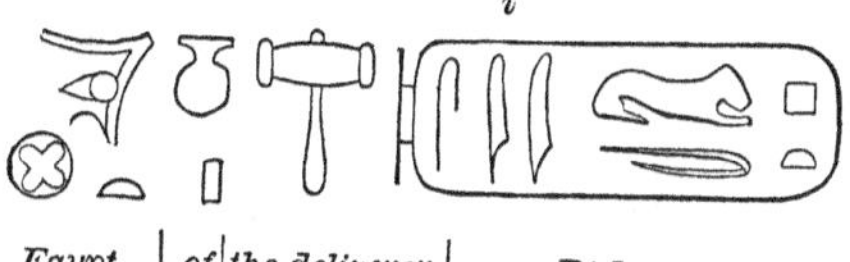

writing | *hard* | *of stone* | *a column* | *On*

PHŒNICIAN AND EGYPTIAN WRITING.

h, Moabite Stone. *i*, Rosetta Stone.

This was soon changed. The era of Leonardo da Vinci, Albert Dürer, Raphael, Michael Angelo, and Vandyck, of Benvenuto Cellini, Galileo, Kepler, Shakspeare, and Bacon, could not long endure mediocrity. The type-founders and printers were worthy of the occasion, and their work leaves little to be desired on the score of sharpness and color. The letters of their books have a vivid blackness that makes one who takes an occasional excursion into *black-letter* wonder where they obtained their ink. The *color* of our pages is gray and rusty in comparison.

In celebrating the achievements of the century we will not claim that we print better, but we do it more easily and much faster; while we handle with great appreciation and respect the works of our worthy, patient, and persevering predecessors, they would view with admiration mixed with awe the towering structure of Hoe, or the compact perfecting presses which print from a web of paper from one to three miles long, and deliver in piles at the rate of 12,000 per hour. They might think, as the doctors of Paris did of Faust, when they considered, from the cheapness of his books and the exact correspondence of their pages, that he was in league with the Evil One.

The art of printing was scattered over Europe when the city of Mentz was taken and plundered by Archbishop Adolphus, of Nassau, in 1462. Within the next decade the Caxton press was set up at Westminster, and that of Theobaldus Manutius at Venice. Æsop's Fables, by Caxton, is supposed to have been the first book with its leaves numbered.

Italic, Greek, Roman, and Hebrew fonts were cast, letters were pruned of their irregularities and excrescences, and order was gradually introduced and concurred in.

The *Aldine* classics are celebrated in prose and verse; in the latter by Alexander Pope among others. The Aldine "Livy" was perhaps the first perfect book, as a modern printer might say. This press was in the hands of the descendants of Aldus for nearly a century.

Catch-words at the foot of the page were first used in Venice by Vindeline di Spori. They have but lately been abolished. *Signatures* to sheets were used by Zorat at Milan in 1470.

A new light dawned upon the nations of Europe. The avidity with which the pages of the printer were seized and read shows that an unsuspected yearning for knowledge possessed the minds of the people. From this time the current was uncontrollable, and the refuges of lies being undermined, commenced to totter and fall, and some others are yet toppling and falling from time to time.

Germany had taken the lead in the invention of printing, as it did seventy-seven years afterward, when the deputies of thirteen imperial towns protested against the decree of the Diet of Spires. The previous attempts at reform in England and Bohemia were before the invention of printing, and, though not fruitless, were apparently quelled. Italy during the Renaissance, at the beginning of the sixteenth century, was the home of arts and letters. Of the various editions of books published in the sixteenth century one-half were Italian, and one-half of these Venetian. One-seventeenth were English.

At Venice was printed the first newspaper, the *Gazette de Venise,* about 1563, during the war with the Turks; the *Gazette de France* appeared in April, 1631; the *London Gazette* in 1642; the Dublin *News-Letter*, 1685; the Boston *News-Letter*, 1704; the first German newspaper, 1715; the first in Philadelphia, 1719; in Holland, 1732. The growth, mission, and power of the press are to be considered elsewhere.

The first press in America was in Mexico. The *Manual for Adults* was printed on it about 1550, by Juan Cromberger, who was probably the first printer in America. The second press was at Lima, in 1586. The press at Cambridge, Massachusetts, was established in January, 1639, by Stephen Daye. The college was censor till 1662, when licensers were appointed. In 1755 the press was free. A psalter in the English and Indian languages was printed upon this, 1709. The press still prospers as the "University Press."

Printing-presses were established at New London, Connecticut, in 1709; Annapolis, Maryland, 1726; Williamsburg, Virginia, 1729; Charleston, South Carolina, 1730; Newport, Rhode Island, 1732; Halifax, Nova Scotia, 1751; Woodbridge, New Jersey, 1752; Newbern, North Carolina, 1755; Portsmouth, New Hampshire, 1756; Savannah, Georgia, 1763; Quebec, Canada, 1764. The first press west of the Alleghanies was at Cincinnati, 1793; west of the Mississippi, at St. Louis, 1808.

TYPE.

The fonts of the earlier printers, as we have said, had a quaint old Gothic character, with various curious tails and inflections, in imitation of the secretary hand of the period. Schoeffer took the best handwriting of his time for his model. The letters gradually became more formal and compact, with fewer exuberances of flourish and abbreviations. It was some time before Italian taste triumphed over German quaintness; but the change was made with more speed than one might suppose would have been the case, considering what a close corporation it was that owned the art of printing in the tight little city, with its tall houses, dark, narrow streets, and its strongly built bastioned walls frowning upon the River Rhine and the adjacent hill. When the archbishop with weapons of this world scattered the coterie of printers it was like the sending forth of the foxes and firebrands of Samson, which carried conflagration into the fields of the Philistines.

In 1465 Schweynheym and Pannartz, who printed first at Subiaco, and afterward at Rome, introduced a new type, very closely resembling Roman. It was professedly derived from the best handwriting of the age of Augustus; and in their *Commentary of De Lyra on the Bible*, 1471, are to be found the first Greek types worthy of the name. Subiaco was the first place in Italy where printing was practiced. In 1468 Ginther Zainer printed at Augsburg the first book in Germany with Roman type.

Roman letters were first used in England by Wynkyn de Worde, Caxton's foreman and successor. He employed them for distinguishing remarkable words or passages, as is now done with *Italic*.

Theobaldus Manutius (Aldus) introduced the *Italic* about 1476: this is believed to have been imitated from the handwriting of Petrarch. This type was first known as *Venetian;* by the Germans as *Cursive.* The first book printed in Italic was in 1501, with the title, *Virgilius; Venet; apud Aldum.*

In 1476 Aldus cast a Greek alphabet, and printed a Greek book. The Pentateuch was printed in Hebrew at Soncino, in the Duchy of Milan, 1482. Irish characters were introduced by Nicholas Walsh, chancellor of St. Patrick's, in 1571.

Aldus's Greek type and books were made by the assistance of Greek fugitives from Constantinople, which had been captured by Mohammed II. in 1453, since which the area of Turkish domination had been continually extending. Aldus finished the publication of his Latin classics in 1494. Some of his Greek works were interleaved with Latin translations.

In 1500 he printed the first part of his polyglot Bible, the Hebrew, Greek, and Latin being on the same page.

The first book printed in the English language was a translation of the *Recueil des Histoires de Troyes* of Le Fevre, by Margaret, sister of Edward IV. of England. When the princess married Charles the Bold, William Caxton was one of her household, and is understood to have assisted in the translation, as also in the setting up and printing, which were done at Cologne, 1471. Caxton moved a few years afterward to England, where, in 1474, he printed the *Game of Chesse,* the first book printed in England.

For some centuries each printer was a law unto himself as to forms and face sizes of letters, height of type, relation of face to body, and composition of type-metal. In course of time the most tasteful superseded those which had less excellence, and something like order was initiated. Without citing the successive changes and attempts at uniformity, it may be stated that the American and English practices approximate in the names of the various fonts and the sizes of body, from the small diamond, which has 205 ems to a foot, to canon, which has $18\frac{1}{3}$ ems in that length. The agreement is not absolute, nor do even the American type-foundries have precisely the same standard. The French standard was established in 1730. The height to paper of the Bruce type is $\frac{92}{100}$ of an inch; other foundries make the height about the same.

The number of punches in the Imperial Printing-office at Paris was 361,000 in 1860. It has fonts of fifty-six Eastern languages, and sixteen European languages which do not use the Roman character.

The "Spécimen Album" of Monsieur C. Derriey, of Paris (1862), affords the most beautiful and graceful examples of the art of the type cutter, founder, and printer. It may fairly be said that the forms, disposition of parts, accuracy of apposition and register—the latter especially noticeable in the chromo printing—have never been excelled.

The scheme of a font is the proportion of the respective *sorts;* an approximate estimate may be given, but different kinds of work require different proportions; for instance, indexes, dictionaries, and directories are *hard on sorts,* as they require so unusually large a proportion of capitals and points.

In a font of 500 pounds:

Lower-case letters	264	pounds.
Points and references	20	"
Figures	14	"
Capitals	37	"
Small capitals	17	"
Braces, dashes, and fractions	13	"
Spaces and quadrats	98	"
Italic	37	"

For French or Italian the above would be deficient in accented letters. Fonts for special work also contain numerous sorts not in the above, such as superior and inferior letters in capitals and lower-case, superior figures in Arabic or Roman, prime letters, arbitrary signs used in arithmetical, astronomical, botanical, chemical, classic, commercial, mathematical, musical, and other works.

Almost every science has symbols of its own. Algebra has one set, chemistry another. For a dictionary which attempts to represent the minute shades of pronunciation a great number are required. Thus in Webster or Worcester, what with letters with dots above and dots below, lines above, below, and across, there are probably 100 additional characters. Some foreign languages have very complicated alphabets. The Greek, with its "accents" and "breathings," requires about 200. Formerly there were so many logotypes and abbreviations as to require 750 sorts. The Oriental alphabets are complex. The Hebrew, with the Masoretic points, requires about 300 sorts, many differing only by a point, stroke, or angle. The Arabic has quite as many. In Robinson's Hebrew lexicon eight or ten Oriental languages appear, and required 3000 sorts, distributed through at least forty cases.

The Chinese dictionary shows 43,496 words; of these 13,000 are irrelevant, and consist of signs which are ill formed and obsolete. For ordinary use 4000 signs suffice. Kung-fu-tze can be read with a knowledge of 2500. There are 214 root-signs, so to speak, which indicate the pronunciation and form *keys* or *radicals*, called by the Chinese *tribunals*. Each character is a word, and the actual number is vastly increased by tones which give quite a different value and meaning.

The number of letters in the following alphabets is thus given in Ballhorn's *Grammatography* (Trubner and Co., 1861):

Alphabet	Letters	Alphabet	Letters
Hebrew	22	Ethiopic	202
Chaldaic	22	Chinese	214
Syriac	22	Japanese	73
Samaritan	22	Dutch	26
Phœnician	22	Spanish	27
Armenian	38	Irish	18
Arabic	28	Anglo-Saxon	25
Persian	32	Danish	28
Turkish	33	Gothic	25
Georgian	38	French	28
Coptic	32	German	26
Greek	24	Welsh	40
Latin	25	Russian	35
Sanskrit	328		

TYPE-FOUNDING.

Type-founding is the invention of Peter Schoeffer, and no important improvement on his mode seems to have occurred to the printers for several centuries. In early times all the operations, from the engraving of the punches, striking the matrices, and casting the type, down to the binding of the book, were carried on within the same establishment. Caxton seems to have regarded himself as well supplied, having five fonts. Type-founding was a separate business in England in 1637.

The "Caslon" type-foundry, established in London in 1716, is still known by that name.

The first type-founder in America was Christopher Saur, of Germantown, Pennsylvania, and the first font cast was of German type, about 1735. In 1768 a foundry was established in Boston, but did not succeed. Abel Buell, of Killingworth, Connecticut, succeeded so far as good work was concerned, but was prevented by a turbulent disposition and by the war of Independence, which supervened, and in which he took an active part, from pursuing the business to a successful issue. Just before the war of the Revolution he was one of the party who destroyed the leaden statue of George III. in the Bowling Green, New York, and was discovered at his house melting up the lead into type-metal, so as to put his Majesty to work disseminating information. A piece of the head of this statue, with some punches and matrices, was found many years afterward in the ammunition chest of an old field-piece to which Buell had been attached during the war.

The American provinces had a hard and generally unsuccessful struggle for independence in business before the idea of political independence seems to have occurred to them. No venture in type-founding was successful till about 1798, when Binney and Ronaldson established themselves by State aid in Philadelphia. The type-founding tools and materials imported by Dr. Benjamin Franklin from France for his own use fell into the hands of Mr. Binney and partner.

The old hand-mould and spoon reigned supreme till 1838, when the first successful type-casting machine was invented by David Bruce, Jun., of New York. Machines for casting a number of types simultaneously, projecting from a common sprue like the teeth of a comb, had been invented in America and in Europe, but no success attended them.

David Bruce's machine is the model of all American and many European type-casting machines. The great difficulty experienced in the development of the machine was in the fact that the resulting type was porous and about fifteen per cent. lighter than the hand-made, each of which was formed by a peculiar spasmodic jerk given by the founder to the mould as he poured in the metal. The effect of this was to condense the metal and expel air. In the Bruce machine the

BRUCE'S TYPE-CASTING MACHINE.

metal is kept fluid by a gas jet beneath, and is projected into the mould by a pump, the spout of which is in front of the metal pot. Each revolution of the crank brings the mould up to the spout, where it receives a charge of metal; it flies back with it; the top of the mould opens, and the type falls out. The matrix containing the letter is held by a spring against the mould opposite to the opening at which the metal is injected, and the rate of making is about 100 per minute for average-sized type.

After casting, the *jet* or surplus metal at the foot of the type, and which formed the ingate of the mould, is broken off, the sides of the type are rubbed on a grit-stone, they are set up regularly in sticks, corrected for inequalities, a groove planed in the middle of the base, forming what are known as *feet.* The proportion of each letter for a font of given weight is arranged in a galley six by four and a half inches, and forms what is known as a type-founder's page. This is papered and marked with the kind of letter contained.

Printing types were first electrotyped with copper in 1850, and have lately been nickel-plated.

TYPE SETTING AND DISTRIBUTING MACHINES.

It is now just about fifty years since the first type-setting apparatus was invented, and a thoroughly successful machine has not yet been introduced. Great hopes have been formed from time to time as one machine after another has been announced, and several of these have done very fair work. As mechanical contrivances they have been quite ingenious, and have worked with a degree of precision which made us think again and again that the goal had been reached at last. And yet to-day but few such machines are in use, and they only on a class of plain work where the number of sorts is limited. A machine must of course include capitals, lower-case, points, and figures; it can not be very efficient without small capitals and italics, but each addition to its capability for variety of work adds greatly to its complexity. After all, it is a race between fingers traveling from the stick to the boxes of the case and back again, and fingers beating upon the keys of the machine. The latter would of course carry the day, as the average travel of the hand after a letter is twelve inches from the stick, and the travel on the key-board of the machine is considerably less than one-half this, but there are so many little niceties to be observed in spacing the words and justifying the lines, work which is done by the skillful printer as he sets up the line, but which, with machine-set type, must be done afterward, when the line of type is broken into lengths for the measure of the work, and then justified by *spaces.* Type-setting machines have separate pockets or galleys for each *sort,* and the mechanical arrangement is such that on touching the key, arranged with others like the key-board of a piano or concertina, the end type of the row is displaced, and is conducted in a channel or by a tape to a composing-stick, where the types are arranged in regular order in a line of indefinite length, and from whence they are removed in successive portions to a justifying-stick, in which they are spaced out to the proper length of line required.

Three machines of this character were exhibited at the Paris Exposition in 1855.

Of the American machines that of Alden has perhaps excited most attention. The persistence of the inventor for seventeen years in the endeavor to perfect his invention, and his death, in 1859, when success appeared to be crowning his efforts, afford one more interesting item to the history of invention when it shall come to be written. His machine has types arranged around the circumference of a horizontal wheel, which rotates slowly, carrying with it fingers which pick up the proper types from their respective cells. The ordinary types are used, with the exception that each has its peculiar nick on one side, which will enable the fellow-machine to discriminate when *distributing* the type.

In the distributing process the *dead matter* is placed on a bed to the right of the key cylinder, and is taken up line by line as each is exhausted. The types are taken up by distributing transits in the revolving wheel, selected by means of the nicks, and then transferred by way of the channels to the respective type pockets. Extra spaces, etc., are tipped out at the end of the channel. Unnicked type are thrown into a separate box, italics into another.

Another instance may be given: the Kastenbein composing machine, in which common types are used, each sort being arranged vertically in a series of tubes, like the pipes of an organ. As a letter key of the key-board is struck, the lever connecting with the particular letter tube opens the lower end of the tube, and allows the lowest type in the rank to fall into a groove which conducts it to the slide where the letters are assembled in a long line, and whence they are taken by the compositor's rule and justified.

The distributing machine reverses this method. The *dead matter* is placed on a bed, each line is cut off and the types raised *seriatim* so that they can be read by the observer. The corresponding key on the key-board being depressed, the type is pushed into its appropriate tube, ready for supplying the composing machine.

Printers have been wont to boast that a practical type composing and *justifying* machine presented a problem which even Yankee ingenuity and persistence could not solve; but in view of the progress made in this direction during the last decade, it can hardly be doubted that complete success will be achieved in the near future.

Still later machines for composing and distributing, the invention of Mr. Paige, were recently exhibited in New York, and worked well. It remains, however, to be determined whether or not the capital invested in them and the casualties incident to complicated and delicate machinery will discourage their use in place of compositors, who own themselves, are always ready, and for whom substitutes can be found if one or another prove ailing or erratic.

STEREOTYPING.

The art of casting solid metallic plates from type was invented by William Ged, a goldsmith of Edinburgh, in 1731. The plates ordered by the University of Oxford for an edition of the Bible were mutilated by jealous printers and thrown aside—the old tale of narrow-minded prejudice and ignorance. Ged's plan was the *plaster process*, but after its abandonment several other means were tried before the plaster was resumed.

Carez (France, 1793) had a plan of dashing down the inverted form upon a surface of hot lead just in the act of solidifying. The cast thus obtained was used in the same way to obtain a cameo impression for a printing surface. Didot's plan consisted in casting types of a hard alloy, and pressing them into a surface of pure lead. This was brought down upon a paper tray of molten type-metal just in the act of solidifying. The *English Monthly Magazine* of January, 1799, comments on this plan. Herham set up the form in copper matrices, and took a cast therefrom in type-metal. These three plans were French.

Stereotyping was introduced into the United States by David Bruce, of New York, in 1813. The first work cast in America was the New Testament, in bourgeois, in 1814.

In the *plaster process* of stereotyping the type is set up with spaces, quadrats, and leads which come up to the shoulders of the type. Guard-lines and bearers are placed at the top of the page and at intervals of the type lines to support the plate during finishing. The type is then oiled, and inclosed by a flask to hold within bounds the fluid plaster, which is poured upon the face of the form, and worked in between the letters by a roller covered with flannel and leather. The plaster soon sets, and the mould is carefully raised by screws which lift it vertically from the form. The stereotype plate is then cast from the plaster mould, which is done by inclosing the mould in a box and plunging it into the bath of molten metal. The casting pan is

CASTING PAN.

of iron, consisting of a tray and a lid, the latter having at its corners gaps for the metal to flow in. Each pan has an iron plate or floater three-eighths of an inch thick, which fits within it. Upon this plate the mould is laid face downward. The cover is chalked and secured by a yoke and screw. The pan is swung over the pot, and lowered on to the metal so as to become heated, then depressed so that the metal flows in at the corners and forces itself between the *floater* and *mould*. When the pan is filled it is submerged, and left till the bubbling has ceased. It is now swung over the water-trough and cooled. The cast is knocked out of the pan, the surrounding metal broken off, and the stereotype freed from the plaster.

The plate is then finished by trimming the edges, laying it on its face, and shaving off the back to bring it to an even thickness. The bearers are cut away with a chisel and mallet, the heads trimmed, and the sides beveled with a plane upon the

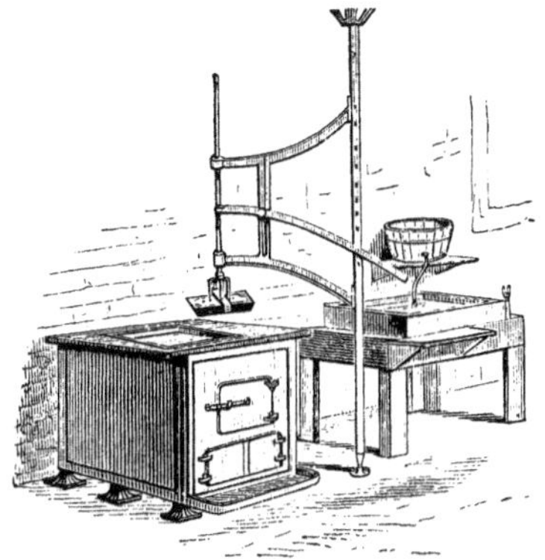

STEREOTYPE CASTING APPARATUS—PLASTER PROCESS.

shooting-board. The plate is then carefully examined and faults repaired.

In the *clay process* a plastic composition of fine clay and plaster of Paris, with a small quantity of gum-arabic water, is spread with a trowel to the thickness of a quarter of an inch upon a plate which is secured to a frame shown in the drawing as hinged like a tympan to the press bed. The form is laid face upward on the bed, the face of the type is brushed over with benzine, covered with a cloth and paper, the tympan is turned down upon the form, the bed run under the platen, and an impression taken sufficiently deep to cause the clay to flow into the blank spaces and give the general outlines of the type. The press is then opened, the cloth and paper removed, and also any superfluous material which has been thrown up by the first pressure, and would be likely to bind. The press is again closed, and a complete impression taken, imbedding the type in the plastic material to the desired extent. This process is usually repeated one or more times in order to give a sufficient depth to the *cups* of the letters. The metallic plate carrying this mould is removed from the press, and the mould hardened by drying. When dry it is set afloat

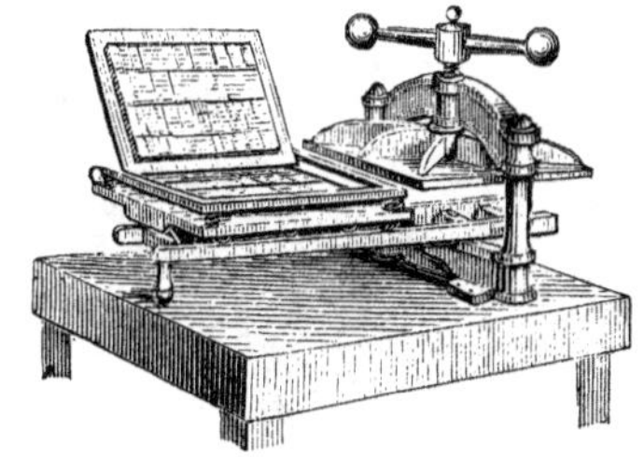

MOULDING PRESS—CLAY PROCESS.

face upward in a vat of melted type-metal in order to bring it to the same temperature as the metal. A wire somewhat thicker than a finished stereotype plate, and bent so as to surround three sides of the mould, is placed on the plate, and a second plate is clamped over the wire, as in a moulder's flask. The whole is then put in a trough, the open edge of the mould upward, and the metal poured in. The casting is cooled by pouring water on the plate containing the mould. When the flask is opened the metal adheres to the mould, which is removed by wetting and brushing. The plate is then planed, trimmed, and dressed up for use.

Curved plates for cylinders are made from a flat form by using a sheet of spring steel of the desired curvature for a mould plate, which is spread flat on the tympan, and the plastic material is applied upon what is to be the concave side. After the impression is taken the sheet is released, and resumes its normal curvature, bending the plastic mould with it. The face of the plate is, of course, somewhat distorted, the stereotype appearing as if taken from type a little more condensed one way than that actually employed in the form.

The *papier-maché* process is very expeditious, and is generally used on daily papers of large circulation. A paper matrix is formed by spreading paste over a sheet of moderately thick unsized paper and covering it with successive sheets of tissue-paper, each carefully patted down smooth; the pack is then dampened. The face of the type is oiled, the smooth surface of the paper treated with powdered French chalk, and laid upon the type. A linen rag is wetted, wrung out, and laid over the paper, and dabbed on the back with a beating brush so as to drive the soft paper into all the interstices between the letters of the form. Remove the cloth, lay a reinforce sheet of damp matrix paper upon the back of the matrix, and beat again to perfect the impression and unite the surfaces of the two. For large establishments a matrix rolling machine is used. A double thickness of blanket is placed upon the matrix, the form and matrix laid in a press, and screwed down tight. The lighted gas heats the press and the form, and dries the paper matrix. The press is unscrewed, the matrix removed, and it is warmed on the moulding press. The matrix is then placed in the previously heated iron casting mould, and a casting gauge to determine the thickness of the stereotype plate is placed upon it. This extends around three sides of the matrix, the other being left open to serve as a gate at which the molten metal is poured in. The cover is screwed tight, the mould tipped to bring the mouth up, and the metal poured. When the metal is *set* the mould is opened and the matrix removed. The plate is then trimmed and otherwise prepared in the usual manner.

BEATING-TABLE—PAPIER-MACHÉ PROCESS.

STEREOTYPE MOULD-DRYING PRESS—PAPER PROCESS.

ELECTROTYPING.

Electrotyping is an application of the art of electroplating, which originated with Volta, Cruikshank, and Wollaston about 1800–01. In 1838 Spencer, of London, made casts of coins and impressions in intaglio from the matrices thus formed. In the same year Jacobi, of Dorpat, in Russia, made casts by electro-deposition, which caused him to be put in charge of the work of gilding the dome of St. Isaac's at St. Petersburg. Electrotyping originated with Mr. Joseph A. Adams, a wood-engraver of New York, who made casts in 1839–41 from wood-cuts, some engravings being printed from electrotype plates in the latter year. Many improvements in detail have been added since to the process as well as the appliances. Murray introduced graphite as a coating for the forms and moulds.

The process of electrotyping is as follows: The form is locked up very tight, and is then coated with a surface of graphite, commonly known as *black-lead;* but this is a misnomer. This is usually put on with a brush, and may be done very evenly and speedily by a machine in which the brush is reciprocated

BLACK-LEADING MACHINE.

over the type by a band wheel, crank, and pitman. A soft brush and very finely powdered graphite are used, the superfluous powder being removed, and the face of the type then cleaned by the palm of the hand. Knight's wet process of black-leading, as practiced at Harper and Brothers' establishment, is, however, much to be preferred, and will be described presently.

A shallow pan, known as a moulding pan, is then filled with melted yellow wax, making a smooth, even surface, which is black-leaded. The pan is then secured to the bed of the press, and the form placed on the bed, which is raised to deliver an impression of the type upon the wax.

ELECTROTYPING PRESS.

The pan is removed from the head of the press, placed on a table, and *built up*, as it is termed. This consists in running wax upon the portions where large spaces occur between type, in order that the corresponding portions in the electrotype may not be touched by the inking-roller, or by the paper sagging down in printing.

The wax mould being *built*, is ready for black-leading, to give it a conducting surface upon which the metal may be deposited in the bath. The wax mould is laid face upward on the floor of an inclosed box, and a torrent of finely pulverized graphite suspended in water is poured upon it by means of a rotary pump, a hose, and a distributing nozzle, which dashes the liquid equally over the whole surface of the mould. Superfluous graphite is then removed by copious washing, an extremely fine film of graphite adhering to the wax. This is Silas P. Knight's process, and answers a triple purpose. It coats the mould with graphite, wets it ready for the bath, and expels air bubbles from the letters. This process prevents entirely the circulation of black-lead in the air, which has heretofore been so objectionable in the process of electrotyping. Black-lead being nearly pure carbon, is a poor conductor, and in the usual process a part of the metal of the pan is scraped clean to form a place for the commencement of the deposit, and the back of the moulding pan is waxed to prevent deposit of copper thereon. When the dry black-leading is used the face of the matrix is wetted to drive away all films or bubbles of air which may otherwise be attached to the black-leaded surface of the type.

The mould is then placed in the bath con-

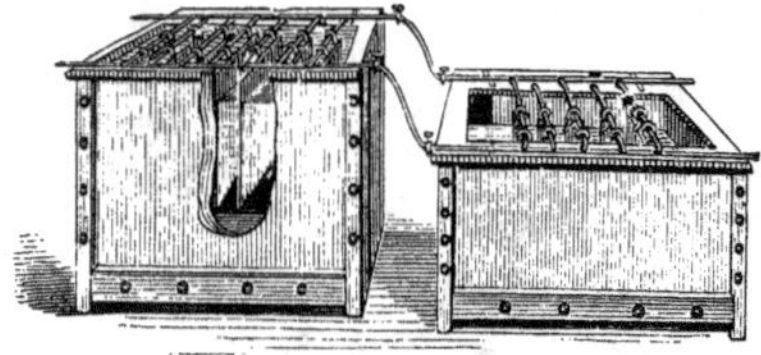

ELECTROTYPING BATH AND BATTERY.

taining a solution of sulphate of copper, and is made part of an electric circuit, in which is also included the zinc element in the sulphuric acid solution in the other bath. A film of copper is deposited on the black-lead surface of the mould, and when this shell is sufficiently thick, it is taken from the bath, the wax removed, the shell trimmed, the back tinned, straightened, backed with an alloy of type-metal, then shaved to a proper thickness, and mounted on a block to make it type-high.

Knight's expeditious process consists in dusting fine iron filings upon the wet graphite surface of the wax mould, and then pouring upon it a solution of sulphate of copper. Stirring with a brush expedites the contact, and a decomposition takes place; the acid leaves the copper, and forms with the iron a sulphate solution, which floats off, while the copper is freed and deposited in a pure metallic form upon the graphite. The black surface takes on a ruddy tinge with marvelous rapidity. The film is afterward increased in the usual manner in the electro bath, but the deposit takes place immediately and regularly over the whole surface. The saving in time, acid, copper, and zinc is very great.

THE PRINTING-PRESS.

The *printing-press* in its earlier forms was but an adaptation of the ordinary screw-press. The form was locked up in a tray and placed on a platform, upon which the platen was brought down by a screw traveling in a cross-bar above. The screw was moved by a lever, which was shifted into holes in the boss of the screw.

BENJAMIN FRANKLIN'S PRESS.

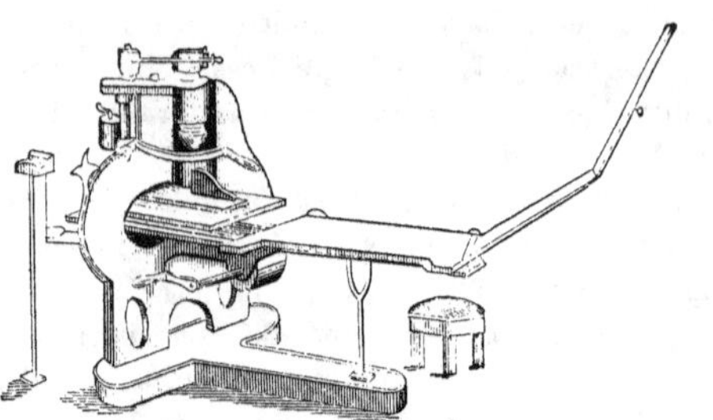

LORD STANHOPE'S PRESS.

The Blaew was the first patent press, 1620. The carriage was rounced in beneath the platen; the pressure was given by a handle attached to a screw hanging from the beam, and having a spring which caused the screw to fly back as soon as the impression was given. Blaew was a very ingenious and versatile man, and was for some time, in the earlier portion of his career, associated with Tycho Brahe, at the observatory of the latter in Denmark, in contriving instruments and reducing observations. Subsequently he was in Amsterdam, where he made globes and maps, and invented his improvements in printing-presses. He died there in 1638.

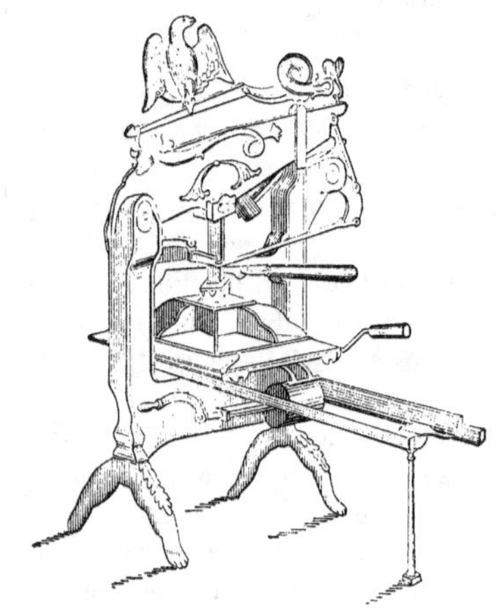

"COLUMBIAN" PRESS.

The Franklin press, one hundred years afterward in London, was a Blaew press with some minor improvements.

To this succeeded the Stanhope press, about the end of the eighteenth century. The oscillating handle operates a toggle to force down the platen upon the paper on the form. The bed travels on ways, and the tympan and frisket are hinged to lay back in elevated position.

The "Columbian" press, by George Clymer, of Philadelphia, was invented about 1817, and was perhaps the first important American contribution to the art of press-making. The power is applied to the platen by a compound lever consisting of three simple levers of the second order. Peter Smith's hand-press soon succeeded the "Columbian," and in 1829 the "Washington"

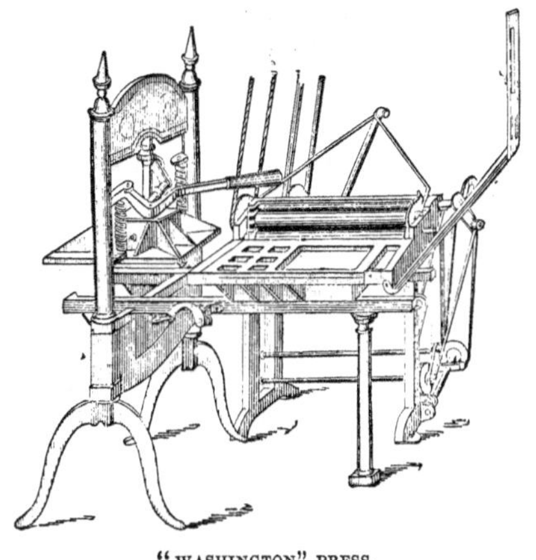

"WASHINGTON" PRESS.

was patented by Samuel Rust. The pressure in this is obtained by a compound lever applied to a toggle-joint, and the platen is lifted by springs on each side. The frame is made in sections, and the bed is run in and out by turning a crank which has a belt attached to its pulley or *rounce*. The tympan and frisket are held up by the nature of their hinges, which allow only a certain amount of swing.

Power-presses or *printing-machines*, as they are indifferently called, belong exclusively to our century. Nicholson obtained a patent for a cylinder printing-machine (1) in 1790. It is not known that it was ever brought into use, but several of its features have survived in later and successful machines. The ink was applied by a roller; the types were made narrower toward the foot, so as to fit against each other snugly when attached to the exterior surface of a cylinder. The type cylinder revolved in gear with a leather-covered impression cylinder, and at another part of its rotation with an inking cylinder, to which inking

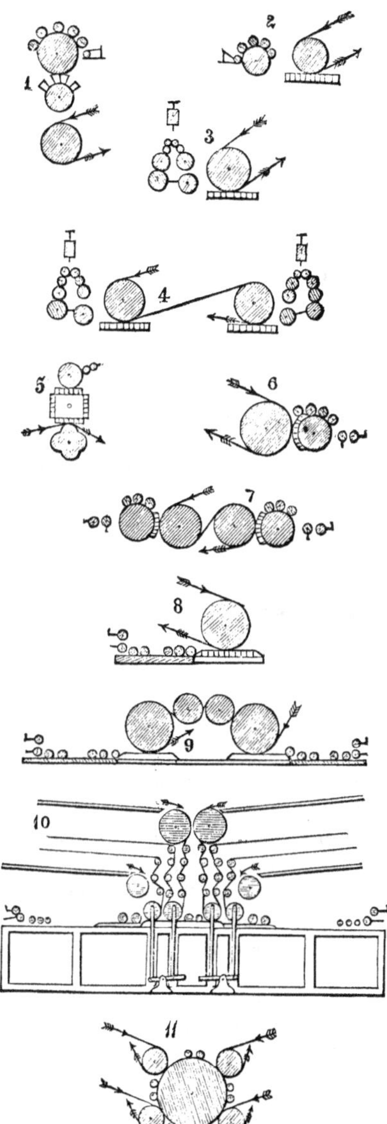

PRINCIPLES OF ACTION OF POWER-PRESSES.

apparatus was applied. The arrangement was modified (2) for a flat bed.

König, a German, constructed a printing-machine (3) for Mr. Walter, of the London *Times*, in 1814. The issue of the 28th of November of that year was the first newspaper printed by machinery driven by steam-power. It gave 1100 impressions per hour, and subsequently was worked up to 1800. The paper was held to its cylinder by tapes; the form was reciprocated beneath the inking apparatus and the paper cylinder alternately. To double the rate, a paper cylinder was to be placed on each side of the inking apparatus. The ink was placed in a trough, and ejected upon the upper of a series of rollers, passing downward in the series; and here first occurred the distributing roller with end motion.

König's press (4), which consisted of two single machines acting in concert and consecutively upon the two sides of the sheet, was perhaps the first attempt at a perfecting press. It was erected in 1818, but did not prove successful.

Donkin and Bacon's machine (5), 1813, was built for the University of Cambridge, England. Several forms were attached on the sides of a prism, and were presented consecutively to the inking cylinder and paper cylinder. In this machine were first used the composition inking-rollers, of glue and molasses.

In 1815 Cowper obtained a patent for curved stereotype plates, to be affixed to a cylinder (6). By duplication of parts the machine (7) was designed to become a perfecting press. The greater portion of the cylinder forms a distributing surface for the ink, the remainder is occupied by the stereotype plate.

Applegath and Cowper's single machine (8) went back again to the flat reciprocating bed, the double machine (9) being a perfecting press. This machine was the first to have diagonal distributing rollers to spread the ink smoothly by sliding on the reciprocating inking-table.

Applegath and Cowper's four-cylinder machine (10), 1827, superseded König's in the *Times* office, and printed at the rate of 5000 per hour on one side. It had four printing cylinders, one form of type on a flat bed, and the paper cylinders were alternately raised and depressed, so that two were printed during the passage one way, and the other two on the return passage. A pair of inking-rollers between the paper cylinders obtained their ink from the table.

Applegath's machine, 1848, was long used upon the *Times*. It introduced one novelty —placing the whole series of cylinders on end. On the vertical type cylinder the type were arranged in upright columns, forming flat polygonal sides to the drum. Arranged around it were eight sets of inking apparatus alternating with eight impression cylinders, and the paper, fed from eight *banks*, was delivered upon as many tables. The paper fed from each feed-board was carried by tapes and rollers, and passed on edge to the type and impression cylinders, was carried off, thrown over flatwise, caught by a boy, and placed upon the table. The number of sheets per hour worked upon this machine rose from 8000 in 1848 to as high as 12,000, printed on one side.

The Hoe type-revolving printing-machine (11) is made with two to ten printing cylinders arranged in planetary form around the periphery of the larger type-carrying cylinder. The type is secured in *turtles*, or the stereotype is bent to the curve of the cylinder. The circumference of the central cylinder has a series of binary systems, the elements of which are an inking apparatus and an impression apparatus, the paper being fed to the latter and carried away therefrom by tapes to a flyer, which delivers it on to a table. It has as many banks as feeder or impression cylinders.

There are numerous modifications of the flat-bed and type-revolving machines for more or less rapid work, perfecting or for one side only; for fine wood-cut work, book-work, or job-work; with continuously revolving cylinders or stop-cylinders, which pause while the bed returns; with inking-rollers varying in number with the kind of work required; and with many variations in size for posters, handbills, and cards.

The first flat-surface printing-machine was made by Daniel Treadwell, of Boston, in 1822. His machines, first used in Boston, were afterward used by Daniel Fanshaw in New York in printing the Bibles and tracts for the "American Bible Society" and the "American Tract Society." The machines for the former society were driven by a steam-engine, and those for the latter by two mules in the upper story of the Tract-house building, using an endless-track power. In this press the platen comes down on the type. These were the first printing-machines in America driven by other than hand-power, and were long used by Gales and Seaton in Washington in printing the Congressional reports, etc.

Next was the Adams press, which was introduced in 1830, has been since much im-

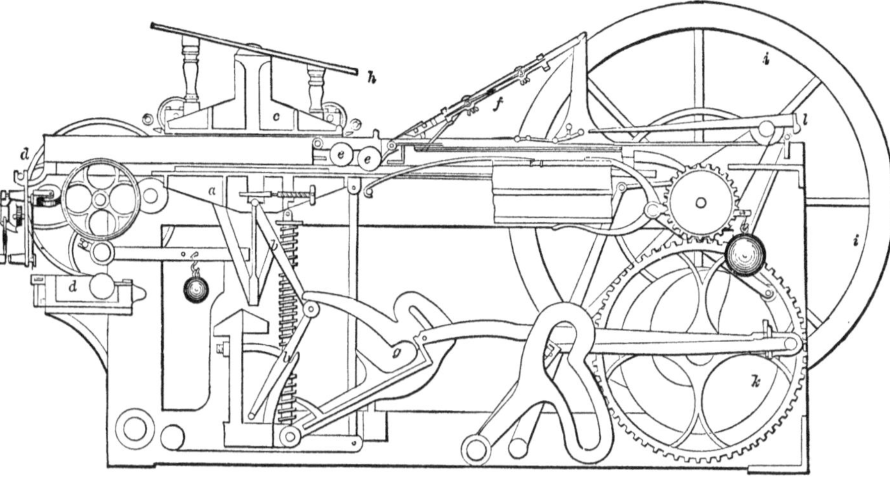

ADAMS PRESS.

proved, and still has a high reputation. Its movement is based on that of the hand-press, and gives a perfectly flat impression by lifting the bed of the press and its form against a stationary platen. Sheets are fed to the press by hand, and taken away by tapes and a fly. One thousand sheets an hour is a full speed for a large Adams press on book forms. It is shown in the figure by a longitudinal vertical section: *a* is the bed, which is raised by straightening the toggles, *b b; c* is the platen, *d* the ink fountain and ink-distributing apparatus. The inking-rollers, *e e*, pass twice over the form, and are attached to the frame of the tympan, *f*. The segment *g* serves to straighten the toggles, and cause the impression; *h* is the feed-board, *i* the drive-pulley, and *k* a gear wheel, with a pitman rod to *g; l* is the fly.

Single-cylinder presses, such as Hoe's, Potter's, Campbell's, etc., have a flat bed, which is geared to reciprocate at an even speed with a revolving cylinder. Sheets of paper are fed to the cylinder, which carries a prepared tympan. The inked form runs along with the sheet until it is printed, when the form is retracted and inked again. In some machines the cylinder stops after the impression is delivered.

The Campbell press is remarkable for several fine points of adjustment. The operation is controlled by the sheet, which, when

CAMPBELL'S SINGLE-CYLINDER PRESS.

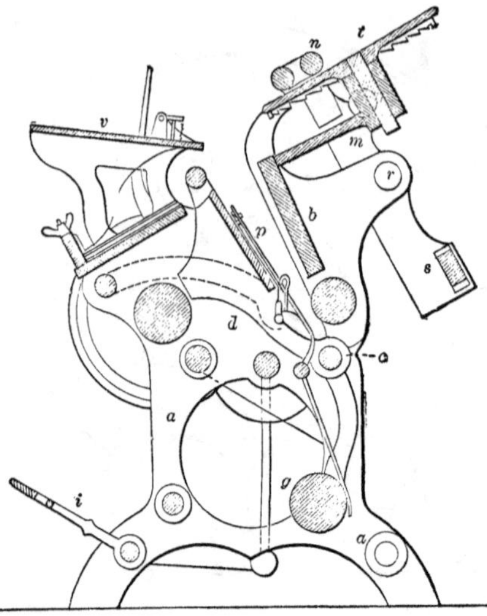

GORDON JOB PRESS.

badly fed, is thrown out. The registering is operated by a small valve through the agency of points, making an electric circuit through point-holes in the sheet. When the press *fails to point*, the exhaust apparatus is brought into action, operating a bolt attached to a diaphragm, which locks up the impression. It has other peculiar features well worth mentioning if space permitted.

America produces a remarkable variety of handy job presses, known by the name of the makers, as the "Gordon," or by names which constitute trade-marks, as the "Globe," "Liberty," "Universal," etc.—a favorite device both with books in the early days of the art and with presses for a hundred years past; witness the "Columbian" and "Washington" hand-presses. One instance may be given.

The form in the "Gordon" press is secured in a chase, which is clamped to the bed, *b*, of the press. This bed rocks on a pivot at *c*, and comes into parallelism with the platen, *p*, when the impression is about to be given. The platen rocks on the main shaft, *d*, which is propelled by pitman and intermediate gearing from the treadle, *i*. The arm, *m s*, is the roller-carrier, which swings on a pivot, *r*, and carries the rollers, *n n*, alternately over the form and the revolving disk, *t*, which distributes the ink: *g* is a counter-weight to balance the swinging bed and attachments, and operate the movable fingers by a spring bar, *a*: *v* is the feed-board.

The *web press* is a later thought, and bids fair to supersede all others for large editions and long numbers, where great nicety is not required. It is not yet expected that for fine work and cuts it will supersede the flat-surface and reciprocating-bed presses.

The "Walter" press prints the London *Times* and the New York *Times*. A roll of paper, *a*, three miles long, reels off over the pulley, *b*, which serves to keep it taut. It then passes by the wetting rollers, *c c*, and over the cylinder *d* to the first type cylinder, *e*, between which and the blanket cylinder, *f*, it receives its first impression. Following the direction of the type cylinder, it passes between two blotting cylinders, and is then delivered to the second printing cylinder, *g*, receiving the impression at *h*. It is then cut by a knife on the

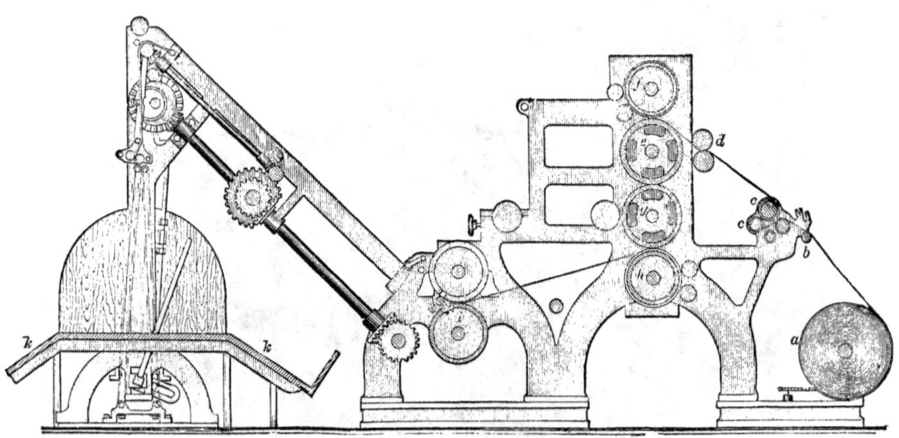

WALTER'S PERFECTING PRESS.

"BULLOCK" PERFECTING PRESS.

cylinder *i*. The sheets are finally piled by two persons on the paper-boards, *k k*. The speed of the Walter press is 11,000 printed sheets per hour.

The "Bullock" press, so named from the inventor, the late William Bullock, of Philadelphia, carries the forms upon two cylinders, requires no attendants to feed it, and delivers the sheets printed on both sides. The paper, in the form of an endless roll, is moistened by passing through a shower of spray. A single roll will contain enough for several thousand sheets, and the printing operation, including the cutting of the paper into proper lengths, proceeds uninterruptedly until the roll is exhausted. The roll of paper having been mounted in its place, the machinery is started, unwinds the paper, cuts off the required size, prints it on both sides at one operation, counts the number of sheets, and deposits them on the delivery board at the rate of 6000 to 8000 per hour. The roll of paper, *a*, is cut into sheets by a knife on roller *b* acting against the cylinder *c*. The sheets are seized by grippers, carried between the impression cylinder, *g*,

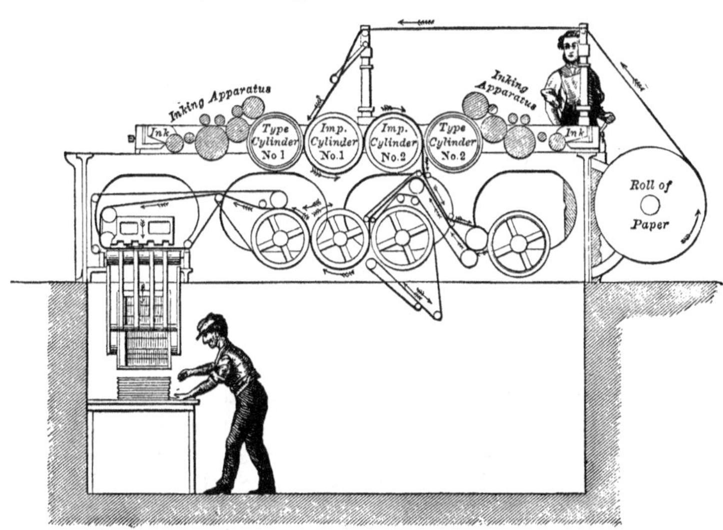

"VICTORY" PERFECTING PRESS AND FOLDING MACHINE.

"HOE" WEB PERFECTING PRESS.

and the form, *e*, receiving the first impression. The printed sheet then follows the large cylinder, *g*, to the second form, receiving its second impression from this form acting against the large drum, *g*. From the large cylinder the sheets are automatically delivered to the receiving board: *i* is a counting device or arithmometer. The inking-rollers are shown above the inking cylinders, beneath which are the ink-troughs. The starting lever is shown on the right.

The "Victory," like those just described, receives its paper from a roll. The names on the parts will obviate the necessity of specific description. The paper is led over two wetting boxes, and then over two hot copper cylinders, and entered between the first type and impression cylinders. Here one side is printed, and it thence goes to the second type and impression cylinder, where it is backed. It then travels to the cutting and folding cylinders, where it receives a transverse fold, and meantime the doubled paper is passed to a serrated knife, which cuts the first printed sheet from the web. A second blunt knife again folds the double sheet, which is carried by grippers to a vibratory frame, entering each alternate sheet to the respective pairs of cross-folding rollers, which deliver the sheets to tapes, which carry them to a swinging delivery frame, by which they are deposited in a pile on the table.

This machine will damp, print, cut, fold, and deliver about 15,000 per hour of an eight-page newspaper of fifty inches square; or it will damp, print, cut, fold, and paste a cover of four pages on a twenty-four page paper at the speed of 7000 per hour.

The "Hoe" web perfecting press is one of the lately established and successful candidates for public favor. The paper is printed from a roll containing a length of over four miles and a half, equal to 10,000 papers. The machine has three pairs of cylinders geared together. A roll, having been previously damped, is lifted into place by a small crane, and the paper from it passes between the first pair of cylinders, the circumferences of each of which are just equal to the required length of the sheet. One of these cylinders has its periphery covered with stereotype plates of the matter to be printed, and is supplied in the usual manner with an ink fountain and distributing rollers, which, as the cylinder revolves, apply the ink to the stereotype forms. The other cylinder is covered with a blanket, and as they revolve together, with the paper between them, they print its first side. The paper then passes on between the second pair of cylinders, and presents its blank side to the stereotype plates of the second type cylinder. It next passes to the cutting cylinders, the periphery of one of which has a vibrating and projecting knife that at each revolution enters a groove in the opposite cylinder and severs a sheet from the roll. The sheets are successively conveyed by two series of endless tapes to a revolving cylinder, which retains them until six (or any desired number) are collected upon it, when they are delivered in a body to the sheet flyer. A circular cutter cuts the double sheets into single copies.

A counter is attached which shows the number of sheets printed. The machine occupies a space of about twenty feet long, six feet wide, and seven feet high, and delivers 12,000 to 15,000 perfected sheets per hour.

These machines have a reputation on both sides of the Atlantic, being used by the London *Lloyds' News*, *Standard*, and *Telegraph*, while five of them are now building for offices in the United States and two for Australia.

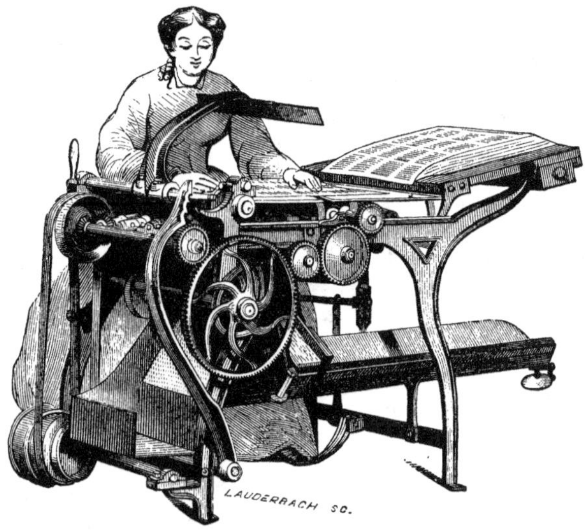

CHAMBERS'S FOLDING MACHINE.

FOLDING MACHINES.

As an improvement occurs in one of the machines of a series, every other one has to mend its pace to keep up. So we found it with the ginning, carding, spinning, and weaving of fibre; so it was with the smelting, puddling, rolling, forging, turning, and planing of iron: one improvement begets another, and a halting member of a series which retards the speed becomes the object of so much solicitude that it shall go hard but he ere long outstrip his brethren in the race.

Machines for folding newspapers and sheets for books follow naturally in the wake of the presses. They are made of various kinds for octavo, 16mo, and 32mo; also for folding 12mo, cutting off, pasting, and inserting the inset; in some cases placing it in a cover, and doubling it up into compact shape for the mail wrapper.

The book-folding machine illustrated is for octavo work, sixteen pages on a sheet, eight pages on a side.

The sheet is placed on the table so that two register points pass through two holes in the sheet previously made on the printing-press. The folder comes down upon the folding edge, the pins give way, and the sheet passes, doubled edge first, between a pair of rollers, which compress it; tapes deliver it to a second table beneath, where a second and a third folder act upon it in turn, and it is delivered into a trough at the rate of 1500 per hour.

With 12mo work imposed in two parts of sixteen and eight pages respectively, the machine cuts them apart, and folds the larger part like an octavo; the smaller folds but once, and is then "inset" into the octavo portion, which forms the "outset."

The two-sheet folder and paster, for large twenty-four-page periodicals, folds one sheet of sixteen pages, 30½ by 45½ inches, insetting the eight pages within the sixteen, and pasting and trimming all, delivering a complete copy of twenty-four pages ready to read at the rate of 1200 per hour. It will fold eight pages alone, sixteen pages alone, with or without pasting or trimming, or will fold, paste, and trim the eight pages, insetting without pasting them in.

Machines of this general character are also made for folding, pasting, and trimming, or for folding, pasting, trimming all around, and putting on a cover of different-colored paper. The *Christian Union* is folded, inset, and covered in this manner, four of these machines being attached to a four-cylinder "Hoe" press.

ADDRESSING MACHINES.

Addressing machines are of two general kinds; one cuts the addresses from printed and gummed strips and attaches them to the paper. The Dick machine works in this way.

The other mode is to set up the addresses in a galley, and bring them successively to a spot at which the enveloped papers are consecutively presented.

The machine illustrated is one of many of

ADDRESSING MACHINE.

the latter class. It prints with ink on the papers or wrappers at the rate of 3000 per hour. The names are set up in long narrow galleys holding fifty or seventy-five each, and after inking with a hand-roller, these are placed successively in the channel of the table, and are pushed along by the apparatus till each name in turn has come under the impression lever, which is worked by the treadle. The motion of the galley is automatic, and the machine indicates a change of post-office by the stroke of a bell, so that the papers may be thrown into separate piles to be bundled for mailing.

The "Forsaith" addressing machine also operates in a very satisfactory manner.

PRINTING FOR THE BLIND.

The art of printing in raised letters which may be distinguished by the touch originated and has been developed within the century. The first successful efforts in this direction were made at Paris in 1784 by the Abbé Valentin Haüy, who in the same year founded "L'Institution Royale des Jeunes Aveugles," the first institution ever established for the instruction of the blind.

Various systems of forming the embossed characters have since been introduced, which may be divided into two classes—the *arbitrary*, arranged exclusively with reference to the supposed greater facility with which their forms may be distinguished by the touch, no attempt being made to imitate ordinary printing; and the *alphabetical*, in which the letters resemble those ordinarily employed.

Prominent among the first are those of Lucas, Frère, Moon, Braille, and Carton. Lucas's system is composed of a series of dots, curves, and straight lines, each of which represents a letter, distinguishable by its form or the position in which it is set. Many contractions and abbreviations are employed, and though it is claimed to be easily read by the touch, its bulk and the frequent ambiguities arising from the peculiar system of abbreviations are objectionable. Thirty-six volumes are required to contain the Scriptures, which in the American lower-case alphabet are comprised in eight.

Frère's system is phonetic, thirty-six characters being employed, each representing a simple sound.

Moon, himself a blind man, represents the letters of the ordinary alphabet by characters, each composed of but one or two lines. The printing is read alternately from left to right and from right to left.

Braille's system is that generally employed in France: the letters are formed by combinations of dots varying in number from one to six.

Carton's system also employs dots, but arranged to more nearly resemble the letters of the Roman alphabet.

Among those known as alphabetical are—

The French, a combination of lower-case and capitals.

Alston's, English, has modified Roman capitals.

Friedlander's, American, Roman capitals of the kind known as block letters.

That of Dr. S. G. Howe, principal of the Institution for the Blind at Boston, Massachusetts, employs an angular form of lower-case for all the letters except G and J, which are capitals. This character is used at most of the institutions in the United States, and many valuable works have been printed in it.

Mr. N. B. Kneass, of Philadelphia, himself a blind man and a publisher of works for the blind, employs lower-case like that of Dr. Howe and block capitals, under the title of "Kneass's improved combined letter."

ENGRAVING.

The early history of engraving concerns the inscriptions on stones; the "iron pen," and inlaid "leaden letters" in the rock, referred to by Job, if that be a fair understanding of the passage. Contemporary with this are the carved and lettered obelisks of Egypt, the tablets of Assyria and Etruria, the engraved gems in the breastplate of Aaron, perhaps the leaden plates inscribed with Hesiod's "works and days," which were so long preserved at the fountain of Helicon, in Bœotia, as recorded by Pausanias.

From inscriptions the Greeks proceeded to engraving maps on metallic plates; and the brass plates containing the Roman laws were complete enough for printing, but it does not seem to have been thought of. The history of engraving is the history of printing; but we must not repeat it here.

The art of engraving is naturally divisible into three orders—metal, wood, stone; the latter better known as lithography, and considered separately.

Engraving on metallic plates originated with chasers and inlayers. It can not but be that such artists took proof in dirty oil on rag or leather, but no impression of intrinsic value was had until the time of Finiguerra, a Florentine artist, in 1440. Euclid was printed with diagrams on copper in 1482. The copper-plate press was invented in 1545. Etching on copper by means of aquafortis was invented by F. Mazzuoli, or Palmegiani, in 1532; mezzotint engraving by Von Siegen in 1643; improved by Prince Rupert, 1648, and by Sir Christopher Wren in 1662.

Stipple engraving—also called "chalk engraving," from the resemblance of the work to crayon drawing—was invented by Jacob Baylaert in London in 1769; engraving on steel as a substitute for copper, by Jacob Perkins, of Philadelphia, in 1819.

The present century has not devised much that is new except the ruling machine by Wilson Lowry.

Plate engraving flourished in England from 1800 to 1850, but photography and lithography have gradually pushed it aside, since which the skill has decayed and the demand fallen off. Until this decadence persons of average taste would claim that though our predecessors excelled in rude vigor, our execution was as good as that of the earlier masters, and our effects better, the connoisseurs in the antique to the contrary notwithstanding. Nor will it avail for such to quote Gifford's sarcasm,

"We want their strength: agreed; but we atone
For that and more by sweetness all our own."

Wood-engraving originated in China, as we have had occasion to observe before; its first uses in Europe were in ornamenting paper and fabrics, afterward for making playing-cards.

The earliest known wood-cut with a date—the St. Christopher of 1423—is in the Althorpe Library, England, which, it may be stated in passing, contains the most valuable single volume in the world, an edition of Boccaccio printed at Venice by Valdarfer in 1474, of which no other perfect copy is known. It sold at the Duke of Roxburgh's sale in 1812 for £1260. The art of wood-engraving was much improved by Dürer, 1471–1528; by Bewick, 1789. It has gone on improving ever since, by fits and starts, but always onward. The great use made of it by the *Illustrated London News* is an era; its advance over the *Penny Encyclopedia* affords a good means of judging the rate of progress. Our best illustrated periodicals and books are triumphs of the art.

LITHOGRAPHY.

The art of engraving or drawing on stone, so that printed copies may be obtained therefrom in the press, originated with Alois Senefelder, of Munich, 1796–1800. The invention was not a mere accident, as recounted in the common myth of an absent-minded man, a piece of limestone, and a waiting washerwoman, but was the result of earnest, persistent, and intelligent work directed to an object kept steadily in view.

The stone used for lithographic work is a compact sedimentary limestone of a yellowish or bluish-gray color, which comes from

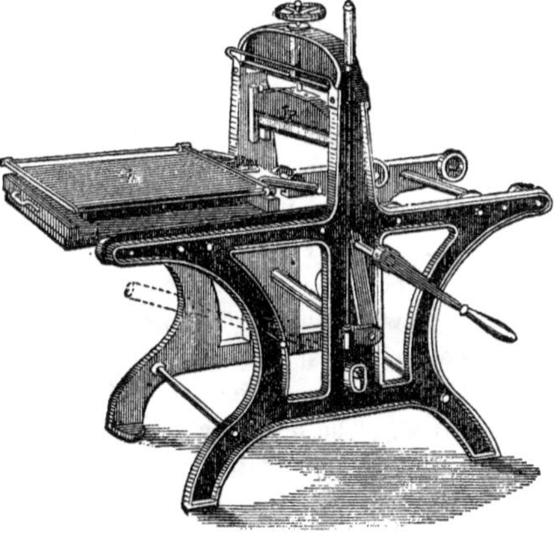

LITHOGRAPHIC HAND-PRESS.

the Solenhofen quarries in Bavaria. It is ground by moving one stone upon another with sand between them, and then polished with pumice-stone.

Upon the stone thus prepared the design may be produced in four ways:

1. It may be done with a fluid, watery ink.

2. With a solid crayon.

3. By a transfer from an inky design on paper.

4. By engraving with an etching point.

1. The *ink* is essentially a soluble soap colored with lamp-black, applied with a pen or hair-pencil. The stone is then *etched* with a weak acidulous solution, decomposing the soap, combining with its alkali, and setting free the fatty acid in contact with the particles of carbonate of lime of which the stone consists, forming an insoluble lime soap which no washing or rubbing can remove and no fatty matter can penetrate. The stone is then flooded with gum-arabic water to incapacitate the clear parts from receiving ink when wetted. The stone is now placed in the press and made ready. With a sponge and abundance of water excess of gum is washed off, and, while still wet, the drawing is *washed out* with turpentine applied with a rag. This appears to obliterate every thing, but a close inspection shows the work as a pale white design on the face of the stone. The stone is now *rolled up* by passing a roller charged with printing-ink over its face, which is still damp; the greasy ink adheres to the white design, while the clear gummed damp face takes no ink. A sheet of paper is laid upon it, the tympan closed, and the stone pulled through. The operations of damping, inking, and printing are then repeated in succession.

2. The work by *lithographic crayon* is upon a *grained* stone, the surface of which is evenly roughened by grinding with very sharp and even sand of a grade according to the fineness of grain required. The crayon is of soap, wax, and tallow, and it is used on the stone as a drawing chalk is upon rough Whatman paper. The subsequent processes in preparing the stone are the same as those before described. The process gives opportunity for much artistic taste and display, the broken surface of the stone preventing the continuity of the lines, whose depth of color will depend upon the pressure of the crayon upon the rasping surface.

3. The *transfer method* consists in placing the design on paper and then transferring it to the stone. The writing, for instance, is done on ordinary sized paper, but preferably on paper prepared with a coating of gelatine, which may be colored with gamboge. The written sheet is damped, laid face down on the stone, and pulled through. The ink adheres to the stone, which is treated as before.

4. The *engraving method* differs from the preceding. The surface of the stone is treated with gum-arabic water, which, when dry, is colored to allow the succeeding work to show. The design is then scratched in with needles or diamond points, and the face of the stone flooded with oil, which is absorbed by the stone where the etching points have laid it bare. The coloring matter and excess of gum are washed off, and the lines are filled with ink, the gum protecting the clean surface. The paper is laid on, and the stone pulled through the press, the sheet lifting the ink out of the lines. It is not usual to print from the engraved stone, but to transfer an impression therefrom to another one and print in the usual way.

There are many modifications of the art: a tint is rubbed on dry, and distributed or rubbed off according to the lights and shades of the design; by another mode the surface is covered with a solution of asphalt and crayon, and scraped off for the lights. The list might be much extended.

Until a comparatively recent period all lithographic printing has been upon hand-presses, but lately a successful lithographic printing-machine has been made. Hoe's machine is a stop-cylinder press, that is, one in which the cylinder comes to a stop pending the adjustment of the sheet. The paper is fed to grippers on the cylinder from the inclined table above. The traveling bed on which the stone rests is drawn under the cylinder by a crank and connecting rod from the end of the frame below, and the cylinder, after being thrown into gear, is rotated at the same time (carrying the sheet with it) by a rack attached to the side of the bed. At the end of the stroke the cylinder goes out of gear, and remains stationary and locked during the return of

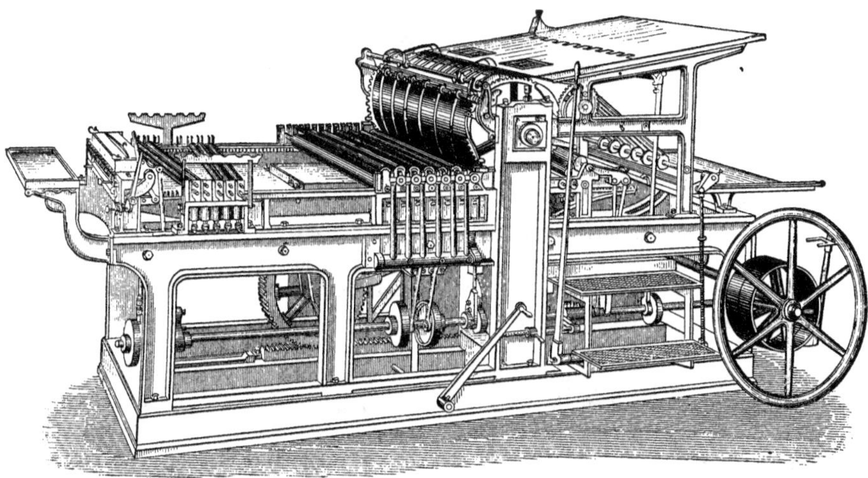

HOE'S LITHOGRAPHIC PRINTING-MACHINE.

the bed and stone, the latter passing under a cut-away part of the cylinder, so as not to come in contact with it. In place of a tympan the cylinder is covered with a thin rubber blanket. The inking of the stone is effected by parallel rollers (from three to six) in front of the cylinder, upon which are heavy riding rollers of iron, the latter being made to vibrate laterally to aid the distribution of the ink. These inking-rollers are covered with leather, like the ordinary hand-rollers for lithographic printing; they receive their ink from a table which travels with the bed, and are driven by a rack or friction pieces on the sides of the bed. The ink is fed to the table from a fountain at the end of the press, and distributed by a number of oblique-lying rollers, also covered with leather. The automatic damping arrangement is at the back of the cylinder. It consists of a shallow trough containing water, partially immersed in which a cylinder of wood is made slowly to revolve. An absorbent roller is held in contact with the surface of this roller for a longer or shorter time, according to the amount of water required upon the stone, after which it carries its increase of moisture over to a heavy riding roller, which again gives it up to two damping rollers covered with linen, which traverse the stone as it passes beneath them, just before it meets the inking-rollers near the cylinder; the feed of water admits of adjustment as to quantity while the press is in motion.

The pressure in this press is adjusted by means of butting screws, which lift or lower the bed in the traveling carriage; these screws are turned by a key from above. When the sheet is printed it is conveyed by an intermediate cylinder provided with grippers to the fly at the end of the press, and there deposited, face up, on the pile of printed work.

This press, though by no means identical with European machines of the same class, may be regarded as furnishing an illustration of the essential features of them all.

The introduction of the lithographic power-press has totally remodeled the lithographic trade throughout the world within the short period of six years (1868–74), increasing the possible production about tenfold. It has lowered the cost of, and in fact rendered possible, large editions from stone which in former times found their way to the type press, with very inferior results. By this change the general public have profited largely.

Chromo-lithography, the highest development of the lithographic art, differs only from the ordinary processes in the imposition of a number of impressions in different colors from as many different stones upon a sheet of paper, the combination of colors making a finished picture. An outline drawing is transferred to each stone required to complete the picture, so as to secure exactness in the co-relation of all parts on each stone. Upon these stones the artist draws the different tints and colors, the number varying with the character of the picture. Mr. Prang's famous chromo, "Family Scene in Pompeii," occupied forty-three stones. An artist must have a high degree of skill in drawing, a fine feeling for and thorough knowledge of color, and must be able to tell what number of stones will be required, what the order of the tints and colors, what effect one tint will have upon the succeeding ones. Careful *register* is required, so that each color may fall in its proper place in the picture.

Senefelder died in 1834. Every phase of the lithographic art described in the foregoing was indicated, originated, or practiced by him. The development and perfection of the present day, in every branch of his great invention, would gratify and astonish him infinitely. He would gaze in amazement at the lithographic power-press printing thousands of sheets daily, and would be lost in admiration at the sight of a chromo which he would confound with the original painting, and which his art has placed within the reach of every one. All this he would readily comprehend; *photo*lithography alone would be to him a mystery and a revelation.

PHOTOGRAPHY.

The art of photography is entirely embraced within the century. The solitary fact bearing upon the subject, and known to the world previous to 1776, was that *horn-silver* (fused chloride of silver) is blackened by exposure to the sun's rays. It is now known that many bodies are photo-chemically sensitive in a greater or less degree, but some of the salts of silver and chromic acid in conjunction with organic matter are pre-eminently so, and are used practically to the exclusion of all others.

Scheele in 1777 drew attention to the activity of the *violet* and *blue* rays as compared with the rest of the spectrum; and Ritter in 1801 proved the existence of *dark rays* beyond the violet end of the visible spectrum by the power they possessed of blackening chloride of silver. Wollaston experimented upon gum-guaiacum. Wedgwood, previous to 1802, was the first to produce a photograph, in the technical sense of the word; this was a negative of an engraving which was laid over a sheet of paper moistened with a solution of nitrate of silver. Such a picture had to be carefully preserved from daylight, or the whole surface would blacken. Neither Wedgwood, nor Davy, who accompanied with observations the memorandum of Wedgwood to the Royal Society, devised any mode of fixing the image.

From 1814 to 1827 Joseph Nicéphore Niepce, of Chalons on the Saône, experimented on the subject. In the latter year he communicated his process. He coated a plate of metal or glass with a varnish of asphaltum dissolved in oil of lavender, and exposed it under an engraving or in a camera; the sunlight so affected the bitumen that the parts corresponding to the white portions of the picture or image remained upon the plate when those not exposed to light were subsequently dissolved by oil of bitumen and washed away. This was a permanent negative picture. In 1829 Niepce associated himself with Daguerre.

In 1834 Fox Talbot commenced his investigations, and in January, 1839, announced his *calotype* process. He prepared a sheet of paper with *iodide of silver*, dried it, and just before use covered the surface with a solution of *nitrate of silver* and *gallic acid*, and dried it again. Exposure in the camera produced no visible effect, but the latent image was *developed* by a re-application of the gallo-nitrate, and finally *fixed* by *bromide of potassium*, washed and dried. A negative so obtained was laid over a sensitized paper, and thus a *positive print* was obtained. This was a wonderful advance.

In the same month, January, 1839, Daguerre's invention was announced, but was not described till July of that year. In the *daguerreotype*, which has made the name of the inventor a household word, and furnished a test of skill in all the spelling schools of the United States, polished silver-surfaced plates are coated with iodide of silver by exposure to the fumes of dry iodine, then exposed in the camera, and the latent image developed by *mercurial fumes*, which attach themselves to the iodide of silver in quantities proportional to the actinic action. The picture is fixed by *hyposulphite of soda*, which prevents farther change by light.

Goddard in 1839 introduced the use of *bromine* vapor conjointly with that of iodine in sensitizing the silver surface.

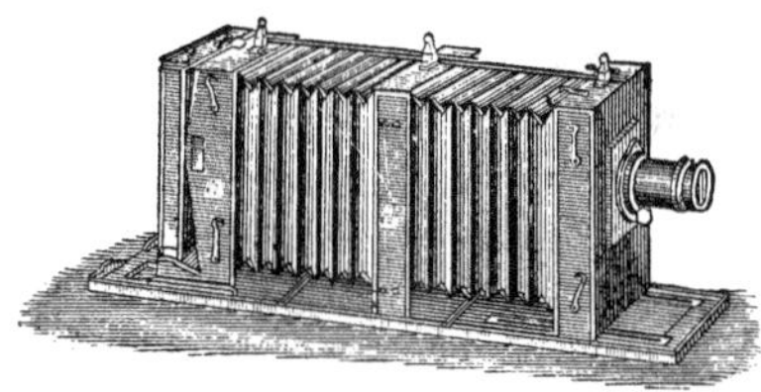

BELLOWS CAMERA.

The addition of chlorine was by Claudet in 1840. M. Fizeau applied the *solution of gold*, which combined with the finely divided mercury, and in part replaced it.

In 1848 M. Niepce de St. Victor coated glass with *albumen*, and treated it with nitrate of silver to sensitize and coagulate it. The film hardened in drying and furnished a negative from which pictures might be printed by light.

The *collodion process*, by Scott Archer, of London, was one of the most remarkable inventions of the series, and has made photography the most important art industry of the world. A plate of glass is cleaned, floated with collodion, sensitized with iodides and bromides, usually of potassium. It is then plunged in a solution of nitrate of silver. Metallic silver takes the place of the potassium, and forms insoluble iodide and bromide of silver in the film, which assumes a milky appearance. The plate is exposed in the camera, and the latent image developed by an aqueous solution of protosulphate of iron, the picture gradually emerging by a dark deposit forming upon those places where the light has acted, the density of this deposit being directly proportional to the energy of the chemical rays. When sufficiently developed, the plate is washed with water, and fixed by washing away the free silver salt by a solvent, such as the cyanide of potassium or hyposulphite of soda. This removes the milky character of the film, and leaves the picture apparently resting on bare glass.

To produce *positive photographic prints* from such a negative a sensitized sheet of paper is placed beneath the negative, and exposed to the sun's rays. The light passes through the negative in quantity depending upon the transparency of its several parts, and produces a proportionate darkening of the silver salts in the albuminous surface of the paper. The paper is now washed to remove the unaltered nitrate, *toned* by a salt of gold, *fixed* by hyposulphite of soda, washed, dried, mounted, and glazed.

The *solar camera* is used for making enlarged prints from a negative. *a* is an adjustable portion, having a central aperture at which the negative is exposed to the rays entering at the window, *b*; *c* is the lens; *d* the board for the paper enlargement.

Space can not be spared for even the recitation of the names of the various processes which have from time to time been prominently before the public. Some of these were invented in the infancy of the art, and have been long superseded by more perfect methods; others yet survive for certain purposes.

The *ambrotype* is a thin collodion negative on glass made by a short exposure, and developed so as to produce as white a deposit as possible on the lights. Such a picture is not looked at by transmitted light, nor is it valuable as a negative; it is to be backed up with a black surface, generally a black varnish, and regarded by reflected light only. Under these circumstances it appears as a positive, the deposit reflecting and the black backing absorbing the light. Pictures of this kind are rapidly made, and finished direct from the camera, as is the case with the daguerreotype, while the cost is very much less. They are, however, very inferior to

ENLARGING SOLAR CAMERA.

good positives on paper, and had to make way for the latter as the negative process improved.

Ambrotypes are rarely to be met with now, but *ferrotypes*, or *tintypes*, as they are sometimes called, are produced by a perfectly analogous process, the substantial difference being that the collodion picture is made directly upon a thin iron plate covered with a black enamel or lacquer, which protects both its surfaces from the action of the negative bath, and acts the part of the black backing used in the ambrotype.

Ferrotypes are still in vogue, the quickness with which they can be produced and their exceedingly small cost making them popular with the public. Cameras provided with a large number of lenses are employed in their production.

The trouble and difficulty in the efficient working of collodion negatives out-of-doors created a desire for a means of preserving a collodion plate in a sensitive condition, so as to render it unnecessary to coat, sensitize, and develop the plate where the landscape is taken. Accordingly a number of preservative and dry-plate processes have been invented. No dry process, however, gives results fully equal in quality to the work from wet plates, but they offer other advantages which can not be ignored.

The stereoscopic camera used for field work has an arrangement for instantaneous exposure of the two lenses, which admit pencils of beams to the plates in the binary chamber. Shutters are placed in front of each tube, so arranged that by touching a spring they are simultaneously rotated, bringing for an instant of time a hole in each shutter in correspondence with the tube, admitting rays of light from the object to the sensitized surfaces in the interior.

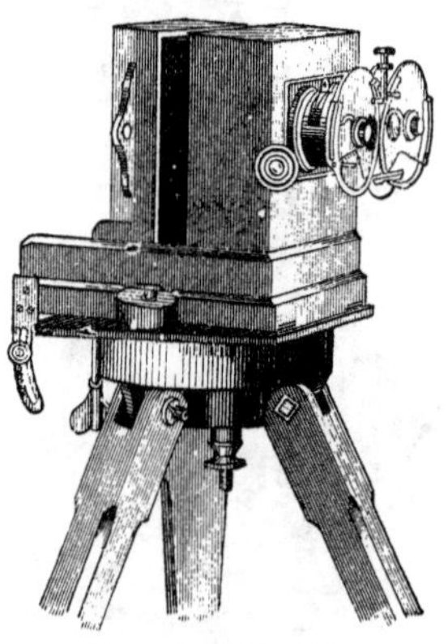

STEREOSCOPIC CAMERA.

The first daguerreotype portrait from life was taken by Professor John W. Draper, of New York, in 1839. An announcement of it was made in the *London and Edinburgh Philosophical Magazine* in March, 1840. A full account of the operation was subsequently published in the same journal. He also took the first daguerreotype view in America, a view of the Church of the Messiah, from a window of the New York University. In his laboratory Professor Morse learned the art.

Daguerre made an unsuccessful attempt to photograph the moon. Dr. J. W. Draper succeeded in 1840 in obtaining a photograph of the moon on a silver plate with a telescope of five inches aperture. He presented specimens to the New York Lyceum of Natural History in 1840. Professor G. P. Bond, of Cambridge, Massachusetts, made photographs of the moon in 1850 with the Cambridge refractor of fifteen inches aperture. Many others followed. Mr. Rutherford's photographs of the moon are most excellent. Mr. Delarue, in England, must also be mentioned.

PHOTOLITHOGRAPHY.

Photolithography is a mode of producing by photographic means designs on stone from which impressions may be obtained in the ordinary lithographic press.

The first attempts in this line were by Dixon, of Jersey City, and Lewis, of Dublin, in 1841; they were followed by several inventors in Paris, Vienna, and Rome.

Their experiments were with resins directly upon stone. Joseph Dixon, 1854, was the first to use organic matter and bichromate of potash upon stone to produce a photolithograph. Poitevin was the first to recognize the fact that bichromated organic matter altered by light took the greasy ink from the roller. No great measure of success was attained by operations with resins and directly upon stone. The various gelatine processes have been more successful. Without ignoring the value of some of these, not particularly described here, it will be well for brevity's sake to describe the best process, and but one.

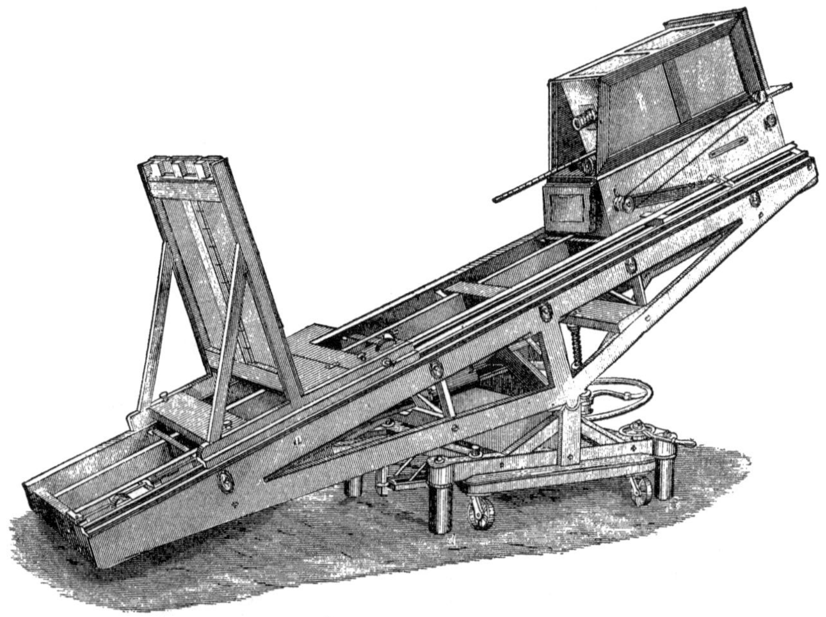

OSBORNE'S COPYING CAMERA AND TABLE.

J. W. Osborne patented in Australia September 1, 1859, and in the United States June 25, 1861, a transfer process, in which he prepares a sheet of paper by coating one side with a mixture of albumen, gelatine, and bichromate of potash, and dries it in the dark. This is exposed under a negative, whereby a visible change is produced, the brilliant yellow of the sheet, due to the salt of chromium, being changed to a chestnut-brown. In addition to this visible change, the organic matter becomes insoluble. A coating of transfer-ink is now applied to the whole exposed surface by passing the sheet through the press, face down, upon an inked stone. When the sheet is removed the photographic picture is almost invisible. The sheet is then floated, ink side upward, upon hot water, the action of which is to coagulate the albumen, rendering it insoluble, and to swell and soften the gelatine, causing the part affected by light to appear depressed by contrast. The sheet of paper so floated is next placed upon a slab, and the superfluous ink rubbed off by a wet sponge. This operation develops the picture. The sheet is then washed, dried, and transferred to the stone in the usual way. The coagulated albumen forms over the whole surface of the paper a continuous film, which adheres strongly to the stone during the transfer process, preventing any shifting and consequent doubling of the lines. This is, for all practical purposes, the first successful photo-lithographic process, and has been used in the Crown Lands Survey Office of Victoria since September, 1859, in the publication of maps. Substantially the same process is used in the Ordnance Survey Office of England. The duplication and copying of drawings for the United States Patent-office has been for some years performed by this process, which, in accuracy and speed, leaves nothing to be desired.

The copying camera employed in making negatives from drawings is shown in the figure. The camera (containing the negative plate) and the plan-board, on which is tacked the drawing to be copied, are adjustable on a table, which is tilted on its truck to give the drawing a good presentation to the light. The focusing is done by a thin metallic belt, giving a rapid and positive movement on either side of the problematical focus. The table is always brought into a horizontal position in focusing, the end of the camera box being covered by a hood, under which the operator stands. So placed, he controls the positions both of the plan-board and the lens, and has the ground glass always at a convenient distance from him. In copying at or near full scale the position of the lens affects the size of the picture, making little change in the sharpness of the focus, which latter operation is then done with the plan-board. When a large reduction is required, the position of the plan-board affects the size, and the focusing is done with the lens.

MISCELLANEOUS PHOTO PROCESSES.

Besides the processes which have been described under the titles *Photography* and *Photolithography*, there are a number of others which should not be entirely overlooked. The processes yet remaining to be stated depend upon the use of gelatine.

Mungo Ponton in 1839 first discovered the sensitiveness to light of a sheet of paper treated with bichromate of potash. Becquerel in 1840 determined that the sizing of the paper played an important part in the change. Fox Talbot in 1853 discovered and utilized the insolubility of gelatine exposed to light in the presence of a bichromate. Dissolve gelatine in hot water, add to the solution some bichromate of potash and dry it; the compound is sensitive to light in a way different from ordinary photographic paper. If a photographic negative on glass be laid over a sheet of this prepared gelatine, the portions shielded from light by the dark parts of the picture will dissolve as readily as before, while the parts acted on by light will form a tough tawny substance unaffected by hot water.

From this point the gelatine processes naturally divide into two groups.

1. The first group includes *carbon printing.* Poitevin, in 1855, was the first to use carbon combined with gelatine as a vehicle, availing himself of its insoluble character after exposure. This process is as follows: Paper is coated with a compound of bichromate of potash, gelatine, and lamp-black dissolved in cold water. This paper is dried in a dark room, exposed beneath a negative, and the parts not affected by the actinic action of the light dissolved off by hot water. The resulting picture is a positive print in black and white, of which the shades are produced by the carbon of the lamp-black, blackest where the light acted most freely, and with all the various shades according to the relative translucency of the different portions of the negative. Poitevin subsequently introduced a process for carbon printing under a positive. The process was materially improved by Swann about 1861. He transferred the film, after exposure, to another surface with the face downward, so that the dissolving was effected from its back, after which it was retransferred to the paper, on which it remained.

2. The picture is produced by the action of light on bichromated gelatine, and is made (*a*) to produce a print capable of being transferred; or (*b*) to serve as a printing matrix, from which impressions may be taken by the ordinary lithographic means; or (*c*) to obtain an impression in relief which may be printed from in the ordinary printing-press.

(*a*) The first success in this line resulted in the process of photolithography, which has been considered.

(*b*) Paul Pretsch in 1854 discovered and utilized the quality which a sheet of bichromated gelatine possessed of not swelling in water after exposure to light. Poitevin, 1855, was the first to recognize the fact that bichromated organic matter altered by light took greasy ink from the roller. Tessié du Motay and Maréchal, in 1864, were the first to print from a photographic image on bichromated gelatine as from a lithographic stone.

The *Albert-type*, named from Albert, of Munich, the *autotype*, the *heliotype*, by Edwards, now worked by J. R. Osgood, of Boston, and many others might be cited, differing in minor respects. Edwards, in the *heliotype*, produced a movable film; by the addition of chrome-alum to the gelatine a tough, tawny, insoluble sheet is formed, capable of standing rough usage, and yet retaining its property of being acted on by light in the presence of a bichromate, and of receiving and refusing greasy ink. The sheet is exposed under a negative, mounted on a metallic plate, the superfluous chemicals washed out, and then printed from with lithographic ink on an ordinary platen printing-press, being damped between each impression, as in ordinary lithographic printing.

(*c*) *Relief-work* is produced in several different ways, but can not here be described. Niepce de St. Victor in 1827 led the way by an asphaltum and etching process.

The *photoglyptic* process of Fox Talbot,

1852, was another etching process. The *photogalvanograph* of Pretsch, 1854, depended upon the swelling of the gelatine after exposure; a matrix was taken in gutta-percha, and from this a cameo plate was obtained by electro-deposit. The *phototype* belongs to this sub-class. Poitevin in 1855 had a process somewhat resembling this, in which he obtained a cast by the use of plaster hardened with protosulphate of iron. Osborne in 1860 transferred the inked gelatine sheet to zinc, and etched to make a relief.

In the *Woodbury process*, from which such excellent results have been obtained for illustrating the *Medical and Surgical History of the War*, the gelatine picture in relief, obtained by light, is placed in contact with a sheet of soft metal, and subjected to heavy hydraulic pressure. This gives a picture in reversed relief and depression. Such a mould is deeper in the places answering to the shades in the original picture, and conversely, shallower in the lights. It is filled with a solution of colored gelatine in hot water; a piece of paper is placed on top and pressed down with a level lid, so as to squeeze out the superfluous gelatine. The paper is then lifted, bringing with it the colored gelatine, which forms the picture.

PHOTO-MICROGRAPHY.

The co-application of the microscope and photographic process has led to wonderful results, which we may briefly illustrate by an example. Merely referring to the early attempts of Donné, and the experiments of Gerlach, Albert, and Maddox in Europe, and of Rood and Rutherford in America, we may describe the plan adopted by Colonel J. J. Woodward, M. D., of the United States Army Medical Museum in Washington. He dispenses with a camera and ground glass. The operating-room has two windows, through one of which sufficient yellow light is admitted to enable the operator to work; the lower part of the other window is provided with a shutter fourteen inches high, the upper part being blackened. In the shutter is a hole in which is inserted a tube, *a*, through which the solar light reflected from a plane mirror, *b*, or, preferably, a heliostat, is thrown upon the achromatic condenser of the microscope, *c*, which is placed on a shelf at the window of the dark room. The light reflected through the tube, which is provided with an achromatic lens of about ten inches focal length, is thrown upon the achromatic condenser. *d* is the focusing device; *g f*, the negative holder and its stand.

For powers from 200 to 500, a $\frac{1}{8}$-inch objective without an eye-piece is used, the power being varied by increasing or diminishing the distance of the sensitized plate from the instrument. A cell filled with ammonio-sulphate of copper, which absorbs the non-actinic rays, is interposed between the large lens and the condenser, and a hood is drawn around the instrument to prevent any loss of light.

For objects magnified less than 500 diameters the time of exposure, being less than a second, is regulated by a sliding shutter placed before a slit in front of the microscope, the width of the slit being adjusted to correspond with the required length of exposure. For powers between 500 and 1500 a $\frac{1}{16}$-inch objective is employed, dispensing in general with an eye-piece or amplifier, and placing the sensitized plate at a distance not exceeding three to four feet from the microscope. In the case of objects having very minute details, however, it is frequently advantageous to employ an eye-piece or amplifier rather than enlarge a negative taken with a smaller power.

Though natural sunlight is to be preferred, it may be sometimes necessary, when this is wanting, to employ artificial illumination. For this purpose the electric, the magnesium, and the oxy-calcium lights have been used with success. Of these the

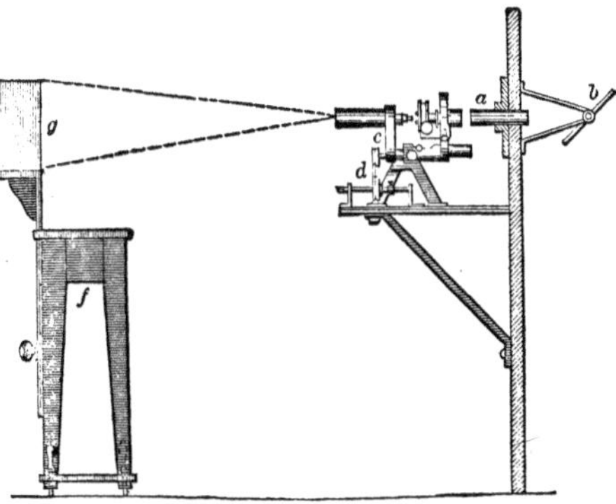

WOODWARD'S MICRO-PHOTOGRAPHIC APPARATUS (WITH SOLAR LIGHT).

electric light is the best, and for its production Dr. Woodward employs a Duboscq lamp, operated by a battery of fifty small Grove elements, ten in a cell.

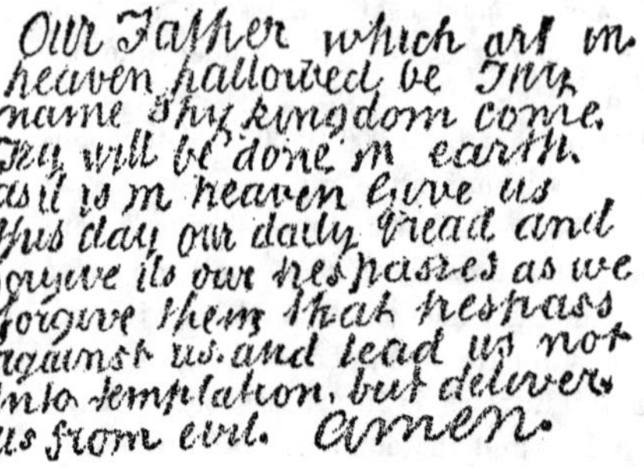

Our Father which art in
heaven hallowed be Thy
name Thy kingdom come.
Thy will be done in earth
as it is in heaven Give us
this day our daily bread and
forgive us our trespasses as we
forgive them that trespass
against us. and lead us not
into temptation, but deliver
us from evil. Amen.

THE LORD'S PRAYER.

The accompanying figure is a fac-simile of a photograph obtained by the instrument just described. It is an enlargement on a scale of 617 diameters from a writing on glass by Webb, of London, for the United States Army Medical Museum. The writing was executed with a diamond point by an instrument of Mr. Webb's invention, and known as a micro-pantograph.

The glass slip also contains the following inscription in a larger writing: "Webb's Test. The Lord's Prayer. 227 letters in the $\frac{1}{294} \times \frac{1}{441}$ of an inch, or the $\frac{1}{129654}$ of a square inch, and at the rate of 29,431,458 letters to an inch, which is more than 8 Bibles, the Bible containing 3,566,480 letters."

The area within which the prayer was written was micrometrically verified by Dr. Woodward, who found that it and the above inscription were contained within a space $\frac{1}{75}$ of an inch square.

According to a statement made in 1862 by Mr. Farrants, president of the Microscopical Society of London, Mr. Peters has succeeded in writing the Lord's Prayer so as to be distinctly legible, with sufficient magnifying power, within the space of $\frac{1}{356000}$ of a square inch.

III.

PROGRESS IN MANUFACTURE.

WHAT ARE MANUFACTURES?

IN a general but correct sense all products suitable for use, resulting from the applications, through human hand or brain, of the forces of nature to matter are *manufactures*, and each person who takes part in effecting or directing such applications is a *manufacturer*. Thus the laborer in the field who prepares the soil, scatters the seed, and harvests the grain, the wagoner, the railroad employé, or the sailor who transports it to the mill, are, in truth, as much the makers (*facturers*) of the flour as the men who, standing at the door of the mill, receive the grain, pass it through machinery, and when changed in form pack and deliver it to the consumers. No one of all these intermediaries between the first step in the so-called process of *production*—*i. e.*, the leading or drawing forth (*pro* and *duce*)—and the final use of the product, which we call *consumption*, at any time makes any thing in the sense of creating, but is only the agent, more or less skilled, for directing one or more of a series of movements, each of which differs from the other in degree, but not in kind. For convenience, however, all these movements are economically divided into groups or classes, under such general names as *agriculture, mining, commerce, the fisheries*, and *manufactures*—the last name being more especially applied to designate those movements which have reference to the changing or elaborating, through the aid of machinery, of those forms of product which have been the result of previous movements effected under the departments of agriculture and mining, and to some extent also of the fisheries.

SOURCES OF INFORMATION.

In the sense of the definition, as thus given, there are no available data for making any thing like a complete exhibit of the gradual development of the manufacturing industry of the American people, not only, as might be expected, for so much of the period of their history as is antecedent to the adoption of the Federal Constitution and the full organization and adjustment of the affairs of the new nation, but what is more remarkable, and at the same time not generally known, for so much of the present century also as is antecedent to the year 1850, at which date the government of the United States for the first time, through the census, attempted to ascertain, with even approximative accuracy, the exact industrial statistics of the country. The requirement of the Federal Constitution (adopted in convention in 1787) that an "enumeration" (of the people) "shall be made within three years after the first meeting of the Congress of the United States, and within every subsequent term of ten years"—being the first provision of the kind instituted in connection with the constitution of any government[1]—only contemplated the obtaining of information respecting population for the ulterior purpose of apportioning representation and direct taxation. The returns, accordingly, of the first census, taken in 1790, and of the second census, taken in 1800, afforded no information whatever concerning either the aggregate wealth of the country, the occupations of the people, or the nature and value of their annual product. It is to be noted, however, that previous to the enactment of the census law of 1800 some public citizens, engaged in scientific and philosophical pur-

[1] Moreau de Jonnés, a distinguished French economist, refers to this provision of the Constitution of the United States in the following language: "The United States presents in its history a phenomenon which has no parallel. It is that of a people who instituted the statistics of their country on the very day when they formed their government, and who regulated in the same instrument the census of their citizens, their civil and political rights, and the destinies of the country." This eulogium was, however, hardly warranted; for there is no evidence that the framers of the Constitution in creating a census ever contemplated any other object than an enumeration of the people, as furnishing a basis for the apportionment of representation and direct taxes. But "they builded wiser than they knew," inasmuch as they provided an instrumentality by which in the future the most vital questions pertaining to the political and social interests of the state could alone be answered.

suits, sought to prevail on Congress to make the census of that year something more than a mere enumeration of the population; and two learned societies, namely, the American Philosophical Society, of which Thomas Jefferson was then president, and the Connecticut Academy of Arts and Sciences, Timothy Dwight, president, sent in memorials on the subject; but beyond referring the memorials to a committee there is no record on the part of Congress of any further action.

In ordering for the third census, that of 1810, Congress, however, for the first time enacted that, in addition to enumerating the people, it should be the duty of the marshals to take also, under the direction of the Secretary of the Treasury, an account of the "several manufacturing establishments and manufactures within their several districts," and set aside for this service the sum of $30,000, out of an aggregate of $150,000 previously appropriated for the general purposes of taking the census. This latter sum, although seemingly small, was nevertheless considered to be amply sufficient to cover all the expenses of the *third* census; and in comparison with an expenditure of nearly three and a half millions authorized by Congress in connection with the taking in 1870 of the ninth census, strikingly illustrates the change in all the elements of national development effected between the two periods. As further illustrating the same point, it may be also interesting to note that the report of the first census was comprised in an octavo pamphlet of fifty-two pages, and that of the second census in a folio of seventy-eight pages, while the report of the ninth census required three large quarto volumes of 679, 851, and 806 pages respectively, besides a statistical atlas.

As the first attempt to set forth the condition of American manufacturing industry in detail, the results of the third census were looked for by Congress and the country with no little of interest; but when the industrial returns were sent in they proved so imperfect and discordant that the Committee of Commerce and Manufactures on the part of the House of Representatives, to whom they were referred, reported, through one of its members, that it was impossible to arrange them in any form which would be "alike useful and compendious." In accordance with a joint resolution they were therefore referred to the Secretary of the Treasury—then Mr. Gallatin — with instructions to place the entire returns in the hands of some person competent to make a digest of them; and for this purpose the Secretary subsequently selected Mr. Tench Coxe, of Philadelphia, who in 1813 submitted a report, which, although from necessity most imperfect, was nevertheless of great interest and value. How imperfect the material placed at the disposal of Mr. Coxe really was may be inferred from the circumstance that not even an attempt was made under the census of 1810 to take an account, under the head of manufactures, of the capital employed, raw material, number of hands, or cost of labor; but only the number of manufacturing establishments, the character of the machinery used, and the quantity and value of certain staple products, and of even these last the statistics collected were so irregular as to be nearly worthless.

In 1820, on the occasion of the taking of the *fourth* census, an effort was again made to obtain statistics of industry; but when the returns came in they were again found so discreditable that the Secretary of State was only constrained by the mandatory character of the law to permit their publication; and the House of Representatives, after debating the propriety of suppressing the entire document, refused to pass a resolution providing for its public distribution.

The result of these two unsuccessful efforts was that in providing for the taking of the *fifth* census the attempt to collect any industrial statistics whatever was wholly abandoned; and although in 1840 schedules for obtaining statistics of industry were issued to the marshals engaged in taking the *sixth* census, the results obtained were regarded as of little or no importance.

The act of 1850, however, under which the *seventh, eighth,* and *ninth* censuses of the United States were taken, in the years 1850, 1860, and 1870 respectively, marks an era in the history of American statistics, inasmuch as it not only incorporated provisions of law looking to the obtaining of results of substantial value relative to domestic industry, but also for the first time so insured the official observance of the law that it became possible to recognize the returns to a certain extent as standards for making comparisons and deductions in the future. And for such a result a debt of national gratitude is due, more than to all others, to the Hon. Joseph G. Kennedy, under whose superintendence the work of the censuses of 1850 and of 1860 was chiefly performed.

But commendable as were the returns of the census of 1850, those of 1860 were much more comprehensive and accurate; while the *ninth* census, taken in 1870, under the superintendence of Hon. F. A. Walker, was not only very far superior in every respect to any previous census of the United States, but also compares favorably with any work of the kind previously executed in any country. At the same time it ought to be known that the returns of the ninth census were very far from being as complete and useful as they could and would have been had not personal and partisan spirit, overruling all considerations of national good, mainly on the part of one man, prevented Congress from adopting a new law, carefully prepared by a committee of the House of Representatives (with the assistance of the best statisticians of every department in the country), and subsequently passed by the House almost unanimously, and so compelled the performance of the work under the old law, one of whose provisions required the enumeration and valuation of slaves, when the institution of slavery had for years been abolished.

But in addition to the reports of the census, the materials available for the preparation of a history of American manufacturing industry are exceedingly varied, and if not complete, exact, and accordant, are at least invested with a high degree of interest. For the earlier periods, or for the first one hundred and fifty years of our national history, the few particulars which can now be gathered are to be sought for mainly in colonial statutes and records, private correspondence, minutes of councils and assemblies, local histories, and individual biographies. In 1791 Alexander Hamilton, then Secretary of the Treasury, in obedience to a resolution of Congress, submitted his famous report on domestic manufactures and their relations to the new Federal government, in which, without entering into details, he gave an enumeration of such branches of industry under this head as seemed to him at that time to be permanently established in the country. Hamilton's report was followed in 1813 by the work of Tench Coxe, of Philadelphia, above referred to; while in 1816 Timothy Pitkin, a Representative in Congress from the State of Connecticut from 1808 to 1819, published, under the title of *A Statistical View of the Commerce of the United States, including also an Account of Banks, Manufactures, and Internal Trade,* what at the time of the appearance of the first edition, and long subsequent also to the second edition in 1835, held rank as the most comprehensive and authoritative commercial and statistical work of American origin. At present the most complete repertory of facts concerning the rise and progress of American manufactures is to be found in the work of the late Dr. J. L. Bishop, of Philadelphia, entitled *A History of American Manufactures from* 1608 *to* 1860—three volumes; in addition to which there have also been from time to time important publications by various authors on specialties of manufactures and the mechanic arts, as Thomas's *History of Printing,* White's *Memoirs of Slater,* Batchelder on the *Cotton Manufacture of the United States,* Munsell's *Chronology of Paper and Paper-making,* as well as numerous statistical reports from special industrial associations, as the American Iron and Steel Association, National Association of American Cotton and Woolen Manufacturers, etc., etc. Within a comparatively recent period, also, many of the States have prepared and published, every five years subsequent to the national census, very full details of their local domestic industries; and as the principle that healthy legislation can only flow from an exact knowledge of the condition and wants of the people has gradually obtained public recognition, the establishment of distinct bureaus of statistics, reporting every year with great minuteness of detail the particulars of all important industrial occupations, is beginning to be regarded as an indispensable adjunct of all State governments.

With this brief review of the sources of information available for studying the history of our national industrial progress, attention is next asked to the subject of the origin and development of American manufactures from the period of the first settlement in Virginia, in 1607–8, to the dissolution of the colonial system by the Declaration of Independence and of nationality, in 1776.

PROGRESS FROM 1607 TO 1776.

And in reviewing the pertinent facts of this period the circumstance that in the first instance most forcibly arrests attention is the strong natural tendency exhibited from the very outset by the people who colonized and built up the American States to multiply and diversify their industries—a fact in striking contrast with and in opposition to the opinion so assiduously maintained by a school of American economists that such a result, among an intelligent people, inhabiting a country of varied resources, does not tend to occur naturally, but is rather the direct offspring of legislative direction and interference.

Thus, for example, the second vessel dispatched by the London Company, in 1608, to the settlement at Jamestown, Virginia (founded the previous year), brought numbers of persons skilled in manufactures, of whom says the historian (Stith), "No sooner were they landed, but the President dispatched as many as were able, some to make glass, and others for pitch, tar, and soap-ashes;" and the very first manufactory established within the territory now controlled by the United States was a "glass-house" (furnace) in the woods of Virginia, about a mile from the settlement of Jamestown. And it is further interesting to note that, with the exception of a cargo of "sassafras" gathered in the vicinity of Cape Cod in 1608, the first export from the British North American colonies consisted in great part of what in the most technical sense are termed "manufactures;" or, to use the quaint language of Captain John Smith in his letter which accompanied the invoice, "of trials of pitch, tar, glass, frankincense, and soap-ashes, with what wainscot and clapboard as could be forwarded." Beverley in his *History of Virginia*, writing of the condition of affairs twelve years later, or in 1620, also says: "Many of the people became very industrious, and began to vie with one another in planting, building, and other improvements. A salt-work was set up on the eastern shore and an iron-work at Falling Creek, on Jamestown River, where they made proof of good iron ore, and brought the whole work so near a perfection that they sent word to the company in London that they did not doubt but to push the work, and have plentiful provision of iron for them by next Easter."

From the very first, under the popular impression probably that the country was particularly adapted to the production of silk, special efforts were made in nearly all the colonies to direct and divert the attention of the people to this particular industry; and it is recorded that the first Assembly that convened in Virginia under a written constitution, in 1621, especially occupied itself with considering "how best to encourage the silk culture." In 1662 also the Virginia Assembly, with a view of encouraging manufactures, offered prizes for the best specimens of linen and woolen cloth, and a special prize of fifty pounds of tobacco for each pound of wound silk produced in the colony; and it was also enjoined that for every hundred acres of land held in fee, the proprietor should be required to plant and fence twelve mulberry-trees. Silk culture in Georgia also so largely occupied the attention of the first colonists that a public seal was adopted bearing as a device silk-worms engaged in their labors; while bounties for the encouragement of the same industry were repeatedly offered by the colonies of Connecticut, New York, New Jersey, North and South Carolina. The extraordinary efforts thus made resulted in some degree of success. Small lots of Virginia silk were sent to England as early as 1660, and, according to tradition, formed part of the coronation robes of Charles II. Raw silk for a considerable number of years became also one of the regular exports from Georgia, and for the eighteen years next subsequent to 1750 the amount so exported averaged about 550 pounds per annum. In Connecticut the production and manufacture of silk was made a matter of special legislation as early as 1732; and in 1747 it is recorded that the Governor, Mr. Law, had a silk coat and stockings entirely of domestic manufacture. It is, however, a most interesting and suggestive circumstance that this specialty of employment, which from the first settlement of the country was particularly selected as worthy of attention, and as such did receive for nearly two hundred years from the various colonial and State authorities an amount of encouragement, through special legislation, greater than was bestowed on any other interest, is the only one of the great industries which has never been able to attain to a healthy condition of existence on the North American continent, and to-day only exists in the United States in virtue of a degree of legislative encouragement far in excess of that demanded and received by any other industrial interest.

But zealously as did the first settlers of Virginia engage at the outset in manufactures, the characteristics of the territory upon which they located, in respect to fertility of soil and mildness of climate, proved antagonistic; and obeying the promptings of self-interest, which are always a far better and surer guide than legislation for determining what occupations individuals as well as communities can best follow, they in common with the population of all the other Southern colonies early became planters rather than artisans. And from that day to this American manufacturing industry has found its greatest development in other and less fertile localities. It has also been noted as somewhat prophetic of the tastes and tendencies of the different sections of the future nation into which all the colonies were subsequently blended, that the first book written and the first book printed in what is now the United States were in verse—the one a translation of Ovid's Metamorphoses, by Mr. George Sandys, Treasurer of Virginia, and the other the *Bay Psalm-Book*, in New England.

Strenuous efforts were indeed made by the authorities to arrest the tendency of the people of Virginia to engage in agriculture rather than in manufactures or commerce, and in 1689 it was even ordered that all the tobacco grown in the colony in excess of a certain quantity should be destroyed. But this and other efforts, like the offering of prizes for the encouragement of the production of textile fabrics, proved of no avail. Tobacco grew most luxuriously, and in 1617 readily commanded three shillings per pound, and the Virginians soon found that it was, at least for the time, more advantageous to buy manufactured articles with the proceeds of their crops than to manufacture for themselves.

On the other hand, in New England the circumstances of a sterile soil and a harsh climate were antagonistic to agriculture and in favor of commerce and manufactures, and from a very early day powerfully contributed to give to this section of country a supremacy in respect to the two last-named branches of industry which no subsequent influences have ever seriously impaired or threatened. The branch of manufacturing industry to which the attention of the New England colonists was first, and as it were naturally, directed, by reason of the inexhaustible wealth of their forests, was the manufacture of lumber, for which there was a constant and remunerative demand in England and throughout the West Indies. Ship-building commenced in the Plymouth Colony within three years after the landing, and the business subsequently received a great impulse by the overthrow of the monarchy under Charles I. and the establishment of the Commonwealth, which led the colonists to apprehend that the incentive to emigration, and the consequent sailing of ships from England, being diminished, they would be thereby left dependent on their own resources for interoceanic communications. "The general fear," says Governor Winthrop, in his journal, "of a want of foreign commodities, now our money was gone, and that things were like to go well in England, set us on work to provide shipping of our own;" and the business was prosecuted with such vigor that within ten years after the launching of the first vessel ever built in Massachusetts, namely, on the 4th of July, 1631, the General Court passed the following resolution: "Whereas, the country is now in hand with the building of ships, and therefore suitable care is been taken that it be well performed, it is therefore ordered that surveyors be appointed to examine any ship built, to see that it be performed and carried on according to the rules of the art." In the year 1676, just a century before the Declaration of Independence, 550 vessels are reported to have been built in Boston and the vicinity, of which 230 ranged from 50 to 250 tons burden; and in 1731 the trade of Massachusetts alone employed 600 sail of ships and sloops, having an aggregate of 38,000 tonnage—one-half of which traded to Europe—in addition to over 1000 sail and from 5000 to 6000 men employed at the same time in the fisheries.

In 1640 the General Court of Connecticut enacted as follows: "It is thought necessary for the comfortable support of these plantations that a trade in *cotten wooll* be sett upon and attempted, and for the furthering thereof it has pleaced the Governor that now is (Edward Hopkins, Esq.) to undertake the finishing and setting forth a vessell with convenient speed to those ports where the said commodity is to be had, if it be pheasable," etc.; and in 1642 the Court further apportioned the amount of *cotten wooll* that each town should take from Mr. Hopkins, the share of Hartford being £200 worth. In 1666 also the Assembly of Connecticut, with an exceptional degree of wisdom, which Great Britain long afterward imitated, as did the State of Pennsylvania in a degree in 1772, exempted ship-building from all local taxation. The business of constructing ships for home use and for sale in foreign countries was also extensively followed in nearly all the other colonies, and in Maine and New Hampshire especially the manufacture of spars, masts, and ship timber for export early became a leading and profitable industry.

The first saw-mill in New England is believed to have been erected as early as 1634 or 1635 on the Salmon Falls River, New Hampshire, near to the site of the present city of Portsmouth. The first water-mill in New England is supposed to have been put up at Dorchester, Massachusetts, as early as 1628; and in 1633 another was erected in the Plymouth Colony by one Stephen Dean, which he engaged should be sufficient to "beat" corn for the whole colony. The number of mills of various kinds that existed in that part of Massachusetts which is now Maine as early as 1682 may be inferred from the circumstance that a tax was imposed that year on mills for the defense of Fort Loyal against the French and Indians. The first Van Rensselaer sent from Holland to Albany as early as 1631 a master millwright and two small millstones for a small grist-mill. The first grist-mill in Pennsylvania was erected by Colonel John Printz, Governor of what was then called New Sweden, in 1643. Virginia as early as 1649 had four windmills and five water-mills, besides many "horse-mills," and for a considerable number of years exported large quantities of breadstuffs to her sister colonies and to the West Indies.

The first printing-press in what is now the United States was set up at Cambridge, Massachusetts, in 1638, only eighteen years subsequent to the landing of the Pilgrims in the wilderness. The first thing printed was *The Freeman's Oath*, a broadside; the second, an almanac, in 1639; and in 1640 the first book, "the Psalms newly turned into metre," or *The Bay Psalm-Book*, as it was called—a work which is said to have gone through seventy editions. William Penn landed in his new territory of Pennsylvania in 1682, and four years later a printing-press —the third in the colonies—was at work in Philadelphia. The first press established in the Province of New York was in 1693, none having been allowed there during the rule of the Dutch. In Virginia the art of printing was not encouraged, and in 1683 is said to have been actually prohibited, while in 1671 Sir William Berkeley, of Virginia, returned thanks to God that there were neither free schools nor printing in the colony. "For learning has brought disobedience and heresy and sects, and printing has divulged them, and libels against the best government." The same year Governor Dongan, of New York, on the renewal of his commission, was instructed "to allow no printing-press." The first printing-press in Connecticut was established at New London in 1709; in Rhode Island, at Newport, in 1713–14; in Delaware, at Annapolis, in 1726; in South Carolina, at Charleston, in 1730; in New Hampshire, at Portsmouth, in 1756; in North Carolina, at Newbern, in 1757; in Georgia, at Savannah, in 1762; and in what is now the State of Maine in 1780. The first printing-press in the territory west of the Alleghanies was set up in Kentucky in 1786; the second, at Knoxville, Tennessee, in 1793; and the third, probably, at Marietta, Ohio, in 1795.

The number of printing-presses in the colonies at the time of the Revolution is believed to have been about forty. The number of separate works printed in the provinces up to this period can not now be ascertained; but the Philadelphia Library contains as many as 459 works printed in that city alone prior to the Revolution.

The first book-binding in this country appears to have been an edition of 1000 copies of the Bible, published at Cambridge in 1663, which was followed by a second edition of 2000 copies in 1685. The work was performed by one John Ratliffe, who came from England expressly for this purpose. His price was about 3*s.* 4*d.* per volume, and one Bible was as much as he could bind in one day.

The manufacture of paper of any description was not established in any of the colonies until full fifty years after the introduction of printing, the first paper mill having been erected in the vicinity of Philadelphia by one William Rittenhousen, a native of Germany, about the year 1690. The first paper mill in New England was established in the town of Milton, near Boston, in 1730, by Daniel Henchman, Peter Faneuil, and others, with a privilege in the nature of a patent for ten years from the General Court of Massachusetts, on condition that they should make in the first fifteen months 115 reams of brown paper and sixty reams of printing-paper, and the third year writing-paper of a superior quality. In 1732 the following advertisement appeared in the weekly *Rehearsal*, of Boston:

"Richard Fry, Stationer, Bookseller, Paper-maker, and Rag merchant, from the city of London, keeps at Mr. Thomas Fleet's, printer, at the Heart and Crown, in Cornhill, Boston, where said Fry is ready to accommodate all Gentlemen, Merchants, and Tradesmen with setts of Accompt books after the most acute manner for twenty per cent. cheaper than they can have them from London. I return the Public Thanks for following the Directions of my former Advertisement for gathering rags, and hope they will continue the like Method, having received upward of Seven thousand weight already."

The early scarcity of paper in the colonies is illustrated by the following curious advertisement, which appeared in the Boston *Evening Post* in 1748:

"Choice Pennsylvania Tobacco paper is to be sold by the publisher of this paper at the Heart and Crown, where may be also had the Bulls or Indulgencies of the present Pope, Urban VIII., either by the single Bull, Quire, or Ream, at a much cheaper rate than they can be purchased of the French or Spanish priests."

The explanation of this was that several bales of "indulgencies," printed upon very good paper and only on one side, had been captured by an English cruiser from a Spanish vessel, and being offered at a very low price, had been purchased by the Boston printer, who saw an opportunity for profit by printing ballads or other matter for his customers upon the backs of the pontifical documents in question. It is also to be noted that about this time Robert Saltonstall was fined five shillings by the General Court of Massachusetts for presenting a petition on a small and bad piece of paper.

In 1768 Colonel Christopher Leffingwell erected at Norwich the first paper mill in the colony of Connecticut, under the promise of a bounty from the General Assembly. Two years after he was accordingly awarded twopence a quire on 4020 quires of writing-paper, and one penny each on 10,600 quires of printing-paper. Having attained such a degree of success, it is recorded that the government patronage was soon afterward withdrawn.

In Pennsylvania the Dunkers, who settled in Lancaster County, very early gave their attention to the manufacture of paper, and also set up a printing-press. During the Revolution, and just previous to the battle of the Brandywine, messengers were sent to their mill for a supply of paper for cartridges. The mill happening to be out of unmanufactured paper, the fraternity, who held their property in common, sent back as a substitute to the Continental army several wagon loads of an edition of Fox's *Book of Martyrs*, and from the paper supplied by the pages of this work the cartridges used in the battle were in part manufactured.[1]

About the year 1770 the number of paper mills in the provinces of Pennsylvania, New Jersey, and Delaware was reported to be forty, this department of manufacturing industry having especially developed in the vicinity of Philadelphia, which was at that time the centre of literary activity for the colonies. It was a business, moreover, in which Dr. Franklin was greatly interested; and he told De Warville, a French traveler who visited America in 1788, that he had himself established as many as eighteen mills.

The business of the manufacture of "paper-hangings" commenced in the colonies

---

[1] Bishop's *History of American Manufactures.*

about the year 1760, and in 1791 it was one of the branches of domestic industry, according to the report of the Secretary of the Treasury, which were well established. Samples of home manufacture, which were highly approved of, and which found a ready sale, were exhibited to the New York Society of Arts and Manufactures as early as 1765.

The household manufacture of textile fabrics—of cotton-wool, linen, and silk—was almost coeval with the settlement of the continent, and the same circumstances which have been before noted as favoring the building of ships also greatly encouraged the development of these other industries. We are accustomed, and with good reason, to regard the tide and volume of immigration which has flowed from the Old World to the New since 1850 as something most remarkable, but the largest *comparative* immigration which this country has ever experienced occurred during the first half of the seventeenth century, between 1630 and 1640, when nearly every year added a number of individuals nearly or quite equal to the previously existing population. The result was an extraordinary demand for provisions, not only for home consumption, but also for the West Indies, with which trade had been greatly fostered by the enterprise of ship-building and the exportation of lumber, and the attention of the colonists, especially in New England and in New York, was largely directed to the raising of cattle, and in the former also to the prosecution of the fisheries. Governor Hutchinson, indeed, records that at one time the price of cattle in the colonies rose as high as £25, and even £28, per head. The cessation of immigration in 1640, consequent upon the cessation of persecution in England for religious non-conformity, caused an immediate and excessive decline in the price of cattle, and as suddenly cut off a leading source of provincial revenue. At the same time, with their thus impaired means of purchase, the diminished intercourse with England also caused great uncertainty in respect to the supply of clothing, for which the colonists had been up to this time almost wholly dependent upon the mother country. What next happened, as told with quaint simplicity by the early historian of New England (Hubbard), strikingly illustrates the state of things in which a resort to manufactures becomes a necessity in a new country. After describing the manner in which their necessity first came upon them, he continues:

"Now the country of New England was to seek of a way to provide themselves with clothing, which they could not obtain by selling cattle as before, which were now fallen from that huge price forementioned to five pounds apiece; nor was there at that rate a ready vent for them neither. Thus the flood which brought in much wealth to many persons, the contrary ebb carried all away out of their reach. To help themselves in this their exigent, for the necessary supply of themselves and their families, the General Court made order for the manufacture of woolen and linen cloth, which with God's blessing upon man's endeavor in a little time stopped this gap in part, and soon after another door was opened by special Providence; for when one hand was shut by way of supply from England, another was opened by way of traffic, first to the West Indies and Wine Islands, whereby, among other goods, much cotton-wool was brought into the country, which the inhabitants, learning to spin and breeding of sheep and sewing of hemp and flax, they soon found out a way to supply themselves of cloth."

The first regular or systematic attempt to manufacture cloth, particularly woolen, was made by a company of Yorkshire immigrants who settled at Rowley, Massachusetts, where in 1643 was erected the first fulling-mill in the North American colonies. The manufacture of cordage was entered upon in Boston as early as 1629. In the New Netherlands (New York), although the primary object with the mercantile company which planted and governed that colony was trade with the Indians, yet the characteristic industry of the Dutch prompted to a very extensive household manufacture of linens, woolens, and hosiery; and Denton, the earliest writer in that province, says (1670) of them, "Every one make their own linen and a great part of their woolen cloth for their ordinary wear." Under the auspices of William Penn, the manufacture of (linen and woolen) cloth was one of the first branches of industry undertaken in his new colony; and among the articles mentioned as produced in Pennsylvania as early as 1698 (which daily improved in quality) were druggets, serges, camblets, and a variety of other stuff, giving employment to dyers, fullers, comb-makers, card-makers, weavers, spinners, etc. The general progress made in the manufacture of fabrics during the first century of the existence of the North American colonies is also indicated by a report which Colonel Heathcote, a member of the Council of the Province of New York, made to the English Board of Trade in 1708, in which he says that he had labored to divert the Americans from going on with their woolen and linen manufactures, which are already so far advanced that three-fourths of the linen and woolen used was made among them, "especially the coarse sort; and if some speedy and effectual ways are not found to put a stop to it, they will carry it on a great deal further, and perhaps in time very much to the prejudice of our manufactures at home." And a letter written from New England to the Board of Trade in 1715 dwells particularly on "the very considerable manufacture" (in the colonies) "of kerseys, linsey-woolseys, flannels, buttons, etc., by which the importations of these provinces has been decreased fifty thousand pounds per annum."

The smelting of iron ore was one of the industries attempted by the first settlers in Virginia; but both the iron-works and the "glass-house," which had been erected, were early destroyed by the Indians, who, although not versed in any system of political economy, nevertheless ever showed themselves the most persistent enemies of diversified employments. In New England preliminary attempts to establish the manufacture of iron were made in 1630, and in 1645 regular works were established at Lynn. Of these last the old historian (Hubbard) says, contemptuously, "That instead of drawing out bars of iron for the country's use, there was hammered out nothing but contentions and lawsuits;" but, notwithstanding this disparagement, the operations commenced in this locality are believed to have been conducted with a degree of success for a period of more than one hundred years.

One of the first, if not the very first patent granted in this country was by the General Court of Massachusetts, in 1646, to one Joseph Jencks, of Lynn, "for ye making of Engines for mills to goe with water, for ye more speedy dispatch of work than formerly, and mills for ye making of Sithes and other Edged Tooles," the Court having previously passed a law that there "should be no monopolies but of such new inventions as were profitable to the country, and that for a short time only." The same Mr. Jencks, who is claimed to have been "the *first* founder who worked in brass and iron on the Western Continent,"[1] also made for Massachusetts, at his iron-works, the dies with which the "pine-tree" shillings and other coins of the colony were stamped; and for the city of Boston "an ingine to carry water in case of fire," which last construction was years in advance of any use of fire-engines on the continent of Europe.

Pig-iron began to be exported from the American colonies to England as early as 1718, when a record is made of a small lot of three and one-half tons received from Virginia and Maryland. By 1728, however, pig-iron had become a regular and important article of colonial export, and some years later the exportation of *bar*-iron also commenced, and from this time both pig and bar iron continued to be annually exported from the North American colonies until after the breaking out of the Revolution.

From the official returns of the British Custom-house (which are still extant, and have been published) the exact amount of such exports received in England at different periods from 1728 to 1776 was as follows:

Years.	Pig-Iron.	Bar-Iron.
	Tons.	Tons.
1728–29	1127	....
1732–33	2404	11
1745	2274	196
1754	3244	389
1764	2554	1059
1771	5303	2222
1775	2996	916
1776	316	28

In addition, there was also some pig and bar iron exported from the colonies during the same period to both Scotland and Ireland, though probably in no very considerable quantities.

Contemporaneously with the manufactures above noticed there were also established throughout the provinces manufactures of leather, of bricks, pottery, and glass, of distilled and fermented liquors, of hardware in various forms, of candles, snuff, gunpowder, copperas, and a multitude of other articles, so that at the close of the first century of their existence there was hardly a branch of useful industry common in Europe which was not practiced with more or less of success in the British North

[1] Lewis's *History of Lynn.*

American colonies. In fact, so successful had been the attempts of the colonists to manufacture that the jealousy of the mother country began to be awakened at a period considerably anterior to that mentioned, for Sir Josiah Child, although a much more liberal and intelligent politician than many of his countrymen at that day, in a discourse "on trade," published in 1670, describes New England as having come to be the most prejudicial plantation of Great Britain, and gives for this opinion the singular reason that they are a people "whose frugality, industry, and temperance, and the happiness of whose laws and institutions, promise to them a long life and a wonderful increase of people, riches, and power."

TRUE CAUSE OF THE AMERICAN REVOLUTION.

And here we come for the first time upon the true cause of the American Revolution, which is now well understood to have been not so much that the colonists were denied representation in the central government, or that they were unduly restrained in respect to any liberty of their persons, but rather that their rights to property were continually interfered with, that they were denied the privilege of freely buying and selling wherever and whenever they might see fit, and of following the occupations which seemed to them most remunerative. On the other hand, the acts of Great Britain, viewed in the light of the investigations and experiences of another century, are susceptible of a much less harsh interpretation than it has been the custom to put upon them. Thus England, during the whole of the seventeenth and eighteenth centuries, and even later, held, in common with the rest of the civilized world, a most firm belief in the doctrine, which had come down from the Middle Ages, that no one nation or individual could get gain from commerce or trade except at the expense of some other nation or individual, and that therefore the surest way for a nation or individual to prosper and grow rich was to sell as much and buy as little as possible, and to endeavor to obtain gold and silver in exchange for what they did sell in preference to any other products. Stated in the abstract, and in this last third of the nineteenth century, these doctrines seem very strange and most absurd; and yet the United States is the one nation of all others claiming to be enlightened which to-day by her commercial system fails to recognize or practically denies the great economic axiom that no nation or community can sell to any great extent except in proportion as it is willing to buy; that all trade and commerce must be mutually advantageous, or it would not exist; and that after every fair mercantile transaction both parties, however varied their nationality and residences, are richer than before.

It is also a mistake to suppose that the American colonies were planted with the least reference to the pecuniary or personal benefit of the colonists themselves. The mode was simply this: The King of England, on payment to himself of a certain sum, granted a tract of land of American territory, together with a charter, to a joint-stock company of English merchants and adventurers, who sent out a colony to cultivate the lands and gather their products for the pecuniary benefit of the stockholders. It was clearly an enterprise for making money—as much so as are the railroad and other corporations of the present day—and the colonists were regarded as merely the hired servants of the company. This was the method after which all the colonies were established, and if the colonists possessed any political privileges it was because they wrenched them from the unwilling hands of the corporators. For proof of the correctness of this position reference is made to the pages of all the American historians, and to the still stronger testimony of the great Adam Smith, of Scotland, who, while the American Revolution was progressing, declared that England had founded an empire on the other side of the Atlantic for the sole purpose of raising up a people of customers—a policy which he denounced as fit only for a nation of shopkeepers.

Entertaining such views respecting the nature of trade and commerce and the use of colonies, nothing, therefore, was more natural and legitimate than that England should regard her transatlantic plantations as instrumentalities for the promotion of her own interests and aggrandizement exclusively, and that when the enterprise of the

Americans in respect to certain branches of manufacturing industry seemed likely to be prejudicial to similar industries of her own, she should attempt to shackle and restrain their progress. It ought also to be borne in mind that if Great Britain acted unjustly toward the colonies, she was at least consistent in both her home and her colonial policy, and framed the former, equally with the latter, in strict accordance with the then narrow commercial spirit of the age. Thus, if it was forbidden to the colonists to export woolen goods, or transport wool from one "plantation" to another, there was at the same time on the statute-book of England a law which made it felony for any Englishman to export any sheep from the kingdom, or to purchase or transport any wool within fifteen miles of the sea without permission of the king, or to load or carry any wool within five miles of the sea, except between sunrising and sunsetting. And again, if the colonists were not permitted to carry any article of produce on the seas except in British ships, the necessity was about the same time announced in Parliament by the Lord Chancellor of going to war with the Dutch, and of destroying their commerce, because "it was impairing ours."

On the other hand, in respect to all those colonial industries which were not regarded as antagonistic to British interests, the action of Parliament was generous and considerate. For example, the cultivation of tobacco was forbidden in England by highly penal enactments, for the sake of securing a monopoly of that product to the Southern colonies. Liberal premiums were also offered and awarded for the cultivation and exportation of colonial silk, indigo, hemp, flax, and for the promotion of the fisheries; and in 1750 an act passed Parliament to encourage the exportation of pig and bar iron from his Majesty's plantations in America, whereby all duties on the import of the same into Great Britain were removed, although maintained in respect to the imports from all other countries. Nevertheless, the one most important fact in connection with this topic is that it was the rapid growth of colonial commerce and manufactures, conjointly with the attempt of Great Britain to interfere with and suppress them, which led to a gradual and increasing alienation and final violent separation of the two countries.

The first important act which operated as a restriction on the industry of the colonists was the so-called "Navigation Act" of 1650, which, although primarily intended, to use the words of Sir William Blackstone, "to mortify our sugar islands, which were disaffected to Parliament, and at the same time clip the wings of our opulent and aspiring neighbors," the Dutch, nevertheless struck a heavy blow at one of the foremost industries of the colonies, namely, ship-building. By this act and its extensions in 1661 and 1663 it was provided that no article of colonial produce or British manufacture should be carried in any but British ships, and that the colonists should not be allowed to purchase in any but British markets any manufactured article which England had to sell. Following the enactment of these purely commercial restrictions, it soon also became a policy on the part of Great Britain to discourage all attempts at manufacturing by the colonists in competition with similar British industries; and it was in pursuance of this policy that in 1696 the management of the affairs of the colonies was by royal order committed to a Board of Trade, under the title of "The Lords Commissioners for Trade and the Plantations." Henceforth the vigilant nation of shop-keepers would not be content with watching and controlling the shipping and trade of American ports, but must lay its hands on all the manufacturing industries of the colonies. The royal governors were required to report yearly to the board on the state of the provinces, and to do all in their power to divert them from setting up and carrying on manufactures. But reports and recommendations were not sufficient to repress the industrial enterprise of the Americans, and three years after, the board having received complaint that the wool and woolen manufactures of the North American plantations began to be exported to foreign markets formerly supplied by England, an act was passed by Parliament which, after declaring in its preamble "that colonial industry would inevitably sink the value of lands in England," prohibited thereafter the movement of any American wool or woolen manufactures not only to foreign countries, but also as between one colony and another. And in 1731, as complaint of the increasing divergence of trade from its prescribed channels by the action of the colonists continued to be made by British merchants and manufacturers, the House of Commons again took up the subject, and ordered, through the Board of Trade, an inquiry "with respect to laws made, manufactures set up, or trade carried on" (in the colonies) "detrimental to the trade, navigation, and manufacture of Great Britain." The report made in pursuance of this order in 1731–32 furnishes some curious particulars respecting the state of manufactures at that time in America, although it was known to be so incomplete that the concealment practiced was made the subject of complaint in England. The return of one officer, for example, stated that it was extremely difficult to obtain any true information, and, furthermore, that the Assembly of Massachusetts Bay had had the boldness to summon him to answer for having given any evidence whatever to the British House of Commons respecting the trade and manufactures of that province. The Governor of New Hampshire reported that there were no settled manufactures in that province. The Governors of Connecticut and the Carolinas made no returns, and the Governor of Rhode Island confined his report to matters not connected with manufactures. Massachusetts was reported as having manufactures of cloth, a paper mill, also several forges for making bar-iron, some furnaces for cast and hollow ware, one slitting-mill, and a manufacture of nails. The Surveyor-General of his Majesty's Woods wrote that they have in New England six furnaces and nineteen forges for making iron; that many ships were built for the French and Spaniards; and that great quantities of hats were made and exported to Spain, Portugal, and the West Indies. They also make all kinds of iron for shipping, and have several still-houses and sugar-bakeries.

Immediately after the reception and publication of this report, or in 1732, it was enacted by Parliament that "no hats or felts should be exported from the colonies, or be laden upon any horse or carriage to the intent to be exported from thence to any other plantation or to any other place whatever;" limiting also the number of apprentices at the business, and forbidding any black or negro from making hats under any circumstances. Nor was this all, for in 1750 a bill was introduced into Parliament decreeing that every slitting-mill in America should be demolished; and although this bill failed of passing the House of Commons by only twenty-two votes, a subsequent act did pass, that no new mills of that description should be erected.

It is most important and instructive to diverge for a moment at this point from tracing the development of American manufactures, and briefly notice the effect of the long-continued restrictive legislation of Great Britain on political and commercial morality. The multitude of arbitrary laws enacted to force the industry and commerce of the colonies and the British people into artificial and unnatural channels created a multitude of new crimes; and transactions which appeared necessary for the general welfare, and were no way repugnant to the moral sense of good men, were forbidden by law under heavy penalties. The colonists became thenceforth a nation of law-breakers. Nine-tenths of the colonial merchants were smugglers. One-quarter of the whole number of the signers of the Declaration of Independence were bred to commerce, to the command of ships, and the contraband trade. John Hancock was the prince of contraband traders, and, with John Adams as his counsel, was on trial before the Admiralty Court in Boston at the exact hour of the shedding of blood at Lexington, to answer for half a million dollars' penalties alleged to have been by him incurred as a smuggler. And if good old Governor Jonathan Trumbull, of Connecticut (Brother Jonathan), did not walk in the same ways as his brother patriot in Massachusetts, then tradition, if not record, has done him very great injustice. There is also on record a letter of Alexander Hamilton, written in 1771, at the time he was in mercantile business as a clerk in the West Indies, indicating an entire familiarity with a contraband trade carried on by his employers with the Spanish colonies. But men like Hancock and Trumbull had been made to feel that government was their enemy; that it deprived them of their natural rights; that in enacting laws to restrain them from laboring freely, and freely exchanging the fruits of their labors, it at the same time enacted the principle of slavery, and that therefore every evasion of such laws was a gain to liberty.

Furthermore, the continuance of such a policy as was adopted by Great Britain toward the colonies, and the spirit of resistance which was as naturally evoked in turn on the part of the colonists, could tend to but one end, namely, war and revolution; and in 1775 war and revolution came.

The population of the colonies at about the time (1670) that their progress in manufactures began to excite the jealousy of Great Britain was probably a little less than 200,000.

In 1714 the Board of Trade, for the purpose of aiding their judgment in respect to the condition of affairs in America, caused a census to be taken of the colonies, which returned a population of 434,000; and another in 1727, which gave an aggregate of 580,000. Mr. Bancroft estimates the total population of the colonies in 1750 to have been 1,260,000; and in 1770, five years previous to the outbreak of the Revolution, at 2,312,000; of whom 1,850,000 were white and 462,000 black.

PROGRESS SINCE THE REVOLUTION.

The immediate effect of the war of the Revolution, by cutting off all except casual and uncertain commercial intercourse with Europe and other countries, was to impart a fresh impulse to such manufactures in the colonies as were then established, and to call into existence some new ones. The immediate effect of the return of peace (in 1783), on the contrary, was most disastrous to nearly all business interests, and more especially to the mechanical and manufacturing industries. But such a result could not well have been otherwise. The country had been subjected to a long and impoverishing war; it was exhausted of men as well as of means; labor was scarce and high, and the burden of debt, both public and private, was most onerous. It has been the custom of many writers in treating of this period to attribute the disastrous condition of affairs which was immediately incident to the close of the Revolution to an unrestrained influx of foreign commodities; but that this agency was not in a high degree potential for mischief is proved by the circumstance that the average imports of British manufactures into the country for several years previous to 1789, notwithstanding a great increase to the population of the States, was considerably less than the average of several years preceding the war; and also that when the first tariff on imports came to be enacted under the Constitution, the rate established on all textile fabrics was only five per cent., and on all manufactures of metal but seven and a half per cent. But the manner in which importations were then made was undoubtedly most mischievous. There was no national government, and the division of the powers of government among thirteen petty sovereignties rendered the adoption of uniform laws impossible. Each State accordingly had its own tariff and regulated its own trade. What was binding in Massachusetts had no validity in Rhode Island, and what was subject to duty in New York might be imported free into Connecticut or New Jersey. Practically, therefore, no revenue could be collected on imports. Great Britain, also, seeing that as a nation we were commercially helpless, not only refused to negotiate a commercial treaty with us, but by an Order in Council excluded our ships from their ports in the West Indies, and, as the government of the States was then constituted, we had no power through retaliation to compel reciprocity. Yet, according to one who participated in the acts of the Revolution, and was one of the most sagacious observers and writers of the period—Peletiah Webster, of Philadelphia—*all the sufferings and evils which the country endured* from all other agencies were insignificant in comparison with the misery that resulted from the introduction and use of an irredeemable paper money, and the consequent irregularities of the entire American fiscal system, his exact language being as follows: "We have suffered more from this cause than from any other cause of calamity. It has killed more men, perverted and corrupted the choicest interests of our country more, and done more injustice, than even the arms and artifices of our enemies." And again he says, "If it saved the state, it has violated the equity of our laws, corrupted the justice of our public administration, enervated the trade, industry, and manufactures of our country, and gone far to destroy the morality of our people."

But let the causes have been what they may, there is no doubt that for a brief period subsequent to the close of the war the industry of the country was greatly depressed. The establishment of a stable government, however, by the adoption of the Constitution at once gave to affairs a new aspect. The wretched system of distrust, jealousy, and weakness, which had before paralyzed all enterprise, and sunk the revenues and credit of the Confederation to the lowest point, disappeared, and fresh energy was infused into all departments of business. "American labor," says Dr. Bishop, "at this period began steadily to change its form from a general system of isolated and fireside manual operations—though these continued for some time longer its chief characteristic—to the more organized efforts of regular establishments, with associated capital and corporate privileges, employing more or less of the new machinery which was then coming into use in Europe."

The population of the country increased from an estimate of 2,945,000 in 1780 to 3,924,000 in 1790; and it is curious to note that the percentage of decennial increase of thirty-three per cent. thus established in this decade maintained itself with approximative uniformity for each subsequent decade from 1790 to the breaking out of the rebellion in 1860.

In an address before the "Pennsylvania Society for the Encouragement of Manufactures," August, 1787, by Mr. Tench Coxe (afterward Assistant-Secretary of the Treasury under Hamilton), the great progress in agriculture and manufactures "since the late war" was particularly dwelt upon. In Connecticut, at this time, according to this authority, the household manufactures were such as to furnish "a surplus sold out of the State. New England linen had affected the price and importations of that article from New York to Georgia." In Massachusetts the importation of foreign manufactures was less by one-half than it was twenty years before, although population had greatly increased, and considerable quantities of home-made articles were shipped out of the State. In one regular factory of the latter State there were made as much as 10,000 pairs of cotton and wool cards, 100 tons of nails in another, and 150,000 pairs of stuff and silk shoes in the single town of Lynn. In the course of the address, pattern cards, embracing thirty-six specimens of silk lace and edgings from the town of Ipswich, Massachusetts, were exhibited. In Rhode Island the number of regular factories was stated to be "great in proportion to its population." Mr. Coxe, however, greatly deprecated the wasteful use of foreign manufactures, and as an illustration stated that the importation into Philadelphia alone of the finer kinds of coat, vest, and sleeve buttons, buckles, and other trinkets cost the wearers annually sixty thousand dollars. The sale of spinning-wheel irons from one shop in Philadelphia in 1790 amounted to 1500 sets, an increase of twenty-nine per cent. over the sales of the previous year. In Lancaster, Pennsylvania, then the largest inland town in the United States, there were in 1786 about 700 families, of whom 234 were manufacturers, in which number were included 14 hatters, 36 shoe-makers, 25 tailors, 25 weavers of cloth, and 4 dyers. Within ten miles of the town were four oil mills, five hemp mills, one fulling-mill. Frederick and Elizabeth, towns in Maryland, and Stanton and Winchester, Virginia, were also important centres of domestic industry, the last-named being famous for its manufacture of hats. There was also a manufactory of glass at Alexandria, Virginia, which, according to the French traveler, De Warville, exported in 1787 glass to the amount of 10,000 pounds, and employed 500 hands. In 1789 Mr. Clymer, of Pennsylvania, stated in Congress that there were fifty-three paper mills within range of the Philadelphia market, and that the annual product of the Pennsylvania mills was 70,000 reams, which was sold as cheap as it could be imported, and that, too, in the absence of any duty. The compiler of the *Bibliotheca Americana*, published in London in 1789, states that the people of North America manufactured their own paper in sufficient quantities for home consumption; and the report of Secretary Hamilton the following year also represents the paper manufacture as one of the branches of American industry which had arrived at the greatest perfection, and was "most adequate to national supply." And yet De Warville a few years previous wrote that on account of the scarcity and dearness of labor and of rags, the Americans could not for many years to come furnish sufficient paper for the prodigious consumption caused by the increase of knowledge and the freedom of the press.[1]

An estimate made by Mr. Coxe in 1790 fixed the annual value of the manufactures of the United States for that year at more than $20,000,000. It is also curious to note that he took as the basis of his computation the returns of the manufacturing industry of Virginia, which then included Kentucky. As Assistant-Secretary of the Treasury, Mr. Coxe also asserted, about this period, that the manufactures of the United States were certainly greater than double the value of their exports in native commodities, and much greater than the gross value of all their imports, including the value of all the goods exported again.

In January, 1790, President Washington delivered his first annual message to Congress, and it is noted that he was dressed at the time in a full suit of broadcloth, manufactured at the woolen factory of Colonel Jeremiah Wordsworth, at Hartford, Connecticut, "where all parts of the business are performed except spinning." In this message the subject of the promotion of manufactures was commended to the attention of Congress; and acting upon the suggestions of the President, Congress thereupon ordered that the Secretary of the Treasury "prepare and report a proper plan or plans for the encouragement and promotion of manufactories as will tend to render the United States independent of other nations for essential, particularly for military, supplies;" and in accordance with this order Mr. Hamilton in the following year (1791) submitted his famous report, twice printed by order of Congress, on American manufactures.

In this report the Secretary, after discussing at length the relations of agriculture and manufactures to each other and the state, the importance of manufacturing establishments as agencies for augmenting the produce and revenue of society, the then existing obstacles in the way of the extension of American manufactures, the necessity of the adoption of a policy of encouragement toward them by the state, and the unity of interest between the different sections of the country, presents in general terms an exhibit, classified under seventeen heads, of the manufacturing industries in the country, which had at that time made such progress as in a great measure to supply the home market, and which were also carried on "as regular trades." Among these the Secretary enumerates manufactures of skins and leather, including under this head leather breeches and glue; flax and hemp, but not cotton; iron, and most implements of iron and steel; bricks and pottery; starch and hair-powder; manufactures of brass and copper, particularly specifying utensils for brewers and distillers, andirons and philosophical apparatus; tinware "for most purposes;" carriages of all kinds; "lamp-black and other painter's colors;" refined sugars, oils, soaps, candles, hats, gunpowder, chocolate, silk shoes, and "women's stuffs;" snuff, chewing tobacco, etc., etc. "Besides these," he continues, "there is a vast scene of household manufacturing, which contributes more largely to the supply of the community than could be imagined without having made it an object of particular inquiry." But as indicating how limited an idea of the actual and future resources of the country was even then possessed by a mind so intelligent and comprehensive as that of Alexander Hamilton, the following memoranda from this report are also exceedingly curious and pertinent. Thus, for example, under the head of coal, he notes "that there are several mines in Virginia now worked, and appearances of their existence are familiar in a number of places." "There is something," also says the Secretary, "in the texture of cotton which adapts it in a peculiar degree to the application of machines," and in a country in which a deficit of hands constitutes the greatest obstacle to success, this circumstance particularly recommends its fabrication. American cotton, he adds, can be produced in abundance; and "a hope may be reasonably indulged that with due care and attention" its quality will greatly improve.

[1] Bishop's *History of American Manufactures.*

Under the head of "the means proper to be resorted to" by the government for the promotion of manufactures, the Secretary, after enumerating and discussing the various agencies "which have been employed with success in other countries," gave his recommendation in favor of a system of "*pecuniary bounties*," and offered in support of the same the following reasons:

"1. It is a species of encouragement more positive and direct than any other.

"2. It avoids the inconvenience of a temporary augmentation of price, which is incident to some other modes.

"3. Bounties have not, like high protecting duties, a tendency to produce scarcity.

"4. Bounties are sometimes not only the best but the only proper expedient for uniting the encouragement of a new object of agriculture with that of a new object of manufacture. The true way to conciliate these two interests is to lay a duty on foreign manufactures of the material the growth of which is desired to be encouraged, and apply the produce of that duty, by way of bounty, either upon the production of the material itself, or upon its manufacture at home, or upon both. In this disposition of the theory the manufacturer commences his enterprise under every advantage which is attainable as to quantity and price of the raw material, and the farmer, if the bounty be immediately to him, is enabled by it to enter into a successful competition with the foreign material."

He accordingly recommended the imposition of additional duties on imports, the proceeds of which, after satisfying the national pledges in respect to the public debt, he proposed should constitute a fund for paying the bounties which might be decreed, and for the operations of a board to be established for promoting arts, agriculture, manufactures, and commerce. The members of this board were to consist of certain officers of the government, and were to apply the funds derived from the sources indicated to assist the immigration of artists and manufacturers, to promote the discovery and introduction of useful inventions and improvements, and "to encourage by premiums, both honorable and lucrative, the exertions of individuals and of classes in relation to the several objects they are charged with promoting." The bounties thus recommended were not, however, intended by the Secretary to be permanent; for, as he remarks, their "continuance on manufactures long established must always be of questionable policy, because presumption would arise in every such case that there were natural and inherent impediments to success."

He also dwells at considerable length on a topic too often overlooked, namely, that it "is not merely necessary that the measures of government which have a direct view to manufactures should be calculated to assist and protect them, but also that those which collaterally affect them in the general course of administration should be guarded from any particular tendency to injure them;" and under this head especially asks attention to "the unfriendly aspect of certain species of taxes toward manufactures." Among such he enumerates, *first*, all poll and capitation taxes, which, if levied according to a fixed rule, operate unequally and injuriously on the industrious poor; "*second*, all taxes which proceed according to the amount of capital supposed to be employed in a business, or of profits supposed to be made on it, are unavoidably hurtful to industry: men engaged in any trade or business have commonly weighty reasons to avoid disclosures which would expose with any thing like accuracy the real state of affairs, and allowing to the public officers the most equitable dispositions, yet when they are to exercise a discretion without certain data they can not fail to be often misled by appearances;" and finally, continues the Secretary, in words that deserve to be printed in gold on the walls of every legislative assembly, "arbitrary taxes, under which denomination are comprised all those that leave the *quantum* of the tax to be raised by each person to the discretion of certain officers, are as contrary to the genius of liberty as to the maxims of industry."

Although this celebrated report of Alexander Hamilton both at the time it was made and since has been regarded as a model of clear and unanswerable reasoning, and was also unquestionably of great service to the country, yet it is well known that his specific recommendations of bounties in preference to protective or prohibitory duties, and also for the repeal of all duties on imported cotton as a raw material of manufactures, were not complied with; but that, on the contrary, the system of protective duties on imports which then prevailed in Europe was gradually established in its place, and from that day to this has been continued.

The period of the adoption of the Federal

Constitution, in 1789, marks also the period of the commencement of the manufacture of cotton in the United States, as a regular and systematic in contradistinction to a domestic and irregular business. Cotton had indeed been grown for many years previous throughout the Southern sections of the country, but its use up to 1789–90 had been almost exclusively domestic, and even for this purpose the quantity produced was inadequate to supply the home demand. In fact, so little suspicion was entertained of the particular adaptability of the soil and climate of the Southern States for the culture of cotton, that when in 1784 an American ship entered Liverpool with eight bags of the fibre as a part of her cargo, the same was regarded as an unlawful importation, on the assumption that so large a quantity could not have been the produce of the United States. And as late, furthermore, as 1792 the cotton product of the United States was regarded as of so little value commercially that John Jay consented to the incorporation of a provision (afterward rejected by the Senate) in the treaty that he negotiated with Great Britain that "no cotton should be imported from the United States," the design on the part of Great Britain being not to interfere with the cotton culture of the United States, but to secure for her own mercantile marine the exclusive movement of cotton from the West Indies. Mr. Tench Coxe, in common with other members of the "Pennsylvania Society for Encouraging Manufactures," seems, however, to have early foreseen the future importance of cotton to both American agriculture and manufactures, and when the Convention for framing the Constitution assembled in Philadelphia his earnest recommendations to the Southern delegates on the subject induced many of them, on their return home, to make personal efforts to interest their constituents in extending the cultivation of the fibre.

The inventions of Hargreaves, Arkwright, Compton, and Cartwright for carding, spinning, and weaving cotton by machinery were introduced in England between the years 1768 and 1788; and although at first were so much opposed that the inventors were afraid to work openly, and had in some instances their lives threatened and their machinery destroyed, yet Parliament very early appreciated the national importance of the several inventions, and in accordance with the narrow spirit of the age, enacted in 1774, and subsequently, most strict prohibitions of the export of any textile machinery from the kingdom. These statutes, which were vigilantly enforced by the British government, together with a law against enticing artificers to emigrate, for a time proved most serious obstacles in the way of the introduction of the new English textile machinery into the United States, although many most ingenious efforts to evade the law were made by our countrymen. Mr. Tench Coxe, who omitted no opportunity to promote the cotton industry, at one time, for example, succeeded, after no little trouble and expense, in having secretly made in England models of a full set of Arkwright's machinery, but they were unluckily seized and confiscated as they were on the point of shipment. The information sought for was, however, gradually obtained, and in 1786 Hugh Orr, of Bridgewater, Massachusetts, a pioneer in American manufactures, notified the Legislature of Massachusetts that he had in his employ two Scotchmen, brothers, by the name of Barr, who had some knowledge of the new cotton machinery. Thereupon the Legislature appointed a committee to examine the men and find out what they knew, which committee subsequently reported in favor of a grant of £200 to the Barrs to enable them to complete certain machines, and also as a gratuity for "their public spirit in making them known to the public." Six tickets in a State Land Lottery, which had no blanks, were accordingly voted to the Scotch brothers by the Legislature, and out of the proceeds the first "stock card" and "spinning-jenny" made in the United States were constructed. These machines were deposited by the order of the General Court with Mr. Orr, who was allowed to use them, as some compensation for his exertions in the matter, and was also requested to exhibit them and explain their principles "to any who might wish to be informed of their great use and advantage in carrying on the woolen and cotton manufacture." The subsequent year, 1787, a company to manufacture cotton was organized at Beverly, Massachusetts, with one or more spinning-jennies, imported or made from the State's models, and a carding-machine, imported at a cost of £1100; and about the same time also several other cotton manufactories were projected or started—at Worcester, Massachusetts; Providence, Rhode Island; Paterson, New Jersey, and other places; none of which, however, for want of skill or proper machinery, appear to have been successful.

Meanwhile (1789) there arrived in New York a young Englishman, not twenty-two years of age, whose name, Samuel Slater, was destined to become famous in the manufacturing annals of the United States. He had been apprenticed at an early age to Jedediah Strutt, a partner with Sir Richard Arkwright in the cotton-spinning business, and had afterward served the firm as clerk and general overseer, until he had rendered himself perfectly familiar with the manufacture of cotton as it was then carried on in the model establishments of Great Britain. The reason which has been assigned for his emigration to the United States was a notice in the newspapers of a grant of £100 by the Legislature of Pennsylvania for the introduction of a new machine for carding cotton, and of the establishment of a society for promoting the manufacture of cotton. But be this as it may, the 18th of January, 1790, found him at Providence, Rhode Island, entered into partnership with the firm of Almy and Brown, under an agreement to construct the Arkwright series of machines, and carry on with his partners the manufacture of cotton by the improved methods. In consequence of the restrictions on the emigration of artisans and the exportation of models and machinery from Great Britain, Mr. Slater did not on leaving home inform his family of his destination, or take with him any patterns, drawings, or memoranda that could betray his occupation, and so lead to his detention. But so thoroughly was he master of his profession that by the 20th of December of the same year, having discarded all the old machinery previously used by Almy and Brown in their attempts to manufacture cotton, he had constructed, chiefly with his own hands, the whole series of machines on the Arkwright plan, and had started three cards, drawing and roving frames, and two frames of seventy-two spindles. The machinery was first set in motion in an old building which had been used as a clothier's establishment; but in 1793 the new firm built a small factory, which may be considered as the first really successful cotton mill in the United States.

The only thing then wanting to insure the rapid development of the cotton manufacture not only in the United States, but throughout Europe, was an abundant supply of the fibre at a cheap rate; and this the invention of the cotton-gin by Eli Whitney in 1793 at once supplied. For some years previous to this the price of cotton in the United States was about forty cents per pound, and it required oftentimes a day's labor to separate a pound of the clean staple from the seed. In 1795 Georgia cotton of good quality was offered in New York at 1*s.* 6*d.* (thirty-six cents) per pound; and at that time cotton continued also to be imported. When Slater first began to spin he used Cayenne cotton, but after a few years he began to mix about one-third of Southern cotton, the yarn produced being designated as second quality, and sold accordingly. The total cotton product of the world in 1791 has been estimated at about 490,000,000 pounds, or about a million bales, apportioned as follows: United States, 2,000,000 pounds; Brazil, 22,000,000 pounds; West Indies, 12,000,000; Africa, 46,000,000; India, 130,000,000; the rest of Asia, 190,000,000; Mexico and South America, 68,000,000. Of the product of the United States at that time Georgia supplied about half a million pounds, and South Carolina a million and a half. In 1801 the product of the United States was estimated at 48,000,000 pounds; and from that time the progress of the culture of cotton is indicated by the following table:

Years.	Pounds.	Years.	Pounds.
1801......	48,000,000	1839–40...	834,000,000
1811......	80,000,000	1849–50...	958,000,000
1821......	180,000,000	1859–60...	2,241,000,000
1831–32...	355,000,000	1872–73...	1,824,000,000

It will thus be seen that the largest crop of cotton ever grown in the United States was in the year 1859–60, just previous to the outbreak of the rebellion; yet it has been demonstrated by Mr. Atkinson that in that year the amount of land occupied by the growth of cotton was less than two per cent. (1.634) of the territory of the United States which is especially adapted to its cultivation.

In 1799 Mr. Slater built his second cotton mill, on the east side of the Pawtucket River, in the limits of Massachusetts, the first mill ever erected in the State on the Arkwright system; and by act of the Legislature the same, with all its appurtenances, was for a period of seven years exempted from taxation. Until this date the improved methods of manufacture had been confined to Mr. Slater and his associates, but after this men who had been in their employ, and had learned the construction and operation of the machinery, left them, and commenced the erection of mills for themselves or other parties, and before the year 1808 fifteen cotton mills on the Arkwright basis were in successful operation in different sections of the country. The first cotton mill west of Albany was erected in the neighborhood of Utica, Oneida County, New York, in 1807–8. In 1807 the whole number of spindles in the United States was estimated at 4000; in 1808 the estimate was 8000; and in 1809, 31,000. From this time until 1840, apart from the annual estimates of the domestic consumption of cotton for all purposes, the statistics of the growth of the cotton manufacture in the United States are very deficient and unreliable. In 1815 the three States of Massachusetts, Rhode Island, and Connecticut had 165 factories and 119,510 spindles. In 1831, 795 factories and 1,246,500 spindles were reported for the whole country. In 1840, by the census, 2,285,000 spindles; in 1850 (for New England only), 2,728,000 spindles. After this the data are reliable, and are as follows: 1860, 5,035,798 spindles; 1870, 7,114,000; 1874 (July 1), 9,415,383, of which 8,927,754 were returned for the Northern States, and 487,629 for the Southern. The recent rapid progress of the Southern States in the manufacture of cotton is indicated by the fact that in 1869 this section of the country had 225,063 spindles in operation, and in 1874, 487,629. The progress of the whole country in spinning spindles from 1870 to 1874 was about thirty-three per cent. The aggregate and average *per capita* manufacturing consumption of cotton in the United States since 1827 is shown by the following table:

Years.	Pounds.	Consumption per Capita.
1827..........	49,489,796	4.22
1835..........	79,597,896	5.31
1840..........	113,058,919	6.68
1845..........	161,435,000	8.15
1850..........	263,190,642	11.34
1855..........	306,582,808	11.40
1860..........	450,877,823	14.32
1865..........	145,935,000	5.21
1869..........	447,216,000	11.57
1874..........	567,583,873	13.50

In 1794 the price of Slater's cotton yarn, No. 20, was $1 21 per pound. In 1808 the price of the same number was $1 31. Power-loom weaving was first successfully introduced into Great Britain in 1806, previous to which time all weaving had been performed upon hand-looms. The first power-looms in the United States were put in operation at Waltham, Massachusetts, in 1814, and it was at the mills of the company at this place, also, that the spinning and weaving of cotton were for the first time combined in any large establishment. In this same year the price of cotton yarn was reduced by the operations of the Waltham Company to less than one dollar per pound. In 1823 the "domestics" of the Waltham Company—which at about this time extended its operations and built the first mill at Lowell—had become so popular that they were counterfeited by foreign manufacturers, and in 1827 it is recorded that the demand for American cottons in Brazil was considerably affected by imitations of them made at Manchester, England, and offered there (in Brazil) "at lower prices, although they could be made as cheaply in the United States as the same quality could be produced in Manchester." It is also a noteworthy circumstance that in 1850 in New England the ratio of cotton spindles to population was that of 1008 spindles to each 1000 inhabitants, while in Great Britain for the same year the ratio was 1003 spindles to 1000 inhabitants, so that at this period New England in respect to cotton had comparatively exceeded Great Britain in its manufacturing industry. From 1850 to 1860 and from 1860 to 1870 the number of spindles in New England increased much faster than the population, averaging in 1860 1265 and in 1870 1478 to each 1000 inhabitants.

The most important cotton manufacturing States of the Union, arranged in the order of their consumption of cotton for the year 1874, were as follows: Massachusetts,

New Hampshire, Rhode Island, Connecticut, Pennsylvania, Maine, New York, Maryland, Georgia, New Jersey, South Carolina, North Carolina, Alabama, Tennessee, and Virginia. Few or no cotton factories exist in the States of Illinois, Iowa, Michigan, Wisconsin, Kansas, Nebraska, California, or Oregon. The following table exhibits the amount and character of the principal products of the cotton manufactories of the United States for 1874:

STATEMENT OF THE KINDS AND QUANTITIES OF COTTON GOODS MANUFACTURED IN THE UNITED STATES FOR THE YEAR ENDING JULY 1, 1874.

	New England States.	Middle and Western States.	Total Northern States.	Total Southern States.	Total United States.
Threads, yarns, and twines............lbs.	32,000,000	99,000,000	131,000,000	18,000,000	149,000,000
Sheetings, shirtings, and similar plain goods............yds.	520,000,000	90,000,000	610,000,000	97,000,000	707,000,000
Twilled and fancy goods, osnaburgs, jeans, etc. ....yds.	204,000,000	80,000,000	284,000,000	22,000,000	306,000,000
Print cloths............yds.	481,000,000	107,000,000	588,000,000	......	588,000,000
Ginghams............yds.	30,000,000	3,000,000	33,000,000	......	33,000,000
Ducks............yds.	14,000,000	16,000,000	30,000,000	......	30,000,000
Bags............	5,000,000	1,000,000	6,000,000	......	6,000,000

Besides the above, there is a large production of articles, like hosiery, etc., composed of mixed cotton and wool, for the details of which there are no satisfactory statistics.

Among other notable improvements which were invented and brought into use about the time of the adoption of the Federal Constitution were those of Oliver Evans, of Pennsylvania, in respect to the manufacture of flour, the importance of which may perhaps be sufficiently indicated by saying that in all the subsequent progress of invention no radical change has ever been made in the system of "milling" machinery as Mr. Evans devised it, and that it constitutes to-day the mechanical basis upon which all the extensive flour mills of the United States and Europe are operated. The more special results of the invention were a saving of one-half the labor of attendance, a better product of manufacture, and an increase of about twenty-eight pounds of flour to each barrel above the method previously in use.

As has been already stated, the value of the product of American manufactures for the year 1790, as estimated by Mr. Tench Coxe, was about $20,000,000.

The census of 1810 fixed the total value of the manufactured products of the country for that year at $127,000,000, but Mr. Coxe, to whom the returns were referred by resolution of Congress for revision, was of the opinion that the aggregate, exclusive of all products closely allied to agriculture, such as lumber, sugar, ashes, wine, bricks, indigo, hemp, and the products of the fisheries, was at least $172,000,000, or including products of the nature specified, $198,000,000. In 1810, also, Mr. Gallatin, then Secretary of the Treasury, reported to the House of Representatives that the following manufactures were carried on to an extent which might be considered adequate to the requirements of the United States for consumption, as the value of these products annually exported exceeded that of the foreign articles of the same general class annually imported, viz., manufactures of wood, leather and manufactures of leather, soap and tallow-candles, spermaceti oil and candles, flaxseed oil, refined sugar, coarse earthenware, snuff, hair-powder, chocolate, and mustard. The following branches were also reported as so firmly established as to supply in several instances the greater and in all a considerable part of the consumption of the country, viz., iron and manufactures of iron, manufactures of cotton, wool, and flax, hats, paper, printing types, printed books, and playing-cards, spirituous and malt liquors, gunpowder, window glass, jewelry and clocks, several manufactures of hemp and of lead, straw bonnets and hats, and wax-candles.[1]

Accepting the estimates of Mr. Coxe, it also appears that the annual value of the manufactured products of the 8,500,000 population of the United States in 1810, less than thirty years after the close of the Revolution, was in excess of that of Great Britain, with her accumulated capital and experience, in 1787, when the population of the United Kingdom closely approximated to the same figure.

The immediate effect of the war of 1812, by increasing demand for all necessary products, and at the same time cutting off all

[1] Bishop's *History of American Manufactures.*

foreign imports and competition, was to impart a most unnatural and unhealthy stimulus to American manufacturing industry. Capital, especially under the form of joint-stock companies, and often without the exercise of the most ordinary prudence or forethought, hastened to inaugurate a host of new industrial enterprises. Mill privileges readily commanded most extravagant figures, wages rose from 30 to 50 per cent., and raw materials and manufactured goods from 50 to 200 per cent. Cottons which had sold before the war at from 17 to 25 cents per yard, found purchasers by the package at 75 cents per yard; and salt, which was, in 1812, 55 cents per bushel, commanded in October, 1814, $3 per bushel. The number of cotton mills in Rhode Island and in Massachusetts within thirty miles of Providence, at the commencement of the war in 1812, was about seventy; at the close of the war, in 1815, this number had increased to ninety-six.

So long as the war continued there was for nearly all these enterprises an apparent great prosperity, to magnify and inflate which an almost unlimited issue of paper money also powerfully contributed. All the banks in the country, save those in New England, suspended specie payments in 1814; and the Federal government, finding itself short of revenue, early in the course of the war commenced the issue of Treasury paper. But as specie disappeared and redemption was abrogated, not only public and private banking associations, but manufacturing and bridge-building associations, and even individuals, issued paper notes, which rapidly passed into circulation, and were largely taken by the public. In one session, that of 1813–14, the Legislature of Pennsylvania chartered forty-one new banks, with $17,000,000 of capital; and according to one writer of the time, "the *plenty of money* was so profuse that the managers of the banks were fearful that they could not find a demand for all they could fabricate, and it was no infrequent occurrence to hear solicitations urged to individuals to become borrowers, under promises of indulgences the most tempting." The result was that the money of the country in a great degree lost its value, and its depreciation, enhancing the prices of every species of property and commodity, appeared like a real rise in value, and induced all manner of speculations and extravagance. The editor of *Niles's Register* characterized "the prodigality and waste as almost beyond belief," and speaks of the furniture of a single private parlor in one of the Eastern cities as costing upward of $40,000. On the other hand, Mr. Mathew Carey, of Philadelphia, writing in 1816, called this period "the golden age of Philadelphia," and says, "The rapid circulation of property, the immensity of business done, and the profits made on that business produced a degree of prosperity which she had perhaps never before witnessed." And in another portion of the pamphlet from which the above language is quoted he further declared "that never was the country in a more enviable state."

With the return of peace, and the consequent cessation of demand for commodities on the part of the government, the fall of prices, and the resumption of importations, all this bubble of prosperity, however, collapsed with great rapidity, and the country entered upon a period of prostration and stagnation of all industrial effort which has had no parallel in all its history except possibly during the darkest hours of the Revolution. Expecting large demands and high prices for commodities, English and American merchants imported enormously as soon as practicable after the ports had been opened; but the markets becoming soon overstocked, prices, under forced sales, declined to such an extent as to prove ruinous not only to the importers, but also to a large proportion of the injudicious or high-cost manufacturing establishments which the war had stimulated into existence. To remedy this state of things, Congress in 1816 enacted the first strong protective tariff, although the average rate of duty imposed by it on all imports was only about twenty-five per cent., and on only a few articles was in excess of thirty per cent. It is interesting also to note that this measure was proposed and mainly supported by Southern members of Congress—especially on the ground of encouraging the manufacture of our own cotton—and met with decided opposition from the people and Representatives of the North, whose capital and labor were at that time largely interested in commerce and navigation.

But whatever may have been the ultimate effect of this tariff, its immediate beneficial influence in restoring prosperity to the manufacturing and other interests of the country proved far less than what was anticipated. On the contrary, the stagnation of every kind of trade and industry, instead of diminishing, continued to increase, and did not reach its maximum until four years after the war, or in 1819. Specie payments were resumed in 1817; and as a legitimate consequence no small proportion of the paper promises to pay, which had been so recklessly issued and so profusely circulated as money, without security behind them for their payment, rapidly became worthless in the hands of the holders. The United States Bank, which at that time was the great financial regulator of the exchanges of the country, became also involved, through imprudent or dishonest management—losing through its Baltimore branch alone $1,671,000—and in attempting to save itself wrought such new mischief that the previous financial and industrial disasters of the country became almost insignificant in comparison. Rents and values of all real estate and merchandise were enormously depreciated. The population of Philadelphia decreased 10,000 between 1815 and 1820. At Pittsburg flour was one dollar per barrel, boards twenty cents per hundred, and sheep one dollar per head. Farms were mortgaged and sold every where for one-half to one-third of their value. Factories and workshops were every where closed; and in August, 1819, it was estimated by some authorities that as many as 260,000 persons, formerly dependent on manufactures, were absolutely without means of support.

After 1819, although the depression of prices continued through 1820, affairs began to improve. In this latter year the site for the city of Lowell was purchased, and between 1821 and 1827 it is noted that *thirty* new cotton factories were erected in the State of New York alone. But from the epoch of the great financial and industrial revulsion following the war of 1812 down to the year 1850 there are no reliable data for exhibiting by decades, or for shorter periods, the aggregate progress and results of American manufacturing industry. Some specific details of interest may, however, be mentioned.

Thus, in 1821 the value of the manufactured products of the United States exported was equal to 28 cents per head of the entire population. In 1825 this value had risen to 51 cents, from which it declined in 1830 to 41 cents. In 1835 it was again 51 cents; in 1840, 58 cents; in 1845, 53 cents; in 1850, 60 cents; and in the period from 1851 to 1861 it attained the highest figures in our industrial history, namely, $1 40 in 1854 and $1 53 in 1860. Since the outbreak of the war, however, this representative value of exports of manufactures has not in any one year risen as high as $1 *per capita* for our entire population.

In 1820 the total value of the books published in the United States was estimated at $2,500,000, and the relative proportion of British and American books consumed was estimated by S. C. Goodrich (Peter Parley) at *seventy* per cent. of the former to *thirty* of the latter; but before 1850 the proportion of foreign books to American consumed in the country had become very inconsiderable.

The mechanical inventions by which the cost of the manufacture of paper was greatly reduced, through the substitution of machinery producing a continuous sheet, in place of the old hand process by which single sheets were made successively and slowly, had their inception unquestionably in Europe at about the commencement of the present century, but the credit of so simplifying and enlarging the machinery as to make it practical and thoroughly efficient undoubtedly belongs to American paper-makers, John Ames, of Springfield, having been especially noted for his useful inventions. In 1800, "by the hand process, it took three months to complete the paper, ready for delivery, from the time of receiving the rags into the mill."[1] At the present day twenty-four hours are amply sufficient. In 1820 the annual value of the product of the paper manufacturing industry of the United States was estimated at $3,000,000; in 1829, $7,000,000; in 1844, $16,000,000, by 600 mills; in 1854, $27,000,000, by 750 mills;

[1] Munsell's *Chronology of Paper and Paper-Making.*

in 1860, $39,428,000; and in 1870 (exclusive of paper-hangings), $48,675,000.

The iron industry of the United States divides itself into two periods, one dating from the first settlement of the country to the end of the year 1862; the other extending from 1863 to the end of 1873. The first period was one of gradual but continuous growth; the second was that in which the iron industry was stimulated into an extraordinary growth and activity, first by the war, and then by railroad building on the most extensive scale.

The fact that both pig and bar iron were included among the regular exports of the country for many years prior to the Revolution has been already noticed. After the war the progress of this industry was for a time very rapid, and in 1791 Mr. Hamilton in his report says, "Iron-works have greatly increased in the United States, and are prosecuted with much more advantage than formerly." We find it also recorded at about this time that "a dangerous rivalry to British iron interests was apprehended in the American States, not only in the production of rough iron, from the cheapness of fuel and the quality of the iron, but also in articles of steel cutlery and other finished products, from the dexterity of the Americans in the manufacture of scythes, axes, nails, etc." In 1810 Mr. Gallatin, Secretary of the Treasury, in a report on manufactures, classed that of iron as firmly established, and estimated the quantity of bar-iron produced to be 40,000 tons, against about 9000 imported. According to the census of 1810, there were 153 furnaces in the United States, producing 53,908 tons of iron, and four steel furnaces, producing 917 tons of steel, the importation of steel for the same year being reported at only 550 tons. The commercial and financial revulsions which followed the war of 1812–15 affected disastrously the iron manufacture in common with all other industries; but that it did not entirely interrupt it is shown by the fact that some new establishments of great importance went into operation at the time of the greatest depression; and in 1816 the total import of pig-iron was but 329 tons. By 1824 the iron production and manufacture were both very active, and the pig-iron product of this year undoubtedly exceeded 100,000 tons. For 1832 it was reported at 200,000 tons. The first furnace for smelting with anthracite coal was built in 1837, but at the close of 1843 there were twenty anthracite furnaces in successful operation. The first important demand for iron in the United States for railroad purposes commenced in 1835, during which year 465 miles of road were constructed, followed by 416 in 1838, 516 in 1840, and 717 in 1841. In regard to the production of pig-iron in the United States during the decade from 1840 to 1850, a period characterized by extreme variations in the tariff policy of the government, there has been no little of controversy; but the most careful investigation yet made into the subject (that of Hon. W. M. Grosvenor) leads to the conclusion that the product of 1840 was about 347,000 tons, and that it increased from that figure to an aggregate of not more than 551,000 tons in 1846, and 570,000 in 1848. Subsequent to this date the progress of the pig-iron industry may be accurately indicated as follows: 1850, 564,755 tons; 1855, 784,178; 1860, 919,770; 1865, 931,582; 1870, 1,865,000; 1873, 2,695,000.

In 1865 the production of cast steel in the United States was 15,262 tons; in 1873, 28,000 tons.

In 1868 the production of pneumatic or Bessemer steel was 8500 tons; in 1873 (estimated), 140,000 tons. The recent progress of that department of the iron industry of the United States engaged in the manufacture of rails for railroads is also indicated by the following statistics of annual product: 1849, 24,314 tons; 1855, 138,674; 1860, 205,038; 1865, 356,292; 1870, 620,000; 1872, 941,000; 1873, 850,000.

In 1840 the consumption of iron in the United States for all purposes was estimated at about 40 pounds *per capita*; in 1846, at about 60 pounds; in 1856, at 64; and in 1867, at (approximately) 100 pounds. The *per capita* consumption of Great Britain and Belgium alike for this latter year was 189 pounds; and of France, 69½ pounds. For the years 1872–73 the *per capita* consumption of iron in the United States has been estimated as high as 150 pounds; and that of Great Britain, at 200 pounds.

It is more difficult to present the details of the growth and development of the woollen manufacture of the United States than those of almost any other great domestic industry; and this, in a great degree, for the reason that no other industry has been subjected to such violent and radical disturbances by reason of financial and commercial revulsions, and by the frequent changes in the fiscal policy of the government in respect to the tariff. Previous to the Revolution this branch of manufacturing was so successfully established that its progress was regarded with probably more of jealousy and apprehension by Great Britain than that of any other colonial industry, and most stringent efforts were made by Parliament to check or suppress it. After the war the business generally changed its "home" or "domestic" character, and became more and more of a "factory" enterprise, and developed rapidly, down to the period of the "embargo" of 1808. Before the "embargo" American woolens were made for $1 06 per yard, equal in fineness and quality with British goods of double the width, costing $3 50 per yard.

The immediate effect of the embargo and of the subsequent war was to greatly stimulate the manufacture of woolens; but wool was so high and scarce as to command in 1815 $4 per pound, while broadcloths were as high as $18 per yard. The detailed accounts of one factory established at Goshen, Connecticut, in 1813, which have been preserved, show that the proprietors purchased wool at $1 50 per pound, and sold cloth of a quality which at the present time would not command over $1 per yard, for $10; and, further, that the ultimate end of that factory after the war was an entire loss of the original capital, and three times as much more in addition.

In the prostration of all business interests that followed the war the woolen industry participated, but yet not more largely than did that of cotton; and it recovered so vigorously that the capital invested in it was reported to Congress to have more than doubled between 1815–16 and 1827. From this time, although the woolen manufacture has continued to increase, and at the present time has attained to a large development in almost every department, its record on the whole has been one of disaster rather than of success; and the annals of Congress from 1827 onward are filled with applications by representatives of the woolen interests for legislative relief, and with most pitiful statements of lack of profit, loss of capital, and abandonment of business. The explanation of this curious result in great part is that no one country produces all the different kinds of wool, which in variety of character may be said to range from the coarsest hair to the finest and most glossy silk; and that in order that the manufacture of woolens may be conducted successfully, it is absolutely essential that the manufacturer should be allowed to freely select his raw material from the peculiar products of every climate and soil, and at prices common to all competitors. But such a condition of things, through legislative interference, has not been given to American woolen manufacturers in one single year since 1827; added to which there has been no stability in the duties imposed on imported fabrics of wool, the tariff on the single article of blankets, for example, having been subjected to five radical and sudden changes during the period from 1857 to 1867 inclusive. The extreme and rapid variations in the price of American wool (upon which the American manufacturer has been obliged to mainly rely) since the year 1827 also strikingly illustrate how unstable have been what may be regarded as the fundamental elements of the business. Thus the average price per pound of common "fleece" in New York for the year 1825 was 33 cents; in 1830, 22 cents; in 1835, 33¾ cents; in 1839, 38 cents; in 1842, 19 cents; in 1850, 35 cents; in 1853, 41 cents; in 1858, 30 cents; in 1863, 67 cents; and in 1873, 40 to 90 cents.

By the census of 1840 the capital invested in the manufacture of woolens in the United States was returned as in excess of $15,000,000, employing 21,000 persons, and producing goods to the value of $20,696,000. Since 1850 the progress and condition of this industry as returned by the census are shown by the following table:

	1850.	1860.	1870.
Number of establishments	1,559	1,260	2,891
Hands employed	39,252	41,360	93,108
Capital invested	$28,118,000	$30,862,000	$108,998,000
Value of product	$43,207,000	$61,894,000	$177,963,000

In 1850 the Federal government for the first time attempted to ascertain through the machinery of the census with any approach to accuracy the exact condition and annual product of all the various industries of the country, not, however, including any establishment the value of whose annual product was not in excess of $500. The amount of capital at that time invested in manufactures in the whole country was returned at $553,123,822, and the value of the annual product (including fisheries and the products of the mines) at $1,019,106,616.

By the census of 1860 the aggregate capital employed in manufacturing for the whole country was returned at $1,009,855,715, and the gross value of the total annual product at $1,885,861,676, an increase as compared with the aggregate of 1850 of about eighty-eight per cent. By the census of 1870 the aggregate manufacturing capital returned was $2,118,208,000, and the gross value of the total annual product of manufactures $4,232,325,442. Reducing the census statements of these values of the annual product to equal terms respectively, the increase in the reported values of the products of manufacturing industry for the decade from 1860 to 1870 was *one hundred and eight* per cent. But of this increase *fifty-six* per cent. was computed to represent merely the enhancement of prices in 1870 over those of 1860 by reason of the inflation of the currency and other general causes, leaving *fifty-two* per cent. as the actual increase in the value of production. Of this latter increase it was further estimated that about *twenty-eight* per cent. was due to increase during the decade in the amount of labor employed, and *twenty-four* per cent. to the application of steam or water power, the introduction of machinery, and the perfecting of processes.

But the evidence is unquestionable that the returns of both the census of 1860 and that of 1870 in respect to the aggregate value of the annual product of our manufacturing industries were much less than the actual facts warranted, and that if proper account had been taken of the omissions and deficiencies in the estimates of the periods above given, the true value of the annual manufacturing product for 1860 would have been about $2,325,000,000 in place of $1,885,000,000, and for 1870 $4,839,000,000 in place of $4,232,000,000.

Careful investigation has also shown that the data upon which the amount of capital invested in manufactures in the United States has from time to time been estimated under the census have been too unreliable and imperfect to authorize any but the most general conclusions; and furthermore that the results of any inquiry by Federal or State officials looking to the obtaining of accurate information respecting invested capital must, from the almost universal unwillingness of persons interested to give information, be ever most unsatisfactory, if not wholly worthless. Thus the estimate under this head, based on the official returns of the census for 1870, was, as before shown, $2,118,000,000; but this sum, in the opinion of the Superintendent of the Census, Hon. F. A. Walker, did not in fact truly represent more than one-fourth of the capital which actually contributed to make up the gross annual value of the manufactured product returned for the year 1870.

RELATIVE IMPORTANCE OF THE MANUFACTURING INDUSTRIES OF THE UNITED STATES.

The following detailed statements, compiled from the returns of the census of 1870, indicate the relative importance of the great manufacturing industries of the country:

Leather (including the dressing and tanning of skins, the manufacture of boots and shoes, saddlery, harnesses, belting, hose, pocket-books, trunks, bags, and valises, but excluding all other manufactures).—Hands employed, 202,613; capital invested, $133,902,000; value of annual product, exclusive of value of material used, $162,872,000.

Lumber (planed and sawed).—Hands employed, 163,511; capital invested, $161,406,-000; value of annual product, exclusive of value of material used, $120,201,000.

Flouring and Grist Mill Products.—Hands employed, 58,448; capital invested, $151,565,-000; value of annual product, exclusive of value of material used, $77,593,000.

Pig and Bar Iron Manufacture (including pigs, blooms, and iron forged and rolled).—Hands employed, 78,347; capital invested, $119,860,000; value of annual product, exclusive of value of raw material used, $70,272,000.

Clothing (ready-made).—Hands employed,

118,824; capital invested, $52,743,000; value of annual product, exclusive of value of material used, $69,600,000.

Manufactures of Cotton (including batting and wadding, thread, twine, and yarns).—Hands employed, 136,763; capital invested, $140,906,000; value of annual product, exclusive of value of raw material used, $64,828,000.

Manufactures of Wool (including woolen and worsted goods, wool carding, and cloth dressing).—Hands employed, 93,108; capital invested, $108,998,000; value of annual product, exclusive of value of material used, $66,745,000.

Machinery.—Hands employed, 83,514; capital invested, $101,181,000; value of annual product, exclusive of value of material used, $57,597,000.

Carriages and Wagons (including building and repairing of railroad cars, children's wagons, and sleds).—Hands employed, 71,772; capital invested, $53,941,000; value of annual product, exclusive of value of material used, $56,565,000.

Agricultural Implements.—Hands employed, 25,279; capital invested, $34,834,000; value of annual product, exclusive of value of material used, $30,593,000.

Paper (exclusive of paper-hangings).—Hands employed, 17,910; capital invested, $39,362,000; value of annual product, exclusive of value of material used, $18,648,000.

Stoves, Heaters, and Hollow Ware.—Hands employed, 13,325; capital invested, $19,833,000; value of annual product, exclusive of value of material used, $14,345,000.

Hats and Caps.—Hands employed, 16,173; capital invested, $6,409,000; value of annual product, exclusive of value of material used, $12,587,000.

Silk (including sewing and twist).—Hands employed, 6699; capital invested, $6,242,000; value of annual product, exclusive of value of material used, $4,415,000.

It thus appears that the preparation and manufacture of leather ranks *first* in importance of the various manufacturing industries of the United States, and that the industries represented by the planing and sawing of lumber, and by the "milling" of cereals, take precedence over the primary manufactures of iron and over the great textile industries of cotton and of wool.

NUMBER OF PERSONS EMPLOYED.

By the census of 1870, 11,155,240 persons, twenty years of age and upward, were returned according to occupations. Of this number 2,500,189 were engaged in manufactures and mining, being a gain of *twenty-eight* per cent. since 1860, or *five and one-half* per cent. more than the ratio of decennial increase in population. The number employed in agriculture was at the same time returned at 5,151,767, and in trade and transportation at 1,117,928.

SOCIAL CONDITION OF LABORERS.

The data and material for describing the condition of laborers engaged in the manufacturing industries of the United States at different periods are very meagre. During the colonial period and the early days of the republic there was but little accumulated national wealth, but what there was was probably distributed with more of equality than has ever prevailed in any other large community of which we have a correct history for any lengthened period. At the commencement of the present century there were probably a smaller number of individuals in the country, in proportion to the whole population, who possessed an accumulated capital of $5000 than there are at the present time who possess $100,000. But if there was but little accumulated wealth in the early days of our national history, there was but little poverty, and consequently but few social distinctions, and the natural resources of the country then as now afforded remarkable facilities to all who were willing and able to work for earning a comfortable livelihood. With the gradual accumulation of wealth, the utilization of natural forces through the agency of machinery, and the great improvements in the means of transportation, the consuming power of the masses has also greatly increased, and many things which were once regarded as luxuries have come to be considered by even the humblest in the light of necessities. But it can not, at the same time, be doubted that the general tendency of events during the last quarter of a century of our national history has been to more unequally distribute the results of industrial effort, to accumulate great fortunes in a few hands—in short, to cause the rich to grow richer and the poor poorer. Such results, however, can not be referred to any one cause, but they are primarily due to an abandonment of that spirit of economy which so pre-eminently characterized our ancestors; to a marked decrease in the efficiency of labor; to a continual, if not increasing, use of artificial stimulants; to the crowding of population in large industrial and commercial centres; to war; to the interference of legislation with the freedom of trade; and latterly, to the use of an unstable, fluctuating medium of exchange, which all experience shows is one of the greatest curses that can befall the laboring population of any country.

As elements for estimating the social condition of laborers in the manufacturing industries of the United States, the statistics of the wages paid in different occupations are most important; and from the great mass of information on this subject which has recently been collected and published the following general items have been selected. Thus in Pennsylvania, the leading State in the production and fabrication of iron, the average earnings per annum in the different manufacturing establishments of the State for the years 1872–73 (as reported by the State Bureau of Statistics of Labor) were as follows: foremen, $638 per annum; skilled workmen, $536; laborers, first-class, $402; laborers, second-class, $332; females above sixteen, $228; youths, apprentices, etc., $150.

In Massachusetts for about the same period the average wages reported in the cotton-manufacturing industry were, for men, $403 per annum; women, $268; children, $134.

In the silk industry the average earnings per hand in the most prosperous establishments probably approximate $335 per annum as a maximum.

In the woolen industry the average daily wages of 5500 operatives in the mills of Massachusetts were reported for the year 1871 as follows: men, $1 62 per day; women, $1 12; young persons, 94 cents; children, 64 cents.

In any limited review of the progress of a great nation for a period of one hundred years, in respect to any one of its leading departments of industry, much that is interesting and suggestive must of necessity be wholly omitted, and many things treated most superficially. But a general conclusion to which a study of all the facts connected with our national development from the time of the founding the first colonies in the wilderness to the epoch of the Declaration of Independence, and from the establishment of peace and the adoption of the Federal Constitution to the present hour, is that the progress of the country, especially in respect to its manufacturing industry, and through what may be termed its element of vitality, is independent of legislation, and even of the impoverishment and waste of a great war. Like one of our mighty rivers, its movement is beyond control. Successive years, like successive affluents, only add to and increase its volume, while legislative enactments and conflicting commercial and fiscal policies, like the construction of piers and the deposits of sunken wrecks, simply deflect the current or constitute temporary obstructions. In fact, if the nation in all respects has not yet been lifted to a full comprehension of its own work, it builds steadily and determinately, and, as it were, by instinct.

IV.

AGRICULTURAL PROGRESS.

THE early colonists of the United States were largely agriculturists, or became so within a very few years after their arrival. A hundred and fifty years before our Independence, agriculture had already a promising foot-hold in several places within our present domain; a full century before the same date in our history the settlements were quite widely extended, nearly all the useful domestic animals and cultivated plants of Europe had been tried on our soil, and most of those we now have were already in successful use.

New and peculiar problems were presented to the new settlers. In the New World they found every thing new. The wild plants were new to them, and the good or bad qualities of each could only be learned by experience, for whether a plant was to be a valuable forage plant or a pestilent weed could not be foretold. Their crops as well as their flocks were subject to ravages by new enemies. Emigrants from nearly every part of Europe brought with them the useful plants they had known at home. But from whatever country they came, and wherever they settled here, they found a climate unlike any they had known before. In the North they encountered a most trying climate, where an almost arctic winter was followed by a semi-tropical summer; the severity of the winter prevented the success of some of the crops which flourished well during summer, while the drier air, clearer sky, and more fervid sun of summer proved unpropitious to others. The warmer parts, too, were unlike the warmer parts of Europe. As a consequence, the adaptability of each crop to our climate had to be tried for itself in each locality. This great experiment went on until one by one these questions were settled. Some crops, after repeated failures, were abandoned, and others found their appropriate localities. Hemp, indigo, rice, cotton, madder, millet, spelt, lentils, lucern, sainfoin, etc., were tried and failed in New England, as did other crops in the Southern colonies. Not only the plants of Europe, but many from Asia and the East Indies, were tried, including such spices as cinnamon, also various commercial plants. Some of these crops, on experiment, failed entirely. Others flourished after a fashion, but proved unprofitable; others flourished with peculiar luxuriance, and with characters unchanged; and still others, under the new conditions, assumed new characters or excellences. Before the war of the Revolution these trials had been made along or near the coast from Maine to Texas, and so completely had this century and a half of experiments solved the great problems of adaptation, acclimation (and often naturalization), that not a single important species of domestic animal has been profitably introduced since, and but one plant, *sorghum*, since added is of sufficient importance to be recognized in our official statistics.

The agriculture of most civilized countries is based on the rearing and use of certain domestic animals, and these in turn depend on the pastures and meadows. The only exception to this is where the cultivation of commercial plants greatly predominates over all other crops. The forage grasses used in Europe were practically indigenous there, and were such as ages of cultivation or use had adapted to the conditions there found. In Great Britain, and perhaps also throughout Northern Europe, the actual cultivation of their native grasses only became common toward the close of the last century. Before that they knew little or nothing of seeding lands to grass, and their pastures and meadows were fostered rather than cultivated. Such cultivation, however, had sprung up in the colonies much earlier, and from dire necessity. Of nearly 300 species of grasses now known to be indigenous to some part of the United States, very few indeed seem well adapted to cultivation. Perhaps more than nine-tenths of the forage of to-day in the cultivated parts of this country is furnished by plants introduced. How and why the artificial production of pastures and meadows and the cultivation of the true grasses sprung up in the American colonies north of the Chesapeake, how the grasses which we derived from Europe, half wild, were caught and tamed, as it were, and sent back for cultivation, is an interesting chapter in the history of American agriculture in colonial times, but it requires more space than we can give it in this review, and is only alluded to because of its relation to stock-raising, to be noticed later.

Agriculture as an *art* had reached nearly as high a point a hundred years ago as it occupies to-day, but agriculture as a *science* has nearly its whole history in the century we are to consider. Science belongs to no particular nation; and thus it is that we can not consider the agricultural progress of the United States entirely independent of that of other lands: it forms too intimate a part of the agricultural progress of the age.

The century is especially characterized in history by mechanical invention and by the growth of the so-called natural sciences, these two being intimately related; and it is through them that all the greater changes have occurred.

The mechanical progress of the century has been so fully treated in previous papers that its relations to agriculture will in this be treated only incidentally; but all improvements in tillage, in planting, in harvesting, in preparing for market, and in transportation are related to the subject under consideration.

The "Centennial of Chemistry" was celebrated in both Europe and America in 1874. The specific branch of that science, agricultural chemistry, belongs properly to this century only. Through its influence have come more philosophical theories of the rotation of crops, of the nature and use of manures; and the whole commerce in and manufacture of "commercial fertilizers" is the direct result of this science. It has, moreover, thrown great light on the nature of the soil and its tillage, on draining and irrigation, on the nutrition and fattening of animals, and the production of wool, flesh, butter, and cheese. Moreover, chemistry, in its extensive applications in various manufacturing processes, has introduced new uses for agricultural products as raw material.

The biological sciences have aided in their way. The laws of vegetable and animal growth are better understood, and by the application of this knowledge old varieties and breeds are improved with more ease and certainty, and new ones are made at pleasure for specific uses.

In noting our agricultural progress along the three ways indicated, that produced by mechanical invention comes naturally first, but the three classes of improvements are parallel, and each blends with the other along nearly the entire course.

The first and most obvious aid of mechanical invention has been to lessen the amount of human labor required to produce a given amount of agricultural product. For many of the processes new machines have been devised, and in those cases where old kinds of implements or tools have remained in use, they have been improved in quality, and usually cheapened in price. The simpler tools of a century ago were made mostly on the farms where they were to be used, or by the neighboring mechanic. They were usually heavy and costly to use, that is, costly in labor. With the specialization of labor, and the use of special machinery for the purpose, the manufacture of agricultural implements has become a great industry, the last national census enumerating over 2000 establishments, the value of whose products for that year amounted to over $50,000,000, the value of the product in 1850 having been less than $7,000,000. The value of the farming implements in use on the farms in 1870 was about $337,000,000, while in 1850 it was only about $152,000,000. These figures of manufacture and use at these two periods indicate extraordinary progress in agricultural operations in those twenty years.

This will be more apparent if we consider, in a general way, the different processes. First, as regards the implements of tillage, we may say that either old ones have been improved or new ones devised. Scarcely one remains in its old state. Some of the improvements economize power, others material, and others time; and what the aggregate cheapening of labor in tillage actually is it is impossible to say. A single laborer can certainly till more than twice the acreage, and with some crops three, four, or five times as much. Beginning with the improvement in hoes and simple tools, then passing to iron or steel plows, cultivators, horse-hoes, pulverizers, crushers, etc., the entire process of tillage has been modified, and animal power performs much that was then done by human muscle. Steam tillage is on trial, or at least steam plowing is, but is not yet common enough to be considered more than a limited experiment.

Drilling machines for planting certain crops were used to a limited extent before the Revolution. In Eliot's "Fifth Essay on Field Husbandry," published in 1754, he says:

"Mr. Tull's Wheat Drill is a wonderfull Invention, but it being the first invented of that Kind, no Wonder if it be intricate, as indeed it is, and consists of more Wheels and other Parts than there is really any Need of. This I was very sensible of all along, but knew not how to mend it. Therefore I applied myself to the Reverend Mr. *Clap*, President of *Yale* Colledge, and desired him for the regard he had for the Publick and to me that he would apply his mathematical Learning and mechanical Genius in that Affair; which he did to so good Purpose that this new modelled Drill can be made for the fourth Part of what Mr. *Tull's* will cost."

We find that a drill for spreading manure was soon afterward devised, and various drills have been in use ever since. The history of the above drill has been repeated in numerous instances. The more intricate and expensive machines of Europe have been simplified and cheapened here, and thus brought into quicker use. The threshing machine and reaper were both undoubtedly invented in Great Britain, but in America they were simplified, cheapened, and, to use an Americanism, were made *handier*, hence more practical. Although drills thus early came into use, nearly all the planting was done by hand until less than forty years ago, particularly for the cereals. Now drills or sowers of some kind are in almost universal use on the larger farms.

The improvement for harvesting has been much greater than for either tillage or planting. Previous to 1850 the scythe and sickle were the almost universal tools for cutting, and the common use of the modern reaper and mower dates back but about twenty years. Labor has always been dearer here than in Europe, hence the sickle was never so much used as was the scythe. As to what its capacity was here we have no precise data. Experiments and estimates published by the Highland Agricultural Society in Scotland in 1844, and approvingly quoted by standard authorities on British agriculture later, give "the average quantities of ground reaped by seven persons, on an average of ten hours' work," as one to one and a half acres of wheat, and two to three acres of oats and barley. (A *bandwin* of reapers consists usually of seven persons, who cut, bind, and stook the grain.) By the use of the cradle in this country, one and a half acres of wheat was not a large day's work to be cut by one man, raked, bound, and stooked by two others, but this was doubtless above the average. With hay, two acres per day is a reasonably large amount. At a recent meeting of a certain State Board of Agriculture, in a discussion concerning hay, the belief was concurred in that "hired labor with a scythe mows much less than one and a half acres per day per man on the average." It is safe to say that a man with a team of horses and modern mower or reaper will average about six times as much as with a scythe. Under the best conditions more is done (we hear of fifteen or twenty acres sometimes), but the *average* would be not far from this estimate. With our hay crop nearly every step in the process has been changed. The horse-rake came into general use before the reaper, the tedder and horse-fork later. A century ago all the processes were by hand labor; now the only labor performed in the old way is pitching on the load, loading, hauling, and stowing or stacking, and each of these is done with improved tools.

To obtain the most profitable yield of hay or grain, it must be cut and secured at just the right time, hence with most crops this has always been considered the most critical period, and the labor then required brings the highest wages. If cut too early, it is immature; if too late, it deteriorates or wastes. Moreover, it is then especially subject to damage by unfavorable weather. Taking all these into account, it is seen that the actual gain to agriculture by the use of the various harvesting machines can not be measured by merely noting the relative areas operated on by a man in a given time by the old methods compared with the new.

With the great crops of cotton, Indian corn, potatoes, and tobacco there has been no such great advance. With cotton, the nature of the crop and the prolonged harvest forbid hope for much improvement, and a similar condition exists in the case of tobacco. With potatoes and Indian corn there have been many attempts, with but very moderate success as yet.

Intimately connected with the harvest is the preparation for market; and in this the progress, as a whole, has been even more marked than in either of the processes already noticed. The most illustrious example is seen in the cotton crop. In no other case has the cultivation of a great staple by people of European civilization depended for its success upon the solution of a single and simple mechanical problem. We hear of cotton being planted in our colonies as early as 1621, and again, in the Carolinas, in 1666, and during the century after the last date it is often spoken of. It was tried over and over again along nearly the whole extent of the colonies. Eliot, in his "Second Essay on Field Husbandry," published in 1749, tells of his experiments with it in Connecticut. It appears to have been, however, a rather rare garden plant until just after the close of the Revolutionary war, when it was introduced anew, and soon after that its field cultivation began. But its production was extremely limited by the cost of getting it ready for market. Hand labor was expensive; and so long as a laborer could prepare but a single "pound per day" there could be no great breadth of culture, no matter how fertile and cheap the soil, how favorable the climate, or how complete the means of tillage. The invention of the cotton-gin in 1793 placed it on the same level with other field products. Since then the rapid increase of its production is one of the marvels of the century. A single generation saw the crop grow from nothing to be the great commercial plant of the world, constituting, some years, five-sixths of our entire agricultural exports. The relations of this growth to the civilization and prosperity of many countries, and especially its relations to our own social and political history, furnish perhaps the most romantic chapter in the retrospect of agriculture.

Threshing machines for our cereals were practically unknown here before the present century. We infer from the journals of that day that they came into somewhat common use in Great Britain between 1810 and 1820; their universal use there was still later by some years, the flail continuing to be a common implement down to 1850.

The dearness of labor and other reasons caused the flail to be used relatively less in this country than in Europe, yet it was not a rare implement by any means down to 1830 or later. Grain was, however, usually trodden out with horses, or threshed by dragging over it a great roller armed with large wooden pins. This was an approved implement, and received the official recommendation of at least one agricultural society as late as 1816, and the writer has seen it in use as late as 1835. In the better farming regions of the Middle States, early in the present century, eight to twelve bushels of wheat per day were considered a good average for a man to thresh with a flail. Threshing was largely done in the winter, and where horses were used to tread out the grain, twenty-three to thirty bushels per day for three horses and a man and boy were common results. The average was perhaps not much above the lowest figures here given. To illustrate: in a specific case in 1826, on one farm in a prosperous and old farming region, 1300 bushels of wheat were threshed, the grain winnowed, and the straw drawn from the barn to a neighboring field, in twelve weeks, two men and five horses performing the labor. This was considered, in that neighborhood, good work. Before 1825 threshing machines were very rare in this country, but between that date and 1835 their use spread rapidly, and before 1840 comparatively little of the cereal grains was threshed by other means. For cleaning grain the hand fan was extensively employed in 1776, but fanning-mills came into common use long before threshing machines. The first threshing machines merely threshed, next separators were added, and then "cleaners;" and now the grain is threshed and cleaned for market in one operation. Horses were the universal power applied until quite lately. Now steam-power is extensively used, particularly in the Western States and in California. Horse-power, however, is still in general use.

What the possible capacity of the modern thresher is, when working under the most favorable conditions, although an interesting question, is not the one we have to consider here, but rather what is the average of good work, or work that can be commonly hoped for by good farmers. The larger machines are mostly employed in doing custom work, and time is lost in passing from farm to farm, and in the delays which are unavoidable in work affected by so many conditions. A steam-thresher, under such conditions as they have in California, will thresh, in actual practice, from 40,000 to 100,000 bushels of grain in a "season" of three months. With such a machine, operated by a gang of eighteen hands, whose combined wages (in the year 1874) would amount to forty-three dollars per day, 2000 bushels of wheat per day is fair work. A recent agricultural journal states of the actual practice that the "full capacity of such a machine is 1500 sacks a day, the average work about 1000, holding over two bushels each." This means that the grain is threshed, cleaned, put in sacks, and the sacks piled up ready for removal by cars or team, and amounts to over a hundred bushels per day per man. Vastly larger figures are cited for short periods under exceptionally favorable conditions. The agricultural papers of the same State mention incidentally, as a local news item, a horse-power machine which averaged 1500 bushels of wheat per day for thirty-one successive days, moving on twenty-eight different farms in that time, and speak of another (also horse-power) which in 1874 threshed and cleaned 80,400 bushels in fifty-two days, of which 11,300 bushels were threshed in five and a half days.

The effect of these improved methods is best seen by noting the total saving of the several processes. A hundred years ago, to cut a hundred bushels of wheat required about three days' work (which could not be delegated to other power); to bind and stook it, four days; to thresh and clean it, five days, which, with the other processes between the standing grain and the merchantable product, would amount to some fifteen days' actual manual (and mostly very hard) labor for each hundred bushels. The average was doubtless more than this, that is, a day's labor would not get more than six or seven bushels of grain through these processes.

The president of an agricultural society in California in 1866 stated that on his farm that year 40,318 bushels of grain (three-fourths of it wheat) were harvested, threshed, cleaned for the market, and stored in the granaries in thirty-six days, including all delays, with an average of twenty-two hands. This is an average of about fifty bushels per man per day for the entire crop. Much larger figures are reported in other cases of later date; but the exact data are not at hand.

While such progress has not marked the gathering and preparing of *all* the crops, yet it has extended to so many of them that all the more laborious processes have been revolutionized.

It must be borne in mind that mechanical invention has not only aided agriculture, but that in turn it has been stimulated by the wants of agriculture, and some of the most profitable patents have been in this direction, and we get a vivid idea of the demand and supply of new methods and appliances in the fact that the Patent-office issues about twelve hundred patents per year relating to agriculture.

It is through the aids of mechanical invention, including the means of transportation, that what is known as "the Great West" has been so rapidly settled and its products made accessible to the world.

That soils became exhausted by cropping, and that the exhaustion could be checked by manuring, were facts well enough known from remote antiquity: the philosophical reason why was left for agricultural chemistry to discover. So soon as chemical analysis became established on a reasonably sure foundation, and chemistry began to assume the character of an exact science, practical applications to agriculture began to follow. Chemical experiments relating to this art had been made earlier by Arthur Young and others, but agricultural chemistry, as the science we now know it, began with Sir Humphry Davy. He first lectured before the English Board of Agriculture in 1802. He experimented on guano, phosphates, and various other manures, and analyzed them. He lectured again before the Board of Agriculture in 1812, and these lectures furnished the basis of his *Elements of Agricultural Chemistry*, published in 1813. This work was extensively read, and was translated and printed in several languages. During the next thirty years there were numerous experimenters, and it was a period rich in discoveries in chemistry. Sprengel made many analyses of the ashes of plants about 1832, and then came the works of Johnston, Mülder, and others; but it was left to Liebig to bring order out of the great mass of experiment and theory which had accumulated, and to really place agricultural chemistry on its present foundation. His *Chemistry in its Applications to Agriculture and Physiology* appeared in 1840, and soon after Boussingault published his *Économie Rurale.* Johnston published his *Lectures on the Applications of Chemistry and Geology to Agriculture* in 1844, since which time works on this department of science have been particularly numerous. While the science has had most of its development in Europe, America has not been without its workers, and the later writings of Professor Johnson have been republished in Europe in the English, German, Swedish, and Russian languages.

"The art of manuring" was a favorite theme in olden times, and it was an art brought to high perfection; but it followed experience only. With the aid of chemistry the art assumed the features of a science. Manures known before were used to better advantage, rare ones brought into greater prominence, and new ones devised. The introduction of turnips and clover into extensive cultivation in England about the time of the American Revolution, and the great rise in rents soon after, produced a radical change in the systems of rotation and tillage, and the discoveries in chemistry came in at just the right time to supplement this. Bones had long been used, but their special merits were pointed out by Davy, and soon their use became very extensive. Then followed the manufacture of superphosphates. To show what great and speedy changes were wrought through these means, where mechanical invention had but little to do with results, a single illustration may be given. A light-house, known as the Dunston Pillar, was built on the Lincoln Heath, in Lincolnshire, about the middle of the last century. This was said to be the only land light-house known. It was built to guide travelers over the barren and dreary waste, and it long fulfilled its useful purpose. This pillar, no longer a light-house, now stands in the midst of a fertile and wealthy farming region, where all the land is in high cultivation. For twenty-five years no barren moors have been in sight even from its top. Turnips and phosphates were the principal means through which this great change came. In this country the abundance of fertile soil and its cheapness, and the cost of labor, while inducing the use of improved implements and machines earlier than in Europe, hindered rather than accelerated the use of chemical aids. It was easier to break new land, particularly if it were prairie, than it was to renovate the old. For a long while bones were extensively exported from this country to England, but since the year 1850 the use of commercial fertilizers has been rapidly increasing, until now it has reached immense proportions.

The history of the use of guano is somewhat similar to that of the phosphates. This material has been in use as a manure on the western side of South America for centuries, and from time to time its merits were spoken of in European publications.[1] Its use, however, remained local until it was prominently brought into notice by the modern agricultural chemists. How early it was brought to Europe can not now be ascertained. Sir Humphry Davy experimented with it as early as 1805; but it was not until after the recommendations of Liebig that it began to be an article of commerce. A few casks were imported into England in 1840 "as an experiment." It was followed by 2000 tons the next year, and in sixteen

[1] In *The Art of Metals*, written "in the kingdom of Peru, in the West Indies, in the year 1640," translated and published in London in 1674, it is said that "out of the Islands of the South Sea, not far from the City of Arica, they fetch earth called *Guano*," etc. And then follows a description, and the statement that it is used for manure, and that the fields are "put in heart thereby for 100 years after."

years its aggregated sales in Great Britain were reported at 100,000,000 of dollars. Its use began in this country somewhat later, the aggregate imports previous to 1850 amounting to less than 30,000 tons. At present it supports a vast commerce, regulated by special national treaties, and employs hundreds of ships and millions of capital in its transportation.

Along with the importation of guano and the development of beds of mineral manures and their preparation, comes the manufacture of commercial fertilizers, one of the most rapidly-growing of our industries. This enterprise is of very recent origin in this country, but in 1870 more than four millions of capital were employed in this branch of manufacture, and the value of the products amounted to $6,000,000. The official estimates place the present product several times higher. Gypsum, which was not included in the above estimate, was used sparingly in colonial times, but to most farmers it was then an unheard-of substance. It was prominently brought into notice by Benjamin Franklin, after his return from France, but its rapid spread kept pace with that of the cultivation of clover between 1810 and 1830. At the last census there were 321 mills, the value of the ground product amounting to about $2,500,000, a part of which, however, is applied to other uses in the arts.

From the nature of the case, the actual value of these new aids to American agriculture can not be shown statistically. For obvious reasons, their greatest effect is as yet seen only in the older States and in the South. Throughout the North, where the farm-yard is, and perhaps always will be, the great source of farm fertilizers, these commercial manures come in as an auxiliary; but farther south, and in those regions where the cattle roam the fields throughout the year, preventing farm-yard accumulations to any considerable extent, the case is quite different. As cotton and tobacco, the two great commercial crops, have been heretofore cultivated, exhaustion was inevitable. The history of a region comprised, of necessity, first the settlement, then its rise and wealth during the increasing growth of the crop, then a period of prosperity of longer or shorter duration, regulated by the original fertility of the soil, and finally the inevitable decline. In actual history, many great plantations became so completely impoverished by cropping with tobacco that they were abandoned and returned to forest again, and more to sparsely peopled, impoverished places. The exhaustion by cotton-growing was similar, although not always so complete. The necessity of new lands for this crop when it was "king," and the connection of this necessity with political events, are familiar to every student of our history, while its relation to fertilizers was generally ignored. Here, as in Southern Europe, "great political and social events had their foundation in the dunghill."

The theory and largely the practice of tobacco and cotton cultivation are now changed, and we see no reason why, by the new methods, the profitable fertility of the soil may not be maintained indefinitely. Official reports in Georgia estimate that "the planters of that State pay over $10,000,000 for fertilizers" annually; and single towns in the Connecticut Valley, where tobacco is the leading crop, in addition to the home fertilizers, pay from $30,000 to $50,000 a year for those from outside sources.

To follow up this subject in its relations to the price of real estate, to vegetable or "market" farming near our cities, to other manufactures whose waste products are utilized, to the great question of the use of sewage and its relations to public health, would lead us entirely beyond the limits of this paper.

Draining and irrigation, although strictly mechanical processes, have been the subjects of much chemical investigation. Thorough under-draining was practiced to some extent long ago, but has only come into extensive use during the last sixty or seventy years even in Great Britain. In this country its use is more modern. Noah Webster, in an agricultural address published in 1818, speaks of "the art of draining wet lands, which is now in its infancy in this country." John Johnston, a Scottish farmer still living near Geneva, New York, was the first in the United States to use tiles, about 1835, making the tiles by hand after Scotch models. The few under-drains made earlier, as indeed many made since, were of stone. John Delafield, a neighbor of Mr. Johnston, and a man noted for his interest in agriculture, imported a tile machine in 1848, the first one in this country. The practice is now common enough, but there are no statistics to show the amount of land drained.

Irrigation has only come into any considerable use in those Western regions where the rain-fall is insufficient for all the purposes of agriculture. It is as yet carried on, for the most part, on a small scale and by private capital. Vast schemes are discussed or projected, but we must leave their results to the future.

We have already alluded to the class of improvements introduced through or aided by the biological sciences. We have already said that a hundred years ago all our *species* of field crops, except sorghum, were already in cultivation here. While this is true, the number of *varieties* of these crops then was less. A neighborhood would know perhaps three or four varieties of each species, rarely more. About that time many farmers began to grow more kinds, in order that if one failed because of a bad season, others might succeed. Old varieties were slowly improved by careful selection of seed, but the occurrence of new ones depended on accident, or on causes not then understood. Late in the last century and early in this the facts relating to the production of new varieties of cultivated plants began to be studied by new methods, and, through the observations and experiments of botanists and gardeners rather than by farmers, the laws came to be better understood. As a result of this knowledge, varieties are now multiplied almost at pleasure, and the kinds in cultivation, or at least known, amount to hundreds or even thousands for each species. As an example, we may mention potatoes. Deane, in his *New England Farmer*, a dictionary which professes to contain "a compendious account" of "the Art of Husbandry as practiced to the greatest Advantage in this Country," published at Boston in 1790, says, "No longer ago than the year 1740 we had but one sort, a small reddish-colored potato, of so rank a taste that it was scarcely eatable." He then enumerates twelve varieties known up to the date of writing, which had originated in various countries, some in the Old World. The paucity of kinds was often spoken of by writers before the Revolution. Guided by the knowledge since gained, a single American experimenter claims to have produced and tested 6000 different varieties. Other crops have a similar but not quite so striking a history. Several hundred varieties of wheat were grown and tried by one farmer in the Genesee Valley all in thirty years. This has given so ample means of selection, of choosing just the best kind for each soil and condition, that there is doubtless a great actual increase in production due to it, but its most obvious effect is to give us a choice as to quality. With fruits this application of science has had even more remarkable results than with grains.

Although but few field *crops* have been introduced since 1776, this is not true of field *weeds*. Some which actually came earlier only became numerous and troublesome later, and others were then introduced. Several local traditions exist in the New England and Middle States of weeds introduced by the British armies and their allies during that war, which have spread and maintained a foot-hold ever since. On the other hand, it is questionable if science has aided in the suppression of weeds except in a very general way.

Columbus, on his second voyage to America, brought various kinds of domestic animals with him, and importations have been frequent nearly ever since. In our own colonies there were many importations, and from several countries, from the north of Europe direct and from Southern Europe by way of the Spanish-American colonies. The live stock in existence at the time of the Revolution was the mongrel progeny of these numerous importations. There is no question but that the domestic animals introduced from Europe rapidly deteriorated here. Various travelers have borne testimony to this, and indeed it was to be expected. The pastures of Europe were such as fostering care for ages had made them, and, as already said, of peculiarly nutritious grasses. The early colonists found only crude grasses, and no natural meadows better than the salt-marshes near the coast or the coarse sedges by some of the streams. The pasturage in the forests was meagre. In the winter, straw, corn stalks, or in places wild marsh hay and the *browse* of the woods, were all the miserable animals had. Spring usually found the flock or herd reduced in numbers, poor, and weak. Too often the farmer's first work of the spring morning was to assist the weakened creatures to rise to their feet, and several native plants had reputation for strengthening cattle so that they could get up alone when weakened by the winter's starvation. The colonists early learned to plant grass seed from Europe, and to plant corn for the animals. Turnips, so valuable in the north of Europe, were of little value here. In the South they did not flourish well; in the North they grew well enough, but being very watery in their nature, and the winters being so cold, they froze very readily, and thus their value was greatly diminished. Maize was made to take their place, and sometimes beans were sparingly cultivated; but with this crop, again, we had to learn by experience and disappointment. The field bean of Europe did not thrive well here. It struggled for cultivation for more than a century, and was finally abandoned as a field crop. Other kinds of beans, however, partially took its place. Clover was introduced from England quite early last century. Eliot speaks in its praise as early as 1747, but for some reason it did not come into common use until sixty or seventy years later. It is, therefore, no wonder that all kinds of live stock deteriorated, that they fell an easy prey to the wolves, and that they only began to thrive successfully after so long experiment and so bitter experience. It must be remembered, too, that the laws of breeding were not then well understood; but special attention was given to this practical question during the last half of the last century. Sebright published about 1773, and Bakewell's experiments were then in full progress; and although he died without giving the secret of his successes to the world, the results were seen and many of the conditions known. In this period the breeding of all kinds of animals received special attention, and while the more scientific problems were being solved abroad, the colonists here had solved those of forage, acclimation, and adaptation.

Several of the more valued breeds of neat cattle were established early in the Old World, and improved during the period spoken of. Pedigrees began to be carefully looked after. The first volume of the *English Short-horn Herd-Book* appeared in 1822, but its pedigrees began at about this period, or a little earlier. Only thirty animals are recorded that flourished in 1780 and earlier; and while the blood of unrecorded animals afterward came in, for present purposes the pedigrees of all the thousands of thorough-bred short-horns date back to about that time, theoretically at least. Precisely when the first importations of this breed were made to this country is uncertain. It is now believed that they occurred very soon after the Revolutionary war, and there are traditions of several importations before 1800. Soon after that date importations began in earnest, and have gone on ever since. The first volume of the *American Short-horn Herd-Book* was published in 1846, the thirteenth in 1874, and in the series are recorded some 33,000 pedigrees. Certain strains of this breed have thrived peculiarly well here, and the sale of one herd, September 10, 1873, at New York Mills, was doubtless the most extraordinary cattle sale that has ever taken place any where. At this sale 109 head sold for about $382,000, or an average of over $3500 per head, the higher prices being $40,600 for a cow, and several sold for over $20,000 each, a calf but five months old selling for $27,000. The Devons were also introduced early, and previous to 1840 were imported more abundantly than the short-horns, and have perhaps had as wide an influence on the improvement of American cattle as the last-named breed, or even a wider. Now all the more distinguished breeds of Europe are successfully bred here, and some five or six of the more numerous or important have American herd-books now published.

The effect of all this has been to enormously elevate the quality of American cattle; and so completely has the mongrel or "native" stock been improved through these that in certain agricultural societies where premiums are offered for the best "natives" it is found that all that are offered as such are, in fact, "grades," having had an infusion of better blood within three or four generations. Even the Spanish cattle of Texas and California are being rapidly changed and improved through and by these better breeds.

The history of American horses is in most respects similar to that of the cattle. There was at first deterioration, but in a less degree, then a slow improvement through selection and better feeding, then a more rapid improvement through better breeding and the importation of better stock. The race of trotters is peculiarly American. It originated here, and is here found in its greatest development. It appears to have followed and been caused by the introduction and improvement in light carriages. The thorough-breds of Europe, the race-horse and the hunter, are essentially *running* horses. For American uses trotters were needed; various causes tended to make them popular, and in the last fifty years the breed has been made. It has a large infusion of the English thorough-bred in it, yet few noted trotters are thorough-breds. The gait and speed are in part the result of training, and are in part hereditary. There has been a constantly augmenting speed and a great increase in the number of horses that are fast trotters. But a few years ago the speed of a mile in two and a half minutes was unheard of; now perhaps 500 or 600 horses are known to have trotted a mile in that time.

There is no question but that, as a whole, the quality of American horses has greatly improved in the hundred years. It was believed that the great increase of railroads would diminish the number required, but, as a fact, the reverse is true.

American sheep before 1776 were all coarse-wooled and mostly very inferior animals. In Europe the fine-wooled breeds were shut up in Spain, and various causes prevented the exportation of the English improved coarse-wooled breeds. Eliot, in his "First Essay" (1747), says: "A better *Breed of Sheep* is what we want. The *English* Breed of *Cotswold Sheep* can not be obtained, or at least without great Difficulty: for Wool and live Sheep are contraband Goods, which all Strangers are prohibited from carrying out on Pain of having the right Hand cut off." Before 1800 there were a few importations of improved coarse-wooled sheep, and very many importations since. Merino sheep were carried into Saxony from Spain in 1765, into France about 1776, and England about 1790. Three merinoes were brought into the United States in 1793, but the person to whom they were presented not knowing their value, they were eaten for mutton. In 1801 or 1802 a few more came, and there were several small importations from Spain and France before 1815. The Saxon merino was introduced in 1824. Various causes led to wild speculation more than once in fine-wooled sheep in the United States, but they have increased now to many millions, and some of the most noted flocks of the world have been or are here. Individual animals have sold as high as $10,000 and even $14,000. Both for fineness of fibre and weight of fleece the American wool is celebrated, and the finest fibre yet attained was from sheep bred in Western Pennsylvania about 1850. Since that time weight of fleece rather than excessive fineness has been bred for. The great pastures of Texas and California at home, and of Australia and South America, are now in competition in the markets of the world, but the wool produced in some of the older States, particularly in the Ohio Basin, is especially sought after by the manufacturers of the finer goods.

The statistics of live stock in the United States as given in the last census are confessedly very imperfect, hence no numbers are here quoted except the aggregate value, which was estimated as amounting to upward of $1,500,000,000.

Incidental to this branch of our subject, we may mention an American invention, the cheese-factory system. This was first put in operation in 1851 by Mr. Jesse Williams, in Oneida County, New York. Down to April, 1860, twenty-one factories had been started. Then the increase was so rapid that by the end of 1866 there had been 500 factories erected in the State of New York alone, and the capital incidentally employed in the farms and stock amounted to at least $40,000,000. In 1870 there were over 1300 factories in operation in the country, producing about 55,000 tons of cheese. The system is still growing here, and has extended to foreign countries.

The great improvements that have taken place in transportation, which make it possible for the wheat of Iowa and California to compete in the English markets with that raised on the Atlantic sea-board, and which place Iowa in competition with New England, have operated to *specialize* farming. The large farmer of to-day raises fewer kinds on his farm than did the small farmer of the last century. This specialization allows the use of the higher appliances and the use of capital as the former system could not. The true farms have doubtless grown in size, on the average. The early settlers of necessity could till but small farms. The tax lists of Long Island for years between 1675 and 1685 show that in nine English towns the average land-holding was about twenty-two acres, and in the five Dutch towns about thirty-seven acres, or for the whole fourteen towns it was twenty-five and one-third acres, and at that time over ninety per cent. of the tax-payers were land-holders. The national census of 1870 enumerates 2,660,000 farms, only six and a half per cent. of which were of less than ten acres, and more than half of the whole number contained over fifty acres. The cash value of the farms, implements, and live stock was placed at upward of $11,000,000,000, and the total estimated value of all the farm productions at about $2,448,000,000. Of the 12,500,000 persons "engaged in all classes of occupations," 6,000,000 were engaged in agriculture. We have absolutely no statistics of the agriculture of the colonies at the time of the Revolution; therefore the actual figures of progress can not be given, and we refrain from estimates.

Agricultural newspapers, societies, schools, and literature hardly had an existence before 1776. Less than forty newspapers were then published in the colonies, none of them agricultural. In 1870 there were ninety-three agricultural and horticultural newspapers and periodicals, with an aggregate annual issue of 21,500,000 copies.

Agricultural societies were organized just after the Revolution; exhibitions or "fairs" began between 1810 and 1820. It is believed that there are now 2000 agricultural societies, clubs, and boards of agriculture organized and in operation. Their annual "reports" amount to very many volumes. A few tracts and essays, which altogether would make but a single small volume, were the entire special agricultural literature the colonies produced. The agricultural literature of to-day is confusing by its quantity and variety.

Agricultural professorships were established in Europe some time last century, and the first agricultural school began in 1799. In this country, Samuel L. Mitchill was made "Professor of Chemistry and Agriculture" in Columbia College, New York, in 1791, but there is no record that he gave special instruction in agriculture. In various colleges professors of general chemistry treated more or less of agricultural chemistry. After special preparation for the office, John P. Norton was appointed "Professor of Agricultural Chemistry and Vegetable and Animal Physiology" in Yale College in 1846, perhaps the first actual professor of agriculture in an American college. His instruction began in 1847, since which time numerous other similar professorships have been established.

Agricultural schools and colleges were talked of for many years, and a few made an actual or nominal beginning before 1850, and several before 1860. In 1862 Congress appropriated certain lands to establish or aid schools in the various States, "without excluding other studies," to "teach such branches of learning as are related to agriculture and the mechanic arts." Stimulated by this, and aided by private and State aid, about forty schools are now in existence, trying in various ways to fulfill the purposes for which they were established. The most of them are recent, and they are mainly important, in this account of progress, because of what they indicate rather than what they have yet accomplished. A few of the older ones have, however, already had considerable influence, and all are ready for the coming century's work.

V.

THE DEVELOPMENT OF OUR MINERAL RESOURCES.

TO write the story of the development of the mineral resources of the United States during the last century would demand a volume. The whole history of the new States and Territories beyond the valley of the Mississippi is little else than that of the opening and the working of their rich mines of gold and silver since 1849. But this region was not a part of the national territory at the time when our survey commences. While the Spaniards, greedy for that wealth which proved their ruin, planted their colonies from Mexico to Chili along the western portion of the continent, rich in precious metals, our English ancestors fixed their homes in a portion which, though not destitute of mineral resources, offered no tempting prizes to the miners of that early day. The records of our colonial period have little to tell beyond the working of some iron ores along the sea-board, and attempts on a small scale to mine ores of copper and of lead. The first half century of our national existence does not add much to this record, and the history of the marvelous developments in the working of the coal, petroleum, iron, and copper in our Eastern regions, and in the mining of gold and silver in the West, belongs to the present generation.

It will be found convenient in our inquiry to follow, with a few exceptions, the geographical division just indicated, and to point out for each of these regions separately the general results already obtained in the development of its mineral wealth, considering in the first place the territory which stretches from the eastern base of the Rocky Mountains to the Atlantic. It is in this division of our territory that are found the great stores of coal and iron, besides vast supplies of petroleum, salt, copper, and other minerals of less importance. Geologically described, this eastern half of the United States is essentially a great basin of paleozoic strata nearly encircled with azoic crystalline rocks, and has been aptly described as a great bowl filled with mineral treasure, the outer rim of which is formed by the mountains of Northern New York, the hills of New England, the Highlands of the Hudson, and their southward continuation in the Blue Ridge nearly to the Gulf of Mexico. Thence, passing to the eastern base of the Rocky Mountains, it extends northward, and by the Great Lakes around the northern rim of the bowl to the point of departure. Within the area thus inclosed lies the vast Appalachian coal-field, with its dependent areas of anthracite and semi-bituminous coal, the lesser coal-fields of Michigan and Illinois, and the still more western one to which the coals of Iowa, Missouri, and Arkansas belong. It includes, moreover, formations containing petroleum, salt, and lead, besides much iron, though not less abundant stores of the latter metal are found in the surrounding crystalline rocks.

The coal deposits of the great paleozoic basin furnish the mainspring of our principal mechanical and commercial enterprises, the great source of motive power, and the chief means of reducing and manufacturing our iron. If to this we add that the value of the coal now mined in the United States is equal to that of all the iron, gold, and silver produced in the country, we have said enough to justify us in assigning it the first place in a survey of our mineral resources. The forest growth supplied the demands for fuel of the early English colonists, to whom the treasures of the great basin were little known, and the first attempts at mining mineral fuel were in the coal-field near Richmond, Virginia, one of several small areas which lie over its eastern rim, or between the Blue Ridge and the sea. This coal of Eastern Virginia occurs in what are known to geologists as mesozoic rocks, and belongs to a later age than the bituminous coal of Pennsylvania, which, however, it resembles in quality. It was probably first mined as early as 1750, and after the war of the Revolution was exported to Philadelphia, New York, and Boston, until within the last thirty years. Other coals have since replaced it in these markets, and it is now mined chiefly for local use.

The anthracite of Eastern Pennsylvania was first discovered, it is said, in 1770. In 1775, just a century since, a boat-load was taken down to the armory at Carlisle, and in 1791 the great open quarry of this fuel near Mauch Chunk was made known. From its unlikeness to the Virginia coal, and the difficulty of igniting it, the Pennsylvania anthracite encountered much opposition. Tradition tells us that a boat-load taken to Philadelphia in 1803 was broken up and used to mend the roads. But it slowly found its way into use; and from a pamphlet published in 1815 we learn that the coal from the Lehigh had been several years on trial in Philadelphia, where it had been compared with the Virginia bituminous coal, and, from the testimony of iron-workers, distillers, and others, was to be preferred to it for durability and economy. Oliver Evans had, moreover, at this time tried the anthracite with success under the boilers of his steam-engine, and had also insisted upon its advantages for domestic purposes. Notwithstanding these results, the new fuel found its way very slowly into use, and in 1822 the total production of the anthracite mines was estimated at 3720 tons, against 48,000 tons of the coal from Richmond, Virginia, then its only rival. Fifty years later, or in 1872, the official returns give for the exportation of coal from the anthracite region not less than 19,000,000 tons, besides about 2,500,000 tons for local consumption, while that of the Virginia coal-field for the same year is estimated at 62,000 tons. The late Professor Silliman, who visited the anthracite region in 1825, and published his report of it in the following year, was the first to appreciate the real value and importance of this deposit of fossil fuel, which he then spoke of as a great national trust.

The small detached basins of the anthracite region have together an area of only 472 miles; but the immense aggregate thickness of the seams of coal, varying in different parts from fifty to one hundred feet, and estimated at an average of seventy feet for the whole, makes this wonderful region of greater value than Western coal-fields whose extent is measured by many thousands of square miles. Mr. P. W. Shaeffer, who has calculated the cubic content of these anthracite beds, estimates it to have been at the time when mining was commenced equal to 26,361,070,000 tons, from which one-half may be deducted for waste in mining and breaking for market, and for losses from faults and irregularities in the beds, giving of merchantable coal 13,180,535,000 tons. If from this we subtract the amount produced by the mines from 1820 to 1870, estimated at 206,666,325 tons, we had still in store at the latter date a supply of 25,000,000 tons a year, or more than the present rate of consumption, for 525 years. The large waste in mining this precious fuel is due in part to the difficulty in working seams of unusual thickness, often in highly inclined positions. Moreover, the loss in breaking and dressing for the market, which demands the anthracite in regularly assorted sizes, is very great, and the waste from these two causes amounts to about one-third the entire contents of the veins, while in Great Britain the average loss in mining and marketing ordinary coals is not over one-fifth. The great value of our American anthracite is due in part to its peculiar qualities, its hardness, density, purity, and smokelessness, which render it pre-eminently fit for domestic purposes and for iron smelting; but in part also to its geographical position. Its proximity to the Atlantic sea-board, which is almost destitute of coal, to our great cities and wealthy and populous districts, and, moreover, to some of the most important deposits of iron ore in the country, has already led to an immense development of mining in the anthracite region. The New England States, Eastern New York, New Jersey, and Eastern Pennsylvania look to it for their chief supplies of fuel; great systems of railways and canals have been called into existence by it; and a vast iron-producing industry has grown up, dependent upon the anthracite fields, which now furnish nearly one-half of all the coal mined in the United States. It results from the course of trade that large quantities of anthracite find their way westward by railways, canal-boats, and lake steamers, freights in that direction being very low at certain seasons of the year. Thus there were brought to

Buffalo in 1873 about three-quarters of a million of tons of anthracite, the greater part by railway, of which Chicago received over half a million, or nearly one-third of its entire coal supply. Smaller quantities of anthracite find their way down the Ohio River to Cincinnati and beyond.

The chief coal supply of the regions to the west of the meridian of Washington comes, however, from the great Appalachian basin, which, underlying much of the western half of Pennsylvania and of the eastern third of Ohio, West Virginia, and a part of Eastern Kentucky, stretches through Eastern Tennessee as far as Alabama, embracing an area of coal-bearing rocks estimated at nearly 58,000 square miles. Along the eastern border of this vast field of bituminous coal there are in Pennsylvania and in Maryland several small areas which furnish a semi-bituminous coal, intermediate in composition, as in position, between it and the anthracite of the East, and now very largely mined. The best known of these outlying basins are the Blossburg, on the north, and the Cumberland, in Maryland, on the south; but there are between these other similar areas of considerable importance, such as the Broad Top, Johnstown, Towanda, and Ralston, the production of the whole being about 5,000,000 tons of coal annually, of which nearly one-half comes from the Cumberland and about one-fifth from the Blossburg. This latter was first opened by a railway in 1840, while an outlet from the Cumberland field to the sea-board was established by the Baltimore and Ohio Railroad in 1842, thus bringing for the first time the bituminous coal of the interior to tide-water, and displacing in Eastern markets the coal of Virginia. These semi-bituminous coals, very rich in carbon, and yet possessing the property of coking in the fire, are much esteemed for iron-working and for generating steam, for which they are largely used on our railways and ocean steamers, besides which great quantities are converted into coke for iron smelting. These valuable coals, like the anthracite, are confined to small areas, and will be exhausted in a few years, or at most a few generations. The Cumberland basin, at its present rate of working, will not last thirty years, and the time is not far distant when both the anthracite and the semi-bituminous coals of Pennsylvania will become augmented in price from their rarity. Its geographical position has led us to mine and consume first the most valuable portion of our coal, which, under different circumstances, it would have been wise to have replaced in part by other and more abundant varieties.

In this connection it should be mentioned that on the southeastern border of the Appalachian coal-field, in Montgomery County, Virginia, are found small deposits of semi-bituminous and anthracite coals, both of good quality, which were mined to a considerable extent during the late civil war. Another area of anthracite demands our notice, which, like the coal of Richmond, Virginia, is outside of the great basin. It is situated in Rhode Island and Massachusetts, where it occupies an area estimated at not less than 500 square miles, and includes, in various parts already explored, beds of anthracite from ten to twenty feet in thickness. This coal-field was discovered in 1760, and attempts at working it were made as early as 1808. The geological peculiarities of the region, the somewhat broken condition of the coal, and, above all, the competition of the anthracite of Pennsylvania, have retarded its development, so that the total production was estimated in 1872 at 14,000 tons, being from a single mine at Portsmouth, Rhode Island, where this coal is employed for copper smelting. There is no doubt that this important field of anthracite will one day be found of great value to New England.

The supplies of true bituminous coal which are found in the great Appalachian field are practically inexhaustible, and the mining of it is rapidly assuming proportions second only to those of the regions along its eastern border, which it is destined before long to surpass in its production. The bituminous coals may be divided into three classes, close-burning or coking coals, free-burning splint or block coals, and cannel. Of these the former are the most abundant, and for the greater number of purposes are used in their raw state. Unlike the anthracite, however, they are not fitted for iron smelting and for many other metallurgical operations unless previously converted into coke, for the production of which they are not all equally adapted. While some are too sulphurous, others contain too much ash, are too poor in fixed carbon, or yield a coke deficient in weight and in solidity. In view of all these circumstances, the value of a superior coking coal is very great, and a striking example of this appears in the Pittsburg seam, as it is called, of Western Pennsylvania. This remarkable coal seam, to the south of the city whose name it bears, attains near Connelsville an unusual thickness, and yields a coke of unsurpassed quality, which is not only the foundation of the iron-smelting industry of the western part of the State, but finds its way in large quantities to Cleveland, Chicago, Cincinnati, and St. Louis, and even as far as Utah, where it is used to smelt the silver-lead ores of that region.

Pittsburg is at present the great centre of the Western coal trade, and in addition to the large amount consumed in its own manufactures, distributes coal in various directions by railway and river, sending vast quantities down the Ohio to supply the cities on its banks, and even to the Lower Mississippi. The amount of coal received at Pittsburg in 1872, in great part by the Monongahela, was over 115,000,000 bushels, which, at twenty-eight bushels to the ton, is considerably over 4,000,000 tons, and the annual increase for three years up to that time was at the rate of thirty-five per cent. To this we must add the amount of coke received, which doubled annually for the same three years, and equaled in 1872 nearly 44,000,000 bushels, the product from coking about 2,600,000 tons of coal. The total estimated production of bituminous coal for Pennsylvania in 1872 (including about 3,000,000 tons of semi-bituminous) was 10,442,000 tons, and if to this we add the 21,500,000 tons of anthracite, we shall find that this State alone furnished in that year more than two-thirds of all the coal mined in the United States. The figures from official sources fail to give the full amount of coal used for local consumption, but the entire production of the United States for 1873 is estimated by Macfarlane at not less than 50,000,000 tons. The check which all our industries, and especially the working of coal and iron, sustained throughout the year 1874 has produced a temporary falling off in production, so that the figures for 1872 and 1873 are really a fairer index of our progress than those of a later date.

Next in importance to that of Pennsylvania is the coal production of Ohio, which was estimated in 1872 at 4,400,000 tons. Owing to the want of proper railway communications the coal deposits of this State have as yet been but little worked. It is in Ohio that the free-burning splint or block coal (which appears to a limited extent in the Chenango Valley, on the western frontier of Pennsylvania) finds its greatest development. This coal, which is extensively mined in the adjacent parts of Ohio, chiefly in the valley of the Mahoning, is prized not only on account of its freedom from ash and sulphur, but from the fact that it can be directly used in the blast-furnace for smelting iron ores without previous coking, and it has given rise to an important iron industry in its vicinity. The supply in Northern Ohio is, however, limited, and it is rapidly becoming exhausted. A much more abundant deposit of a similar coal, under very favorable conditions for mining, has lately been made known farther southward in the State, in the Hocking Valley, where it is, moreover, accompanied by large beds of coking coal. The coal of Ohio is destined from its geographical position to become of great importance: lying on the northwest border of the Appalachian field, as the anthracite and semi-bituminous coals of Pennsylvania do upon its northeast border, it has to the north and west of it a vast, wealthy, and populous region, with growing industries, and demanding large and increasing supplies of coal.

The extension southward of the Appalachian coal-field through West Virginia and parts of Kentucky, Tennessee, and Alabama is known to abound in valuable beds of bituminous coal, which have lately attracted considerable attention. Since the opening of the Chesapeake and Ohio Railroad the coals from the valley of the Kanawha are finding their way, to some extent, to the seaboard and into Eastern markets, but with this exception the vast coal deposits of this great Southern region are as yet mined only to supply the limited local demands.

Among the important uses of bituminous coal is the manufacture of illuminating gas, for which purpose immense quantities of coal are distilled. The annual consumption for this purpose in the cities of New York and Brooklyn is estimated at about 400,000 tons. Those coals which yield large quantities of pure gas of high illuminating power are greatly prized. The Eastern cities are in part furnished with gas coal from Cape Breton, but the greater part of the coals for this purpose is got from Western Pennsylvania. Excellent gas coals are, however, obtained in Ohio and in West Virginia.

The State of Michigan includes a coal basin with an area of not less than 6700 square miles, but the beds of coal which it contains are few, thin, and of inferior quality. For this reason, and from the fact that the State is cheaply supplied with superior coals from Pennsylvania and Ohio, the coal of Michigan is worked only to a small extent for local consumption, the estimated production for 1872 being but 30,000 tons. The Illinois coal basin, which underlies the greater part of that State, and extends into the western parts of Indiana and Kentucky, has an area of not less than 47,000 square miles. Along its eastern and western borders in Clay County, Indiana, and near St. Louis, are found deposits of an excellent block coal like that of Ohio, adapted for iron smelting; but with this exception the coals of this great basin are generally sulphurous and inferior in quality, and command in the market of Chicago a price much below those of Pennsylvania and Ohio. Chicago received in 1873 over 1,600,000 tons of coal, of which about two-fifths only were from the adjacent coal-field, the remainder being brought from the two States just named. The first working of coal in Illinois dates from 1810, and the production of the State for 1872 was equal to 3,000,000 tons, while Indiana furnished 800,000, and that portion of the coal-field which lies in Western Kentucky 300,000 tons.

The coals of the great field west of the Mississippi, which extends through Iowa, Missouri, Kansas, and Arkansas, are mostly of inferior quality and in thin beds, but are of great local importance in these sparsely wooded regions. In the State of Arkansas, moreover, there is found a superior semi-bituminous coal, approaching to anthracite in its character. Further westward, in the Rocky Mountains and thence to the Pacific coast, from the confines of Mexico to Canada, are extensive deposits of tertiary coals or lignites, which, though inferior in quality to the coals of the Appalachian basin, are, in the absence of better fuel, employed for generating steam and for domestic purposes. They are, however, very variable in quality, and some beds have of late been found which are fit for the manufacture of illuminating gas, and are even capable of yielding a coke suitable for metallurgical processes. These coals are mined in Utah, Colorado, and Wyoming, and again on the Pacific coast in California, Oregon, and Washington Territory. Of the coal supply of San Francisco in 1873, which equaled 441,000 tons, about sixty per cent. came from these deposits along the western coast, the remainder being from Australia, England, and the Eastern States.

The petroleum industry of the United States was in its beginning closely connected with coal, since it was the production of oils from bituminous coals which led the way to the utilization of the native mineral oils. It had long been known that tar and oily matters could be extracted from coals and from shales impregnated with coaly matter by subjecting them to a high temperature, these substances, although not existing ready-formed in the coals, being generated by the decomposing action of heat. A product thus obtained was known to apothecaries more than a century ago by the name of British oil; and in 1834 experiments on a large scale were made in France by Selligue to manufacture illuminating oils by the distillation of shales, with partial success. In 1846 similar results were obtained by Gesner in New Brunswick; and in 1850 Atwood, of Boston, prepared a lubricating oil from coal-tar. At the same time Young, of Glasgow, was experimenting, and in 1850 introduced into the market, under the name of paraffine oil, a product from cannel-coal. The first works for this manufacture in the United States were established on Long Island in 1854, under Young's patents for manufacturing oils from the Boghead coal brought from Scotland, or from American coals. From this point the industry spread rapidly, and in 1855 and 1856 works for the distillation of oils from coals were erected in Kentucky, Ohio, and Pennsylvania, as well as along the Atlantic sea-board, where the principal material employed was the mineral from Scotland just named. In January, 1860, there were in the United States not less than forty factories, the total daily production of which was about five hundred barrels, chiefly of burning oil. This was sold in the market with the trade name of kerosene, or simply as coal oil; and lamps suitable for burning it having been devised, it became widely used. But this industry of the distillation of coal was destined to have a very short duration, for the oil wells of Pennsylvania, opened in 1859, furnished in 1860 not less than 500,000 barrels of petroleum—a production far exceeding that of the coal distilleries. It was soon found that from this mineral oil products could be extracted in all respects similar to those from coal, and the result was that from this time the manufacture of coal oil was abandoned, and the works which had been erected for this purpose were changed to petroleum refineries.

The early history of petroleum is curious. Known and employed for burning from remote antiquity in the Old World, no process for its purification had been devised, and it was therefore at best but an indifferent and cheaper substitute for animal and vegetable oils. The first attempts to refine it for commercial purposes are believed to have been made by Young, of Glasgow, in 1847, on petroleum got from Derbyshire, in England, from which he prepared a lubricating oil, and it was the exhaustion of this supply which led him to improve the methods for the extraction of oils from coal.

Meanwhile, in the United States, the existence of sources of mineral oil had been known to the Indians of New York and Pennsylvania, who prized it as a medicine, for which purpose it became familiar to the early European colonists under the name of Seneca-oil. It appears to have been an object of research to the aborigines ages ago, since in the oil regions of Western Pennsylvania are found pits or wells apparently dug for the purpose of collecting the oil, carefully timbered, and affording from the growth of the forest upon the site evidences of an antiquity of from 500 to 1000 years. As early as 1819, in boring for brine on the Muskingum River, in Ohio, from a depth of 400 feet were obtained large quantities of mineral oil, which was a source of great annoyance to the salt-makers. At this time attempts were made to use the oil for illumination, but, from the want of proper lamps, it was not found to be adapted to the purpose. In 1854 the successful manufacture of oils from coal caused attention to be drawn to the possibility of utilizing these native oils, and the Pennsylvania Oil Company was formed for the purpose of manufacturing the petroleum found at Oil Creek, in Venango County, Pennsylvania. The chemical investigation of the material was committed to Professor B. Silliman, Jun., and his report to the company, which appeared in April, 1855, has been the point of departure for the immense industry of petroleum which has grown up within the last twenty years. In this report was described the conversion of the crude petroleum by fractional distillation into products differing in density and in volatility, the manufacture from it of a burning oil of great illuminating power, of an oil capable of supporting a low temperature and fitted for lubrication, and also of paraffine. He farther showed the importance of distillation in a current of highly heated steam, and noticed the breaking up of heavier into lighter oils by continued heat—processes which have since assumed a great importance in the manufacture of petroleum.

Notwithstanding these remarkable results, little was effected for some years; the supply of petroleum was limited to that which could be gathered from the surface of the water in the locality, and from its cost it could not compete with the product of the distillation of coal. At length an attempt was made to repeat the early experiment of the Muskingum salt-works, and a well was bored by Drake, the superintendent of the Pennsylvania Oil Company, from which, at a depth of seventy-two feet, a supply of oil amounting to ten barrels or 400 gallons a day was obtained, which was sold for fifty-five cents a gallon. This was in August, 1859, and the successful trial was soon followed by many others not less so. The history of the wild excitement and speculation which followed this discovery, and the great accession of wealth to the region, is familiar to all. Wells were sunk which yielded from 100 to as much as 2000 barrels of oil daily, often without the labor of pumping. Of one well it is recorded that it afforded 450,000 barrels of oil in a little over two years, while another is said to have given not less than 500,000 barrels in a twelvemonth. Petroleum was soon discovered not only over a wide district in Pennsylvania, but in Eastern Ohio and in parts of West Virginia and Kentucky, and even in Indiana, as well as in Western Canada. In 1860 the production rose to 500,000 barrels of forty gallons each, and for the decade ending with 1870 it amounted to not less than 35,273,000 barrels of crude oil. Of this by far the greater part came from Pennsylvania, for of the 6,500,000 barrels produced in 1870, not less than 5,569,000 were from that State, the production of about 3000 wells, which is an average of only about five barrels daily for each well.

The wells in Venango County, where this industry began, were generally from 600 to 800 feet in depth, but with the partial exhaustion of these the scene of operations has been removed to more southern districts, where the oil supplies are found at greater depths; and the wells in Butler County, now the great seat of production, are from 1200 to 1500 feet deep. The crude oil is carried from the wells to the points of refining or of shipment through iron pipes. Some of these lines are fifteen and twenty miles in length, and one is in process of construction from Butler County to Pittsburg, a distance of about forty miles. It has even been proposed to convey the oil by a series of conduits and reservoirs across the mountains to Philadelphia.

The processes for refining the crude petroleum and preparing from it various commercial products have been perfected by much chemical skill. The loss in refining amounts to about ten per cent., and the average product of illuminating oil from the crude petroleum of Pennsylvania is about sixty-five per cent. The other products are dense lubricating oils, light naphthas, and paraffine or mineral wax, of which a barrel of crude cil yields about five pounds.

The abundance of the Pennsylvania petroleum and the skillful manner in which it is refined have led to a general exportation of these products to every part of the civilized world. Already in 1861 we find the shipments of petroleum from the United States to foreign ports equal to nearly 28,000 barrels of forty gallons each, and for the ten years ending with 1870 the exportation was 14,465,000 barrels. By far the greater part of this was shipped in the refined state, and its average price for the term of ten years was estimated at twenty-five cents a gallon, thus representing an aggregate value of over $144,000,000. The increase in the amount exported has been regular and constant. That for the calendar year 1870 was 3,495,800 barrels; for 1872, 3,754,060; for 1873, 5,937,041; and for 1874, 5,878,578 barrels, of which about nine-tenths were refined oil.

This large increase in the exports of 1873 and 1874 shows the very considerable augmentation in production which has followed late discoveries of new and productive oil districts in Pennsylvania. These have been attended by a great reduction in price. From fifty-five cents the gallon, at which the first crude oil from the wells was sold, it soon fell to twenty cents, and to sixty or seventy cents for the refined oil. In 1872 its price in New York had fallen below twenty-four cents, in 1873 to below nineteen, and in 1874 to a small fraction over thirteen cents, the crude oil in New York having fallen in the same three years from about thirteen to less than six cents the gallon. Of crude oil forty-three and a half gallons are counted to a barrel, yet its price in Western Pennsylvania in 1874 was from sixty to seventy-five cents a barrel at the wells, and from eighty cents to a dollar at the delivery pipes. Even at the present reduced prices the annual value of the petroleum product of the country is very great. The export for 1874, chiefly of refined oil, at the mean price of 13.09 cents the gallon, equals $30,825,268. The present annual consumption of the United States is estimated at 1,500,000 barrels of refined petroleum, which, added to the export for 1874, gives a total of 7,378,000 barrels of refined oil. The estimated production of crude oil for 1874 was not less than 10,687,930 barrels, or 29,282 daily. Already in 1870, when the production was considerably less than at present, it was said that the petroleum wells of the United States yielded in a week an amount of oil greater than the entire annual production of the whale-fisheries of New England at the time of their greatest prosperity. American petroleum has now almost entirely replaced the products of these fisheries, and furnished to the whole world a cheap and admirable means of illumination. Petroleum abounds in many parts of the Old World, but attempts to compete with the product of Pennsylvania have not hitherto been very successful. The same remark will apply to the petroleum found in Santa Barbara County, California, which is refined there to a limited extent for domestic use, and yields, besides a good burning oil, one peculiarly fitted for lubricating purposes.

We now proceed to notice the history of the iron industry of the United States, which is as yet confined to the region east of the Rocky Mountains, and must be considered in connection with the coal upon which it is to a great extent depėndent. The great supplies of iron ores to the east of the Appalachian coal-field are, first, from the beds, chiefly of the magnetic species, but occasionally of red hematite, which abound in the Adirondack region of New York, extending northward into Canada (which furnishes a considerable quantity of ore to the American market); while southward, in the mountain belt from the Highlands of the Hudson to South Carolina, are great deposits of similar ores, extensively mined in New York, New Jersey, and Pennsylvania. Within the eastern rim of the basin and parallel with it is, in the second place, a belt of iron ores, chiefly brown hematite, which is traced from Vermont along the western border of New England, and assumes a great development in parts of Pennsylvania, Virginia, Tennessee, and Alabama. Further westward, within the great basin, are found the red fossiliferous ores which lie near the summit of the Silurian series, and are traced from Wisconsin eastward through Ontario and Central New York, and thence southward, parallel with the Alleghanies and in proximity to the coal, through Pennsylvania, as far as Alabama. Besides these are to be considered the great deposits of iron ores belonging to the coal measures, including those of the lower carboniferous. These ores, which are carbonates and limonites, occasionally with red hematite, abound in Western Pennsylvania, Ohio, and West Virginia. They are wanting or rare in the middle and western coal-fields of the great basin; but between these, in Missouri and Arkansas, there rise from the thinly spread out paleozoic strata mountains of crystalline rocks, which include immense deposits of red hematite and magnetic ores of great value. Farther northward these crystalline rocks, with their metallic treasures, are concealed beneath newer strata, but they re-appear, charged with great quantities of these same species of iron ore, in the northern peninsula of Michigan, whence, sweeping eastward through Canada, the chain of crystalline rocks bearing these ores is continued to the Adirondack region of New York.

In the colonial period, and even during the first years of the republic, the smelting of iron ores was confined to the eastern rim of the great basin, and indeed the first furnaces erected were for the reduction of the limonite ores which occur in small deposits along the Atlantic border and outside of the limits above defined. We find an attempt to make iron at Jamestown, in Virginia, as early as 1619, and a little later a furnace was erected at Lynn, Massachusetts. As early as 1717 pig-iron was exported from the colonies to England, and the increase of the iron industry excited the jealousy of the British iron manufacturers, so that in 1750 an act of Parliament forbade the erection of rolling or slitting mills in the colonies. Before the time of the Revolution we find numerous blast-furnaces from Virginia as far as Western Massachusetts, smelting the limonites, and in New Jersey and Pennsylvania the magnetic ores of these regions.

A considerable portion of the iron of this early time was, however, made in bloomary furnaces, by means of which malleable iron is obtained directly from the ore, a method of no little interest in the history of our manufacture. A similar process belongs to the infancy of the metallurgic art, and is still practiced among barbarous nations, where the mode of making pig-iron in the blast-furnace is unknown. A modification of this direct method survives in the

Catalan forge of Western Europe, and in the last century another form was known in Germany, where it is now forgotten. The German bloomary furnace found its way to America, and was employed in New Jersey and Pennsylvania at least as early as 1725. This furnace had the great advantage that its construction required but little skill and little outlay. A small water-fall for the blast and the hammer, a rude hearth with a chimney, and a supply of charcoal and ore, enabled the iron-worker to obtain, as occasion required, a few hundred pounds of iron in a day's time in a condition fitted for the use of the blacksmith, after which his primitive forge remained idle until there was a farther demand. To this day such furnaces are found in the mountains of North Carolina, and furnish the bar-iron required for the wants of the rural population.

An interesting episode in the history of American iron manufacture is afforded by the attempts of the early explorers to utilize the black iron sand which is found at many points along our sea-board, from the Gulf of St. Lawrence to the Capes of the Chesapeake, and early in the last century, under the name of the Virginia sand iron, was the subject of unsuccessful attempts to treat it for the extraction of iron. At length the Rev. Jared Eliot, of Killingworth, Connecticut, grandson of John Eliot, the apostle of the Indians, after many experiments on the iron sand which is found in considerable quantities on the south coast of that State, succeeded by the aid of the German bloomary in resolving the problem, and made blooms of malleable iron of fifty pounds weight, for which discovery he was in 1761 awarded a medal by the Society of Arts of London. He informs us that his son had, moreover, been able to convert this iron into steel of superior quality, and would have established a manufactory of it but for the act of Parliament passed at that time prohibiting the production of steel in the colonies. It is curious to see this forgotten discovery brought up again in our day, and applied to these sands on the southern shore of Long Island, and more successfully at Moisie, in the Lower St. Lawrence. Still more worthy of note is it that this primitive bloomary furnace, discarded in Europe, has been improved by American ingenuity, enlarged, fitted with a hot blast, water *tuyères*, and other modern appliances, so that in the hands of skilled workmen in Northern New York it affords for certain ores an economical mode of making a superior malleable iron, of which about 50,000 tons are thus produced yearly. A large part of this product is consumed at Pittsburg for the manufacture of cutlery steel of excellent quality.

The first half century of the republic saw but little progress in the manufacture of iron, and the total amount produced in 1810 is estimated at only 54,000 tons, which is not equal to the present annual yield of four or five of our modern blast-furnaces. During this period charcoal was the only fuel employed, and the first great step in our iron manufacture was the use of anthracite. Attempts were made to employ a mixture of this fuel with charcoal at Mauch Chunk, Pennsylvania, in 1820, and at Kingston, Massachusetts, with the anthracite of Rhode Island, in 1827, but the way to the solution of the problem was finally prepared by the introduction of the hot blast in 1831, and in 1833 a patent was granted in the United States for the smelting of iron with anthracite by the aid of a blast of heated air. The first successful attempt to use anthracite alone in this country seems to have been in 1838, near Mauch Chunk, with a furnace twenty-one and a half feet high, producing two tons of iron daily. From this the industry spread, and in 1840 there were six furnaces employing this fuel, and making each from thirty to fifty tons weekly of pig-iron. To-day our anthracite furnaces are many of them sixty and even eighty feet in height, producing from 250 to 300 tons of iron in a week. Of 680 furnaces in the United States in 1873, 226 consumed anthracite, and produced nearly one-half of all the pig-iron made.

From its purity, hardness, and ability to resist the weight of the charge, this fuel is unrivaled for the purpose of iron smelting. This coal supplies the furnaces of Eastern Pennsylvania and New Jersey, and to a great extent those of Eastern New York and of Maryland; but as we approach the central region of Pennsylvania its use is gradually replaced by that of charcoal and of coke from the semi-bituminous coals, while further westward the coke of the true bituminous coals, of which that of Connelsville is the type, is the principal fuel, until we reach the western border of the great Appalachian field, where, in Ohio, are found the free-burning splint or block coals, which can be used in the smelting furnace in the raw state either alone or with an admixture of coke. The ores of the coal measures of Southern Ohio, known as the Hanging Rock district, have hitherto been smelted with charcoal, which is now being replaced by the block coal of the region. Similar coals on the eastern and western borders of the Illinois coal-field are also used for iron smelting.

The relations of the ore to the fuel are of great importance to the development of the iron industry. Thus of the ores of Lake Superior a small portion only is smelted with charcoal in the region, and by far the greater part is brought southward by the lakes—some to Chicago to be smelted with the coal of Indiana, and much more to Cleveland, where it is met by the block coal of Ohio, and in still larger quantities is carried southward to the mines of this coal, chiefly in the Chenango and Mahoning valleys, or as far as Pittsburg, to be smelted with the coke of that region. In like manner the rich ores of Missouri find their way to the block coals of Indiana, to Southeastern Ohio, and even to Pittsburg, filling the returning vessels which have gone down the Ohio River laden with coal. In the East the iron furnaces consuming anthracite are not directly in the coal region, but scattered through the eastern part of Pennsylvania, and the adjacent portions of Maryland, New Jersey, and New York, sometimes, moreover, at points more or less remote from the ore beds which supply them. In the valley of the Hudson the anthracite comes half-way to meet the rich ores of Lake Champlain, and even on the shores of this lake may be seen large blast-furnaces smelting the ores of the vicinity with the help of the anthracite brought as back freight by the vessels carrying the supplies of ore southward. The ores from the crystalline rocks, on account of their greater richness, can support the cost of a longer freight than the poorer ores found within the paleozoic basin, and they have, moreover, the advantage in many cases of yielding a purer iron. The early manufacturers of Bessemer steel in this country were under the necessity of bringing their supplies of pig-iron from Cumberland, in England, and ores have even been brought from Spain and Algeria to be smelted with anthracite for the manufacture of Bessemer pig metal. Recently, however, it has been found that by careful selection the crystalline ores from our Eastern regions may be made to yield a pig-iron suitable for this purpose, while the region beyond the Alleghanies gets its supply of Bessemer metal from the ores of Lake Superior or of Missouri. The iron ore shipped from the northern peninsula of Michigan in 1873 amounted to 1,178,879 gross tons, in addition to about 100,000 tons smelted in the region. This, at an average of sixty per cent. of metal, equals considerably more than one-fourth of the total iron product of the country.

The history of the growth of the iron manufacture in the United States within the last fifty years exhibits a remarkable progress. From a production of 54,000 tons in 1810, it had become 165,000 tons in 1830, 347,000 tons in 1840, and 600,000 tons in 1850, as near as can be estimated. In 1860, it had reached 919,870; in 1870, 1,865,000; and in 1872, 2,880,070 tons; while the diminished production of 1873, 2,695,434 tons, shows already the effect of the depression under which the iron interest of the country still suffers. Of the production of 1873, very nearly one-half was made in Pennsylvania, and not less than 1,249,673 tons with anthracite, while the total amount of charcoal-made pig-iron was only 524,127 tons, to which is to be added 50,000 tons of malleable iron made by the direct process in bloomaries. The importation of foreign iron and steel for 1872 was 795,655 tons; for 1873, 371,164 tons; and for 1874, less than 200,000 tons. From the figures for 1872 and 1873 we may conclude that the consumption in the United States was then equal to about 3,500,000 tons of iron yearly.

The great demand for iron in this country for the purposes of railway construction, together with the high prices in Great Britain in 1872 and 1873, led to a large increase in the number of blast-furnaces. In the two years just named eighty-three furnaces, some of them among the largest in the country, were finished and put into blast, and the whole number in operation in the autumn of 1873 was estimated at 636, having a capacity of producing not less than 4,371,277 tons of pig-iron, while a later estimate from the same source, the American Iron and Steel Association, gives in July, 1874, a capacity of 4,500,000 tons, or about 1,000,000 more than the greatest consumption yet reached. Even at the previous rate of increase, many years must elapse before the country can consume such an amount of iron, and with the general prostration of business, and especially of the iron trade, in 1874, we are not surprised to find that a very large proportion of these furnaces is now out of blast, and that the selling price of pig-iron at the beginning of 1875 was below that at which it could be made at some of the furnaces. For the future the iron manufacturers of our country must strive for progress not only in the selection of ores and fuels, but in improvements in the construction and the management of furnaces, in all of which directions great economies remain to be effected, as the results obtained in late years by the skill and high science of British iron-masters abundantly show. In this way we may hope before long to rival not only in quality but in cheapness the iron products of other countries. With the boundless resources of coal and iron which our country affords, it is only a question of how soon we can successfully contend with Great Britain in foreign markets. The entire iron production of the world was in 1856 about 7,000,000 tons, and in 1874 it was estimated at 15,000,000 tons, of which, at both of these periods, about one-half was furnished by Great Britain. It is supposed by Mr. A. S. Hewitt that at the end of the century the demand will amount to not less than 25,000,000 tons. The present immense production is already taxing heavily the resources of England, which obtains a large proportion of its purer ores from foreign countries, and a period will soon be reached when she can no longer meet the world's increasing demand, for the supply of which no other country offers advantages comparable with the United States. The day is therefore not far distant when, in the words of Mr. Hewitt, all rivalry between the two nations in iron production must pass away.

So long as the business of iron smelting was prosperous, and the profits were, as has been the case for the past few years in most parts of the country, very large, considerations of economy in the production of iron were too much neglected, but for the future all this must be changed. It is probable that before long we shall see some of the old furnaces and furnace sites abandoned, and a transfer of capital and skilled labor from many of the present centres of production to points where iron can be made at lower rates. Questions of freight of the raw materials will be closely considered, and new fields will be sought where the associations of ores of iron with coal suitable for smelting them will enable pig-iron to be produced more cheaply than where both the ore and the fuel are brought from afar. In districts like Fayette County and the Johnstown and Broad Top coal-fields in Pennsylvania, and along the western outcrop of the great Appalachian coal-field in Eastern Ohio, where the characteristic iron ores of the coal measures are more abundant than farther eastward, and are accompanied with coals suitable for their reduction, these conditions for the cheap production of iron exist. While the ores thus found in proximity to the coal are adapted for the production of all the ordinary qualities of iron, the increasing export of coal from this western border to the regions northward and westward permits the bringing back at low rates of freight of the rich ores of Missouri and Michigan, which are adapted to the making of Bessemer steel. The southward extension of this great coal-field into West Virginia, Eastern Kentucky and Tennessee, and Northern Alabama also offers great facilities for the cheap manufacture of iron from native ores, which will at no distant day be utilized.

The copper mines of the United States next claim our attention. Throughout the crystalline rocks which form the eastern border of the paleozoic basin ores of this metal are pretty abundantly distributed, and are now mined and treated for the extraction of the copper in Vermont, Pennsylvania, North Carolina, and Eastern Tennessee, besides which ores from other localities along this belt, and from various regions to the westward of the great basin, are brought to Baltimore and to the vicinity of Boston for reduction. The total production from all these sources, which has never been greater than at present, is, however, estimated at less than 2500 tons—an amount inconsiderable when compared with the production of the mines of Lake Superior. In these, unlike the mines just mentioned, and, indeed, unlike most others in the world, the copper, instead of being in the condition of an ore—that is to say, mineralized and disguised by combination with sulphur or with oxygen and other bodies, from which it must be separated by long and costly chemical processes—is found in the state of pure metal, and needs only to be mechanically separated from the accompanying rocky matters previous to melting into ingot copper. The history of the copper region on the south shore of Lake Superior is famous in the annals of American mining. The metal, which in many cases is found in masses of all sizes up to many tons in weight, was known and used by the aboriginal races, and the traces of their rude mining operations are still met with. The first modern attempts at extracting this native copper, in 1771, were unsuccessful, and it was not until 1843 that the attention of mining adventurers was again turned toward this region. Numerous mines were opened, and a period of reckless speculation followed, which ended, in 1847, in the failure and abandonment of nearly all the enterprises which had been begun. They were, however, soon resumed under wiser management, and have been followed up with remarkable success. At first the operations were chiefly directed to the extraction of the great masses of native copper which were found distributed in an irregular manner in veins or fissures in the rocks, and yielded in some cases large profits; but with the exhaustion of these a more abundant and regular source of supply has been found in layers of a soft earthy material, known as ash beds, containing metallic copper finely disseminated, or in beds of a conglomerate of which pure copper forms the cementing material. The successful working of these two kinds of deposits has been arrived at only by well-directed skill in management, and by mechanical appliances which diminish the costs of mining, crushing, and washing the rock, and reduce to a minimum the inevitable loss of copper in the waste material. No mining industry illustrates more strikingly than this the importance of such economies. A rock which may be made to yield one part in a hundred of metallic copper can, under favorable conditions, be treated with profit, and the residue in such a case may still contain one-half as much more copper, which is lost. A mine in this region a few years since yielded annually, from the treatment of 1,200,000 tons of rock, 800 tons of metallic copper, being at the rate of two-thirds of one per cent., and this amount, at the price of copper then prevailing, was just sufficient to pay all the costs of extraction. The residues showed by assay the presence, in a finely divided state, of as much more copper, and it is evident that a greater perfection in the process of extraction, by which one-half of the copper thus lost could have been saved, would have yielded 400 tons additional, which, inasmuch as the costs of mining, crushing, and washing were already paid by the first 800 tons, would have been clear profit. One of the best-known mines in the region, which has been worked with continued success since its opening, in 1849, produced, in 1872, 1138 tons of fine copper, to obtain which over 100,000 tons of rock were mined, and over 60,000 tons of this selected for stamping and washing, so that the copper yielded was only 1.12 per cent., yet the profits of the year's working were $200,000. It would be foreign to our plan to describe modes of treatment, but statements of results like this serve to show what may be obtained by the application of skill and science to mining industry. At the Calumet and Hecla mine, the most remarkable one of the Lake Superior region, from 700 to 800 tons of rock are now treated daily, and yield about four per cent. of metallic copper, which, when converted into ingots, costs about thirteen cents the pound —a price far below that at which it can be extracted from the less rich deposits of the region or from the ores of the metal by the ordinary process of smelting. This mine produced of ingot copper, in 1872, 9717 tons, and in 1874, 9918 tons, of 2000 pounds. The crude copper from these mines, as delivered to the refiners, who melt it into ingots, yields on an average about eighty per cent. of metal—a fact to be borne in mind in consulting the statements of production, which are generally given for the unrefined product. The amount of copper yielded by the Lake Superior region from its opening, in 1845, to 1858 is estimated at 18,000 tons. From about 4100 tons in the latter year the production has shown a progressive increase, with some slight fluctuations, to the present time. It equaled, for 1873, 18,514 tons, and for 1874 not less than 22,235 tons, making an aggregate for the past thirty years of 217,134 tons, which at eighty per cent. equals 173,704 tons of ingot copper. The total yield of ingot copper for the lake region in 1874 is estimated by Caswell at 17,327 tons, to which he adds for the production from the ores of the metal 2375 tons, making a total production for the United States of 19,702 tons of copper. This exceeds considerably the domestic consumption, and accordingly we find that there were exported in 1874 not less than 4500 tons of copper. The supply of native copper from the mines of the lake region will probably continue to increase, and in years to come the working of the great deposits of copper ores which abound both in the Eastern and Western portions of our country will add largely to the production, so that henceforth the United States is destined to furnish considerable quantities of copper to foreign markets. The price of this metal is subject to remarkable fluctuations. Thus from fifty-five cents the pound in 1864 it gradually fell to nineteen in 1870, rising again to forty-five cents in 1872, and, falling once more to nineteen in the summer of 1874, rose to twenty-four cents at the close of the year.

It yet remains to speak of our mines of gold and silver. Although gold is distributed in greater or less quantity throughout the mountain ranges which form the eastern rim of the great basin, its presence was not made known till 1799, when it was discovered in the soil in Cabarrus County, North Carolina. For the next twenty-five years small quantities of gold were gathered by washing from the earth at various points from the Potomac to Alabama; but it was not until 1825 that the precious metal was found in veins of quartz both in North Carolina and Virginia. The whole amount of gold got from this Southern region up to 1827 is estimated at only $110,000; but with the opening of the gold-bearing veins a rapid increase in production took place, and in 1837 branch mints were established by the government in North Carolina and in Georgia, where they existed up to the time of the late civil war; before which, however, the gold production of the region had greatly fallen off, these mines having been deserted for the richer ones of the western coast. The whole amount of gold from this region for three-quarters of a century up to 1873 is estimated at about $20,000,000; but for the last year mentioned it amounted only to $160,000, the chief part of which was from North Carolina.

The great supply of precious metals has come from the western half of our territory. The vast region from the eastern base of the Rocky Mountains to the Pacific presents geographical features very different from those of the great Eastern paleozoic basin. Its numerous nearly parallel mountain ranges, to which the collective name of the Cordilleras has been applied, are rich in mineral treasures, which, as pointed out by Blake and by King, may be described as arranged in parallel zones, coinciding with the mountain belts. Along the Pacific coast range are deposits of quicksilver, tin, and chrome, while the belt of the Sierra Nevada and the Cascades carries a range of copper mines near its base, and a line of gold-bearing veins and gold alluvions on its western flank. Along the eastern slope of the Sierra lies a zone of silver mines stretching into Mexico, and including the great Comstock lode of Nevada, while silver ores abound in the subordinate ranges between the Sierra and the Wahsatch. The silver-lead ores of New Mexico, Utah, and Western Montana, and the still more eastern gold deposits of New Mexico, Colorado, Wyoming, and Montana, follow the same general law of distribution. We can, within our present limits, do little more than note some of the principal points in the history of the opening of these mining regions, and give some figures which serve to show the vast mineral wealth of the Cordilleras.

The gold of California was noticed by early Spanish explorers, and was again discovered on the Colorado River, just a century since, in 1775, but attracted no attention till its rediscovery early in 1848, when the existence of very rich gold alluvions was made known. A rapid immigration to the region at once followed, and it was reported in August of that year that the daily production of gold was from $30,000 to $50,000. It was not until 1851 that the gold-bearing veins were discovered, and the larger part of the gold of California has been got from the placers, as the alluvions are called. It is from the partial exhaustion of these that the production has of late years considerably diminished. In 1848 it was estimated at $10,000,000, and reached its maximum of $65,000,000 in 1853. In 1870 it had fallen to $25,000,000, and reached $19,000,000 in 1873, but rose again in 1874 to $20,300,000. The total yield, since the opening of the mines in 1848, amounts to more than $1,000,000,000. The working of the gold-bearing veins and of the deeper alluvions or placers has of late been systematized and greatly improved, and from the abundance and richness of these, and the persistence of the veins in depth, this region may be expected to produce great amounts of gold for generations to come.

From California explorations were soon carried both northward and eastward, and in addition to the gold of Oregon, Idaho and Washington Territories, the vast silver deposits of Nevada were made known. It was in 1859 that silver ore was first discovered on what has since been known as the Comstock lode—a vein which, viewed in the light of recent developments, is one of the most remarkable known in the history of mining. This lode, of great breadth, has been traced for a length of over five miles, and worked for more than four miles, in some places to a depth of 1500 feet. The ore has not been rich, seldom yielding over fifty dollars to the ton, and often less than one-half that amount, yet such has been its abundance that the production of the vein from its first working, in 1860, up to 1868 was $81,500,000, and up to the close of 1874 it had yielded a total amount of about $180,000,000, with very large profits to the miners. The bullion extracted from these ores contains an amount of gold equal to about one-third of the entire value. Other silver producing districts, second only in importance to that of Virginia City, which is the site of the Comstock lode, have since been discovered in Nevada, and the value of the bullion from the State in 1872 amounted to not less than $25,000,000, of which $13,500,000 were from this lode. For the calendar year 1873 it equaled $31,666,000, of which $21,756,000 were from Virginia City; and the returns for the first half of 1874 showed a still increasing production. During the latter months of that year remarkable discoveries were announced in the Comstock lode, which surpassed all previous developments in that region. An enormous mass of ore, in great part below a depth of 1500 feet, was exposed, far richer than any thing hitherto found in the lode, and said to yield an average of many hundred dollars to the ton. Some of the published estimates of the value of this discovery were probably exaggerated, but there seems little doubt that the amount of treasure revealed exceeded the whole production of the lode up to that time.

The existence of silver-bearing lead ores in Utah was known as early as 1863, but the first attempt to develop them was made in 1870, when a few thousand tons of ore were shipped from the Emma mine eastward over the Union Pacific Railroad. In 1872, however, the production of this region had reached a value of $3,250,000; in 1873, of $3,750,000; and in 1874, very nearly $6,000,000. The ores are in great abundance, but are often not rich enough to support the cost of transportation, while, on the other hand, the rarity and high price of fuel render their treatment on the spot very costly. The average value of the ores exported, chiefly to the eastern and western sea-boards, in 1873 was $115 a ton, besides which a large quantity was reduced in the region, yielding what is called base bullion, that is, lead carrying silver and some gold, and valued at from $200 to $250, the lead being there estimated at about $50 the ton. In some establishments in Utah the precious metals are extracted from the lead before shipment. The fuel there used is in part charcoal and in part coke sent from Pennsylvania. The lead furnished to the United States markets from the silver-lead ores of Utah and Nevada in 1874 is estimated at 26,000 tons, while the lead production of Missouri was 15,000, and that of Iowa, Illinois, and Wisconsin only 5500 tons.

The silver production of the United States was altogether insignificant until 1861, when the Comstock lode gave $2,000,000 of silver, since which time there has been a steady increase to $36,500,000 in 1873, giving a total production of $189,000,000. It is probable that for some years to come the supply of silver from the mines of the Cordilleras will be much greater than in the past. Already within the last four years the immense production of silver in this country has considerably reduced its price in the markets of the world, and the effect of recent discoveries can not fail to be a still farther depreciation of its value.

The history of the mining of our gold and silver would be imperfect without a notice of the quicksilver of California, as it is by its aid that nearly the whole of these precious metals, with the exception of the silver of the lead ores, is extracted. Quicksilver ore was discovered in California as early as 1849, and the mines opened soon after have not only continued to supply the wants of the immense gold and silver industry of the West, but since 1852 have furnished large quantities for exportation to Mexico, South America, China, and Australia. This amounted in 1865 to 44,000 flasks of seventy-six and a half pounds each, or 3,366,000 pounds of quicksilver. The increased demand for this metal for the treatment of our silver ores, and the diminished production of the mines, have since reduced considerably the exportation. In no other region of the globe, however, is the ore of quicksilver so widely distributed as in California, and there is reason to believe that from the opening and working of new deposits the production will soon be much increased—a result which will be stimulated by the present high price of quicksilver and its scarcity in foreign markets.

We have noticed the falling off in the yield of gold from California which began in 1853. It was not until 1860 that supplies of this metal from other districts appeared, rising from $1,000,000 in that year to $28,000,000 in 1866, since which time there has been a gradual falling off from these also, so that while for 1873 the gold of California equaled $19,000,000, that from other sources in the Western United States was $17,000,000, making a production of $36,000,000, that of the entire world being estimated at $100,000,000. Dr. R. W. Raymond, to whom we are indebted for these figures, gives the entire gold product of the country from 1847 to 1873 inclusive at $1,240,750,000; and if to that we add his calculation of the silver produced up to that date, equal to $189,000,000, we shall have $1,429,750,000. Adding to this the figures for 1874, which exceed a little those of 1873, we have a grand total of over $1,500,000,000 of gold and silver as the production of the territory between the eastern base of the Rocky Mountains and the Pacific since the opening of the mines of California in 1847.

There are many mineral resources in the United States besides those already mentioned which might justly claim a place in a sketch like the present. Among them are the ores of chrome, zinc, lead, and nickel, now extensively mined; the extensive salt deposits in New York, Michigan, Pennsylvania, Ohio, Virginia, and West Virginia, which now supply to a great extent the markets of the country; the mineral phosphates of the vicinity of Charleston, South Carolina, which are not only manufactured into fertilizers for domestic consumption, but largely exported to Great Britain; and the granites, marbles, sandstones, roofing slates, and other materials of construction, which are now the objects of large and profitable industries. We have, however, selected, in preference to any of these, coal, petroleum, iron, copper, silver, and gold, which, from their great pecuniary value and their direct connection with material progress, have been among the most important elements in our national growth and prosperity.

VI.

COMMERCIAL DEVELOPMENT.

WHOEVER desires to understand the commerce of this and other lands, and to perceive its true order and meaning, must first consider what words stand for—what commerce and manufactures really are in their simplest form. One to whom the word "manufactures" brings only the conception of vast factories for the working of cotton, wool, or iron has but the faintest idea of what constitute the true manufactures of the nation; and one to whom the word "commerce" brings up only the image of an ocean steam-ship laden with goods and wares from distant ports, or a train of cars drawn by a powerful engine bearing many tons of merchandise to far-away places, has an equally faint impression of the vast scope even of our inland traffic.

Commerce is an occupation in which men serve each other; it is an exchange in which both parties in the transaction gain something which they desire more than the thing they part with. It may sometimes be that the desire which is satisfied on the one part or the other is one that had better not be served: that is a question of morals with which we are not now dealing. Such exchanges are, however, the exception. The traffic in commodities that work permanent injury constitutes but an insignificant proportion of the vast exchanges of the world; true commerce in useful things lies at the very foundation of human welfare. Unless a good and wholesome subsistence is possible there can be neither spiritual, intellectual, nor æsthetic culture, and such a subsistence is only possible to the mass of men by means of an exchange of products. All commerce is the aggregate of small transactions. The milkman who brings the daily portion of milk to him who dwells in city or town represents a commerce of vast proportion, almost equal in this country, in its aggregate value, to the whole sum of our foreign importations. The value of dairy products consumed in the United States or exported in the form of cheese and butter is more than four hundred million dollars. The milkman is the representative of one of the branches of commerce which has grown to this vast proportion during the century, and in which the people of the United States have shown the greatest originality. The cheese factory represents a manufacture born of thrift and enterprise only, and our exports of cheese exceed ninety million pounds a year.

How little the true function of commerce has been understood may be proved by the fact that only within the century has it been admitted among English-speaking people that there can be any mutual service in the matter. In this country even to this day this truth is but obscurely perceived, and hence the nation with which we have our largest transactions, our mother country, is often called our natural enemy by otherwise intelligent persons, because she tries to supply some of our needs at a low cost to us; yet had the true nature of commerce been comprehended a hundred years ago, war between us and England would have been as impossible then as it would now be infamous and absurd. It was a want of knowledge as to the true function of trade that caused the Revolution.

The year 1776 witnessed the publication of two documents of very great importance to the welfare of humanity, one of a purely public character—the Declaration of Independence of the United States of America; the other, the work of a single man, a poor Scotch professor, a treatise on the causes of the wealth of nations, by Adam Smith. It may be affirmed almost with certainty that had the book been printed fifty years earlier, the Declaration of Independence would never have been issued, because the wrongs which made it necessary would have been remedied without resort to war. Had the simple principle of mutuality of service been accepted, had it only become a part of the common knowledge of the English and the colonists that all commerce, whether among the people of the same state or between different states and nations, only exists and can only be maintained because it is profitable and beneficial to both parties, no English ministry could have been supported in the measures which were undertaken to prevent the establishment of manufactures and to restrict the commerce of America. It was the enforcement of these measures through a long series of years that gradually sapped the allegiance of the people of America, and finally led to the violent resistance of acts of minor importance, which in themselves would have been insufficient to provoke rebellion. The colonists were ready to pay money, but resisted the perversion of the power of taxation.

Viewed from a commercial stand-point, the war of the Revolution, therefore, was a terrible blunder, caused by a series of erroneous theories as to the true nature and function of trade on the part of the English statesmen who had controlled the government of Great Britain during the previous century.

They were imbued with the false idea that in commerce what one nation gained another must lose, and their policy in dealing with their colonies was controlled by the same false assumption. Their great navigators had been many of them only buccaneers under another name, their merchants and ship-owners found no infamy in the slave-trade, and their conquests in the East had begun in motives of personal and selfish aggrandizement. Throughout their history it had become apparent only to a few obscure students or to one or two enlightened merchants that there could be greater gain in liberty than in restriction or slavery. How much of the true spirit of liberty our Puritan ancestors gained from the Dutch among whom they dwelt so many years might be a question well worth investigating. The policy of the rulers of England in regard to their own people was of the same character as toward us, and it may not be charged against them that they enforced upon us any more injurious or unjust measures than they inflicted upon themselves. To the student of political science no lesson is more clearly indicated by the acts of Great Britain during the eighteenth century than the extreme danger and unfitness of restricting the control of government and the right of suffrage to the possessors of property only. Through a long series of years England was governed by those whose claim to rule was based mainly upon the possession of property; during this period war was chronic, the profession of arms the one that gave the most influence and distinction, and the theory of government was the rule of the few for the alleged protection of the many, but the result was the privation of the many and the aggrandizement of the few.

The profession of the merchant and the tradesman was considered ignoble, and many of the great commercial and manufacturing cities were not represented in the government. Even the rude lesson imposed upon England by the success of the American colonies in achieving their independence was not at once comprehended, and for fifty years more she struggled with economic error, and under a false system of social philosophy sought to regulate and control the commerce of the world by restrictive statutes, carrying on gigantic wars, and burdening the English nation with the larger part of that enormous debt which even to this day retards its progress, and is one of the main causes of the poverty of so large a portion of the inhabitants of the British Isles. Not until 1824, or nearly fifty years after the publication of the *Wealth of Nations*, did its truths become so well understood as to cause even the beginning of reform; at that date, under the lead of Huskisson, began the series of changes which have relieved English commerce from the shackles of meddlesome legislation, but only within ten years has even her commerce been truly free and prosperous. In 1820 there were over two thousand acts on the statute-book of Great Britain unrepealed, which had been enacted at various dates for the regulation of commerce.

It seems passing strange that England should have maintained her false theories in the face of such evidence as was presented in the history of the Dutch Republic. A century before Adam Smith's work was published the great merchant of London, Sir Josiah Child, gave his list of reasons why the Dutch were more prosperous than the English. His reasons sound strangely modern, and are even in advance of our thought. He gave them in the following order:

Firstly. "They," the Dutch, "have in their greatest councils of state *trading merchants* that have lived abroad in most parts of the world, by whom laws and orders are contrived and *peaces* projected, to the great advantage of all men."

Have the United States yet learned this first rule of prosperity during our first century of life as a nation?

Secondly. "Their law of *gavelkind*, whereby all the children possess an equal share of their father's estate."

Thirdly. "Their exact making of all their native commodities, and packing of their herrings, cod-fish, and all other commodities."

Fourthly. "Their giving great encouragement and immunities to the inventors of new manufactures and the discoverers of new mysteries of trade, and to those that shall *bring* the commodities of other nations first in use and practice among them."

Fifthly. "Their contriving and building of great ships to sail with small charges."

Sixthly. "Their parsimonious and thrifty living."

Seventhly. "The education of their children, as well daughters as sons; all which, be they of never so great quality or estate, they always take care to bring up with perfect good hands, and to have the full knowledge of arithmetic and merchants' accounts; and in regard the women are as knowing therein as the men, it doth encourage their husbands to hold on to their trades to their dying days, knowing the capacity of their wives to get in their estates or carry on their trades after their death."

Eighthly. "The lowness of their customs and the height of their excise, which last is certainly the most equal and indifferent tax in the world."

Ninthly. "The careful providing for and employing the poor."

Tenthly. "Their use of banks, which are of so immense advantage."

Eleventhly. "Their toleration of different opinions in matters of religion."

Twelfthly. "Their *law-merchant*, by which all controversies between merchant and tradesman are decided in three or four days."

Thirteenthly. "Their law for the transference of bills of debt from one man to another."

Fourteenthly. "Their keeping of public registers of all lands and houses sold and mortgaged."

Lastly. "The lowness of interest on money with them."

The jealousy on the part of England of the prosperity of the Dutch had, prior to the date of the last publication by Sir Josiah Child in 1691, caused them to enact the navigation laws, and these laws had then already caused two wars, as the result of which the first funded debt of Great Britain took form. The same jealousy continued, and the same ignorance of the true theory of trade led to the enforcement of the navigation acts and the restrictions upon the trade of the American colonies. Resistance ensued, and the colonies became a nation. But the people of the mother country failed yet to see the error of their system, and again attempted to enforce the same bad laws against us, thus leading again to the last war with Great Britain. At last, slowly and surely, the English people learned the lesson that the malign effect of such restriction was as injurious to themselves as to the people whom these acts had made their enemies. One by one they were repealed, and with each repeal England went onward toward the end she had failed to compass before. In liberty she has supremacy over every sea.

We also have succeeded in what we aimed at; we have maintained our navigation laws; but our ships are few and scattered, our steam marine has mainly existed through subsidies, and our flag is unknown in harbors and cities where the flag of other nations daily comes and goes at the mast-head of a gallant ship or a noble steamer.

We have the lesson yet to learn. A hundred years hence, by which time it is to be hoped the people of this nation will have intelligently grasped the simple theory of trade, it is not to be doubted that the declaration of principles by Adam Smith will be recognized as of supreme importance to the human race, while the Declaration of Independence will be looked upon even by the citizens of this country only as an important incident in the history of the Anglo-Saxon people, and the war which then ensued will be proved and acknowledged to have been caused mainly by a want of knowledge of that economic science of which Adam Smith was the first great expounder. If the people of this nation could but now respond to the grand forecasting of that true and humane statesman W. E. Forster, who lately visited us, and form an Anglo-Saxon alliance for the liberty of commerce, for the repression of slavery, for the doing away of privateering or piracy upon the seas, the end of all war among civilized people would be at hand, and the grand vision of the prophet would be realized—"They shall beat their swords into plowshares, and their spears into pruning-hooks."

To him who shall among us succeed in making this vision a grand and living truth will come deserved fame as great as ever yet belonged to any one among us; but that good time has not yet come, and will not come until the simplest principles of political science are made a part of common education.

We do not undervalue the Declaration of Independence when we recognize the fact that the vast material progress in this country during the century now about ending has ensued from only a partial realization of the principles of liberty therein contained. Our fathers threw off the fetters of British domination, but continued the restrictions of English thought, and they thus hampered themselves and us from within with the very trammels they had resisted from without.

It was not until the framing of the Constitution in 1787, and the adoption of the provision that no State should enact any law restricting commerce between the States, that even a true union was established.

Never before that time had commerce upon a grand scale, and through vast regions differing widely in soil, climate, and condition, been freed from restriction. And because of this partial liberty has the material welfare of the people of this country been so well assured as to blind them to the evils of the system that has prevented an extension of our foreign commerce on an equally grand and profitable scale. Although the framers of the Constitution itself may not have fully comprehended the importance of this act, or the truly scientific basis on which they built, they did so organize and assure a system of absolute free trade between the States that even the corruption of slavery failed to break the union.

The Union exists to-day partly because the people of the West would not permit the traffic of the great Southern water-way of the continent to be under the control of a foreign nation, lest it should be obstructed by custom-houses. When they presently realize the other fact that it is as important to them to have the traffic of the great Northern water-way through Canada as free from obstruction as the Southern water-way now is, another onward step will be taken, and another barrier to our full prosperity will fall—not this time, however, by violent means.

In treating the subject of our commercial progress during the past century, it is not worth while to waste time and space upon mere commercial statistics which any one may compile, but rather to note the changes in policy and method that have occurred, and to see how far we are behind the position we might have held had we not been in some measure blinded to our opportunity by the very ease with which we have achieved great though but partial success.

As was once said of the policy of Austria in its treatment of Hungary, the bad line of custom-houses with which we have surrounded ourselves has caused us "to be smothered in our own grease." Long anterior to the year 1776 the infant manufactures of America had come into existence, and had obtained such a vigorous growth as to cause the utmost jealousy in the mother country. In 1750 the production of iron and steel and the manufacture of steel tools and iron wares had become so well established in America as to induce hostile legislation, and England prohibited the erection of rolling-mills and steel furnaces, and attempted to stop the domestic commerce in and the export of their products. This was one of the many acts which culminated in the separation of the colonies from England. The records of the owners of the Cornwall Iron Mountain, in Pennsylvania, prove the working of the ores long anterior to the Revolution, and one of the carefully treasured documents now preserved in the office of the mine is the account current between the former owners and the commissary-general of the patriot army, wherein they are credited by the government with shot and shell, and charged with Hessian prisoners at thirty pounds a head, whose services they bought for the term of their being held as prisoners of war.

Our ancestors were clothed in homespun, and the endeavor to stop commerce in wool and woolen cards was one of the most vexatious restrictions imposed by the mother country.

Our forefathers established a prosperous traffic among themselves, and sent commercial ventures in their small vessels to various ports of the world. But this was not to be permitted. The laws of England forbade her colonies to trade with the colonies of France and Spain. The power of taxation was invoked to prevent it. Naval officers were made custom-house officers, not so much to collect revenue as to stop traffic altogether, just as the civil officers had previously attempted to stop our manufactures.

What we have failed to perceive is that the measures which only provoked animosity when imposed from without are equally mischievous when enacted within.

We have not yet learned that restrictions upon commerce are most injurious to those who enforce them, and by continuing the same navigation acts we have compassed the very result that Great Britain failed to accomplish by war. In one century we have reduced ourselves from the position of a dreaded maritime people to a position of comparative insignificance upon the sea. At the end of a century of vigorous life and effort we remain but a province, unable to keep our own flag at the mast-head of any fleet of modern vessels.

But let us turn from this sorry picture of perverted force and ignorant striving to imitate the long since discarded methods of England, to the far more satisfactory consideration of the result of our domestic commerce and the prosperity that has ensued from its unrestricted character. It has been fortunate for us that within our own limits we possess such diversity of soil, climate, and condition as to have prevented the restrictions upon foreign commerce from producing the same bad results as the restrictive policy caused and culminated in in Great Britain in 1841. At that time "the system which was supported with the view of rendering the country independent of foreign sources of supply, and thus, it was hoped, fostering the growth of home trade, had most effectually destroyed that trade by reducing the entire population to beggary, destitution, and want. In the manufacturing districts mills and workshops were closed, and property daily depreciated in value; in the sea-ports shipping was laid up useless in the harbor; agricultural laborers were eking out a miserable existence upon starvation wages and parochial relief, and the country was brought to the verge of national and universal bankruptcy."

As we are now about to enter upon the hundredth year of our existence as a nation, this dark picture will only partially apply to those identical branches of industry which the government has especially attempted to promote by restrictive statutes. Depression rules the hour among the mills, the mines, and the iron-works; strikes prevail in the factories; bloodshed is common at the mines; but the stove-maker, the wood-worker, the tinsmith, the wagon-builder, the blacksmith, the plow-maker, the millwright, the harness-maker, and their companions are busy and tolerably well employed, and these are the ones who constitute the vast army of manufacturers who must exist in every civilized community.

It is true that the depression in a few great branches of industry more or less affects all others, but it is also true that those special branches of industry are now the most depressed that have been most protected, as it is called, by the government during the last half of the century just ending.

We have only to glance at the vast force of free and industrious manufacturers and artisans, who are to be found in every corner of our fair land, to perceive how a free inland commerce thrives and how true manufactures flourish in spite of and not because of the restrictive statutes.

The great centres of manufacture and of agriculture are not to be found where they are usually sought, and the true and great diversity of our industry and the extent of our commerce may be most fully realized by tracing them out. The census of 1870 gives us the data, and by it we find that the centre of manufacturing industry is in the city and county of New York, whose product of manufactures in the year 1870 exceeded $332,000,000 in value; next comes Philadelphia, $322,000,000; next, St. Louis, $158,000,000 (in 1870, since increased to $239,-000,000 in 1875); and then follow Middlesex County, Massachusetts, $113,000,000; Suffolk County, Massachusetts, $112,000,000; Providence County, Rhode Island, $85,000,000; Hamilton County, Ohio, $79,000,000; Baltimore County, Maryland, $59,000,000; Essex County, New Jersey, $52,000,000; San Francisco, California, $37,000,000; and in smaller sums we find the manufacturing arts wherever cities, towns, or villages exist.

Again, in agriculture the pre-eminence is not to be found in the West, where it would usually be sought, but in the list of counties producing the largest aggregate value each in its own State we find that Pennsylvania is at the head, while others follow in the following order:

Lancaster Co., Penn.	950 sq. miles	...	$11,815,008
St. Lawrence Co., N. Y.	2900 " "	...	9,508,071
Worcester Co., Mass.	1500 " "	...	6,351,411
Hartford Co., Conn.	807 " "	...	6,220,911
La Salle Co., Ill.	1050 " "	...	5,502,502
Oakland Co., Mich.	900 " "	...	5,154,231
Burlington Co., N. J.	600 " "	...	4,908,839

Then follow the rest of the champion counties in agriculture, indicating as little of the commonly assumed order as to position and section as the manufacturing and mechanic arts.

The exchanges of the products of these counties and States constitute our national commerce. It has been estimated that the aggregate of values moved over our seventy thousand miles of railroad in a year is over ten thousand million dollars, and for this service and for the transportation of passengers the sum of five hundred and twenty-six million dollars was paid in the year just ended. Yet all this vast movement is but for the supply of the simplest wants, and the utter futility of attempting to regulate or direct it by statute can be fully realized when we consider that it only exists because men choose to exchange bread for boots, beef for hats, pork for clothing, timber for dwellings, or the like. Thus commerce between States differing as widely as almost any section of the earth's surface in soil, climate, and condition, also differing widely in the rate of interest, in the incidence of local taxation, and in the wages of labor, has yet called into existence our seventy thousand miles of railway, costing nearly four thousand million dollars, by means of which exchanges of goods were made last year estimated at two hundred million tons. Free commerce between the states of a great continent has induced this diversity of employment, and this establishment of manufactures in the immediate neighborhood of agriculture which assures prosperity to the mechanic, the manufacturer, and the farmer alike, while at the same time progress in the method of transportation has caused neighborhood to consist not so much in proximity as in the elimination of time. This freedom of commerce, and the division of labor that ensues from it, have led to certain results in the distribution of population which call for a passing notice. The production of the cereal crops upon which our whole prosperity now depends has ceased to be a matter of manual labor to any great extent, but is carried on by means of machines of complex character requiring few hands to tend them in proportion to their product. Had it not been for these new methods the war for the preservation of the Union would have been almost impracticable, because the million of men who were at one time in the loyal army could not have been spared without risk of famine; but in fact such had been the increased power of production and transportation that during the war, had the crops alone been considered, it would not have appeared that a single man had left his home upon the fields.

A further result has come in this, that as a less number of hands are needed in the field, a greater number may be employed in the arts, and herein is an explanation of the greater relative increase in the manufactures of the country than in the products of agriculture. This, again, has led to a far greater concentration in towns and cities. The tendency to concentration has been to some extent counteracted by the homestead and land-grant system under which the public lands have been distributed, but it is to be doubted if even this cheap land has caused any great increase in the relative number of the agricultural population; the new lands have been settled by a portion only of the immigrants from abroad, and by the farmers from the East, who have only changed their place and their method of work.

Men who have once been engaged in the arts or manufactures seldom return to the field, but the country lad does seek the town or city. It can not be doubted that this concentration in cities and towns will continue, and that population will be more and more condensed in narrow spaces, drawing their subsistence from long distances, and exchanging, in ever-increasing abundance, the comforts and luxuries which they produce, for the food and fuel they consume; and with this condensation will come the more pressing need of solving the method of governing and administering great cities; of draining and ventilating, and of providing for the imperative necessity of parks, play-grounds, commons, and other wide, open areas, in order that, with these vast material gains that accompany free commerce and the division of labor, there may not be a grave loss in the moral welfare and in the physical vigor of the race.

The interdependence of our States and the service which each renders to the other find most homely illustration in a subject not fitted for poetic treatment, nor likely to appeal to the imagination—*commerce in hogs.*

The great prairies of the West grow corn in such abundance that even now, with all our means of intercommunication, it can not all be used as food, and some of it is consumed as fuel.

It often happens that the farmer upon new land, remote from railroads, can get only from fifteen to twenty cents per bushel for Indian corn, at which price, while it is the best, it is also the cheapest fuel that he can have, and its use is an evidence of good economy, not of waste. Upon the fat prairie lands of the West the hog is wholesomely fed only upon corn in the milk or corn in the ear; thence he is carried to the colder climate of Massachusetts, where by the use of that one crop in which New England excels all others—ice—the meat can be packed at all seasons of the year; there it is prepared to serve as food for the workman of the North, the freedman of the South, or the artisan of Europe; while the blood, dried in a few hours to a fine powder, and sent to the cotton fields of South Carolina and Georgia to be mixed with the phosphatic rocks that underlie their coast lands, serves to produce the cotton fibre which furnishes the cheapest and fittest clothing for the larger portion of the inhabitants of the world.

Here, then, is commerce, or men serving each other on a grand scale, all developed within the century, and undreamed of by our ancestors. The vast plains of the West, enriched by countless myriads of buffalo, can spare for years to come a portion of their productive force. Commerce sets in motion her thousand wheels, food is borne to those who need it most, and they are spared the effort to obtain it on the more sterile soil of the cold North. Commerce turns that very cold to use. The refuse is saved, and commerce has discovered that its use is to clothe the naked in distant lands. Borne to the sandy but healthy soils of Georgia and South Carolina, it renovates them with the fertility thus transferred from the prairies of Illinois and Indiana, and presently there comes back to Massachusetts the cotton of the farmer, the well-saved, clean, strong, and even staple which commerce again has discovered to be worth identifying as the *farmer's*, not the planter's, crop, made by his own labor and picked by his wife and children, to whom only a few short years since such labor was ignoble, and because thus well saved worth a higher price.

Had the custom-house officer stood upon the Hudson River and said to the farmer of Illinois, "Your corn and meat must not come here, lest by your cheap labor you ruin our farmers," as the custom-house officer of the United States now says to the farmer and miner of Canada, when they try to send food and fuel to New England; had the tax-gatherer watched at the bar of the harbors of Charleston and Savannah to make the obstruction greater, lest the meat packed in New England should affect the price of the poor freedman's pigs, and lest the fertilizers made in Boston and Philadelphia should stop the phosphate works of those cities, as the custom-house officer of the United States now attempts to stop the refuse salt of foreign production, even when only needed as a manure; had the revenue official of Massachusetts stood ready to make the cotton more costly, as the custom-house officer of the United States now doubles the price of the wool of Canada—this commerce could not have existed, the men of the West could not have rendered service to New England, nor they to their Southern brethren, nor they again to the people of all lands and all climes.

The century has witnessed the establishment of the culture and exchange of cotton, the extension of civilization over the prairies of the West, and the infinite and complex movements which we feebly try to grasp throughout all their ramifications, whereby the hungry are fed, the naked clothed, and the soil that has been burned over and scathed by slavery renewed and made more productive than ever before; yet one of the chief instruments in this vast benefit, by which the general struggle for life has thus been made less arduous, has been nothing but a *herd of swine.*

Turning a moment from this homely phase of progress, let us glance at another vast change. Early in the century a few small ships or barks sailed from New England, laden with muskets, beads, tobacco, and bales of red flannel, their destination the Northwest coast. Upon the voyage the goods were made up into packages containing each one musket, a few yards of flannel, and a small portion of beads and tobacco, each package the price of a bale of fur skins. Arriving at their destination, the vessel was laden with the furs thus bought, and then she slowly wended her way to China, where teas, purchased at about the same ratio of profit, were taken on board, and, after a long period passed without being heard from, the ship returned to Boston or Salem. Under this system tea was the luxury of the few; now it is the comfort of the million. And how does it now reach the consumer? A telegram from St. Petersburg to New York or Boston calls for supplies of wheat or barley for the Russian troops on the Amoor River, the merchant in Boston or New York sends the message to San Francisco, the grain is laden upon a vessel there, the banker's credit furnished by the Russian government is transferred in a moment to China or Japan, and within a few weeks the tea of China or Japan, brought over the Pacific Railroad, is being consumed in Chicago in exchange for the wheat or barley of California, of which the rations of the Russian troops may at the same moment consist.

Were it not for the barriers that we maintain between ourselves and other nations, by which most of our manufactures are made more costly than those of other countries, orders not only for wheat and cotton and other crude products of the soil, but for the finer products of manufacturing industry, would be telegraphed for in the same manner, and we should serve the need of untold millions now almost unknown to us, receiving back that abundance of foreign comforts and luxuries of which we are in part deprived by the folly of economic superstition.

We are deprived of them under the pretense that our laborers can not afford the consumption of foreign luxuries, but that all such importations impoverish the country.

The end of all commerce is an abundant and general *consumption* not only of the necessary articles of subsistence, but of the comforts and luxuries of life; and the material prosperity of the country is to be gauged by the amount of its annual consumption more than by the magnitude of its accumulations.

The figures of the census, by which it is attempted to measure the wealth and progress of the people, are utterly fallacious if taken by themselves, the true measure of material prosperity being the amount of comfort and of luxury that the wages of workmen, relatively equal in intelligence and skill, will purchase at different dates and in different places.

A century since the man who now enjoys leisure and abundance, and whose hours of labor are not overlong, would have been forced to work the livelong day for a bare and coarse subsistence, while many of the ignorant emigrants who now swarm throughout our land would have starved had they then attempted to come into the colonies.

The great difference in the condition of the mass of the people a century since and at the present time consisted in this, that then nearly all knew how to get moderate comfort from little means, partly because the labor of that day was nearly all of a kind that stimulated intelligence; there was much drudgery, but not the routine and monotony which now mark the condition of those who do the commoner sort of work. The Irish servant of to-day can obtain for her wages better clothes and more of them, is furnished with better food and more of it, and is better and more comfortably housed than the mistress of the house a century since; and these changes have come because the division of labor, the extension of commerce, and the improvements in means of transport have brought distant places near, and have increased production. The workman in the iron furnace, the weaver in the mill, the man who tends the machine in the boot factory, earns higher wages and may be able to live far better than the blacksmith, the cobbler, or the carpenter of old time. But he earns his subsistence in a far different way, and the abundance that he may enjoy may not be an unalloyed benefit. Why is not the man or woman of to-day who performs the drudgery of the world equal in thrift and intelligence to those who once did the work which they now do?

The reason is not difficult to find. The cobbler then used his brain as well as his lapstone; the blacksmith was an artisan, a leader in the church choir, and a chief speaker in town-meetings; the carpenter of that day was a craftsman; with poor tools, unaided by machinery, he was compelled to hew out his dwelling-place, and he built it firmly and well; the house and the man were built up together, and each was strong and true.

The housewife spun and wove the very cloth in which the family was clad, and as the web was woven, thrift and intelligence made part of the warp and woof. Each man and woman was the "builder of a brain" as well as of a home, and there could be no comfortable subsistence without true manhood and true womanhood.

Commerce has changed these conditions, and we are now at one of the half-way places. The same labor and the same intelligence that then gave but a subsistence, gained with arduous toil, but with much mental vigor, will now suffice to procure an ample competence and exemption from toil. The craftsman of the old time is the master of to-day, the housewife has become the mistress of a mansion; but the toiler of to-day is not the equal of the toiler of old time, and he could not then have subsisted at all. Commerce, invention, and the division of labor have increased abundance, but have also, to a considerable extent, separated the functions of those who work with the head from those who work with the hand; they have raised a large portion of the community to a higher plane of comfort and luxury than could have been even dreamed of a century since, and in so doing have made a place and created occupations for those who could not then have existed at all in regions or countries which now have a dense population; but these occupations are of a new kind, and many of the methods by which this comfort and abundance are obtained tend to deaden the intelligence and to promote a merely animal existence. May it not be that one of the causes of the uneasiness of those who toil, and who constitute the laboring classes of some sections, comes from the monotony of their work rather than from the want of material comfort? Man can not live by bread alone, and ten or eleven hours a day spent in watching a machine, while they may yield more bread and meat than the hand spinner and weaver of a century since ever earned, may yet be devoid of that use of the mental faculties that alone makes existence tolerable.

Where the operation of the machine tends to relieve the operative of all thought, the man or woman who tends it risks becoming a machine, well oiled and cared for, but incapable of independent life. The culture of the past was more diffused, but it was obtained by means of the very toil that was needed to gain subsistence, because the work itself called upon all the faculties, and was not a matter of routine; the culture and refinements of to-day come from leisure and opportunity more than from the development of men in the necessary work of their lives. May it not be possible that one of the causes of the great demand which exists for bad and sensational books and for exciting amusements comes from the dreary monotony of many of the necessary occupations of men and women, and that one of the most essential developments of commerce or of mutual service in the future will be in the direction of more ample provision for wholesome amusements? As has been well said by an eminent and truly orthodox divine, "Amusement is a force in Christian life;" and unless this need is well served by the saints, we may be very sure that it will be ill served by those whose title is not saintly. How to provide cheap and wholesome amusements for those who toil is one of the great problems of commerce which must be solved.

We have said that much of the necessary work of the laboring people fails to develop character. In a higher walk of life, even the merchants of former days, though their ventures were small, their vessels of but few tons, and though their gains would only have been those of the small shop-keepers of the present time, yet seem to have been men of a larger type and of finer mould than the great tradesmen of our time. The merchant's work then called for foresight, energy, and a wide comprehension; but steam and the telegraph are great levelers, and the success of the merchant of to-day depends more on routine, method, and capital.

The grander men of this time, who would once have been great merchants, are now the builders of railroads and great works, the tool-makers and the machine-builders, the masters of the arts of all kinds.

On the other hand, the theory of Malthus that population gained faster than the means of subsistence, and that men must die of war, pestilence, and famine in an ever-increasing ratio, finds as yet no warrant in the experience of men. Commerce has eliminated time and distance, while invention and discovery have yielded greater and greater abundance for each given portion of time devoted to the work of procuring subsistence; and the one great fact which especially indicates the progress of commerce in the century just ending is this, that more men may now live, and need not die, on any given area in the civilized world than was possible a century since. This is as true of parts of our own country as it is of other countries.

The "progressive desire" which distinguishes men from brutes has been met by ever-increasing power of satisfaction. But it is not sufficient to have achieved only the means of living: life must be made worth living to each and all.

We have said that the nation is at one of the half-way points: division of labor and the extension of commerce have increased the supply of all that men need for subsistence, while altering the conditions of much of the work, so that it has become monotonous drudgery. On the other hand, the uses that have been found for refuse and offensive substances have led to inventions that have removed the degrading conditions from many kinds of necessary labor.

If we consider society as a pyramid, the constant rising of the apex has opened the way for a broader and firmer base of useful employment, and it can not be questioned that the constant tendency is toward a steady reduction of the necessary hours of labor, and a constant increase of the opportunity for mental stimulus in the hours of leisure; hence, as the labor of production becomes more and more a matter of machinery and apparatus rather than of individual exertion of brain and muscle, the capability for enjoyment which all covet but few attain will surely come for the mass of men, but it must come from culture and education outside their work, and not in the work itself. Hence it follows that the need of our time is not so much the promotion of greater abundance of material things, because the abundance exists even at this very moment to the extent of plethora, but the removal of the obstacles which exist in the form of meddlesome statutes and constant attempts to hinder, by restrictive methods, that free exchange by which alone can even abundance be made a blessing.

It is a fact not to be gainsaid, that even at this moment the only conditions requisite to a comfortable subsistence for man or woman in this country are prudence, intelligence, health, and integrity. The question is not one of the supply of the things needed, but of the method of obtaining them; and yet our ever-increasing wealth is accompanied by increasing poverty; the attempt to protect, foster, and promote certain specified branches of industry by restricting exchange has enervated and emasculated those to whom the artificial stimulus has been given, and has obstructed the progress of those whose occupations could not from their very nature be included in the attempt to protect.

Added to these removable causes of harm we have another more subtle and vicious cause of a false and unjust distribution of the abundance of material things that we produce. We shall enter upon our second century of life as a nation under the curse of bad money. The most essential tool of our trade, the medium by which all the exchanges that constitute our commerce are made, is the dishonored promise of the nation. Issued under the stress of war, it continues to inflict the curse of war long after peace and plenty have become assured. Of it may be said, as was said of the legal-tender paper money of the Revolution, that it has polluted the equity of our laws, and turned them into engines of oppression and wrong; that it has corrupted the justice of our public administration; that it has enervated the trade, husbandry, and manufactures of our country; that it has gone far to destroy the morality of our people; and that it has done more injustice than the arms and artifices of the enemies of the Union for whose subjugation it was issued.

Thus does it appear that the century just ending, the first of the strictly commercial age, has been marked by greatly increased power over the productive forces of nature, and that the promises of the future material welfare of the nation are grand indeed. What we now need is greater liberty and a broader education, with instruction in what constitutes the true use of leisure, in order that there may not be the shadow of truth in the charge sometimes made that for a large portion of the community leisure is now but another name for license.

The legal obstructions to our true prosperity are maintained by the influence of the rich, and not of the poor; not willfully in the face of better knowledge, but because they are still misled as to the true function of commerce. We have provided well for the common education of the poor, and that provision is now our salvation. When we shall have as fitly provided for the higher education of the rich, when we shall have reversed the old order, and it shall be the conviction of every man born to fortune that only the idle man is ignoble, then will the merchant, the tradesman, and the manufacturer fill their true places in the order of events. Then will come the time when peace and good-will may reign among the nations of the earth, and when by means of free commerce there shall be for the millions yet unborn not only material comfort and welfare, but the opportunity fully enjoyed for general culture and refinement, coupled with mental and spiritual progress never yet attained.

VII.

GROWTH AND DISTRIBUTION OF POPULATION.

OF the five maps which illustrate the present paper, the first exhibits the acquisition of territory by the United States from 1776 to the present time. The second shows the areas actually covered by population at each alternate decennial census from 1790 to 1870. The third presents the movement of the centre of population, the "star of empire," if the reader please, across the face of the country from east to west, upon the line of the thirty-ninth degree north latitude, from its first recorded position, twenty-three miles east of Baltimore, in 1790, to its resting-place in 1870, forty-eight miles east by north of Cincinnati. We said its resting-place: we should have said its last recorded position, for the time has not yet come for it to stand in its place above any favored town or city in the land. Its course is still westward; and while we write it is pressing on with an equable motion of seventy or seventy-five feet a day in a direction generally west, but also slightly north. The fourth map is illustrative of interstate migration; showing the *habitat* at 1870 of the natives of New York and of South Carolina severally. The fifth exhibits in three degrees the density of population within the area settled at 1870 east of the 100th meridian.

If we examine the first of these maps, we shall find ten divisions of the existing territory of the United States noted thereon; but these, for our present purpose, may be consolidated into seven, namely: the original thirteen States; the original Western Territory (embracing the territory northwest of the river Ohio, Kentucky and Tennessee, and the Mississippi Territory); the French cession of 1803 (called Louisiana); the Spanish cession of 1819 (Florida); the Texan annexation of 1845; the Mexican cessions of 1848 and 1853; and last, though, perhaps unfortunately, not least, the Russian cession of 1868 (Alaska).

Of these the first comprises 420,892 square miles, and contained in 1870 about eighteen millions of inhabitants; the second comprises 406,952 square miles, with thirteen and a half millions of inhabitants; the third, 1,171,931 square miles, with five and a quarter millions of inhabitants; the fourth, 59,268 square miles, with less than two hundred thousand inhabitants; the fifth, 376,133 square miles, with about eight hundred and thirty thousand inhabitants; the sixth, 591,318 square miles, with about the same population as the fifth; the seventh, 577,390 square miles, with but four or five hundred white inhabitants.[1]

Although the Spanish and Mexican cessions comprise towns which far antedate the earliest settlements within the original thirteen States, it is to the latter that we must first turn in any attempt to broadly grasp the history of population within the United States. But we shall fail to reach the full significance of the situation if we only give to ourselves, as reasons for treating this portion of territory first in order, its present population, exceeding that of any other section, its earlier political development, or its more conspicuous figure in American history. It is not more, but rather less, on account of these than on account of the actual contributions which this section has made to the population of each one in turn of the other geographical divisions of the United States, early or recent, that the writer on population must turn first to Jamestown and Plymouth, or he will read his theme backward. St. Augustine (1565) and Santa Fé (1582) were, indeed, planted before English Cavalier or English Puritan sought the more northern lands for settlement; but St. Augustine and Santa Fé were a barren stock, and the populations that to-day occupy the regions in which these were planted in the sixteenth century

[1] These statements of population are exclusive of Indians, who are not embraced in a census of the United States. On their account there should be added to No. 1 about six thousand souls; to No. 2 about twenty-six thousand; to No. 3 about one hundred and sixty thousand; to No. 5 perhaps thirty thousand; to No. 6 about eighty thousand; and to No. 7 about seventy thousand.

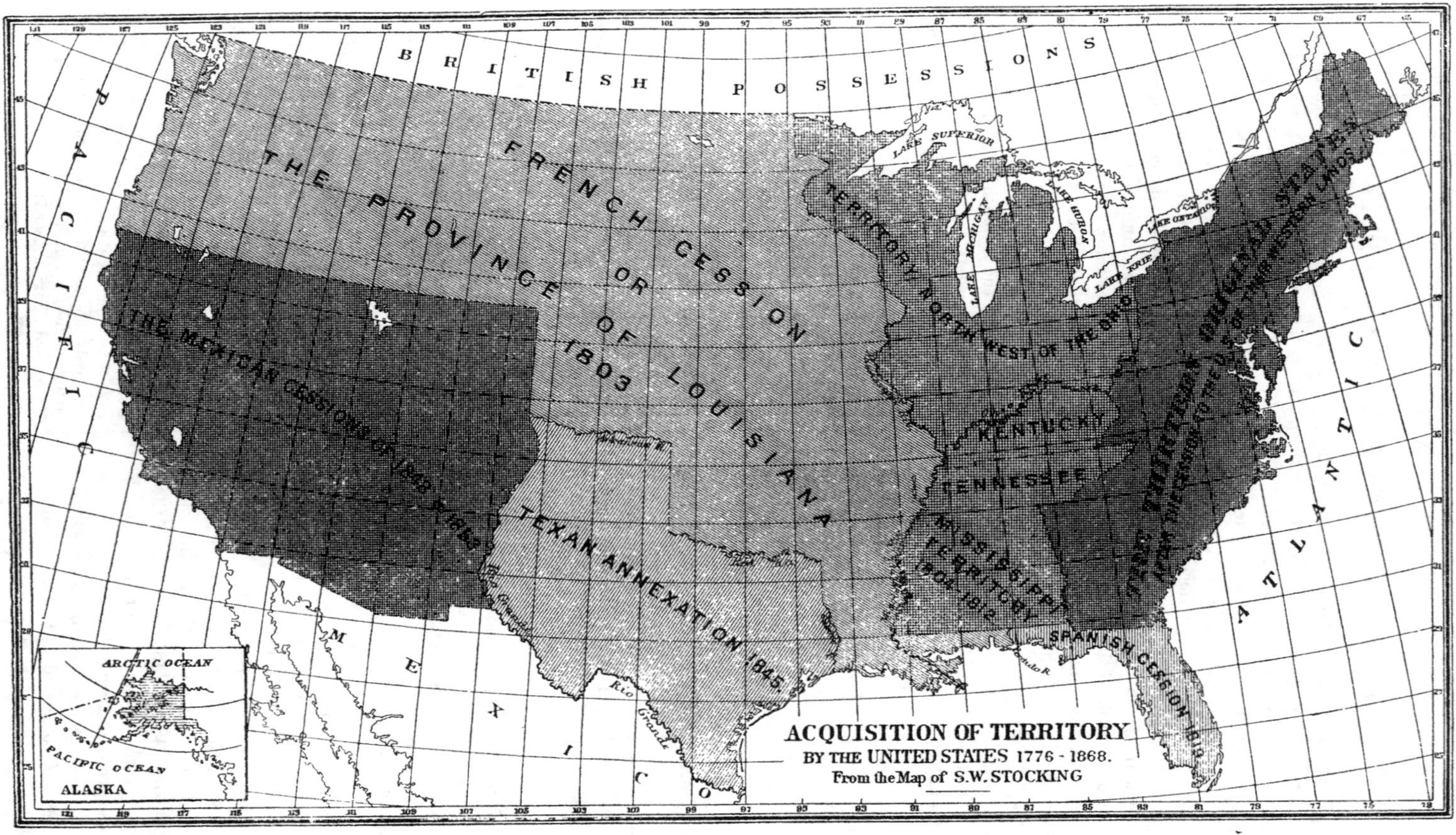
ACQUISITION OF TERRITORY
BY THE UNITED STATES 1776 - 1868.
From the Map of S.W. STOCKING
BRITISH POSSESSIONS
ATLANTIC
PACIFIC
MEXICO
THE PROVINCE OF LOUISIANA
FRENCH CESSION OR 1803
TEXAN ANNEXATION 1845.
THE MEXICAN CESSIONS OF 1848 & 1853
SPANISH CESSION 1819
MISSISSIPPI TERRITORY 1804-1812
TENNESSEE
KENTUCKY
TERRITORY NORTH WEST OF THE OHIO
LAKE SUPERIOR
LAKE MICHIGAN
LAKE HURON
LAKE ERIE
LAKE ONTARIO
Rio Grande
ARCTIC OCEAN
PACIFIC OCEAN
ALASKA

have poured forth from States founded in penury and neglect long afterward. When the great province of Louisiana came to us, in 1803, more than three centuries after the discovery of the main-land of America, it contained, from the delta of the Mississippi to Puget Sound, scarcely twenty thousand white inhabitants. That this vast territory now contains more than five millions of inhabitants, who will by 1880 be eight millions or ten, is not due to the robustness of the stock which Jefferson annexed with the soil, or mainly to direct immigration.[1] In like manner, when we received Florida from Spain by the treaty of 1819, not consummated, however, until 1821, the white population was but twelve or fifteen thousand, so slight had been the fecundity of the Spanish settlements. And when, in 1822, Congress directed the Postmaster-General to make provision for a post-route from St. Augustine to Pensacola, that officer was obliged to report the next year as follows:

> "Diligent inquiry has been made, and it does not appear that there is a road between these places on the route designated on which the mail can be conveyed. There are Indian paths which pass through different Indian settlements, but none, it is understood, that extend for any considerable distance in the proper direction."

And so late as 1850, the first date for which we have the statistics of nativity in the United States, it was found that of the free inhabitants of Florida more had been born in the original thirteen States than in Florida itself, while less than six per cent. of the free inhabitants were of foreign birth. The Texan annexation, again, now contains about 830,000 souls; but when Texas revolted from Mexico, it contained probably not more than 40,000, of whom by far the greater part had come, in anticipation[2] of "manifest destiny," from the States. In 1850, of the free inhabitants scarcely more than one-third, including, of course, an undue proportion of children, were natives of Texas.

In the same way the first Mexican cession, when taken possession of by the United States, embraced but a small white population. Of this tract it is true that, in the furious excitement caused by the discovery of gold at Sutter's Mill in 1848, it was settled more largely than any other had been by direct immigration. Yet of the first eighty thousand eager gold-hunters who pressed into the valleys of California, more than three-fourths were born in the East, of whom one-half, as nearly as might be, were natives of the original thirteen States, while probably not less than two-thirds of the remainder would be found to be cis-appalachian in their origin, could we go but thirty years further back.

Of the second Mexican cession, the Gadsden purchase of 1853, embracing the territory south of the river Gila, in Arizona and New Mexico, little can be said any way. Two or three hundred whites, insecurely guarded by perhaps as many soldiers, as yet constitute the population of this treeless, trackless desert.

Twenty-three degrees to the north, under the very "shadow of the pole," lies, securely frozen up, the latest purchase of the United States, a region as large as Great Britain, France, Spain, and the German Empire combined, all the eligible portions of which are now devoted to the preservation in theory and extermination in fact of fur-bearing seal.

It is not so easy to show statistically the derivation of the people of the original territory of the United States from the original thirteen States, but it is, at the same time, less needful. Our history from 1763 onward is full of the migrations from the Atlantic slope into the Ohio and Mississippi valleys, at first through the passes of the Alleghanies, and later by the lakes and around the southern extremity of the great coast chain. And even of the vast immigration from Europe which has helped to build up these nine interior States between the mountains and the river, no small part, perhaps the greater part, has been received from the original States, not merely through their ports, but after a period of residence, acclimation, and often even of naturalization at the East.

So incessant had been the fresh supply of Eastern blood, so little had the "Great

---

[1] At the southeastern extremity only are the effects of direct immigration traceable in any marked degree. New Orleans has been to some extent supported by arrivals from Mexico and the West Indies, as well as from France, Ireland, and Germany.

[2] Indeed, the immigration into Texas had been largely for the very purpose of wresting the country from Mexico.

West" of two or three generations ago been left to the propagation of the stock then planted there, that, so late as 1850, seventy-five years after Kentucky was founded, more than one-fourth of the free inhabitants of these nine States had been born east of the mountains, while, if the adult inhabitants only had been taken into account, the proportion must have greatly exceeded one-third, if, indeed, it did not reach nearly to one-half.

If thus the early settlements in what we shall always know as the "Thirteen States" were vastly more prolific than those made by the Spaniards and French at the south and southwest, they also greatly surpassed in the vigor of their growth the settlements to the north and northeast, whether by the French or the English. In 1754, when the thirteen colonies aggregated of whites and blacks nearly a million and a half, New France, though planted at the same time with Virginia, had scarcely a hundred thousand people, mainly collected on the St. Lawrence, between Quebec and Montreal.

"At the time of Queen Elizabeth's death (1603)," writes the annalist of America, "which was 110 years after the discovery of America by Columbus, neither the French, Dutch, nor English, nor any other nation excepting the Spanish, had made any permanent settlement in this New World. In North America to the north of Mexico not a single European family could be found."[1]

Between 1607 and 1733 were founded all the original States of the American Union. The order of their settlement and the main facts of their growth in population while colonies of Great Britain are, if not essential, at least important to a comprehension of their history as independent States, and still more to an understanding of the origin of the twenty-four equal members of the Union which have come into existence since 1789.

1607–1660.

By a natural grouping of the facts of our early settlement, one who chooses to regard the growth of population merely, irrespective of grants, charters, and political institutions, may consider the colonies in three classes—those of New England, the middle colonies, and those to the South, from and including Maryland.

The first permanent settlement within the territory of the original States was at Jamestown, Virginia, on the James River, 1607, by a colony of about 100 English. For twelve years the colony grew slowly, so that but 600 persons, men, women, and children, were counted among the inhabitants at the beginning of 1619. During the two years which followed, however, the number was increased nearly sixfold. At the outbreak of the civil war in England the population was estimated at 20,000, which was probably in excess of the true number.

Mr. Bancroft explains as follows the liability to "glaring mistakes in the enumerations" in the Southern provinces: "The mild climate invited emigrants to the inland glades;" "the crown-lands were often occupied on warrants of surveys without patents, or even without warrants;" "the people were never assembled but at muster."

The settlement of Maryland was closely connected with that of Virginia. In 1631–32 Captain William Clayborne established small settlements on Kent Island, in Chesapeake Bay, and also near the mouth of the Susquehanna. In 1634 a colony of about 200 English was planted at St. Mary's, on the mainland, under Leonard Calvert, brother of the proprietary, Lord Baltimore. Virginia and Maryland were the only colonies of the Southern group which were planted prior to the restoration of the Stuarts in 1660. At that date they were estimated to contain respectively 30,000 and 12,000 inhabitants.

Passing northeastward to New England, we find the first settlement made in 1620 by a body of about 100 English at Plymouth, within the present limits of Massachusetts, constituting what was, until 1692, known as the "Plymouth Colony." In 1643 this colony had grown to contain seven townships.

In 1628 a colony was planted at Salem, on Massachusetts Bay; in 1630 and 1633 large accessions were received; in 1634 the settlements were reported as extending thirty miles from the capital; 1635 was a year of rapid extension; by 1636 population had reached the Connecticut, and

[1] Holmes's Annals, i. 123.

Springfield was settled. There were now twenty "towns," and the colony was divided into three "regiments." During the summer of 1638 twenty ships arrived with 2000 persons. The colony was divided into four counties. In 1640 it was at its highest point of prosperity within the period we are considering. "The number of emigrants who had arrived in New England before the assembling of the Long Parliament is estimated to have been 21,200; 198 ships had borne them across the Atlantic."[1] Hildreth adds: "The accessions which New England henceforward received were more than counterbalanced by perpetual emigration."[2]

The Puritans in England, instead of fleeing before Acts of Conformity, were now engaged in reforming church and state to suit themselves.

In 1660 there were three towns on the Connecticut River within the jurisdiction of Massachusetts.

For the first settlement of New Hampshire, Mr. Bancroft assigns the date 1623, permanent plantations being then established on the Piscataqua. Dover and Portsmouth are among the oldest towns in New England. The province grew at first very slowly.

Of the first settlements within the State of Maine, Bancroft remarks (i. 331): "It is not possible, perhaps, to ascertain the precise time when the rude shelters of the fishermen on the coast began to be tenanted by permanent inmates, and the fishing stages of a summer to be transferred into regular establishments of trade. The first settlement was probably made 'on the Maine,' but a few miles from Monhegan, at the mouth of the Pemaquid." The probable date assigned is 1626.

In 1636 Providence, in the present State of Rhode Island, was planted by Roger Williams and five companions. In 1638 the "Rhode Island Colony" was established on the Isle of Rhodes by William Coddington and eighteen associates. Six years later Rhode Island and Providence plantations were united in self-government.

In 1633 trading posts were established within the limits of the present State of Connecticut, both by Dutch from New Netherlands (New York), and by English from Plymouth, the former at Hartford, the latter at Windsor.

During 1635 removals took place from Massachusetts to Wethersfield and Windsor, and in 1636 these towns, with Hartford, were occupied, constituting the "Connecticut Colony." In 1645 there were eight taxable towns within the colony.

In 1633 a settlement was made at New Haven, which, with its adjacent towns, constituted the "New Haven Colony," until it was united with the Connecticut Colony by charter of Charles II. The consolidated colony contained nineteen towns, distributed among four counties.

We have thus shown the beginnings east of the Hudson of four of the original thirteen States, prior to 1660. At 1640 these contained twelve independent communities, with not less than fifty towns or distinct settlements; but before the Restoration a consolidation had taken place, which reduced the separate jurisdictions to six.[1]

Of the central group of colonies New York was first settled. The Dutch had for some years maintained trade with the natives at Manhattan and up the Hudson River. In 1623–24 "New Netherlands" was planted, and a permanent settlement, called New Amsterdam, was made at Manhattan, the site of the present city of New York. By 1656 the village had been laid out into several small streets; 1660 found the Dutch still in possession, as well as disputing the title to Western Connecticut. The population at that date of New Netherlands, which in 1647 was hardly 2000 or 3000, even including the Swedes on the Delaware (Hildreth, i. 436), had risen to about 10,000, of whom 1500 resided in New Amsterdam.

One part of the present State of New York, however, has a history which directly connects its settlement both with New England and with the central group of colonies.

Long Island was first settled at its western end, under the protection of the Dutch, and a number of towns were a little later

[1] Bancroft, *United States*, i. 415.

[2] *Hist. United States*, i. 267.

[1] Hildreth, *United States*, i. 267.

planted there by this people.[1] The eastern portion of the island was settled about 1640 by Puritans from Lynn, Massachusetts, and from the New Haven Colony, and these settlements grew rapidly to meet those advancing from the west. The island was partitioned by the treaty of 1650 between the Dutch and the English, and so remained until the fall of the Dutch power in 1664.

In 1631 a small settlement had been made by the Dutch near Lewistown, within the present State of Delaware, but the young colony was entirely cut off by Indians a year later. In 1638 a company of Swedes and Finns, under the then renowned flag of Sweden, arrived in Delaware, and built a fort near the mouth of the creek, which they called Christiana. The Swedish settlements soon extended northward almost to the present site of Philadelphia. In 1655, however, the fear of Swedish arms had so far abated that the Dutch from Manhattan accomplished the subjection of Delaware to the dominion of Holland.

This completes the tale of colonies planted within the limits of the thirteen States prior to the Restoration. Thus at 1660 the only English colonies were those of New England, Virginia, and Maryland, estimated to contain in all not more than eighty thousand inhabitants.

1660–1688.

Within a few years from the Restoration the Dutch colonists of New Netherlands (New York), as well as the Dutch, Swedish, and Finnish residents of Delaware, were brought under English dominion, and the colonies of New Jersey and Carolina were planted.

Settlements had been made in what is now New Jersey very early in the seventeenth century. Dutch, Swedes, and Finns, English, Dutch again, and again English, had successively appeared and disappeared in the course of the early contests for the sovereignty of the soil. "Here and there," says Bancroft,[2] "in the counties of Gloucester and Burlington a Swedish farmer may have preserved his dwelling on the Jersey side of the river, and before 1664 perhaps three families were established about Burlington; but as yet West New Jersey had not a hamlet. In East Jersey......a trading station seems in 1618 to have been occupied at Bergen. In December, 1651, August Herman purchased but hardly took possession of the land that stretched from Newark Bay to the west of Elizabethtown; while in January, 1658, other purchasers obtained the large grant called Bergen, where the early station became a permanent settlement. Before the end of 1664 a few families of Quakers appear also to have found a refuge south of Raritan Bay."

In 1664 the settlement of New Jersey began under conflicting grants. There were soon four towns—Elizabeth, Newark, Middletown, and Shrewsbury. In 1676 New Jersey was divided as East and West New Jersey, the latter being purchased by the Quakers, who settled Burlington the following year. In 1682 the towns of East Jersey were supposed to have 700 families; those of West Jersey perhaps as many persons.

In 1663 Carolina was granted to eight proprietors; but it would appear that Albemarle had been settled already[1] by the growth southward of the Nansemond settlement just on the borders of the Virginia grant.

Two or three years prior to the grant, moreover, it would appear that a settlement had been effected by men from New England on the southern bank of Cape Fear River. Whatever remained of this settlement was, however, absorbed by a colony planted near the same spot in 1665 by the exertions of the proprietary, and which so prospered that in 1666 it embraced 800 persons.

In 1670 a company, brought out in three

---

[1] Anabaptist refugees from Massachusetts settled Newtown and Gravesend, under Dutch protection. So numerous were the English-speaking inhabitants of the Dutch part of the island that an English secretary was appointed.—Hildreth, i. 417.

[2] *Hist. United States*, ii. 316.

[1] "Perhaps a few vagrant families were planted within the limits of Carolina before the Restoration."—Bancroft, ii. 134, 135.

The historian Grahame charged that scarce any historian at his day had correctly given the facts relating to the early settlement of Carolina. "Even that laborious and generally accurate writer, Jedediah Morse, has been so far misled by defective materials as to assert (*American Gazetteer*) that the first permanent settlement in North Carolina was formed by certain German refugees in 1710."—*Hist. United States in North America*, ii. 111, n.

ships, settled on the Ashley River, at "Old Charlestown."

In 1671–72 Dutch both from New York and from Holland arrived at the Ashley River settlement. Subsequently, it would appear, to both these dates—perhaps 1679 or 1680—the colonists generally passed over to the west bank of Cooper River, and settled on Oyster Point, which became the city of Charleston.

In 1681 Pennsylvania was planted. The growth of this colony was rapid. In the first three years "fifty sail" arrived with settlers.

Thus, prior to 1688, the period of the great Revolution in England, we see settlements made within the territory of all the original thirteen States except Georgia. The whole population of the colonies at this time was about 200,000, "of whom," says Bancroft,[1] "Massachusetts, with Plymouth and Maine, may have had 44,000; New Hampshire and Rhode Island, with Providence, each 6000; Connecticut, from 17,000 to 20,000—that is, all New England, 75,000 souls; New York, not less than 20,000; New Jersey, half as many; Pennsylvania and Delaware, perhaps 12,000; Maryland, 25,000; Virginia, 50,000 or more; and the two Carolinas, which then included the soil of Georgia, probably not less than 8000 souls."

1688–1754.

In 1733 Georgia was settled and Savannah founded by Oglethorpe, with about one hundred and twenty persons. In 1734 Augusta was laid out. The immigrants of this year were computed at six hundred. In 1835 a colony of Highlanders planted New Inverness, in Darien. In 1736 Oglethorpe brought out three hundred emigrants.

But though perhaps the most auspiciously founded of all the colonies except Pennsylvania, the growth of Georgia was not rapid, and more than twenty years after its settlement we find the Board of Trade estimating its white inhabitants at but 3000.[2]

Meanwhile we find the other twelve colonies growing very unequally, both as we compare one colony with another and as we compare one epoch with another.[1]

In Virginia the number of "tithables" (*i. e.*, free males above sixteen years, and slaves above that age of both sexes) had been estimated in 1691 at 14,000; in 1703 the number was computed at 25,023; in 1754 the "tithables" had increased to nearly 100,000.

In the Carolinas the growth had been rapid in both the white and the black population. In 1700 5500 white inhabitants were counted. In 1723 the white inhabitants of that part alone which became South Carolina were estimated at 14,000; the slaves (negroes and a few Indians) at 18,000.[2] In 1729 the crown, having bought out the proprietors, formed Carolina into two distinct royal provinces, North and South Carolina. In 1730 the negroes of South Carolina were estimated at 28,000. This sudden increase in the estimate of their number may have been in some measure due to the alarm

---

[1] *Hist. United States*, ii. 450.

[2] Grahame (*Hist. United States*, ii. 403, n.), referring to the many inconsistent statements of the population of the colonies at different dates, says: "Even writers so accurate and sagacious as Dwight and Holmes have been led to underrate the early population of North America by relying too far on the estimates which the provincial governments furnished to the British ministry *for the ascertainment of the numbers of men whom they were to be required to supply for the purposes of naval and military expeditions.*" The reason suggested for the probable disparagement of the early population of the colonies has not a little force.

[1] In his *History of the United States*, vol. iv. p. 128, Mr. Bancroft expresses the opinion that "he who, like H. C. Carey, in his *Principles of Political Economy*, Part iii. p. 25, will construct retrospectively general tables from the rule of increase in America since 1790, will err very little." The writer must dissent from this opinion. The approximate regularity of increase from 1790 to 1860 was due to the fact that the accession by immigration bore a very small proportion to the total population. Thus, Professor Tucker places the foreign arrivals at 50,000 for the period 1790–1800, 70,000 for 1800–10, 114,000 for 1810–20, and this with an aggregate population rising meanwhile from four to nine and a half millions. Moreover, that immigration tended more and more to uniformity as between individual years. In the period before the Revolution, however, to which Mr. Bancroft refers, the average annual foreign arrivals unquestionably bore a much higher ratio to the existing population, and the immigration was very spasmodic and without system. Thus in 1750, when the total population of the thirteen colonies was, by Mr. Bancroft's estimates, a million and a quarter, we have an account of 5317 persons arriving in that single year in the single colony of Pennsylvania; and in 1729, when the total population must have been about 650,000, we find 6208 persons arriving in the same colony. Where disturbing elements of such magnitude enter, subject to no law that any one can presume to state, such computations as Mr. Bancroft suggests become most fallacious.

[2] Hewatt, i. 308, 309.

aroused by a plot for a servile insurrection.[1] In 1738 there was another attempt at servile insurrection, and the negroes were now estimated at 40,000.[2] Mr. Bancroft makes the number but little greater in 1754. Both the Carolinas meanwhile received large accessions of Irish and of French Protestants from Europe, of Puritans from New England, and of Dutch from New York, so that in 1754 the white inhabitants of the two colonies were estimated at twenty-two times the number stated for 1700.

If we follow Mr. Bancroft's classification, and place Maryland with the middle colonies, we find this group in 1754 exceeding New England in the ratio nearly of five to four. Of the middle colonies, Pennsylvania had, in the sixty years since its settlement, become by far the most populous.

New England, during the period we are considering, had increased nearly fivefold. Maine, Rhode Island, and New Hampshire had now considerable populations; and the beginnings of a new State, though not to be reckoned among the immortal "Thirteen," had been made, in 1724, by the establishment of Fort Dummer, on the site of Brattleborough, within the present State of Vermont.

It is natural that on the verge of the Seven Years' War, which broke the power of France on the American continent, the historian should pause to review the progress of settlement; and accordingly we find Mr. Bancroft summing up thus, for the year 1754, the population of the several colonies:

"Of persons of European ancestry perhaps 50,000 dwelt in New Hampshire, 207,000 in Massachusetts, 35,000 in Rhode Island, and 133,000 in Connecticut: in New England, therefore, 425,000 souls.

"Of the middle colonies, New York may have had 85,000; New Jersey, 73,000; Pennsylvania, with Delaware, 195,000; Maryland, 104,000: in all not far from 457,000....To Virginia may be assigned 168,000 white inhabitants; to North Carolina scarcely more than 70,000; to South Carolina, 40,000; to Georgia not more than 5000: to the whole country south of the Potomac, 283,000....

"Of persons of African lineage the home was chiefly determined by climate. New Hampshire, Massachusetts, and Maine, may have had 3000 negroes; Rhode Island, 4500; Connecticut, 3500: all New England, therefore, about 11,000. New York alone had not far from 11,000; New Jersey about half that number; Pennsylvania, with Delaware, 11,000; Maryland, 44,000: the central colonies collectively, 71,000. In Virginia there were not less than 116,000; in North Carolina, perhaps more than 20,000; in South Carolina, full 40,000; in Georgia, about 2000: so that the country south of the Potomac may have had 178,000."[1]

These estimates yield totals of 1,165,000 whites and 260,000 negroes.

1754–1790.

Pitt's war with France ensued. In 1763 his Most Christian Majesty by treaty relinquished to England all his rights to territory east of the Mississippi and north of thirty-one degrees north latitude. Population had gone on increasing all the time in spite of the war, but the triumphant conclusion was instantly followed by an extension of settlement in every direction. The presence of the French military posts in an unbroken chain from the Atlantic through the valleys of the St. Lawrence and the Mississippi to the Gulf of Mexico, and the fear of the Indian allies of the French, had repressed in a degree even the adventurous courage of the English-Americans. When once this pressure was removed, population bounded forward with astonishing alacrity.

On the extreme Northeast, in Maine, where settlement had been retarded by six successive Indian wars, "old claims under ancient grants began now to be revived, and new grants to be solicited."[2] The counties of Cumberland and Lincoln were erected in the year following the peace. Settlements stretched unrestrained along the coast toward the Penobscot, and population soon became almost continuous, even to Nova Scotia. To the North, the New Hampshire side of the Upper Connecticut witnessed a rapid immigration; while the other bank, contested then between New York and New Hampshire, became the scene of a petty warfare between rival patentees, possession and law being generally invoked against each other. Population also began to seek the borders of Lake Champlain, and to force its way through the forests to the lakes of Central New York.

To the South again, Georgia and South Carolina were now increasing in population and extending their settlements with unexampled rapidity. In 1752 the population

[1] Holmes, i. 547. [2] Holmes, ii. 10, 11.

[1] *Hist. United States*, iv. 127–129.
[2] Hildreth, *Hist. United States*, ii. 510.

of Georgia had been computed at 9000. In 1775 it was estimated to be 75,000. About the latter date the colony was divided into eight counties—four along the coast and four up the Savannah River.

But it was to the West, between the parallels which embraced the colonies of North Carolina and Virginia, and upon lands included within their charters, that the greatest movement in this period took place. Notwithstanding the exclusively agricultural character of the industry of these colonies, inviting a wide extension of population, the Blue Ridge had been, so late as 1731, the western boundary of settlement. From that time forward, however, settlers gradually penetrated the mountains north of the James River, and found homes in the valleys beyond, until in 1751–52 the furthermost wave of population had reached the base of the Alleghanies, and here for a time was stayed. But the Virginians and North Carolinians of that day knew better what lay beyond that mountain barrier than did the British Board of Trade when they sent Captain John Smith up the Chickahominy to discover the Pacific Ocean. By the explorations of Colonel Wood in 1654–64 several of the branches of the Ohio River had been made known, though for fifty years it still remained the general belief that the Alleghanies themselves were impassable. In 1714, however, Lieutenant-Governor Spottiswoode, of Virginia, led in person, "with great parade and solemnity," an expedition for the discovery of a passage across the mountains, which was crowned with such complete success that Spottiswoode was hailed by the Virginians with acclamations "of grateful and, indeed, hyperbolical praise, which exalted him to an approach to the glory of Hannibal."[1]

The statesmen of Virginia early saw that the long French line might be thrust through with fatal effect if settlements properly covered with military force were pushed across the mountains. It was the attempt of Governor Dinwiddie to seize the junction of the Alleghany and Monongahela in 1754 which brought on the war which ended in the conquest of the Ohio Valley.

Yet even after the peace of 1763, which gave all this country into the undisputed possession of England, subject only to Indian claims (and curiously enough, and in this connection importantly enough, it happened that no Indian tribe at any time had title to the territory immediately west of Virginia, which subsequently became the State of Kentucky), the home government persistently discouraged emigration to the West; and by proclamation of October 7, 1763, "it was ordered that, except in Quebec and West Florida, no public lands should be taken up *beyond the heads of the rivers which flow into the Atlantic.*" Thus the Alleghanies were set as the boundary of American enterprise; and the valleys of the Ohio and the Mississippi were to be locked against the intrusion of the pioneer.

But little did the pioneer reck of proclamations. His axe and rifle were his patent, and, looking down on the richest soil of the world, he was not likely to be long hindered by minutes from the Board of Trade.

Hardly was the proclamation issued when the banks of the Monongahela were occupied by emigrants from Pennsylvania, Maryland, and Virginia. In 1768 James Robertson planted his North Carolina colony on the Watauga, in the present State of Tennessee, and soon the Clinch and Holston valleys experienced the influx of emigrants from across the mountains.

In 1769 began the romantic exploits of Daniel Boone upon the "dark and bloody ground" later to be known as the State of Kentucky. Boonesborough, Harrodsburg, and Lexington appear to have been founded by 1776. In 1788 the settlement of Ohio was begun by the establishment of Marietta on the left bank of the Muskingum. In two years 20,000 persons were reported to have passed the Muskingum on their westward way.[1]

The surrender by France of the territory east of the Mississippi had brought within the jurisdiction of England in 1763 not a few settlements whose age, while it can not always be precisely ascertained, gives them still most respectable standing among the present towns of the United States.

There was Detroit, in the present State of Michigan, reported, though erroneously,

[1] Grahame, iii. 69.

[1] Holmes's Annals, ii. 370.

to contain in its immediate vicinity as many as 2500 Europeans, destined to become in the very year of the surrender the prime object of the famous "conspiracy of Pontiac."

The non-Indian population within the present State of Illinois was, according to Mr. Bancroft, not more than 1358 persons, of whom more than 300 were Africans.

Indiana had but one settlement, Vincennes, of nearly equal age with Detroit, with 400 to 500 inhabitants.

To the loyalty of the people thus transferred by the fortune of war, Mr. Jefferson bears the following testimony:

"Having been Governor of Virginia when Vincennes and the other French settlements of that quarter surrendered to the arms of that State twenty-eight years ago, I have had a particular knowledge of their character....I have ever considered them as sober, honest, and orderly citizens, submissive to the laws, and faithful to the nation of which they are a part."—*To William M'Intosh, January* 30, 1808.

Nor was the settlement of the newly acquired territory limited to the northern portions. President Stiles preserves account of extensive migrations in 1773 to reinforce the existing settlements on the Mississippi at and about Natchez.

But while population was thus spreading over the vast territory opened up by the peace of 1763, the older settlements, especially at the South,[1] were also growing rapidly, and even the war did not suffice to check the progress of population in communities where but a small proportion of the fertile lands was yet taken up, and where every added man was added strength to the State.[2]

"From many returns and computations," says Mr. Bancroft, "I deduce the annexed table as some approximation to exactness:"

Year.	Whites.	Blacks.	Total.
1750	1,040,000	220,000	1,260,000
1754	1,165,000	260,000	1,425,000
1760	1,385,000	310,000	1,695,000
1770	1,850,000	462,000	2,312,000
1780	2,383,000	562,000	2,945,000

At the first glance it will seem incredible that in the decade which bore almost the entire brunt of the Revolutionary struggle against England population should have held its own not only, but have made an advance of nearly thirty per cent. Yet much can be said in favor of this estimate for the period 1770–80. 1770–73 witnessed a rapid and continuous immigration, especially from Ireland and Germany, which provided a great resource during the long-continued drain which followed in the years of war. In 1773 especially we have accounts of wholesale immigration from Ireland into Pennsylvania, New York, and the Carolinas.[1]

The outbreak of the Revolution and the union of the colonies, which, in 1776, declared themselves States, required that the population of each should be at least approximately ascertained for the apportionment of the fiscal burdens of the war. The numbers, as then settled, "exclusive of slaves at the South," Pitkin gives as follows:

New Hampshire[2]	102,000	Delaware........	37,000
Massachusetts...	352,000	Maryland........	174,000
Rhode Island....	58,000	Virginia.........	300,000
Connecticut.....	202,000	North Carolina..	181,000
New York.......	238,000	South Carolina..	93,000
New Jersey.....	138,000	Georgia.........	27,000
Pennsylvania....	341,000		
Total..............	2,243,000		

The slaves being then estimated at 500,000 (*ibid.*), the total estimated population at this time was 2,750,000. In the Convention of 1787, which framed the present Constitution of the United States, it became necessary to use the estimated population of each State for another purpose, namely, that of determining provisionally its representation in Congress pending an actual enumeration. Mr. Curtis, in his *History of the Constitution*[3]

[1] Mr. Hildreth calls the years immediately succeeding 1763 "the golden age of Maryland, Virginia, and South Carolina."

[2] Our fathers very early set themselves to figuring out their coming greatness through this rapid increase of population. The works of Franklin and Jefferson abound in allusions to the growth of the past and predictions of corresponding growth in the future. Mr. Jefferson especially delighted to dwell on the possibilities of increase. "A duplication in little more than twenty-two years," he writes in his first annual message as President after the second census. "In fifty years more the United States alone," he writes to Humboldt in 1813, "will contain fifty millions of inhabitants." In 1815 he states it to Mr. Maury as forty millions in forty years, and in sixty years eighty millions. The time is already up, but the eighty millions are not forth-coming. The truth is that no expectation is so unreasonable respecting a geometrical ratio of increase as that it will continue.

[1] Holmes's Annals, ii. 183.

[2] New Hampshire complained that her number was too high, and in 1782 caused an actual enumeration to be made, by which it appeared that the number of her inhabitants was only 82,000. Congress, however, refused to alter her proportion of taxes on that account. —*Pitkin's Statistics.*

[3] A statement differing from this slightly in respect to several of the States, and decidedly in respect to

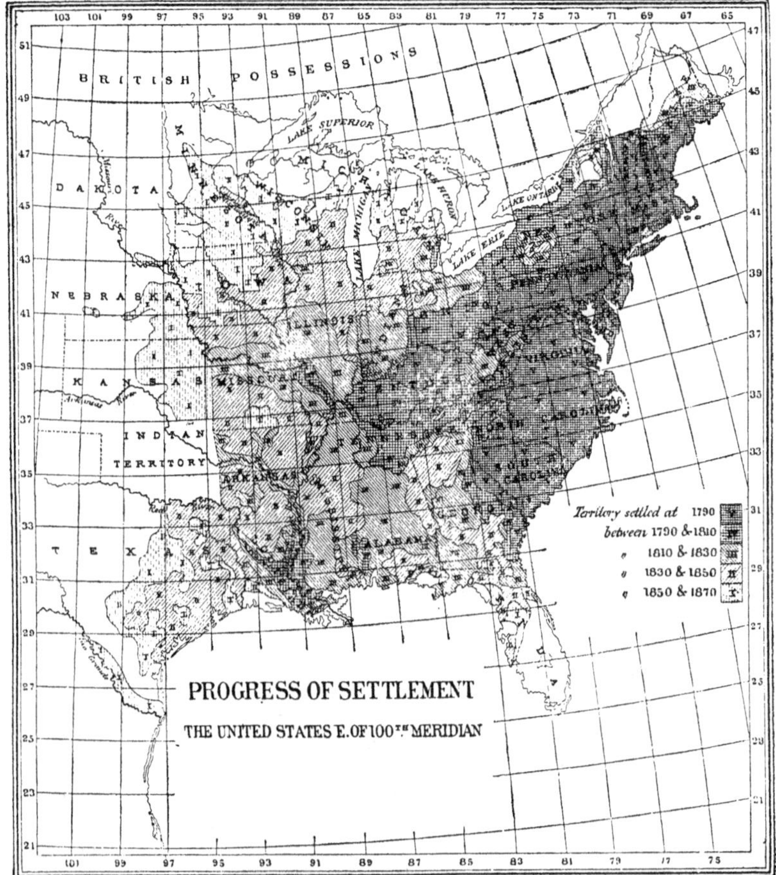

(vol. ii. p. 168, 169), gives the following table as that "used by the Federal Convention:"

New Hampshire	102,000
Massachusetts[1]	360,000
Rhode Island	58,000
Connecticut	202,000
New York[1]	238,000
New Jersey	138,000
Pennsylvania	360,000
Delaware	37,000
Maryland, including three-fifths of 80,000 negroes	218,000
Virginia,[1] including three-fifths of 280,000 negroes	420,000
North Carolina,[1] including three-fifths of 60,000 negroes	200,000
South Carolina, including three-fifths of 80,000 negroes	150,000
Georgia, including three-fifths of 20,000 negroes	90,000
	2,573,000
Add for negroes omitted	208,000
Total estimated population	2,781,000

1790–1870.

The first census of the United States was taken in 1790, fourteen years after the Declaration of the Independence of the States, and determined the population to be 3,172,006 whites, and 757,208 blacks.

Pretty much as a matter of course, great disappointment was felt at the result, and dissatisfaction at the methods of enumeration was loudly expressed. Mr. Jefferson, then Secretary of State, in sending copies of the published tables to our representatives at foreign courts, was careful to impress it on the minds of his correspondents that the returns fell far short of the truth, and even went so far as to supply the omissions which he assumed by entries "in red ink" (see letters to William Carmichael, August 24, 1791, and to William Short, August

Georgia and New Hampshire, is given in Elliott's *Debates* (i. 194), as found among the papers of Mr. Briarly, a delegate to that convention.

[1] Massachusetts, it will be remembered, then comprised the territory which in 1820 became the State of Maine; New York that which in 1791 became the State of Vermont; Virginia that which in 1792 became the State of Kentucky; North Carolina that which in 1796 became the State of Tennessee.

29, 1791). The results of later censuses, however, substantially establish the accuracy of the first enumeration, and show that the dissatisfaction was due to overstrained anticipations. The following table (anticipating the formation of State governments in Maine, Vermont, Kentucky, and Tennessee) exhibits the result by States:

Maine............	96,540	Delaware.........	59,096
New Hampshire..	141,885	Maryland.........	319,728
Vermont.........	85,425	Virginia..........	747,610
Massachusetts....	378,787	North Carolina...	393,751
Rhode Island.....	68,825	South Carolina...	249,073
Connecticut......	237,946	Georgia..........	82,548
New York........	340,120	Kentucky........	73,677
New Jersey.......	184,139	Tennessee........	35,691
Pennsylvania.....	434,373		

The second map which we present exhibits the areas actually covered by a population of two inhabitants or more to the square mile at each alternate decennial census. The deepest shading (No. 5) indicates the settlements of 1790. The aggregate area covered by population at that time was 239,935 square miles, which,[1] with the population then returned, would yield an average of 16.4 inhabitants to the square mile. This inhabited area stretched from the thirty-first degree north latitude in the south of Georgia to the forty-fifth degree north latitude in Maine, while its extent inland was comparatively insignificant. The following table shows the number of miles on each parallel of latitude occupied by population at each alternate decennial census, measuring from the Atlantic coast westward to the 100th meridian.

Degree of North Latitude.	1790.	1810.	1830.	1850.	1870.
47	0	0	0	79	209
46	0	0	15	50	230
45	30	392	392	437	858
44	226	279	299	404	777
43	339	425	485	816	1137
42	234	568	691	984	1248
41	238	471	663	1107	1325
40	358	584	912	1140	1252
39	270	565	1038	1043	1224
38	425	707	871	1032	1193
37	344	706	797	1018	1134
36	462	682	878	1057	1057
35	384	391	961	1030	1030
34	302	362	707	938	938
33	175	230	554	989	1055
32	30	227	742	929	1008
31	10	240	634	860	991
30	0	150	323	725	785
29	0	0	0	255	372
28	0	0	0	80	140
27	0	0	0	0	25
26	0	0	0	0	65

[1] *Statistical Atlas of the United States*, 1874: article, "The Progress of the Nation." We shall, from this point forward, freely use the statements made in that article without the affectation of an acknowledgment.

Examining the figures for 1790, we find the average settlement inland, along the fifteen degrees of latitude on which there was then population, to be but 255 miles, while if we exclude the forty-fifth and the thirty-first and thirty-second degrees, which were most scantily populated, we shall still have an extent inland of but 313 miles, one-half at least of which, the writer is disposed to believe, had been covered with population[1] since 1763.

We have said little of charters and constitutions, and have sought to carry forward our account of the growth of population in the American colonies without much regard to the greater or the smaller politics of the time. But one effect, of a political character, due to the geographical relations of the population just noted, fairly comes within the scope of this paper. It is that, by reason of the location of settlements coastwise, the tendency toward a union of the colonies under a common government had, from the first, been reduced to a minimum. If, on the other hand, we imagine the colonies to have been originally planted on the Mississippi and its principal tributaries, the Red, Arkansas, Missouri, and Ohio, we can not but be struck with the reason, and almost the imperative necessity, for an early union, which would have been found in their geographical relations alone. Especially as we recall how quickly the free navigation of the Mississippi became a vital issue with the first few thousands of pioneers who pushed across the Alleghanies after the peace of 1763 to make their homes in the valley of the Ohio, how constantly ever after, until the final adjustment of the question, that region was embroiled by contests arising out of disputed rights, and how ready these sons of Massachusetts, of Virginia, and of Carolina were reputed to be to fling away even their allegiance before submitting to be "cabined, cribbed, confined, bound in," by the grasp of another sovereignty upon their only outlet to the sea, it becomes scarcely possible to believe that the thirteen colonies, had they been planted in any order within the great Mississippi system, could, even under the tempering and con-

[1] That is, to the degree necessary to allow of its representation on this map, namely, with at least two inhabitants to the square mile.

trolling supervision of the crown, have remained for so much as one human generation at peace with each other without some common form of government representing their own free and perennial consent. War must, in spite of all the restraining influence of the crown, have furnished the only relief for the stifling sensations of the interior colonies, or else, as with English good sense and good feeling would have been more likely, some form of union for general purposes would at an early date have been resorted to.

But the colonies were not planted upon the Mississippi, which for more than two hundred years after the discovery of the mainland remained, we can not say unknown, but avoided by immigration, its difficult approaches and its tedious navigation below the Isle of Orleans giving it the unpromising name of "Malbouchia." It was on the coast, from Georgia to Maine, that colonies were planted in the seventeenth century. Now the Atlantic slope is made up of scores of distinct river basins, within each of which colonies might have been planted in practical independence of each other. As matter of fact, the malignant force of circumstances[1] and the more effectual ignorance and stupidity of the home government combined to involve the colonies in many disputes; yet still it remained true that each colony had its own coast-line and harbors and its own water-courses, sufficient to enable it to maintain its communication with the outer world without the leave of any other colony. Massachusetts and Connecticut did, indeed, quarrel for a while (1647–50) over the dues levied at the mouth of the Connecticut River (Saybrook) on goods destined for Springfield, and retaliatory measures were for a short time resorted to. New York, Connecticut, and New Jersey might quarrel, as, indeed, they have, in a feeble way, even since the adoption of the Constitution,[2] over the navigation of the waters of New York Bay. Virginia and Maryland had cause of dispute, traditions of which survive even to our day, in the petty war of oyster-men over their conflicting rights upon the Chesapeake, Potomac, and Pocomoke; and several of the colonies had reason to complain that their neighbors took advantage of superior power and better geographical location to tax their products.[1] But in none of these, or other instances that might be cited, were the actual or possible injuries of a vital character, tending to destroy the existence,[2] or even in an appreciable degree to impair the growth, of the colonies suffering them.

It is in this attitude of natural independence that we find the explanation of the fact that no popular sentiment in favor of an American nationality appeared in the early days of our colonial history. Even the ever-dreaded hostility of the French and their Indian allies was insufficient to furnish a motive to union. Virginians were content to be Virginians, Carolinians to be Carolinians, New Yorkers to be New Yorkers. None seemed to aspire to be Americans. The partial confederation of New England in 1643, an occasional joint expedition or contribution,[3] and the abortive convention at Albany in 1754 were all that came of the common needs and common dangers of the colonies, until the one overwhelming necessity of a common resistance to the wrongs of the mother country, which should have been the common protector, assembled the Continental Congress of 1774.

THE EXTENSION OF SETTLEMENT SINCE 1790.

Group No. 4 on the map already referred

[1] Such as the cutting into two of the Massachusetts and Connecticut grants by the Dutch occupation of New York.

[2] Over the matter of the exclusive right of certain patentees of New York to navigate the waters of New York with vessels propelled by steam. Mr. Webster summed up the situation as it existed in 1824 as follows: "The North River shut up by a monopoly from New York; the Sound interdicted by a penal law of Connecticut; reprisals authorized by New Jersey against citizens of New York."—*Argument in "Gibbons and Ogden."*

[1] Virginia had taxed the tobacco of North Carolina; Pennsylvania had taxed the products of Maryland, of New Jersey, and of Delaware.—Curtis, *Hist. Const.*, i. 290.

[2] Delaware would seem to afford an instance in contradiction of this remark. But Delaware originally formed a part of Pennsylvania, being known as "the lower counties on the Delaware." From 1703 it enjoyed a separate Legislature; but it continued to have the same Governor as Pennsylvania—a fact which generally sufficed to prevent that antagonism of interests which otherwise might have arisen from the geographical relations of the two colonies.

[3] Maryland was the most southern colony which contributed to the defense of New York in 1695.—Bancroft, iii. 34.

to exhibits the settlements of 1810; group No. 3, those of 1830; group No. 2, those of 1850; and group No. 1, those of 1870. The following table shows the areas which are thus represented on the map, reduced to figures, in square miles. For 1850 and 1870 we have, however, for convenience of comparison, added the settled areas west of the 100th meridian, which are not on the map.

Year.	Total Area of Settlement.	Population.	Average Density of Settlement. Persons to a square mile.
1790	239,935	3,929,214	16.4
1810	407,945	7,239,881	17.7
1830	632,717	12,866,020	20.3
1850	979,249	23,191,876	23.7
1870	1,272,239	38,558,371	30.2

This table excludes the nearly eighteen hundred thousand square miles of territory belonging to the United States (without reckoning the area of Alaska), which have either no population at all, or else are so sparsely populated that the settlements can not be exhibited on the scale taken for our map. The following table shows the degrees of latitude and longitude within which the *solid body* of settlement was at each period comprised, the plan of constructing it being to exclude all patches of settlement, or even considerable tracts, which were separated from the main body by vacant spaces, leaving thus only the solid mass of continuous settlement reaching from the Atlantic westward to the frontier for the time being.

Year.	EXTENT OF CONTINUOUS SETTLEMENT.	
	North Latitude.	West Longitude.
1790	31° —45°	67°—83°
1810	29° 30′—45° 15′	67°—88° 30′
1830	29° 15′—46° 15′	67°—95°
1850	28° 30′—46° 30′	67°—99°
1870	27° 15′—47° 30′	67°—99° 45′

CITIES.

The population of 1790 was very largely rural. Of the 226,085 square miles which were covered with population, 166,782 had between 2 and 18 inhabitants to the square mile; 59,282 had between 18 and 45; and but 13,871 had over 45.

Of cities of 8000 or more inhabitants, there were at this date but six: Philadelphia, with a population of 42,520; New York, with 33,131; Boston, with 18,038; Charleston, with 16,359; Baltimore, with 13,503; Salem, with (in round numbers) 8000.

Of the six cities named only three had been the first-chosen seats of population. Salem had been settled in 1628 in preference to Boston; Calvert's company sought St. Mary's, and not Baltimore; "Old Charlestown" had to be abandoned to found modern Charleston.

Of the six, Philadelphia, though founded nearly sixty years after New York, early took the lead, remaining the chief city until nearly 1810. As early as 1696 it is described as containing 1000 houses, mostly of brick, and doubtless all then as decorous in aspect, and appearing as incapable of being out of the way, as their successors at the present time. At 1750 the population of the city is put at 13,000.[1]

New York, which had grown out of a few trading huts on Manhattan Island, had come in 1677 to be a smart village of 350 houses, with perhaps 3000 inhabitants. In 1696 the number of houses had increased to 594. In 1759 there were 2000 houses, with perhaps 12,000 inhabitants. By the colonial census of 1773 the population was determined to be 21,363.

Boston had a rapid growth at first, which was checked by the almost entire cessation of immigration about 1670. In 1700 1000 houses are reported; in 1765 the number had increased only to 1676, the number of inhabitants being 15,520.

Baltimore had not been laid out until 1729. It was incorporated 1745. It remained, says Hildreth, but a petty village for twenty years afterward (ii. 414).

Of cities now noted, Providence, Portland, Albany, and Richmond were then smart towns. Newport, though past its greatest prosperity, was still a considerable place. Norfolk was coming to be known for its export trade. Savannah was as yet of little account. It was described in 1754 as containing "about 150 houses, all wooden ones, very small, and mostly old."[2] The beginnings of Detroit have already been spoken of. Mobile, New Orleans, and St. Louis were as yet foreign territory. Mobile was little more than a Spanish garrison. The site of New Orleans, a pestilential swamp, had been cleared in 1718 by the Mississippi Company, under "the reign of Law" in France. In 1769, after the transfer of Louisiana to Spain, New Orleans was found to

[1] *European Settlements in America*, ii. 254.
[2] Hildreth, ii. 454.

contain 1801 whites, 99 free colored, 60 domiciliated Indians, 1225 slaves.[1] St. Louis had been founded in 1764 as the emporium for the fur trade of the Missouri and Mississippi valleys. President Jefferson, writing of it to Colonel (afterward President) Monroe, May 4, 1806, says, "St. Louis, where there is good society, both French and American, a healthy climate, and the finest field in the United States for acquiring property."

The aggregate population of the six cities at 1790 was 131,472, being 3.4 per cent. of the total population of the country. There are now twenty-nine cities which have a larger population than the largest at 1790; 226 cities and towns as large as Salem then was; the aggregate city population of to-day is 8,071,875, being 20.9 per cent. of the total population.

The following table shows the growth of the city system from 1790 to 1870:

Year.	CITIES BY CLASSES, ACCORDING TO SIZE.								
	8000 to 12,000.	12,000 to 20,000.	20,000 to 40,000.	40,000 to 75,000.	75,000 to 125,000.	125,000 to 250,000.	250,000 to 500,000.	500,000 and over.	Total.
1790	1	3	1	1	..	..	..	..	6
1810	4	2	3	..	2	..	..	..	11
1830	12	7	3	1	1	2	..	..	26
1850	36	20	14	7	3	3	1	1	85
1870	92	63	39	14	8	3	5	2	226

The next table exhibits the aggregate city population at each specified date, in comparison with the total population of the country:

Year.	Population of United States.	Population of Cities.	Inhabitants of Cities in each 100 of the total Population.
1790	3,929,214	131,472	3.4
1810	7,239,881	356,920	4.9
1830	12,866,020	864,509	6.7
1850	23,191,876	2,897,586	12.5
1870	38,558,371	8,071,875	20.9

Speaking roundly, it may be said that at 1790 one-thirtieth of the population was in cities; at 1810, one-twentieth; at 1830, one-sixteenth; at 1860, one-eighth; at 1870, one-fifth and more.

[1] Bancroft, vi. 296.

THE CENTRE OF POPULATION.

It has been said that the average extent inland of population at 1790 was 313 miles, if we exclude the three parallels then most scantily populated. If the density of population over the settled area had been every where uniform, the centre of population[1] would have been easily found. But, in fact, so irregular was the settlement of the Atlantic slope, so far as it was occupied at all, that very elaborate calculations require to be made in order to ascertain even approximately the point at which the population would, so to speak, have *balanced*. Entering into these calculations, we find the denser settlements immediately on the coast, and especially the sea-port cities, drawing the centre of population far to the east of the geographical centre of the then populated tract, and fixing it about twenty-three miles east of Baltimore. Since that date the centre of population has moved a total distance of 399 miles, being, as nearly as possible, an average of fifty miles every ten years. The following table exhibits the position, by latitude and longitude, of the centre of population at the beginning of each decennial period, with its location approximately by reference to important towns, and indicates the number of miles which had been traversed in the westward movement of the preceding decade:

Year.	POSITION OF CENTRE OF POPULATION.			Westward Movement during preceding Decade.
	North Latitude.	West Longitude.	Approximate Location by important Towns.	
1790	39° 16.5′	76° 11.2′	23 miles E. of Baltimore.	
1800	39° 16.1′	76° 56.5′	18 " W. of Baltimore.	41 miles.
1810	39° 11.5′	77° 37.2′	40 " N.W. by W. of Washington.	36 "
1820	39° 05.7′	78° 33′	16 " N. of Woodstock.	50 "
1830	38° 57.9′	79° 16.9′	19 " W.S.W. of Moorefield.	39 "
1840	39° 02′	80° 18′	16 " S. of Clarksburg.	55 "
1850	38° 59′	81° 19′	23 " S.E. of Parkersburg.	55 "
1860	39° 00.4′	82° 48.8′	20 " S. of Chillicothe.	81 "
1870	39° 12′	83° 35.7′	48 " E. by N. of Cincinnati.	42 "
				Total..399 "

[1] By the phrase "centre of population" is commonly intended the point at which equilibrium would be reached were the country taken as a plane surface, itself without weight, but capable of sustaining weight, and *loaded* with its inhabitants, in number and position such as they are found at the period under consideration, the individuals being of equal gravity, and each consequently exerting pressure on the pivotal point proportioned to his distance therefrom.

The tremendous leap from 1850 to 1860, eighty-one miles, is due to the sudden transfer of a considerable body of population from the Atlantic to the Pacific coast, consequent on the gold discoveries, twelve individuals in San Francisco exerting as much pressure at the pivotal point, say, the crossing of the 83d meridian and the 39th parallel, as forty individuals in Boston.

The third map exhibits to the eye the movement of population which is stated in figures in the foregoing table.

THE ARITHMETICAL PROCESS OF THE NATIONAL GROWTH.

The arithmetical process of the national growth has been so fully set forth by a score of writers on population that we shall give but little space to its exposition here. The table following exhibits the ratio of increase, by ten, twenty, and thirty year periods, from 1790 to 1870:

Year.	INCREASE PER CENT.		
	In Ten Years.	In Twenty Years.	In Thirty Years.
1800	35.1	....	....
1810	36.3	84.2	....
1820	33.1	81.5	145.1
1830	33.5	77.7	142.3
1840	32.6	77.2	135.8
1850	35.8	80.2	140.7
1860	35.6	84.2	144.4
1870	22.6	66.2	125.9

THE GEOGRAPHICAL PROCESS OF THE NATIONAL GROWTH.

We find in a recent review so good a generalization of the process of our national growth geographically that we can not do better than quote it, premising that the description has reference to a series of maps like No. 5 of the present series (following), one for each census of the United States, showing the location and density of population at each date by shades of the same color. The writer says:

"The feature which this series of plates brings to view most strikingly is the constant tendency to the formation beyond the general frontier line of detached patches of color in localities favorable to population, at first of insignificant proportions, but increasing during each decade; the subsequent projection of branches toward the main body, which itself seems to develop sympathetically in the direction of these outlying masses; the formation of a broad connecting band; and finally the complete absorption of the outlying groups by the advancing main body, which in the mean time has been deepening in tint simultaneously with the extension of its area. The foregoing process, in continuous action, seems to be the normal law of growth of our population, and its operation can be distinctly discerned to-day in the feelers cautiously thrown out from the east along the lines of the Missouri, the Platte, and the Arkansas rivers toward the Rocky Mountain settlements in Colorado and New Mexico."[1]

The process may perhaps be illustrated by supposing an overflow from one of the banks of a lake of a definite volume of water, the overflow then to cease. The ground beyond the bank may seem to be level, but the water quickly discovers a slight depression through the middle of the plain, and flows out along this as a channel until, sooner or later, it finds a shallow basin, into which it drains, leaving perhaps here and there a small pool along its former channel.

Now let us suppose a second overflow to take place: the water pours as before into the interior basin, but that basin now begins to lose its original shape. By little and little, broad shallow tracts upon one side of it are covered with water, while on all the other sides narrow arms are stretched out, marking certain natural channels whose depression below the general surface the eye perhaps could not detect; and as we pass back along the path of the overflow to the lake we find the few pools become many. Now let a third overflow take place: new shallow expanses will be added to the original basin; some of the arms will be extended around to meet each other, embracing spaces which still remain dry; new arms will be stretched out in new directions, and the channel by which the water overflows from the lake will now stand full, and even begin to overflow *its* banks in turn, send out its arms, and annex broad shallow expanses of water on either hand. Still another overflow, and the whole land would lie under water, and the margin of the lake be carried clear across the plain and established, for the time at least, on the other side.

Such we conceive to be the process by which the geographical extension of our population has taken place, and had a census been taken every two or three years, and the results carefully noted down, we do not doubt that this process would be shown in almost uninterrupted action from 1776, or even from 1660, to the present time.

[1] *International Review*, Jan.-Feb., 1875, p. 133.

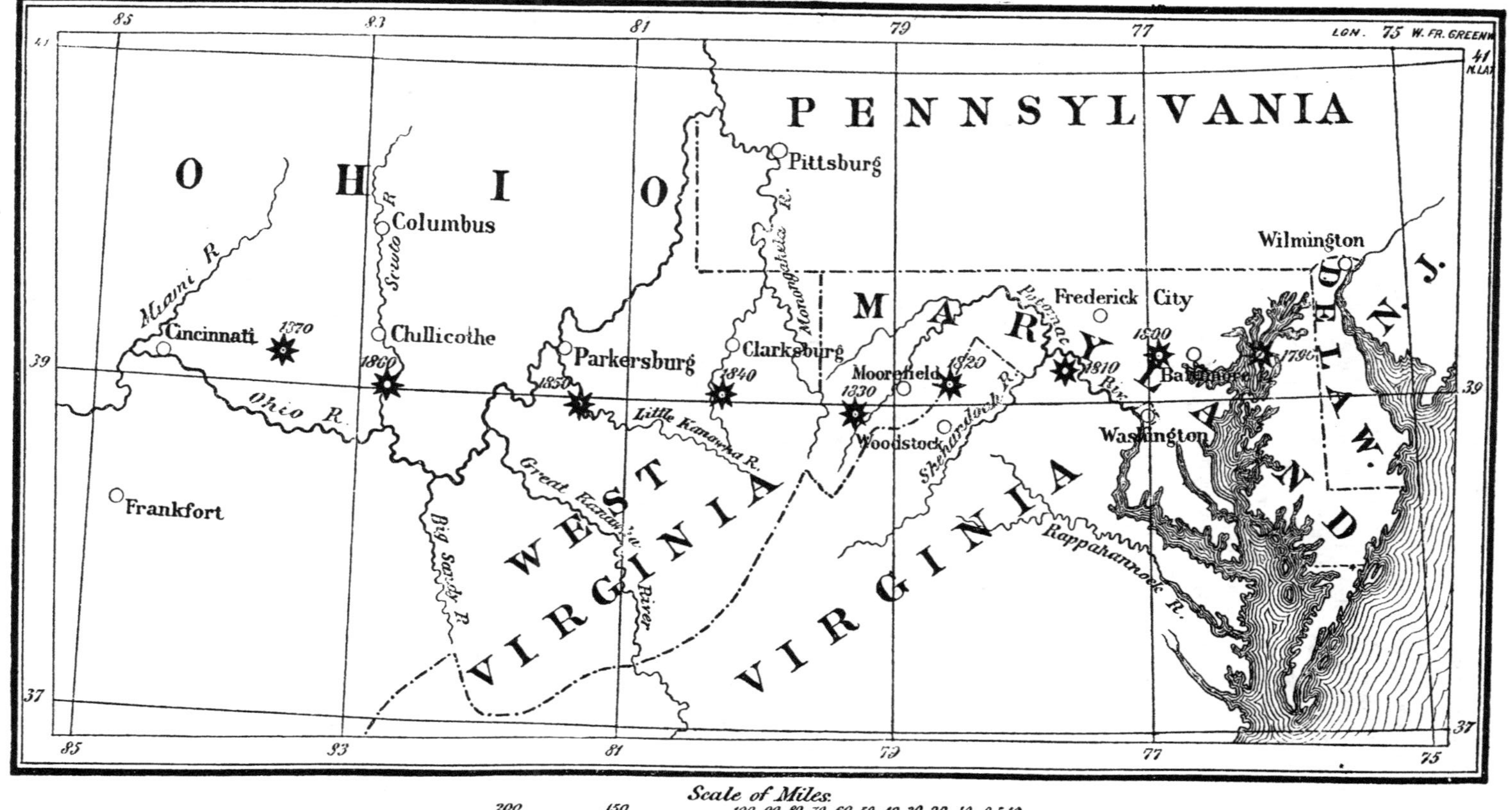
OHIO
PENNSYLVANIA
WEST VIRGINIA
VIRGINIA
MARYLAND
DELAW.
N.J.
Frankfort
Cincinnati
Columbus
Chillicothe
Parkersburg
Clarksburg
Pittsburg
Moorefield
Woodstock
Frederick City
Washington
Baltimore
Wilmington
Miami R.
Ohio R.
Scioto R.
Big Sandy R.
Great Kanawha River
Little Kanawha R.
Monongahela R.
Shenandoah R.
Potomac River
Rappahannock R.
1870
1860
1850
1840
1830
1820
1810
1800
1790
LON. 75 W. FR. GREENW.
41 N. LAT.
Scale of Miles.
200 150 100 90 80 70 60 50 40 30 20 10 0 5 10

THE PACIFIC COAST SETTLEMENTS.

But while the description thus given of the formation of bodies of population outside the general frontier and their ultimate absorption in the mass of settlement applies with substantial accuracy even in such extreme cases as the Tennessee and Kentucky groups of 1790 and the Mobile and New Orleans groups of 1810, the settlements on the Pacific coast followed another course, and have never come within the scope of this law.

The "Louisiana" which Jefferson purchased in 1803 embraced, as appears on our first map, not only a vast extent of territory on this side of the Rocky, or, as they were then known, the Stony, Mountains, but also the present Territories of Washington and Idaho and the State of Oregon beyond. There were then no white settlements in Oregon outside of the trading stations, nor was there any population worth regarding until the gold discoveries of 1848.

In 1824–25, however, a strong effort was made in Congress to secure this territory as against the conflicting claims of Great Britain by both a military occupation and a political organization, settlement to be encouraged by grants of public lands. It is not our purpose to trace the history of this bill, which was lost in the Senate, but the course of debate elicited expressions of opinion from honorable members which are not without interest and instruction to us to-day.

In the House, Mr. Smyth, of Virginia, combated the notion that the limits of "the federation" could ever be safely extended beyond the Stony Mountains. He conceived that the principle of union from mutual interests might bind together all those who should inhabit the Mississippi Valley, as their produce would all seek the same outlet. He would concede that the federation might ultimately be made to embrace "one or two tiers of States beyond the Mississippi," but, in his judgment, the federative system ought not to be extended further.

In the Senate, Mr. Dickerson, of New Jersey, offered a slashing opposition to the bill. The project of a State upon the Pacific was an absurdity. "The distance that a member of Congress from this *State of Oregon* would be obliged to travel in coming to the seat of government and returning home would be 9200 miles......If he should travel at the rate of thirty miles per day, it would require 306 days; allow for Sundays, forty-four, it would amount to 350 days. This would allow the member a fortnight to rest himself at Washington before he should commence his journey home......It would be more expeditious, however, to come by water round Cape Horn, or to pass through Behring Straits, round the north coast of this continent to Baffin Bay, thence through Davis Strait to the Atlantic, and so on to Washington. It is true, this passage is not yet discovered, except upon our maps, *but it will be as soon as Oregon shall be a State.*"

Mr. Dickerson's geographical eloquence was too much for the friends of the bill, which, on his motion, was laid upon the table.

About 1850, however, the United States government was brought to provide for four longitudinal bodies of settlement west of the 100th meridian. But though these groups of population came at about the same time under the control of the United States, they were of widely different age and history. The easternmost (in the present Territories of New Mexico and Colorado, between the 103d and 105th meridians) represented the old Spanish settlements on the Rio Grande, extending to its source in the Rocky Mountains, and containing about 50,000 whites, of very various degrees of whiteness, now brought by cession, as the result of the Mexican war, under the flag of the United States. The second line of settlement (in the present Territory of Utah, along the 112th meridian) was the result of the flight of the Mormons across the plains in 1847–48. The remaining two lines of settlement were drawn west of the Sierra Nevada, close by each other, being scarcely distant a degree in longitude, the one at the foot of the Sierra, the other at the base of the coast range. These settlements were the result of the gold discoveries in California in 1848. Two years sufficed to fill the valleys of the Sacramento and San Joaquin and the Willamette with a population of 100,000 of all races and conditions of men. Though these two lines of settlement were in their general course distinct, they were yet united by one broad band of population reaching from San Francisco to Sacramento and Stockton.

Such were the settlements west of the 100th meridian in 1850. They then comprised about 33,600 square miles, occupied by a population of an appreciable degree of density. Ten years later their population had risen to about 620,000, covering about 100,000 square miles. In 1870 the population west of the 100th meridian had risen to a full million, covering about 120,000 square miles. Each of the four lines of settlement still remains distinct, though each has grown greatly since 1850. The easternmost now stretches from the Mexican border, across the whole extent of New Mexico and Colorado, into Wyoming, in a narrow, irregular fashion, embracing in all about 140,000 souls. The Utah group now extends from the northern border of Arizona, a little way across the northern boundary of Utah, into Idaho. The population, Saints and Gentiles, has now risen to 90,000. The two California groups have extended themselves longitudinally—the westernmost from the thirty-ninth degree of latitude south to the thirty-third; the other from the thirty-fifth parallel, with but slight interruption, northward to Puget Sound.

In addition to these four longitudinal belts of population there are at the present time perhaps 150 patches of settlements, comprising each from 100 to 300 souls, with a few of even greater importance, scattered over the face of the vast region west of the 100th meridian. A little ingenuity and the use of a somewhat heroic method of treatment would undoubtedly suffice to refer nearly all of these to one or another of the seven longitudinal zones or chains of mineral deposits[1] which are recognized by our explorers and geologists.

THE POST-OFFICE.

Perhaps no better illustration could be found of the increase of population and the extension of settlements than is afforded by the history of the Post-office in the United States.

In 1692 a royal patent constituted Thomas Neale Postmaster-General of Virginia and other parts of North America. Holmes says that under Neale's patent nothing whatever resulted, on account of the "dispersed situations of the inhabitants."[1] Hildreth says, "A colonial Post-office system, though of a very limited and imperfect character, was presently established under this patent."[2] In 1695, says Bancroft, letters might be forwarded eight times a year from the Potomac to Philadelphia.[3]

In 1710 Parliament passed "an act for establishing a General Post-office for all her Majesty's dominions." The Postmaster-General was authorized to keep "one chief letter office in New York, and other chief offices at some convenient place or places in each of her Majesty's provinces or colonies in America." A line of posts was established from the Piscataqua to Philadelphia, "irregularly extended a few years after to Williamsburg, in Virginia, *the post leaving Philadelphia for the South as often as letters enough were lodged to pay the expense.* The postal communication subsequently established with the Carolinas was still more irregular."[4]

In 1753 Dr. Franklin was appointed Postmaster-General[5] for America, and held the office till 1774. Of his administration of the office he writes in his autobiography:

"The American office had hitherto never paid any thing to that of Britain.... Before I was displaced by a

---

1 This generalization was first made by Professor Blake, and has been more minutely brought out by Mr. Clarence King, as follows:

"The Pacific coast ranges upon the west carry quicksilver, tin, and chromic iron. The next belt is that of the Sierra Nevada and Oregon Cascades, which upon their west slope bear two zones—a foot-hill chain of copper mines and a middle line of gold deposits. These gold veins and the resultant placer mines extend far into Alaska, characterized by the occurrence of gold in quartz, by a small amount of that metal which is entangled in iron sulphurets, and by occupying splits in the upturned metamorphic strata of the jurassic age. Lying to the east of this zone, along the east base of the Sierras, and stretching southward into Mexico, is a chain of silver mines, containing comparatively little base metal, and frequently included in volcanic rocks. Through Middle Mexico, Arizona, Middle Nevada, and Central Idaho is another line of silver mines, mineralized with complicated association of the base metals, and more often occurring in older rocks. Through New Mexico, Utah, and Western Montana lies another zone, of argentiferous galena lodes. To the east, again, the New Mexico, Colorado, Wyoming, and Montana gold belt is an extremely well defined and continuous chain of deposits."

1 Annals, i. 444.

2 *Hist. United States*, ii. 181, 182.

3 *Hist. United States*, iii. 34.

4 Hildreth, ii. 263.

5 At first jointly with William Hunter.

freak of the ministers, we had brought it to yield *three times* as much clear revenue to the crown as the Post-office of Ireland."

In 1774 William Goddard, a printer, of Baltimore, proposed a plan for a "Constitutional American Post-office," and, after much agitation of the subject, a service was actually inaugurated under Goddard's management; but it had brief continuance.

After the outbreak in 1775 the colonies were for a time driven to their own individual efforts for maintaining the Post-office.[1] On the 26th of July, 1775, however, the Continental Congress resolved that a Postmaster-General be appointed for the "United Colonies," who should hold his office at Philadelphia, where the Congress was sitting. We ask special attention to the phraseology of the resolution fixing the general scope of the postal service:

"That *a line of posts* be appointed, under the direction of the Postmaster-General, *from Falmouth, in New England, to Savannah, in Georgia, with as many cross posts as he shall think fit.*"

The expression shows the situation of the population as stretched along the coast, with but little extent inland.

In 1790 the number of post-offices in the United States was seventy-five; the aggregate length of the post-roads, 1875 miles; the amount paid for transportation of the mails, $22,081; the gross postal revenues were $37,935, and the expenditures $32,140. Mails were conveyed but three times per week between New York and Boston in summer, and twice in winter, occupying five days in transit.[2] Only five mails per week were exchanged between New York and Philadelphia, requiring two days in each direction, the weight rarely, if ever, exceeding the capacity of horseback mails. The number of letters transported during 1790 probably did not exceed 300,000, and the annual transportation (counting every trip) was about 350,000 miles. In 1870 there were 28,492 post-offices; the length of post-roads was 231,232 miles; the amount paid for transportation was $10,884,653; the postal revenue was $19,772,220; the expenditures, $23,948,837. In 1870 the number of letters carried in the mails was not less than 590,000,000, and the aggregate of distances traveled amounted to 97,024,996 miles.[1] In 1870 the letter-carriers of Manchester, New Hampshire, delivered more letters than constituted the whole burden of the postal service in 1790.

In 1835 the total steamboat transportation of the mails aggregated 906,959 miles, the railroad transportation, 270,504 miles.[2] In 1850 the steamboat transportation was 2,659,656 miles, the railroad transportation, 604,396. In 1870 the steamboat transportation had risen to 4,122,385 miles, the railroad transportation[3] to 47,551,970 miles.

The following table exhibits the growth of the postal system, by five-year intervals, from 1790 to 1870:

Year.	Number of Post-offices.	Length of Post-routes in Miles.	Year.	Number of Post-offices.	Length of Post-routes in Miles.
1790	75	1,875	1835	10,770	115,176
1795	453	13,207	1840	13,468	155,739
1800	903	20,817	1845	14,183	143,940
1805	1558	31,070	1850	18,417	178,672
1810	2300[4]	36,406	1855	24,410	227,906
1815	3000	43,748	1860	28,498	240,594
1820	4500	72,492	1865	20,550[5]	142,340
1825	5677	94,052	1870	28,492	231,232
1830	8450	112,774			

1 The Provincial Congress of Massachusetts, May 13, established a postal system, with routes from Cambridge to Georgetown, in Lincoln County, Maine; to Haverhill; to Providence; to Woodstock (Connecticut) by way of Worcester; and from Worcester, by way of Springfield, to Great Barrington; and to Falmouth, in Barnstable County. Fourteen post-offices were set up. New Hampshire, May 18, established an office at Portsmouth. In June, Rhode Island established post-routes and post-offices.

2 In 1792 we find Mr. Jefferson, as Secretary of State, writing to Colonel Pickering respecting the practicability of sending the mails 100 miles a day. Op., iii. 344.

1 Postmaster-General's Report, 1870.

2 Transportation by four-horse post-coaches and two-horse stages, 16,874,050 miles; on horseback and in sulkies, 7,817,973 miles.

3 We find General Jackson's Postmaster-General, Amos Kendall, engaged in 1835 in the same warfare with the railroads which so enlisted the passions and the energies of Mr. Creswell. Mr. Kendall, in his report of that year, informs Congress that he does not propose to pay the exorbitant rates demanded by the companies. "He will sooner put post-coaches or mail-wagons on the old roads, and run them there until public opinion or the force of superior authority induces the associations which have been permitted to monopolize the means of speedy conveyance on their routes to abate their terms."

4 This and the two following entries have much the appearance of guess-work, and are perhaps explained by the following somewhat remarkable expression occurring in the report of the Postmaster-General for 1823: "*As near as can be known from the records of this department,* there are about 5142 post-offices established. Means have been taken to ascertain the exact number."

5 The reduction is explained by the war of secession.

THE CONSTITUENTS OF OUR POPULATION.

It will have been noted that the result of the national enumeration at 1790 showed the proportion of whites to blacks to be a little more than five to one. The following table shows the number of parts in each 100 of the total population sustained by the colored element at each successive census under the Constitution, and, secondly, the decennial rate of increase within the colored element itself:

Year.	COLORED.	
	Percentage of total Population.	Percentage of Increase during preceding Decade.
1790	19.3	
1800	18.9	32.32
1810	19	37.05
1820	18.4	28.58
1830	18.2	31.44
1840	16.8	23.40
1850	13.3	26.60
1860	14.1	22.07
1870	12.7	9.21

The rapid falling off in the rate of increase from 1860 to 1870 is the feature of this table which will at once arrest attention. Unfortunately we can not know how much of this is due to the effects of war from 1860 to 1865, when a violent and unprepared emancipation was wrought, not so much by the proclamation of the Executive as by the operations of armies, drawing after them vast bodies of the blacks to be crowded into camps and cities, uninstructed and unprovided, to perish by disease and privations in uncounted thousands; how much to the effects of emancipation upon habits of life, occupation, diet, and location during the period following the return of peace. Had Congress in a proper view of the prodigious change which had passed upon the United States, and of the especial need of statistical information for directing the reconstruction, social, political, and industrial, of the South, provided for a census in 1865, we should have been able to see just where and in what condition the war left this race, and where and how the state of peace took them up. But that opportunity has gone by.

The number of colored persons counted in the census of 1870 was 4,880,009. Few of these were found north of the forty-first degree of latitude.

OUR FOREIGN ELEMENTS.

The statistics of the foreign elements in the United States are historically very incomplete. For only three censuses, 1850–70, has the "place of birth" been returned with enumeration. From the former of these dates backward to 1820 we have only the tables compiled from the passenger lists of vessels bringing immigrants—data notoriously imperfect. Before 1820 we have only scraps of evidence on the subject.

In one sense, substantially all the white inhabitants within the present United States were at one time foreigners. But in the days when the population was mainly recruited by immigration the word "foreigner" was never applied to an Englishman, nor generally to a Scot or Welshman, nor always to an Irishman. Thus we find it recorded of the Rhode Island Colony in 1680: "We have lately had few or no new-comers, either of English, Scotch, Irish, or *foreigners*."[1]

The population of the thirteen States was mainly composed of Englishmen. Mr. Bancroft (vol. vii. 355) speaks of the colonies in 1775 as inhabited by persons "one-fifth of whom had for their mother-tongue some other language than the English." The order in which other nationalities contributed to the numbers of that population the same writer indicates as follows: "Intermixed with French, still more with Swedes, and yet more with Dutch and Germans."

The French were mainly Protestant refugees. After the revocation of the Edict of Nantes, William III. dispatched to the colonies large numbers of those who had sought a home in England. A few of these came to Massachusetts,[2] where some of the most illustrious names of subsequent history speak of the virtues of the Huguenots. In 1690 a large number of these refugees were sent out to Virginia, and in the same year many arrived in Carolina. In 1698 another considerable body arrived in Virginia. Even prior to these dates the French had appeared in New York. "When the Protestant churches in Rochelle were razed," says Mr. Bancroft (ii. 302), "the colonists of that city were gladly admitted, and the French Prot-

[1] Chalmers, i. 282–284.

[2] Holmes cites an act of the Legislature of 1692 prohibiting any of the French nation to reside in any of the sea-ports or frontier towns within the province without license, the reason assigned for the rule being that with the French Protestants "many of a contrary religion and interest" had obtruded themselves.—*Annals of America*, i. 441.

estants came in such numbers that the public documents were sometimes issued in French as well as in Dutch and English."

The persons of Swedish stock referred to by Mr. Bancroft as found in the colonies in 1775 were largely the descendants of those who settled Delaware. Of these Mr. Bancroft says, in another part of his history (ii. 297, 298): "The descendants of the colonists, in the course of generations widely scattered and blended with emigrants of other lineage, constitute probably more than one part in two hundred of the present population of our country. At the time of the surrender they did not much exceed seven hundred souls." The fecundity which Mr. Bancroft thus assigns these Swedes is only surpassed by that which Mr. Hildreth (i. 267) assigns to the twenty-five thousand, or fewer, original emigrants into New England prior to 1640—"a primitive stock from which has been derived not less, perhaps, than a fourth part of the present population of the United States." Mr. Hildreth must have formed his notions of the average capabilities of the early New Englanders from the contemplation of exceptional cases like that of Obadiah Holmes, the Anabaptist, who was publicly flogged about 1651, and is reputed to have had five thousand descendants in 1790.

But of all the European nations outside the British Isles, "the chief migration," says Mr. Bancroft (i. 450), "was from that Germanic race most famed for love of personal independence."

The commercial enterprise of Holland had already planted many thousands of her subjects in the "New Netherlands" when the dominion of the last of the colonies passed to England; nor did Dutch or German emigration cease, but it rather increased, when New York lost scout, burgomaster, and schepens, to gain mayor, aldermen, and sheriff.

We have said that South Carolina, in its earliest settlement, received accessions of Dutch both from New York and from Holland. Before the downfall of the power of Holland on the Continent the Dutch had also appeared in Connecticut, and for a time disputed with the English the sovereignty of the soil even to the Connecticut River, but their few colonists were overwhelmed by the rapid invasion of the English.

To Pennsylvania the Germans resorted, until, in 1764, Durand, in a report to Choiseul, wrote that "Germans weary of subordination to England, and unwilling to serve under English officers, openly declared that Pennsylvania would one day be called Little Germany." "Like Pennsylvania and the Carolinas," says Mr. Hildreth of New York in 1749, "it contained a great admixture, but those of Dutch origin still constituted a majority."

Of all the German states, the misfortunes of the Palatinate made it the largest contributor to the population of the New World. When Hunter came out in 1710 as Governor of New York, we find notice of his bringing with him 2700 of this unfortunate people. Large numbers of the Palatines settled also in Carolina, upon the Roanoke and Pamlico, and many were cut off by the Tuscaroras in the savage rising of 1712. "We shall soon have a German colony," wrote Logan of Pennsylvania in 1726, "so many thousands of Palatines are already in the country."

Even after the adoption of the Constitution, and the removal of the seat of government to the banks of the Potomac, we find a proposition seriously entertained for bringing over Germans to furnish the labor for building up Washington city.[1]

The Swiss also appeared in considerable force among the early settlers of America. Newbern (as we now write it), on the Neuse, speaks of old Bern, on the Aar. In 1730 Swiss immigrants founded Purysburg, the first town on the Savannah; and Grahame speaks of considerable accessions to the same State from the same source in 1733.

"Asylum for the oppressed," of all nations and all religions, as America had become, the Moravians found their way in large numbers to our shores. Of Oglethorpe's 300 recruits in 1736 more than one-half were of this faith, to which their brethren who preceded them had already witnessed by raising their "Ebenezer" on the banks of the Savannah. Pennsylvania, however, was their chosen country of refuge during the eighteenth century.

It will readily be believed that help in building up so many youthful colonies, from whatever quarter it came, was eagerly welcomed by the English population, and that

---

[1] Washington's works, xii. 305, 306.

foreigners were not long excluded from the full privileges of citizenship. The first colonial naturalization act of which we find notice was that of Maryland in 1666. Virginia followed in 1671. Pennsylvania naturalized the Swedes, Finns, and Dutch of Delaware. Carolina naturalized the French refugees she received in 1696.

The English Privy Council was long troubled by the scope and effect given to the colonial acts of naturalization, by which aliens were vested with the power of exercising functions which they were disabled from performing by the Navigation Acts. At last, by act of Parliament in 1746, a uniform system of naturalization was established, on the basis of seven years' residence, an oath of allegiance, and profession of the "Protestant Christian faith."

Of the inhabitants of the British Isles by far the largest contribution, next to that of England, was from Ireland. This immigration, though somewhat spasmodic, had reached a vast though indeterminate total before the Revolution. The Irish settled all the way from New Hampshire, where Londonderry was founded in 1719 by a colony of about 100 families from Ulster, to Carolina, where a colony of 500 arrived as early as 1715.[1] The author of *European Settlements in America* speaks of the population of Virginia in 1750–54 as "growing every day more numerous by the migration of the Irish, who, not succeeding so well in Pennsylvania as the more industrious and frugal Germans, sell their lands in that province to the latter, and take up new ground in the remote counties of Virginia, Maryland, and North Carolina.[2] These," he adds, "are chiefly Presbyterians from the north of Ireland, who in America are generally called the Scotch-Irish" (ii. 216). It is probably to some colony thus planted that Jefferson referred when he wrote (Op., vi. 485) of "the wild Irish who had gotten possession of the valley between the Blue Ridge and the North Mountains, forming a barrier over which none ventured to leap, and could still less venture to settle among."

[1] A small colony under Fergusson had preceded them, arriving as early as 1683.—Bancroft's *Hist. United States*, ii. 173.

[2] Especially in the northwestern counties.—Hildreth, ii. 416.

But Pennsylvania was still the especial centre of attraction to the Irish before the Revolution. In 1729 there was a large Irish migration to Pennsylvania. The years 1771–73 appear also to have witnessed a wholesale movement of population from Ireland, especially the northern counties, into this province. Of these large numbers found their way to the region of the Monongahela and the Alleghany, and formed the pioneers of a vast population in Western and Southwestern Pennsylvania. We get a lively impression of the importance of this element a little later, when we find in the letters of that vehement Federalist, Oliver Wolcott, Jun., the formidable "whisky insurrection" of 1794 attributed almost wholly to the Irish of Pittsburg and vicinity. Thus: "The Irishmen in that quarter have at length proceeded to great extremities;"[1] "Pennsylvania need not be envied her Irishmen,"[2] etc. They might be in a strange land, but in making war upon the excise they found no unfamiliar or uncongenial occupation.

The Scotch were then, as they are now, every where, though not largely in New England, nor generally *in colonies* any where.

In New Jersey,[3] Georgia, and North Carolina we find, perhaps, the most prominent mention of the Scotch as a distinct element of the population. One exception to the rule that the Scotch did not tend to settle in colonies was found in the case of Highland soldiers of the British army discharged from service in America.

New York, as the only considerable State of the thirteen which was originally formed under any other flag than that of England, might be supposed to have possessed the largest foreign element, proportionally, of all; and, indeed, from the first, not only was New York "a city of the world," with a citizenship "chosen from the Belgic provinces and England, from France and Bohemia, from Germany and Switzerland, from Piedmont and the Italian Alps,"[4] but the Hudson, from

[1] Gibbs, *Adm. Washington and Adams*, i. 156.

[2] Gibbs, i. 157.

[3] In 1686, in defending their charter, the proprietors of East Jersey urged that they had sent out several hundreds of persons from Scotland.

[4] Bancroft, ii. 301. The Bohemians survive unto this day.

the bay to Albany, was settled with a most motley population.

But Pennsylvania long disputed with New York the honor of having the most curiously and variously composed population, and at the date of the Revolution indisputably carried off the palm. Chalmers says that Penn found the banks of the Delaware inhabited by 3000 persons, Swedes, Dutch, Finlanders, and English. Those he brought with him and drew after him were only more widely assorted. "The diversity of people, religions, nations, and languages," says the author of *European Settlements*, "here is prodigious. Upward of 250,000 people," is his summary for 1750, "half of whom are Germans, Swedes, or Dutch."

At a little later date within the century General Washington wrote: "Pennsylvania is a large State, and from the policy of its founder, and especially from the great celebrity of Philadelphia, has become the general receptacle of foreigners from all countries and of all descriptions" (Op., xii. 324).

The large accessions from other countries than England, received by the Southern colonies from Maryland to Georgia, have already been sufficiently noticed. The States which now represent these colonies are those which have fewest foreigners.

On the other hand, of all the colonies, those of New England received the smallest proportional accessions from nationalities other than pure English, and earliest experienced the cessation of immigration, even from England.

"The policy of encouraging immigration from abroad," says Hildreth (ii. 312, 313), "which contributed so much to the rapid advancement of Pennsylvania and Carolina, never found favor in New England. Even the few Irish settlers at Londonderry became objects of jealousy."

In 1796 we find Washington writing to Sir John Sinclair as follows (Op., xii. 323, 324):

"Their numbers are not augmented by foreign emigrants; yet from their circumscribed limits, compact situation, and natural population, they are filling the western parts of the State of New York and the country on the Ohio with their own surplusage."

It is to this long cessation of immigration into New England that Madison refers when, writing after the fourth census (1820), he says:

"It is worth remarking that New England, which has sent out such a continued swarm to other parts of the Union for a number of years, has continued at the same time, as the census shows, to increase in population, although it is well known that it has received but comparatively few emigrants from any quarter" (Op., iii. 213).

Of the immigration between 1790 and 1820 we know little precisely. Dr. Seybert estimates the total arrivals at 250,000, but the very form of the estimate reveals the inadequacy of the data from which it was constructed. With 1820 begins the record of arrivals at our ports. The following table shows the immigration for the period 1820–50:

Year.	Total.	From Germany.	From British Isles.
1820–30	151,000	8,000	82,000
1830–40	599,900	152,000	283,000
1840–50	1,713,000	435,000	1,048,000

With the seventh census begins our exact account of foreigners in the United States. From this it appears that of the total population at 1850 nine and a half per cent. were of foreign birth, at 1860 thirteen per cent., at 1870 fourteen per cent. At the several dates named the several specified nationalities contributed as follows to the total foreign population:

Nationality.	1850.	1860.	1870.
	Per cent.	Per cent.	Per cent.
Irish	43.5	38.9	33.3
Germans	26.4	30.8	30.4
English and Welsh	13.9	11.5	11.2
British Americans	6.7	6.0	8.9
Swedes, Norwegians, and Danes	0.81	1.7	4.4

The foreign immigrants to the United States have placed themselves mainly between the thirty-eighth and the forty-sixth degrees of latitude.[1] The meridian of the western boundary of Pennsylvania divides this foreign population into an eastern and a western half.

---

1 The geographical relation of the foreign and colored elements of the population is complemental in a high degree. Taking the States of Delaware, Maryland, West Virginia, Kentucky, and Missouri as constituting a central zone neutral to the two elements, we have the following numerical proportions for each 1000 of the population:

	Colored.	Foreign.
Northern and Northwestern States	14	197
Central States	132	91
Southern and Southwestern States	415	22

Some of the foreign elements are themselves in turn complemental in their location. Thus two-thirds of the Germans are found west of Buffalo, two-thirds of the Irish east of it; the Scandinavians are mainly west of Lake Michigan, the British Americans east of it.

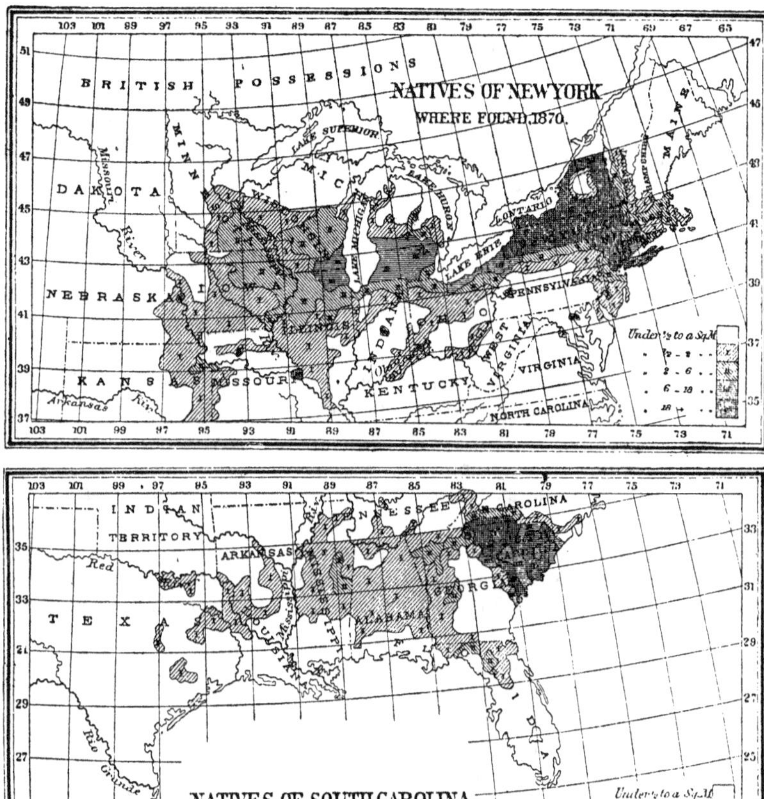

THE FECUNDITY OF THE FOREIGN ELEMENTS.

In addition to the 5,500,000 foreigners residing in the United States, there are 4,167,616 both of whose parents were foreign, 786,388 more who had a foreign father and a native mother, 370,782 who had a native father and a foreign mother, and by consequence there are 5,324,786 who have one *or* both parents foreign.

Very grave statistical blunders have been committed by some very pretentious writers on population, who have sought to establish the comparative sterility of the native white population of North America. The following sentence, quoted from a paper read before the British Association in 1856, contains in substance a doctrine which was for a long time generally accepted in Europe, and has even been repeated on this side the Atlantic:

"From the general unfitness of the climate to the European constitution, coupled with the occasional pestilential visitations which occur in the healthier localities, on the whole, on an average of three or four generations, *extinction of the European races in North America* would be almost certain, if the communication with Europe were entirely cut off."

Our space would not serve for the discussion of this question did it require to be argued at length; but Dr. Edward Jarvis, of Massachusetts, has so completely exposed[1] the successive mistakes in figures and fallacies in reasoning by which this most disparaging conclusion[2] was reached, that it is only necessary to refer to the subject here

[1] *The Atlantic Monthly*, April, 1872.

[2] Mr. Frederick Kapp, formerly of New York, now of Germany, who has perhaps done more than any one else to give currency to these views in Europe, reached the conclusion that of the free population of 1850 but thirty-six per cent., and of that of 1860 but twenty-nine per cent., was American in the sense of being derived from inhabitants of the country at 1790. No result on this subject has been too monstrous to receive credence from the press of Europe.

in order to assure our readers, who are liable at any time to meet statements of this character floating through the press or stranded in the proceedings of scientific associations, that there is not the shadow of a statistical reason for attributing to the native American population prior to the war of secession a deficiency in reproductive vigor compared with any people that ever lived upon the face of the earth.

INTERSTATE MIGRATION.

It will have been observed that the early colonists did not wait for a common form of government before inaugurating that system of internal migration which has been one of the most marked features of our national history. Almost as if from love of change, they moved up and down the coast by turns, or from a half-settled East to a wholly unsettled West. We have already had so many occasions to notice these movements of population that under the present title we will speak only of those wholesale migrations which are revealed by the census since 1850, when the "place of birth" came first to be recorded. The *Edinburgh Review* of July, 1854, so well summarizes the results of the seventh census in this respect that we condense the statement for insertion here.

1. In the Free States the movement was generally due west—from New York, for instance, to Michigan and Wisconsin, and from Pennsylvania to Ohio. And so strong was this passion that the West itself supplied a population to the further West. Ohio had sent 215,000 to the three States beyond her; Indiana had retained 120,000 from Ohio, but had sent on 50,000 of her own; Illinois had taken 95,000 from Ohio and Indiana, and given 7000 to Iowa.

2. The migration from the central Slave States had followed the same general law of a westerly movement; but it had taken also a partial northwest direction into the Free States.

3. In the planting States the movement had been mostly within themselves, taking a southwesterly and westerly direction.

4. The American-born population of Texas had come principally from the Slave States; that of California from the Free States; that of the Territories more from the Free than from the Slave.

The census of 1870 shows the internal movements of population to be not less but more wholesale and incessant than at 1850. Our fourth map shows where the natives of New York and of South Carolina severally were found within the United States at the date of enumeration. The reader will be struck by the conformity to the rules laid down by the Edinburgh reviewer in his Nos. 1 and 3. A map showing the *habitat* of the Kentucky-born population, which our space does not allow us to introduce, shows that this one of the former "central Slave States" still conforms in its emigrations to the rule laid down in No. 2.

The following table shows *by even thousands* for each State at 1870 (1) the number of persons residing in the State who were born therein; (2) the number residing in the State who were born in other States and Territories of the Union; (3) the number born in the State who were residing in other States or Territories. The figures on the left indicate the rank of the States in population.

	State.	(1)	(2)	(3)
16	Alabama.......	744,000	243,000	230,000
26	Arkansas	233,000	247,000	55,000
24	California......	170,000	181,000	12,000
25	Connecticut....	350,000	73,000	137,000
34	Delaware	95,000	21,000	39,000
33	Florida	110,000	73,000	15,000
12	Georgia........	1,034,000	139,000	274,000
4	Illinois.........	1,190,000	835,000	290,000
6	Indiana........	1,049,000	491,000	321,000
11	Iowa...........	429,000	561,000	89,000
29	Kansas	63,000	253,000	11,000
8	Kentucky......	1,081,000	177,000	403,000
21	Louisiana......	502,000	163,000	63,000
23	Maine..........	551,000	27,000	149,000
20	Maryland	630,000	68,000	176,000
7	Massachusetts..	903,000	201,000	244,000
13	Michigan	507,000	409,000	66,000
28	Minnesota	126,000	153,000	13,000
18	Mississippi.....	564,000	253,000	139,000
5	Missouri	874,000	625,000	171,000
35	Nebraska	19,000	74,000	5,000
37	Nevada	3,000	20,000	2,000
31	New Hampshire	242,000	46,000	125,000
17	New Jersey	575,000	142,000	149,000
1	New York	2,988,000	257,000	1,074,000
14	North Carolina.	1,029,000	40,000	307,000
3	Ohio...........	1,842,000	450,000	807,000
36	Oregon	37,000	42,000	6,000
2	Pennsylvania ..	2,727,000	250,000	675,000
32	Rhode Island ..	125,000	37,000	45,000
22	South Carolina.	679,000	19,000	246,000
9	Tennessee	1,028,000	212,000	404,000
19	Texas..........	389,000	368,000	26,000
30	Vermont.......	244,000	40,000	177,000
10 27	Virginia..... West Virginia }	1,545,000	91,000	584,000
15	Wisconsin	450,000	240,000	97,000

THE POPULATION OF 1870.

The *situs* of the thirty-seven and a half millions of our people who at 1870 were west of the 100th meridian is shown sep-

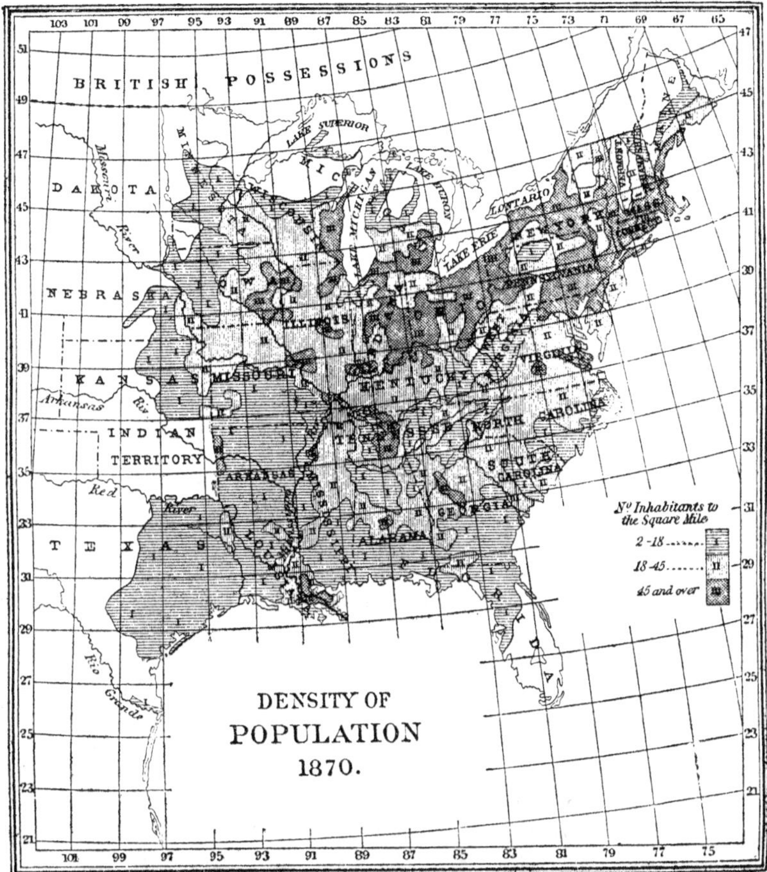

arately in our fifth map. The solid mass of continuous settlement here represented covers more than 1,150,000 square miles, lying between 27° 15′ and 47° 30′ north latitude, and between 67° and 99° 45′ west longitude. The average density of population over this vast tract is 32.7 inhabitants to the square mile. This population is, however, shown not as an average, but in three degrees of density of wide range.

Of the four great river systems, the Atlantic system, with 304,538 square miles, contains 14,207,453 inhabitants, or 46.6 to the square mile; the northern lake system, with 185,339 square miles, 4,399,604 inhabitants, an average of 23.7; the Mississippi or Gulf system, with 1,683,303 square miles, 19,111,804 inhabitants, an average of 11.3; the Pacific system, an average of but 0.98 inhabitants to the square mile.

Such is the story of our population, told with more figures of arithmetic than figures of speech. Speculation on the future would here be alike impertinent and vain. Whether the writer who tells of the increase and territorial expansion of our population at the second centennial of independence shall describe the settlement of six hundred thousand, or twelve hundred thousand, or the whole of the vast domain yet uninhabited—whether the flag of the Union shall wave over fifty States and a hundred millions of people only, within our present borders, or over a territory co-extensive with the continent and populous as Europe, may be left in all trustfulness with the Power that hath thus far guided the career of this young nation. As I write, my eye falls on the motto of Connecticut, lifted up first in a savage wilderness, and lifted up since in many a day of battle: *Qui transtulit, sustinet.* Yea, and will sustain.

VIII.

MONETARY DEVELOPMENT.

EMIGRANTS are never of the capitalist class, while the great need of settlers in a new country is capital. All forms of capital are required, and the only question is what make-shift will do to-day, and what requirement can be postponed until the morrow. Value money is that form of capital which, under such circumstances, seems to be the most dispensable; but it can not be disposed of, any more than a community could sell all its wagons, boats, scales, measures, and other tools of transportation and exchange, unless some substitute is provided. Hence various substitutes are adopted whenever they can be devised, and the monetary history of the United States from the first colonization until now is a history of experiments with cheap substitutes for money.

Barter currency was adopted very generally in the colonies from the first, rates at which goods should exchange being fixed by law. Taxes were collected in kind, and fees were established in barter. In New England the aborigines had a currency of beads made from clam shells (wampum or peag, or wampumpeag), which the whites adopted and used among themselves and with the Indians, the rates being fixed by prices demanded in wampum by the Indians for furs, and by the prices which the furs would bring in England. Wampum became overabundant, depreciated, became broken, and was abolished as a nuisance about 1650. In 1652 a mint was established at Boston, which went on coining "pine-tree" coins for over thirty years, although, as the mint was illegal, its coins were all dated 1652 to conceal the continuance of its operations. The charge for minting was exorbitant, and the English mint law of 1663 having made the importation and exportation of coin free, and the law of 1666 having abolished all charge for coining, the Massachusetts mint law served to drive the precious metal away. The coins were called shillings, etc., but were twenty-five per cent. below sterling of the same denomination, giving par of silver 6*s.* 8*d.*, New England currency, per ounce. This became the standard, but the barter currency being still legal, the silver coins which were not exported (and there was a severe law against exportation) were all clipped.[1]

In 1704 a proclamation of Queen Anne fixed the rates of Spanish and other foreign coins for the colonies. The Spanish dollar, or piece of eight, was rated at 4*s.* 6*d.* Hence sterling was changed into dollars at two-ninths of a dollar for a shilling, or $4 4/9 for £1, which remained the "par" until January 1, 1874. New England currency being twenty-five per cent. worse, £1 in New England currency was $3 33. A Spanish dollar, or piece of eight, in New England currency was 6*s.*

In 1686 a bank was proposed in Massachusetts, but its history is obscure. In 1690 paper notes were first issued by that colony to pay for an unfortunate expedition against Canada.[2] The issue was moderate at first, and canceled year by year. In 1704 the redemption was postponed two years, and after that there was no stopping. Issues were made to pay the expenses of government, and other issues to loan on mortgage, carrying out the scheme for getting rich by printing and borrowing, which starts up every generation over again. There were special "hard times" in Massachusetts in 1715,

---

[1] A mint was established in Maryland in 1661, but nothing is known of its history.

[2] Among the authorities on the colonial currencies should be mentioned the following: Hutchinson's *History of Massachusetts Bay* (very intelligent and correct on finance); Douglas's *Summary* (unequal, but valuable); Holmes's *Annals*. Other old histories are generally occupied with other than financial interests. Arnold's *Rhode Island* takes full account of trade and finance. A pamphlet published at Boston in 1740, and republished in Lord Overstone's tracts, 1857, *Discourse concerning the Currencies of the British Plantations*, is of great value. Special works are Felt on Massachusetts currency, Bronson on Connecticut currency, Hickox on New York currency, and the collection in Phillips's *Colonial and Continental Paper Currencies*. These last all pursue chiefly the antiquarian interest. Bronson's is the only one which shows a knowledge of financial science.

1720, 1727, 1733, 1741, 1749. Rhode Island, Connecticut, New York, and New Jersey first issued bills in 1709 for the second expedition to Canada. In 1714 New York issued £27,680 in bills of credit as a "back-pay grab." Pennsylvania first issued paper in 1723. Franklin urged more issues, and wrote in favor of them.[1] Maryland issued bills in 1734, to be redeemed in sterling in three payments, at fifteen, thirty, and forty-five years. These payments being discounted, exchange rose to 250. Virginia used tobacco-warehouse receipts as currency until 1755, when she issued paper, and pushed it to great excess. North Carolina was a very poor colony, and her currency was greatly depreciated, although not over £52,500 in 1740. South Carolina issued for war purposes in 1702. Rice was a barter medium.

The only colony which ever resumed was Massachusetts. In 1745 the New England colonies made an expedition against Cape Breton, and took Louisbourg. The issues to pay for this rose to £2,466,712, nominal value in New England currency, in Massachusetts alone. Parliament ransomed Cape Breton, and Massachusetts imported her share of the ransom in silver and copper, redeemed her notes at eleven for one, and became "the silver colony." In 1751 Parliament forbade legal-tender non-interest-bearing notes for New England, at the prayer of Massachusetts, and in 1764 for all the colonies. Gold circulated by weight, not being legal tender until 1762, when a law was passed in Massachusetts making it a tender at 2½*d.* silver per grain. This was five per cent. more than it was worth, and silver being unjustly rated, was exported, and became scarce.

Issues within the act of Parliament continued to be made in the older colonies, and in 1775, when the representatives of the New England colonies met to prepare for war, Massachusetts agreed to allow their bills to circulate in her territory, because they had nothing else.

The First Continental Congress met at Philadelphia September 5, 1774. Its first measures were not military, but renewed the commercial war which the colonies had tried before, which was believed in long afterward, but which always accomplished

[1] See vol. ii. of his works.

harm to the enemy at the expense of tenfold harm at home in local and class bickerings. Trade was thrown away just when wise policy dictated to keep it, and even fight for it. After December, 1774, nothing was to be imported from any part of the British Empire; and after September, 1775, nothing was to be exported to the same. English goods were needed for the army, and came by way of the European continent and the West Indies; and lumber and tobacco went out the same way.

The Second Congress, May 10, 1775, set about making war, but it had no power to tax, and therefore no power to borrow. New York proposed bills of credit of the old kind, to be redeemed by taxes, and this plan was adopted. The first issue was ordered June 23, 1775—promises to pay 2,000,000 Spanish dollars. The issues were apportioned among the colonies on an estimate of population, and they were called upon to redeem the quotas assigned them by taxes. Rhode Island, Massachusetts, and New Hampshire alone did this entirely; New York, Pennsylvania, New Jersey, Maryland, and Virginia did so in part. The issues went on, however, and in January, 1777, the depreciation began, although it was not admitted by Congress until September.[1]

During 1777 all means of coercion by public officers and private committees were used to enforce the legal-tender character of the bills and to keep down prices. Some crimes were perpetrated in the name of liberty in this connection. In September, 1779, the issues were $160,000,000, and Congress promised that they should not exceed $200,000,000. The depreciation was twenty-eight for one (silver, 2800). In March, 1780, silver was at 6500.[2] Congress recognized a depreciation of forty for one, and recommended the repeal of all tender laws, and issued six-year six per cent. notes. The Register of the

[1] Monographs on the Continental currency have been published by Henry Phillips, 1866, and J. W. Schuckers, 1874. See also the article in *Harper's Magazine* for March, 1863. On the social effects, see Pelatiah Webster's *Essays*, 1791. He gives the depreciation from a merchant's books. Another table is given in *Niles's Register*, November 23, 1833.

[2] In 1780 and 1781 an officer's mess bill included sugar at $14, $16, and $18 per pound; twist, $10 per yard; three brushes and a blackball, $95; a black silk handkerchief, $75; eggs, $12 per dozen.—*Niles's Register*, August 5, 1826.

Treasury made a report to Congress in 1828,[1] in which he put the sum of the issues at $241,000,000 of the first tenor. Jefferson says $200,000,000,[2] and he puts the value at $36,000,000 in specie. He estimated the cost of the war at $140,000,000. Another statement from a Treasury report of 1790 gives $357,400,000 old tenor and $2,000,000 new tenor. These were partly re-issues. The same report estimates the cost of the war at $135,100,000 in specie.[3] In fact, as John Adams wrote to Niles,[4] the history of the Revolution [especially of its finances] is lost beyond recovery. The bills went on depreciating, being really only negotiable paper, until the spring of 1781, when Morris took charge of the finances on condition that he might conduct them in specie. Then the notes became waste paper. Some were redeemed at one hundred for one in Hamilton's funding scheme. These notes were a greater obstacle to independence than the British arms; so much so that the enemy counterfeited them as a war measure. The French money was a greater aid to independence than the French fleets and forces. After the paper money had exhausted the patience of the people, Congress had to collect taxes in kind to supply the army. It could not have been worse off for money at the outset, and would have had enthusiasm to help. The miseries of those days were enhanced by the failure of the crops of 1779 and 1780.

The war was now carried on by loans from France, Holland, and Spain, which were obtained on French credit. Specie brought by the French and English came into circulation as soon as the paper was dropped, and trade with the English was winked at because specie was obtained by it. So much for non-intercourse.

In 1780 a company of gentlemen in Philadelphia took government bills of exchange, and issued notes to purchase supplies for the army. December 31, 1781, they were incorporated by resolution as the Bank of North America, Congress having finally organized, November 1, under the Articles of Confederation. The validity of this act being questioned, the bank obtained a charter from Pennsylvania in 1783 for ten years, with a monopoly; capital, $400,000. In 1785 the State charter was repealed, on account of political and business jealousy. In 1787 it was renewed, without the monopoly. This was the first bank which issued convertible notes. It was of great use as a fiscal agent of the government, and very successful in its operations. Gouge says that it put on false pretenses of strength, but its history is so obscure that it is impossible to verify or refute these charges.

The peace found the finances of the Confederation and of the States in confusion. The Confederation was a shadow which no longer had dignity. It could not collect revenue or adjust its accounts, which were found in inextricable confusion, showing recklessness and carelessness, or worse, as a result of the numerous boards and officers among whom the responsibility had been divided. The States were likewise struggling with paper issues, which they retired by taxes, heavy in nominal amount, but small in value. In Massachusetts Daniel Shays led a body of armed men to Worcester, and from there to Springfield, to prevent the court from sitting. This body was dispersed by force, but leniently treated.

In the same year (1786)[1] Rhode Island issued paper, as a measure of bankruptcy, with a stringent tender law. In 1789 the paper was at fifteen for one, and the State debt had been called in, and either paid in this currency or forfeited. Then the assumption by the general government being assured, the State stocks were returned to the holders who had been paid off, and in 1791 and 1795 they all participated in the stocks allotted to the State.[2]

The war-protected industries were now prostrated. Commerce was restricted by the English navigation laws from its old path to the British West Indies, contrary to

---

[1] Twentieth Congress, First Session, State Paper 107.

[2] Works, ix. 259.

[3] Pitkin, *A Statistical View*, etc. (New Haven, 1835), p. 27.

[4] *Register*, January 18, 1817.

[1] In a speech in the Senate, March 24, 1838, Judge White, of Tennessee, described the currency of "Franklin" (East Tennessee and West North Carolina) at this time as consisting of raccoon-skins. Counterfeiting consisted in attaching raccoons' tails to opossums' skins. The collectors practiced this fraud on the Treasury.

[2] Arnold's *Rhode Island*, ii., at the end. Richmond, *The Revolutionary Debt repudiated by Rhode Island.*

Pitt's policy.[1] The commercial treaty proposed by Adams in 1785 was refused, and so both from within and without the necessity of union and nationality was enforced.

The first measure of Congress was for taxation. The act of July 4, 1789, specified protection as one of its objects. It laid duties of five per cent., fifty cents per ton on foreign ships, and ten per cent. discriminating duty. Thus the United States failed to take the enlightened position on foreign trade which consistency with their other doctrines seemed to prescribe. Other acts followed on an average every other year for the next thirty years, by which the duties were increased and extended.

September 2, 1789, the Treasury Department was established,[2] and Alexander Hamilton was appointed Secretary. He made a report on the finances January 14, 1790. The Confederate debt was $42,000,000 domestic and $11,000,000 foreign, and the debt of the States $25,000,000. The Confederate domestic debt, including officers' half-pay commutation (a very unpopular thing), was funded at par, the market price being 15. The State debts were assumed, and funded against strong opposition, the location of the capital on the Potomac being assured in order to gain the consent of Virginia. Pensions and the funding of crops of exchequer bills had been two great abuses in England for a century, and were regarded with dread here.

Hamilton next proposed a national bank, which was established by act of March 3, 1791, with a capital of $10,000,000, $8,000,000 subscribed by individuals (one-quarter in specie, three-quarters in United States stock), and $2,000,000 by government. Its charter was for twenty years. It issued no notes under $10. Eight or ten years later the government sold its stock for twenty-five, twenty, and forty-five premium. A bubble speculation followed the founding of the bank.[3]

[1] Pitkin, 189.

[2] A full history of the finances would include tonnage, post-office, and tariff. These, however, are excluded, except in cases where they affect the finances generally, from the present account. The only attempt to deal thoroughly with the financial history of the United States is Von Hock's, *Die Finanzen und die Finanzgeschichte der Ver. St.* (Cotta, Stuttgart, 1867.)

[3] *Niles's Register*, May 9, 1835.

March 3, 1791, an excise was laid on spirits, which led to a rebellion in Pennsylvania in 1794. In 1794 other direct taxes were laid, and in 1797 stamp taxes. July 14, 1798, direct taxes were apportioned on land, houses, and slaves. These taxes were all repealed in 1802.

Questions of coinage were taken up as early as 1781. January 15, 1782, Robert Morris made a report (said to have been prepared by Gouverneur Morris) proposing a coinage.[1] July 6, 1785, the "dollar" was adopted. August 8, 1786, a mint law was passed, which was modified October 16, 1786. During 1790 both Hamilton and Jefferson[2] prepared papers on coinage, and September 2, 1792, the mint law was approved. Silver was first coined in 1794, and gold in 1795. The silver dollar was to weigh 371.25 grains pure metal, and the gold dollar 24.75 grains pure metal, thus rating the metals as 15 to 1. Silver was to gold in England as 15.2 to 1, and here it was probably as 15.5 to 1. Little gold circulated here before 1820, and after that none. The silver dollar having less value than the gold dollar, was the only one which debtors paid.

The calamity of Europe in the wars from 1791 to 1815 was the opportunity of America. It could not be enjoyed without experiencing the usual fortune of neutrals, nor without in its final results showing that the best gain of a nation comes not from the quarrels of its neighbors, but from their peace and prosperity. We were led to try another commercial war, and finally to undertake actual hostilities "for free trade" (*i. e.*, of neutrals during war) "and sailors' rights," being forced to this by votes from south of the Delaware, while the ships and sailors in the North and East asked only to take their own risks. April 14, 1814, the restrictive acts were finally repealed. Daniel Webster characterized the whole system in a sentence when he said it was "pernicious as to ourselves, and imbecile as to foreign nations."[3] The idea was by withholding trade to get a consideration in hand, viz., the promise to restore it, and then to offer this to either belligerent to induce him to

[1] Sparks's *Diplomatic Correspondence*, xii. 81. *American State Papers*, vii. 101.

[2] *American State Papers*, vii. 105; xx. 13.

[3] Speech in the House, April 6, 1814.

relax his hostile regulations. Mr. Canning treated this with thinly veiled contempt. His position was, If it is a threat, I do not notice it; if it is something to sell, I decline to buy.

The embargo and war had "encouraged domestic industry," and had come to be considered by some as beneficent forces. Commerce had developed in an unexampled manner. The customs revenue fluctuated greatly, but rose from $3,400,000 in 1792 to $13,300,000 in 1811, actual receipts, long credit being given from the time of importation. Lands figure as a source of income from 1796; $21,000,000 were due on arrears (credit being given) in 1820,[1] of which $14,900,000 were canceled before 1830 by surrendering lands. The Post-office was established May 8, 1794. A single letter cost six cents for thirty miles; over 450 miles, twenty-five cents. Between 1794 and 1830 the Post-office produced revenue except in 1808, 1820, 1821, 1822, 1823, 1828, 1829, 1830.[2] Between 1837 and 1874 it produced revenue only in 1837, 1848–1851, and 1865.[3]

January 1, 1791, the foreign debt was $12,800,000; the domestic debt, $62,600,000; total, $75,400,000. The act of August 4, 1790, set apart the surplus revenue from duties to pay the debt. The act of May 8, 1792, appropriated the revenue from lands to that purpose. The act of March 3, 1795, increased this fund, and named it the "sinking fund." The act of April 29, 1802, raised the sinking fund to $7,300,000 per annum. Two acts of November 10, 1803, raised loans of $13,000,000 to pay for Louisiana, and increased the sinking fund to $8,000,000 per annum. By the treaty of January 8, 1802, in fulfillment of section six of Jay's treaty, the United States agreed to pay £600,000 (at $4 44) to discharge ante-Revolutionary debts of Americans to Englishmen. The foreign debt increased until 1795, but was extinguished in 1810. The domestic debt increased until 1801. The Louisiana purchase carried it to its maximum in 1804 (January 1, total, $86,400,000). It was reduced to $39,000,000 September 30, 1815.[4]

A bankruptcy law was passed April 4, 1800, but it was repealed December 19, 1803.

[1] *Niles's Register*, February 5, 1820.

[2] Pitkin, 338. [3] Postmaster-General's Report, 1874.

[4] Treasury Report, 1815.

The following table shows the development of banking,[1] the Bank of the United States being omitted:

Year.	No.	Capital.	Circulation.	Specie.
1791	3	$2,000,000	....	....
Jan. 1, 1811	88	42,600,000	$22,700,000	$9,600,000
" 1815	208	82,200,000	45,500,000	17,000,000

Banks at this time were political engines. Niles often says that the old United States Bank gave favors only to black-cockade Federalists in and after 1798. Pitkin says that bank was Federalist, and finds it natural that the Jeffersonian Democrats would not recharter it. McDuffie[2] repeats the assertion of political character in the old bank. Clay said that its stock was largely held by foreigners and noblemen,[3] which proves that it brought capital here which, at that day, would not otherwise have come. The charter expired March 3, 1811. The recharter was lost in the House, January 24, by one vote, and in the Senate, February 20, by the casting-vote of the Vice-President. The bank closed up its affairs, and paid back its capital at 108½.[4] A large number of State banks at once sprang up. February 12, 1820, Secretary Crawford estimated the paper in circulation in 1813 at $62,000,000, and the specie at $8,000,000; the paper in 1816 at $99,000,000, and the specie at $11,000,000. For the latter year Gallatin estimated the banks at 246, with $89,800,000 capital, $68,000,000 circulation, $19,000,000 specie.[5]

Duties in 1804 were twelve and a half, fifteen, and twenty per cent. The "Mediterranean Fund" was then raised by addition of two and a half per cent. April 3, 1812, in preparation for war, an embargo was laid for ninety days. The exportation of specie was forbidden, all duties were doubled,

[1] Gallatin, *Considerations on the Currency and Banking System of the United States* (Carey and Lea, Philadelphia, 1831). Others give four banks in 1789, counting one in Maryland.

[2] Report on United States Bank, April 13, 1830.

[3] Clay's report against the first bank (Senate, March 2, 1811) would have made a good Jackson document in 1832.

[4] Pitkin, 421. The last dividend was in 1834 (*Niles's Register*, September 13, 1834).

[5] The best account of this period is given by William Gouge, *History of Paper Money and Banking* (Philadelphia, 1833). Historically very correct and trustworthy, but theoretically marred by indiscriminate hostility to banks. See also Condy Raguet's *Currency and Banking*, 1840, Appendix H.

an additional duty of ten per cent. was laid on foreign ships, and a tonnage duty of $1 50. This made the duties twenty-seven and a half, thirty-two and a half, and forty-two and a half per cent. The Mediterranean Fund expired in 1815, and the duties were twenty-five, thirty, and forty per cent. until July, 1816. July 22, 1813, a direct tax of $3,000,000 was laid. July 24 excise taxes and licenses were laid, which were extended by acts of January 18 and February 27, 1815, but an income tax was defeated January 18, 1815. Another direct tax of $6,000,000 was also laid. On December 23, 1814, postage was raised to twelve cents for one sheet less than forty miles; this was repealed February 1, 1816. The internal taxes were repealed in 1817.

The loans contracted were:

Date of Act.	Interest.	Amount authorized.	Amount issued.	Rate.
March 14, 1812	6	$11,000,000	$7,860,500	Par.
February 8, 1813	6	16,000,000	18,109,377	88
August 2, 1813	6	7,500,000	8,498,581	88¼
March 24, 1814	6	25,000,000	15,661,818	80
March 3, 1815 (for funding interest-bearing Treasury notes)	6	12,000,000	9,745,745	90 to par in Treasury notes.
February 24, 1815 (for funding non-interest-bearing Treasury notes)	7	....	3,268,949	Par in Treasury notes.
Total funded debt on account of the war			$63,144,972	

Five and two-fifths per cent. Treasury notes outstanding September 30, 1815	$14,686,600
Non-interest-bearing Treasury notes, about	1,500,000
Temporary loans	1,150,000
Total cost of the war, ascertained to September 30, 1815, about	80,500,000

These items, with the temporary loans, made the debt for the war $80,500,000, and the total public debt, September 30, 1815, $119,600,000.[1]

These loans were contracted at 80–90 in paper, depreciated twenty per cent., and after 1814 all the income of the government was in the same paper.[2]

March 19, 1813, Governor Snyder, of Pennsylvania, vetoed twenty-five bank charters; March 21, 1814, forty charters were passed over his veto. Banks multiplied on every hand, especially in the Middle States, where they speculated in government stocks. The system was generally to deposit stock notes for the capital, issue notes even beyond this, and loan them on accommodation paper. Bridge and other companies in this way got their capital from the public.

The New Orleans banks suspended in April, 1814; the banks of the District during the invasion, August 27; those of Philadelphia, August 30, 1814; those of the Middle and Southern States, within a fortnight later; those of Ohio and Kentucky paid specie until January 1, 1815; the only one in Tennessee went on until July or August, 1815; a few in Maine stopped early in 1814; the rest in New England did not suspend at all.[1] Banks now multiplied faster than ever, and the old ones increased their issues. The notes required elaborate quotations, and brokers had a rich harvest in negotiating them. *Niles's Register* from 1814 to 1820 is filled with complaints and objurgations about the "shavings." The Secretary of the Treasury found the greatest embarrassment from this state of things. The New England people paid all their dues to the government in Treasury notes worth 90. The government had to pay in New England in specie all that it owed there, while it nowhere received a specie revenue. At the same time the Boston merchants found that the Baltimoreans had the advantage of them in trade, for while the Bostonians paid duties in Treasury notes at 90, the Baltimoreans paid in their own bank-notes at 80. So little was the "exchange" understood that the Secretary (Dallas) complained because he got bids for the loan of March 3, 1815, which "varied according to the arbitrary variations of what is called the difference of exchange." The object of this loan was to fund Treasury notes. The Secretary fixed the price of his bonds at 95, either in Treasury notes or "cash," *i. e.*, bills of suspended banks. The result was that the large subscriptions were made where the currency was most depreciated, and were made in "cash." Where the currency was

---

[1] Treasury Report, 1815, with review of the finances of the war. See also Treasury Report for 1827, and a letter of Gallatin in *Niles's Register*, February 21, 1846, on the finances of the second war.

[2] Crawford's Report, February 12, 1820.

[1] Gouge's *Journal of Banking*, quoted in Macgregor's *Commercial Statistics*, iii. 987.

about at 95, the subscriptions were paid half in "cash," and half in notes. Where the currency was worth more than 95, the subscriptions were all in Treasury notes. The Secretary's own table shows this at a glance.[1]

In the disorder of the currency, Eppes (on behalf of Jefferson) proposed a government paper money fundable in stock, such as was issued in January, 1815, and never circulated. Dallas, the Secretary of the Treasury, October 17, 1814, proposed a national non-specie-paying bank. Calhoun proposed a bank on Treasury notes, but which should never suspend specie payments. Dallas's scheme passed the Senate, but was defeated in the House by the double vote of the Speaker (Cheves). A plan for a bank to be prohibited from suspending passed, and was vetoed January 30, 1815. Dallas's paper scheme passed the Senate again, but was defeated in the House by one vote on February 17, the day the news arrived of the Peace of Ghent. It was heard of no more.

At the next session Calhoun re-introduced the bank, the charter being Dallas's work. It was passed April 10, 1816. The bank was to have $35,000,000 capital, $7,000,000 to be subscribed by government in five per cent. stock, $28,000,000 by the public, of which $7,000,000 was to be in specie and $21,000,000 in six per cent. United States stocks. It was to pay a bonus of $1,500,000 in one, two, and three years. It was to issue no notes under $5, and was forbidden to suspend under twelve per cent. penalty. Votes were to be given at elections of bank officers by an intricate limitation, varying according to the number of shares held, and directors could serve only three years out of four.

This bank was to correct the currency and to control the exchanges, which no bank can do or ought to do. It was to be the financial Providence of the country, bring exchange to par, and keep it there in an immense sparsely settled country with defective means of communication. Its capital was far too large, and there was no reason for putting part of the capital in stocks. Finally, there was no reason why the government should have shares in it.

April 30 Congress voted that specie payments ought to be resumed February 20, 1817, and that government ought to accept only specie or its equivalent in payment thereafter. The banks refused to resume before July, 1817. The stock of the Bank of the United States was taken in July in such a way that a Baltimore clique, taking advantage of the rule about voting, got votes enough to control the organization.[1] By subscribing as attorneys they got 22,187 votes out of 80,000, and they subscribed only $4,000,000 out of $28,000,000. In November the stock was at $42.50 for $30 paid. The organization took place October 28, fifteen directors being Democrats and ten Federalists. The directors allowed, December 18 and 27, discount on the pledge of stocks, by which the specie payment in the second installment (January 2) was evaded. Wild stock-jobbing now began, especially among those inside. After February 20 all stock was discounted at par (65 paid). "The discounts, the payment of the second installment, the payment of the price to the owner, the transfer, and the pledge of the stock were, as it is termed, simultaneous acts." August 26, 1817, they voted to discount on the stock at 125. The third installment was partly paid in bank-notes because government stock was at a premium in notes. August 28, 1818, the bank refused to receive or pay its notes except at the offices specified on the note, and also refused to collect drafts, etc., except for exchange rates, thus abandoning the attempt to "equalize exchange." In April, 1819, it refused to transfer funds for the government except at exchange rates, thus disappointing another expectation in regard to it.

The bank was going on just after the prevailing fashion. Instead of restraining, it joined the race. The Secretary in 1817 said that he had paid off *all* the United States stock in the capital of the bank, and he paid off $13,000,000, which seems, therefore, to be the amount paid in, instead of $21,000,000. The rest was bank-notes or stock notes. This redemption turned the whole capital into a shape demanding use, and led to a prodigious expansion of credit. The State banks agreed to "resume" if the bank would extend

[1] This report (1815) was very correctly criticised by Mr. Nathan Appleton: *On Currency and Banking* (Boston, 1841), Appendix D.

[1] The story is told here consecutively. The doings inside the bank were not made known until the inquiry in 1819 and Cheves's report in 1822.

its discounts at New York $2,000,000, Philadelphia, $2,000,000, Baltimore, $1,500,000, Virginia, $500,000. There never was any resumption in fact.[1] August 8, 1817, the president and cashier were authorized to discount $500,000, and subsequently to discount $2,000,000, between discount days, in their discretion. September 30 they were authorized to renew notes so discounted. The stock was then at its highest, 155–156½. From July, 1817, to December, 1818, the bank imported $7,300,000 in specie, at an expense of over $500,000. Congress appointed an investigating committee, on the rumor that things were not all right, and because the bank had not helped the currency. They reported[2] January 16, 1819, exposing the facts here detailed. The president of the bank and the managers at Baltimore resigned. March 6, 1819, Langdon Cheves became president. He found the bank bankrupt, but already engaged in vigorous efforts to contract its obligations. These measures were continued. The loss at Baltimore was $2,000,000, the whole loss $3,000,000. February 25 Congress refused to order a *scire facias* for the forfeiture of the charter.

Maryland, Ohio, and Kentucky had attempted to tax the bank, but the tax was declared unconstitutional.[3] In Ohio a tax of $100,000 was collected by force September 16, 1819, but ordered restored, after long litigation, in September, 1821.[4]

Meanwhile the commerce, industry, and finance of the world had been finding their way back to the ordinary natural forms and channels of peace, and away from the unnatural developments of war. This did not take place without shocks and confusion throughout the commercial world. The United States had, for insufficient reason, plunged into the general *mêlée*, and the result was that not only was their commerce first unnaturally distorted and then crushed, but also their home industry had sought unnatural developments, and their finances had been thrown into confusion. In 1816 paper money yet prevailed in Europe, and was depreciated more than ours. The exchanges were favorable to the United States, and a golden opportunity was offered for resumption. In 1819 efforts were being made all over Europe to resume, and masses of metal were moving from country to country. In the midst of this state of things came the real, though not publicly known, break-down of the bank. Its efforts to recover itself prostrated the whole industry of the country. Prices, which had risen fifty or one hundred per cent. since 1814, fell even below the former level, and a grand liquidation set in, which ran through some three or four years.

In 1820 exchange on England rose to 105 and 106, which carried off gold, the par of gold being 102.72, or, with expenses, 105. Par of silver was 106 (at 15½ to 1), or, with expenses, 108. In fact, silver was then depressed to 16 for 1 by the demand for gold in England, and it took 110 to draw silver from here. Exchange rose at a leap from 106 to 110, and then to 112—rates which the living generation could hardly remember. Every gold coin here was drawn away, for there was no such profit on any thing else exported. The re-adjustment was not complete before 1822 or 1823, and it was not brought about without great suffering.[1]

In 1823 land was worth forty or forty-five per cent. less than in 1806, and sixty or seventy per cent. less than in 1817;[2] thousands in actual suffering; families living on one dollar per week;[3] women earning six and a quarter cents per day. The distress was all used as an argument for protection.

The indiscriminate rage of men like Gouge and Niles against "banks" dates from this period. Niles again and again speaks of banks just as one would speak of gambling hells. There were three kinds of paper afloat in 1819: first, notes of incorporated banks with more or less pretense to solvency; second, notes of banks which had no other reality than a counting-room, books, and a plate—their notes were circulated at a distance, and when they came home the bank ceased to be; third, counterfeits in enormous quantities, though they differed from the second kind only in stealing a name

1 Crawford's Report, February 12, 1820.

2 See the report and documents in *Niles's Register*, vols. xv. and xvi., series 1.

3 4 Wheaton, 316.

4 Final action and history of the case, 9 Wheaton, 739.

1 Valuable reports on coinage, etc., by Lowndes, H. R., January 26, 1819, and J. Q. Adams, February 22, 1821.

2 *Niles's Register*, August 23, 1823.

3 *Niles's Register*, May 17, 1823.

some one else had invented, instead of inventing a new one. The amount afloat can not be guessed at. Niles[1] said the number of banks was put at 397 on unknown authority. The homilies about extravagance and protecting home industry, and the praise of the old simple times, then began. These times have never been since the earliest colonial days, when people were so poor that they could buy nothing. Since then they have bought all they could, and as they have been getting rich fast, they have always had far more good things at the end of any twenty years than at its beginning.

In 1817 the sinking fund was raised to $10,000,000 per annum, and more, if possible, leaving $2,000,000 in the Treasury. In 1816, 1817, 1818, and 1819 this sum was paid, and in some years much more; but in 1820, the revenue having declined, $2,000,000 were borrowed from the sinking fund, with many apologies. In 1821 it was curtailed over $3,000,000, but without any apologies. It showed that the sinking fund is simply what can be saved and paid, nothing more or less.

During the next decade the scene of interest is in the West. Kentucky, Tennessee, Illinois, and Missouri tried stay laws, tender laws, property laws, and paper issues in every form. Kentucky tried the experiment most thoroughly; the others desisted sooner. A history of Tennessee banking was given by Judge White in a speech in the Senate March 24, 1838.[2]

In the East things soon returned to order, and the next years were generally quiet financially. The agitations were in regard to protection. The revenue was good, the public debt was being paid, canals were being built, and although there was, in regard to all these things, much which a conservative economist would disapprove, yet there was perhaps nothing but what must be tolerated in a new and poor country. It may suffice here to mention the following important incidents: In 1819 it was proposed to issue a government paper money. Secretary Crawford reported against it February 12, 1820. In 1820 a loan of $3,000,000 was contracted, and in 1821 a loan of $5,000,000. July 2, 1821, a committee of stockholders of the bank reported its losses at $3,547,838 80. October 1, 1822, Mr. Cheves reported on the state of the bank when he took it, and his efforts to save it. The Suffolk bank system was organized in New England in 1824. The investments of foreign capital here, 1823–1825, were estimated at from $30,000,000 to $38,000,000.[1] The great crisis of 1825 in England did not have great effect here. In 1826 there was a great collapse of unsound banking institutions in various parts of the country. Many such had been organized at New York, and in New Jersey opposite. Several of the projectors were condemned to the penitentiary.

Andrew Jackson became President March 4, 1829, and proceeded to reform the government. In the summer of that year complaints were made by New Hampshire politicians that the branch of the bank at Portsmouth was presided over by Mr. Jeremiah Mason, a friend of Mr. Webster. The administration sought to induce Mr. Biddle (president of the bank since January, 1823) to remove Mr. Mason. He refused, and this is the earliest germ we can find of a great war. Mr. Biddle was in the position of resisting an alliance of Bank and State.[2] The Message of 1829 astonished the nation by questioning the constitutionality and advantage of the bank, whose charter would not expire until March 3, 1836, and proposing a bank on the revenues and credit of the nation. The bank had lived down the odium of its early history. The Committee of Ways and Means reported April 13, 1830 (by McDuffie), in favor of rechartering the bank at the proper time. The Committee of Finance of the Senate reported March 29, 1830, that the currency was good, and in a fair way to improve. "They deem it prudent to abstain from all legislation, to abide by the practical good which the country enjoys, and to put nothing to hazard by doubtful experiments." In November, 1830, Mr. Gallatin published the article on the currency above referred to, in which he showed that

[1] August 29, 1818.

[2] A short history of banking in the separate States is given in a series of articles in the *Bankers' Magazine*, vol. xi.

[1] Niles, November 22, 1823; June 12, 1824; January 22, 1825.

[2] J. Q. Adams's Report, 1832. The history is given consecutively; incidents which did not become publicly known until later are put in their proper place.

the bank had been very useful. These documents no doubt represented the opinions of the educated and business classes at that time.

The revolution of 1830 in France, political disturbances elsewhere on the Continent, and the disturbances which preceded the Reform Bill in England were then causing much capital to be sent to this country. The new canals just opened, the railroads just beginning to be built (for horse-power), the application of anthracite coal to the arts, and numerous improvements in all branches of production afforded ample opportunity of applying this capital here to advantage. The same improvements in England tended to an unprecedented increase of capital, which sought investment here for the next eight or ten years.

It was under these circumstances that the President set about an "experiment" with the currency. The Message of 1830 repeated the opinion of 1829 in regard to the bank; that of 1831 was milder. January 9, 1832, the petition for a recharter was presented. A special committee having been appointed in the House, a majority reported against the recharter; McDuffie and Adams both made counter-reports. The charges against the bank were, first, that its assets consisted largely of accommodation loans in the West, which were created by "race-horse" bills, and were worthless. (There was too much truth in this; the branch drafts since 1827 had been mischievous.) Second, extending favors to Congressmen. (This was admitted and defended.) Third, using political influence. (It appeared rather that the administration had tried to use the bank politically.) The recharter passed, but was vetoed July 10, 1832.

In 1830 $3,000,000 of the $7,000,000 five per cent. stock of the United States which was in the capital of the bank was redeemed, and in 1831 the remaining $4,000,000.

By treaty of July 4, 1831, France agreed to pay the United States 25,000,000 francs as indemnity for spoliations after 1806. The Secretary drew on the French Finance Minister for the first installment, due February 2, 1833, and sold the bill to the bank. The French Chambers had made no appropriation to carry out the treaty, and the bill was protested, but taken up by Hottinguer for the bank. The bank claimed fifteen per cent. damages, and reserved the sum with interest ($170,041) from dividends due the government July 17, 1834. The government gained the suit to recover this in 1847.[1]

The government desiring to pay off the three per cents in 1832, the bank assumed and carried them a year longer. The President expressed his fears that the public deposits were unsafe in the bank, in his Message, 1832. The majority of the Committee of Ways and Means found the deposits safe, but the minority made a strong attack on the bank on account of the Western loans. These were rapidly reduced.

During the summer of 1833 overtures were made to the State banks to receive the public deposits. August 19, 1833, the government directors of the bank made a report showing large expenditures by the bank for printing and distributing documents during the campaign of 1832. These consisted of Gallatin's article, the minority reports of Adams and McDuffie, *et al.*[2]

Meanwhile the national debt was being rapidly paid, and a surplus was to be expected after 1835. The opposition desired to divide the public lands, in order to cut off revenue, and to go into internal improvements, in order to increase expenditures, but not to reduce the protective tariff. The tariff of July 14, 1832, was finally modified by the act of March 2, 1833, to reduce duties until 1842. The pound sterling was rated at $4 80 for customs purposes, standard weights and measures were distributed,[3] and the credit on duties was shortened.

September 18, 1833, the President read in his cabinet an argument against the bank, showing why the deposits ought to be removed. Duane, who had only been Secretary since May 29, refused to remove them. He was dismissed, and Taney appointed,[4] by whom they were transferred. The amount

[1] 2 Howard, 711, and 5 Howard, 382.

[2] Report of directors on "A Paper read in the Cabinet," December 3, 1833. (*Niles's Register*, December 14, 1833.)

[3] The weights in use at the various custom-houses varied sixteen per cent. The proportion of the bushels in use was: Bath, 74; Portland, 76; Saco, 80; Boston, 78; New York, 78¾; Philadelphia, 78¼; Baltimore, 77½; Newbern, 87½; Charleston, 78; Savannah, 76. (*Niles's Register*, January 5, 1833.)

[4] He was not confirmed.

was $9,800,000. The Secretary of the Treasury is in an ambiguous position, being dismissible as a cabinet officer, and yet charged with independent responsibility. The sixteenth section of the bank charter gave to him power to remove the deposits. This act caused great alarm, being apparently a bold and self-willed, but not intelligent, act. Credit was disturbed, and the winter passed in commercial distress. In February, 1834, the President, in answer to a deputation from Philadelphia,[1] sketched his new programme. He would crush the bank, try the plan of using State banks as fiscal agents, introduce a metallic currency, and use specie only for the government. The radical weakness of this plan was that he could in no way control the State banks, though they should do far worse things than the Bank of the United States had done.

Bank of the United States.

January 1.	1831.	1832.	1833.	1834.
	$	$	$	$
Loans	44,000,000	66,200,000	61,600,000	54,900,000
Circulation	16,200,000	21,300,000	17,500,000	19,200,000
Deposits...	17,200,000	22,700,000	20,300,000	10,800,000
Coin.......	10,800,000	7,000,000	8,900,000	10,000,000

Small banks now sprang up in great numbers to claim the deposits, and they urged political reasons generally for being granted a share.[2] December 3, 1833, Taney gave the reasons for removing the deposits: First, the Exchange Committee of the Board of Directors governed the bank. (This was a well-founded complaint. It was the arrangement which made the final catastrophe of the bank possible.) Second, the bank had meddled in politics. Third, selfishness in deferring the three per cents and demanding damages on the French draft. December 9, the government directors reported that they were excluded from knowledge of the affairs of the bank. March 28, 1834, the Senate resolved that the President had "assumed upon himself authority and power not conferred by the Constitution and the laws." April 15, the President sent in a protest against this resolution, which the Senate refused to register (27 to 16). The resolution was "expunged" January 16, 1837. April 4, 1834, the House resolved that the bank ought not to be rechartered nor the deposits restored, and raised another committee. Of this the majority reported, May 22, that the bank had refused to submit to investigation; the minority reported that the committee had made unreasonable and improper demands.

February 4, 1834, the Senate appointed a committee which reported, December 18, favorably to the bank. The Message of 1834 reviewed the controversy and renewed the old charges.

June 28, 1834, the coinage was altered so that the silver dollar should weigh 412½ grains, 371.25 grains pure, and the gold dollar 25.8 grains, 23.2 grains pure, rating the metals as 15.99 to 1. The standard for silver was 0.900 fine; for gold 0.89922. This expelled silver, rating it as much too low as it had before been too high. Another mistake was made at the same time by rating foreign coins too high, so that they were a cheaper tender than American coin. This prevented them from being sent to the mint. The act of January 18, 1837, brought both metals to the standard 0.900, and made the gold dollar 23.22 grains fine. From this time par of exchange with England was 109½, or £1=$4.8665. A gold eagle, coined before July 31, 1834, was worth $10.668 in eagles coined after that.

The new banks opened a period of speculation in 1834, which went on through 1835, growing wilder and wilder, seizing on cotton lands and negroes, city lots, Western lands, and every form of stocks.[1] The administration, it is true, prevailed on the following States[2] to forbid notes under $5: Pennsylvania, Maryland, Virginia, Georgia, Tennessee, Louisiana, North Carolina, Indiana, Kentucky, Maine, New York, New Jersey, Alabama. Connecticut had forbidden $1's and $2's; Mississippi and Illinois had no notes under $5; and Missouri had no bank of issue; but the exchanges were kept favorable by exporting securities (importing capital), and the position was one of unstable equilibrium. The specie in the country was $64,000,000. The prevailing belief was that bank issues could be extended to any amount, if only there was one-third the amount in specie behind them.

[1] Niles, March 1, 1834.
[2] See *Niles's Register*, April 8, 1837.

[1] Niles, May 9, 1835.
[2] Treasury Report, 1835.

The directors of the bank[1] ordered the Exchange Committee, March 6, 1835, to loan the funds of the bank on stock as fast as it was called in, in order to facilitate the winding up. The branches (of which there were twenty-five) were sold, and bonds taken payable in from one to five years. In the winter of 1835–36 it was suddenly proposed that Pennsylvania should grant a charter to the bank, and a bill was passed February 13, 1836, doing so, but joining the charter with internal improvement schemes and a repeal of some taxes. The conditions were very onerous. Thus instead of winding up March 3, 1836, the bank went on as the United States Bank of Pennsylvania. Under the resolution of March 6, 1835, $20,000,000 of its capital had been loaned on stocks, and it had its bonus to the State to pay, the shares of the government to pay back, and the circulation of the old bank to redeem. The Exchange Committee had complete control of the bank.[2]

In the winter of 1835–36 the rates for capital advanced under great fluctuations, such as always occur on a bank-note currency with an inadequate coin basis. The great fire of December, 1835, at New York led some to propose a bank of $5,000,000 for the sufferers. Niles said, "To make a bank is the grand panacea for every ill that can befall the people of the United States, and yet it adds not one cent to the capital of the community."[3]

During 1836 speculation went on, although rates for loans were twelve to twenty per cent. per month throughout much of the year. Prices were so high that wheat came here from Europe. It was said that the canals, etc., had drawn laborers away from agriculture. In the fall the Bank of England refused to discount for bankers who were granting American credits, and those houses reduced their acceptances from £20,000,000 to £12,000,000 during the winter,[4] producing still greater distress here, both directly and indirectly, by the fall in cotton.

The public debt was all paid January 1, 1835, and a surplus of over $40,000,000 accumulated during 1836. The administration having done all the harm it could by scattering this over the Union in forty banks, the opposition now undertook to withdraw it from the banks and distribute it to the States in the ratio of Congressional representation. The bill passed June 23, 1836. It ordered the surplus over $5,000,000 January 1, 1837, to be *deposited* with the States. The Message of 1836 contained a criticism of this proceeding which was unanswerable, although the three great men, Clay, Calhoun, and Webster, all favored the scheme.

July 11, 1836, the Secretary of the Treasury issued a circular forbidding the receipt of any thing but specie for public lands. Congress passed a resolution practically rescinding this. It was sent to the President March 2, and he sent it to the State Department to be filed at 11.45 P.M., March 3, 1837.

February 25, 1837, the United States Bank offered to pay off the public shares at $115 58 per share, in four installments, September, 1837, 1838, 1839, and 1840. March 3 Congress ordered this offer accepted, and it was fulfilled.

Early in March Herman Briggs and Co., of New Orleans, failed, on account of the decline in cotton. J. L. and S. Joseph and Co., of New York, failed as soon as the news reached New York. This was the beginning. The whole Southwest was prostrated. At New York one failure followed another among those who held Southern funds. Mr. Biddle had before acted as financial Jupiter, and to him prayers were now addressed. He came, March 28, and sold post-notes for mercantile paper at 112, which notes brought in cash 95. They were payable in Europe, and were remitted to settle, instead of shipping specie. In April news came that three great houses granting American credits, Wilson, Wildes, and Wiggins, had become dependent on the Bank of England, and were being carried on a guarantee from the City. The panic now recommenced, and ran on increasing until May. May 8 a run on the Dry Dock Bank caused its suspension. The other banks were forced to suspend on the 9th and 10th. The Philadelphia, Baltimore, and other banks followed as the news spread. Each city professed that it could have held out,

[1] Report of 1841.
[2] Ibid.
[3] *Register*, January 2, 1836.
[4] *Morning Chronicle*, in *Niles's Register*, April 29, 1837.

but was forced to yield in the general interest.

In May news reached England of events here in March, and post-notes instead of money. The great question was: Can the Americans pay? The amount of American debts falling due June 1 was, to the three W.'s, £3,800,000; to other English houses, £5,000,000; to France, £1,500,000. Total, £10,300,000. The American houses were allowed to fall June 1. They failed for £2,000,000; £1,300,000 was covered by the guarantees, and £700,000 fell on the bank.[1] An arrival of $100,000 in specie sufficed, however, to restore American credit and to turn the tide. Extensions were granted, securities were negotiated, and in general long credits secured.

On the suspension gold went to 107, all specie disappeared, and the country was flooded with shin-plasters. The premium on gold was greater in the South and West, being 120–125 in the Southwest. There were said to be $80,000,000 in specie in the country, which Benton said would be its "bulwark" against financial disaster. Thus, between those who misused paper and those who held the superstition of gold, the advocates of sound doctrine were either wanting or their voices were drowned.

May 3 a committee of New York merchants went to Washington to ask the recall of the specie circular, delay in collecting duty bonds, and the calling of an extra session of Congress. The first the President (Van Buren) would not do, the second he could not do, and the third he thought useless; but the necessities of the government forced the last. Congress met September 4, and passed bills to collect the deposits of the suspended banks, to delay the collection of duty bonds, and to issue Treasury notes. Three installments of the deposit had been paid. The fourth ($9,000,000) was yet in the banks. As to calling back any of the $28,000,000 which had been "deposited," no one proposed it. It was with great difficulty that the payment of the fourth installment was deferred until January 1, 1839. It was not paid at all. The Treasury Report of 1838 showed $2,400,000 still due from suspended banks.

[1] London *Times*, in *Niles's Register*, July 22, 1837.

The bank had really had very little grounds for the position it had assumed as public benefactor. It was itself a borrower. A ring of officers and their friends were using the funds of the bank, putting securities in the cashier's drawer, and taking out cash. These transactions passed examination day as "bills receivable." In July, 1837, the bank began to speculate in cotton, of course through outside firms, but, as Mr. Biddle said in his letters to Clayton, 1841, it was to meet the post-notes of the bank. He also thought that he could carry cotton to get a price. Mr. Jaudon was sent to London as agent for the bank September 22, 1837. He executed some sensational transactions, the consequence of which was that he was regarded as a reckless and dangerous man.

The New York banks tried all winter to get a general agreement to resume, but without success. The New York law allowed the suspension for one year. May 10, 1838, the New York and New England banks resumed. The New York banks had pursued a policy of contraction on all their liabilities which at the time was regarded with great disfavor, and was unfavorably compared with Mr. Biddle's policy of "repose" under the suspension. It produced health, however, and brought New York out of the troubles of the times at least three years before Philadelphia issued from them, and with far less suffering on the whole. The Philadelphia banks delayed until the Governor forced them to resume, August 13, 1838. Meantime Mr. Biddle was writing plausible letters to Mr. J. Q. Adams to manufacture public opinion. Perhaps his head was turned by the position of financial Providence to the country. It would not be strange. In the summer of 1838 he enjoyed his highest prestige. Mr. James G. King induced the Bank of England to send £1,000,000 in specie here, and some of it was sent, which went into the United States Bank, and was thought a great victory for Mr. Biddle. He was said to have carried the merchants of Philadelphia, the great corporations of the country, and the public improvements of Pennsylvania through the crisis.[1] The great bank was, however, an

[1] New York *Express*, in *Niles's Register*, May 12, 1838.

unwieldy hulk, which was already stranded, and Mr. Biddle's bravado was only preparing a more humiliating downfall. He had become president of the bank at the age of thirty-seven, succeeding Mr. Cheves, who was considered too conservative. He had been urged on to bold methods of banking, flattered as to his success, and encouraged to assume unbusiness-like duties and responsibilities.[1] December 10, 1838, he wrote his last letter to Mr. Adams, in which he finally abdicated for the bank the position of financial Providence. March 29, 1839, he resigned the presidency of the bank, leaving it, as he said, prosperous. During 1838 its stock had reached 123. When he resigned it was 111–113. July 6, 1838, an act was passed by Congress to prevent the bank from re-issuing the notes of the old bank.

The notion of controlling the cotton market, which has been mentioned, was embodied in a circular of June 6, 1839, proposing a grand national combination to "bull" cotton. It was issued by Mr. Wilder, who denied that the bank was in the plot, but it appeared in 1841 that this was a prevarication. The Manchester *Guardian*[2] spoke of it as "the most rash and insane speculation of modern times." The mills closed up, the price fell, and the speculators were ruined. $1,400,000 had been gained previously by the clique, of which $800,000 had been divided. The residue and $900,000 more were now lost.[3] In August Mr. Jaudon was in great straits for money, and was calling on Biddle and Humphreys, of Liverpool, to get money at any sacrifice of cotton. The bank here was selling post-notes in New York, Boston, and even smaller cities. In August it drew all the bills it could sell on Hottinguer, and shipped the proceeds in specie to meet the bills. The object was to force the New York banks to suspend.[4] The drawee had given warning that he would not honor any bill unless he was covered. September 18, 1839, bills for 2,000,000 francs were presented, for which the specie had not arrived. They were refused, but the Rothschilds took them up,[1] and also some 8,000,000 francs more which were out, Mr. Jaudon finding security.

The fact of the protest was known in New York, October 10, 1839, but the Philadelphia banks had suspended the day before. They were followed by all the banks South and West, and by those of Rhode Island. The New York and other New England banks did not suspend. This was the real break-down of credit. There was no recovery from this, except through a liquidation, which went on during 1840. The Pennsylvania Legislature set January 15, 1841, as the day beyond which the penalties of suspension should be enforced. January 1, 1841, the bank published a list of its assets, from which it appeared that its capital was locked up in a lot of the most doubtful securities on the market. A run on the banks began as soon as they opened, January 15. In twenty days the United States Bank paid out $6,000,000, and the other banks $5,100,000. February 4 they all suspended again. The United States Bank had just loaned the State $800,000, and it held over $2,000,000 of Michigan bonds which it had not paid for. It had paid or loaned to Pennsylvania $12,000,000 since the charter was granted.[2] Suits were now brought against the bank in such number that all hope of recovery was destroyed. Three trusts were established to wind it up. A committee of stockholders reported April 3, 1841, and gave a history of the bank for six years, for, as they said, "The origin of the course of policy which has conducted to the present situation of the affairs of the institution dates beyond the period of the recharter by the State." Mr. Jaudon borrowed $23,000,000 in Europe between November, 1837, and July, 1840. After that he borrowed $12,200,000 at an expense of $1,100,000 for discounts, etc., and the expenses of his office were $335,937. The foreign debt of the bank was $15,000,000. One firm had had over $4,000,000 of cash from the drawer between August, 1835, and November, 1837. Jaudon, Andrews (first cashier), and Cowperthwaite (second cashier) had owed the bank $300,000 or $400,000 each, and

[1] Contemporary criticism was all colored by party feeling. The most just and intelligent criticism, combined with sound financial doctrine, is in Mr. N. Appleton's pamphlet *On Currency and Banking*, 1841.

[2] Quoted in *Niles's Register*, July 27, 1839.

[3] Biddle's first letter to Clayton, 1841.

[4] Biddle's second letter to Clayton, 1841.

[1] The *Messager* in *Niles's Register*, November 2, 1839.

[2] Memorial to Pennsylvania Legislature (*Niles's Register*, February 27, 1841).

settled by handing over stocks, etc. The losses on cotton had been repaid to the bank by the clique in doubtful securities. The stock in April, 1843, was quoted at 1⅞.[1] January 1, 1846, the notes still outstanding were $3,400,000. Every one seems to have dropped the bank suddenly in disgust, and it is even more difficult to get information about its obsequies than about its earlier proceedings.

In a Treasury Report of January 8, 1840, it was stated that there were 850 banks and 109 branches, of which, in 1839, 343 suspended entirely, and 62 partially, 56 had failed entirely, and 48 had resumed. The Philadelphia banks resumed March 18 or 19, 1842. a precedent was fortunately avoided. The States and Territories without debt were New Hampshire, Rhode Island, Connecticut, Vermont, New Jersey, Delaware, North Carolina, Wisconsin, and Iowa. Those which at any time failed to pay interest were Pennsylvania, Maryland, Louisiana, Indiana, Illinois, and Arkansas. Those which repudiated part of their debt were Mississippi, Michigan, and Florida. Pennsylvania suspended in 1842.[1] Her debt, January, 1843, was $37,900,000. She resumed in February, 1845. Mississippi plumply repudiated $5,000,000. Louisiana repudiated $20,000,000, but the banks finally assumed or provided for it. Michigan settled up by disposing of her

COMPARATIVE BANK STATEMENTS.

Year.	No.[2]	Capital.	Circulation.	Deposits.	Specie.
1820	308	137,100,000	44,800,000	....	19,800,000
1830	330	145,100,000	61,300,000	....	22,100,000
1834	506	200,000,000	94,800,000	75,600,000	....
1835	704	231,200,000	103,600,000	83,000,000	43,900,000
1836	713	251,800,000	140,300,000	115,100,000	40,000,000
1837	788	290,700,000	149,100,000	127,300,000	37,900,000
1838	829	317,600,000	116,100,000	84,600,000	35,100,000
1839	840	327,100,000	135,100,000	90,200,000	45,100,000
1840	901	358,400,000	106,900,000	75,600,000	33,100,000
1841	....	....	74,300,000	57,000,000	25,800,000
1844	....	....	44,800,000	88,300,000	46,900,000
1845	697[3]	197,000,000	97,000,000	87,300,000	43,200,000
1848[4]	791	200,800,000	125,200,000	....	49,200,000

American credit held good abroad until 1839. Loans were negotiated during 1838 with as much success as ever. The "deposits," however, had seduced the States into great expenditures for improvements, and into debts. The debts of the States were about $200,000,000 in 1840. The amount of American securities held in England was over £20,000,000 sterling in 1837.[5] In 1839 the credits given in 1837 were not all met, and some States defaulted. Doubts of the credit of the States arose. Mr. Webster was in England, and gave the Barings an assurance of the constitutionality of the debts.[6] An effort was made in 1840 to have Congress assume the State debts, but so mischievous public works. Maryland suspended in 1842, but resumed in 1848. The delinquencies of interest in 1844 were over $7,000,000.[2] Some on the other side sneered at republicanism and Yankees on account of these defaults.[3] Some here cared little for the losses of foreigners. They gravely mistook the value to a young new country of its *credit*, its power to borrow capital of old countries.

The debt began to grow again as soon as it was extinguished, and the accounts show indebtedness every year after 1835 (when some $30,000 of old claims were outstanding). After 1837 the Treasury notes, which were authorized from year to year, raised the debt to $32,700,000, January 1, 1843. After that it was reduced to $15,500,000, January 1, 1846. The Mexican war carried it up to $63,000,000, January 1, 1849. The Texan indemnity of $5,000,000 was passed September 9, 1850; $15,000,000 were paid to Mexico in five installments, and $3,250,000

---

1 Table from *Bicknell's Reporter* in *Niles's Register*, September 30, 1843. Twenty-three stocks are given. A share of each would have cost, in 1836, $2839 62; in April, 1842, $708.

2 Branches included. In 1840 one hundred and one banks and branches are estimated. The statistics have value only as general indications.

3 Twelve more, with capital $7,300,000, not reported. Niles, February 7, 1846.

4 *Bankers' Magazine*, in Niles, February 26, 1848.

5 London *Bankers' Circular* in *Niles's Register*, March 25, 1837. Garland's estimate, $110,000,000. Niles, July 21, 1838.

6 Niles, December 28, 1839.

---

1 See Sydney Smith's letter to Congress in *M'Culloch's Dictionary of Commerce*, article "Funds."

2 Niles, October 12, 1844.

3 Webster's letter to Biddle. Niles, September 12, 1840.

of her debts to American citizens, assumed under the treaty of February, 1848; $7,000,000 were paid for the Gadsden purchase of December, 1853. The debt reached $68,300,000 January 1, 1851, but was reduced to $28,600,000 January 1, 1857.

The Sub-Treasury, after having been vehemently discussed thoughout Van Buren's administration, was established July 4, 1840. At the special session which assembled May 31, 1841, the Sub-Treasury was abolished, two national bank bills were passed and vetoed, a bankruptcy act, a revenue act raising duties to twenty per cent. throughout, and a land distribution act, with proviso that it should not be executed at any time when duties were over twenty per cent., were passed. The bankruptcy act was signed August 19, 1841, and repealed February 25, 1843. At the same special session the Secretary reported that $2,620,500 had been lost within twelve years by the defalcations of public officers. At the regular session, 1841–42, a temporary and a permanent tariff were both vetoed because they provided for violating the proviso in the land distribution bill. A third tariff of high protective duties passed, and land distribution was cut off. The duties were to be collected on the "home valuation," and no credit was to be given. In 1842 the pound sterling was rated at $4 84 for customs purposes. August 6, 1846, the independent Treasury was re-established, and the operations of the government were prescribed to be carried on with specie. The result proved the system wise and sound. The government had nothing to do with banking, and very little to do with the money market.

The paper money disease broke out next in Ohio, Indiana, and Illinois. The Fort Wayne *Times*[1] gives a description of the currency of Indiana in 1843, which is instructive as to some doctrines of "redemption." State bank paper was the standard. "Scrip" was issued for the domestic debt of the State, and was receivable for State dues. "Bank scrip" was a State issue to the bank to reimburse it for payments to canal contractors. "White Dog" was a State issue to pay for canal repairs, and was receivable for certain lands at its face and interest. "Blue Dog" was a State issue for canal extension, receivable for canal lands and canal tolls. "Blue Pup" was a shinplaster currency issued by canal contractors, and redeemable in "Blue Dog." Quotations (State Bank being standard): scrip, 85–90; bank scrip, 85; White Dog, 80–90; Blue Dog, 40; Blue Pup—![1] In 1845 the quotations of Illinois currency were, State Bank, 42–45 discount; Bank of Illinois, 50–55 discount; Cook County orders, 18–20 discount; canal indebtedness, 60–75 discount; railroad scrip, 60–75 discount; Bank of Michigan, 85 discount; Michigan or Indiana State scrip, 10–15 discount.[2]

In the summer of 1845 the business status was said to be: stocks neglected, much building going on for the "new communities" which were coming across the water, money abundant, exchange at par.[3] In 1846 and 1847 the potato famine in Ireland sent us thousands of emigrants, and in 1848 the revolutions on the Continent sent thousands more. The potato famine also gave us a market for grain, and saved us from a share in the financial troubles of 1847. The repeal of the Corn Laws in 1846, and our own more liberal tariff of that year, gave wider scope to industry. Railroads were extended already, both here and in Europe, far enough to affect production and exchange. The telegraph was just coming into general use. Ocean steam navigation was rapidly extending. Upon this set of circumstances came the discovery of gold in California in 1847. At once a great emigration thither of adventurous men began, and also a great speculation in exports thither. The gold diggers found that they ran into hardship, danger, and toil to pursue an industry which was precarious at best, and that the same amount of sacrifice would have gained more comforts at the East. Their industry nourished the gambling spirit, and their gains changed hands first over the gaming table.

The traders were little better off after a few years. The market was alternately glutted and empty, and the gains of one period were swallowed up in the losses of

[1] *Niles's Register*, September 30, 1843.

[1] The Ohio nomenclature was wider still. "Yellow Dog," "Red Cat," "Smooth Monkey," "Blue Pup," and "Sick Indian" (*Niles's Register*, June 28, 1845). More particular descriptions are wanting.

[2] Niles, June 28, 1845. [3] Niles, June 14, 1845.

another. It was the great industrial world which gained by this new supply of the medium of exchange, which came just when it was needed to sustain the new development of industry and commerce. The first exchange of the metal was for food and manufactured articles. It presented a new and sharp demand for agricultural and manufactured products. New fields were opened, new factories built, not here only, but in all the commercial countries. The new and enlarged industries brought richer returns than before both of wages and profits, not on account of the money, but on account of the whole industrial expansion which the new supply of money facilitated, and the possibilities of which already lay in the improvements mentioned. The returns in all these industries being large, the demand for luxuries was extended, and the importations of wines, cigars, silks, etc., rapidly increased. The accumulation of capital was also rapid, and credit institutions which sought to facilitate its transfer sprang up in all civilized countries. They never have been able, under such circumstances, to refrain from credit creations in addition to the capital which passes their hands, and they did not refrain in this case. In the United States all the old tendency to over-issues, heightened, as it unquestionably was, by the usury law, and also the general use of accommodation paper, were at hand to assist such a movement.[1]

After two or three years of low discount rate and cheap food, there followed in 1853 rumors of war and a bad crop in England. This caused high prices for wheat here and a renewed speculation in Western lands and railroads, which issued in 1854 in a formal crisis and panic in Wall Street. Some California traders also found their affairs at a crisis, but generally the mercantile community held firm. The indebtedness for foreign importations was large, and the investments of foreign capital here were rapidly increasing. The Secretary of the Treasury estimated them at $200,000,000.

During 1856 the discount rate of the Bank of England was high, the harvest being poor and the importation of wheat great. In the spring of 1857 it was feared that the harvest here would not be good, but during the summer it turned out so well that the fear was lest it might not bring a price. Suddenly, on the 24th of August, the failure of the Ohio Life and Trust Company, of Cincinnati, an old and highly esteemed institution, with liabilities for $7,000,000, was announced. It had loaned its means to new railroads, and then borrowed more to lend. This incident passed, however, without causing general alarm. The banks knew best what it meant. They reduced their loans in New York city from $120,000,000, August 22, to $67,000,000, October 17. This produced a crisis. The whole fabric had been built up on bank credits, and it was ruined when they were withdrawn; but the banks feared for themselves, so it was said that the panic broke out in the bank parlors. On the 12th and 13th of September the Philadelphia banks and others of the South and West (except of New Orleans) suspended. Mercantile failures now commenced, and followed day by day, the panic increasing, as money was locked up by any one who could get and keep it. The run on the New York city banks for note redemption began on the 9th. On the 13th an agreement was made to open a run on them for deposits in order to force them to suspend. Eighteen succumbed on that day, and thirty-two more the next day. One did not suspend. The New England banks followed immediately. The Constitution of New York forbade the Legislature passing any law to allow a bank suspension, but the judges of the Supreme Court agreed to grant no injunction against a bank unless there should appear to be fraud. The Northern and Eastern banks resumed in December. The Pennsylvania Legislature authorized suspension until May. Of nine banks at New Orleans only four suspended for a few days.

This crisis was short, sharp, and severe. It never touched the productive powers of the country. It is the only one in our history on a currency approximately of specie value. The recovery was rapid, and the reaction healthful. The losses were very great, but it was only a bad stumble in a

[1] As an example of the comprehensive and philosophical study of commercial crises, from which alone any correct knowledge of them can be derived, mention should be made of Max Wirth's *Geschichte der Handelskrisen* (Frankfort, 1874), from which some suggestions are here adopted.

career of great prosperity, and it simply taught sobriety and care. The number of bankruptcies in the United States and Canada was 5123; liabilities, $299,800,000; 3839 bankrupts, with $197,000,000 liabilities, were expected to pay forty cents on the dollar; 435 resumed, and paid in full $77,100,000; $143,700,000 were a total loss. Fourteen railroads[1] suspended payment on $189,800,000. Cotton manufacturers suffered severely by the fall of cotton (sixteen cents to eight and a half cents) and by the depreciation of stock. The American securities held in Europe at this time amounted to $400,000,000.

The tariff had been lowered by act of March 3, 1857, and the revenue suffered, of course, from the financial crisis. Indian wars had also increased the expenditures. Treasury notes were issued by act of December 23, 1857; loans were authorized June 14, 1858, and June 22, 1860. The debt January 1, 1861, was $90,500,000. There were on the same date 1605 banks, with $429,600,000 capital, $207,200,000 deposits, $91,300,000 gold, $202,000,000 circulation, and $696,700,000 loans.

The election of Mr. Lincoln was followed by movements toward secession and political alarms. There ensued limitation of business, contraction of credit, reduction of enterprise, and some hoarding of gold. Prices were reduced, the foreign exchanges fell, gold began to be imported. During the winter the Southern States seceded, and the political excitement increased. Southern collections became difficult, and then ceased. The failures during the year 1861 were 5935, for $178,600,000.

The Morrill tariff had passed the House May 10, 1860. Protection had been adopted in the Chicago platform. After the departure of the Southern Senators the tariff passed the Senate, and was approved March 2, 1861. It was soon buried deep under the financial legislation of the war.

Part of the loan of June 22, 1860, had been offered in October, 1860, but some of the subscribers withdrew after the election. December 17, 1860, $10,000,000 Treasury notes were authorized: $5,000,000 brought 88; in January $5,000,000 more brought 89 and 90. February 8, 1861, a loan of $25,000,000 was authorized; on March 2, another loan of $10,000,000 was voted, or Treasury notes to the amount of this and all unissued loans: $35,300,000 were issued. In March Secretary Chase refused bids under 94. In May $5,000,000 Treasury notes were sold under onerous conditions, and May 25 the banks took $6,400,000 in bonds at 85 to 93, and $2,200,000 Treasury notes at par. July 4 Congress met in extra session. On the 17th they voted to issue $50,000,000 non-interest-bearing demand notes, receivable for all dues; also 7.30 notes; also a loan at six per cent. to fund the same; and August 5, another loan. The Secretary proposed a direct tax of $30,000,000. Congress voted and apportioned $20,000,000, of which $8,000,000 fell on the seceded States. August 5 the tariff was extended. After Bull Run the six per cent. stocks were at 88½. August 19 the banks agreed to take $50,000,000 Treasury notes under conditions unfavorable to the government, and two months later to take $50,000,000 more. In November they took six per cent. bonds at 89, under still harder conditions.

The *morale* of the nation was now high. The war feeling was strong, and the enthusiasm had only settled down into determination. The Secretary of the Treasury reported an enormous deficit, and did not propose any way to deal with it. He looked wistfully toward paper issues, but rejected that plan. He proposed a national bank system, but such a moment did not seem propitious for reconstructing the banking system of the country. A run on the banks and an export of specie began in December. On the 30th all the banks suspended. Specie was at one or two per cent. premium.

December 24, 1861, duties on tea, coffee, and sugar were raised. February 12, 1862, $10,000,000 demand notes were issued, like those of July 17, 1861. February 25, 1862, $500,000,000 of 5–20 bonds were authorized. The same act established a sinking fund of one per cent. on the debt, and provided for the issue of $150,000,000 of non-interest-bearing notes ("greenbacks"), legal tender, con-

---

[1] Wirth treats his readers to an account of the purchase of the Wisconsin government for $872,000 by the La Crosse and Milwaukee Railroad (p. 341), and he translates a number of confessions of American rascality from the newspapers of the post-panic period, when extravagances in that direction were in order.

vertible into six per cent. bonds. This was the Legal Tender Act. It was passed as a temporary war measure, under the stress of necessity. There was necessity for money, a necessity which had been neglected three months too long, but there was no necessity for a legal tender law. It was another illustration of Daniel Webster's saying, when a paper bank was proposed in 1815, "A strong impression that something must be done is the origin of many bad measures." The old demand notes were to be withdrawn. As they were received for duties, they bore the same premium as gold. The Secretary was also authorized to receive deposits at five per cent. to the amount of $25,000,000, raised March 17, 1862, to $50,000,000, July 11, 1862, to $100,000,000, and June 30, 1864, to $150,000,000, and six per cent. interest allowed. July 11, 1862, $150,000,000 more legal tenders were voted, and the provision of the act of February 25 for funding them in six per cent. bonds was omitted. Those of February 25 were to be recalled. The first issue of legal tenders was in April, 1862. As they were issued, gold rose and all specie disappeared. An effect was produced at first just like that noticed above as following the opening of the California mines, but the paper did not distribute itself over the world. It threw American prices out of relation to those of the rest of the world; that is to say, it disturbed all the relations of value and exchange, both internally and externally. July 1, 1862 (just a year too late), an act was passed laying internal taxes. This was extended by acts of March 3, 1863, June 30, 1864, March 3, 1865. The last provided for a commission to investigate the subject of internal revenue.

March 17, 1862, an act was passed authorizing the purchase of coin, which was necessary until the "old demand notes" were all paid in. The act of March 1, 1862, authorized certificates of indebtedness. July 14, 1862, duties were raised "temporarily."

The act of July 17, 1862, provided for an issue of stamps to be used as "change," but they were inconvenient, and the act of March 3, 1863, provided for $50,000,000 of fractional notes.

February 25, 1863, the National Bank Act was passed, authorizing $300,000,000 of bank capital, to be distributed, half of it by banking capital, and half of it by population. An act approved July 12, 1870, added $54,000,000, and provided for withdrawing and redistributing an excess above the quota held in New York and the East. This last was found impracticable. The act of January 14, 1875, removes all restriction on the amount of capital. The $54,000,000 were never taken up by those who had not their "quota," but are now in a fair way to be taken up by those who before had an excess. Banking capital does not go by heads nor by square miles.

October 5, 1865, there were sixty-six national banks in operation. The system rapidly absorbed nearly all the banks. The law required that country banks should hold fifteen per cent. of their circulation and deposits in greenbacks, and that the banks in the large redemption cities should hold twenty-five per cent. The banks were afterward allowed to count their reserves with their redemption agents as part of this reserve up to three-fifths of the required amount. The act of June 20, 1874, did away with this reserve, as far as circulation is concerned, and substituted a five per cent. reserve to be kept at Washington, where the redemption takes place.

The Comptroller of the Currency reported, December, 1874, that 2200 banks had been organized, 35 had failed, 137 wound up, 2028 remained. December 31, 1874, there were 2027 banks in operation; capital, $495,800,000; loans, $955,800,000; bonds to secure circulation, $412,900,000; specie, $22,400,000; United States Treasury certificates of deposit, $133,500,000; legal tenders, $82,700,000; five per cent. redemption fund, $16,900,000; circulation, $332,000,000; deposits, $682,800,000.

In his report for 1862, the Secretary sustained his legal tender paper money by all the old paper money fallacies. He set his face against the "gold speculators." March 3, 1863, a tax of one-half per cent. was laid on time sales of gold, and six per cent. per annum also for the time the contract had to run. June 20, 1864, gold trading was forbidden. Gold rose from 199 on the 21st to 230 on the 23d, and fell to 207 again. The act was repealed July 2. Nevertheless Mr. Stevens introduced a bill, December 6, 1864, declaring gold and paper equal, and laying a fine equal to the amount of the proposed transaction, and imposing six months' imprisonment on any one who should contract to sell notes for gold. This was tabled, but, January 5, 1865, he tried to introduce the bill again. The opposition was so great that he withdrew it. It was not because he did not know of the English acts of 1811 and 1812, and the fame of Mr. Vansittart. He did know of them. He specified those acts as laudable precedents, and wanted to imitate them, and he called Mr. Vansittart "the great financier."

Gold reached its highest point, 285, in July, 1864. Sales of American government stocks in Germany began in the summer of 1864. Loans were being contracted continually which it is not thought necessary to enumerate here. They were being "floated" by the redundant paper in the hands of the people. The debt, June 1, 1866, was $2,800,000,000. The greenbacks out were $402,100,000. The national bank notes were $280,000,000. The fractional currency was $27,300,000. In May, 1865, gold fell to 140.

The act of June 30, 1864, limited the amount of greenbacks to $400,000,000, and such part of $50,000,000 more as might be needed to redeem temporary loans. A general resolution in favor of contraction and resumption passed December 18, 1865, by 144 to 6; but a measure allowing the Secretary to withdraw $10,000,000 in six months, and thereafter $4,000,000 per month, was lost, and only passed, on reconsideration, by 83 to 52, April 14, 1866. This stiff and arbitrary measure had no principle of sound finance in it except that it went in the right direction. If the Secretary had been allowed a tithe of the immense discretion allowed in creating debt and issues two years before, he could have withdrawn $200,000,000 in two years without annoyance, for at that time every one expected it, and there was no credit structure yet built on the inflated paper. The crisis in England in the spring of 1866, and the war on the Continent in the summer of that year, caused some stringency here, and set the gold premium in activity. In February, 1868, McCulloch's contraction was suspended by order of Congress. He had reduced the greenbacks to $356,000,000, at which point they stood until October, 1872, when Mr. Boutwell, who affirmed that the $44,000,000 so withdrawn were under his control, issued $5,000,000 of them to correct a stringency in Wall Street. It took him all winter to get them back. The sum remained $356,000,000 until the crisis of 1873, when it was raised to $382,000,000. The act of January 14, 1875, set that sum as the limit, allowed national banks to be formed to any extent, and to issue notes for ninety per cent. of the bonds deposited, and greenbacks to the amount of eighty per cent. on the additional notes issued are to be withdrawn until greenbacks are reduced to $300,000,000.

March 2, 1867, for the third time in our history, a general bankruptcy law was passed.

March 3, 1865, the tariff was raised to compensate for internal taxes. July 13, 1866, internal taxes were re-arranged and somewhat reduced. This is the act under which Hon. D. A. Wells became special commissioner. The office expired by limitation June 30, 1870. Internal taxes were reduced by the acts of March 2, 1867, which exempted incomes under $1000; February 3, 1868, which repealed the tax on cotton; July 20, 1868, which reduced and re-adjusted the taxes; and by the act of July 14, 1870, which was a grand reduction. The income tax expired by limitation in 1871. The act of July 14, 1870, also reduced duties somewhat (pig-iron $9 to $7 per ton). Up to this time the protective system had been steadily extended by acts which have been left out of the present review as belonging more to commerce than finance. The duty on tea and coffee was repealed in 1872, and a ten per cent. reduction over a number of important articles was made. In the session of 1874–75 two acts were passed increasing and extending duties. The result is that the balance which should exist between internal and customs duties in a sound system of taxation has been more and more destroyed, that the customs duties have been placed too high and on too many articles to be productive of revenue, and that there is no system or principle in the present taxes at all. They weigh very heavily on the people without furnishing adequate revenue to the government.

The act of March 3, 1865, provided for funding Treasury notes in 5–20's. This went on through 1865, 1867, and 1868. Hence the 5–20's of those years. The act of July 14, 1870, provided for issuing $200,000,000 in bonds at five per cent., $300,000,000 in bonds at four and a half per cent., and $1,000,000,000 in bonds at four per cent., in order by exchanges to reduce the interest paid. This is now being partly carried out through the "Syndicate." March 30, 1867, $7,000,000 were paid for Alaska, and July 8, 1870, four per cent. certificates for $678,000 were issued to pay Massachusetts her old claims against the United States from the war of 1812. The principal of the debt January 30, 1875, was $2,242,301,082 43, besides $64,623,512 issued to railroads.

By the act of March 3, 1863, the Supreme Court was to have ten members, and a new judge was appointed. The act of July 23, 1866, provided that no new appointments should be made until the number of judges was reduced to seven. By the act of April 10, 1869, to take effect the first Monday in December, the court was to consist of eight judges and a chief justice. The case of Hepburn *v.* Griswold,[1] involving the constitutionality of the Legal Tender Act as to contracts made before its passage, was decided in conference November 27, 1869, by the Chief Justice and seven associates. One of these, Judge Grier, resigned February 1, 1870, and the decision *against* the constitutionality of the act as applied to the contracts mentioned was announced February 7. Judge Strong was appointed February 18, 1870, and Judge Bradley March 21, 1870. The re-argument of Knox *v.* Lee, involving the decision just mentioned, took place in December, 1870.[2] Judge Miller read the decision of the majority *affirming* the constitutionality of the law, Chase, Nelson, Clifford, and Field dissenting.[3]

In September, 1869, a corner in gold was made which belongs to the financial history of the country, for it was the legitimate fruit of the existing financial system. It issued in a panic September 23 ("Black Friday"), when the Secretary of the Treasury intervened by a sale of gold to put a stop to the proceedings of a clique of characterless speculators. A panic in stocks followed, and a number of important failures.

[1] 8 Wall., 626.

[2] 12 Wall., 457.

[3] See 12 Wall., 528, note.

The coinage law of February 21, 1853, fixed the weight of silver coins for fractional parts of a dollar at 384 grains to the dollar, 0.900 fine; legal tender for five dollars. It also put a seigniorage of one-half of one per cent. on gold coined. The effect was to send gold to England or France, where there was no seigniorage and lower mint charges.[1] The act of February 12, 1873, reconstructs the coinage and mint laws entirely. The only silver dollar is the trade dollar of 420 grains standard, not meant to circulate here, but in the East. It is worth one dollar when silver is at $1.14285 per ounce standard, which is just about the present price. The fractional coins were made to weigh 385.8 grains to the nominal dollar, so that two halves should just equal a five-franc piece. These coins are issued at $1.24414 per standard ounce, or 803¾ ounces for $1000, and are legal tender for five dollars. The gold dollar is yet the dollar of 1837, 23.22 grains fine, 25.8 grains standard.

The act of 1873 made the charge for coining gold one-fifth of one per cent., but the second section of the act of January 14, 1875, repealed this, and left coinage of gold entirely free. The law of March 3, 1873, fixes the pound sterling for customs purposes at $4.8665, and prescribes that exchange be quoted $4 86, $4 87, etc.

The stringency which had occurred in the fall of 1871 and 1872 was significant of the approaching absorption by expanding credit of the legally limited amount of paper currency. In the summer of 1873 the Granger agitation at the West frightened investors from railroad bonds, and crippled the enterprises which depended on the continuance of these investments for funds. The rebuilding of Chicago and Boston had also caused a great absorption of circulating capital. September 8 the New York Warehouse and Security Company failed, followed by one or two firms involved in railroad construction. Confidence in persons known to be burdened in this way was impaired, and a run on them for deposits began. September 18 Jay Cooke and Co. succumbed to this demand, and a panic followed. The country depositors began to

[1] The best criticism on this is in Ernest Seyd's *Suggestions in Reference to the Metallic Currency of the United States.* London, 1871.

run on their banks, though without panic. The country banks called for their balances, and the city banks called their funds in from the brokers. On the 20th the Union Trust Company suspended, followed by two or three other banks and trust companies. The panic on the Exchange was so great that the Exchange was closed, and remained closed for ten days. The Gold Exchange closed on Monday the 22d, gold at 112. On the 20th the Associated Banks formed an alliance by which seven per cent. certificates were issued for seventy-five per cent. of the value of securities deposited by any bank, which certificates were good for Clearing-house balances; $22,000,000 of them were issued before the tide turned. The President and Secretary were in New York on the 21st, but refused to draw on the $44,000,000. The Secretary ordered bonds to be bought as a measure of relief, and $12,000,000 were bought. This depleted the cash on hand, and before January 1 he was obliged to issue over $26,000,000 of the $44,000,000 for current expenses. This carried the greenbacks up to $382,000,000. The suspension of paper payments by the banks lasted until November 22. Meanwhile the crisis was affecting industry in all forms. It produced a general doubt of the status and of the future. Hours of labor and wages were reduced and workmen discharged. The lack of reviving courage and enterprise has been very marked, and is due to nothing else than the general feeling that there can be no permanent cure until the financial problem is solved. The failures in 1873 were 5183, liabilities, $228,100,000; those in 1874, 5830, liabilities, $155,200,000. The act of January 14, 1875, specified January 1, 1879, as the day for resuming specie payments.

The people of a new country are not likely to be very careful financiers. They have no traditions to carry down the warning of the past. They are not trained to look back or to look forward. They do not look back, because the great achievements of yesterday only provoke a smile to-day. They do not look forward, because they trust their power to deal with whatever may come. We must not expect what is inconsistent with the conditions. If we look to the past, there has been great progress. The theories on which the colonists based their paper "banks" obtain attention from no sober men to-day. The banks, whatever their faults, are not like those of 1816, nor yet like those of 1836. On the other hand, we are still struggling with the problems of currency and taxation and debt. A student of our past history can hardly expect that these will be solved by a heroic effort, but by a long and painful growth up to the conviction that financial make-shifts do not pay, and that the first condition of dealing successfully with difficulty is to get free exercise of the national productive powers.

IX.

THE EXPERIMENT OF THE UNION, WITH ITS PREPARATIONS.

THERE are some states and forms of government which have been slowly building themselves up for ages, while others are the artificial results of political theory. The first find support in historical causes and in past political habits. Having grown with a people, and being expressions of their national life, they are in little danger of overthrow from within, and present so great a resistance to aggression from without that nothing but a very superior force can destroy them. The states which are constructed on theory or after an approved model, without being rooted in old habits, are much less sure of continuance. If enacted constitutions do not meet the wants of the nation, they have little self-preserving power, they awaken no enthusiasm, they point back to no history on which a people's pride loves to dwell. Especially is the life-power of institutional nations great. Those ancient institutions which are connected with the habits and affections of a people, and those local ones which carry the spirit of self-government into the smallest territorial divisions, and which are at the opposite pole from centralization—these possess a tenacity of life to which no constitutions founded on the rights of man and on the almost mechanical working of functions of government can possibly attain. If in the course of time it should be found necessary to make changes in the form of government, such institutional nations can make them without changing their political habits. The state puts on another dress, and seems to have passed through a revolution, but the revolution is confined to form; the essential spirit of the polity remains as before.

Yet even a nation wonted to self-government and to political reflection can not hope to escape changes of a different kind from those that generally give birth to revolutions in free communities. The changes to which we refer do not proceed from political causes in the first instance, although such causes may help them in their growth; but they are to be ascribed to moral and social changes affecting large masses in the society. They resemble, on the great scale, those silent alterations in individual character when a man finds his old ways of thinking not so satisfactory to himself as they once were, or when he acquires the means of pleasure or of show of which in his youth he was destitute, or when he forms relations and enters into intimacies with men of a class or of habits to which he was a stranger before. By-and-by he finds his old principles giving way; he was not aware of the direction in which he was drifting until, perhaps, the work on his character or his faith is nearly done. In the same way the influences of changes in the relations of property when there is immense capital in the hands of a few by the side of a great proletarian class, or of a transition from simplicity of life and habits to showiness and expensiveness, or of changes of religious faith and moral principles undermined by social or philosophical causes, and giving way to skepticism or profligacy on the part of many—these influences may go on without being noticed or feared for a long time, but are really more to be dreaded than political revolutions. Changes from causes like these are hard to be estimated, not only because they are slow and silent, but also because the people themselves are the subject of the change, and the new generations have no exact standard within their reach by which they can compare the present with the past. Their effects, again, on political institutions as well as on social life can not be prevented. You might as well try to keep a stream from running downward as to prevent these consequences altogether. Take an example: the feudal system could keep its sway over a nation as long as the feudal lords held all the land, and there was no, or next to no, personal property; but as soon as the towns became great centres of manufacturing and commerce, as soon as large merchants could lend money to kings and so turn the fortune of war against the nobles, so soon a new estate was in its germ, which, in the nature of the case, would demand a place in the political system, and could not long be kept out. Such an instance is a plain one, because the external side of life is visible to all, and is easily measured by the historian. But what shall we say of a general loss of religious faith in a nation, of the decay of simplicity, of integrity in public and private affairs, of honor, of respect for the institutions or habits of forefathers? Shall we not say that these changes in a people's moral principles must have an effect upon their capacity to endure political restraints, to bear political freedom, to deal soberly with obstacles in the way of prosperity, to respect the relations of private life, to be orderly and contented amidst the inequalities of fortune?

In forecasting the dangers to which national union or liberty is exposed, in estimating the probabilities for the future of good or evil growing out of causes already active or now beginning to act, in endeavoring to form a judgment on the continuity of political habits, in discussing the question whether a community has a self-reforming power when evil is already admitted into its system—we must look at moral and historical influences both. These may be coeval and concurrent at their origin, while afterward a new set of causes may come in and act either together or on opposite sides. If they are found in decided conflict—the historical, for instance, being conservative, and those of a moral nature destructive—the tendency will be toward national weakness and decay, unless there is life enough left to reform the body-politic. Or they may come into existence at different epochs; and in general it is true that new moral influences, themselves the results, in part, of changes in society, appear after states are fully organized, and amidst great public as well as private prosperity.

Bearing these remarks in mind, let us look at the development of our institutions from the time of the first English colonies onward. For one of the most hopeful things to be said of these United States is that we are what we are not chiefly by any forecast of our own, still less by any intention to form a great English-speaking nation on this side of the water, but because historical causes which could not be foreseen shaped and moulded us into a tolerably homogeneous and compact people. This is the only nation of civilized men of which it can be said that we passed through all the stages of our life, from birth onward, through revolution to self-government and political greatness, in a natural progress, so that what some call historical accidents stand out, in our case most especially, to a man who sees a God in the world, as His guidance and purpose to make something good out of us: which purpose we can thwart, but one is filled with hope by believing that it is real.

Among the advantages which the English colonies had at their commencement deserve to be mentioned the nationality of the first colonists, the time at which they emigrated, and their general character.

We are not disposed, on the score of race, to claim a superiority for the Anglo-Saxons over the inhabitants of other parts of Europe; nor can we believe that if there had been no Norman conquest, no check on the kings by the nobles, no parliaments, no opposition to papal interference by statutes of *præmunire* and against provisors, no Protestant Reformation, the English race would have of course developed itself by its inherent energies into something great and good. It was, in fact, owing to national decline that William of Normandy succeeded in his conquest of Saxon England. But we rejoice that the first colonies were composed chiefly of Englishmen, because they brought with them the habits and traditions of a land

> "Where freedom broadens slowly down
> From precedent to precedent."

It was not in England, as on the Continent, that the towns needed to conspire with the kings against an oppressive nobility, or that the nobility gained privileges exclusively for their own order, leaving the others to take care of themselves, but the Magna Charta and all the securities of freedom that followed it were for the benefit of all. There the Parliament at an early day separated into two Houses, and by its power of granting or withholding taxes, which was derived from feudalism, came to have a material part in making the laws. It was there that the town privileges and habits of local self-government maintained themselves with more permanence than on the Continent. There arose a numerous yeomanry, holders of small portions of land in their own rights—a class which since the emigrations has almost disappeared in the old country. There, too, the freemen were called to act on juries, and felt that they were part of the power of the country. Thus the colonists brought with them habits of self-government and the spirit of free Englishmen, which were not likely to fade out of their characters in the new wilderness life where they were forced, in great measure, to model their own institutions.

The time of the emigrations was the best possible for the formation of new self-governing communities. If they had begun in the century before the Reformation, when the civil wars of England had destroyed a large part of the upper classes and barbarized the people, the star of empire setting its way westward would have shed a baleful light. Little intelligence, no learning, small acquaintance with the arts, no religious thoughtfulness, and an ill-defined feeling of political rights would have presided over the birth of the new settlements. If they had begun in the middle of the eighteenth century, when England had fallen to its lowest degree of moral and religious degeneracy, and when the old yeomanry were beginning to disappear, these States would have been founded by a less hardy class, with purposes in changing their homes that were less noble, and with less of the vigorous manhood required in the conquest of nature. It is a remark of the political economists that the best prospects for successful colonization belong to an age anterior to division of labor on a great scale. Men whose lives are spent in one process of manufacture are not well fitted for all the various employments of a settlement in the wilderness, where every one must know a little of the numerous arts of life, or succumb in the conflict with unsubdued nature. The time which determined the character of the American colonies was prior to the great modern triumphs of mechanical invention.

We have also great reason to be thankful for the average character of the early colonists. M. Guizot, in speaking of the English and French revolutions, contrasts them in this respect: that the English occurred in a religious age among a religious people, while the French broke out in an age when the human mind doubted, or denied with extreme boldness, every thing that had been settled before. The first colonies belonged to that religious age, and though it would not be true to say that religious liberty was the only motive of even the Puritan colonists, yet it was a very strong motive, and it furnished the best conditions for the rise of a God-fearing and liberty-loving nation. For they who planted first of all the church, and the school by its side, who within a few years founded a college, as a pattern for all that should afterward arise, might indeed be narrow in some of their views and practices, but they were the best possible pioneers of a coming host of freemen. So, also, the Quaker settlements were dictated by the desire to enjoy their religion in peace, away from the oppressive laws of England and of its colonies; their leaders were among the best men of the mother country. The Catholics of Maryland founded their colony for the sake of religious freedom. The Dutch of New Netherlands did not, indeed, emigrate for this purpose; but they belonged to a noble race, in whose memories the times of William the Silent were still fresh, and their settlements at the end of his son Maurice's life were favored by the more liberal of the two political parties. The more southern colonies did not, it is true, have motives in their emigrations much beyond the ordinary ones that lead people away from their homes. Some, moreover, who joined them at an early time added any thing but character and strength; yet the chivalrous spirit and the attachment to English institutions which animated the best of the settlers in that quarter were to become valuable elements in the formation of the national character.

Besides the classes of colonists just mentioned, two others deserve to be spoken of, although, on account of their small number and the later date of their emigration, they contributed comparatively little to the qualities which mark the American people. One of these were the Huguenots, who came in the greatest numbers soon after the revocation of the Edict of Nantes, and who, making small settlements in New York, Massachusetts, Virginia, and South Carolina, have given to the country a number of honorable and important families. Larger and more compact settlements were made by the Scotch-Irish Presbyterians of Ulster in New Hampshire, Western Pennsylvania, and North Carolina—a class of inhabitants of whom their descendants have a right to be proud.

Another most fortunate circumstance in the early history of the country was the substantial equality of the early settlers. They nearly all belonged to that industrious middle class which is the strength of a nation. A few servants came with the more opulent of the colonists, and a few younger branches or near connections of noble families established themselves both in the Northern and the Southern settlements, but not enough to have any sensible influence either on the spirit or the destinies of the land. It was fixed well-nigh a century before the Revolution that if such an event should happen, and the colonies become self-governing, there could be no strife of orders to add complexity to the struggle with the mother country.

Still, again, it deserves notice that the slowness with which population and wealth increased during a century and a half contributed to the steadiness, the simplicity of manners, and sobriety of judgment of the people. The colonies went into the war of independence with a population of less than three millions. There were no towns containing twenty-five thousand inhabitants at the peace in 1783. There were no centres of business in the last century such as now exist. Merchants in some of the smaller villages of the Eastern States imported their goods directly from England; as, indeed, it was the custom in parts of the South for the planters of a district to receive their annual supplies from the old countries and send back their tobacco and other commodities in the same vessel. In regard to social distinctions it may be said that they were more marked than now. Certain families here and there had a pre-eminence conceded to them, which rather grew out of old ancestral respectability than out of wealth, which was acknowledged willingly and accepted without pride. In a few large places a style prevailed which wanted the show and expense of our times, but approached nearer to the style of true gentlemanly living. This was a tradition from the usages of the upper middle class in England, which was as natural, as much expected from persons of a certain standing, as plain living was from the mass of the people. In those families, however, who set the mode, thrift, domestic economy, a training of the daughters for housekeeping, are believed to have prevailed which are now passing away. As there was slow growth, with no perceptible change, steady habits grew up in political as well as in social life. Take the colony of Connecticut for an example. Three Wyllyses of the same family were Secretaries of State in succession all the time from 1712 to 1810, and the middle one of the three for sixty-one years. One member of what is now called the House of Representatives was elected by his town to seventy-two Legislatures in succession, that is—since there were two annual elections—through a period of thirty-six years. It was comparatively rare for a minister to leave his parish until death called him away. Capital accumulated so slowly, and families were in general so large, that strict economy, the parent of many civic virtues, was almost a necessity. Men were free, and felt themselves to be equal, but marks of respect were voluntarily rendered to persons in public stations. When on Sunday the service was over, the minister and his family went out of church first, the congregation all rising, and in some places bowing until they had passed through the aisle. The display in dress was very small, but if the thick brocades which are now shown here and there as having belonged to a grandmother or a great-grandmother afford a criterion for judgment, materials were chosen which would last almost a lifetime, while the ordinary household garb was very simple. If habits such as particulars like these show to have existed did indeed prevail, they mark a character contented with the present, averse to innovation, neither anxious nor speculative—the best possible character for hardening and toughening a people in preparation for future struggles. And here, again, our good fortune in having had no aristocratic class in the proper sense of the term may be referred to as another cause of simplicity of manners. For if there had been but a moderate number of noble families with large incomes and domains distributed through the colonies, their mode of living and dressing would have been the ideal, and would have made many dissatisfied with their moderate means. It might have been as it has since been in the new settlements of some of the Western States, where a very small percentage—say, five or eight per cent.—of slaves was diffused through the district. This small ratio was enough to bring white labor into disrepute. So, in the case supposed, a sprinkling of persons belonging to a noble class might have been enough to affect injuriously those solid and homely virtues which are the strength of a country.

And here we are reminded of the one bitter drug poured into our cup—the institution of slavery and the importation of blacks from Africa. The bringing over of indentured apprentices, of convict laborers, and of "redemptioners" was a small evil, for in fifty years they were lost in the population. But when, in 1620, a Dutch vessel brought twenty negroes for sale into James River, a new element of race and population was introduced, which has had, and may yet have, a vast and disastrous influence on our history. This is not the place to pursue this gloomy subject to a great length. We simply remark that the separation in interests and traits of character between the Northern and Southern States was intensified by slavery far beyond the bounds of a healthy difference; that the uniformity of interests produced by it in States where it existed gave them the power of combination, made them the political masters of the country, and opened the way for burning jealousies; that the wearing out of the soil by the agriculture of slavery demanded new lands for its spread; that it tended to degrade the lower class of whites where it was predominant; and that it was destined to come inevitably into conflict with ideas of personal rights and with those religious feelings which demanded security for the sacredness of family ties in the negro race as well as for their mental and moral elevation. The conflict came, and was indeed awful. Had there been less blindness and more trust in the final triumph of justice, it would have been earlier and less severe.

But that which more than all things else determined the future of this country was the number of colonies, together with their general similarity and their important differences. If there could have been one vast colony, under one government, extending along the whole line of coast from the French possessions to the Spanish settlements in Florida, it might have been strong and prosperous possibly, but the present United States would not have grown up on such a foundation. There was a necessity of just such a series of colonies as were actually planted, all animated by a common English feeling, and speaking the common English tongue, yet settled for different reasons, and, in a course of many years of self-government, developed into different entities, as well as having distinctive characteristics. The Northern and Southern groups of these colonies, alike among themselves, yet differing each from the other in their climates, industries, institutions, and religious peculiarities, might have formed the nucleus of two nations if English feeling, influences from the mother country, trade, and many common interests had not brought them together more than the causes of an opposite nature tended to keep them apart. The colonies lying between these extremes had no common likeness; indeed, before the cession of New Netherlands to the English they had no common bond of union, and afterward, although best situated for purposes of commerce, were more fitted for some time to follow than to lead. We will make the supposition that when the Southern colonies admitted slavery, New England had thought it a sin and a shame; even such an opinion could easily have prevented the two extremes from meeting. As it was, slavery existed every where, and not being regarded as a wrong or an evil until the Quakers began to teach a higher morality, no such cause of separation existed. We will make another supposition, that the colony of New Netherlands, lying like a wedge on the coast, with the best sea-port within its borders, settled originally by colonists not understanding the English tongue and not educated under English political institutions, could have retained its nationality until no power could have conquered it. In this case a most serious problem would have offered itself in the course of time—either the Eastern and Southern English colonies would have pursued their destinies apart, or, if they could have acted in conjunction with the Dutch colony, difficulties from language and institutions might have prevented a perfect union. Thus we see that the colonies were pointed toward confederation by their history, and were almost prevented from establishing any other kind of government throughout the course of centuries. One cluster of confederates, or more than one, seems to have been the only possible political alternative if they were ever to separate from the mother country. Two or more clusters, so far as we can interpret the probabilities of things, would have been most disastrous, as containing the seeds of strife, and sowing them for all the future.

Another point connected with our colonial history deserves notice. We were not only prepared by the circumstances of our history for a confederation or union of States, but were educated for it by our relations to the mother country. The colonies all had law-making assemblies formed somewhat after the pattern of the Houses of Parliament, and the larger part of them chief executive officers holding their places, without any popular election, by appointment of the king. At first, indeed, several colonies chose their own chief magistrates, but on various pretenses they were divested of this power, until at last two of the colonies subsisted under what was called a proprietary government, and two of the smaller alone retained their original free choice of all public officers. The royal Governors certainly did not tend to establish friendly relations between the crown and its American subjects: witness the strifes between these magistrates and the Legislatures in Massachusetts and Virginia. The proprietary government in Pennsylvania was perhaps less acceptable, as placing it in the hands of a private man by hereditary right to fill a kind of secondary throne, with the power of vetoing the acts of the Legislature. The two chartered colonies of Connecticut and Rhode Island certainly had no occasion to find fault with their independence; but they were brought up by their very privileges to be on their guard against any invasion of them, and could see little use in their distant connection with the crown.

The exigencies of self-defense often called for common counsels on the part of neighboring colonies, so that the minds of the people were accustomed to congresses gathered for objects in which all shared alike. The great contest between England and France for supremacy in North America excited the liveliest interest through the colonies; they looked on the French not only with the eyes of Englishmen as hereditary foes, but as allies also of the red men, and as willing to incite them to any treacherous act against the frontier English settlements. The prelude to the seven years' war was marked by the unfortunate expeditions of the Virginians and of Braddock, in which Washington was schooled for his future post. The critical years 1757–1758 saw regiments from the Northern colonies joining Abercrombie and Lord Howe in their expedition against Ticonderoga and Crown Point, while large quotas were sent from New England to aid General Amherst in his attack on Louisbourg. There were thus scattered through the colonies numbers of officers and soldiers who had seen service. When the critical blow was struck, and Quebec became English—when, finally, by the peace of 1763, all the French territory in the North changed hands, and in the West the Mississippi nearly to its mouth became the boundary between the two nationalities, we may easily believe that the colonies felt an increase of security, and would be the more ready to resist aggressions from the mother country because they stood in no fear of the power of France.

Thus far we have seen historical causes preparing the colonies for self-government, on a certain plan, if ever the connection with the mother country should be broken. The declaration of independence and the war of the Revolution, after this preparation, were owing to faults and blunders of the mother country, and to the political doctrines of the eighteenth century. Of this breach we will forbear to speak. To say little of it would be to do injustice to events so supremely important in our history; to say much of it would turn us aside from our main subject. The colonists had as much loyalty to the mother country as could justly be expected from men who had chiefly protected themselves, who had been denied their privileges as Englishmen, and had been used rather as sources of commercial benefit for Great Britain than helped in their progress toward becoming self-sustaining parts of the empire. The war was undertaken soberly, regretfully, with no side issues in view, and with no rancor toward England in the hearts of the people. This want of rancor is shown by the fact that many of the best officers, Washington himself, Hamilton, Knox, and a host of others, remained English in their feelings, and were attached to the traditions of the mother country; and that the leading civilians who had urged on rebellion, and had been the counselors of the country in the war, were afterward charged with undue partialities toward England. Probably no revolution did its work with more conscientiousness, and fuller persuasion of its rightfulness on the part of the people, with less of a spirit of blood, with fewer bitter remembrances of the enemy, than this. It deserves to be noticed, as showing the sober temper of the war, that a regiment formed from volunteers in one part of a county took one of the parish ministers with them as their chaplain, as if it had been a church meeting adjourned to another place.

It was a blessing for which we can never be too thankful that an experiment at constitution-making was set on foot in the war, and was tried long enough to show its defects, and point the way toward something better. It was nothing but a league of States, with no Executive, with one House in Congress, without a Supreme Court, without the power of regulating commerce with foreign countries or between the States. This last defect especially it was that demanded a new instrument. This new instrument was made to remove difficulties which were felt; and, as Mr. Edward A. Freeman, in his history of confederations, justly remarks, was made in no conscious imitation of any other constitution. This learned and able historian of federal governments, writing in 1863, when he looked on the Union as permanently dissolved, says of it: "The American Union has actually secured for what is really a long period of time a greater amount of combined peace and freedom than was ever before enjoyed by so large a portion of the earth's surface. There have been and still are vaster despotic empires, but never before has so large an inhabited territory remained for more than seventy years in the enjoyment at once of internal freedom and of exemption from the scourge of war. Now this is the direct result of the federal system." If we have succeeded in making it clear that our present Constitution was almost an inevitable result of historical causes—that is, of Divine Providence—we shall be led to value it more than if we were to look on it as a product of successive workings of human wisdom.

It is impossible that any constitution should at all times be equal in its bearing upon all interests and all parts of a country, and equally impossible that it should not admit in some points two interpretations. The parts of the country which were more devoted to trade wanted a strong government; the parts where the people lived within themselves, in the pursuits of agriculture, felt in general less zeal for some improvement on the old Confederation. There grew up naturally a jealousy of powers conferred on the common government as restricting and opposing the powers of the separate States; with this the principle of strict construction of the Constitution of the United States was united; and thus two parties coeval with our present government arose—the Federal, and the Republican or Democratic. The former had a certain leaning toward England, and dreaded the principles of the French revolutionists; the other admired France and distrusted England. After twelve years of control over public affairs, during the Presidencies of Washington and the elder Adams, the very upright party of the Federalists was driven out of power, partly in consequence of blunders and dissensions within itself, partly because it did not fully understand the temper of the people, while a still greater blunder on the part of leading members of it in the Eastern States led to its final extinction.

The Democratic party, under Southern leaders, held the government from the beginning of the century for sixty years, not without internal differences and divisions, arising from sectional interests and other causes. As it often happens, the name rather than the essence of the original party was preserved; new issues had driven out the old ones from the field of politics. Tariffs were altered from time to time, the Southern States being almost unanimous for free trade, and the North preponderating toward protection. Through all the changes the country flourished by emigration, by the rise of manufactures, in its marine, in its wealth. The great West, growing vaster in its dimensions, from the time of the purchase of Louisiana until it reached the Pacific coast, began to give signs of grasping at the hegemony and controlling the policy of the country. But meanwhile a spiritual cause, without power at first—a cloud no bigger than a man's hand—arose above the horizon. Slavery had been preached against by a few, protested against by the noblest of the Quakers from the days of John Woodman, acknowledged by all to be unrighteous in itself, and yet was endured in the hope that emancipation at length would quietly dissolve a structure which ages had built up, and which could not fall without a reconstruction of society. The cotton-gin and the ample lands of the Gulf States, including the latest acquisition, Texas, offered it a boundless field to spread over, and opened the prospect, whenever a new State should be formed in which there was an appreciable infusion of the slave element, of new strength added to the Southern supremacy. In the extreme South this was a smooth path toward supremacy, but was not so easy on the borders, where slave and white labor came together. As early as 1820 the problems of the future developed themselves, at which time a dividing line was drawn by the Missouri Compromise between the two interests. Next appeared the doctrine of nullification, and the attempt of the leading Southern State, South Carolina, to establish a practical check on the action of the general government by that of one of the States. It was maintained at first that there resided a power in each State of the confederation to judge whether a law of the United States was constitutional, and to resist within its own territory the operation of such laws as were judged to be otherwise. In 1832 an ordinance was passed declaring the tariff law "null, void, and no law," and forbidding duties on imports to be paid within its jurisdiction after a certain day in the near future. It so happened that the President at this time was a Southern man of great popularity and of singular energy, who not only felt that such a doctrine of nullification, if carried out, would be a death-blow to any union, and was entirely unconstitutional, but had personal reasons for doing his utmost to oppose it. In his opposition he carried for the time the greater part of the South with him; it was understood that he was ready to use all the forces at his disposal in executing the law; and the message on nullification which was issued in his name in 1833 was a most valuable state paper in refutation of the doctrine that a State has a right to decide for itself that the Constitution has been violated, and so deciding, to secede from the Union or to declare a law void.

The storm thus raised was blown over by the help of a tariff compromise, but the opinions already spoken of spread through the Slave States more and more, in a greater ratio of increase, perhaps, than the principles of abolition and the political party founded upon them grew at the North and West. Here a controversy began which nothing—no prudence at the North, no denunciation, no interests of traffic—could put down. Every fugitive slave reclaimed added to the force of the feeling against slavery. Formerly it had been hoped that in time slavery would give way to serfdom, and in the end to full freedom; but as the abolitionists appealed to the conscience and to our American theory of human rights, it was necessary to construct moral defenses on the other side. Instead of confessing the wrong of the institution, and asking for time to prepare for its abolition, it was supported by the authority of Scripture; it was the redemption of men from heathenism in Africa; it brought with it relations most kindly and humane between an abject race and an enlightened one; it kept out much of the vice too easily discoverable in the cities of the Free States. This was the beginning, evidently, of the last phase of the controversy between the two parts and two interests in the country; for how could there be any compromise when such diametrically opposite sides were taken? And as the foes of slavery grew bolder, the apprehension of what might come to pass at some future day grew stronger among its friends. Perhaps, too, they must have been aware, and have half confessed to themselves, that whether their pleas on behalf of their institution were tenable or not, there was an inconsistency between the apologies and those fundamental notions which the whole Union once avowed. It was too evident also that there must be a division, affecting all questions of politics, and becoming more pronounced from year to year, growing out of this question of questions, which could be neither settled nor avoided.

We pass by transactions of great importance, such as the affairs in Kansas and the question of slavery in the Territories, and come down to the opening of the war. Why was it, when Southern men and Southern interests had controlled the country for generations, when the North and West were divided, and probably would always continue so, that the die was cast in 1860 for secession and dissolution? The Presidential election had been far from a decided expression of public will, and wise adjustments taken in time might at least have delayed a disruption. There were, as it seems to us, two leading causes. First, the progress of ideas, and the prospect of an increase in the future of the number of Free States, without any counterbalancing weights in the other scale, were sure to fix the policy of the country for the future. Secondly, the temper of the Northern States was not well understood, just as at the North the South was thought to be threatening rather than purposing. It was supposed that the North could not act as a unit nor by great majorities, and that a party against the war would paralyze the movements of the government. Even the North had some distrust of itself. This is not the first instance in which great masses of men have failed to comprehend each other or themselves, nor will it be the last. But it was found that the preservation of the Union, all over the North and West, had an importance attached to it in men's minds which had not been thought to exist. Nor was it the commercial value of the Union that seemed so precious, as if the navigation of the Mississippi, the free intercourse, as before, in every direction through the whole territory, needed to be maintained at all hazards, but it was the Union as an idea, and as involving the future peace of this land for generations. In the spring of 1862 the writer of these words was standing on the highlands above Cincinnati, and looking over toward the Kentucky side of the Ohio. Then first a deep impression was made on his mind of the terrible results likely to follow disruption, for the line of that great river would divide free soil from slavery for hundreds of miles. And when the boundary should be fixed, who would or could prevent fugitive slaves from crossing it? Who would not resist their pursuing masters? Who could prevent a thousand border difficulties which might give rise to war? Wherever the two republics met there would be desolation or chronic warfare, obstructing the prosperity of some of the fairest regions in the world; there would be bitterness and national hatred; a blight would come over vast tracts, unless, perhaps, by slow degrees, slavery should restrict its limits, and allow its antagonist to encroach on its domains. Nor were such evils in the future worse than the loss of a great Union over which one constitution reigned, where common principles of justice were supreme. Such feelings were found in multitudes of minds; but *they* could not partake of them who had clung to their State as the highest object of their pride and allegiance.

The war had its course. At its close the problems offering themselves for solution were nearly as grave as the problem with which it began, and more difficult. The Union had been saved at the cost of overthrowing society at the South, and now the question of reconstruction came before the country under conditions which demanded the highest wisdom and moderation. A new race was called into political existence: the slaves had been turned into freemen. What was to be their political status? If they should have no voice in public affairs—if they, while acquiring civil rights, should stand by and see the most ignorant of the whites voting and determining State politics and making constitutions, what would be their security for the future?

If, on the other hand, political power were given to all indiscriminately, blacks and whites, the evil might be as great. What a strange state of things to bestow the franchise on immense multitudes who had not the knowledge requisite to vote intelligently for the lowest local magistrates, who could be combined into a party which black or white demagogues could mould and guide according to their will, and against whom it might be necessary for the whites to form an opposite combination in order to save themselves from ruin! Never, perhaps, since the world began was there such a dreadful alternative on so large a scale. Above all was this true in those States where the numbers of the races were nearly equal, or where the blacks were even in a majority. In the process of reconstruction it was managed that the suffrage should be granted to this race wherever States containing slaves had joined in the secession; and a new motive for conceding the suffrage was supplied by the Fourteenth Amendment to the Constitution, which provides that representation in Congress shall depend on the number of active or fully qualified citizens. Thus suppose the number of male inhabitants of a State over twenty-one years of age to amount to 150,000, and one-third of them to be disfranchised by an amendment of its constitution on account of want of sufficient property—which disqualification would chiefly affect the negroes—the representative quota for Congress must be diminished by one-third. Few States would be willing to submit to this reduction of political power in the general government, and so, probably, it will never take place, if otherwise it were practicable. We regard the Fifteenth Article of the Amendments as most just and desirable, namely, that rights shall not be abridged on account of "race, color, or previous condition of servitude;" but in the constitutions of the restored States, and by the Fourteenth Amendment, universal suffrage in its worst shape, with its worst consequences, is fastened, perhaps necessarily, but unfortunately, on these restored republics.

This condition of things is now one of the worst evils that we suffer. We concede that it may have been necessary, but that does not take from the dangers which attend upon it. We will look at some of these dangers, disclaiming most solemnly all party motives or wishes in what we are to say. The greatest of them all is that the two races, through the States where slavery formerly existed, will be separated by party lines, and will look on one another with reciprocal distrust. Sectional differences are bad enough, as we have found in our past history, even when able men managed the parties; but differences of race, intensified by the jealousies and distrusts of politics, are tenfold worse. In the present case they tend to increase in intensity and bitterness, because the ignorant mass that has just been rescued from slavery must fall under the influence of fear of what will happen if the management of State affairs passes over permanently into the hands of their adversaries. They feel their weakness; they have inferior power of combination; they have small means of self-protection. They are also to a considerable extent under the influence of cunning leaders who seem to have unlimited power of acting on their fears. Brawls will unavoidably break out in many neighborhoods, which will grow into feuds and local quarrels, and will in report be magnified or extenuated, as it may happen, in their importance, so that the country will not know what to believe or disbelieve in regard to them. As for the blame to be imputed to the one or the other side, that is a small matter. We do not believe that the colored race or their leaders of like origin would be or have been the first to encroach on the rights of the white race. And we wish that one could not believe that there has been a policy or understanding on the part of many leading whites in some of the States in question to the effect that the colored people must be prevented by terrorism from enjoying the benefits granted to them in the new amendments. But the evils to which we refer lie outside of the immediate occasions of strife between the races; it will reach beyond existing parties. How can there be harmony between them under any future division of parties, when, in addition to difference of race, distrust, suspicion, past feuds and antagonisms, will continually foment disquiet? If it be said that unprincipled whites are corrupting the blacks and poisoning their minds, it may be very true, but how is the nuisance to be abated? Will not the eagles be gathered together where the carcass is? In brief, the cause of all that has taken place or is to be apprehended lies not in particular or local provocations, nor in the leaders of to-day, nor in the imbittering of a most mild and inoffensive race by the war, but it is one that is likely to last as long as measures, now never to be set aside, shall have run their course and borne their fruits. "The end is not yet."

Until this state of things shall end, if end it can, this unhappy part of our Union, injured in its property, with its old landholders impoverished or driven from their homes, with its institutions shattered, must lag far behind the other parts in most of the essentials of prosperity. That section is full of undeveloped resources; its exhaustless beds of iron and coal, its soil yet unbroken, or capable of vastly increased production, its mild climate, must invite capital and labor, if those timid forces could be assured of safety and protection. Perhaps the solution of the problem for the South may come from this source, from a new emigration not compromised in old strifes, and able to act in the end as a mediating and a reconciling power.

We pass on to another source of danger which the late war has opened up, or at least made more apparent—to the increased power of the general government. We have already had occasion to speak of the subject of the powers given by the present Constitution to the United States as exciting alarm in many, and as giving occasion to the birth of the old Republican or Democratic party. But, as it often happens in politics, that party, when it came into power, was not faithful to its convictions or principles. Thus, when the purchase of Louisiana was opposed by the Federalists as being a stretch of the Constitution, this was not wholly denied by the Democrats, but justified by the circumstances of the case. Thus, too, in the war of 1812, when the Federal Governors of the New England coast States, while consenting to furnish the quotas of militia called for, claimed to judge when an actual invasion of their soil had taken place, and refused to put the troops under officers of the United States, pleading their unquestioned rights under the Constitution and the law, the anti-Federal party, then having the government in their hands, denounced this action as disloyal and unconstitutional. Further, the Hartford Convention—an innocent scheme with an ugly look—was taxed with treasonable or disloyal designs, although without good reason; and yet the secession in 1861 justified itself by this unwise measure of a party which the States joining in the secession had for that very measure strongly denounced. But after the Peace of Ghent the parties returned to their original principles, or, rather—as one of them had nearly expired, and the other was divided within itself on questions of sectional interest—the parts of the country where they had respectively predominated went back to the old positions of a stricter and a freer interpretation of the Constitution, to the Federal and the States-rights theories. In the interval between that peace and the attack on Fort Sumter things ran commonly in the States-rights channel. The general government seemed to be weak; and foreigners, as they speculated on our government in those days, thought that the great danger was that State power weighed most in the balance. It is true that the Supreme Court put a curb on the acts of several of the States, and that General Jackson would undoubtedly have crushed nullification by armed force if necessary; but his vigorous measures only put off the operation of a theory which even then involved the power of a State to secede from the Union.

Yet even while the general government was regarded as weak in conflict with the State power, it showed an increase of strength of an indirect sort in the way of patronage and of influence on private persons. The appointments within the gift of the Executive grew in value and number, and already, if we mistake not, members of Congress had begun to regard it as their right to nominate to offices within their districts, to be the President's almoners, if we may give that name to their business. Still this accumulating power was rather political than governmental; it would not have excused the Executive of the United States from transcending the constitutional limits; it was strictly constitutional, although used for party purposes. If the framers of our instrument for uniting the country could have had a vivid impression of its vast extent, they would perhaps have put some check on the appointing power. But they built the house without dreaming how many servants the large family would require.

The appointing power is a means to an end, to the reward of partisans, and those the neediest generally and the most selfish. As such it is corrupting, and the interests involved in it are strong enough to resist all attempts at reformation. Its bad influences on party and on personal honor can not be removed without some change in the Constitution, and such change party feeling itself would resist. The ill success of civil service reform is mortifying enough, and disheartening for the future.

The strength of the government, looked at apart from its indirect influences, never appeared formidable until the war called it fully forth. Then first the Executive seemed to have a new quality, which might be compared with the dictatorial power conferred by the Senate of Rome on the consuls in the well-known formula that they do their best to prevent the republic from suffering any detriment. Then first the command of immense armies, the arrests of suspected persons, the control over vast sums of money, the arbitrary use of telegraphs, and, after the war was over, the government of the Southern States by military officers, and the reconstruction of those States, revealed an accumulation of authority which was unsuspected before, and pointed to a possible military despotism in the future. Then, too, the power that Congress authorized of suspending specie payments and issuing legal tenders showed that in emergencies financial measures could be set on foot which could involve the country in untold distress, and even in bankruptcy. Since the war, also, the disturbed condition of one of the Southern States has induced the President, on his own responsibility, to use military power in a case of very doubtful constitutionality, to say the least, and to interfere for the restoration of order in a way that can not be justified. The upright intentions of the Chief Magistrate we do not intend to question; the subject, interesting as it is, concerns us only because a very dangerous precedent may be set for the future. The question may be asked, and is asked, whether there is any danger of military despotism. And as this could not exist without consolidation, it can be asked, also, Is not consolidation, which, at the founding of the republic, one party dreaded, and would have prevented by constitutional limitations if the other had thought it more than a bare possibility—is not this to be the ultimate goal of our Union? This is what those who look at us with no sympathy for our institutions profess to regard as a future probability. Within a few months we have seen the following expression in a foreign paper commenting on affairs in Louisiana: "The President is exhibiting how easily a military despotism could be built on American institutions." Thus the same Constitution which a few years ago, as looked at through foreign spectacles, could not resist the weak power of the States, or bring back a recalcitrant Governor into his proper relations to the general government, is now allowing, it is said, the general government and the "one-man power" in it to trample on the rights of the States, and to threaten the extinction of liberty. Do these opposite charges, made at different times, refute one another, or is there a real and a new danger before us, and that, too, when the army of the United States does not contain one soldier for every thousand of the inhabitants of the country?

So great a change as that from our present Constitution to an imperial despotism, or, in other words, to an absolute democracy under one man, may not seem to many worthy of serious apprehension; and we share this opinion so far as to think that, in itself considered, a revolution so great, so without precedent in the English race, is entirely improbable. Before it could be effected there would need to be a strong party in favor of it diffused through all quarters of the Union. No sectional dissatisfaction would be adequate to bring it about. To attempt it would involve the probability of two or more confederacies, and of a war between them with an uncertain issue. To effect it would require taxation on a vast scale, or the borrowing of money to such an extent as would involve speedy bankruptcy. There are now no questions on which the

Union could be territorially divided without the uprising of a great majority against a small minority. Capital, in its connections all over the land, is a bond of union. The mouth and course of the Mississippi, the avenues to the Pacific, the communication with Europe by Atlantic ports, must be open to all. An empire on the coast seems equally impossible with a great interior empire. The only cause of essential change that seems deserving of being taken into account is a general loss of reverence on the part of thinking men for the institutions of the country, a wide-spread conviction that we have failed in our experiment. Whenever such a humiliating day shall arrive, the same conviction might lead toward peaceable reforms and modifications; but a military despotism, after the experience of France and Rome, and with the political leanings of our race, is not likely to be one of them.

It is, however, possible, we admit, that attempts may be made to substitute laws of the Union for State laws in some very important departments of legislation, and that in case of their success the prestige and efficiency of the general government would be greatly increased, to the detriment of State power. Some of us are old enough to remember the time when the Cumberland Road was a bone of contention between strict and free constructionists; but now the talk is to put all telegraphs and all railroads under the supervision of the United States, as, with far less constitutional objection, banks of issue sustain relations to the States no longer. It might also be highly advantageous if in the department of international (or, if such a word might be allowed, interstate) private law harmony could be introduced, which could be effected only by general agreement between the States, or by an alteration of the Constitution which should invest Congress with new law-making powers. The laws concerning marriage, legitimacy, divorce, bequests, guardianship, the rights of married women, and the rights of aliens ought rationally to be uniform through the Union. This is the direction, as we understand, that the constitution of Switzerland is taking. From a loose confederation it became a strict one, a "Bundesstaat," and now still newer powers in legislation are to be or have been conferred on the central government. But what we dread is that the Union is becoming so great a tree, with such thick foliage, that the States, like shrubs, will lose their healthy growth under its shade; that instead of being protected, they will wither. If we look at government patronage, already so vast a factor in all political calculations and bargains, and add the possible enlargement of the sphere of United States law, demanded with the more reason on account of the great number of the States, and then bring into account the sway of an ambitious man at the head of the government taking advantage of some local difficulty, we shall not regard the anti-Federalist dread of consolidation as wildly unreasonable. Washington and Hamilton, with their compeers, were right in wanting a stronger government in place of the shackling old Confederation. That was the only sound statesmanship at that time. But when a measure of Mr. Jefferson's enlarged our domain, and set the precedent for an immense further enlargement, the danger took another direction. The very party which felt the apprehension set causes at work which alone made it to be reasonably apprehended. There is now possibility enough of such enormous powers being accumulated at Washington as ought to make men look narrowly at that tendency. For our part, at the present, we should rather endure some inconveniences from hasty or ill-considered laws of some State or States than seek a cure which might itself be a source of ill. We would print E PLURIBUS in as large letters as UNUM.

At this point of our progress we pause a moment to make the remark that we owe our protection against the tendency to consolidation to our historical development. The settlement of the country in the first instance by separate colonies, which were kept apart long enough to form distinct characteristics and to feel their independence each of the rest—*this* is obviously the force that resists perfect fusion and compactness. The nice balance aimed at in the Constitution may not last through all changes in society and in public interests; the scale that holds the rights of the Union and that which holds State power may alternately outweigh each other; but the true lover of his country will aim to keep them as far as possible in equipoise. Meanwhile, if uniform legislation is demanded on points where all the States ought to have one policy, let it be reached by a common understanding. But surely the end of a war, when State power fell into the background, and the Union was, as it ought to have been, prominent before the eyes of all, is no time to carry the old Federal principle to an extreme which the venerated founders of the Union never contemplated.

The danger of consolidation, if there be any, is future, and must be the result of slowly moving causes, of long misgovernment, and of a demand for more energy and uniformity in our system. The dangers which many fear and have feared from the democratic cast of our institutions are, if real, more immediate, because universal suffrage is upon us, and can never be gotten rid of as long as the country shall endure. The history of the extension of the suffrage in this country since the independence is a very instructive one, if it could be set forth in detail. It is sufficient here to say that most, if not all, the older colonies had at that time in their laws a qualification for voting based on the possession of land, which continued in many of them long afterward. By degrees this became a form, that is, young men who wished to become qualified for voting received deeds of land, which were reconveyed soon after the election to the friend who had helped them. At length all native-born white males twenty-one years old could vote, on taking the freeman's oath, after a certain brief term of residence in a State or town. Then naturalized citizens received the same privilege. Meanwhile free blacks, who at one time could vote even in some of the slave-holding States, as North Carolina, were deprived of their privileges in some of those which held no slaves; such was the case in New York and Connecticut, in the latter of which States a colored man of great personal worth, the owner of a considerable property, was disfranchised by the constitution of 1817. Now at length every where, if we mistake not, colored persons are put on an equality with whites, and naturalized foreigners with persons native born. The single exception known to the writer is the limitation of suffrage in Connecticut to those who are able to read—a rule by which almost no one is excluded. So generally is it held that citizenship and the right of suffrage are co-extensive that the first now passes with the greater part of Americans as a natural right, like the right of property or of contract. There are very many who believe that the earlier state of things was far better, but very few who believe that the present state of things will ever be altered. We must carry it with us through all our national existence, and endeavor to educate all voters into the ability to judge what is best, and into the spirit of conscientious citizenship; meanwhile, accepting the situation, we may look at the evils which it brings with it. These are more apparent in large towns, while in the country a restriction of the suffrage would make little difference. They are increased by the habit of many substantial citizens of staying away from the polls, either owing to a kind of despair on account of the small influence of a single vote, or to the engrossing interests of business. And thus whatever be the bad results, the higher classes of society are in a good degree responsible for them. They are increased also by the number of foreign-born voters, who can be led in masses by their more intelligent countrymen, and who thus render possible a number of inferior demagogues ready to sell votes for offices, and able to make themselves necessary to their parties. In this way differences of nationality are perpetuated long after aliens have become naturalized; and even the divisions in their old homes across the water survive their changes of abode. It is surely a most unnatural thing that there should be in communities where rights are the same for men of every kind of nativity these political sects, depending on something renounced and abandoned. Nor could we find such parties within parties, carried down even to the second or third generation, unless the means of combination lay within the power of men who have their own ends in view. The voters themselves have no need to unite for self-protection against native-born Americans, either for relief in taxation or for securing their privileges in other respects. It is the interest of all that these foreign-born citizens should grow rich, that their children should be well educated, that all places of trust should be open to them, when they are found worthy of political or social honors.

Here, then, is one danger and source of peril, that while native Americans act politically as individuals, the naturalized citizens act in masses under demagogues as their leaders, as if they were invading armies rather than men seeking for homes and for quiet. Only in one instance have native-born citizens formed a political party, and the ignominious failure in this case showed that it was unnatural and outlandish. Of the religious factor in massing certain classes of men together we have a word to say soon; we add at present the single remark that these demagogical influences retard the assimilation of the new-comers to the old, and prevent the complete harmony of the people.

In this state of things, to which universal suffrage gives rise, one party, at any one given time, will naturally attract the demagogues more than the other; that is, one will be, or affect to be, more in sympathy with the foreigner or the poor, or with liberty and equal rights; the other, more in sympathy with the interests of property and civil order. Both may be intensely selfish and equally one-sided. But they can not co-exist without acting on one another. They discover each the other's arts, means of success, and projects. Naturally they try to counteract plans by similar plans of a questionable character. They make platforms on which they do not intend to stand. They propose candidates who are ignorant or pliable, instead of those who are sturdy and experienced in legislation. There must be understandings that such and such persons of service to a party are to be rewarded in due time. These and many more of the obvious evils of parties, such as the caucus system, unanimity forced by the whip, as it were, discreditable compromises, are either owing to the universality of suffrage or are greatly increased by it; and there is no present prospect of their discontinuance. We make no complaint of parties as such; they are necessary and useful in a free state; they act as watchmen and as checks upon each other; but we maintain that the more ignorant the constituencies are, the greater is the tendency on their part to misplaced confidence in designing men, to jealousy and strife of classes, to the election of inferior politicians, to the turning of politics into a trade, to misgovernment, and, in our case at least, to the banding together of emigrants into factions founded on their nationalities. Nor do we mean to charge the mass of voters in the country with political corruption, which would be a slander. They want good government; they are ready for sacrifices, as we saw only a few years since; they have no direct interest in the results which they procure; they are in great measure far less open to bribes than the political leaders themselves. The great evil is that, without intending or foreseeing it, they raise up a crop of politicians who are strikingly unlike the mass of such as elect them, and who are fast bringing the name and work of a statesman into contempt.

But if the extent of the suffrage has so much to do with the degeneracy of political men, and if this can never be abridged, what remedy is there, and what need to talk of the evils? The remedies must be applied in detail, or they must be such as will grow out of a greater general intelligence, especially on subjects of political science, or there must be an increased moral and religious purity, which will work a cure of our evils in an indirect way. Of these general remedies we don't intend to speak. We simply remark that here and there a cure can be applied to some of the most glaring evils. If our Legislatures have been exposed to temptations by special legislation, a remedy can be applied, as has been done in the amended constitutions of several large States, by taking away to a great extent from these bodies the power of granting special incorporations; if the towns, as has been done, abuse their charters, and come under the control of venal, corrupt men, their powers can be abridged or controlled; if judges, as now elected in many States, are inferior men, for this too, it is to be hoped, a cure may be provided. The whole power of burdening States and towns with debt, as well as the taxing power, ought to have limits set for them in the States by public law.

We are reminded here of another danger which is thought to be threatened by an influx of foreigners. This land, once almost exclusively Protestant, is the refuge now of five millions of Catholics, more or less. It is odd enough that some of those very people who saw in four millions of slaves a providence bringing them within the influence of Christianity, now see a frowning providence providing these Catholics a home in a land founded and nourished by Protestant principles. There may be great hopes of converting this country to the mediæval religion. That religion will, of course, grow by natural increase, and causes new in our age may aid it, although what the Pope's newly developed infallibility will have to do with it we fail to see. Of this we are sure, that if any new vigor and spread of the Catholic faith, any aggressive action, should appear in this country, it would unite all Protestants of all hues more than any thing else could do, and would probably promote among them a *catholic* spirit far more than it would promote *Catholicism* outside of them.

Other evils which usher in this second century of our national existence arise from the late war and the financial measures of the government. The war was undertaken, we are proud to say, without bitterness, in a spirit of loyalty toward the Union, and with a deep sense of the immense evils of a permanent disruption. Never was a war marked to a greater degree by compassion for the wounded or by a more merciful treatment of prisoners than this of ours. And when did a nation, of its own accord, without the force of treaty, forgive the authors of a war more generously—we might say, with more dangerous forgetfulness of injuries? All classes who are not ordinarily roused to excitement by a sense of wrong joined in supporting it. The vast body of the religious people of the North and West felt its necessity and justice. Never did prayer for the country arise to the God of nations more unceasingly and more fervently; never did men, especially at the West, risk their lives with a fuller conviction of the rightfulness of the struggle. Such a war, like all wars, might have evils attending it. Some of the officers may have entered the service to better their political chances in the future; looseness of life and of principle may have been learned by a few; the obligations of the citizen may have been unlearned by a few more. But it is certain, we think, that if the war had ended without leaving any other besides its own direct evils, its bearing on life and manners would have been, on the whole, good. Certainly the winning side, as it looks back on the morality of its cause and of the measures for making it victorious, has no reason for shame.

But war can not stand alone: Mars and Mercury must go together; and the contrivances of the latter to raise money are more than a counterbalance to the blunt honesty of the former. Whether the war could have been waged without a suspension of specie payments, whether there were not reasons which justified that measure, aside from the financial ones, we will not stop to ask. Our work is to look at facts and their issues. The fact is that irredeemable paper and a vast debt, beyond all power of payment for years to come, were introduced; and as the ease of carrying on the measures of government for the time banished anxiety, the ultimate difficulties were not duly weighed. At the beginning of the war there was a general settling of balances between debtor and creditor; the money so returned to its owners was lent to the government; and when the bonds of the public debt had increased in value, and the confidence of capitalists abroad in our securities was restored, these were sold at an advantage to parties across the water. Meanwhile, especially after the end of the war, new enterprises were begun, some of them immense in extent; new debts between individuals were contracted; private persons were eager to go into enterprises which promised large returns; banks were willing to lend to speculators and stockjobbers; every body wanted to get rich without labor or capital. Had there been no suspension of specie payments, but little of all this could have taken place; had there been an honest, intelligent attempt after the return of peace to resume specie payment at some future day, with the right machinery for it, instead of the puerile measures that were actually adopted, the country might now be rejoicing that the unavoidable crisis had passed over, and might look with rational confidence toward the future. But this was too great an effort for a speculating generation, too great for political leaders. Nearly the whole of our present evils, except those which arise from the reconstruction of the Southern States and the character of political adventurers in that uncertain field, are the direct or indirect results of the condition of the currency, of the fluctuations in the value of specie as measured by the legal tender. To this we must ascribe a large part of the speculations of recent years, the necessary reactions, failures, and shrinking of values, the depression of the mercantile community in consequence of greater economy on the part of consumers, and the dread of the future. To this are owing in a measure the vast fortunes acquired since the war began, the power of great houses to depress and drive out of the field smaller ones, the immense extravagance and show, the almost contempt for the virtues of thrift, moderation, and forethought—virtues so important and efficient as even in heathen lands or under bad governments to secure a happy, unaspiring middle class. To this, again, we must refer the uneasiness and strikes of laborers, at least in part, and the general feeling pervading the producers in one section of the country that they are oppressed by transporters, and can by legislation change the laws of profits. To this, too, in large part, we must attribute that intensely excited worldliness which appears on all sides; those frequent outbreaks of crime, especially of dishonesty, which will soon be regarded as matters of course; that venality, that want of honor, which are injuring our principles as well as our reputation.

These last vices call for more extended consideration, for just now they are imputed to the legislature of the nation. Formerly if there was a member of Congress who came there with "itching palms," he could do but little in the way of gratifying his propensity. There was nothing to steal; there was no chance for corrupt bargains, and there was little suspicion of corrupt practice. Our poverty was our integrity. The new state of things is mainly owing, not to a lower set of men brought into the service of the country as legislators, not to the unwillingness of Congress itself to ferret corruption out, but to the means held in the hands of great corporations to influence votes. These means, again, are owing mainly to the financial condition of the country; and if there be increased venality—that is, if Congressmen half a century ago would have resisted similar temptations—this, again, is mainly owing to the overstimulus of the covetous spirit which the last ten or twelve years have engendered.

The suspicions felt in regard to the honesty and honor of Congress have derived strength from what has become known and what has not been discovered. At first there seemed to be an unwillingness to probe an ulcer; then the facts that came to light, while revealing crime on the part of a few, involved many in suspicion; and finally the disclosures of the winter of 1874–75 made it seem as if the money paid to agents at Washington for a subsidy to a line of steamboats must have passed into many hands. Here, then, we have guilt charged on a very few, suspicion resting on many: and this is just the worst state of things possible. If forty members of a political body were found to have taken bribes and were expelled, it would be better for the country or State than if five were detected and two hundred were under suspicion, although the suspicion might be wholly groundless; for a general distrust of men in public stations is most disheartening and demoralizing. Unjust doubt of human character in general destroys the motives to probity arising from example, if it be not already the fruit of a corrupt heart.

And here we can not refrain from saying a word on the conduct of public journals as it respects the charges against public men. Our leading journals contain men in their editorial corps who may compare advantageously with any members of Congress. But some of them, in their anxiety to give the first news, are not equally anxious to find out whether it be true or not; they trust too implicitly to the reports of correspondents; or they have, perhaps, grudges which make them unfair. To be fair would be to be moderate. It would not do to be gentlemanly, for strong words would need to be weighed. When we read the vilifications of Congress and other political bodies, one thing at least we are sure of, that the writers ought to be believers in the doctrine of total depravity, for seldom were such charges made even by stiff Calvinists against individual men as these journals, otherwise most respectable, sometimes make upon large bodies of leading politicians. It is much to be regretted that individual character should be attacked without the best reasons; for while it is of very little importance that this or that man keeps his hold on the public confidence, it is of immense importance that our representative system should be trusted in. When that is thought to be venal we lose the hope of good government, and our reverence for institutions, so much prized once, vanishes; we become ashamed of our country, make a feebler resistance to causes of disorganization, and fall into despair.

In asking ourselves what means lie within our reach that we may recover ourselves from evils partly temporary, partly arising out of our political system, we look first at the possibility that the sentiment of honor may be purified and quickened. It has been thought by De Tocqueville that for the growth of honor in a country there must be men of rank and birth, who are enabled by their position and traditions to know what is honorable, and who would sink into contempt within their own class if they fell below the standard. To the English idea of honor belong especially the virtues of courage, truth, and straightforwardness; or more generally honor consists in a nice sense of personal rights, of that which is due to others and owed by them to ourselves. Is it too much to hope that a noble and manly literature in the future may raise the standard of character through the whole people, so that a truckling, deceitful, dodging politician shall be thoroughly despised on all sides, and be obliged to renounce his political hopes on account of his meannesses? Is it too much to hope that such a principle of honor, without the pride that often goes with it, may be incorporated into our law of social morality; and that religion, which has a most intimate and inseparable connection with genuine morality, may take up this principle also, and may leaven society with it, so that a trick or a lie may be utterly abhorred by merchants, by politicians, by young men entering into life, by all who can corrupt others or be corrupted themselves? O for more men in public life with the character of him of whom the poet speaks:

> "Who never sold the truth to serve the hour,
> Nor paltered with Eternal God for power;
> Who let the turbid streams of rumor flow
> Through either babbling world of high or low;
> Who never spoke against a foe!"

And even if this sentiment should not always put on its most spiritual and ideal form, if reputation rather than character and reality of life should be its aim, if it should occasionally resort to that barbarous, revengeful, and unmeaning practice of dueling which has now happily become almost obsolete, could this be a worse evil than that truth and honesty should not be brought into greater respect than they seem to have now?

Of course, with the feeling that there must be a higher tone of character, in case our politics are to be redeemed from their degradation, must be united the removal of those demoralizing influences growing out of the war, of which we have already spoken at length. When the time will come for this reform is still uncertain. Such is the want of uprightness at present in making pledges that we can put no full confidence, either in the party heretofore dominant or in that which expects soon to be dominant, that opinions or platforms or declarations of Congress and of law in regard to specie payments will be respected. But a time for this must come, we know, first or last. When that time comes, and when the race difficulties shall be settled, much of our ground of fear for the future will be removed. The question then remaining, which can not be settled now with entire certainty, because we can not accurately separate temporary political evils from permanent ones, is no less a one than this, Is there such a poison in the political system that there is no cure for it? Must the Union, made less than a hundred years ago, go to pieces or run into a degenerate form of polity within the next hundred years? The question depends upon the general good sense and uprightness of the people, whether, if evils arise that can be removed, they will remove them, or, if those evils are owing to some radical cause, they will be ready for a radical cure. All our future, then, hangs on the strength of the moral and religious causes at work or that can be used for the elevation of the American character. And in the prospect there is, aside from religious faith and hope, the consoling thought that the great mass of the people is not corrupt; so that, as a good constitution of body resists and overcomes disease, so a sound general character of the nation may contain in itself a self-reforming power. No one, we think, ought to doubt that there is a latent force that can resist political evils and preserve the system who thinks what was endured in the late war, and with what readiness the people bore their burdens. We are more afraid of the centres of wealth than we are of the scattered country population, of the temptation to be rich than of the middle and poorer class, of the half-cultivated and self-indulgent than of those whose advantages for education have been small, of morals imported from Europe than of emigrants from Europe. Dangers we have of our own, together with some of those that stand in the path of older communities, and seem to threaten the very existence of modern society. But we have hopes, too, of our own which the rest of the world does not share. God grant that these hopes may not be mere visions, and that no new darkness may cloud our future!

X.

EDUCATIONAL PROGRESS.

THE conception of a community so generally educated that each one of its members should know and fulfill all the duties of a good citizen, should obey the laws without constraint, and practice humanity, honesty, and propriety, should be trained to virtue, and cultivate self-control, is one that has suggested itself to most eminent legislators from the dawn of history, and is, indeed, so engaging a notion as to commend itself to every intelligent mind. The ignorant must be governed by rude violence; the cultivated rule themselves; and the fertile fancies of the Greek thinkers were early filled with projects for enforcing a universal education. None of them, however, succeeded except perhaps the Spartan legislator.[1] The idea made no strong impression upon the Romans. It was adopted by the Israelites and the early Christians, and was almost perfected in China. The Arabian caliphs founded a school in every village.[2] Charlemagne and Alfred strove to teach the savage Germans and Saxons. The Papal Church of the Middle Ages taught in its monasteries; and the private schools of Erigena, Gerbert, Abelard, Duns Scotus, and a series of early school-masters saved education from sinking into monastic dullness. But the true parent of the modern system of teaching was the Reformation. Luther urged upon Germany the necessity of general instruction,[3] Calvin filled his followers with mental activity, and it was in the Protestant states of Germany that the governments first assumed the task of educating all the people, and of fulfilling that conception of the duty of legislators which had dawned upon the active intellects of Greece. The government became the school-master, the nation a community of pupils. Prussia, Saxony, and several of the lesser states have carried on the theory to a wide limit. No one is suffered in Prussia to go without an education. In many districts it is impossible to find a person who can not read and write. Yet it must be remembered that it is only since the beginning of the present century that Prussia has made its chief advance in education; that it was after the disasters and the shame of the Napoleonic invasion that the king, the queen Louisa, and the minister Stein renewed the public schools, emulated the zeal of Pestalozzi and Zeller, and forged that intellectual weapon which was to cleave the armor of their triumphant foes, for it is allowed that the common schools and their teachers have chiefly produced the unity and progress of the German race.

The idea of popular instruction was brought to the New World by our ancestors in the seventeenth century, and has here found its most appropriate home. Puritan, Hollander, Huguenots, and Scots or Scottish-Irish, they had seen that most of their sufferings and persecutions had sprung from ignorance and blind fanaticism. They had become in Europe the most intellectual and studious of its people, and, amidst the bleak forests of New England and the middle colonies, planted almost at their first landing the printing-press and the school. Knowledge they thought the proper cure for social evils. It was the school-master and the school-house, they believed, that could alone save them from sinking into barbarism, and revive a more than Attic refinement in the dismal wilderness. Massachusetts and Connecticut early passed laws that might seem severe even to our present conception of the duties and powers of the State. Every

---

[1] Plutarch, Numa, asserts that "the fair fabric of justice" raised by Numa passed away rapidly because it was not founded upon education. Education was the leading principle of the institutions of Zaleucus and Pythagoras. Plato in the Republic, Aristotle in his Politics, enforce the same conception.

[2] Renan, Averroes, chap. i., describes the flourishing literary condition of Spain under the Arabs. And Charlemagne perhaps emulated the free schools of Haroun-al-Raschid. See Eginhard, Vita Caroli Imp., c. 33.

[3] Luther said if he were not a preacher, he would be a teacher; and he thought the latter the more important office, since, he lamented, it was easier to form a new character than to correct one already depraved.

father of a family was obliged under a considerable penalty to see that his children were taught to read and write, and were instructed in the elements of morals and religion. The provision was apparently enforced, and it is possible that the people of New England in the seventeenth century were better educated than those of any European nation. In the present century Germany has outstripped Massachusetts. But the honorable race is still to be run, and it may be hoped that the next and all succeeding centuries will witness a generous strife among the nations which can do most to cultivate the popular intellect. As school-masters alone can legislators hope to be successful. Mental equality is the foundation of popular sovereignty, and we must conclude with the Greek philosopher that no political institutions can be made lasting without the cement of a common education.

In the American plan of education the national government has no further share than to give liberally from its public domain to the State or Territorial schools, and by its Educational Department at Washington to collect and distribute important information.[1] Each State controls its schools in its own way, directs the course of education and the formation of the school-districts, sometimes prescribes what is to be taught, provides the way in which the school funds are to be raised, and governs by general laws. The local municipalities levy the school taxes and elect the school officers. These officers appoint the teachers and fix their salaries, build school-houses, govern and support the schools. Thus the people of each school-district choose their own school officers, and the schools are wholly under popular rule—the true source of their rapid growth and general excellence.

In no part of the Union has education been so carefully and assiduously cultivated as in New England, and nowhere have its results been so important and remarkable. Wealth, industry, and good order have followed in its train. Massachusetts, although its soil is sterile and its climate severe, maintains a larger population in proportion to its territory than any other State. All New England is prosperous beyond example; and it has ever been the custom of its chief statesmen to attribute this rapid progress and general activity to the common schools. Of the early New England teachers Ezekiel Cheever, almost in the dawn of its history, holds a conspicuous place. Cotton Mather compliments him as the civilizer of his country. He was a scholar, learned, accurate, judicious; a severe and unsparing master, tall, dignified, and stern. He taught in the middle of the seventeenth century in Connecticut, and was afterward transferred to Boston, where he died at ninety-four. He was the founder of schools, and three generations of intelligent men were formed by his careful hand. He gave the Latin school at Boston its early excellence, and his ardent labors as a school-master for seventy years justify Cotton Mather's unstinted praise. "Educated brain," we are told, "is the only commodity in which Massachusetts can compete with other States," and to its long line of eminent school-masters New England owes its wealth and progress. Yet it has only been by a slow and often doubtful toil that in its natural home American education has attained its final excellence. The wild new land before the Revolution was incapable of reaching more than the elements of knowledge. When it became free, its eminent men were all the firmest friends of education. The two Adamses and their associates in all the New England States felt that their labors in the cause of freedom were incomplete, and even useless, unless they could teach all the people the duties of good citizens. But even in Massachusetts until 1834 the common schools had been comparatively neglected, their means of support were insufficient, the teachers were often incompetent, the school-houses rude and inconvenient. But in New England the principle had always been admitted that it was the duty of the State to educate its children, and in 1834 a fund of $1,000,000 was raised in Massachusetts to aid the towns in their educational labors. From that time a steady progress has been observed not only in Massachusetts, but through all New England. Gifted and laborious educators have

[1] Theory of Education, Washington, 1874, p. 10, etc. The generosity of the general government to the public schools has never wavered, and but for its foresight and liberality they could never have spread so rapidly over the new Territories.

given their lives to the perfection of the common-school system. Mann, Barnard, and their able coadjutors have raised the New England States to a high rank among the communities that teach the people. A normal school was opened in 1839 at Lexington; Massachusetts has now six. Connecticut and Rhode Island have made equal progress. Yet it was only a few years ago that Connecticut still demanded *rates*, and that the school-houses of Rhode Island were still imperfect.[1] In some districts of New England poverty and the thinness of the population prevent the perfection of the system. In Madawaska, Maine, where the currency is in articles of trade, and the brief summer scarcely supplies the people with necessary food, they are aided by the generosity of their fellow-citizens and are wholly exempted from school taxes.

Massachusetts expends more money upon its schools than any other State in proportion to its population. Its teachers are better paid, its school buildings generally more complete, and its people more carefully instructed. Of 292,481 persons in the State between the ages of five and fifteen in 1873, the average attendance at school was 210,248, or more than seventy per cent.[2] The rate of attendance constantly increases, new schools are founded every year, new buildings provided, and the normal schools and colleges send out annually a succession of well-trained teachers. The whole population of Massachusetts is probably a million and a half. They laid out last year in the various expenses of the public schools $6,180,848 64, or about twenty-one dollars for each person of school age. A cheaper mode of education could in no way be devised. In private schools the cost of instructing as many children would be four or five fold, and the public schools of Massachusetts are already better than any private schools, or are rapidly becoming so. But even in Massachusetts a rigid compulsory law is plainly necessary. Its uneducated population give rise to three-fourths of its crime, and an influx of foreigners has

[1] The fine engravings of new school buildings that adorn the latest educational report from Connecticut are worthy of general study. In fact, all the educational reports of the various States are full of interest.

[2] Secretary's Report, 1873–74, p. 113.

already filled it with a dangerous, because uncultivated, class. Connecticut, which has recently set in action its compulsory law, is probably in advance of any other State in the rate of attendance.[1] It has long been a centre of manufactures and of inventive progress. Its wealth and influence increase rapidly, and its capitalists have discovered that the public school is the sure path to good morals and order among those who labor. Hence they encourage education, and press on the improvement of all the instruments of public teaching.

In New York the growth of the common-school system has been slow, and its advantages only reluctantly admitted. I shall review its progress briefly, since in no State has the struggle for victory been more laborious or the triumph of the friends of knowledge more complete.[2] There was always a desire for education prevalent among its people, even when they were no more than a band of trappers and traders, and an accomplished school-master was one of the earliest importations from the shores of Holland. The free school still exists, founded by the Reformed Dutch Church, in the city of New York, not long after Boston had been planted on its three mountains. The Dutch clergyman usually kept a school, and the Dutch immigrants were probably not altogether illiterate. But in the opening of the seventeenth century the idea of a common education for all the people was still a phantasm and a Utopian vision; it was scarcely thought possible, or even desirable, to teach the laboring classes or to raise a whole nation to an equality of knowledge. Through the colonial period, and for a long time after the Revolution, the people of New York possessed no means of education except a village school and an incompetent teach-

[1] Connecticut attributes its inventive genius to the public schools established by its "fathers." See Report of the Commissioner of Education (Eaton), 1872, p. 47, and Connecticut Report of Board of Education, 1874. Of the effect of the compulsory law, says one school visitor, "In one of the largest villages I found the increase" (in attendance) "was sixty-seven per cent."

[2] Randall, Hist. Common Schools of New York. Boese, Hist. School System of the City of New York. New York State Reports. New York City Reports.

er, a college and a few classical seminaries, and its chief political leaders, as the State increased rapidly in wealth and population from 1787 to the close of the century, felt the pressing want of some method of general instruction.

George Clinton, Governor of New York in 1795, suggested and laid the foundation of its common schools. He was one of those discreet and rational intellects that had sustained his country through the Revolution with unchanging firmness, and had learned amidst its perils the value of mental progress. Like Washington, Jefferson, or Adams, he had discovered that an ignorant people could not be a free one; that the education of the wealthy class alone was fatal to human equality; and in his message to the Legislature of 1795, Clinton recommended to the people "the establishment of common schools throughout the State." It was a period when such a suggestion was so new and so surprising as to have little chance of general approval, and the conception of a State expending its revenues in teaching was scarcely heard of out of Saxony and Prussia. New England had in part developed the idea, but to the people of New York it was altogether novel. The State was poor, and still in its feeble infancy; the savages still occupied a large part of its domain west of Albany; its chief city was yet a small though rapidly advancing town; no great canal had joined the Hudson to the lakes, and the wealth of a continent had not yet found its natural outlet to the sea. But Clinton's suggestion was at once adopted by the intelligent Legislature, and a sum of $50,000 was set aside to be divided among the towns and counties in proportion to the number of their electors, and each county was required to raise by taxation a sum of money from every town equal to one-half the amount allowed by the State. Such was the foundation of the common-school system, and for a time it flourished with singular success. In 1798, in sixteen of the twenty-three counties, 1352 schools were already opened, and 59,660 children had received in them at least some share of the public tuition. But the limit of the appropriation expired in 1800, the schools were suffered to languish, and the system was practically abandoned.

Soon, however, two remarkable men took up the cause of education, and forced it upon the attention of the people. Jedediah Peck, of Otsego, a native of Connecticut, and Adam Comstock, of Saratoga, deserve to be remembered among the chief benefactors of New York. Peck was a plain uneducated farmer, a religious enthusiast, who exhorted and prayed with the families he visited; was modest, meek, diminutive in size, and almost repulsive in appearance; yet his active labors in the cause of knowledge show that he had not only cultivated himself, but was incessantly teaching others. Comstock, not more highly educated, aided him with equal zeal. They asserted every where that freedom, morality, and religion could only be supported by general intelligence. They pressed their theme upon the Legislature and the people. Peck was anxious that a school fund should be provided, like that of his native State, Connecticut, and he found a ready ally in Governor Clinton, who in 1802 again urged upon the Legislature the renewal of the common schools. But the people were no longer willing to be taxed for the diffusion of knowledge. Political troubles were impending, the State was poor, and all that the friends of education could obtain was a grant of the proceeds of certain lotteries, known as "Literature Lotteries," or the sales of the State lands, and three thousand shares of the capital of the Merchants' Bank of the city of New York, to found the nucleus of the common-school fund. Twice Mr. Peck's bill to authorize the towns to tax themselves for school purposes failed in the Legislature. But a strong impulse toward general education had now been awakened in England by the success of the Lancasterian system: the Dissenters, and chiefly the Methodists, had lent their influence to a new effort to teach the poorer classes, and the movement was already felt in the New World. The city of New York in 1805 founded its free-school society, and the Mayor, De Witt Clinton, with many other patriotic citizens, gave his aid to the cause of the popular education with valuable assiduity. The Lancasterian system was introduced, and the free schools made considerable progress. De Witt Clinton, whose sincere zeal for science, art, literature, and freedom has affected the prosperity of his native State more, perhaps, than any other cause, and who lived to prepare and perfect a great engineering work, which for that early period seems almost incredible, must also be ranked among the most eminent of the friends of the common schools. He was never weary of urging forward mental progress, and filling the minds of his contemporaries with the conception of a complete form of national education.

Peck, Comstock, and Clinton at last, after a brave contest against ignorance, were successful, and in 1812 a bill passed the Legislature of New York founding anew a common-school system that was to remain in action until 1842. A sum was given to every town for school purposes. The town was obliged to raise an equal amount by taxation. No district was to be left without its school-house, and no village without its teacher. The commissioners recommended the plan to the people by pointing to the necessary connection between knowledge and virtue, and by invoking the sacred name and authority of Washington. It was, in fact, in a period of singular gloom and public danger that the machinery of public education was first set in motion in New York. A barbarous war was raging on the frontier and over the seas; English cruisers swept the commerce of the republic from the ocean, and American privateers retaliated with more than common success. Poverty once more pressed upon the people. Yet in periods of public danger men see more clearly their true interests, and amidst the perils of war our ancestors founded the fairest of the fabrics of peace. Peck, Clinton, Comstock, were sustained by their fellow-citizens, and in 1813 Gideon Hawley became the superintendent of the common schools of New York. He was a young lawyer, active, intelligent, and cultivated in letters; and for eight years his energy and zeal kept alive the onward progress of education. Peace had returned; the vast resources of the State were slowly developed; the savages were removed from the interior counties; the famous wheat fields of the Mohawk and the Genesee rose into wonderful productiveness; a vast system of internal improvements was projected by Clinton that was to prove the source of boundless progress to the nation as well as the State. Yet the labors of the friends of education will probably outlive the material achievements of this busy period. And it is as educators that Hawley, Peck, and Clinton may be remembered in distant ages as the founders of the prosperity of New York.

The common schools advanced in general favor amidst much opposition. Hawley's vigorous hand kept them from falling into decay, as they had fallen in 1800. In 1819 there were already nearly 6000 school-districts, and it was estimated that almost 250,000 children had been placed upon their lists. In 1820, of 302,703 children of the proper age, 271,877 were taught in the schools. The number was still greater in 1821. Yet here the valuable labors of Gideon Hawley came to an end; a political opposition removed him from office, a person of inferior talents was put in his place, and thus New York repaid the services of its great benefactor by a cruel ingratitude. But the immense fabric which he had helped to rear could not now be torn down, and De Witt Clinton, the Governor of the State, resolutely pressed on the cause of education. The control of the schools was transferred to the Secretary of State, Yates, an intelligent and able man. The number of districts in 1822 was 7051, and 351,173, out of 357,000 children, had been taught during the year in the public schools. Joseph Lancaster visited the United States in 1818, and had been received by De Witt Clinton with signal interest, and his method of teaching was at that time the popular one; his presence at least gave new courage to the friends of knowledge, and the genius of Pestalozzi and the example of European educators were felt in New York. It was said that its education was even more general than that of Connecticut, which had a larger school fund, and where the common-school system had been longer in use.

Yet the idea of a free and public education for all classes of the people, a common source for all of equality and union, had not yet been openly avowed, and the division of castes was still maintained in the public schools. Those children whose parents were too poor to pay the rates were called charity scholars; in some districts they seem not to have been admitted at all to the schools. The right of every child to a free and full education by the community was seldom allowed. It may well be supposed, too, that the instruments of education were at this early period in its course (1822) very imperfect and rude. The school-houses were often bare log-huts in the country, or narrow and pestilential rooms in the cities and towns; the teachers were uncultivated and incompetent; the school-books worthless and worn; the whole fabric of education a vast misshapen pile that needed the skill of a master-architect to found it securely. Such a man was De Witt Clinton. To no single intellect is New York so widely indebted for its progress, vigor, and refinement; and in every part of his native State some trace of Clinton's energy and foresight may be found. He had just completed the great canal which had tested for so many years his courage and endurance amidst ceaseless opposition and unsparing assaults; he had seen the waters of Lake Erie mingle with the Hudson; he had been every where the founder of libraries, colleges, academies of design, and centres of art; and now he had been chosen Governor by a spontaneous impulse of a grateful people. One of his latest labors was to perfect the public schools. He urged (1826) the founding of schools for teachers, the extension of the course of study, the creation of school libraries, the increase of teachers' salaries, careful inspection, the higher education of women. None of those improvements that have since been adopted seem to have escaped his clear perception; and he founded all his projects upon a single principle. "I consider," he said, "the system of our common schools the palladium of our freedom."

Not long after, Clinton died suddenly. But his ideas live among us, and his successors have seldom shown any indifference to the cause of popular education. The statesmen of all parties have united in advancing the popular intellect. Spencer, Marcy, Dix, Flagg, aided in the organization of that immense scheme of public instruction which has ruled the fortunes of the State, and successfully resisted the assaults of various foes. In 1832 there were 9690 school-districts, and 514,475 children had been taught in the public schools. Only about ten thousand of the school age seem to have lost the advantages of education. But in the city of New York the extraordinary growth of the foreign population now began to lead to a struggle that was to rise into singular importance. For many years Ireland had poured out its excess of population upon New York, and the Irish immigrants had at first seemed willing and even eager to become thoroughly American and republican. They sent their children to the public schools, and were liberal and patriotic in politics. But unhappily a less discreet policy was advocated by their priests, who founded a number of private schools, and required that they should be supported by a donation from the public funds. The Irish population do not seem to have followed their guidance implicitly, and have always profited largely from the system of common schools. But Bishop Hughes urged on the sectarian contest with unyielding rigor, his priests and many of his people followed him, and already in 1840 that violent struggle had begun which seems fated to extend throughout the whole Union wherever the indiscreet counsels of the papacy can drive its Church into an opposition to the civil administration.

The question was whether the public schools should be converted into a series of sectarian institutions, whether each sect should have its own schools, whether the Bible should at least be excluded from the public teaching, or whether the common schools should resemble the government under which they had grown up, and take notice of no difference of religious or secular opinion. In the one case they must be remodeled upon the plan pursued in Europe; in the other, they must remain wholly American. In one, separate churches or sects would be recognized and maintained by our government; and in the other, the sects would be held in complete obedience to the civil law. The question was debated with earnestness. A single sect alone demanded a change in the principle of free education, and even of that one many of the most intelligent members were satisfied with the equity and liberality of the American system, and the common schools have retained their unsectarian character in spite of the ceaseless and often dangerous assaults of their foes. Still more important advances were now made in the material and nature of public instruction. From 1842 the system rose rapidly to a completeness which had scarcely been looked for. The cultivated zeal of the Hon. Horace Mann, from Massachusetts, lent new ideas and a fresh impulse to education in New York; and at a distinguished convention of superintendents and others, held at Utica in 1842, the various topics of the important theme were discussed with fresh animation. It was shown from recent statistics that crime decreased with the advance of education, and that the more perfect the schools, the less costly would be the prisons and the almshouses. It was shown that knowledge should be free to all the people, and that all the people should, if possible, be educated in the same schools. The defects of the common schools were pointed out—their imperfect buildings, uncultivated teachers, worthless books. Emerson, from Massachusetts, told of the value of the normal school which had been established in his own State, and showed that the teacher should be the highest and most cultivated of his contemporaries. Horace Mann enlarged with all the eloquence of his intellect upon the grandeur of the work in which they were engaged. And from the convention of 1842 education began to assume a more scientific form among us and to penetrate more deeply among the people.

A normal school was now (1844) established at Albany, the first of those excellent institutions which have raised our public teachers to a high standard, and which seem capable of being made the source of a great moral advance. The aim of the normal school is to produce a perfect teacher, to soften the manners, refine the taste, and cultivate the faculties of those intrusted with the care of children. Time has proved their usefulness, and may raise them to a still higher excellence. It is not impossible that our normal schools may at last educate our professors, and produce our most active men of letters. District libraries began now to be improved and widely extended, teachers' institutes were formed, the fabric of education was enlarged and amended; but the system was still in its infancy, and the principle of a common education provided by the state, and possibly enforced by it, had not yet become familiar to the people. The school-houses were still, in many districts, painfully rude; of 7000 only 2000 had more than one apartment, and in some counties they were wholly unfit for scholastic purposes. Instead of being the finest and most imposing building in every town and village, the school-house was often one of the rudest and least convenient. In many counties the school rates were still exacted, and parents refused to send their children to schools where they were looked down upon by their wealthier neighbors. The principle of free education had not yet been admitted in New York; and when the friends of education pressed upon the State Convention of 1845 the duty of the Legislature to provide for the instruction of the community by a general taxation, the motion was defeated, and the system of charity schools was maintained for another twenty years. It was not until the rebellion and the disasters of the civil war had forced men to see more clearly their own interests that an efficient and universal system of common schools was extended over the State.

For fifty years the idea of public education had been slowly unfolding itself in New York. The finest intellects of the State had been employed upon its development; from Peck and Clinton to Dix, Spencer, Seward, Young, Flagg, Greeley, Morgan, an endless array of accomplished citizens had joined in the school conventions, and lent aid to the growth of the intellect. Already in 1845 the Hon. Horace Mann could say, "The great State of New York, by means of her county superintendents, State Normal School, and otherwise, is carrying forward the work of public education more rapidly than any other State in the Union or any other country in the world." And the Hon. Henry Barnard, of Connecticut, thought its system superior in many particulars to any other he knew of. But the county superintendents were abolished in 1847, and the common schools began at once to decline. Their enemies were active, and a violent struggle arose upon the question of free education. A free-school act was passed in 1849, yet still clogged by rate bills and assessments.

In many instances in the country wealthy property owners refused to be taxed for education. The free schools were assailed with new energy by their opponents, and the Roman Catholic editors demanded the repeal of the free-school law. They required the schools "to be subject to the clergy;" otherwise, said their leading paper, they will be "a source of demoralization and public nuisances." A large party joined the opposition to the schools. But the people rose in their defense. Fish, Hunt, Phelps, Wool, Nott, Greeley, and a throng of able men led the party of education. The elections of 1850 decided the question in their favor, and in 1851 the principle that the State must educate all its children was sanctioned in theory by the popular vote.

Meantime—for I must pass rapidly over the history of this great struggle of the intellect—within the next ten years the school-houses grew into convenient and costly buildings, supplied with all the requirements of careful tuition. The normal school gave out a succession of intelligent teachers. In 1861 there were 11,400 school-districts and 872,854 pupils; but it was noticed that the school libraries were neglected, and the books often wasted and destroyed. One normal school was not sufficient to supply with teachers ten thousand schools, and the odious rates were still exacted. The war came, and the graduates of the common schools were found among the foremost defenders of the Union; and amidst the terrors of a civil convulsion, roused by heroic ideas, the people of the State in 1862 threw off forever all the lingering prejudices of the past, and declared education free to all as the light of heaven. The common-school idea was adopted in all its limitless expansion, and the State proclaimed itself the mental parent of all its children. The people admitted that they had no higher duty than to see that no one should live among them without an education; but it was some time before they could learn that ignorance was a crime against society. From the declaration of the principle of universal public instruction the schools of New York have flourished in the midst of a thousand foes. The great influx of uneducated foreigners has exposed them to a mass of hostile voters. They have been assailed by secular and clerical influences, and have sometimes suffered from indifference and neglect. But the abolition of the rates and the improvement of the system have drawn in a growing throng of pupils, and already in 1869, 1,161,155 children had been taught in the normal schools, academies, colleges, and private schools of the State, and, what was somewhat disheartening to the friends of education, 300,000 between the ages of five and twenty-one had attended no school at all. An ominous cloud of ignorance had gathered under the very shadow of the common schools.

A compulsory law, passed by the Legislature of 1874, has completed, at least in theory, the public-school system of New York; and it is probable that succeeding generations will see nearly all their children gathered in the school-house and the academy. Nor does any where a more effective and imposing machinery for general education exist, nor does any community expend its money more bountifully upon the elevation of the popular intellect. New York gives $11,000,000 annually to public instruction. A free college in the city of New York is filled with the best students of the public schools. A fine normal school for female teachers adorns the metropolis; and in every part of the State the normal colleges produce every year a great number of accomplished instructors. The school-houses in the cities are often palaces of education, filled with the latest improvements in the art of teaching. The teachers' salaries are slowly advancing; the reputation of the profession rises with the higher cultivation of its members. Yet it must still be allowed that some errors have crept into the system, and possibly the whole theory of education may yet be in its infancy. The school-houses in the country districts are too often imperfect, unadorned, and rude. They should always be centres of taste, comfort, and convenience. In the city schools too many branches of knowledge are taught at once. It would be wiser to perfect each scholar in the simpler elements. If religion can not be taught in the schools, the moral nature should be especially instructed, and no pupil should leave the public care without having acquired the conception of kindness, gentleness, modesty, as well as mental power. In this the example of the teacher is the chief guide, and the highest literary culture and the purest characters should alone be suffered to form the dispositions of the young. Republican simplicity should be inculcated from the cradle—a contempt for European follies and the glitter and display of foreign barbarism. It may be hoped, too, that, through special schools, trades, industry, and all branches of labor will form at last a part of the education of every American.

Pennsylvania, like New York, has passed through a long struggle to reach its present educational advantages. It has also adopted the common-school system in its widest limit.[1] Its school property is of great value; it expends more than $8,000,000 annually upon its schools; it has no general school fund, and derives all its school moneys from taxation. It has seven State normal schools and a great number of excellent technical schools and private colleges. This wonderful community, enriched by the boundless gifts of nature, is also one of the most widely educated. The spirit of Franklin has ever filled it with mental activity. New Jersey is already emulating Pennsylvania and New York. Its common schools are fast rising in excellence. The four Middle States (for even Delaware has shown marks of progress) have already joined in a generous enthusiasm for knowledge.

But if we turn to the Southern portion of the Union, the prospect is less encouraging. It is not that the first settlers of the South were less intelligent or cultivated than those of the North. Some of them were Huguenots, learned, thoughtful, heroic in their devotion to their faith; some were Scottish-Irish; some Quakers, or Friends. The most intellectual races of Europe were represented on our Southern coasts. And after the Revolution, Washington, Jefferson, Henry, Lowndes, Gadsden, and Rutledge would have held it their noblest mission to spread knowledge among the people. But slavery intervened. The great designs of Jefferson and Gadsden were never to be perfected. With slavery a notion grew up that knowledge was only the privilege of the ruling class, and that tradesmen, mechanics, and slaves were better left in ignorance. While the Northern States seized upon the mighty engine of education to win ease and industrial progress, the Southern States suffered their free schools to perish, and even for their higher education looked to the North or to Europe. The rebellion threw open the South to a new intellectual movement; a system of common schools has been introduced into every Southern State; the colored and even the white laborers of the South are said to be anxious to make use of this opportunity to raise themselves by an intelligent education to the condition of men. Yet we are told by the report of the Commissioner of Education that the common schools are not favored by an influential class of the people. They seem to languish in most of the Southern States.[1] The condition of the Southern people is one of extreme ignorance. Of the 5,643,534 persons in the Union wholly "illiterate," 4,117,589 are found in the Southern States. Of course these "illiterates" are nearly all native born. The subject is one that may well employ all the intelligence and observation of the South, for it is education alone that can give good order and prosperity to its people. Virginia, Tennessee, and Kentucky are already laboring to provide a general and effective system of instruction. It is certain that the extension of common schools over the whole South and a general education of its people would double the value of its lands, and foster more than any thing else foreign immigration.

But if the common-school system has been forced to make its way slowly against the opposition of caste and sectarianism in the North and East, and was nearly banished from the South by the long prevalence of slavery, in the new States and Territories of the West and the Pacific coast it has won an almost immediate popularity.[2] Here among the settlers of the wilderness its value was at once perceived. The school-

[1] Pennsylvania Report, 1873, p. 12. Only one district, a small one, was without its common schools in a population of 4,000,000. Pennsylvania has adopted the system of free education in its widest extent.

[1] So in Georgia they were closed in 1872. Report of the Commissioner of Education (Eaton), 1873, p. 69. And in Texas in 1873 they were "abolished," and have scarcely been re-established.

[2] Yet even in the Western States the labors of a series of patriotic men alone have saved the common school and university funds, and made education free. See Tenbrook, American State Universities, p. 141, and p. 118–120.

house, the church, the newspaper, telegraph, and railway have grown up together. Nowhere has the American plan of education been found so perfectly suited to the wants of a progressive people. Nowhere were ever such vast and complete educational systems so rapidly perfected as in Ohio, Indiana, Illinois, Michigan, or in the newer States of the northwest. Through all this wide, populous, and productive territory, the granary of half the world, caste and sectarianism have been laid aside forever; by a spontaneous movement of the people education has been made free to all; such great sums are lavished upon the teachers and their schools as naturally startle our European contemporaries, and the money of the people, which in Europe has been expended usually upon priests and kings, has here been devoted to the cultivation of those who earned it. Ohio spends nearly ten millions of dollars annually upon its public schools, Indiana and Illinois together a sum not much less. The fair, convenient, primary school house shines out upon the prairie and in the forest; the higher school houses of Chicago or Cincinnati are unsurpassed in New York or Boston; the science of teaching is carefully studied in a host of teachers' institutes, and with republican liberality the West and the great Northwest care for all their children.[1] This remarkable enthusiasm for education penetrates all the nation; it has become the distinguishing principle of American progress.[2] In the heart of the Rocky Mountains, and in the midst of the gold and silver bearing peaks of Arizona and Colorado, the free school is the sentinel of civilization. In Tucson or Denver the love of knowledge has survived the prevalence of what is usually thought the stronger passion, and the cities of the miners are seldom without their public school. The most splendid of our high school buildings is said to be that of Omaha, seated on a lofty bluff over the Missouri. California has produced a system of education so complete and valuable as may well serve as a model for all older communities; its teachers are made examples of propriety and tenderness, its scholars are taught integrity and moral excellence; sectarianism and caste are forbidden to divide the people, and the prosperous State is already feeling in all its industrial pursuits the happy influence of the common school.

Thus the American system of education pervades and covers every section of the Union. By the spontaneous impulse of the people it has been made the foundation of our political institutions. It has grown up with little direction from the general government. It has flourished in the cities and in the wilderness; it spreads its golden links from ocean to ocean, and holds in its embrace the destinies of the republic. A few statistics will show how immense is its influence and how important its results. By the census of 1870 it appears that an army of nearly 200,000 teachers conduct the public schools of the Union; of these, 109,000 are females. The number of schools was 125,000, and has no doubt largely increased. Fifty-eight millions of dollars[1] were raised in 1870 by taxation to educate the people—a sum nearly as great as the annual cost of a European army. There are also endowments and other sources of revenue, making the whole amount spent upon the common schools $64,000,000. The number of pupils in 1870 was more than 6,000,000. Thus the annual cost of each scholar enrolled was apparently only about ten dollars. Many of these pupils have attended only for a few months at the schools, others have been irregular and inattentive. Yet the fact that 6,000,000 children were brought under the control of the common-school system in one year, and learned some, at least, of the proprieties of life, is sufficient to show its immense influence upon the young; and it may be estimated that at least half the number were thoroughly instructed in the common branches of knowledge.

When we look over the returns of our illiterate population, of the great mass of ignorance that has grown up at the side of the common schools, we might at first conclude that our popular system of education had

[1] In all these States a sectarian party exists, but the majority favor free education.

[2] See Ed. Report, 1873. Minnesota and Iowa are filled with the educational spirit.

[1] These figures must now (1875) be largely increased, and it is probable that $70,000,000 yearly are raised for school purposes by taxation alone, and the number educated has risen in proportion.

wholly failed. Few civilized countries present a more lamentable scene of intense and almost savage dullness. Our illiterate population over ten years of age numbers 5,600,000. And an unfriendly critic, the *London Quarterly Review*, April, 1875, seizes upon this singular contrast as a ground of attack upon the American system of teaching. Yet the assault fails wholly. The great mass of our illiterates are in the former slave territory, where the common schools were never suffered to come, and where a large part of the people were forbidden by law to learn even to read and write. Slavery has produced more than 4,000,000 of our illiterates.[1] Of the remainder, who live in the Northern and Western sections of the Union, one-half are due to the neglect of England to educate its poorer classes. Our German immigrants are nearly all well educated. The English and Irish can seldom read or write. Of the 1,300,000 illiterates in the Northern States, 665,000 are foreign born, and they come chiefly from Great Britain. Thus, excluding the former slave territory, we have only 690,000 native-born illiterates, and of these a large number are the children, no doubt, of foreign parents. If we allow 500,000 as the number of native-born Americans who have escaped the influence of the common schools, we shall not possibly fail in liberality. The people of the Free States number at least 26,000,000. Only one person out of fifty, therefore, among us has been untouched by the influence of the public school. Reaching over the wild wastes of the new States and the thick crowds of our cities, the common-school system, often imperfect and rude, has been almost as thorough and effective as the older systems of Germany and Holland.

Wherever it extends, crime diminishes, the morals of the community improve, and taste and culture flourish even in the wilderness. An absurd charge is sometimes raised against the public schools that they are "godless and immoral." Some recent statistics taken in Massachusetts show that eighty per cent. of its crime is committed by persons who have had no education, or a very imperfect one, that a still larger proportion have learned no trade, and that not far from seventy-five per cent. of its criminals are of foreign birth;[1] intemperance, the natural resource of ignorance, is the parent of the greater part of this crime, and ninety-five per cent. of it is hereditary, transmitted from depraved and uncultivated homes. A similar condition of things exists in New York and the Western States. If all the children of the community could be well educated and taught productive trades, crime would be diminished by more than one-half; and so effective already have been our common schools that they have reduced the criminal class among the native population to a small figure, and secured the peace of society. The reports show that uneducated foreigners produce three-fourths of the crime and pauperism of our large cities. It is plain that the money expended upon the public schools is not laid out in vain. The seventy millions we give annually to education is the wisest outlay a nation ever entered upon.

The influence of the common schools penetrates through all our social system, teaches equality and republican principles, offers the elements of commercial knowledge, and creates the reading public. The press plainly lives in the rapid progress of the teacher. Our common schools have produced a throng of readers, such as was never known before—countless, bountiful, and never satisfied. The periodicals and newspapers printed in the United States very nearly equal those of all the rest of the educated world. In 1870 it was estimated that 7642 were published in Europe, Asia, and Africa, and in our own country 5871.[2] Since that time our publications have increased, it is supposed, nearly to an equality with those of all the world besides, and our forty millions of people read as much as all the rest of the hundreds of millions upon the same globe who can read at all. To our free institutions much of this in-

[1] Compendium of the Ninth Census, p. 456, and Report of the Commissioner of Education (Eaton), 1872. In 1870, of 28,238,941 persons of age to read and write, more than one-fifth were illiterate.

[1] Report of the Commissioner of Education (Eaton), 1871, p. 549. Rep., 1872, p. 589. Rep., 1873, p. 173. Of 102,855 criminals in England only 4297 could read and write well; only 206 had had a "superior" education.

[2] Hudson, Journalism in America, p. 773, 774.

quisitive spirit is due; but to the common-school system we owe the capacity of gratifying our curiosity and cultivating a general knowledge of the condition of our fellow-men. It is estimated that the number of copies of newspapers and periodicals printed in Great Britain in 1870 was 350,000,000, and an equal number in France.[1] The census returns show that in the same year 1,500,000,000 copies were printed in the United States. Our readers consume and pay for a periodical literature twice as great as that of the two populous centres of European civilization; and the census reports show how closely the progress of a demand for newspapers is connected with the advance of the common schools. Where there are no public schools, there are no newspapers; where the teacher leads the way, the press follows. In uneducated Georgia, for example,[2] with a population of nearly 1,200,000, there are only 123 newspapers and periodicals; in Massachusetts, with a population of nearly 1,500,000, there are 280. The circulation of the newspapers of Georgia is 14,447,388; of Massachusetts, 107,691,952. In educated Ohio the annual circulation was, in 1870, 93,000,000 in a population of 2,662,681. In uneducated Texas, fivefold as large as Ohio, with a population of 885,000, the circulation was 5,813,432. Only seven copies of a newspaper are printed yearly in Texas for each inhabitant; in Ohio, 35; in Massachusetts, 74; in Alabama, 9; in Pennsylvania, 67. The total number of publications in North Carolina, we are told, would allow only one paper to each inhabitant every three months;[3] New York prints 113 copies a year for each of its people.

California stands next in this proportion, and allows eighty-two copies a year to each inhabitant. Its people probably consume at home more newspapers in proportion to their numbers than any part of the world—a proof that the emigrants to the Golden State have been well educated, and their common schools effective. It would, indeed, be ungenerous to pursue further this contrast between the literature and intelligence of the different portions of our country. Temporary obstacles have divided us in this particular. We may reasonably trust that the common schools will win at last an equal victory and control in every section of the Union.

These two great intellectual agents, the schools and the press, indissolubly united, have produced the physical progress of the country. They have built railways, canals, steamers, telegraphs. Our people converse with each other through their newspapers, and hold their consultations in open day. Publicity has become a part of our national life. Like the Roman patriot who desired all his acts to be seen and known by his countrymen, we throw open all our doors and windows to the public. All is activity with us, curiosity, and vigilance. It would be quite impossible, indeed, to trace in a few pages the achievements of the common schools. They have extended the duration of human life among us,[1] checked disease, cultivated cleanliness, founded new States, planted cities, indicated the sites of future capitals. The publisher finds the purchasers of his books in their graduates, the merchant and manufacturer depend upon their silent energy, the churches are filled with their pupils, and the lecture-rooms gratify the curiosity excited in their midst. Millions of active intellects, the offspring of the public schools, listen to the sweet strains of Bryant, Longfellow, and Whittier, muse with Bancroft on the thrilling exploits of freedom, or wait to hail the new bard and the rising thinker, whether he comes from the Sierras of Nevada or the crowded cities of the East.

That the common-school system is still imperfect no one can doubt: it is a vast machine, whose various parts are capable of ceaseless improvements. Truancy prevails to a great degree, and can only be removed by a general compulsory law. The teachers in many parts of the country are themselves imperfectly trained, their salaries are often miserably low. Men have not yet learned

[1] Hudson, p. 774.

[2] Report of the Commissioner of Education, 1871, p. 561–563. See Compendium of the Ninth Census, p. 510.

[3] Report of the Commissioner of Education, 1871, p. 559.

[1] So Haushoffer, Statistik, p. 200. Wo die Civilization die grössten Fortschritte macht, beobachtet man auch die grösste Abnahme der Sterblichkeit. We want more careful statistics on this nice point, as on many others.

that it is cheaper and safer to build school-houses than ships and forts, and that good schools are always profitable. But the idea is rapidly spreading, and it can not be long before our school-houses will be every where models of neatness, and our teachers at least as well paid as our judges or constables. In one direction the system is destined to make an extraordinary advance. The plan of technical and industrial instruction is already beginning to make great progress among our educators. It has long been found in Europe that the elements of a trade could be rapidly acquired in childhood. Germany, Austria, and Belgium have all their industrial schools, where manufacturing, masonry, building, carpentering, engineering, are taught practically, and where young men, while they study history and geography, may also learn a trade.[1] The educated artisans of Germany already surpass those of all other countries. If we wish to preserve our equality with the European workman we must turn the vast powers of the common schools to industrial instruction. Already the subject has met with careful attention among us. Schools of science have long been in use, but they scarcely reach the industrial classes. In 1862 Congress gave a liberal endowment of land to each State to establish these schools of labor.[2] New York received 990,000 acres, Ohio 630,000, and every State its share, proportioned to its population. Various excellent institutions have been founded. Illinois has a flourishing industrial university. Michigan led the way in opening these schools.[3] Nearly all the States have employed the national gift in some useful manner. But the chief problem of our future educators will no doubt be how to make every common school the means of spreading a knowledge of the arts, and to join invariably with every education some useful pursuit. There is no reason why our working classes should not also be our most highly educated classes, the most intelligent, the most refined. What the republic requires is the healthy mind in the healthy body; and regular physical labor should always be joined with mental. To unite these conditions in our national education will no doubt be more than ever the aim of the teacher. Gymnastic sports are useful; riding, leaping, rowing, are not to be neglected;[1] but labor on the farm, in the factory, with the mason or the mechanic, will prove of signal value in producing health of mind and body, and the experience of foreign schools shows that children learn with eagerness and pleasure the elements of all industrial pursuits. Every child must at last be taught some useful trade.

In the higher grades of education our system is capable of a wide improvement. Our method of grading the schools is every where imperfect. Mr. Matthew Arnold presents an attractive picture of the organization of the higher schools of Prussia.[2] Step by step they rise from the primary schools, through a course of instruction suited to every pursuit in life, until they blend with the Berlin University, the most perfect, it is supposed, of all the means of intellectual improvement.[3] The gymnasia, pro-gymnasia, real schools, and upper burgher schools afford instruction for the merchant and the scholar. The gymnasia prepare the students for the university, the real schools for other pursuits. In the latter the modern languages take the place of the ancient. The thoroughness of the Prussian system is due to the strictness of the examinations, the regular promotion from grade to grade, the necessity of a university degree to the acquisition of a profession: and it is certain that our own schools may well borrow the strictness of the Prussian. No one should be permitted to take what is called a "degree" without proper preparation. To win a degree should be made an object of real value and interest. It should be part of the duty of government, if it assumes the charge of our national education, to see that it is

[1] J. W. Hoyt, Report on Education, 1870, p. 118-127, notices the "building schools," agricultural, commercial, etc., of the Continent. Lace-making, clock-making, and all the arts are taught.

[2] See Report of the Commissioner of Education, 1871, p. 425.

[3] See a careful account of the Western higher schools, Tenbrook, American State Universities.

[1] In London it is even proposed to teach swimming to the school-children.

[2] Higher Schools and Universities in Germany, p. 7. "I believe," he says (p. 44), "that the public schools are preferred in Prussia on their merits," etc. This feeling must also become prevalent with us.

[3] "The most distinguished and influential university in the world," says Mr. Hoyt. Report, p. 349.

well done, to enforce thoroughness, and provide for an adequate return for its outlay; and this in Prussia is secured by a system of rigorous examinations.

It is somewhat mortifying to be assured that, after all our generous outlay upon our common schools, we are still surpassed in some particulars by the Europeans, and that even our costly school buildings in Boston and New York are excelled by those of Berlin, Vienna, and London.[1] The village school-houses of Switzerland are said to be unequaled in grace and simplicity. They are surrounded by gardens or play-grounds, and imbedded in flowers. In London, where land is cheap, a large play-ground is provided for the children; and several of its new school-houses are so convenient and admirable that they may instruct even our most successful builders. And of the foreign teachers, especially those of Germany, we are told that they are graduates of a university, acquainted with the whole range of letters and science, and carefully instructed in the art of teaching; that they have given themselves to their profession from early youth with ardor, and improve each year by active practice. They form a dignified community of state officials. They have usually, at least in the higher grades, adequate salaries, and a pension in sickness or old age. In Holland the teachers have already become the most respectable class in the community; and in Prussia their value is allowed by a most intelligent government. Yet we can have no doubt that many of our American teachers already equal in attainments even those of Holland, and that our great army of instructors is rapidly improving in discipline and skill. Our teachers are already often the purest and wisest part of our people. When their profession is made a safe and profitable one they will seldom leave it. Our best teachers already give their whole lives to their pursuit, and it is chiefly those who are badly paid who seek some other means of living. It must be the aim of our system to make the teacher's employment permanent.

[1] Massachusetts Report, 1873-74, p. 35. Mr. Philbrick's criticism is often just, but I fear his notion of the happy condition of the European teacher is not well founded. In Prussia the primary teachers are badly paid.

The tendency of American education is evidently to constant and valuable progress. Our schools and teachers are far better than they were ten or twenty years ago. Our school buildings are finer and more complete, in general, than those of any European nation, except, perhaps, Switzerland and a part of Germany.[1] Of infinite grace and variety, these palaces and cottages of education adorn all our land. Normal schools are springing up in all the States with singular rapidity; practical learning is making constant advances among us. We have already discovered the defects of our system, and are laboring to amend them. But the question is already presented to us whether the national government should not provide for the common welfare by insisting upon the general education of the vast mass of our illiterates. In the instance of the colored people, it seems a duty imposed upon the nation to educate them all; and the immense influx of uncultivated foreigners and the large body of uneducated whites at the South demand some immediate remedy for a pressing danger. The safety of the government requires that it should enforce and support every where popular instruction. Where a State fails to educate its people, the national government has plainly a right to interfere, and a general system of public instruction might be formed which would enforce every where thorough and practical teaching, uniformity in study, and mental equality throughout the nation. Our colleges and universities must finally form a part of the national system, and offer a free education in the highest branches to every intelligent citizen.

The extraordinary cheapness of the American school system,[2] its effectiveness, its admirable influence upon morals and public order, its equity and liberality, have been

[1] A great mass of information may be found in the reports of Mr. Eaton, the National Commissioner of Education, and the value of his bureau is already apparent. It has spread many striking facts.

[2] The elegance and convenience of such buildings as the Worcester High School, the Omaha palace, with its Mansard-roof and graceful spires, the New York Normal School, or the infinite series of magnificent school buildings reaching from ocean to ocean, would scarcely seem to admit of the idea of cheapness, yet the cost of a single Versailles or Blenheim would surpass all that we have laid out thus far on school-houses.

proved in every part of the Union, and, like a prudent family, the nation educates its children in common. The chief excellence of our system is that it teaches pure republicanism. In private schools and colleges the principle of human equality upon which our country leans for safety is sometimes forgotten. Foreign impulses, frivolities, fashions, barbarisms, may at times corrupt our youth, and reach even the pulpit and the press. But the public schools bravely repel the wave of European reaction, and are founded upon the immutable principles of 1776. In the public schools Samuel and John Adams, Jefferson, Washington, and Franklin speak to us with the fresh ardor of the dawn of freedom, inculcate a rising humanity, and demand for their new republic a plain advance over the savage blindness of the past. So long as our public schools flourish, the country is safe. So long as American ideas are taught by accomplished and patriotic teachers to each new generation, the republic will ever live. When falls the common-school system, freedom perishes and reason dies. Possessed of this admirable instrument, we may teach with irresistible clearness the principles of 1776, and the second century of the republic may witness a rapid growth of knowledge among us unequaled among nations.

XI.

SCIENTIFIC PROGRESS.

I.—THE EXACT SCIENCES.

THE condition of the British dependencies in North America during the seventeenth and eighteenth centuries was by no means favorable to the growth among their inhabitants of a high order of intellectual culture, whether literary, æsthetic, or scientific. During a large portion of this period, the colonies were but feeble and isolated settlements dotted at wide intervals along a sea-coast a thousand miles in length, and separated from each other by vast stretches of unbroken forest. Even when in the lapse of time these natural barriers had been more or less completely broken down, and the infant communities began to mingle with each other along their boundaries, the territory redeemed to civilization formed still but a narrow fringe along the margin of a wilderness of unknown extent, and its occupants continued every where, except in the immediate neighborhood of the original centres of population, to be subject to all the hardships and privations of a pioneer life. To these natural disadvantages must be added the anxieties and often serious molestations arising out of the immediate contact of the colonies upon their extended frontier with the aboriginal inhabitants of the continent—tribes of savages with whom their relations were always precarious and often hostile; and out of the wars in which Great Britain was more or less constantly engaged with the Continental powers which had also their outposts on these shores. These were strifes in which the colonies became embroiled in spite of themselves, and in which, while they had every thing to suffer, they had nothing whatever to gain. When along with these things we consider the absence upon this continent, during the entire period preceding our Revolutionary struggle, of all the aids indispensable to the prosecution of original research by the scholar or man of science—as, for instance, libraries, archives, collections, museums, laboratories, observatories, universities, and even living expositors of the knowledge already existing—it should surprise us not so much that in the early dawn of the republic our people had not yet won for themselves a lofty name for their achievements in letters or in science as that they should have been, as they were in fact, generally well educated in the rudiments of knowledge, so that such a thing as gross ignorance was hardly known among them.

In any review of the progress of science, therefore, during the first century of the republic, the period which lies between the declaration of independence and the close of the eighteenth century may, without danger of any important omission, be passed over in silence. There were men, it is true, in the colonies and in the newly emancipated States whose native abilities and distinguished attainments as astronomers or physicists won for them a reputation which in their time reached to other lands, and which has since come down to us; but these, though they were masters, were not originators, and their names are but incidentally connected with the history of science. Of this class David Rittenhouse is an honorable example. His scientific activity is illustrated in his numerous communications to the American Philosophical Society, of which he was a member, and in the presidency of which he succeeded Franklin—communications which display not only a powerful but also a remarkably versatile mind; and his singular ingenuity and extraordinary mechanical skill are attested by his orreries, still to be seen in the College of New Jersey and the University of Pennsylvania, which, according to the account given in the Transactions of the Philosophical Society, show the movements of the heavenly bodies for a period of five thousand years, and their positions in each year, month, day, and hour, with such accuracy as not in all this time to differ sensibly from those given by the astronomical tables.

Toward the close of the century the celebrated Priestley, whose discoveries entitle him to a high place among the original investigators of his day, made our country his home; but as the successes to which his fame is due were achieved before he left his native country, and as his later years were mainly occupied with the profitless task of defending a now long exploded theory, which his own discoveries had already rendered indefensible, and which his contemporaries were every where even then abandoning, he can not be counted as having materially contributed to the advancement of science in America. Another illustrious name belongs to this time, which should have been ours, but which was lost to us by influences not wholly unlike those which gained us Priestley. Benjamin Thompson, afterward Count of Rumford, was an American who early in life abandoned a home and a country which his fellow-citizens had made intolerable. Received into the service of a foreign prince, his force of character, activity of intellect, and singularly practical turn of mind at once commanded appreciation, and secured to him a position which enabled him to achieve a noble reputation not only as an efficient administrative officer and a zealous philanthropist, but also as an original and sagacious scientific investigator. To Rumford belongs the immortal honor of having boldly announced, before the close of the eighteenth century, a truth which the world was not very ready to receive till near the middle of the nineteenth, a truth which lies at the foundation of the mechanical theory of heat, and through that theory leads to the grandest generalization in the history of science—the truth that heat is a mode of motion. Now that this truth has come to be universally admitted, America may be justly proud that its discovery was made by one of her own sons.[1]

Before proceeding with the history of science in America during the nineteenth century, it might be proper, would space permit, to notice the extent to which its growth has been encouraged by the fostering hand of the government, and the modes in which this encouragement has been shown, and also to enumerate the principal organizations through which its votaries have endeavored to promote its progress by associated effort, and the channels of publication through which the results of their labors have been given to the world. With these materials an interesting chapter might be written, for which, however, we can find no place here. That the government of the United States, though it has as yet made no systematic and permanent provision for promoting scientific investigation, has not been wanting in liberality when solicited to lend its occasional aid to special objects of scientific interest, will be evident when we call to mind the Wilkes exploring expedition of 1838, the Lynch Dead Sea exploration of 1848, the solar parallax expedition under Gilliss in 1849, the expedition of the *Polaris* in 1871, and the more recent provision for the dispatch of parties to distant parts of the world to observe the transit of Venus of 1874. But besides these instances, in which the advancement of science for its own sake has been the exclusive aim of Congressional appropriations, many other examples may be mentioned in which legislation has been indirectly favorable to the same end. The Coast Survey is, from the necessity of things, a scientific institution and a school for training scientific men. The same is true of the public survey of the great lakes, of the boundary commissions, of the exploring expeditions in the heart of the continent, of the Naval Observatory, of the Nautical Almanac Office, and of the special commissions from time to time created for investigating experimentally certain questions regarded as practical, which have nevertheless important scientific relations, such as the heat developed in the combustion of coal, the tenacity, rigidity, and other useful qualities of different descriptions of iron and steel, the causes producing the explosions of steam-boilers, and others of like character.

Though we can attempt no history of scientific associations or organizations, there is one exception which may properly be made to this rule. The Smithsonian Institution is an organization unique in its character, which for the past thirty years has held a peculiar relation to the science of the country, of which it has been, also, one of the

[1] Bacon and Locke, it is true, spoke of heat as motion; but with them the view was a pure hypothesis; with Rumford it was a demonstrated certainty. Speaking of the paper in which it was communicated to the Royal Society, Professor Tyndall says: "Rumford in this memoir annihilated the material theory of heat. Nothing on the subject more powerful has since been written."

most powerful promoters. In the language of the will of its founder, an English gentleman of wealth who had never visited this country, it has for its large and liberal object "the increase and diffusion of knowledge among men." The fund from which it derives its revenue is bequeathed in trust to the United States of America, and its affairs are administered by a Board of Regents appointed principally by the Senate. During the infancy of the institution there was at one time danger that, instead of being made an instrumentality for the increase of knowledge by the encouragement of original research, it would become merely a depository of objects of interest in natural history or archæology, and of books of general literature, exhausting itself thus in the creation of a museum and a library. To this it was proposed to add a show of diffusing knowledge by means of popular lectures delivered annually in Washington during the winter. Such lectures were, in fact, given down to about 1860; but the danger menaced by the other part of the project was averted by the earnest zeal and conclusive logic with which the purposes of the founder were set forth and defended by the able secretary of the institution, Professor Joseph Henry. Thus for a long period of years the institution has employed all its available income in defraying, in whole or in part, the expense of original investigations, and in publishing the results of these, and of any others independently made which, after careful examination by expert judges, have appeared to be substantially valuable contributions to knowledge. Under the title of *Smithsonian Contributions to Knowledge* there have now been published nineteen large quarto volumes, embracing elaborate monographs on a large variety of subjects in exact science, in natural history, in ethnology, and in linguistics, including among them the important astronomical researches of Walker, Newcomb, and Stockwell, the ingenious discussions of rotary motion by General Barnard, the elaborate investigations of terrestrial magnetism by Bache, the grammar and vocabulary of the Dakota language by Riggs, and the explorations of the North American earth mounds by Squier and Davis.

In addition to its usefulness in provoking scientific research, of which it would be difficult to measure the value, the institution has also fulfilled, and is now fulfilling, a most important function in acting as the organ of a widely extended system of scientific exchanges between our own and foreign countries. Its correspondents and agents are scattered every where throughout the civilized world. Plants, minerals, books, specimens in natural history, objects of archæological interest—every thing, in short, which belongs to the material, or is serviceable for the illustration, of science is through its instrumentality expeditiously forwarded to the remotest destination, without any expense, except that which attends the local delivery, to sender or receiver. No such agency any where else exists. The degree to which it is promotive of scientific activity, not only by stimulating individual effort, but by bringing distant individuals into frequent communication with each other, and inducing systematic co-operation, need hardly be insisted on.

In passing now to the proper history of science itself, it is necessary to remark that of a subject occupying so broad a field only the merest outline can here be given, and that that outline can embrace only such portion of this history as is properly American. Convenience also suggests that each department of science, or group of allied sciences, should be considered separately.

In the pure mathematics our country has an honorable, if not a very extensive, record. The number of men who deserve to be called truly eminent as mathematicians in any country or in any age is always comparatively small, and the number of those whose eminence is due to real originality of genius is smaller still. It accordingly happens that of those who are most spoken of in their own time for the presumed profundity of their mathematical knowledge or their ingenuity in the use of mathematical methods the larger proportion leave behind them no permanent monuments of this imagined and perhaps real greatness. Among the men distinguished for their mathematical ability whom our country has produced there are nevertheless a few whose published works have been substantial contributions to the advancement of their favorite science, and have won for them a celebrity destined to be enduring. In this honorable record no name stands higher than that of Nathaniel Bowditch, whose voluminous and lucid commentary on the *Mécanique Celeste* of Laplace not only eclipsed the multitude of his previous admirable performances, but drew from analysts and physical astronomers of the highest eminence abroad most enthusiastic expressions of commendation. Professor Benjamin Peirce, of Harvard University, a pupil and friend of Bowditch, still in the vigor of life, stands hardly second to his master in the originality and value of his contributions to mathematical literature. His *Analytic Mechanics*, which is professedly an attempt to consolidate the latest researches and the most exalted forms of thought of the great geometers into a consistent and uniform treatise, is more than it professes to be. It is rather an attempt—successfully accomplished—to carry back the fundamental principles of the science to a more profound and central origin, and thence to shorten the path to the most fruitful forms of research. The most remarkable and most original of Professor Peirce's publications is the description of a new mathematical method, called by him "Linear Associative Algebra." This method seems to be a step in the direction of quaternions, but a larger one. It therefore oversteps the power of human conception to grasp its essence, while its visible machinery is algebraic, and in the modes of its use it has analogies both with algebra and with quaternions. The method is of too recent origin to have been largely developed in its capabilities or tested in its applications.

Of other eminent mathematicians whose labors deserve a more extended notice our limits allow but a mere mention. The algebra of Professor Theodore Strong, the memoir on "Musical Temperament" by Professor A. M. Fisher, the essay of Professor A. D. Stanley on the "Calculus of Variations," Professor Patterson's "Calculus of Operations," Professor Newton's memoirs on questions of higher geometry and on transcendental curves, General Alvord's "Tangencies of Circles and Spheres," Professor Ferrel's "Converging Series," and his investigation of the movements of the atmosphere, General Barnard's "Theory of the Gyroscope" and "Problems in Rotary Motion," are all valuable contributions to mathematical science. The "Problems" last named treat chiefly of the earth's rotation, and the resulting precession of the equinoxes, embracing a discussion of the relation to precession of the earth's internal structure, and refuting conclusively the deductions of a very celebrated investigation of this subject by the late W. Hopkins, while demonstrating, on other grounds than his, the existence of a thick rigid crust.

ASTRONOMY.

There are several distinct departments of astronomical science which are often pursued independently of each other. The elder Herschel occupied himself chiefly with discovery; Tycho Brahe, with the accurate determination of the places of known objects. Our gifted countryman, Mitchell, was especially interested in devising new methods of observation and record; our esteemed fellow-citizen, Mr. Rutherfurd, with the application of photography to astronomy. Some astronomers, like Newton, Lagrange, and Laplace at an earlier period, or like Adams, Leverrier, Peirce, Newcomb, and Stockwell in our own time, have engaged in the theoretic investigation of the laws of celestial motion, and of the action of the heavenly bodies on each other. Others—and the number is large, including at present De la Rue, Huggins, Lockyer, Faye, and Secchi abroad, and Young, H. Draper, and Langley among ourselves—have been busied in the fascinating study of solar and stellar physics. Finally, comets and shooting-stars, and the recently detected connection between these two seemingly very different classes of bodies, have been a subject of long-continued study, fruitful of interesting results, to a series of observers, among whom are most prominent at present Professor Schiaparelli, of Milan, and Professor Newton, of our own country.

In connection with *discovery*, an interesting chapter might be written on the history of the agencies to which discoveries are mainly due, that is, of observatories—a history which the limitation of our space necessarily excludes. Half a century ago such a thing as an astronomical observatory was unknown in the United States. At present the number is considerably greater than the necessity. Though the work of the observatory is the basis on which the theory of the existing universe must rest, it is not a work which needs to be indefinitely repeated. With the very superior instruments which the skill of recent times has furnished, a few observatories, judiciously distributed over the earth's surface, are all that the physical astronomer requires. There are at present in the United States not fewer than thirty astronomical observatories, probably more. If so many had been needed, they would still in many cases have been founded in vain, since no suitable provision has accompanied their erection for maintaining them subsequently in use. Some of them, connected with the colleges of the country, have, perhaps, been made sufficiently useful for purposes of instruction to justify their erection; but it is perfectly clear that the founders in general have been laboring under the delusion that an observatory when once brought into existence will somehow work itself. It has accordingly happened that, except in the case of the Naval Observatory, at Washington, that of Harvard University, and, in its earlier period, that of the Cincinnati Observatory, the responsibility for the use of the instruments, provided at great expense in these various establishments, has fallen upon men overburdened with heavy duties as instructors, occupying the greater part of their time by day, and rendering continuous systematic observation by night physically impossible. Notwithstanding these disadvantages, several of the gentlemen here referred to have found time in the midst of their distractions to render so signal services to astronomical science as to connect their names permanently with the history of its progress. There exists, however, no adequate provision, and in general no provision at all, for the training of observers and the support of observation; and hence much of this costly apparatus has been hitherto comparatively useless for the purposes of practical astronomy. Still less has there been a provision for what is now the most urgent necessity of the science—the encouragement and maintenance of a class of astronomers of a superior order of scientific culture, devoted to the study and reconstruction of theory. This is a consideration to which the benefactors of this noblest of sciences, who have provided it with so many instruments of magnificent proportions as monuments of their liberality speaking to the eye, would do wisely in the future to turn their attention.

Some of the most interesting of the astronomical discoveries of the century have been due to the keen-sightedness of American observers. The great telescope of the Cambridge Observatory was mounted in the summer of 1847. On the 16th day of September, 1848, it was the means of rendering for the first time visible to human eyes the eighth satellite of the planet Saturn—the eighth in the order of discovery, though the seventh in the order of distance from the planet. Five satellites of this planet had been discovered in the seventeenth century; two more, very close to the ring, were seen in 1789 by Sir William Herschel, who, as illustrated in this example and in several others, seems to have been endowed with an almost preternatural keenness of vision; but his observations were not confirmed until his son, more than forty years after (1836), rediscovered one of them, and caught a single doubtful glimpse of the other. Ten years later (1846) Mr. Lassell, of Liverpool, recovered the remaining one. The new satellite discovered by the Messrs. Bond is fainter than either of these two extremely difficult objects, though more distant from the planet than any other, except that known as Iapetus. Between this satellite and Titan, the next interior, a wide gap had been noticed to exist, Titan revolving around the primary in a little less than sixteen days, and Iapetus in more than seventy-nine. Bond's satellite, which has received the name Hyperion, has a period of a little over twenty-one days, so that it is comparatively near to Titan, and leaves still a large seemingly unoccupied space between itself and Iapetus. It is remarkable that Hyperion was noticed by Mr. Lassell on the 18th of September, only two days after its discovery by Bond.

The most wonderful object in the universe, as well to the physical astronomer as to the observer who surveys the heavens only for the gratification of his curiosity, is the double or multiple ring surrounding the planet Saturn. The ring is certainly double, a wide space separating the inner, broader, and brighter from the outer, narrower, and less bright. Small stars have sometimes been seen between the ring and the planet. Some very good observers have occasionally noticed what appeared to be lines of division in the breadth of both the rings, and these appearances, together with the deductions of theory as to the conditions necessary to the stability of the system, have led to the general belief that the rings are not rigid solids. Until the year 1850, however, only two rings had been suspected to exist, unless by occasional and temporary subdivision. But on the 11th of November in that year there was noticed by the Messrs. Bond a shadowy appearance interior to the broad ring, which led them to suspect the existence of a third and almost nebulous ring, having a breadth about two-thirds as great as that of the narrow or outer ring. Subsequent observations confirmed them in this belief; and the same appearances were later noticed by Dawes and Lassell in England. An interesting question hereupon arose as to whether this dusky ring was of recent formation, or had been noticed but not understood before. It was ascertained that Galle had mentioned appearances of a similar kind in a memoir published in 1838; and Father Secchi testified that such had been noticed in the observatory at Rome as early as 1828. Mr. Otto Struve also adduced evidences from the observations of J. Cassini in 1715, and those of Halley in 1720 and 1723, that the obscure ring had been noticed by those observers, and assumed by them to be a belt upon the planet itself. Mr. Struve created some excitement in the astronomical world by stating that on a comparison of the measurements of the apparent distance between the inner edge of the broad bright ring and the planet's disk made by his father in 1826 and by himself in 1851, together with an examination of similar measurements by Huyghens, Cassini, Bradley, Herschel, Encke, and Galle, he was satisfied that the inner edge of the bright ring is gradually approaching the planet, while the total breadth of the two rings is constantly increasing. This proposition was too startling to meet with ready acceptance by astronomers generally, and up to the present time the question remains where Struve left it, with, however, an apparently growing disposition to accept his conclusions. If it is true that the ring is slowly subsiding toward the planet, the hypothesis is not without plausibility that Bond's dusky ring may be composed of loosely scattered fragments, which, from causes possible to assign, have been accelerated in their descent beyond the general mass.

The astronomical discovery next in interest deserving mention, as an American contribution to science during the century, was remarkably enough made in the immediate neighborhood of the observatory which the successes of the Messrs. Bond had already made famous. Mr. Alvan Clark had just completed the great telescope of eighteen and a half inches designed for the University of Mississippi, and now at Chicago, when on the night of January 31, 1862, his son, Mr. Alvan G. Clark, directing the instrument toward Sirius, the brightest of the fixed stars, detected almost in contact with it a minute point of light which he recognized immediately as a companion star. Curiously enough, a well-founded suspicion had long been entertained that this star is double. Minute as are the annual proper motions of the fixed stars in the heavens, they are in general uniform and well ascertained. But the motion of Sirius was long ago discovered by Bessel to be affected by an irregularity such as would be produced by the action of some other body revolving with it around a common centre. The orbit of the imaginary attendant star had, in fact, been inferred by Peters, of Altona, and Safford, then of the Cambridge Observatory. No scrutiny with instruments then existing had, however, been successful in detecting this attendant, when the newly finished glass of Mr. Clark made it visible without effort. After its discovery it was seen with the Harvard equatorial and others of less power, but not till 1866 with the 9½-inch Munich glass of the Naval Observatory. This admirable discovery, or more properly the construction of a glass capable of making a discovery so difficult, was rewarded by the Academy of Sciences of France by the presentation to Mr. Clark of the Lalande Medal —a prize annually decreed to the author of the most interesting discovery of the year.

Several comets have been discovered by American astronomers, among which may be mentioned, the first of 1846, discovered February 26, 1846, by William C. Bond, of which the elliptic elements were determined by Peirce, giving a period of ninety-five years. The comet known by the name of Miss Maria Mitchell was first seen by her on October 1, 1847, at her private observatory in Nantucket. Two days later it was also seen by De Vico at Rome, and Mr. H. P. Tuttle at Cambridge. The comet 1862, III., which was discovered by Mr. Tuttle July 18, 1862, and by Mr. Thomas Simons, of Albany, on the same evening, but later, belongs to the August stream of meteoroids. An interesting fact in regard to Miss Mitchell's comet is that, four days after its discovery, it passed centrally over a fixed star of the fifth magnitude without in the slightest degree obscuring it. For a brief time the star was, in fact, so truly in the centre of the nebulosity that it appeared like the proper nucleus of the comet.

Of the swarm of minute planets which occupy the place between Mars and Jupiter, where the law of Bode indicates a member of the solar system to be missing, about one-third have been discovered by American observers. It is remarkable that all of this numerous group, now amounting to no fewer than 153, belong to the nineteenth century, the first to be detected having been discovered on the evening of the first day of the century, January 1, 1801, by Piazzi, at Palermo. Three others were discovered within the seven years next succeeding, after which nearly forty years elapsed without adding to the number. Up to the close of 1850 the total number known amounted to thirteen only. Within the twenty-five years which have since elapsed there have been discovered 140 more, or about six per annum. It is to be observed that discovery in recent years has been greatly facilitated by the Berlin star maps and other celestial charts, in which every star down to the ninth magnitude is set down. When an object is seen which is not in the map, therefore, the probability is great that it is an asteroid, and the question will be settled by a second observation on the following night, or even a few hours later on the same night. The first American astronomer to detect an asteroid previously unknown was Mr. James Ferguson, of the Naval Observatory, by whom the thirty-first of the series, now known as Euphrosyne, was found on September 1, 1854. Two others were subsequently discovered by him, making three in all. Besides these, there have been discovered one by Searle, two by Tuttle, sixteen by Watson, and twenty-two by Peters, making a total of forty-four, all discovered within a period of about twenty years.

Practical Astronomy.—The automatic registration of time observations by means of electro-magnetism is an improvement in practical astronomy due to American ingenuity. The merit of its first suggestion has been somewhat in dispute, but the earliest experimental demonstration of its feasibility was certainly made by Professor John Locke, of Cincinnati, who in 1848 introduced a clock provided with a suitable mechanism into the circuit of the electric telegraph between Cincinnati and Pittsburg. The distance is four hundred miles, and the experiment was continued for two hours, during which the beats were regularly registered at every station throughout the whole line. The application to astronomical observation immediately followed. In recognition of the value of this invention, Congress awarded to Dr. Locke the sum of ten thousand dollars, and ordered a clock of the same description to be constructed for the Naval Observatory. As a recording instrument, the ordinary telegraphic register of Professor Morse was at first employed. More convenient forms of apparatus were subsequently devised by Professor Mitchell, Mr. Joseph Saxton, of the Coast Survey, and Messrs. W. C. and George P. Bond, who introduced the regulator which has since been so almost universally employed in these instruments, known as Bond's spring governor. More recently (1871) a printing chronograph has been invented by Professor George W. Hough, of the Dudley Observatory, which records to the hundredths of a second, and saves to the observer who employs it the labor and time required for deciphering and recording in figures the indications of the register in common use. The electro-magnetic method of recording transits was adopted without delay in the observatories of the United States, and soon after found its way into those of Great Britain and the continent of Europe, where it was known as the American method. Of its great value in promoting accuracy it is not necessary to speak; but only those who have had experience in observation can adequately appreciate the degree to which it has lightened the labor of the observer. Previously to its introduction the clock divided with the object viewed the observer's attention, and the necessity for unceasing vigilance was exhausting in the extreme. If nothing else had been gained by it but this, the benefit would be incalculable.

The introduction of the electric chronograph into observatories furnished a very simple means of determining differences of longitude between any two places connected by a telegraphic wire. These determinations are made by comparing the exact times of transit of a given celestial object over the meridians of both places, a single clock giving the times for both, or by transmitting time signals alternately in opposite directions compared with the clocks at both ends. The earliest observations of this kind were made in January, 1849, between Washington and Cambridge, Massachusetts. The method has since been brought into very extensive use throughout the world. In 1867, and again in 1871 and in 1872, it was employed to determine the difference of longitude between Greenwich and Washington, by means, in the first instance, of the Anglo-American cable, and, in the second and third, of the French, from Brest to St. Pierre, and Danbury, Massachusetts. It may be interesting to compare the results thus obtained with those of the great chronometric expeditions of 1849 and 1855 between Cambridge and Liverpool—expeditions which, in the words of Mr. W. C. Bond, "for the magnitude and completeness of their equipments have not been equaled by any of the similar undertakings of European governments. Even the 'Expedition Chronometrique' of Struve was on a scale much less extensive." In 1855 fifty-two nautical chronometers were transported six times between Cambridge and Liverpool, giving nearly three hundred individual longitude determinations. The difference of longitude obtained was 4*h.* 44*m.* 31.8*s.* Previous expeditions had given 4*h.* 44*m.* 30.6*s.*, showing a difference between the two of 1.2*s.* The cable results (omitting hours and minutes) were: 1867, 31.00*s.*; 1871, 30.96*s.*; 1872, 30.99*s.*, the largest discrepancy being only four one-hundredths of a second.

In observing for longitude, the velocity of propagation of electric impulses in the wires of the circuit becomes a matter requiring attention, and thus the telegraph has become the means of throwing light upon this interesting question in physics. The results obtained have differed very widely, being dependent on difference of material of the conductor, difference of cross-section, and largely upon differences of surrounding conditions. In the ordinary iron wires of the American telegraphic lines the velocity seems not to exceed fifteen or sixteen thousand miles per second.

Improvement of Instruments.—Until about 1850 the observatories of the United States were furnished with instruments of foreign manufacture exclusively. Since that time the telescopes of American opticians have rivaled, if they have not surpassed, in excellence those of the most celebrated constructors of the Old World. The 12½-inch equatorial of the Michigan University is one of many admirable instruments produced by Mr. Henry Fitz, of New York, an ingenious artisan, who was removed by a premature death just as his reputation had been firmly established, and as he was preparing for a bolder attempt than any of those in which he had been previously so successful —the construction of an objective of twenty-four inches aperture. Mr. Charles A. Spencer, of Canastota, New York, in the year 1848 suddenly acquired an extraordinary celebrity for superior skill in constructing objectives for microscopes. Having proved himself to be without a superior in this field, he turned his attention to the construction of telescopes with a success no less signal. One of the most remarkable examples on record of a career commenced without previous preparation, rather late in life, in a most difficult art, and leading in the end to the highest eminence, is to be found in the history of Mr. Alvan Clark, of Cambridge, Massachusetts, who undertook in 1844, without thought of going further, to assist his son, a lad of seventeen, in the grinding of a metal speculum. The earlier years of Mr. Clark had been spent upon a farm. After the age of twenty-two he had occupied himself with engraving for calico-printing, and subsequently with portrait painting, which pursuit he followed for ten years with eminent success. In assisting his son, his object was to further the aspiration of the youth to become a professional optician, and this he hoped to accomplish by himself learning in order that he might teach. After several experiments with metals, he was encouraged by Professor Peirce to undertake a refractor. The son hesitated; the father allowed himself to be persuaded, and his boldness was rewarded by such a degree of success as to lead him gradually to abandon all other occupations and to become a professional optician himself. The great excellence of his work was first justly appreciated by Mr. W. R. Dawes, of Haddenham, England, a distinguished astronomer, possessed of a keen vision, and a critical judge of instruments. Mr. Dawes had purchased two or three glasses of seven or eight inches aperture of Mr. Clark, and had made him well known in England before his own countrymen became aware how superior an artisan they had among them.

In February, 1860, the sum of $10,000 was appropriated by the trustees of the University of Mississippi to defray the expense of an object-glass for an equatorial telescope to be placed in the observatory of that institution. The writer of this article was intrusted with the responsibility of selecting the artisan in whose hands this important work should be placed. His choice fell upon Mr. Clark, and instructions were given that the glass should be made of sufficient size to exhaust the entire appropriation. According to a scale of prices which Mr. Clark had arranged, a glass worth $10,000 should measure about seventeen and a half inches. The diameter was more than twice as great as that of any which Mr. Clark had made before; and it was his preference and his proposition to prepare one of exactly the size of the Munich glass in the Cambridge Observatory, viz., fifteen inches, in order that he might compare it with that by placing it in the same tube and observing the same objects on the same nights. Mr. George P. Bond, then in charge of the observatory, expressed his entire willingness to afford this opportunity of comparison, but advised against the limitation of size, saying, "Always improve if you can upon the last thing done." Mr. Clark finally consented to attempt the larger diameter, and the necessary disks were ordered. They were considerably in excess of the size necessary for the glass proposed, and on careful examination were found to be perfect to the extreme borders, so that Mr. Clark reported that it would be quite possible to grind them to a diameter of eighteen and a half inches, exceeding by an inch the size which the appropriation allowed. It seemed an unjustifiable sacrifice to cut down to such an extent a material so excellent, and Mr. Clark was desired, in reply, to work the disks to as large a diameter as they would bear, and assured that the appropriation would be increased accordingly. Under these circumstances he proceeded with the work with such rapidity that in June, 1861, he was able to give notice that the glass would be ready for a preliminary examination in the month of August succeeding. The troubles of the times prevented such an examination, and no one of those with whom the order for this instrument originated has ever had an opportunity of looking through it. The latest achievement of Mr. Clark has been the construction of the grand 26-inch objective erected in 1873 in the Naval Observatory at Washington.

Some of the most successful constructors of astronomical instruments in our country are to be found among the astronomers themselves. Mr. Lewis M. Rutherfurd, of New York, is the originator of a department of practical astronomy requiring the use of instruments specially adapted to its purposes; and as the most expeditious and satisfactory mode of providing these instruments, he resolved to construct them himself. His idea was to make photography subservient to the uses of astronomy, and especially of uranography. Considering how rare are the occasions in which atmospheric conditions are altogether favorable to the observation of difficult objects in the heavens, and how large is the necessary consumption of time in making measurements of position and distance between the objects observed, it occurred to him that if these favorable opportunities should be seized to make exact photographic maps of the groups under examination, measurements of these maps might take the place of direct measurements of the stars, and that thus a single evening might be made productive of results as numerous and valuable as those obtained in many months in the ordinary course of observation. His first attempts at a practical realization of this idea were made with a reflecting telescope, for the reason that a parabolic speculum is free from aberration both of color and figure. The Cassegrainian form was adopted, as best suited to the purpose; but the tremors produced by passing street vehicles were so largely magnified by the double reflection in this instrument that he was soon compelled to abandon it for the refractor. A little experience, however, taught him that the refracting telescopes in common use, whatever their degree of excellence for purely optical purposes, would not furnish him celestial photographs exhibiting the stars with the degree of sharpness which his plan required. Though the luminous rays are well concentrated, the actinic rays are scattered, giving indistinct images of the larger stars, and failing to exhibit minute ones at all. He therefore undertook the construction of an objective corrected for actinic effect, without regard to color. The whole of the work, theoretic and practical, was done by himself, and about the year 1863 he completed an actin-aplanatic objective of eleven and a quarter inches aperture, which gave results entirely satisfactory. With this he speedily obtained many sharply defined maps of star groups upon glass, and it remained only to effect the intended measurements upon these maps. Here was presented a new mechanical problem of peculiar difficulty. No known micrometric apparatus was adapted either in form or in dimensions to effect these measurements. Mr. Rutherfurd met the difficulty with his characteristic ingenuity, and with his own hands constructed an instrument in which, by means of an observing microscope directed toward the plate, and having motion in two directions at right angles to each other, the co-ordinates of position of the objects observed may be measured with a delicacy which leaves nothing to be desired. In the original form of this instrument a micrometer screw was depended on to give these dimensions, and an immense amount of labor was expended in the construction of such a screw and in determining its error. The investigation resulted, however, in demonstrating that the error of the screw is not constant, no matter how faultless the workmanship or how excellent the material. Discarding the screw, therefore, for purposes of measurement, Mr. Rutherfurd introduces into the instrument, as at present constructed, two auxiliary microscopes traveling with the observing microscope, one in each direction, and reading the distances traveled upon fixed scales ruled on glass. In a paper read before the National Academy of Sciences in 1866 Mr. Rutherfurd gave an account of his method; and at the same meeting a discussion of measurements made at his observatory upon photographs of the Pleiades was presented by Dr. B. A. Gould, who reached the conclusion that the micrometric measurements of a single such plate, with the customary corrections for refraction, etc., would give results about as accurate as those obtained by Bessel with thirteen years' labor—the time employed by him in mapping this group. Though this method has not yet been adopted in public observatories, it can not be doubted that it is destined to be instrumental in the future in largely promoting the advancement of uranographical science.

Another American astronomer, whose ingenuity in the construction of instruments is no less remarkable than his skill in the use of them, Dr. Henry Draper, has devoted himself to the improvement of reflecting telescopes. The use of silvered glass for astronomical specula had been suggested by Foucault, as being a material lighter and less brittle than speculum metal, and as reflecting a larger proportion of the light; and he had practically illustrated the value of this suggestion by actually grinding and silvering one or two such specula with his own hands. With no light to guide him but the knowledge of these facts, Dr. Draper undertook an investigation of the best mode of proceeding in the construction of such specula, recording the results of his experiments as he went on; and having at length attained a triumphant success, he published his method among the *Smithsonian Contributions*, in an elaborate memoir, which has become a standard authority on the subject, and is continually quoted as such at the present day. The telescope described in this memoir is of fifteen and a half inches aperture, and it was for a long time the largest in the country; but it is now surpassed by one of twenty-eight inches, also constructed by Dr. Draper, and mounted in his observatory equatorially under a dome. With both these telescopes Dr. Draper has taken splendid photographs of the moon, one representing the satellite in the third quarter, which has borne an enlargement to fifty inches in diameter; and also the spectroscopic photographs of Alpha Lyræ, mentioned later in this article.

Physical Astronomy.—No incident in the history of astronomy has ever excited more universal interest than the detection, in August, 1846, by a method purely mathematical, of a planet which had been previously lurking unseen upon the confines of the system ever since the creation. This marvelous achievement, of which the history is too well known to need repetition here, was simultaneously accomplished by two foreign astronomers, and does not belong to American science. But it is a curious fact that the planet thus discovered fell immediately after into the hands of American astronomers, and that they have made it practically their own ever since. Owing to the exceedingly slow motion of the body, the elements of its orbit could not be determined from the observations of a few months. Assuming the orbit to be circular, several European astronomers reached early and concurrently the conclusion that its mean distance from the sun is less than the discoverers had supposed by between five and six hundred millions of miles. But the first approximately correct theory of its motions was wrought out by Professor Sears C. Walker, of the Naval Observatory at Washington, in February, 1847. When Herschel discovered the planet Uranus in 1781, Lexell was enabled to determine its orbit by means of observations made of the same body (supposed then to be a fixed star) by Bradley and Mayer nearly thirty years before; and the number of such previous accidental observations of this body which have since been discovered amounts to no less than nineteen. It was naturally hoped that the examination of star catalogues of earlier years would furnish some similar help to the solution of the problem presented by Neptune. Of these catalogues, however, most were for one reason or another useless in this inquiry. One only offered a possibility that the newly discovered body might have been by good fortune recorded in it. This was the *Histoire Céleste* of Lacaille, embracing 50,000 stars; and Mr. Walker soon discovered that Lacaille had swept over the probable path of the planet on two days nearly following each other—the 8th and 10th of May, 1795. Having, therefore, from the observations made at Washington, combined with those received from Europe, computed as well as he could the place of the body for these dates, varying the elements so as to include the entire region within which it could possibly have been at that time, he selected from Lalande all the stars within one degree of the computed path. There were nine of these, but among the nine one only seemed likely to be the planet. The question then presented itself, Is this star still in the place in which Lalande saw it? Two days after this question had been raised by Mr. Walker, the telescope of the Washington Observatory was directed to the spot, and found it vacant. Assuming, therefore, this missing star to have been the planet, Mr. Walker computed an elliptic orbit which represented with gratifying precision all the modern observations. The elliptic elements first obtained were, however, only approximate. In order to their more exact determination it was necessary that the theory of the perturbations should be revised. Here Professor Peirce, of Harvard University, lent his powerful assistance, and with the perturbations furnished by him, and revised normal places, Walker computed an ephemeris of the planet which he published in the *Smithsonian Contributions.* The only attempt at a theory of Neptune made abroad was by Kowalski, of Kasan, Russia, in 1855; but this, though formed on a much larger number of recent observations, did not represent the motions of the body more exactly than that of Walker.

The ephemerides founded on these early theories were affected more or less with error. Toward 1865 the errors were increasing with rapidity, and it was evident that without a new determination of the orbit, they would reach, before the end of the century, the serious amount of 5′ of longitude. Professor Simon Newcomb, of the Naval Observatory, Washington, now addressed himself to the laborious task of reconstructing the theory from the foundation. His results are published in the *Smithsonian Contributions*, and embrace (1) a determination of the elements of the orbit from observations extending through an arc of 40°; (2) an inquiry whether the mass of Uranus can be determined from the motion of Neptune; (3) an examination of the question whether these motions indicate the action of an extra-Neptunian planet; (4) tables and formulæ for finding the place of Neptune at any time, but more particularly between the years 1600 and 2000.

In the computation of the tables the elements adopted are not the mean elements, but their values at the present time as affected by secular inequalities and inequalities of long period, particularly that of 4300 years arising out of the near approach of the mean motion of Uranus to twice and a half that of Neptune, these being adapted to give the place of the planet with the highest degree of accuracy during the period for which the tables are specially designed, *i. e.*, till the year 2000. The work is one involving an enormous amount of labor. As to the mass of Uranus, Professor Newcomb concludes that no trustworthy value can be deduced from the motions of Neptune, nor, had this body been unknown, could even its existence have been detected from all the observations of the exterior planet hitherto made. It results, almost of course, that no evidence yet appears of the existence of any still more distant planet remaining yet undiscovered.

Soon after the publication of Professor Walker's "Elements of Neptune," Professor Peirce, in a communication to the American Academy of Arts and Sciences, after demonstrating that this planet, with the mass deduced from Bond's observations of Lassell's satellite, and with the orbit assigned by Walker, would fully reconcile all the modern observations and all the ancient accidental ones better than the hypothetical planet of Leverrier or Adams (Flamsteed's observation of 1690 being discordant with Adams to the extent of 50″ and with Leverrier to 20″, but harmonizing with the computation from the Walker and Peirce theory within a single second), ventured upon the bold assertion that the planet actually discovered by Galle, searching under Leverrier's direction, was not the planet predicted or expected, but a very different body, which occupied that place at that time only by a happy accident. Leverrier had fixed the distance of his planet from the sun at 36.154 times the earth's distance, and Professor Peirce demonstrated that at the distance 35.3 (at which a planet would have a periodical time equal to twice and a half that of Uranus) so important a change takes place in the character of the perturbations as to make it impossible to extend to the space within that distance any investigations relating to the space beyond. The observed distance is slightly over 30; and it appears that a second similar peculiarity occurs at 30.4, where a planet would have a period just double that of Uranus. The perturbations produced by it on this latter would, therefore, for a twofold reason, be of very different character from those resulting from the supposed planet at the distance of 36. Though these criticisms of Professor Peirce are well founded, and have never been satisfactorily answered, yet they can not materially affect our estimate of the merit of Adams and Leverrier. A planet such as that indicated by their analysis would have produced very nearly the actually observed irregularities of motion of Uranus, and must have been occupying very nearly the place in the heavens of that which was actually found. Any planet capable of doing this must have been in this neighborhood at the time of the discovery, and it was the merit of the analysis that it indicated the quarter in which the disturbing body was to be looked for—a merit which remains, though the actual planet differs from the planet predicted, in mass, distance, and period.

Besides his "Theory of Neptune," Professor Newcomb has made numerous very valuable contributions to physical astronomy. His "Investigation of the Orbit of Uranus," in the *Smithsonian Contributions* for 1873, is a work of great labor, commenced as early as 1859, but necessarily deferred till after the completion of the "Theory of Neptune."

In 1871 he published in Liouville's *Journal*, Paris, a "Theory of the Perturbations of the Moon produced by the Action of the Planets." Of this very able and very original investigation it is sufficient to cite the opinion expressed by Professor Cayley, president of the Royal Astronomical Society of London, who pronounces it, "from the boldness of the conception and the beauty of the results, a very remarkable memoir, constituting an important addition to theoretical dynamics."

Another very interesting memoir by Professor Newcomb embraces an investigation of the secular variations and mutual relations of the orbits of the asteroids, for the purpose of testing the question, from a theoretic point of view, whether the theory of Olbers, that these bodies are the fragments of a single shattered planet, is tenable or not. Twenty-five asteroids are included in the comparison, and the conclusion is unfavorable to the hypothesis in question.

In the Washington observations for 1865 there appeared an investigation by Professor Newcomb of the value of the solar parallax, reached by a discussion of the observations made in 1862 at six observatories in the northern hemisphere and two in the southern, and a combination of these with other results furnished by micrometrical measures of Mars by Professor Hall, the parallactic equation of the moon, the lunar equation of the earth, and finally the transit of Venus of 1769 recomputed by Professor Powalky. The inference is that the true parallax is 8.85″, with a probable error of 0.013″. Apparently the conclusion from the transit of 1874 will not be far from 8.87″, a result very near to that previously obtained by Professor Newcomb.

The great geometers who succeeded Newton in applying the principle of gravitation to the explanation of planetary motions assume that those minute inequalities, of which the effects only become sensible after long intervals, and produce considerable changes only after many centuries, or, perhaps, myriads of centuries, are developed uniformly with the time—a supposition which answered the immediate purpose, though it is by no means true. Yet a knowledge of the laws which govern these inequalities is important to the settlement of a number of interesting questions, especially such as concern the stability of the system, and the vicissitudes of heat and cold to which our own planet has been manifestly subjected in the distant past. Lagrange pointed out the mathematical criterion by which the general question of stability might be determined. Its application required a knowledge of the masses of the planets. These were not accurately known, but by substituting approximate values for them he was able to announce that none of the variations of the planetary elements could go on increasing forever. Laplace went further than this, and proved that, provided the direction of revolution is the same for all the planets, the stability of the system is independent of the masses. In this case he showed that the sum of the products of the several masses by the squares of the eccentricities and the square roots of the mean distances is constant, and that if the eccentricities are small, the variations will be small, so that the system will not only be stable, but will undergo no large departures from its mean condition. This is the state of things in our solar system. The actual condition of physical astronomy at present has seemed to demand a more complete investigation of this intricate subject, and such an investigation has been recently undertaken and successfully accomplished by Mr. J. N. Stockwell, of Cleveland, Ohio, whose elaborate memoir relating to it has been published among the *Smithsonian Contributions to Knowledge*. The object of the investigation has been to determine the numerical values of the secular changes of the elements of all the planetary orbits. The elements considered are four: the eccentricities and inclinations of the orbits, and the longitudes of the nodes and of the perihelia. The fluctuations of value are largest in the case of Mercury, and smallest in the case of Neptune. We are concerned chiefly with what relates to our own planet, and more especially with the fluctuations in the eccentricity of its orbit. This eccentricity may vary between the limits zero and 0.0694, involving a difference between the aphelion and perihelion distance of the earth from the sun of 13,000,000 miles, and also a difference between the duration of the summer and the winter half year, of thirty-two days. It can hardly now be doubted that to these changes of eccentricity have been due the remarkable vicissitudes of climate to which, as geology informs us, the earth has been subjected. At present the winter of the southern hemisphere occurs in aphelion, and is longer than the summer by eight days. The consequence is that the south pole is capped with massive ice, which occupies an area of probably more than 2000 miles in diameter. When the eccentricity is maximum, the hemisphere which has the winter in aphelion is probably ice-bound nearly or quite down to the tropic.

The stability of the Saturnian system and the mechanical condition of the material of Saturn's rings form the subject of an important memoir read by Professor B. Peirce at the meeting of the American Association for the Advancement of Science held at Cincinnati in 1851. The conclusion arrived at is that the rings could not possibly be stable unless sustained by the mutual attraction between them and the inner satellites; and consequently that, in the absence of such satellites, they could have no existence. Also, that inasmuch as no solid material known is sufficiently tenacious to resist without rupture the immense divellent forces to which a solid ring under such circumstances must be subjected, therefore the rings must be fluid, and not solid. Laplace had recognized the difficulty attendant on the hypothesis of a continuous solid ring of such breadth, and had therefore assumed that the rings, though apparently presenting continuous plane surfaces, are nevertheless divided into many concentric and comparatively narrow rings. He also perceived that such rings would necessarily be in a condition of unstable equilibrium with the planet in case their centres of gravity should coincide, as would seem from their appearance to be most probable, with their centres of figure; and he accordingly supposed that there exist irregularities in the disposition of their substance imperceptible to us, which, by displacing the centres of gravity, give them the necessary stability. He failed to show that these two hypotheses can both be true and at the same time consistent with the optical phenomena, and, in fact, left the theory of this system incomplete. In 1857 Mr. J. Clerk Maxwell, in a prize essay presented to the University of Cambridge, in England, investigated these hypotheses of Laplace, and showed conclusively that they are untenable. On the hypothesis of fluidity he investigated the tidal movements which must take place in the rings, and rejected equally this supposition. But his analysis did not extend to the movement of the rings in mass, and therefore it is not in conflict with the view of Professor Peirce. If this be discarded, there remains no other but to suppose the rings to be made up of innumerable small discrete solid masses so near together that, in a zone having the generally admitted thickness of one or two hundred miles, they present to a distant observer the appearance of a continuous solid. This view is that which is held by Mr. R. A. Proctor.

Few of our American astronomers have contributed more abundantly to the literature of the science than Professor Stephen Alexander, of Princeton. In 1843 Professor Alexander presented to the American Philosophical Society an elaborate memoir upon the physical phenomena attending eclipses, transits, and occultations, which excited much interest in the astronomical world. In 1874 there was published among the *Smithsonian Contributions* a paper by the same astronomer, entitled, "Exposition of certain Harmonies of the Solar System." The design is to show inductively a tendency in nature to the arrangement of the planets according to a law of distances from the sun's centre, in which the distance of each succeeding planet is five-ninths of that of the last preceding, and to explain the actual departures from this law in the existing solar system by the supposition that in one or two instances two planets (called, therefore, half-planets) have been formed in the place of one. The earth and Venus constitute a pair of this kind. This ingenious speculation may be classed among the curiosities of astronomy, as it does not appear practicable to test its probability by mathematical analysis. Of the numerous other interesting astronomical papers of Professor Alexander the limitations on our space prohibit us from making mention.

In the year 1849 Professor Daniel Kirkwood, then of Delaware College, Newark, now of the State University of Indiana, announced a remarkable law connecting the masses and distances of the planets of the solar system and their periods of rotation on their axes. To understand this, let it be premised that between any two planets succeeding each other in order as numbered from the sun outward, there is, when the bodies are in conjunction at their mean distances, a point of equal attraction, that is to say, a point in which a body free to move would be held *in equilibrio* by the opposing attractions of the two planets. Suppose these neutral points to be found for all the planets of the system, and the distance between the two neutral points above and below each planet to be called the diameter of the sphere of attraction of that planet, then, according to this law, it will be true that the cubes of these diameters for any two planets will be to each other as the squares of their respective numbers of rotations during one sidereal revolution of each. This law was subjected to a close examination by Professor Sears C. Walker in 1850, with a favorable conclusion. It is to be observed, however, that the uncertainty existing as to the masses of several of the planets, and as to the periods of rotation of some of them, gives to this conclusion the character of a probable rather than of a certain result. In order to extend the analogy throughout the system, Mr. Walker interpolates a planet in the region of the asteroids between Mars and Jupiter, which he places very nearly at the distance given by Bode's law. He finds also that if there exists a planet nearer the sun than Mercury, its distance must be one-fifth that of the earth, or about 18,000,000 miles. For the doubtful masses, Mr. Walker finds that the values demanded by the law are within the limits, often pretty wide, of those actually employed by different authorities in the investigations of physical astronomy and in the construction of tables. It will only be after a higher degree of perfection shall be attained in the theory of every planet than has yet been reached, that the accuracy of Kirkwood's analogy can be conclusively tested.

Solar Physics.—The physical condition of the sun has occupied very much of late years the attention of the scientific world. Ever since the invention of the telescope the solar spots have been observed with careful and curious interest, and these, together with the varying features of the photosphere itself, when minutely examined, led early to a general though hardly universal acquiescence in the opinion expressed by Wilson in the Philosophical Transactions of 1774, and adopted by Sir William Herschel, that the luminous surface which we see is not the surface of a solid. The question what is beneath this surface remained a subject of controversy; and on any hypothesis of the state of the sun's mass, the essential nature of the spots and the causes producing them were matters equally unsettled. The vastly improved instruments of recent years, the employment of photography in aid of observation, and above all, the application of the spectroscope to the study of the chromosphere and the photosphere, have shed a flood of light upon this difficult subject, which is likely soon to harmonize all opinions, though it can hardly be said to have done so yet.

Immediately after the erection of the great Munich achromatic at the Harvard Observatory, this splendid instrument was employed by Mr. W. C. Bond in a continuous series of observations of the solar spots continued for a period of more than two years, maps of the spots being carefully drawn at every observation. The results are published in full in the Annals of the Harvard Observatory, and furnish a valuable means of studying the varying aspects of the spots, their growth, decline, and duration. More recently many foreign observers have devoted themselves to the investigation; among whom may be mentioned Mr. De la Rue, Mr. Balfour Stewart, and Mr. Loewy in England, who have given special attention to the laws governing the variations of the total area of sun spot and its distribution over the solar disk; Mr. Faye, in France, and Father Secchi, in Rome, who have engaged not only in observation, but in speculations on theory. The British observers arrived at the conclusion that the maxima and minima of spot development are periodic, the period coinciding with the synodical revolution of the planet Venus, to the influence of which body they therefore ascribe it. They attribute a similar and perhaps as powerful an effect to Jupiter; but in this case the irregularities are less, on account of the greater distance of the disturbing body. Professor Loomis, of New Haven, investigated the question of the period of maximum, in a paper published in 1870, arriving at the conclusion, somewhat different from that above mentioned, that the period is determined by Jupiter, and is about ten years; the magnitude of the maximum fluctuating, and dependent on Venus, with irregularities unaccounted for still outstanding. As to the sun's physical constitution, Professor Sterry Hunt is the author of a theory which is essentially a part of his theory of chemical geology, according to which the solar sphere consists wholly of matter in a gaseous condition, all the elements being mingled but not combined, their affinities being held in check by the intensity of the heat. The partial cooling of the surface by radiation depresses the temperature to the point at which combination is possible, and thus are formed vast volumes of finely divided solid or liquid matter, which, suspended in the surrounding gases, become intensely luminous, and form the source of the solar light. This view is sustained also by Mr. Faye and by Mr. Balfour Stewart, but is dissented from by Father Secchi, who inclines to believe the luminous envelope to form a kind of liquid or viscous shell. Recent observations by Professor S. P. Langley, with the admirable 13-inch objective of the Alleghany Observatory, have furnished probably the most conclusive evidence on this subject which has yet been obtained, and are entirely favorable to the theory of Professor Hunt. Professor Langley's papers have been published in the *American Journal of Science* for 1874 and 1875, and are full of interest not only as to the phenomena of the spots, but as to the minute features of the sun's general superficies. Accompanying his latest paper is a magnificent engraved illustration from a drawing of a typical solar spot observed in December, 1873. It represents what is commonly called the penumbra as being formed of long-drawn luminous filaments which in their curvature give evidence of gyratory movements, indicating that the spots are formed by tremendous vortices spirally ascending or descending. Professor Langley remarks of the apparently black centre or nucleus of the spot, that he has found it by direct experiment, when all extraneous light is excluded, to be not only intrinsically bright, but insupportably intense to the naked eye.

One of the most interesting contributions to the knowledge of the solar physics was the discovery in 1871 by Professor C. A. Young of that comparatively limited but well-defined solar envelope called the chromosphere, where the lines which in the ordinary solar spectrum are black become reversed, and assume the brilliant tints which characterize the spectra of the elements to which they belong, as seen in experiments artificially instituted. Professor Young's preliminary chart of the lines thus seen and its subsequent extension will be referred to later.

A very ingenious device recently suggested by Professor A. M. Mayer, of Hoboken, for the study of the laws of the distribution of heat upon the sun's surface is the latest addition which has fallen under our notice to the means of investigating the physical condition of that body. The double iodide of copper and mercury becomes discolored when raised to a certain ascertained temperature. Let a thin paper, blackened on one surface and coated with the iodide on the other, receive the solar image on the blackened side, the aperture of the object-glass being reduced to such an extent that no discoloration of the salt may occur. Then let the aperture be gradually enlarged. Presently a spot will appear, which marks in the image the point of maximum temperature in the solar disk. By successive additional enlargements of aperture the spot on the paper will be correspondingly enlarged, and its borders will indicate the isothermal lines of the solar disk. Several interesting discoveries already made by the application of this method our narrow limits will not permit us to notice here.

Comets.—In 1843 Professor Alexander, of Princeton, presented to the American Philosophical Society an investigation of the orbit of the great comet of that year, according to which it appeared that the body must almost have touched the sun, this result being explained on the hypothesis that the centre of gravity of the comet was not coincident with its centre of figure. In 1850 he published in the *Astronomical Journal* a memoir on the classification and special points of resemblance of certain periodic comets, and the probability of a common origin in the case of some of them. Three classes were distinguished. The possible rupture by the planet Mars of a large comet—that of 1315 and 1316—to furnish three of the third class, was suggested as an example. This hypothesis was very lightly treated by Humboldt in his *Cosmos*, but it has found unexpected corroboration in observations of our own time.

The orbit of the second comet of 1840 was computed by Professor Loomis, and the results communicated to the American Philosophical Society, in an able paper, which was published in their eighth volume.

In regard to cometary physics some very important speculations, or, perhaps, more properly discoveries, are due to American physicists and astronomers. The nature of the appendages called tails and the causes producing them have been in all ages subjects of perplexing discussion, and have given rise to a variety of hypotheses, many of which are more or less wild. This character can not be attributed to the theory presented in 1859 by Professor W. A. Norton, of Yale College, in which the formation of comets' tails is assumed to be due to electrical repulsion, exerted both by the nucleus and by the sun, upon the attenuated matter sublimed from the mass by the solar heat. The particles, under the action of these forces, pass off in hyperbolic orbits. An application was made of this theory to the case of the remarkable comet of 1858, known as Donati's, by Professor Peirce. This comet had been continuously observed and mapped through all its varying and wonderful aspects, during the entire five months of its visibility, by Mr. George P. Bond, whose monograph on the subject, published in the Annals of the Harvard Observatory, with its numerous and beautifully executed illustrations, will always make it an authority of the highest character on the subject of cometary changes. Professor Peirce's analysis led to results entirely in harmony with the hypothesis, explaining not only the phenomena in general, but the special aspects, including the simultaneous exhibition of one or more rectilinear tails, along with the principal tail, which was curved in the form of a sabre. He applied a similar analysis to the great comet of 1843, with results equally satisfactory. Here also the investigation explained the existence of two tails, one of which did not reach the comet's head. The theory of electrical repulsion as applied to comets was proposed by some foreign astronomers, perhaps independently, at about the same time with the appearance of Professor Norton's memoir. It is frequently spoken of abroad as Professor Zöllner's view.

Auroras.—The aurora borealis has formed the subject of a pretty voluminous literature, both at home and abroad, during the last half century. All the scientific journals teem with articles on the subject, and the transactions of societies contain numerous elaborate memoirs relating to it. We can mention but a few of these publications, and those only briefly. In the first volume of Transactions of the Connecticut Academy there appeared the results of seventeen years' study of auroras by Edward C. Herrick, of New Haven, an observer unsurpassed for accuracy of observation and soundness of judgment. This paper will ever be a high authority in regard to the facts. Professor Loomis, of New Haven, examined a few years since the question of the periodicity of the aurora, and of its relation to the maxima and minima of solar disturbance as indicated by the spots, with reference to the possibility that both phenomena are dependent on a common cause. He found the periods nearly equal, but the auroral period less regular than the other, and the coincidences in general only approximate. This question was at the same time occupying Professor Lovering, of Harvard University, who has investigated it, so far as records go, to exhaustion. The tenth volume of the Transactions of the American Academy contains a catalogue by him of every aurora to be found in accessible records from the year 502 B.C. down to A.D. 1868. The total number is about 12,000; and this immense catalogue is carefully analyzed with a view to determine the daily, the yearly, and the secular periodicity, if such exists. The results, which are not only tabulated but expressed in curves, do not exhibit all the regularity which might be anticipated, but they show, nevertheless, evidences of a periodicity, subject manifestly to large disturbances from unknown causes.

Meteoric Astronomy.—To American astronomers is due the credit of having first correctly interpreted the phenomena presented by the frequent intruders from the regions of space into our atmosphere called shooting-stars. In regard to the nature of these bodies the most widely various hypotheses had from the earliest times been held by different speculators, none of them supported by proofs, or resting on any systematic observation. Some of the earliest conjectures regarding them seem to have been soundest. Anaxagoras, whose general views of the structure of the universe were so much in advance of his time, supposed that there are non-luminous bodies revolving about the earth, from which meteors may proceed, though this idea is marred by the supposition that such bodies may have been thrown off from the earth itself by centrifugal force. Diogenes of Apollonia, whose own writings are not extant, but who wrote on cosmology, is said to have held that, besides the visible planets, there are other planets which are invisible. These sagacious conjectures, however, were overborne by the later authority of Aristotle, who inculcated the doctrine that shooting-stars are terrestrial meteors originating in the atmosphere itself—a doctrine generally received as the most probable down to the present century.

On the morning of November 13, 1833, there occurred one of the most wonderful displays of celestial pyrotechnics that was probably ever witnessed. As observed in the Eastern United States, it commenced about midnight and continued for some hours, increasing in magnificence until it was lost in the light of the rising sun. It was visible probably over the greater part of North America, and was actually observed at various points from the West India Islands to Greenland, and westwardly to the one-hundredth degree of longitude. From the numerous descriptions of this sublime spectacle with which, immediately after its occurrence, the journals of the day were crowded, it seems to have presented the appearance of a literal shower of fire, the meteors falling on all sides in prodigious numbers, and many of them exhibiting a splendor truly dazzling. An important fact in regard to these meteors noticed by many observers was the apparent divergence of their paths from a single radiant point. All accounts agreed in fixing this radiant in the constellation Leo, and in the statement that it continued to maintain its position unchanged as the constellation advanced with the diurnal motion of the heavens. This fact offered very conclusive evidence that the source of the meteors was foreign to the earth, and that their paths, though seemingly divergent, were actually parallel to each other and to a line drawn from the spectator to the radiant, the divergency being merely an effect of perspective. To Professor Denison Olmsted, of New Haven, belongs the credit of having first pointed out the legitimate conclusions to be drawn from these phenomena, which he did in a paper published in the *American Journal of Science* in March, 1834. Having first demonstrated the cosmical origin of the meteors, Professor Olmsted proceeded, with the aid of such imperfect data as at that time existed, including observations of a similar star-shower observed on the Eastern Continent in 1832, and of a much earlier one witnessed by Humboldt and Bonpland in Cumana, South America, in 1799, to devise upon this basis a theory adequate to account for the facts. The conclusion reached by him was that the meteors must be portions of a nebulous body drawn into the earth's atmosphere at a point of near approach, and inflamed by the heat generated by the resistance of the atmosphere to their motion. Professor Olmsted did not explain the meaning attached by him to the term nebulous. If he meant by it a gas, or a finely comminuted and uniformly diffused solid matter, his theory is inadmissible. But if he meant a congeries of loosely scattered discrete bodies, the phenomena are in harmony with his view; and to this extent the more recent and more exact investigations of Professor Newton, of Yale College, and Professor Schiaparelli, of Milan, have confirmed his conclusions. But in assigning to the supposed nebulous body a period of 182 days, and in his speculations as to the density of the constituent parts of the nebula, he was less happy. He supposed the specific gravity to be very small, whereas the researches of Newton and others conclusively prove that these bodies must have the average density of our harder rocks; and the numerous specimens in cabinets of the fragmentary portions of them which have forced their way through the atmospheric shield by which our planet is protected against their destructive impact are many of them largely or wholly composed of metal. The intense interest excited in all classes of persons by the meteoric display of 1833 turned the attention of a multitude of observers in this and other countries to the study of these phenomena—a study which was pursued both by the careful examination of records for the discovery of past examples of similar occurrences, and by the direct and continuous observation of the heavens themselves. The scientific journals of the period bear striking witness to the activity of these investigators. One of the most successful among them was Mr. E. C. Herrick, of New Haven, at that time, or later, librarian of Yale College, who presently announced the discovery of three or four additional periods of periodical shooting-star abundance or star showers, viz., in January, August, April, and December. In regard to the August period, Quetelet, of Brussels, was afterward found to have anticipated him, but his discovery of the others was original. Since that time observation in many quarters has been so persistent and so fruitful of results as to justify the statement that there are not fewer than fifty different days in the year on which there is a tendency to a meteoric display above the average.

As from the examination of records, ancient and modern, the number of observed returns of the November shower was increased, two very important deductions followed—first, the congeries of bodies furnishing the meteors must extend along its own orbit to a distance equal in longitude to about one-sixteenth or one-seventeenth of an entire circumference; and secondly, there must be a continuous advance or procession of the node, or intersection of the orbit with that of the earth, causing a retardation of the display by about a day at each return. The significancy of the accumulated data was first shown by Professor Newton in 1864, who, from a comparison of observations covering a period of 931 years, determined the length of the cycle to be 33.25 years, the annual mean procession of the node 1.711′, the inclination of the orbit about 17°, and the length of the part of the cycle within which showers might be expected 2.25 years. From these definitely ascertained results he deduced the highly important conclusion that the periodic time of the group of bodies from which the meteors proceed must be one of the five following, and no other, viz., 179.915 days, 185.413 days, 354.586 days, 376.575 days, or 33.25 years. It remained only, by applying the principles of physical astronomy, to compute the amount of annual procession of the node for each of these five orbits, and, by comparing the results with the observed procession, to determine which of the five orbits is the true one. This computation Professor Newton suggested as the *experimentum crucis;* but delaying to apply it himself, the honor was snatched from him by Mr. Adams, of Cambridge, England, who demonstrated that the only orbit of the five which fulfills the conditions is that which belongs to the period of 33.25 years.

Professor Newton followed up his success with the November meteors by investigations hardly less remarkable of the numerous irregularly occurring bodies of this class called sporadic. From a very large number of determinations of the altitudes of these bodies above the earth, he formed a table arranging the observations in groups between limits of altitude regularly increasing, by which it appeared that few are seen at heights greater than 180 kilometers and few below 30 kilometers, the mean altitude on the whole being 95.55 kilometers. He then, by a course of very ingenious reasoning and analysis, proceeded to demonstrate that the number of meteors which traverse some part of the earth's atmosphere daily, and are large enough to be visible to the naked eye (sun, moon, and clouds permitting), amounts to more than seven and a half millions. Including those fainter bodies of this class which escape the unaided eye, but may be detected by the telescope, this number must be greatly increased. Taking as a basis of calculation the number of telescopic meteors observed by Winnecke between July 24 and August 3, 1854, with an ordinary comet-seeker of 53′ aperture, the total number per day would seem to be more than 400,000,000—a number which higher optical power would, of course, correspondingly increase. The following are some of the more interesting conclusions reached in this investigation: 1. It is impossible to suppose that these sporadic meteors proceed from a group or ring at the same mean distance from the sun as the earth. 2. The mean velocity of these meteoroids considerably exceeds that of the earth in its orbit, and hence the orbits are not approximately circular, but resemble the orbits of comets. 3. The number of meteoroids in the space through which the earth is moving is such that in each volume of the size of the earth there are as many as 13,000 small bodies, each one of which is capable of furnishing a shooting-star visible, under favorable circumstances, to the naked eye.

The further contributions to the theory of shooting-stars in which American astronomers have participated are those which connect these bodies with the comets. Near the end of December, 1845, Mr. Herrick and Mr. Bradley, of New Haven, watching the Biela comet with the Clark telescope in the observatory of Yale College, observed a small companion comet beside the principal one. The same was seen two weeks later by Lieutenant Maury and Professor Hubbard at the Naval Observatory at Washington, and two days later than this was noticed in Europe. Professor Hubbard thereafter made this body a special study. At the time of the observations above mentioned the comet was receding, and each day the pair presented some novel phase. At one time an arch of light connected the two; the principal one had two nuclei, and each had two tails. The smaller grew till it equaled the larger in brilliancy, then faded gradually, until, when the comet was last seen in March, it was no longer visible. In 1852 the comet was very distant, but it was still double, the two companions being a million and a quarter miles apart. Since September of that year this remarkable object has never been again seen. At the return in 1859, it was in conjunction, or nearly so, with the sun, and was necessarily invisible. In 1866 every thing favored its visibility, and hundreds of observers swept the heavens in search of it without success. Another return was due in the autumn of 1872. The body was not seen, but countless fragments broken from its mass came pouring into the earth's atmosphere on the night of the 27th of November, producing a star shower which for an hour or two almost rivaled in brilliancy that of the 13th of the same month in 1833. A German astronomer, Professor Klinkerfues, at once conceived the notion that, if this were the comet's following, the main body might be seen in its retreat, though we had not seen it in its approach. But if so, it must be seen in the southern hemisphere. He telegraphed Mr. Pogson, at Madras: "Biela touched earth November 27. Search near Theta Centauri." Mr. Pogson looked, and found the comet. The question is unsettled whether this was one of the two parts into which the comet was divided in 1845. Professor Newton thinks it was more probably a fragment thrown off long—perhaps centuries—before.

The comet of 1862, III., was discovered on the 18th July, 1862, by Mr. H. P. Tuttle, of Cambridge, Massachusetts. It has been proved by Professor Schiaparelli that this comet is only a large member of the August stream of meteoroids. The comet of 1866, I., discovered by Tempel, December 19, 1865, is shown also by Schiaparelli to be a member of the November stream. This comet Professor Newton has identified with one which appeared in 1366. From the evidence furnished in these instances, and for other reasons, Professor Newton and Professor Weiss regard all these meteoroids as sufficiently proved to be made up of countless fragments detached from solid cometary masses, which comets until thus entirely broken up are only large members of the swarms with which they move in company. The cause of the fracture is supposed by Professor A. W. Wright, of Iowa, to be the intense heat of the sun as the body approaches its perihelion. Professor Wright has recently obtained a gas from the Iowa meteorite which has the same spectrum as that of the comets. The comet's tail, therefore, is a gaseous emanation not to be confounded with these meteoroid masses.

Comets and meteoroids having thus been demonstrated to be generally identical, the question of the origin of all these bodies has become one of great interest. A theory on this subject, put forth in 1866 by Professor Schiaparelli, of Milan, assumed that matter is disseminated throughout space in all possible grades of division—embracing, in the first place, immense suns or stars of different magnitudes; secondly, groups of smaller or comparatively minute stars, such as those into which many of the nebulæ are resolved; then bodies so small as to be invisible except when they approach our sun, appearing then as comets; and finally, "cosmical clouds," made up of elements conformable in weight to such as we may handle or transport upon the earth. The elements of these cosmical clouds he supposes to be so distant from each other that their mutual attraction is insufficient to counteract the effect of the sun's unequal action upon their different members, so that when drawn into our system from the regions of space, they lose wholly their globular form, and enter as streams, "which may possibly consume years, centuries, and even myriads of years in passing the perihelion, forming in space a river whose transverse dimensions are very small with respect to its length." This was the essential part of a theory which won for its author the Copley medal from the Royal Society—a theory of which the only part not pure hypothesis is the demonstration that the mean velocity of the meteoroids exceeds that of the earth, and this fact had already been demonstrated by Professor Newton some years before. The rest, viz., all that relates to the different mechanical conditions of matter in space, is mere conjecture, and it is doubtful whether it continues still to be held by Professor Schiaparelli himself. A more probable theory of the origin of comets is suggested by a very significant observation of the sun made by Professor Young, of Dartmouth College, on the 7th of September, 1871. An explosion was seen to take place at that time, by which a volume of exploded matter was driven to a height of 200,000 miles, with a velocity, between the altitudes of 100,000 and 200,000 miles, of 166 miles per second. The visible clouds consisted of hydrogen. The resistance of the solar atmosphere prevented their complete separation from the sun, but should solid masses be projected with an equal velocity, they must be driven off never to return. Professor Young's observation, therefore, suggests an origin of comets which harmonizes with the views of Weiss and Newton as to the source of meteoric streams; and it is in further confirmation of these views that hydrogen was found by Graham in abundance occluded in meteoric masses, and that the gas of the Iowa meteor gave to Professor Wright a cometary spectrum.

METEOROLOGY.

As early as 1743 Dr. Franklin made the important discovery that the atmospheric disturbances known as northeast storms on the Atlantic coast of North America begin actually in the southwest. The first fact which drew his attention to this seeming physical paradox was the occurrence of an eclipse of the moon on the 21st of October in the year just mentioned, which a northeaster prevented him from observing at Philadelphia, although it was seen to its close by his brother, at Boston, before the storm began. This storm did great damage along the coast, and, from the accounts subsequently obtained, it appeared that its effects were felt progressively from Carolina to Massachusetts. Other storms of the same kind were observed to advance in the same manner, whence Franklin inferred the existence of a law, and proceeded to inquire the cause. This he presumed to be the rarefaction of the air by the tropical heats of the far south, producing upward currents, with diminished pressure and a consequent flow of air toward the region of rarefaction. This inference of Dr. Franklin was the first step toward a proper understanding of the law of storms in the temperate zones.

The views then held by Dr. Franklin as to the mechanical action of the air in waterspouts, and as to the identity of the phenomena with tornadoes on the land, were very nearly those at present entertained. He failed, however, to recognize the important agency of the heat set free by condensation in the whirling column in maintaining and promoting the violence of the action, and he supposed that the height of the column of water raised was limited to that which the static pressure only of the atmosphere is capable of sustaining in a vacuum. For a long period after these observations, meteorological science made very little advance either in this country or abroad. The year 1814 was marked by the publication of the well-known essay on dew by William Charles Wells, which has become a classic in meteorological science, and has been pronounced by Sir John Herschel a model of experimental inquiry. Dr. Wells was a native of Charleston, South Carolina, and though his life was principally spent abroad, he belongs in a certain sense to the science of America. In the year 1827 Mr. William C. Redfield, of New York, published the first of a series of papers in which he announced and maintained a theory of the storms of the Atlantic coast, or, as he called them, Atlantic hurricanes, which gave rise to much controversy, but which has since in substance been received as a true statement of the law governing the great progressive storms of the northern hemisphere. Mr. Redfield held—and aimed by a laborious comparison of observations upon the winds, made at numerous and widely distant points on land and at sea during these storms, to prove—that the storm is a vast whirlwind, circular in figure, its motion of gyration being to an observer within it from right to left. While such was supposed to be the internal movement, the whole storm was shown to have a motion of translation along a curved path, convex toward the west, and having usually its vertex in about latitude 37° or 38°, entering upon the continent between Georgia and Texas, and passing off on the coast of New England or of British America. The motion of progress is, therefore, the reverse of that of rotation, and the storm moves on its path in the same manner in which a wheel might be supposed to roll along a curved track. The birth-place of these storms was supposed by Mr. Redfield to be the West India Islands and the Caribbean Sea, and, like Franklin, he supposed them to be caused by uprising currents produced by local tropical heats. As for their progress, he supposed them to be borne along first by the trades, and then by the counter-trades, or prevailing west winds of the higher temperate zone.

To the theory of Mr. Redfield was opposed a rival theory, identified with the name of its originator, Mr. James P. Espy, of Pennsylvania, who published in 1841 an essay entitled, "The Philosophy of Storms." As to the origin of storms the two theories were in harmony; but Mr. Espy supposed the air currents within the storm to follow the direction of radii of the circle from the circumference to the centre, instead of being coincident in direction with the circumference itself. Long-continued and extended observation has shown that in this he was in error; and it is, in fact, capable of *a priori* demonstration that no two opposite atmospheric currents, drawn toward the same point by a local diminished pressure, can approach in straight lines or meet each other directly. From the configuration of the earth, and from its motion of rotation, of which the atmosphere partakes, such currents must necessarily deviate toward the right, producing as a result a motion of gyration. It is evident, however, that Mr. Redfield was not wholly correct. The true motion of the winds within the storm is neither rectilinear nor circular, but spiral, converging to the centre. Mr. Espy made an important contribution to the physics of storms in pointing out the source of the energy which maintains them in action after the merely local cause which originally produced them has ceased to have effect. This is the immense liberation of the heat of elasticity which takes place in consequence of the condensation of the aqueous vapor contained in the ascending air. As the air ascends, it expands from diminished pressure; expansion reduces its temperature below the dew-point; condensation occurs, and the heat released causes further expansion. Thus the process continues till the moisture of the air is exhausted. The storm would soon cease if it were not in this manner continually fed by fresh supplies of uncondensed vapor drawn in with the air from surrounding regions. No such storm can endure upon deserts like those of Northern Africa. Mr. Espy's merits were acknowledged by the French Academy of Science in a formal report. Professor Loomis, of Yale College, has made many valuable contributions to meteorological science in the study of particular storms, and more recently in a careful analysis of the weather maps which have for the last few years been issued daily from the Signal-office of the United States War Department. He has especially shown that while all our great storms are cyclonic, and to that extent conformable to Mr. Redfield's theory, they are not by any means, as Mr. Redfield had supposed, circular. They are rather irregularly elliptical, having their longer diameter generally north and south, inclining most frequently to the northeast and southwest direction, and they have often large sinuosities of outline.

The weather maps of the Signal-office just mentioned, and the system of widely extended telegraphic communication of observations from all points of our national territory to a single central office at Washington, by means of which the material is gathered for their preparation, have furnished admirable means for studying the laws which govern atmospheric changes on this continent. The system originated in 1869, at Cincinnati, with Professor Cleveland Abbe, who now conducts it, under General Myer, chief signal officer. The telegraphic prognostications of the weather daily transmitted for publication from the central office to all the chief cities of the Union have proved to be a very important public benefit. Something similar to this was attempted about twenty years ago by Mr. Espy, who then held an official appointment as meteorologist under the government, but the means at his command were more limited, and his organization less complete. The Smithsonian Institution, ever since its establishment, has been active in promoting meteorological observation, and has maintained constant communication with several hundred observers in all parts of the United States. Previously to the war the secretary, Professor Henry, had planned and had partially put into operation a system of weather bulletins and storm warnings like the present, which, in consequence of the disturbed state of public affairs, was necessarily abandoned after the commencement of hostilities; and for a number of years there was maintained at the institution a large meteorological wall map of the continent exposed to public view, on which were daily exhibited emblems showing the aspect of the weather and the direction of the wind at each of a large number of points of observation distributed widely throughout the country, as communicated by telegraph.

SOUND.

The science of acoustics has been greatly advanced by the labors of the physicists and physiologists of the present century. The mathematical theory of sound, the mode of its generation and propagation, the principles of music, and the laws of harmony had been well established by previous investigators. But the experimental study of the particular phenomena of vibration, of the physiology of audition, of the elementary tones which enter into the ordinary notes of music, of the physical causes of *timbre* or quality in sounds, and of whatever else in acoustics is incapable of being deduced abstractly from definitions or first principles, had received comparatively little attention, or had been pursued with little success. The recent progress of experimental acoustics has been wonderfully promoted by the ingenuity of the methods employed in the study of vibration; some of them graphic, in which the vibrations record themselves, and others optical, in which they present a visible picture of their phases to the eye. The methods strictly acoustic have, moreover, been greatly improved in the hands of modern investigators; as in the case of the *sirene* of Cagniard de la Tour, which has been converted by Helmholtz into an instrument of largely increased capabilities. The vibrating lens of Lissajous, and the revolving mirrors and manometric flames of Kœnig, have furnished admirable means of illustrating the composition and resolution of harmonic vibrations. Professor Tyndall's singing tubes and sensitive flames have shown in a striking manner the power of one vibration to excite or repress another. Recent comparatively simple forms of apparatus contrived by German experimenters have shown that the velocity of propagation of sound in air or other gases can be determined in the space of a few feet with as much accuracy as has been heretofore attained in the most elaborate and protracted observations made in the open air between signal stations separated from each other by some miles.

No single investigator has contributed more largely to the advancement of acoustic science than Professor Helmholtz, of Berlin. In his great work on tone sensation he has given the whole philosophy of composite waves and the theory of audition as founded on the capacity of the ear to resolve these waves into their component elements. He has shown that within a certain portion of the structure of the ear there are found a multitude of microscopic stretched cords, each of which is fitted to respond to a particular vibration, just as in a piano a single string will vibrate when its own note is sounded, while all the rest remain silent. He has also contrived hearing tubes or shells, called by him resonators, which possess this same property of separating an elementary tone out of an ordinary composite musical note, and by means of a series of these he succeeds in discovering all the elements of which such notes are composed. Every such elementary tone when separately heard has precisely the same quality, whether derived from a reed, a stringed, or a wind instrument; and thus it appears that the quality or *timbre* of a musical instrument is an effect of difference of composition, and not of difference of elementary sound.

In the United States the number of investigators who have occupied themselves with this interesting branch of science is small. Professor W. B. Rogers, now of Boston, gave some attention as early as 1850 to the curious phenomena of singing tubes, that is, of tubes which utter a musical note on the introduction within them of a small gas flame. The vibration was imputed by Professor Rogers to a periodical explosive combustion of the gas, extinguishing the flame, which is immediately re-illuminated. For the purpose of demonstrating this latter fact, he employed as his gas jet a tube bent twice at right angles, which, by means of a pulley, he caused to revolve rapidly around its lower limb. When this is revolved it produces an apparent ring of flame so long as the tube is silent; but the moment the sound begins, the ring breaks into a crown of minute flames resembling a string of pearls.

Professor Henry, in the discharge of his duties as chairman of the Light-house Board, has made many experiments on sound, with a view to improve the system of fog-signals. Some of the facts observed by him are interesting contributions to science. One of these is the remarkable property manifested by powerful sounds to propagate themselves laterally, or in directions divergent from that to which they are originally confined. A steam-whistle, for example, blown at the focus of a large parabolic mirror will at moderate distances be better heard in front and in the prolonged axis of the mirror than behind it; but when the distance amounts to several miles, it is heard as well behind as before. In like manner, if a source of sound be near a building, an observer at a distance on the other side of the building may hear it distinctly, and yet may entirely lose it as he approaches the building. Another remarkable observation is as to the effect of winds on the audibility of sounds. At any considerable distance a wind blowing from the observer toward the source diminishes the loudness. This is explained by the consideration that the lower strata of the air are retarded in their movements by the friction of the earth, and consequently that the fronts of the sound waves become inclined to the earth's surface. But as the direction of sound propagation is normal to the wave fronts, it happens that a sound proceeding against the wind is deflected upward so that its force passes above the heads of distant listeners.

The only elaborate continuous series of investigations in acoustics which has been undertaken in this country has been conducted by Professor A. M. Mayer, of Hoboken. The processes of Professor Mayer, which are themselves extremely ingenious, have led to many results of interest and value. It is a proposition deducible from theory, and was so announced by Döppler more than thirty years ago, that the undulations generated by a vibratory body in motion will be effectively shortened in the direction toward which the body moves, and lengthened in the opposite direction. This is true as well in optics as in acoustics, and it is upon the assumption of its truth that Mr. Huggins has founded his inferences as to the absolute velocities with which the fixed stars are approaching the earth or receding from it. It has first been experimentally proved in the researches of Professor Mayer.

The double *sirene* of Helmholtz affords a convenient means of studying the effect of partial or complete interference between sound waves which differ in phase at the point of origin, but there has been hitherto no instrumental means devised for determining the amount of difference of phase which exists between two waves originating in a common phase at the same origin, but brought by different and unequal paths to the point of interference. This want Professor Mayer has supplied, and in doing so has at the same time provided the most exact mode hitherto devised of measuring the wave length corresponding to any pitch, and of ascertaining the velocity of sound in the air or in any gaseous medium. The determinations are made by means of the serrated flames in Kœnig's revolving mirrors, and their precision is secured by what is called a flame micrometer—as ingenious in conception as it is exact in its indications.

The analysis of a composite note which Helmholtz accomplished by the use of his resonators, combined with Kœnig's manometric flames and revolving mirrors, has been effected by Professor Mayer directly, by connecting the arms of a number of steel tuning-forks by means of tightly stretched silk fibres with a membrane forming part of a reed pipe. On causing the pipe to speak, every fork whose tone forms a part of the note immediately sounds.

Professor Mayer has also presented very strong evidence to confirm the opinion which many naturalists have entertained, that the antennæ of insects constitute for them the organs of hearing, or organs, at least, through which they receive impressions for their guidance from the vibrations of the atmosphere; he has investigated and delineated the curves which represent the resultant sound wave of a composite note, and has devised the means of optically representing the movements by which a single molecule of an elastic vibrating medium must be animated under the influence of such complex impulses. The most interesting of his contributions to this department of science is found in his determination of the law which connects the pitch of a sound with the duration of its residual sensation, and in the deductions which flow from this law. It appears experimentally that if a sound of any pitch is suddenly arrested there follows a momentary dissonance, but that if the interruption is regular and periodic the dissonance diminishes with a diminution of the intervals till it finally disappears; also, that a more rapid succession of the impulses is necessary to this disappearance in proportion as the pitch is higher. Professor Mayer finds that for a tone produced by forty vibrations a second, the residual sensation lasts one-eleventh of a second, while for one of 40,000 vibrations per second, it lasts only one-five-hundredth of a second. This difference of duration of the residual sensation is the reason that trills upon the upper notes are pleasing, while those on the lower are not. The application of these principles to the study of harmony and to the means of producing the most agreeable effects in musical composition is important.

LIGHT, HEAT, ETC.

From the time of Newton to that of Young the science of optics made no material progress. The correction by Dollond, in 1758, of one of the few mistaken inferences of Newton, that the dispersive powers of transparent bodies are not proportional to their mean refractive powers, however practically important, was not a large contribution to theory; and Bradley's discovery of the aberration of light belongs rather to dynamics than to optics. It is, in fact, somewhat surprising that this latter phenomenon had not been recognized in anticipation of observation as a physical necessity, since the progressive motion of light had been demonstrated by Roemer half a century before. The first note of returning activity in the field of optical investigation was given by Dr. Young in the memoirs which, in 1800 and the two or three years following, he read before the Royal Society, reviving the hypothesis of Huyghens that light is propagated by undulations and not by the emission of material particles, and supporting this view by evidences and reasonings so cogent as to advance it to the dignity of a theory. It is a remarkable fact, illustrating the tenacity with which even enlightened minds cling to opinions long received without question, that these able and unanswerable papers failed to convince, or even, as is remarked by Principal Forbes, to secure a single adherent among the members of the learned body to which they were addressed. The discovery by Malus in 1808 of the polarization of light by reflection awakened a new interest in optical questions, and a large part of the history of this science during the first half of the nineteenth century is occupied with the development of the consequences of this discovery by Fresnel, Arago, Brewster, Seebeck, and others. Important contributions to the mathematical theory, left in some respects incomplete by Fresnel, were made by Cauchy, Macculagh, and Sir William Rowan Hamilton. No part of this belongs to American science.

Spectrum.—In 1802 Dr. Wollaston, of London, in observing through a prism the image of an elongated and very narrow aperture, perceived it to be intersected by well-defined straight lines perpendicular to its length—lines which Young seems to have regarded at first as boundaries between the several elementary colors of the spectrum. Dr. Brewster subsequently observed that certain bodies, solid, liquid, and gaseous, have the power of producing not lines only, but broad bands in the spectral image of the light transmitted through them. But the most remarkable discovery in this branch of investigation was made by Fraunhofer in 1814, who, employing a telescope to aid the observation, detected and was able to count nearly six hundred lines like those seen by Wollaston, fixed in position—a number which Brewster subsequently increased to two thousand, and which later observations have shown to be practically unlimited. The earliest investigations of this curious, but, as it has since appeared, highly important class of phenomena, undertaken in the United States, were made by Dr. John William Draper, of New York, a man whose name occupies a very conspicuous place in the world as well of letters as of science. Dr. Draper's labors in this department were spread over so large a field that it would be quite impracticable to do them justice in the limited space at our command. They embraced at once the physical, chemical, and thermal properties of light, and the relations of this principle to the organic world and the physiology of vision. He was the first to apply the method of photography to the study of the Fraunhofer lines. A memoir published by him in 1843 describes many new lines in the ultra-red and ultra-violet. The great bands in the ultra-red were first detected by him. Some of these were subsequently rediscovered by the aid of the thermo-multiplier. In 1844 he photographed the diffraction spectrum formed by a *Gitter-platte,* or ruled grating, and published a memoir showing the singular advantages which that spectrum possesses over the prismatic in investigations on radiation. Since the science of spectroscopy (a science of which the foundations were laid in Dr. Draper's early researches) has attained so high an importance in connection with investigations both of celestial and terrestrial chemistry, the spectrum has been photographed upon a much larger scale than was attempted by Dr. Draper.

The most admirable photograph of this kind, so far as the visible spectrum is concerned, was obtained by Mr. Lewis M. Rutherfurd, of New York, in 1866. It was enlarged from an original taken with prisms constructed of plate-glass, hollow, and filled with bisulphide of carbon—a plan first adopted by Professor O. N. Rood, in 1862. To a very powerful train of such prisms, six in number, made effectively twelve by means of a repeating prism, Mr. Rutherfurd subsequently applied a system of mechanical or automatic adjustment for varying the angular position without deranging the regularity of the train, which was the first contrivance of the kind ever invented. Of the map, eighty-two inches in length, and embracing more than 2500 sharply defined lines, Mr. Lockyer, the celebrated spectroscopist of London, remarked recently in a public lecture, it was a thing so admirable that he could not look at it without a feeling of the intensest envy. Still more recently (1873), Dr. Henry Draper, son of Dr. J. W. Draper, has produced a photograph of the ultra-violet rays of the diffraction spectrum which far exceeds in distinctness any thing previously attempted in this difficult spectral region. The gitter from which it was taken was ruled by Mr. Rutherfurd, who had long been engaged in the attempt to perfect plates suitable for this purpose. The earliest gitters were prepared by Fraunhofer, and were ruled through leaf metal or thin coatings of grease on glass. He subsequently ruled with a diamond point on the glass itself; but none of his rulings were closer than about 8000 lines to the inch, and none of over 3500 were regular enough to be serviceable. For the last twenty or thirty years the plates most in use by investigators have been furnished by Mr. F. A. Nobert, of Barth, in Pomeranian Prussia, who has carried his rulings to a degree of fineness far beyond that at which spectra cease altogether to be produced, the object being to provide tests for the resolving power of microscopes. Admirable as these productions certainly are, they are deficient in uniformity, which is the quality of most essential importance in the gratings required for the study of diffraction spectra. Mr. Rutherfurd's finer gratings have nearly 18,000 lines to the inch, and their uniformity, as tested by the sharpness of their definition of the spectral lines, is all but perfect. The delicacy of this ruling operation may be judged by the fact that when the machine which draws the lines is operated by hand, although not touched but only moved by a cord attached, the ruling is liable to be made uneven by the effect of expansion from the radiant heat of the person. In consequence of this, Mr. Rutherfurd resorted to the expedient of driving the machine by a miniature turbine wheel, with very satisfactory results.

The memoir of Dr. Henry Draper accompanying the photograph above mentioned was read before the French Academy of Sciences, and published in their *Comptes Rendus*. It has also been printed in full in the principal journals devoted to physical science in France, England, Italy, and Germany, and the discussion of the photograph has settled the wave lengths of all the ultraviolet rays, and has finally corrected the errors of previous observers.

The first suggestion of the relation between the spectra of incandescent or incandescing bodies and their physical condition or chemical composition was made by Dr. J. W. Draper, in an important memoir "On the Production of Light and Heat," published in 1847. This, among other things, pointed out the means of determining the solid or gaseous condition of the sun, the stars, and the nebulæ. In it the author demonstrated experimentally that all solid substances, and probably all liquids, become incandescent at the same temperature; that the temperature of red heat is about 977° F.; that the spectrum of an incandescent solid is continuous, containing neither bright nor dark fixed lines; that from common temperatures up to 977° F. the rays emitted by a solid produce no effect on vision, but that at that temperature they impress the eye with the sensation of red; that the heat of the incandescing body being made continuously to rise, other rays are added, increasing in refrangibility with increase of temperature; and that while the addition of rays so much the more refrangible as the temperature is higher is going on, there is an augmentation of the intensity of those already existing. In the following year, in a memoir on the production of light by chemical action, Dr. Draper gave the spectrum analysis of many different flames, and devised the arrangements of charts of their fixed lines in the manner now universally employed. The former of these memoirs had a circulation in American and foreign journals proportionate to its importance. An analysis of it in Italian was read in July, 1847, by Melloni, before the Royal Academy of Naples, and this was afterward translated into French and English. Yet, notwithstanding the publicity thus given to these discoveries, the same facts were thirteen years later published by Professor Kirchhoff, under the guise of mathematical deductions, with so slight a reference to the original discoverer that he secured substantially the entire credit of them himself; and in a historical sketch of spectrum analysis subsequently published, he omitted the name of Dr. Draper altogether. This is the more remarkable, as the historical sketch here referred to was professedly prepared because the writer had become aware of the existence "of some publications on the subject which he had not before known, and had found that other publications which had appeared to him to possess no special interest" were not similarly regarded by all. The object, therefore, of this sequel was "to complete the historical survey." It is entirely occupied, nevertheless, with an argument to disprove that any observer had contributed any thing to "the solution of the proposed question whether the bright lines of a glowing gas are solely dependent on its chemical constituents" until 1861, when it was solved by Bunsen and himself—excepting only Swan, who in 1857 identified the sodium line, although "he did not answer the question positively, or in its most general form." The writer considers and passes judgment on the claims of Herschel, Talbot, W. A. Miller, Wheatstone, Masson, Angström, Van der Willigen, and Plücker, all of whom had examined the well-known bright lines in the spectra of flames or of the electric spark, and had made suggestions indicating that this question had been present to their minds; but remarkably omits from the enumeration the name of the only observer whose publications were most directly suggestive of such a course of investigation as that which he himself subsequently pursued. In 1858, three years before the announcement of the results obtained by Bunsen and Kirchhoff, a memoir appeared by Dr. Draper on the nature of flame and the condition of the sun's surface, which was the precursor of the numerous investigations out of which has grown the imposing science of celestial chemistry.

The spectra of the stars were earliest studied by Mr. Rutherfurd, who published in 1863 a comparative map or diagram giving the spectra of seventeen different stars compared with those of the sun, the moon, and the planets Mars and Jupiter. The star spectra were arranged by him in three classes, to some extent corresponding to those since made by Secchi. In 1861 Professor Kirchhoff made public his well-known map of the solar spectrum, in which the very numerous lines given are determined in place by a millimetric scale. To remove the uncertainties attendant on the use of such a system, Dr. Wolcott Gibbs, of Harvard University, proposed, and to a certain extent constructed, in 1866, a normal map of the spectrum founded on wave lengths. His map embraced 187 lines lying between C and G of Fraunhofer. In 1871 a preliminary map or catalogue of the spectral lines of the solar chromosphere was published in the *Philosophical Magazine*, of London, by Professor C. A. Young, of Dartmouth College, which was afterward republished by Schellen in his large work on the spectroscope. This embraced 103 lines, identifying such as had been observed before, and giving the names of former observers. In the following year this number was increased by Professor Young to 273. The most important contribution to stellar spectroscopy yet made is a photograph of the spectrum of Alpha Lyræ taken by Dr. Henry Draper with his great speculum of twenty-eight inches aperture, showing in the invisible region four great groups of lines never before seen. This interesting result has been attained only after seventeen years of persevering effort, and is the fruit of probably the most difficult and costly experiment in celestial chemistry ever made.

The conclusion as to the chemical constitution of the heavenly bodies to which the study of their spectra has led, is that the same elements are found in them as in the earth, and only the same, with the single exception of a supposed element in the sun, called for the present, helium. But it appears that the temperatures of the different bodies must be materially different; and this difference is without doubt the occasion of the varieties of their spectral aspects, and of their very observable differences of color to the eye.

In regard to the distribution of heat in the spectrum, an important discovery was made by Dr. Draper so recently as 1872. He has shown that the observed decrease of the intensity of heat from the more to the less refrangible region is due not to any inherent quality of the rays, but solely to the action of the prism itself, which compresses the less refrangible region and dilates the more refrangible.

Photography.—The sensibility of many chemical compounds to the action of light was very early observed. Attempts were made by Sir Humphry Davy and others early in this century to take advantage of this fact for the purpose of producing copies of prints, leaves, etc., by pressing them under glass against sheets of paper which had been impregnated with silver salts, and exposing them in the sunlight. Imperfect copies were obtained, but they were evanescent, no successful process having been discovered for removing the unchanged salt from the paper. They were counterparts of the originals, but presented, of course, the lights and shades reversed. For a number of years, beginning in about 1830, Mr. Nicephore Niepce and Mr. Daguerre in France, and Mr. Fox Talbot in England, occupied themselves in persevering endeavors to discover some mode by which the fleeting images might be fixed, and to increase the sensitiveness of the chemically prepared surface employed to receive the impression. These efforts were at length crowned with success. In 1839 Mr. Daguerre made public the beautiful process which bears his name, and this was immediately followed by the announcement of the very different one which Mr. Talbot had been engaged in perfecting, and which he was thus constrained somewhat prematurely to disclose. The production of these light-pictures was attributed to the action of a class of rays present in the sunlight, but non-luminous, called, for want of a better name, the chemical rays. For this term Dr. Draper proposed to substitute the name tithonic, from a fancied analogy with the fable of Tithonus, the favorite of Aurora; and somewhat later Sir John Herschel suggested the term actinic—a term which, in spite of its etymological vagueness, has since prevailed. In regard to this class of rays, the researches of Dr. Draper, protracted through a period of ten or fifteen years, commencing about 1835, were more fertile of results than those of any contemporary investigator. Though embracing the class of phenomena on which the art of photography has been founded, their scope was in the largest degree comprehensive. They included, among other things, experiments on the absorption of the chemical rays by solid and liquid media, the decomposition of carbonic acid by light, the interference of chemical rays, the crystallization of substances in the rays of light, the supposed magnetizing properties of the solar rays, which he found not to exist, and the effects of light upon vegetation. The memoirs published by him on these subjects in foreign and American journals amounted to nearly forty. Many of these were collected in 1844 in a large quarto volume, entitled, *A Treatise on the Forces which produce the Organization of Plants.* Particularly noticeable among these are a memoir explanatory of the mechanical cause of the flow of sap in plants, which is ascribed to the carbonization of water on the leaves by the light of the sun; and another, demonstrating that it is the yellow ray which produces the reduction of carbonic acid in plants, and not the violet, as had been previously supposed. The first photographic portraits of the human countenance were taken by Dr. Draper soon after the announcement of Daguerre's discovery, and at a time when such a thing had been pronounced impracticable by so high an authority as Sir David Brewster. He taught the art to Professor Morse, by whom it was long successfully practiced, and who possessed exclusively the secret until it was at length made public by the originator in the *London and Edinburgh Philosophical Magazine.* This consisted essentially in quickening the sensitiveness of the Daguerrean plates by brief exposure to the vapor of bromine. By this treatment they became so extremely sensitive as to receive an impression instantaneously in the open air, and in the light of an ordinary apartment in a very few seconds. About the same time, and while the method of Dr. Draper was still undisclosed, a similar result was attained by the writer of this article by the use of chlorine. Photographs of the moon were taken by Dr. Draper as early as 1840, at a time when the moon's rays were supposed to possess no actinic power, and when, in fact, bright objects strongly illuminated by the intensest light of the full moon failed, after hours of exposure, to produce any trace of an impression on the plates of Daguerre. These photographs showed very well the light and shade characteristic of the different regions of the satellite, though by no means comparable to the magnificent photographs since taken by Dr. Henry Draper and by Mr. Rutherfurd.

The useful applications of the photographic art are very numerous. In portraiture it has created a special industry, large and lucrative, and of world-wide popularity. In mechanical engineering and in every branch of constructive art it furnishes the means of obtaining designs of the most complicated machinery or structures without the expenditure of time and labor necessary for the execution of drawings. It provides a perfect means of cultivating the popular taste or of instructing the popular intelligence by bringing faithful representations of the choicest works of art, or of the most interesting scenes of nature and of human life, within the reach of every one. Aided by the ingenious invention of Professor Wheatstone, the stereoscope, it actually seems to reproduce before us the objects which it represents, with all the aspect of reality. In its later degrees of perfection it has made it possible to prepare plates from which prints in ink can be directly taken; and as an aid to the lithographic art it has substituted a direct impression on the stone for the patient labor of the engraver or the draughtsman. In the magnetic observatories established by the British and other European governments, it traces the record of the daily and hourly fluctuations of the magnetic elements; and it has in some instances been employed to record in like manner the indications of the barometer and the thermometer. Its highest applications are undoubtedly to astronomy, to uranographical measurements according to the method of Mr. Rutherfurd, to the study of the solar and stellar spectra as practiced by Mr. Rutherfurd and Dr. H. Draper, to that of the sun spots so perseveringly pursued by De la Rue, Loewy, and Carrington, and to fixing the phases of solar eclipses, and of still more rare phenomena, like the transit of Venus.

Production of Cold.—One of the most important applications of the principles of physics to a practical purpose is to be found in the various forms of apparatus at present in use for the artificial production of cold. All of these owe their efficacy to the absorption of heat which takes place in the vaporization of highly volatile liquids; and the discovery that this principle can be practically and economically utilized is due to our countryman, Professor A. C. Twining, of New Haven, by whom the first apparatus for the purpose on a working scale ever constructed was put into operation in 1850, and was made the subject of a patent in this country and in England. Professor Twining made use of common sulphuric ether as the liquid to be vaporized. Subsequently Mr. Tellier, an English inventor, substituted for this, methylic ether, which has the advantage of being greatly more volatile; and Mr. Carré, of Paris, employed liquefied ammoniacal gas, which possesses the same advantage in a still higher degree. An important industry has grown out of this discovery, which is every year enlarging the magnitude of its operations.

The Microscope.—The discovery made in 1829 by Mr. J. J. Lister, of London, that every achromatic combination of lenses has two aplanatic foci, and that by the combination of two achromatics the spherical aberration of oblique pencils can be effectually suppressed, formed an epoch in the history of this instrument from which dates an almost miraculously rapid advance toward perfection. Results toward which Chevallier and others had been blindly feeling their way without ever satisfactorily reaching them were now made dependent upon well-ascertained principles; and the question who should produce the best microscope became a question of relative ingenuity in the application of theory no less than of practical skill in producing the curves which theory dictated. In 1846 Mr. Charles S. Spencer, a young, self-taught, and previously unknown optician living in the interior of the State of New York, submitted to the microscopists of the country microscopic objectives exhibiting a sharpness of definition and power of resolution which excited the greatest surprise, and entitled them to be esteemed, for the time at least, as superior to any other known in the world. The great multiplication of microscopic observers produced by the wonderful improvement of the instrument, and the great increase in the demand for objectives consequent upon the multiplication of observers, soon, however, produced the natural effect of rivalry among opticians, and foreign objectives appeared which justly challenged comparison with those of Mr. Spencer. In the subsequent progress of improvement the artisans of England, France, Germany, and the United States have maintained a pretty equal strife. Mr. Spencer still sustains the high reputation which he so early established; and upon the same plane with him may be placed Mr. R. B. Tolles, of Boston, and Mr. William Wales, of Fort Edward, New Jersey. Of the naturalists among us who have devoted themselves to the use of the microscope, none have done more honor to the science of our country than the late Professor Bailey, of West Point, whose contributions to the knowledge of the diatomaceæ are distributed through the journals and Transactions, and Professor H. L. Smith, of Hobart College, one of the highest living authorities upon this order of the algæ, who has now in the hands of the Smithsonian Institution, awaiting publication, a systematic and comprehensive monograph on the subject, founded on the studies and observations of twenty years, and illustrated with numerous original drawings from nature.

ELECTRICITY, MAGNETISM, ETC.

Down to the end of the eighteenth century the science of electricity existed only in a very elementary condition. Its phenomena, so far as they were known, belonged to static electricity only, and were referred to the agency of a subtle fluid or fluids present every where, but becoming manifest only when in a state of disturbed equilibrium. The hypothesis of a single electrical fluid is usually ascribed to Franklin, and passes by his name, though Leslie claims that it had been earlier suggested by Watson, of London. The opposing hypothesis of Dufay presumed the existence of two fluids neutralizing each other in the ordinary condition of bodies by their union, and exhibiting attractions and repulsions when separated. The Franklinian hypothesis is liable to the objection that it necessitates the supposition that material bodies deprived of electricity are mutually repellent. But neither is any longer entertained. Franklin demonstrated the identity of lightning with the ordinary electric spark as early as 1752. It is commonly believed that the first suspicion of this identity originated with him; but it had already been suggested by Nollet in 1746, who compared a thunder-cloud to the prime conductor of an electrical machine (it resembles more nearly one coating of a Leyden-jar), and had been urged in a plausible course of reasoning by Winkler. Franklin's merit was that he suggested the means of setting the question forever at rest by actually drawing electricity out of the clouds. It is a curious fact that he was not the first to try his own experiment. The plan he had publicly proposed was to erect on some eminence a lofty insulated iron rod tapering to a point; and this plan was followed by Dalibard, who drew sparks from such a rod erected near Paris, and even charged from it a Leyden-jar, as early as the 10th of May, 1752. The famous kite experiment of Franklin was performed more than a month later, on the 15th of June; but in those days, in which ocean cables and steamships were equally unknown, he was, of course, ignorant of Dalibard's previous success. It is upon this experiment that the immense reputation of Franklin as a man of science mainly rests. Considering the simplicity of the conception and the still greater simplicity of the apparatus by which it was realized, we can not at this distance of time but be astonished at the profound impression it produced upon the world. Such was his popularity in France that, when he appeared as the representative of the American colonies at the court of Louis XVI., the sale of his portrait made the fortune of the engraver; and beneath this portrait was inscribed, by the minister of a monarch himself a few years later dethroned and executed as a tyrant, the famous legend,

"Eripuit cœlo fulmen, sceptrumque tyrannis."

Not long after this, moreover, the celebrated Erasmus Darwin, writing to compliment Franklin on having united philosophy to modern science, directed his letter merely to "Dr. Franklin, *America*," adding that he was almost disposed to write "Dr. Franklin, *The World*," there being but one Franklin, and that Franklin being known of all men. After making all allowance for the weight of Franklin's political position and the sound practical sense displayed in his writings on subjects of popular interest, there remains no doubt that his singular celebrity was due mainly, after all, to the association of his name with the lightning. The great discovery of Volta, just at the close of the century, originated a new and prolific branch of electrical science, not at first recognized as such. In the infancy of the investigation which this discovery opened, it was a first necessity of progress to improve the means by which the electric current is generated. For the inconvenient pile of the discoverer, trough batteries with immovable plates were soon introduced in England, and it was by means of such that Sir Humphry Davy made many of his very numerous and celebrated electro-chemical discoveries. Dr. Wollaston greatly improved these batteries by giving them a construction which caused both sides of the zincs to be effective, and permitted the plates to be removed from the troughs. But all these forms of apparatus were attended with the serious disadvantage that their power when in action rapidly declined, in consequence of the formation upon the negatives of a coating of minute bubbles of hydrogen gas. This difficulty was first effectually overcome by Dr. Robert Hare, of Philadelphia, who in 1820 introduced the form of voltaic battery which, from the intensity of its effects, he called the deflagrator. The deflagrator was made very compact by forming the metals into coils, their opposed surfaces being very near to each other, but separated by insulating wedges; but its important characteristic consisted of a mechanism by which the entire series of elements could be instantaneously immersed in the liquid or lifted out. For experiments of brief duration, therefore, the battery was always ready to act with its full power. A similar device occurred later to Faraday, but though it was original with him, he very honorably admitted that on examination he found this new battery to be "in all essential respects the same as that invented and described by Dr. Hare." Besides the deflagrator, Dr. Hare constructed another form of voltaic apparatus, designed with low intensity of electricity to generate an enormous volume of heat. This, which he called the calorimotor, was formed by combining many very large plates of zinc and copper into two series, and immersing them at once into a tank of dilute acid. By means of it large rods of iron or platinum are ignited and fused in a few seconds, and its magnetic effects are equally surprising; yet it is hardly capable of producing the faintest spark between carbon electrodes. Dr. Hare was an extremely voluminous writer on subjects connected with voltaic electricity and chemistry. Nearly one hundred and fifty articles from his pen may be found in the *Journal of Science* alone. In invention he was wonderfully fertile, and in the variety of ingenious contrivances devised and constructed by him in aid of investigation or for purposes of illustration, he deserves to be ranked with men like Hooke, Wollaston, and Wheatstone.

The constant battery, the next improvement in voltaic electro-motive apparatus, was produced by Daniell in 1836. It is a battery of four elements, two metallic and two liquid, the liquids being separated by a porous partition. In this arrangement the nascent hydrogen set free on the zinc side, combining with the oxygen of the metallic base of the solution on the copper side, no longer appears in the gaseous form, and the obstruction it had occasioned to circulation is thus suppressed. Daniell, nevertheless, was not the first to suggest a battery of four elements. The credit of this suggestion is due to Dr. John W. Draper, of New York, who, as early as 1834, described such a battery in the Journal of the Franklin Institute.

The relation of electricity to magnetism was a discovery accidentally made by Oersted, of Copenhagen, in 1819. He noticed that if a wire conveying a voltaic current be brought near a suspended magnetic needle, the needle will be deflected from its normal position. This remarkable discovery was followed by one no less remarkable, made simultaneously by Arago and Davy, that the conducting wire itself, whatever may be the material it is composed of, is capable, while conveying the voltaic current, of attracting soft iron. Ampère next discovered that two wires conveying electric currents attract each other if the currents are in the same direction, and repel if the directions are opposite. Upon this he founded his celebrated theory which made magnetism only one of the forms of manifestation of electrical force. This theory suggested to Arago the idea that a steel needle might possibly be magnetized by subjecting it to the action of an electric current passing spirally round it. He tested the truth of this conjecture, and his experiment was a success. A repetition of this experiment in modified form by Sturgeon, of Woolwich, England, in 1825, drew after it important consequences. Bending a piece of stout iron wire into the form of a horseshoe, and coating it with varnish to secure insulation, he wound round this a copper wire, which he introduced into the battery circuit. The iron wire thus treated became temporarily a feeble horseshoe magnet, capable of sustaining a weight of two or three pounds. At this stage of the investigation the subject attracted the attention of Professor Joseph Henry, of Albany, New York, and the next step in the progress of this history—a very large one—was taken by him. Considering that the intensity of the effect must be proportioned to the closeness of the coil, and that with a naked conductor the spirals could not permissibly be brought into contact, it occurred to him to insulate the conducting wire itself, which he did by winding it with silk. This expedient enabled him not only to envelop the iron closely in the first instance, but also to wind several successive coils over each other. The result was to produce an electro-magnet in the proper sense of the word—an instrument not limited in its use to the purposes of lecture-room illustration, but capable of important and largely varied practical applications. Some of the magnets constructed by Professor Henry sustained weights of between one and two tons.

In pursuing his investigations on this subject, Professor Henry ascertained a number of important facts concerning the laws of development of magnetism in soft iron. Having surrounded a given bar with a number of short helices abutting end to end, he tried the effect of first uniting the similar ends of these so as to make one short compound conductor, and of afterward uniting their dissimilar ends so as to make a single continuous conductor of them all. With a battery of a few elements, the first arrangement proved to be most effective, but with one of many, the second was superior. Hence the distinction introduced by him between quantity and intensity magnets.

The possible practical applications of the electro-magnet were not overlooked by Professor Henry, though he contented himself with pointing them out without pursuing them. The practicability of an electric telegraph was illustrated by him in an apparatus fitted up in 1831 in the Albany Academy, by which an electric current transmitted through a circuit of more than a mile was made to ring a bell. The invention of the first recording magnetic telegraph—that is, of the instrument by which signals are actually written down by magnetism, and not merely addressed to the sense of hearing or sight—was made by Professor S. F. B. Morse, of New York. He had conceived it as early as 1832. The instrument did not take form till some years later. It was impossible that either mode of signaling (the mode actually used by Professor Henry in 1831 or that conceived by Professor Morse in 1832) should come into public use or be economically a possibility so long as there existed no form of constant or sustaining battery, and the batteries of Daniell and Grove were only known in 1836 and 1837.

In the construction of long lines of telegraph it became early necessary to devise some practicable means of crossing the larger streams or the narrower estuaries by means of submerged conductors. When this had been successfully accomplished, the same system was naturally extended to the smaller seas or arms of the ocean, such as the British Channel and the Mediterranean. But when, a little more than twenty years ago, it was first proposed to lay an electric cable from continent to continent in the bed of the ocean itself, the audacity of the project was such that, at its first announcement, it struck the world as too visionary to be seriously considered. Even to contrive a form of conductor which should combine the strength and completeness of insulation indispensable to such a purpose, was a problem in applied science of no slight difficulty, and to lay it in its place demanded the exercise of mechanical skill of the highest order. Supposing it to have been laid, science, again, had not yet devised the means of making it available. The exhaustless energy and indomitable perseverance of Mr. Cyrus W. Field nevertheless triumphed at last over all the practical difficulties; and the patient study of the scientific side of the question by the electricians, especially by Sir William Thomson, with his marvelous fertility of invention, was equally successful in overcoming the rest. The electrical telegraph, therefore, one of the most magnificent gifts of science to the world, may be justly claimed as especially a gift of American science, and the energy which was mainly instrumental in giving it its latest and largest availability was no less American.

Professor Henry was the first to point out the practicability of applying electro-magnetism as a motive power, and in illustration of this he constructed an oscillating apparatus, described in the *American Journal of Science* in 1829. The attempts which have been made to turn this power practically to account have been very numerous. Almost or quite the earliest was made by Messrs. Davenport and Cook, of Vermont, in 1836. A machine in model exhibited by them in New York attracted much attention; but a working engine which they subsequently attempted did not meet their expectations. In all these forms of mechanism there is one unavoidable disadvantage, which in the infancy of the science was not known, consisting in the fact that the moving magnets generate in each other currents directly opposed to those from which their own magnetic energy is derived; and hence the dynamic power of the engine is not proportional to the static energy of its component magnets. Electro-magnetic engines of some power have in a few instances been tried, and subsequently abandoned, not on account of any mechanical failure, but for reasons of economy. One of this description, constructed under the direction of De Jacobi at the expense of the Emperor of Russia, was employed to propel a boat on the Neva. Another was the electro-magnetic locomotive of our countryman, Dr. Charles G. Page. This was remarkable for its original and ingenious method of applying the power, which was by means of solid cylindrical steel magnets rising and descending in the interior of a pile of short helices, the helices being successively thrown into and out of the circuit. With two such engines, Dr. Page drove a car weighing eleven tons and carrying fourteen passengers on a level track at the rate of nineteen miles an hour. Electro-magnetic engines can never compete with steam-engines in point of economy until it shall be possible to construct batteries in which the materials consumed shall be, weight for weight, a great deal cheaper than coal. Experimentally it has been proved that a grain of coal consumed under the boiler of a Cornish engine lifts 143 pounds one foot high, while a grain of zinc consumed in a battery to move an electro-magnetic engine lifts only eighty pounds to the same height. But it requires the consumption of a number of grains of coal to produce one grain of zinc.

The applications of the electro-magnet to purposes of use are too various to permit here an enumeration in detail. The astronomical electro-magnetic chronograph has been already mentioned. The instruments for measuring still more minute intervals of time, called chronoscopes, are dependent, in several of their large variety of forms, on similar means of operation. This same remark may be made of numerous very ingenious and very valuable contrivances introduced in recent years for demonstrating the laws of falling bodies, for registering vibrations in acoustics, for recording the indications of meteorological instruments, and for many other purposes auxiliary to scientific investigation.

As more practical applications, there may be mentioned fire-alarms, by means of which information of the exact locality of a fire in any large city may be instantaneously communicated to the central office, and definite orders issued at once to fire-companies how to proceed; burglar-alarms, which instantly indicate the door or window in a dwelling at which entrance has been attempted, and at the same time turn on a light and arouse the sleepers by ringing bells or sounding rattles; time-balls dropped in centres of business or in sea-ports by electrical communication from distant astronomical observatories; and clocks operated by electro-magnetism as a motive power, or systems of dials by which a single clock may show simultaneously the same time in every part of a large business establishment. In the year 1859 a clock of peculiar and original design, operated by electro-magnetism, was constructed, under the direction of the writer of this article, by Mr. E. S. Ritchie, of Boston, for the observatory of the University of Mississippi. The pendulum was entirely free, the force required to maintain its motion being applied by depositing a very light weight (of one or two grains) upon an arm of the pendulum at the beginning of the swing, and removing it in the middle, by an arrangement of electro-magnets. The small weight served itself to make and break the battery connections necessary to actuate the auxiliary mechanism. The intention was, by relieving the pendulum from the work of operating the escapement, and by reducing its swing as low as possible (to a fraction of a degree), to remove every external cause which might interfere with the perfect uniformity of its beat. But a very low power was required to run it. A single cell of Farmer's so-called water battery (pure water next the zinc, and copper sulphate next the copper) was sufficient to maintain its action, but two were commonly used. Mechanically it was a perfect success, but after some months of action it was found that the electric contacts became vitiated by the spark produced, even with that low power, at every rupture of the circuit, and the current ceased to flow. Though the most refractory metals were employed, they were still vaporized and oxidized. The difficulty was at length overcome by introducing Fizeau's condenser into the circuit, by which the spark was effectually suppressed; but owing to the troubles of the times, which prevented the completion of the observatory, it was never brought into use.

Within recent years some interesting contributions to the progress of electro-magnetic science have been made in this country by Professor A. F. Mayer, of Hoboken, New Jersey, Professor John Trowbridge, of Harvard University, and others. Professor Mayer's experiments have led to some very important deductions as to the most effective forms of soft iron core to be given to electro-magnets, and have shown that in general, when such cores are solid cylinders, the central portion is practically ineffective, and may be removed without diminishing the power of the magnet. They have shown also that the inducing action of the enveloping wire on itself, or that of the adjoining spirals on each other, has no effect on their power to magnetize the core, or on the intensity of the current passing through them. We owe also to Professor Mayer one of the most delicate and at the same time simple modes yet devised of investigating the resistance of conductors to electric currents passing through them.

That the molecular changes produced in a bar of iron by magnetization are attended with simultaneous changes of dimensions, was rendered probable by the observation (made many years ago by Dr. Page) that they are attended by audible sounds, and was experimentally proved by Joule and Wertheim. By a very elaborate and carefully conducted investigation, aided by the exceedingly delicate micrometric comparator constructed for the Coast Survey by Mr. Joseph Saxton, Professor Mayer has determined quantitatively the precise character and magnitude of these changes. Professor Trowbridge has also made some interesting discoveries relating to this subject, among which is the fact that if the core of an electro-magnet be made a part of a voltaic circuit, and the magnetizing current be then sent through the enveloping helix by another battery, a magnetic power may be obtained materially greater than that which the latter current is capable of producing alone, but that this effect will not be repeated if the magnetizing circuit be broken and again renewed.

Voltaic Induction.—The power of a voltaic current to induce currents in neighboring conductors was discovered by Faraday in 1831. If both conductors are motionless, the induced current is but momentary, occurring only when the primary current begins or ceases to flow. If they approach toward or recede from each other, the induced current is continuous so long as this movement continues, being opposite in direction to the primary while approaching, and similar in direction while receding. By using helices instead of single conductors, Mr. Faraday succeeded in producing induced currents of great energy. In the same year Professor Henry made the remarkable discovery that a voltaic current induces an extra current in the conductor in which it is itself conveyed, which, however, manifests itself only on making or breaking connection with the battery, the intensity being proportional to the length of the conductor, and being greatly increased by giving the conductor the form of a close spiral. Professor Henry demonstrated later that, if a series of closed circuits be placed side by side, the first receiving a primary current from the battery, then on making or breaking battery connection a series of induced currents will be generated in these several circuits, which will be alternately in opposite directions. The system of conductors best adapted to this demonstration is a series of flat spirals known as Henry's coils, formed of wire, or better of copper ribbon, insulated. Induced currents of the ninth order have thus been demonstrated, and the possible number is theoretically unlimited.

Magneto-Electricity.—The year 1831 was very fruitful of electrical discovery. It was in this year that Faraday detected the power of a permanent steel magnet to induce electric currents in neighboring conductors, and in this year also he succeeded in producing from the induction of such a magnet a visible electric spark. From this memorable discovery the science of magneto-electricity takes its date. Almost immediately after it a powerful magneto-electric machine was constructed by Mr. Joseph Saxton, of Philadelphia, which was almost the first of its kind. Another, still more powerful, was subsequently invented by Dr. Page, who added the simple but ingenious contrivance called the pole-changer, by which the currents, incessantly reversed in the helices of the machine, are transmitted through the circuit in one constant direction. With this improvement the machine may be made a substitute for a galvanic battery in the operations of electrolysis. Magneto-electric machines have consequently in recent years to a large extent superseded batteries for many important practical purposes. The galvano-plastic art, so largely employed in copying in fac-simile objects of ornament and use, in plating and gilding, in duplicating the plates of the engraver, in stereotyping pages for the letter-press, and in a variety of other ways, is now conducted almost entirely by the use of these machines. Constructed on a large scale, they have been employed by the governments of France and England to furnish electric lights for some of their most important light-houses.

Induction Coils.—After the power of a permanent magnet to induce electric currents had been demonstrated, it could not be doubted that electro-magnets would do the same. This was Faraday's inference, and experiment confirmed the anticipation. A secondary coil, surrounding but independent of the coil of an electro-magnet, gave currents whenever the battery connection of the magnet was made or broken. In this discovery is found the first suggestion of a form of electrical apparatus which has in recent years become a powerful instrument of physical investigation, the induction coil. In its earliest form this apparatus was the invention of our countryman, Dr. Page, and was called by him the "separable helix." There was an inner helix, fixed upright upon a support, into the hollow interior of which might be introduced bars or wires of soft iron. An outer helix, which was removable, was designed to convey the induced current. Dr. Page, in the study of this instrument, made several important discoveries. These were, first, that the intensity of the induced current may be greatly increased by making the wire of the secondary coil many times longer, and also very much smaller, than the primary; secondly, that the effect of a number of soft iron wires introduced into the inner coil is vastly greater than that obtainable from the same weight of iron in a single bar; and thirdly, that unless the primary current is broken very abruptly, the induced current of that circuit will leap over the break, neutralizing to some extent, by secondary induction, the induced current in the outer coil. To counteract this he invented an ingenious and successful contrivance called the spark-arresting circuit-breaker. These discoveries date back to 1838 and earlier. In 1853 Mr. Fizeau, of Paris, suggested the use of a condenser constructed on the principle of the Leyden-jar, as a means of absorbing the extra current in the primary; and this has since superseded Page's circuit-breaker. About the same time Mr. Ruhmkorff, of Paris, commenced the construction of the induction coils known by his name, which were in no respect different, except in magnitude, from the separable helices of Page above described, but which attracted much attention in consequence of the length of spark they produced. This, in Page's instrument, had hardly exceeded one-eighth of an inch; but in Ruhmkorff's it was increased to nearly an entire inch, and in his later instruments to two or three inches. A practical limit to increase of power in this direction was, however, found in the liability of currents of high intensity to strike through the insulation from layer to layer of the secondary coil. This liability is the greater in proportion as the points of the wire of the helix which are brought near each other in winding are more distant as measured upon the length of the wire itself. As a means of preventing it, it occurred to Mr. Ritchie to wind the wire in many flat spirals, placing these side by side and connecting them at their inner and outer extremities, so as to form a continuous helical conductor of which no two points should be more distant from each other, measured along the wire, than the length of two such contiguous spirals, developed. The result was a surprising increase in the length of spark, which has been carried up by him to twelve, fifteen, and even twenty inches. One of Mr. Ritchie's coils was exhibited in Paris in 1860, by Professor McCulloh, of Columbia College, New York. By an examination of this, Mr. Ruhmkorff became acquainted with the mode of its construction, which Mr. Ritchie had not previously disclosed, and adopting it, produced others of enormous power—one of which projected sparks two feet in length. For this great success, mainly due to the ingenuity of our countryman, Mr. Ruhmkorff received in 1864 the prize of 50,000 francs offered in 1852 by Napoleon III. for the most important discovery connected with the progress of electricity.

Static Electricity.—Some very interesting discoveries in static electricity were made by Professor Henry as early as 1830. He demonstrated that the discharge of a Leyden-jar consists of a series of oscillations backward and forward, something like the vibration of a spring. The mode of proof employed in this demonstration is at once simple and ingenious. It rests on the two experimentally ascertained facts—first, that a steel needle may be magnetized by surrounding it with a spiral conductor, and sending through the conductor the discharge of a Leyden-jar; and secondly, that there is a point of saturation beyond which the needle will not receive magnetism. By passing successive discharges of gradually increasing intensity through the coil, the needle will undergo changes of polarity, showing that it derives its magnetism alternately from the direct and the reversed movement of the electric force. It follows that the electric spark, though to the eye apparently single, is, in fact, made up of many sparks. This multiplicity has recently been optically demonstrated by Professor Rood, of Columbia College, who, by means of a rapidly rotating mirror, has made the successive component sparks visible. A very striking palpable demonstration of the same fact was also exhibited to the National Academy of Sciences in November, 1874, by Professor A. M. Mayer, of Hoboken, New Jersey. Professor Mayer caused disks of blackened tissue-paper to revolve with great rapidity between the points through which the discharge of the Leyden-jar is made. Subsequent examination of the disk shows it to be perforated with a very great number of minute holes along the circular arc which was passing between the points during the brief continuance of the discharge.

The fact which he had demonstrated of the jar, Professor Henry afterward proved to be true of thunder-clouds. These stand to the earth beneath them in the relation of the coatings of the jar, the stratum of air between being the insulating medium. When the insulation is broken through, the lightning flash which follows is multiple and oscillating, presenting on a grand scale an analogy to the discharge of the jar.

The duration of flashes of lightning, as well as of the spark from the jar, has been the subject of interesting investigations by Professor Rood, in which he has succeeded in measuring more minute intervals of time than have ever before been made the subject of exact determination. By his methods, which appear to be quite unexceptionable, it is proved that a jar of small surface discharges itself in a space of time not greater than forty one-billionths of a second; and that its light, though of inconceivably brief duration, makes surrounding objects perfectly visible. As there is reason to believe that this time is at least tenfold greater than is necessary to impress the retina, it follows that the perfect sensation of vision may be excited in an interval as brief as four one-billionths of a second. The duration of lightning flashes is much greater. Besides investigating the form and nature of the spark by optical methods, as already mentioned, Professor Rood has employed photography in the same research, and has demonstrated marked differences between the positive and negative sparks, as well as between the sparks obtained through the jar from the induction coil and from the common frictional machine.

In thermo-electricity not much has been done by American investigators. In 1840 Dr. J. W. Draper published a memoir on the electro-motive power of heat, with descriptions of improved thermo-electrical couples. A pretty effective thermo-electric battery has been constructed by Mr. Farmer, of Boston, thirty-six elements of which are about equivalent to one of Grove's nitric acid elements. Professor Rood has made an interesting application of a thermo-electrical couple to the determination of the heat produced by percussion when the mechanical force exerted is very small. He has been able thus to demonstrate that in the fall of a weight of a single pound through trivial heights, varying from one to five inches, the amount of heat generated is measurable, and is directly as the amount of living force acquired by the body in falling.

CHEMISTRY.

Chemistry as a science may be said to have been the creation of the century we are reviewing. Many important facts which have now a recognized place in this science had, it is true, been previously gathered; but they were either facts of accidental discovery, or they had been discovered in the course of investigations guided by no intelligent theory. The doctrine of phlogiston, introduced early in the eighteenth century by Stahl, though now usually spoken of as a reproach to the science of that age, was really a step of progress, for it was part of a system which proposed to ascertain by experimental research the elementary composition of natural bodies. But it is also true that the overthrow of that doctrine by Lavoisier, near the end of the same century, forms the epoch from which modern chemistry in a proper sense takes its rise. The contemporaries of this great philosopher, Black, Cavendish, and Priestley in England, Scheele in Sweden, and Wenzel in Saxony, contributed largely by their discoveries, and by their researches on heat and on the laws of chemical affinity, to build up the new science on a rational basis. The doctrine of definite proportions, which had been already substantially established by the labors of Higgins, Proust, and Richter, was formally announced by Dalton in his atomic theory, taught as early as 1804 and published in 1808. The question whether there does not exist, also, a law of definite proportion between the combining or equivalent weights of the different bodies called elementary, was naturally suggested as a consequence of this discovery. When the numbers are compared with the assumption of any particular equivalent weight as unity, while the results are in many cases integral, there remain always some which continue to be fractional. A comparatively recent and laborious investigation of this subject, however, by Dumas, has led to the result that when a unit is adopted which is equal to one-fourth of the equivalent weight of hydrogen, all the numbers are integral. It is, therefore, a view not without plausibility, entertained by some chemists at present, that all the bodies commonly called elementary may be compounds; and even that, on a complete decomposition of them all, there might remain but a single elementary substance. The power of heat, when sufficiently exalted in temperature, to break up all known chemical compounds, has been fully established of late years by Henri St. Clair Deville; and spectroscopic observation has shown that many substances exist as vapors in the sun and the stars which no degree of heat which we can artificially produce upon the earth is competent to vaporize. It is therefore not unreasonable to presume that, if there is such a primitive elementary matter as is above supposed, it may be set free in the intense heat of the self-luminous celestial bodies. And it is an interesting fact that, in the spectroscopic examination of the envelopes of the sun, there are detected lines which belong to no element known upon our planet, and which seem also to indicate the presence of a substance lighter than hydrogen.

Organic chemistry, or the chemistry of animal and vegetable compounds, became early a distinct department of the science. The study of organized bodies led to the discovery of *series*, in which a number of bodies differ from each other only in the number of times a simpler definite combination is repeated in their formulæ. This discovery was first distinctly announced by

Dr. James Shiel, of St. Louis, Missouri. In this same study also was found the conception of types, in which one element may be replaced by another—a conception which lies at the foundation of the chemical science of the present day. This conception, originated by Dumas, and followed up and developed by Laurent and Gerhardt, was first reduced to its most simple and satisfactory form of expression by Professor T. Sterry Hunt, now of Boston, who so early as 1848 demonstrated that all the various saline forms are reducible to two, the types of which are seen in water, and in hydrogen with the equivalent doubled. In a series of papers published subsequently at intervals, Professor Hunt further applied these views and extended them to embrace the multiple or condensed types afterward adopted by Williamson and Gerhardt, to whom the entire credit of these important generalizations has been often ascribed in foreign publications.

So wide is the field covered by the science of chemistry, and so rapid has been the growth of the science during the last half century, that any attempt in the brief space at our disposal to do justice to the numerous laborers to whose activity this great progress is due, would be vain. In this department of science our country has produced a larger number of active investigators than in any other, and of these also a larger proportion have become honorably eminent. We must content ourselves in this place with mentioning a few only of the names which have become worthily identified with the history of American chemistry. Among the early teachers of this science in our country who, without engaging largely in original research, did good service in their enlightened defense of the doctrines of the new school of Lavoisier, may be fitly mentioned Dr. John Maclean, of Princeton College (elected 1795), Dr. Benjamin Rush, of the University of Pennsylvania (1769), Dr. James Woodhouse, of the same institution (1795), and Dr. Samuel L. Mitchill, of Columbia College, New York (1792). Both Dr. Woodhouse and Dr. Mitchill published somewhat largely upon chemical topics. Dr. Mitchill was a man of exceptionally varied attainments, but his favorite studies were in natural history, especially in zoology, in which he was long regarded as the highest authority in the United States.

In 1801 there was read before the Chemical Society of Philadelphia a memoir "On the Supply and Application of the Blow-Pipe," by a young man of twenty years of age, destined subsequently to attain a high celebrity—Robert Hare. In this was described the apparatus long known as "Hare's compound blow-pipe," and more recently as the oxyhydrogen blow-pipe, the most powerful means yet known for generating artificial heat. The apparatus referred to was not so much an invention, in the ordinary sense of the word, as a logical deduction from a consideration of the conditions necessary to secure the maximum effect from a given amount of heat generated. Lavoisier and others had obtained remarkable effects by directing a stream of oxygen upon ignited carbon. In this case, however, though the body to be operated on was raised to a very high temperature on the side which rested on the carbon support, this temperature did not reach the upper surface, and the fusion or volatilization attempted was only partially accomplished. Mr. Hare reflected that this difficulty might be got over if some means could be discovered of "clothing the upper surface with some burning matter the heat of which might be equal to that of the incandescent carbon." It soon occurred to him that a flame produced by the combustion of the oxygen and hydrogen gases ought, "according to the theory of the French chemists" (for this was in advance of any demonstration), to be attended with a higher heat than even that generated by the combustion of carbon. But it was known that a mixture of oxygen and hydrogen in proper proportion to produce a complete combustion is dangerously explosive, and in order to attain the end in view some means of creating the flame had to be devised which should be free from this danger. The expedient actually adopted—that of storing the gases in separate vessels and bringing them together by tubes which meet at the point of ignition—seems simple enough now; but that it was not so obvious as it seems is made evident by the fact that, some fifteen years later, Dr. E.

D. Clarke, Professor of Mineralogy in Cambridge, England, introduced and employed an oxyhydrogen blow-pipe in which the gases were mingled in explosive proportions in the same vessel. If Dr. Clarke, in 1816, knew nothing of what Hare had done in 1802, and had described in the same year in *Tilloch's Philosophical Magazine*, the construction he gave his apparatus proves that the artifice by which the original inventor provided against the possibility of explosion was one which would not readily occur to any but an ingenious mind. If he did possess a previous knowledge of the invention of Hare, his silence in his own paper in regard to it admits of no honorable explanation. The blow-pipe was but one of Dr. Hare's very numerous contributions to the instrumental means of chemical investigation, but we have room for the mention of no other.

Professor Benjamin Silliman, the elder, Professor of Chemistry in Yale College (elected 1802), continued for a long series of years to occupy a very conspicuous position in the world of American science. Though he published a large number of papers on chemical topics, as well as a voluminous systematic treatise on the general subject, his early acquired reputation rested in great measure on his eloquent and forceful presentation of the truths of science to his numerous classes and to popular audiences. The monument which will speak most enduringly of his labors, however, is undoubtedly the *Journal of Science*, one of the most powerful stimulants of the scientific spirit which has existed among us, established by him when this spirit was at a low ebb, and maintained by him almost single-handed for years under discouragements against which few would have had the energy to persevere.

Dr. Samuel Guthrie, of Sackett's Harbor, New York, deserves mention here as the discoverer of the very remarkable anæsthetic compound known as chloroform. It is a little curious that the same discovery was made about the same time by Soubeiran, a French chemist, and that both discoverers were similarly mistaken as to its nature, and both called it chloric ether. Soubeiran published his discovery in February, 1831, and Guthrie his in January, 1832. It was not till 1834 that the true constitution of the substance was understood, when it was analyzed by Dumas, who gave it the name it has since borne.

The numerous and important contributions of Dr. John W. Draper to physical science have been already mentioned. His chemical researches are scarcely less original, though many of them occupy the border region between physics and chemistry. The most noticeable are his ingenious experiments and deductions on osmosis, and on interstitial movements taking place among the molecules of a solid, as in cases of alloys in which the adulterating metals make their way to the surface. Also his beautiful and sensitive photometric apparatus, called by him originally the tithometer, in which chlorine and hydrogen are mingled in combining proportions. In absolute darkness the gases remain free, but on exposure to light they combine with a rapidity dependent on the intensity. One of his later publications is his treatise on *Human Physiology*, which discusses with much originality questions concerning the chemistry of animal life, as well as the chemical and physical functions of the various organs of the body.

Dr. William B. Rogers, of Boston, has published many chemical papers, some of them of special interest. One of these embraces the discovery that the thermal springs of Virginia contain free nitrogen in large proportion, exceeding in quantity the carbonic acid and the hydrogen sulphide. Another describes a method of determining carbon in graphite, which is still one of the best methods of effecting the same determination in the analysis of cast iron.

Dr. Charles T. Jackson, of Boston, has been one of the most active investigators the country has produced. His chemical and geological papers number nearly seventy. What has given him probably a wider reputation than any other of his discoveries has been the efficacy of ether to produce anæsthesia. For this he has been made the recipient of honorable decorations from many European governments, yet his title to the credit attributed to him has been contested by two of his countrymen, both now deceased—Dr. W. T. G. Morton, of Boston, and Dr. Horace Wells, of Hartford.

Dr. James Blake, of San Francisco, is noticeable for his interesting researches in physiological chemistry made by experiments on the living subject. Two of his conclusions are striking: first, that the character of the changes produced in living matter by inorganic compounds depends more on the physical properties of the reagent than on the chemical; and second, that the action of such compounds on living matter appears not to be related to the changes which they produce in the same substances when not living.

Dr. Wolcott Gibbs, now Rumford Professor of the Applications of Science in Harvard University, commenced his career as an investigator while an under-graduate in Columbia College, in 1840, in a description of a new form of magneto-electric machine, and an account of a carbon voltaic battery. This, it will be perceived, was earlier than the date of Bunsen's carbon battery. The contributions of Dr. Gibbs both to chemistry and to physics have been very numerous. The more important relating to chemistry are, "New General Methods of Chemical Analysis," "Theory of Polybasic Acids," "Researches on the Platinum Metals," and, in association with Professor Genth, "Researches on the Ammonio-Cobalt Bases"—a memoir which occupied the authors several years, and is more full of new results than any chemical research before undertaken in this country. This was published in 1857 among the *Smithsonian Contributions to Knowledge.*

Dr. Gibbs has recently announced the empirical discovery of a new optical constant, which may possibly prove to be an important contribution to the resources of the analytic chemist. The number of interference bands produced in the spectrum between two given wave lengths by the partial interception of the light falling on the prism by any transparent substance is different for different substances, and for the same substance diminishes as the density diminishes with increase of temperature. For any given substance, therefore, and for a constant thickness, the actual number of bands produced, divided by the density, gives a sensibly constant quotient; and this quotient is called by Dr. Gibbs the interferential constant. Its value in mixtures is a function of the values belonging to the components, and in compounds a function, apparently, of those of the molecular constituents; hence its probable usefulness in the operations of analysis.

Professor Frederick A. Genth, of the University of Pennsylvania, a native of Germany, was a chemist of distinction before coming to this country. The first ammonio-cobalt bases were discovered by him in 1846. As an analytic chemist he is without a superior. His chemical labors of recent years have been chiefly contributions to the chemical constitution of minerals.

Dr. J. Lawrence Smith, of Louisville, is the author of many valuable researches in chemistry and mineralogy. In 1850 he addressed an important memoir to the Academy of Sciences of Paris on the geology, mineralogy, and chemical history of emery, prepared after a thorough examination of the emery deposits of Asia Minor. This subject had been previously but little understood, and the memoir was received with marks of high approbation. Dr. Smith has made larger investigations upon the physical and chemical constitution of meteorites than any other American chemist. Of his very numerous scientific papers he has recently collected and published forty-seven in a volume.

Professor T. Sterry Hunt, whose name has been already mentioned, has been the most active contributor to theoretic chemistry in the United States. The credit due to him in the construction of the theory of types has been already mentioned. His various memoirs on chemical geology published from 1859 to 1870 have made him, perhaps, the highest living authority upon that subject. In fertility he is unrivaled, having within the last thirty years produced between one hundred and fifty and two hundred scientific papers, many of them elaborate.

Dr. J. P. Cooke, of Harvard University, is another of our prominent chemists whose labors have done much to advance theoretical chemistry. He is the author of *Chemical Physics* and *First Principles of Chemical Philosophy*, both of them profound and admirable expositions of theory, and of other publications of less extent, exhibiting great originality. One of these, a memoir on the numerical relations between atomic weights, and the classification of the chemical elements, elicited expressions of high commendation from Sir John Herschel before the British Association for the Advancement of Science.

The applications of chemistry to the arts are too various, too large, and too multiplied to admit of enumeration here. There is scarcely a department of industry into which they do not enter; while, on the other hand, there are many industries which, without this science, could not exist at all. In the words of Dr. J. Lawrence Smith at the Priestley centennial, "Industrial chemistry links itself with every modern art in such an intimate manner that were we to take away the influence and results of chemistry, it would be almost like taking away the laws of gravity from the universe; industrial chaos would result in one case, as material chaos would in the other." In some instances chemistry has rendered to industry a reduplicated aid—first, by creating or by greatly improving the industry itself; and secondly, by providing in wonderfully increased abundance or at wonderfully diminished expense the material on which or through which the industry is exercised. For instance, the manufactures of glass, of soap, and of textile fabrics, while indebted in a variety of ways unnecessary to specify to chemical science, are largely dependent upon a particular chemical product, the carbonate of soda, commonly called in commerce soda-ash. By the substitution, early in this century, of the manufactured carbonate, derived by a chemical process from common salt, instead of the natural substance previously obtained from sea-weed, the price was reduced to the tenth or twelfth part of what it had been before. By a new and more recently invented process this cost is likely to be reduced still lower. Again, in the manufacture of paper, to which chemistry has in various ways contributed, great embarrassments have in later years been experienced in consequence of the growth of a demand outrunning the supply of the substances out of which paper is made. Chemistry has done much to meet this demand by rendering available vast masses of rags which from discoloration had been previously unavailable, and by converting the fibre of various kinds of wood and grasses into suitable material for the same manufacture. Early in this century the process of bleaching linens occupied many months, and was attended with much labor, and some hazard of loss from mildew. Chemistry has made this a process occupying at present but a few hours. To every department of metallurgy chemistry has largely contributed, as is illustrated by the Bessemer process for steel, and in nearly every economical process in use for the precious metals. To the dyer's art a whole series of the most brilliant colors has been supplied, rivaling and often surpassing the rarest and most costly of those which have been hitherto only obtainable from natural sources. To the miner and the engineer have been furnished, in gun-cotton, nitro-glycerine, dynamite, and other explosive compounds, sources of resistless energy to aid in the prosecution of their often gigantic undertakings. The sources of artificial illumination at present in general use—viz., kerosene, stearine, paraffine, and coal gas—are the gifts exclusively of chemistry to the common uses of life. Fifty years ago the substance known as India rubber had no use but that which its name implies, to efface the marks of the draughtsman's pencil. At present, under the transformations given to it by chemistry, it enters into a larger variety of manufactures than almost any other material, except wood and a few of the metals.

The benefits rendered to the science of medicine by chemical discovery and chemical art are beyond calculation. An entirely new pharmacopœia has been created by it, in which the active principles of the drugs known to the old have been separated from the masses of inert matter with which they are naturally combined; and to these, new compounds have been added of an efficacy in assuaging pain or subduing disease surpassing all former experience. Of the wonderful variety of exquisite perfumes now offered to the choice of the fashionable world, only a very limited number are any longer sought from natural sources. Most are artificial products, in which chemical art has outdone nature. The numerous delicious preparations by which the confectioner succeeds in delighting the palates of the lovers of sweet things are due to a similar origin. Of the different descriptions of strong liquors, of which, to the misfortune of mankind, so incredible quantities are annually consumed as beverages, under the names of rum, gin, choice brandies, superior old Bourbon, Monongahela, etc., probably half or more than half the quantities sold are merely dilute solutions of alcohol, to which chemically prepared essential oils and chemically prepared sugars have communicated so perfectly the odors, flavors, and colors of the liquor imitated, as to defy detection by the most practiced dealer or drinker. In this case it is some compensation to be able to say that the chemical substances employed are entirely innocent, and that the liquors so manufactured, contrary to the popular impression, have nothing in them more noxious than the alcohol they contain; which, however, is just as noxious in the genuine liquors of the same name. Some of the gifts of chemistry to the ordinary uses of life have been so long and so constantly familiar that we habitually forget the source to which we owe them. The adhesive stamp, the gun-cap, the lucifer-match, are used daily and hourly by multitudes to whom it never for a moment occurs that science has had any thing to do with their production. And thus it happens, not only in small things but in great, that precisely in the points in which science has been most serviceable to mankind, her services, for the very reason that they are most constantly in sight, cease to be regarded as services, but are habitually confounded in the common mind with the things which come into existence in the ordinary course of nature's operations.

In closing this cursory sketch of a century's progress in science, a word may not be out of place as to the effect of this progress on the mental characteristics of the race. It is certain that not only has increase of knowledge largely modified prevalent popular opinions in regard to natural phenomena, but also that the modes by which knowledge has been increased have still more largely modified the spirit in which every new question is received which addresses the popular judgment. Even the less educated in enlightened lands no longer tremble at the advent of a comet, or imagine human destinies to be controlled by the stars, or see a mischievous sprite in the Will-o'-the-wisp, or conceive it possible for man by magical arts to subvert the ordinary course of nature. One by one those mysteries in natural things which to the common mind have heretofore from the foundation of the world been associated with the supernatural, have resolved themselves, under the scrutiny of scientific investigation, into their simple natural causes. The rainbow, the lightning, the tempest, the earthquake, the volcano, the aurora borealis, the star-shower, and even the rarer and more startling phenomenon, the shower of seeming blood, by which whole provinces have been occasionally appalled, are no longer regarded as evidences of the arbitrary interposition of invisible agencies, and no longer afford cause for either alarm or encouragement. It is a dogma of modern science that all the phenomena of the natural world, without exception, are subject to unalterable law; and accordingly that mysteries, wherever they still exist, are only evidences of our still existing ignorance. Standing upon this law, the investigator accepts no solution of a difficulty which does not clearly associate the observed effect with its efficient cause. For him authority has no weight whatever. He demands incontrovertible proof for every proposition advanced. The scientific spirit is, therefore, not a spirit of respect for traditions as traditions. It respects them only for the truth they contain. Its motto is, Prove all things —hold fast that which is good.

This spirit, which has been always that of the true investigators of nature, has in past centuries been confined almost exclusively to those who were immediately engaged in such investigation. The popular spirit has been directly opposed to it, even up to the point of hostility and bitterness; so that any man who, like Albertus Magnus, or Roger Bacon, or Baptista Porta, allowed himself to seek for natural causes in natural things, drew upon himself the dangerous suspicion of dealing with spirits of darkness. Those were ages in which authority was all in all; in our own, this matter is entirely reversed, and authority has ceased to be any thing.

The effect of this change is especially noticeable in the discussion of questions which concern education. The ancient learning is no longer respected because it is ancient. Rather, on the contrary, its claim to precedence as the basis of the highest education is prejudiced by the consideration that it was the only learning of the age which gave it such prominence. Larger space is naturally demanded for that new knowledge which is the growth of our own time, and is based on positive demonstration—knowledge which reveals to us the natural laws under the rigorous rule of which we are compelled to live, and which it concerns the immediate welfare of every individual to know. Hence the growing favor for what in recent years has received the name of "the new education." It is a demand that of the three elements, the good, the true, and the beautiful, the second shall have as full a recognition as the other two.

The same effect may be observed in the discussion of religious questions. The basis of belief is investigated with a freedom unknown to other centuries. This is not merely the prompting of a skeptical spirit. If the unbeliever would discredit revelation, the believer no less desires to give a reason for the faith that is in him. There is no ground for the imputation which we hear occasionally expressed, that science is hostile to religion, or that infidelity is more rife in the present age than in the last. Modern science hardly existed when the French Republic, "one and indivisible," abolished religion by public decree. The thing which is true is that the infidelity of our time is open in its utterance, while that of other periods has been restrained by fear of penalties both judicial and social. It is in the nature of things impossible that science and religion should be in conflict, since truth, which is the aim of the one, is also the substance of the other, and truth can never be inconsistent with itself.

A failure to recognize this simple principle has operated more powerfully than any other cause to retard the progress of the world's enlightenment; and it must be counted as the largest of the services which modern science with its methods of free inquiry has rendered to the race, that it has burst at length the shackles by which human thought has been held for centuries in bondage.

II.—NATURAL SCIENCE.

At the commencement of the century which is distinguished by the existence of the United States of America as an independent nation, students of nature had regard almost alone to "natural history," or the observation and description of what in nature immediately appealed to their senses.

At the present time the "natural sciences" are acknowledged constituents of general science, that great superstructure which enables us by a long-established series of observations and assured deductions to predicate the nature of the unseen from what has been observed, and to throw into a few terse general propositions and principles the results of all our studies.

How the several branches of natural history have grown and developed into the natural sciences, and what quota America has contributed to this progress, will be the subject of inquiry in this chapter.

The distinction just indicated between the stages of our knowledge of natural objects in times past and present is exemplified in the relations of the several branches to schemes of classification of general knowledge. In the celebrated synopsis of Bacon, in which the triple division is based on the faculties which are called into activity in the consideration of the various branches, "natural history" is placed with "civil history" as a branch wherein "memory" is chiefly demanded, while the "mathematical sciences" belong to the domain over which "reason" presides—"philosophy." Such was in his time and long afterward, and, in fact, until this century had well advanced, to some extent a true exhibit of the facts and the mode of study of nature. Natural history was, indeed, a mere record of empirical observations and of the crude impressions produced on the senses. The chief aim of the naturalist was then to know the name of a given species, and only long afterward did the name become of secondary importance, and simply a means toward an end, that end being the knowledge of the relations of the forms in question to others, and, *a posteriori*, to the economy and plan of nature.

FIRST STEPS.

It was in 1766 that Linnæus published his last edition of the *Systema Naturæ;* in the earlier editions of that celebrated work he had, in intention at least, incorporated all the species of animals, plants, and minerals which had been made known in a recognizable manner by his predecessors and contemporaries, and, in this final edition published during his lifetime, he had systematically applied the binomial method of nomenclature, which has been so powerful an auxiliary as a method of notation to the naturalist; he also revised, and in a number of cases very materially modified, the arrangement adopted in the previous editions of his work, and he added the species in each department of nature which had in the mean while been described. This, therefore, will furnish a fitting starting-point for our inquiries in each case; and this work, be it observed, was almost the last in which a single naturalist attempted to cover the whole domain of nature, and to recapitulate all known species. The impulse which had been given to the cultivation of natural history, and the zeal with which travelers collected, as well as the researches of the European colonists in the lands of their adoption, soon increased the numbers of species to such an extent that their survey by one man became impossible.

The species of animals and plants—especially the former—known to Linnæus from America, or at least from the limits of the present United States, were comparatively few. It is true that in numerous works devoted to the description of the country or its several parts the characteristic species were enumerated, and even alleged lists of species were published; but in few cases were they scientifically or at all intelligibly described: in default of specimens, therefore, they could not be incorporated in the *Systema Naturæ*. Linnæus was consequently confined in his work to the descriptions or identifications of the species which were in the museums or herbaria of Europe accessible to him, or which had been sent to him by American correspondents, among the most conspicuous of whom were Cadwallader Colden, of New York, and Alexander Garden, of South Carolina. A student of his own, the afterward well-known Kalm, in 1747 and 1748 visited this country and collected especially the plants. The comparative facilities then enjoyed for the manipulation of plants, the tastes of his correspondents, and, indeed, Linnæus's own greater familiarity with the vegetable kingdom, all tended to his acquaintance with our plants rather than animals, and consequently while the number of species of the former attributed by him to North America was considerable, that of the latter was small.

SOCIETIES AND LOCAL DEVELOPMENT.

Although after Linnæus equal individual attention to the several branches became rare, societies devoted to the cultivation of all in common originated, and several of them exercised a notable influence on the development of science in its various branches, either being called into existence in response to an active want for the means of expression for individuals, or being themselves the agents for eliciting communications which might otherwise have never been made known; these, therefore, always demand special notice in a history of science.

The earliest of such societies, founded when the States were yet colonies of Britain—the American Philosophical Society for promoting useful knowledge, held at Philadelphia—was originated by Franklin and some companions as early as 1743; its first volume of Transactions was published in 1771. The American Academy of Arts and Sciences was next established, in 1780, at Boston, and published the first volume of its Memoirs in 1785. Both these societies contributed much in their youth (as they still do) to the cultivation of the natural sciences, and various articles on animals, plants, and minerals were published in their serial volumes. Before the close of the eighteenth century (1799) another society—the Connecticut Academy of Arts and Sciences—was founded at New Haven, but after the publication of one volume languished, or was entirely inactive, till after the establishment of the Sheffield Scientific School, when it awoke to active life, and has since (1866–75) published many excellent memoirs. In 1814 there was founded in New York a society whose existence was ephemeral, but which played a notable part in American science; this association was the Literary and Philosophical Society of New York. In 1815 it published a large quarto volume of Transactions, which contained memoirs by Dr. Samuel L. Mitchill, Governor De Witt Clinton, Dr. David Hosack, and others less known, but the principal article was by Dr. Mitchill, and was a monograph of the fishes of the State, illustrated by six plates, containing sixty figures. For years afterward the society was inactive, and after publishing the first part of a second volume in 1825, dissolved. The year 1814 saw also the birth of a society destined to have an extraordinary connection with the growth of science in the United States generally—the Academy of Natural Sciences of Philadelphia. This body commenced the publication of a Journal in May, 1817, and in this first volume, as well as in all the succeeding ones, were published some of the most important papers on the animals, plants, and minerals of the country. A very considerable portion of our most familiar species of animals was, in fact, first made known in that journal, and in the earlier volumes Say and Lesueur published their classical memoirs. In 1818 the Lyceum of Natural History in the city of New York was organized, and a new impetus was given to the cultivation in that city of the natural sciences, and Mitchill, Leconte, Cooper, De Kay, and others contributed numerous articles to the pages of its Annals. Next, in 1834, the Boston Society of Natural History was established, and soon popularized in the city of its home the several subjects of its preference, which till then had received comparatively little attention. Finally were successively established in Albany, San Francisco, St. Louis, Chicago, Buffalo, Washington, and other cities, active societies devoted to science in several or all of its branches, which have in each case exercised a healthy influence in their several spheres.

All the societies specially noticed have not only continued to live, but are more active now than ever. Their inception coincided with the awakened activity in the several cities where they are located, and thus mark distinct epochs of progress.

Besides these local societies, two national ones, the American Association for the Advancement of Science and the National Academy of Sciences, have accomplished important results. The Smithsonian Institution, established at Washington in 1846, by its policy of facilitating intercommunication between the learned societies and individuals of this and other countries, of seconding the efforts of investigators by collection of materials and publishing the results of such investigations, and in other ways, greatly increased the means for the pursuit of the natural as well as mathematical sciences. To a large extent, too, it has been intrusted by the government of the nation with a superintendence of scientific exploration, and has done much thus to direct expenditure for such purposes in a proper channel.

In this connection may be fitly noticed a journal which is not the organ of any society, but which has, perhaps, exerted more influence on the progress of science in this country than any other. This is the *American Journal of Science and Arts*, commenced by the elder Silliman in 1818 in New Haven, and uninterruptedly continued there to the present time by him or members of his family. Its pages are replete with original and copied articles on the natural as well as the other sciences, and furnish in themselves an epitome of the progress of science in America.

GENERAL EXPLORATIONS.

The general government early adopted the policy of sending, from time to time, expeditions to the comparatively unknown portions of the country for their exploration, and with these in many cases naturalists were connected. Only those most notable from a scientific point of view can be referred to. In 1804–6 Lewis and Clarke traversed the continent, and more or less intelligibly indicated previously undescribed species of animals from the far West, which were subsequently incorporated by Ord, Rafinesque, and others into the zoological system. In 1819–20 S. H. Long (then major) conducted an expedition to the Rocky Mountains, of which Edwin James was the historian (1823), and also detailed the geology and botany, while Say described the new animals, and Torrey enumerated the plants. In 1848, and again in 1852–53, Fremont led expeditions across the continent, and brought back new riches in botany and geology. In 1849 and 1850 Stansbury explored the Great Salt Lake basin; in 1852 Sitgreaves the Zuni and Colorado rivers; and, also in 1852, Marcy the Red River of Louisiana. All of these expeditions were accompanied by energetic collectors, who brought back from the regions in question, whose natural history had been previously almost unknown, many new species, which were described and illustrated by naturalists mostly within the walls of the Smithsonian Institution. In 1854–56 General Emory (then major of cavalry) and Señor Salazar, as commissioners of their respective governments, surveyed and determined on the boundary line between the United States and Mexico. The United States commission was accompanied by a corps of scientists; and the report, published in 1857–59, contained most valuable contributions, richly illustrated, on the zoology, botany, paleontology, and geology of the country surveyed.

But all these must yield in importance to the several expeditions which were sent out by the War Department, under the auspices of the Bureau of Topographical Engineers, for "explorations and surveys to ascertain the most practicable and economical route for a railroad from the Mississippi River to the Pacific Ocean." These expeditions were mostly prosecuted from 1853 to 1856, and were conducted nearly on the parallels of latitude: (1) the 47th; (2) the 38th and 39th; (3) the 35th; (4) the California line; (5) the 32d, (6) under Parke, and (7) under Pope; and (8) the California and Oregon line. All these parties had naturalists attached, and as the natural history of the Pacific slope was almost unknown, a very large proportion of the species brought home for examination were new. These were reported upon by the naturalists of the surveys, but more fully elaborated by Professor S. F. Baird and Dr. Charles Girard. The results were published under a common title in a uniform series of twelve volumes in quarto. Professor Baird undertook the great task of revising, in connection with the new forms studied by himself, all the existing material from every part of North America. The fruits of his researches were issued in two very large volumes, respectively describing the mammals and birds of North America, in which the species were subjected to a critical examination; and for the first time those classes were completely and systematically exhibited according to their affinities, detailed descriptions given of all the species and successively including groups, and clear synoptical tables added. The fishes collected by the expeditions were elucidated chiefly by Girard and Suckley. Plates were published of the reptiles, under the direction of Baird; the coleoptera were partially reported upon by Leconte, and the mollusca by Cooper; the plants were catalogued and described by Torrey, Gray, Engelmann, Newberry, and others; the paleontology was investigated by Hall, Conrad, Agassiz, etc.; and the geology by the several geologists of the survey.

Two other surveys undertaken by the Bureau of Engineers should be noticed in this connection. One was the United States geological survey of the 40th parallel, prosecuted under the charge of Mr. Clarence King in 1867, 1868, and 1869; the other a geographical and topographical survey of certain of the Western and Southern Territories, under Lieutenant George M. Wheeler, still in progress. Both have done much for the furtherance of our knowledge of the zoology and botany, as well as the topography and geology, of the sections explored.

Under the Department of the Interior a geological and geographical survey also originated in 1869, and gradually developed into importance, under the charge of Dr. F. V. Hayden; and recently a second division of the same, with Professor J. W. Powell at its head, has been added to it. These vie with the other surveys in adding information respecting the physical geography and life, past and present, of the Territories under the government.

The geological survey of the State of California, under the superintendence of Professor J. D. Whitney (1861–74), also merits special notice on account of the completeness of its organization and the ability of execution of the work undertaken.

While the knowledge of the natural history of our country was being thus made known, that of foreign lands likewise received attention from American naturalists. During the years 1838–48 an exploring expedition was engaged, under the command of

Admiral (then Captain) Wilkes, in a voyage of circumnavigation, and in the course of its long cruise visited several countries whose natural productions and features were almost or wholly unknown. The expedition was accompanied by several energetic and accomplished naturalists, chief of whom in labors was the versatile Dana. The results of these explorations were most satisfactory, numerous new species were collected, and the publications on the collections were, as a whole, in the highest degree creditable to American science. The mammals and birds were reported on by Peale and Cassin; the reptiles, by Girard; the mollusks, by Gould; the crustaceans and zoophytes, by Dana; the botany, by Torrey, Gray, Eaton, etc.; and the geology of the countries visited, by Dana. The most noteworthy of these were the volumes on crustaceans and polyps, wherein the classification of those animals was entirely revised, and a great mass of new material added.

In the years 1849–52 a "United States Naval Astronomical Expedition to the Southern Hemisphere" was for the most part stationed in Chili, and the commander thereof (Captain J. M. Gilliss) and his assistants paid zealous attention to the natural history of the regions traversed. Collections were made in the various departments, and on the return of the expedition were studied by Baird, Cassin, Girard, Gould, Gray, Wyman, Conrad, J. Lawrence Smith, etc. The collection richest in new forms was of the class of fishes, of which some remarkable new types were described by Girard.

An expedition which was excelled by none, if it did not, indeed, surpass all, in the collections amassed sailed from New York in 1853 for the Northern Pacific, and for about four years cruised in all the great seas, at first under the command of Captain Ringgold, and afterward under Captain Rodgers. In this expedition Mr. Wright was attached as botanist, and Mr. Stimpson as zoologist. The collections made, especially in the department of zoology, were very large. Mr. Stimpson for the first time dredged in many of the harbors visited, and the results, as might be expected, were very rich. Numerous remarkable types of marine as well as other animals were thus discovered. These were partially described in preliminary reports by Stimpson, Cassin, Hallowell, Cope, and Gill, but the final reports were never published, and several of them, with the original illustrations, were consumed in the great fire which destroyed Chicago, and the loss thus incurred is irretrievable.

Such are the principal explorations which have been instrumental in the extension of our knowledge of nature. Numerous others have concurred, but limited space forbids any mention of them. We may now best inquire how each department has been forwarded by American naturalists, commencing with the most simple, and advancing to the most complex.

MINERALOGY.

Linnæus applied the same system of nomenclature to the mineral kingdom, or *lapideum regnum*, as he did to the animal and vegetable, dividing it into three "classes"—*petræ*, or stones; *mineræ*, or minerals; *fossilia*, or fossils; and this exposition alone will give a good idea of the imperfect conception then entertained of the relations of those objects, and especially of the last. Chemistry and crystallography were almost ignored, or made use of in a very crude manner. More than any of his predecessors, however, Linnæus availed himself of the crystallographic characters of minerals in their diagnoses; but their action when subject to friction, fire, and acids was the chief means of determination used. Linnæus was, however, much surpassed as a mineralogist by contemporary investigators, and the status of mineralogy became rapidly improved by the discoveries of chemists, physicists, and crystallographers, and it had assumed the dignity of a science before any native Americans applied themselves with intelligent zeal to the study.

It is true that the occurrences at various places of certain minerals and peculiar conditions of some were noted from time to time, but nothing which deserves special notice was published for a long time. A journal professedly devoted to mineralogy, the *American Mineralogical Journal*, was, indeed, commenced by A. Bruce, but was discontinued with the first volume. In 1816, however, Professor Parker Cleveland published *An Elementary Treatise on Mineralogy and Geology*, whose science was respectable for its day, and gained a demand for a second edition in 1822. In 1832 appeared the first, and in 1835 the second, parts of Shepard's *Treatise on Mineralogy*. This was soon succeeded by a work which was destined to become the *opus magnum* of the science, *A System of Mineralogy*, by James D. Dana. It has passed through five entirely revised editions, and several are, to all intents and purposes, distinct works, and fairly exemplify the several stages of science. In the first (1837) the system of nomenclature introduced by Linnæus was retained, and a modification of the so-called natural classification by Mohs, proposed several years previously (in 1833), was adopted. This system was based chiefly on the consideration of the superficial characters of the minerals, but which were claimed to be true coordinates of the chemical, upon the superior value of which many mineralogists had already insisted. In the second edition (1844) the same system of classification, with some modifications, was retained, but another, "placing the minerals under the principal element in their composition," was added. In the third edition (1850) the old system of nomenclature and classification was discarded, and the author adopted a provisional system in which the chemical constitution of the mineral was taken more cognizance of, the chief aim, however, being to "serve the convenience of the student for easy reference and for the study of mineralogy in its economical bearings, while at the same time it should exhibit many natural relations, and inculcate no false applications or distinctions of species." A more rigid chemical classification, in which the Berzelian method was coupled with crystallography, was appended. In the fourth edition (1854) the arrangement appended in the previous, amplified and corrected, was adopted as the regular system. In the fifth and last (1868) the same method was essentially retained, and in obedience to the necessities imposed by the more detailed study of the subject, and to show the proper subordination of the several characteristics, varieties were recognized.

In the course of time the demands on the other branches of science in behalf of mineralogy had become greater and greater. As we have seen, originally mineralogy was simply the art of identifying mineral forms by reference to their superficial physical characteristics. Gradually the chemist was called upon to tell the constitutions thereof; the crystallographer and mathematician to define and classify their forms; the physicist to answer various questions as to characteristics; the spectroscopist to aid the chemist. Finally the chemist was accorded the rank of prime arbiter, and in most cases his judgment is now accepted as final. In each of these departments America has had and still has most distinguished investigators. Dana's work stands *facile princeps* among mineralogical text-books, and is a true "manual" in the Old World as well as in the New. He ranks pre-eminent in the special department of crystallography. In chemical mineralogy there have been many successful students, chief of whom are T. Sterry Hunt, George J. Brush, F. A. Genth, C. M. Shepard, and B. Silliman. A son of Professor Dana (Mr. E. S. Dana) has, with scarcely unequal skill, begun to continue the work so well commenced by the father, and has been paying especial attention to the physical characters of minerals.

BOTANY.

Devotion to plants has been a favorite source of enjoyment to man. The attractiveness of the objects, the positiveness and superficial concentration of characters, and the ease of preserving have all tended to this bias. As a natural result, to a certain extent the value and characteristics of plants were earlier appreciated than any other group of natural objects. Those of this country were tolerably well known at a comparatively early period. Jean Robin, a Frenchman, as early as 1620 published on the plants of old Virginia; J. Cornuti, a French physician, in 1635, on those of Canada; J. R. Forster in 1771 issued a *Flora Americæ Septentrionalis;* Cadwallader Colden, of Newburgh, New York, communicated to Linnæus a descriptive account of the plants indigenous to Orange County; Mr. Cutler in 1785 published in the Memoirs of the American Academy of Arts and Sciences a catalogue of the New England species; and numerous other works and articles of various degrees of merit were published (some meanwhile, but especially in succeeding years), the most notable of which were the elder Michaux's *Flora Borealis Americana* (1803); Pursh's *Flora Americæ Septentrionalis* (1814); and Eaton's *Manual of Botany for the Northern and Middle States*. In all of these and the minor contemporary productions the artificial sexual system of Linnæus was adopted, and this had a wonderful hold on the affections of the older botanists. A man of remarkable versatility but disordered mind (C. S. Rafinesque), who had come to this country in 1814, had published much on botanical subjects, and had in several of his works suggested and partially carried into execution a quasi-natural scheme of classification; but his influence had no weight, and not until the end of the last half century did any one of recognized standing discard the Linnæan method. In 1823 Dr. John Torrey had published the first part of a *Flora of the Northern and Middle States*, in which he still retained the sexual system; but having become satisfied of its incongruity with the existing state of science, he discontinued the work, and immediately after applied the natural system to the classification of the plants collected on Long's expedition to the far West, and subsequently rendered it more popular by the publication of a catalogue of the North American genera, arranged in accordance with Lindley's classification (1831). Lewis Beck, in a *Botany of the United States North of Virginia*, also adopted this system. The natural system was thus fairly adopted by scientific botanists and those who appreciated the aims of science, but was long in obtaining favor with the masses. The publication of such works as the *Flora of North America*, by Torrey and Gray, in 1838–43, the *Manual of the Flora of New York*, by Torrey, in 1843, *Manual of the Botany of the Northern United States*, by Gray, in 1848, and kindred ones, however, procured its ultimate adoption even in manuals for schools and colleges.

The States of the Atlantic sea-board and the Mississippi Valley were sedulously explored by native botanists, and catalogues, and even extensive descriptive works, of the plants of many of the separate States, as well as sections, counties, and townships, were published. The expeditions that have been already alluded to in connection with natural history generally extended our knowledge of the flora of the extreme West, and the progress of botany advanced hand in hand with that of geography. Private collectors, too, devoted themselves to the search for the plants of various unexplored sections, and among these may be especially enumerated Fendler, who herborized in New Mexico; Lindheimer, who collected in Texas; Wright, Parry, and Vasey, who penetrated to divers places in the Southwestern sections and Rocky Mountains; and Rothrock, who has visited the extreme North (Alaska), and the furthest Southwest (Arizona).

The monographers of groups have also been active. Above all must be mentioned Gray, Torrey, and Engelmann, and during later years Watson, who have studied various groups of phænogams; Eaton has especially attached himself to the ferns; Sullivant and Lesquereux to the mosses; Curtis, of South Carolina, to the fungi; Tuckermann to the lichens; and lately Dr. H. Wood has monographed our fresh-water algæ, and Dr. Farlow has catalogued the marine species.

The consideration of the geographical distribution of plants has also engaged the attention of many students, and the researches of Gray demand especial notice. Pursh had as early as 1814 called attention to the similarity between the flora of North America and Northern Asia. Gray in 1846 pointed out many analogies, and in 1856 insisted on the similarity between the floras of corresponding sides of the Old and New Worlds. He also at the same time recognized that, although the number of tropical types was much greater than in the northern portion of the Old World, "the peculiar and extra-European families do not predominate nor overcome the general European aspect of our vegetation." He has more recently recognized a casual relation in this similarity, and contended that they indicated derivation from a common source.

ZOOLOGY.

Although more or less pretentious lists of the animals of North America were given in many works descriptive of the country, scarcely any are worthy of notice, and so little was known of our species that an extremely small percentage appeared in the

Systema Naturæ of Linnæus. The field in zoology is so vast that none have in this country attempted to do what has been so well done for botany, that is, to prepare compendiums of descriptions of all the known species. From the complete dissimilarity and want of homologies between the great groups of the animal kingdom a peculiar terminology for each is entailed, and consequently the students are more specialists than in botany. Each group of animals, however, has had its devotees. The progress in each, too, has, like that of botany, been to a considerable degree coincident with the growth of our geographical knowledge; and this statement must serve in lieu of particularization in each case. The more difficult groups have been backward in attracting students, and the more pleasing types have received most attention. Thus the birds early excited the admiration of lovers of nature, and numerous works have been dedicated to the portraiture of their beauties, while the worms and other lower invertebrates have only lately attracted the notice science demanded.

Before indicating the progress of our knowledge in the several branches of zoology a notice of one who did much to shape the course which investigation took for some years may be fitly given.

In 1846 Louis John Rudolph Agassiz visited the country, and soon was induced to make it his home, and in 1848 accepted the chair of zoology and geology at Harvard College. Gifted with quick powers of perception and a remarkable memory for specimens, he had early applied himself to the study of fossil fishes, which till then had been nearly neglected. The publication of a very extensive and finely illustrated work gained for him a great reputation in Europe. A peculiarly genial and impulsive disposition procured him the favor of those with whom he came into personal contact. This impression communicated itself quickly to others. He gathered around him a number of young men who were destined to pursue with distinguished success different branches of science. His prestige caused the ready acceptance of his teaching and principles by others, and insured their application to the various branches of zoology. Many of these principles were most sound; others (among them unfortunately were those most frequently applied) were less justified by scientific reason. Such were the views respecting the rigid limitations of species in time and area. He was also prone to differentiate genera because of minor differences, and to trust to intuition rather than to the inexorable logic of facts in the classification of data. His views were generally accepted, as well by amateurs as scientists, in this country, and not for a long time was there any strong counter-current. This subsequently set in, and the present tendency is toward a recognition of species with more variable limits, and with greater extension in time and space. But in spite of the drawbacks indicated the influence of Professor Agassiz was most salutary; he raised the standard of scholarship looked for in the naturalist, incited general respect and even enthusiasm for natural science, and his popularity enabled him to found a Museum of Comparative Zoology which is an honor to Massachusetts and to the country at large, and the best monument to his own zeal and learning.

The United States presented long the anomalous position of being the only great nation which had no public museum. The collections that were brought back from time to time were, after the establishment of the Smithsonian Institution, intrusted to its custody, but only within a few years has it been recognized as a duty to appropriate at all adequate amounts for their preservation and use. But some provision has been made for several years for a national museum; this still remains as an appanage of the Smithsonian Institution, under the charge of its assistant secretary, Professor Baird, and now bids fair to soon rival the most important in Europe in the extent and actual value of its collections.

The most notable accessions to our special knowledge have been as follows:

Some of the more conspicuous quadrupeds of North America had been early described and figured in a recognizable manner by compilers and iconographers, and especially in the works of Catesby, Edwards, and Brisson, and these were incorporated in the *Systema Naturæ* by Linnæus; but, all told, he only attributed twenty-five species to North America, and even of these he does not seem to have had autoptical knowledge of more than two or three. Others were subsequently made known, chiefly by English and French naturalists, and later by Americans (especially Say and Ord), and in 1825 Richard Harlan published a special volume on the class, in which were recognized 147 species, a number of which were, however, synonyms. Soon after (1826–28) John D. Godman issued a corresponding work, in three volumes, containing nothing new. Subsequently Townsend and Audubon obtained from the West many new species, which were described by Bachman, and in 1846–54 Audubon and Bachman published a work on *The Viviparous Quadrupeds of North America*, in three volumes. Finally, in 1859, the great work by Professor Baird, already referred to, appeared, and in this were described a number of previously unknown species, incorporated with others he had previously made known. On the basis thus laid various zoologists have built. Among these have been the natural historians of various regions and the monographers of distinct groups, such as Harrison Allen, J. A. Allen, Cope, Coues, Gill, etc.

The birds have excited the most lively interest, and the works published on the class have been many. The more common and conspicuous species were early introduced into the system, and from the time of John Bartram (1791) and Benjamin S. Barton (1799) to the present there have always been active students of the class in America. The most distinguished of these are Alexander Wilson, a native of Scotland, naturalized in the United States, who published in 1808–14; Charles L. Bonaparte (a nephew of Napoleon, and afterward Prince of Musignano and Canino), who published, besides many other articles, a complementary volume to Wilson's work (1825–33); T. Nuttall, who issued a *Manual of the Ornithology of the United States and Canada* (1832–34); J. J. Audubon, who contributed the most superbly illustrated work to ornithology that had up to that time been seen; and S. F. Baird, who first (1858), in conjunction with J. Cassin and G. N. Lawrence, revised the entire system of North American birds, and very recently (1874), in union with T. Brewer and R. Ridgway, has published the first three volumes of a work which surpasses all others in accuracy of description, philosophical breadth of views, and comparative valuation of characters. Lastly may be mentioned *Birds of the Northwest: a Hand-Book of the Ornithology of the Region drained by the Missouri River and its Tributaries*, by Elliott Coues (1874).

While these general works were in course of publication, many minor works and articles were printed on the general subject, on the species of limited regions, and on the modifications of structure and color induced by geographical and climatic causes, etc. The most successful students of the causes of geographical variation have been Baird, Allen, and Ridgway.

The reptiles and amphibians, although extremely unlike in structure, superficially resemble each other so closely as to have been always confounded together and studied in common under the general head of herpetology. This has been a less cultivated branch than others, but several eminent naturalists have elucidated our species, and more than either of the preceding classes has the present owed its advancement to natives. J. E. Holbrook, of South Carolina, published, in 1843, a *North American Herpetology*, in five volumes, which was then unsurpassed by any similar production in Europe. S. F. Baird, Charles Girard, Edward Hallowell, and Louis Agassiz have done eminent service on different groups, and more recently E. D. Cope has revised the entire herpetological fauna in connection with the general system of reptiles and amphibians.

The students of fishes have been more numerous. In the last century but little was known of these inhabitants of our waters, and even that little was inexact. In 1814 S. L. Mitchill, a man of great eminence in his day, published a valuable though crude memoir on the fishes of New York; in 1839 D. H. Storer reported on the fishes of Massachusetts; in 1842 J. E. De Kay published an important work on the fishes of New York; and in 1855, and again in 1860, J. E. Holbrook commenced an illustrated work on the *Icthyology of South Carolina*, but suspended it with the first volume.

The fishes of the extreme West and of the Pacific coast, almost absolutely unknown till 1854, were in that and in immediately succeeding years described by Agassiz, Girard, Ayres, etc. Among other cultivators of the science may be mentioned Kirtland, Baird, Brevoort, Gill, Putnam, Abbott, Cope, Bliss, Goode, Garman, Milner, Yarrow, and Jordan.

The invertebrates for purposes of study fall into two groups—the air-breathing insects and the marine forms.

The insects soon attracted attention, and the various groups engaged active students. Say (1818 *et seq.*), Fitch, Packard, Walsh, and Riley have described species of almost every group. The coleoptera have been studied by Melsheimer, J. Leconte, Haldemann, and above all by J. L. Leconte and Horn; the lepidoptera have had numerous students—Morris, Clemens, Edwards, Packard, Scudder, Grote, and many others; the hymenoptera, or groups thereof, have been examined by Norton, Saussure, etc.; the orthoptera have been investigated by Scudder, Thomas, and Sydney Smith; the neuroptera by Hagen; the hemiptera by Uhler; and the diptera have engaged the attention of Loew and Osten-Sacken. The myriopods have been described by H. Wood, as have also the pedipalp arachnoids.

The marine invertebrates were almost wholly neglected till Say, in 1818, commenced his investigations, and for some years worked upon several of the groups, describing our most common crustaceans, shells, and other forms. A. A. Gould, in a work on the invertebrata of Massachusetts, made evident the paucity of our knowledge of all except the shells; and a few years afterward (1851) W. Stimpson, then a very young man, commenced his researches, which added very largely to our information. In recent years the work thus commenced has been worthily continued by the two Agassizes, H. J. Clarke, A. E. Verrill, S. Smith, O. Harger, and others.

The mollusks, on account of the beauty of their shells and the ease of preserving them, have, like the birds, been favorite subjects for amateur students, and this has directly and indirectly accelerated our acquaintance with the species. The laborers have been very many. It must suffice to name, besides the general students of invertebrates previously referred to, Isaac Lea, A. A. Gould, Amos and William G. Binney, Thomas Bland, Edward S. Morse, William H. Dall, and George W. Tryon. These have studied, some all the groups, others the land or fresh-water shells, others the anatomy, and still others have especially considered the problems connected with their geographical distribution.

PALEONTOLOGY.

In no department of natural history has progress been so distinctly marked, or the revelations so interesting and unexpected, as in that which takes cognizance of the former life of our globe. The science of paleontology, as this branch has been named, had absolutely no existence or name when the United States became a nation. Fossils were classified by Linnæus not with animals or plants, but with minerals. Their nature was then in doubt. By some they were supposed to be sports of nature, or abortive *simulacra* of what the Deity destined afterward to create. By the best informed and orthodox they were believed to be witnesses of the Noachian deluge. In a number of cases their nature was, indeed, recognized, but by none was it definitely realized that most fossils were the remains of forms that are no longer living. Although this truth became apparent to several at nearly the same time, Cuvier was the first to render it clear and popular by the restoration of numerous fossil remains of the skeletons of mammals found in the tertiary deposits of the neighborhood of Paris. These were so demonstrably different from any animals that were known in a living state, and the improbability of their having remained undiscovered if still living was so extreme, that conviction of the truth necessarily struck every one who considered the evidence. The clew thus gained, although at first imperfectly held, was soon firmly grasped and followed by many interested students, and the present assured superstructure has been the reward of their zeal. In this country the science engaged the attention of many, and Say, Lesueur, De Kay, and Greene were among the earliest. Morton, Conrad, Lea, Hall, Meek, Gabb, White, and Whitfield, besides many others, have described and identified the fossil invertebrates. Hall has especially published a noble work on the fossils of the paleozoic formations of New York. Meek has done more than any one else to illustrate the fossils of the carboniferous and mesozoic beds of the West; and Conrad has excelled in knowledge of and labors on the species of the tertiary rocks. Lea and Gabb have efficiently supplemented the works of the last two.

The vertebrates have received attention from another class of scientists. For their comprehension an exact knowledge of the details of comparative osteology was requisite, and the students have, therefore, been comparatively few. De Kay, Harlan, Godman, Hays, Cooper, Redfield, Warren, and Wyman simultaneously or successively touched the subject, but the great labors have been accomplished by Leidy, Cope, and Marsh. It had by some become supposed that America would furnish no deposits of fossil bones such as had been discovered in Europe, but in 1846 and 1847 Dr. Hiram A. Prout, of St. Louis, and in 1847 Dr. Leidy, published communications on remains found in the Mauvaise Terres of the then Territory of Nebraska, and those deposits have since been a fruitful source of new discoveries. Other regions containing analogous deposits were subsequently made known, and the mammalian faunas of past times, pliocene, miocene, and eocene, have become tolerably well known. Among the most interesting of the types discovered are many forming "connecting links" between the existing ruminants (cattle, deer, etc.) and hog-like animals first made known by Leidy; others lessening the interval between the proboscidians and ordinary pachyderm ungulates, discovered by Cope and Marsh; others demonstrating the line of descent of the horses of the present day, elucidated by Marsh; and still others establishing the former existence in North America of animals most nearly related among living forms to the lemurs of Madagascar, as Marsh was the first to clearly demonstrate. Numerous other almost equally important discoveries have been made, illustrating the structure and range in time and biological generalizations for almost every group of vertebrates; but this is not the place to recount them.

GEOLOGY.

Geology is almost entirely the child of the present century. Its foundations were chiefly laid by Werner, of Freyberg (after 1775), and his school in the clear recognition of the nature and the relations of rocks to each other, and their distribution; by Hutton, of Edinburgh (1788), in the comprehension of the origin and natural causes of the strata and rocks, and in the limitation of cataclysmal agencies; and by William Smith, an English surveyor (1790), and Cuvier (1808), in a general perception of the restriction of fossils to definite horizons, and the value of those fossils in determining the relative age of the strata in which they were imbedded. In each case, indeed, these had been to some extent anticipated in their discoveries, but their ideas were clear and positive, while their predecessors failed to recognize the full significance of the facts in question. The age had also become ripe to apply the truths thus perceived.

Nothing worthy of mention was done for the geology of North America till William Maclure (a pupil of Werner), in 1806, came to this country and undertook a geological survey, traveling in the prosecution of this self-imposed task from our Northern border to the Gulf of Mexico. He was engaged on it for about three years, and in 1809 published the first geological map, and a commentary thereon in a special memoir. As was to be expected, he adopted the Wernerian system of nomenclature, and having been unable to apply paleontological evidence, his work exhibited little more than certain points in structural geology. Lardner Vanuxem (1828) first availed himself successfully of paleontology for the determination of the age of several of our formations and their approximate synchronism with European beds. The natural history survey of the State of New York, commenced in 1836, brought together a great mass of facts, and by the concert of the several geologists and paleontologists, but especially guided by the judgment of Vanuxem and James Hall, a classification of the rocks on sound paleontological principles was instituted, which, as since perfected by Hall, has been adopted as the standard of reference for the paleozoic rocks of the United States and British North America. Henry D. Rogers, in his final report on the geology of Pennsylvania (1858), made evident the skill with which he had disentangled the complications of the geological structure of the Alleghany system. F. B. Meek during a long series of years has acted as the universally accepted arbiter for the determination of the age of the groups of rocks in the far West. Meanwhile the details of the geology of the various geographical sections and States engaged the attention of many laborers, and one after the other almost every State instituted a geological survey, and many of them undertook at intervals two or more. In the order of first publication of results they are as follows: 1824, North Carolina; 1826, South Carolina; 1832, Massachusetts; 1834, Maryland; 1835, Tennessee; 1836, New Jersey, New York, Ohio, Pennsylvania, Virginia; 1837, Connecticut, Maine; 1838, Indiana, Michigan; 1839, Delaware, Kentucky; 1840, Rhode Island; 1841, New Hampshire; 1845, Vermont; 1850, Alabama; 1853, California, Illinois; 1854, Mississippi, Wisconsin; 1855, Missouri; 1858, Arkansas, Iowa; 1859, Texas; 1865, Kansas; 1866, Minnesota; 1869, Louisiana; 1875, Georgia.

The general government also from time to time instituted special geological surveys, independent of the exploring parties mentioned in the first part of this article. In 1834 and 1835 G. W. Featherstonhaugh investigated the elevated country between the Missouri and Red rivers and the Wisconsin Territory. At various times D. D. Owen conducted surveys in several States and Territories of the Northwest, publishing the chief results in 1844, 1848, and 1852. In 1869 the persistent solicitations of F. V. Hayden, already well known as a field geologist and collector, secured a geological survey of Nebraska, under the auspices of the Land-office, a bureau of the Interior Department. For two years this was prosecuted, and the wedge having been thus driven, the survey was continued, and, organized under a more ample scope and with enlarged designs, is continued to the present time. A number of eminent men have availed themselves of the means of investigation and publication presented to them by the survey, and consequently a number of valuable publications have appeared under its auspices. Also productive of similar work have been, or are, the surveys of the 40th parallel, and the Territories west of the 100th meridian, already referred to under the head of general natural history.

In every department of geology America has exhibited efficient works. Stratigraphical, chronological, dynamical, and mineralogical geologies have each had its votaries, and so numerous have they been that the simple mention of their names is precluded.

Such are the principal incidents of progress in the knowledge of the natural history of our land. Many important discoveries have not been even alluded to, and the limitations of space preclude notice of the advance of anthropological science and the general propositions and principles of biology to which American naturalists have contributed.

XII.

A CENTURY OF AMERICAN LITERATURE.

IN a retrospect of what has been done in American literature during the past hundred years, it is of the first importance to draw a sharp line of distinction between the mental powers displayed in literature and those which have been exhibited in industrial creation, in statesmanship, and in the abstract and applied sciences. The literature of America is but an insufficient measure of the realized capacities of the American mind. When Sir William Hamilton declared that Aristotle had an imagination as great as that of Homer, he struck at the primary fact that the creative energies of the human mind may be exercised in widely different lines of direction. Imagination is, in the popular mind, obstinately connected with poetry and romance. This prejudice is further deepened by associating imagination with amiable emotions, regardless of the fact that two of the greatest characters created by the human imagination are two of the vilest types of intelligent nature—Iago and Mephistopheles. When the attempt is made to extend the application of the creative energy of imagination to business and politics, the sentimental outcry against such a profanation of the term becomes almost deafening. Every poetaster is willing to admit that Newton is one of the few grand scientific discoverers that the world has produced; but he still thinks that, in virtue of versifying some commonplaces of emotion and thought, he is himself superior to Newton in imagination. The truth is that, in spite of Newton's incapacity to appreciate works of literature and art, he possessed a creative imagination of the first class—an imagination which, in boundless fertility, is second only to Shakspeare's. In fact, it is the direction given to the creative faculty, and not to the materials on which it works, that discriminates between Fulton and Bryant, Whitney and Longfellow, Bigelow and Whittier, Goodyear and Lowell. Descending from the inventors, it would be easy to show that in the conduct of the every-day transactions of life, more quickness of imagination, subtilty and breadth of understanding, and energy of will have been displayed by our men of business than by our authors. By the necessities of our position, the aggregate mind of the country has been exercised in creating the nation as we now find it. There is, indeed, something ludicrous, to a large observer of all the phenomena of our national life, in confounding the brain and heart of the United States with the manifestation that either has found in mere literary expression. The nation outvalues all its authors, even in respect to those powers which authors are supposed specially to represent. Nobody can write intelligently of the progress of American literature during the past hundred years without looking at American literature as generally subsidiary to the grand movement of the American mind.

It is curious, however, that the only apparent contradiction to this general principle dates from the beginning of our national life. At the time the American Revolution broke out, the two men who best represented the double aspect of the thought of the colonies were Jonathan Edwards and Benjamin Franklin. Both come within the domain of the historian of literature, for both were great forces in our literature, whose influence is yet unspent. Of Jonathan Edwards, the greatest of American theologians and metaphysicians, and a religious genius of the first order, it is impossible to speak without respect, and even reverence. No theologian born in our country has exercised more influence on minds and souls kindred to his own. Those who opposed him recognized his pre-eminent powers of intellect. Every body felt, in assailing such a consummate reasoner, the restraining modesty which a master-spirit always evokes in the minds of his adversaries. His treatise on the Will has been generally accepted as one of the marvels of intellectual acuteness, exercised on one of the most difficult problems which have ever tested the resources of the human intellect. There have been many answers to it, but no answer which is generally considered unanswerable. Such works, indeed, as this of Edwards on the Will are not so much answered or refuted as gradually outgrown. But the treatise has certainly exercised and strengthened all the minds that have resolutely grappled with it, and has aided the development of the logical powers of American orthodox divines in a remarkable degree. Whether a controversialist agrees with its author, or dissents from him, Edwards always quickens the mental activity of every body who strives to follow the course of his argumentation, or to detect the lurking fallacy which is supposed to be discoverable somewhere in the premises or processes of his logic. Perhaps this fallacy is to be found in the various senses in which Edwards uses the vital word "determination." To most readers, who believe the will to be abstractly free, but that the actions of men commonly proceed from the characters they have gradually formed, the most satisfactory explanation of the mystery is that of Jouffroy, who declares that "Liberty is the ideal of the Me." Others may obtain consolation from Gilfillan's somewhat flippant remark, that every thing a man does is not necessary before he does it, but is necessary after he has done it. Essentially the doctrine of Edwards agrees with that of philosophical necessity, and with that so vehemently urged by many scientists, that the actions of men are as much controlled by law as the movements of the planets. The great difference between Edwards's theory and the others is, that he connects his metaphysics with a theological system, and his treatise remains as a kind of practical argument for the everlasting damnation of those who question the infallibility of its logic.

Edwards's large and subtle understanding was connected with an imagination of intense realizing power, and both were based on a soul of singular purity, open on many sides to communications from the Divine mind. He had an almost preternatural conception of the "exceeding sinfulness of sin." His imagination was filled with ghastly images of the retribution which awaits on iniquity, and his reasoned sermons on eternal torments were but the outbreak of a sensitive feeling, a holy passion for goodness, which made him intolerant of any excellence which did not approach his ideal of godliness. But then his spiritual experience, though it inflamed one side of his imagination with vivid pictures of the terrors of hell, on the other side gave the most enrapturing visions of the spiritual joys of heaven. It is unfortunate for his fame that his hell has obtained for him more popular recognition than his heaven. Like other poets, such as Dante and Milton, his pictures of the torments of the damned have cast into the shade that celestial light which shines so lovingly over his pictures of the bliss of the redeemed. True religion, he tells us, consists in a great measure in holy affections—in "a love of divine things for the beauty and sweetness of their moral excellency." "Sweetness" is a frequent word all through Edwards's works, when he desires to convey his perception of the satisfactions which await on piety in this world, and the ineffable joy of the experiences of pious souls in the next; and this word he thrills with a transcendent depth of suggestive meaning which it bears in no dictionary, nor in the vocabulary of any other writer of the English language. He was certainly one of the holiest souls that ever appeared on the planet. The admiration which has been generally awarded to his power of reasoning should be extended to his power of affirming, that is, when he affirms ideas coming from those moods of blessedness in which his soul seems to be in direct contact with divine things, and vividly beholds what in other discourses his mind reasons up to or about. To reach these divine heights, however, you must, according to Edwards, mount the stairs of dogma built by Augustine and Calvin.

Jonathan Edwards may be characterized as a man of the next world. Benjamin Franklin was emphatically a man of this world. Not that Franklin lacked religion and homely practical piety, but he had none of Edwards's intense depth of religious experience. God was to him a beneficent being, aiding good men in their hard struggles with the facts of life, and not pitiless to those who stumbled in the path of duty, or even to those who widely diverged from it. The heaven of Edwards was as far above his spiritual vision as the hell of Edwards was below his soundings of the profundities of human wickedness; but there never was a person who so swiftly distinguished an honest man from a rogue, or who was more quick to see that the rogue was at war with the spiritual constitution of things. He seems to have learned his morality in a practical way. All his early slips from the straight line of duty were but experiments, from which he drew lessons in moral wisdom. If he happened occasionally to lapse into vice, he made the experience of vice a new fortress to defend his virtue; and he came out of the temptations of youth and middle age with a character generally recognized as one of singular solidity, serenity, and benignity. His intellect, in the beautiful harmony of its faculties, his conscience, in the instinctive sureness of its perception of the relations of duties, and his heart, in its subordination of malevolent to beneficent emotions—all showed how diligent he had been in the austere self-culture which eventually raised him to the first rank among the men of his time. Simplicity was the fine result of the complexities which entered into his mind and character. He was a man who never used words except to express positive thoughts or emotions, and was never tempted to misuse them for the purposes of declamation. He kept his style always on the level of his character. In announcing his scientific discoveries, as in his most private letters, he is ever simple. In breadth of mind he is probably the most eminent man that our country has produced; for while he was the greatest diplomatist, and one of the greatest statesmen and patriots of the United States, he was also a discoverer in science, a benignant philanthropist, and a master in that rare art of so associating words with things that they appeared identical. Edwards represents, humanly speaking, the somewhat doleful doctrine that the best thing a good man can do is to get out, as soon as he decently can, of this world into one which is immeasurably better, by devoting all his energies to the salvation of his own particular soul. Franklin, on the contrary, seems perfectly content with this world, as long as he thinks he can better *it*. Edwards would doubtless have considered Franklin a child of wrath, but Francis Bacon would have hailed him as one of that band of explorers who, by serving Nature, will in the end master her mysteries, and use their knowledge for the service of man. Indeed, the cheerful, hopeful spirit which runs through Franklin's writings, even when he was tried by obstacles which might have tasked the proverbial patience of Job, is not one of the least of his claims upon the consideration of those who rightfully glory in having such a genius for their countryman. The spirit which breathes through Franklin's life and works is that which has inspired every pioneer of our Western wastes, every poor farmer who has tried to make both ends meet by the exercise of rigid economy, every inventor who has attempted to serve men by making machines do half the drudgery of their work, every statesman who has striven to introduce large principles into our somewhat confused and contradictory legislation, every American diplomatist who has upheld the character of his country abroad by sagacity in managing men, as well as by integrity in the main purpose of his mission, and every honest man who has desired to diminish the evil there is in the world, and to increase every possible good that is conformable to good sense. Franklin is doubtless our Mr. Worldly Wiseman, but his worldly wisdom ever points to the Christian's prayer that God's will shall be done on earth as it is done in heaven.

One of the most ludicrous misinterpretations of this large, bounteous, and benignant intelligence is that which confines his influence to the little corner of his mind in which he lodged "Poor Richard." It is common even now to hear complaints from opulent English gentlemen that Franklin has done much to make the average American narrow in mind, hard of heart, greedy of small gains, mean in little economies. This is said of a nation the poorer portions of whose population are needlessly wasteful, and whose richer portions astonish Europe annually by the profusion with which they scatter dollars to the right and the left. The maxims of Poor Richard are generally good, and the more they are circulated, the more practical good they will do; for our countrymen are remarkable rather for violating than for obeying them. In all these criticisms on Franklin, however, it is strange that few have observed what a delicious specimen of humorous characterization he has introduced into literature in his charming delineation of Poor Richard. The effect is heightened by the groaning, droning way in which the good man delivers his bits of wisdom, as if he despairingly felt that the rustics around him would disregard his advice and monitions, and pass through the usual experiences of the passions, insensible to the gasping, croaking voice which warned them in advance.

Franklin is probably the best specimen that history affords of what is called a self-made man. He certainly "never worshipped his maker," according to Mr. Clapp's stinging epigram, but was throughout his life, though always self-respectful, never self-conceited. Perhaps the most notable result of his self-education was the ease with which he accosted all grades and classes of men on a level of equality. The printer's boy became, in his old age, one of the most popular men in the French court, not only among its statesmen, but among its frivolous nobles and their wives. He ever estimated men at their true worth or worthlessness; but as a diplomatist he was a marvel of sagacity. The same ease of manner which recommended him to a Pennsylvania farmer was preserved in a conference with a statesman or a king. He ever kept his end in view in all his complaisances, and that end was always patriotic. When he returned to his country he was among the most earnest to organize the liberty he had done so much to achieve; and he also showed his hostility to the system of negro slavery with which the United States was accursed. At the ripe age of eighty-four he died, leaving behind him a record of extraordinary faithfulness in the performance of all the duties of life. His sagacity, when his whole career is surveyed, amounts almost to saintliness; for his sagacity was uniformly devoted to the accomplishment of great public ends of policy or beneficence.

Edwards was born three years before Franklin, and died in 1758, nearly twenty years before the war broke out. Franklin died in 1790. Both being representative men, may properly be taken as points of departure in considering those writers and thinkers who were educated under the influences of the pre-Revolutionary period of our literary history. The writings of Washington, Adams, Hamilton, Jefferson, Madison, Jay, are a recognized portion of our literature, because the hoarded wisdom slowly gathered in by their practical knowledge of life crops out in their most familiar correspondence. A truism announced by such men brightens into a truth, because it has evidently been tested and proved by their experience in conducting affairs. There is an elemental grandeur in Washington's character and career which renders impertinent all mere criticism on his style; for what he was and what he did are felt to outvalue a hundredfold what he wrote, except we consider his writings as mere records of his sagacity, wisdom, patience, disinterestedness, intrepidity, and fortitude. John Adams had a large, strong, vehement mind, interested in all questions relating to government. He was a personage of indomitable individuality, large acquirements, quick insight, and resolute civic courage; but the storm and stress of public affairs gave to much of his thinking a character of intellectual irritation, rather than of sustained intellectual energy. His moral impatience was such that he seems to fret as he thinks. Jefferson, of all our early statesmen, was the most efficient master of the pen, and the most "advanced" political thinker. In one sense, as the author of the Declaration of Independence, he may be called the greatest, or, at least, the most generally known, of American authors. But in his private correspondence his literary talent is most displayed, for by his letters he built up a party which ruled the United States for nearly half a century, and which was, perhaps, only overturned because its opponents cited the best portions of Jefferson's writings against conclusions derived from the worst. In executive capacity he was relatively weak; but his mistakes in policy and his feebleness in administration, which would have ruined an ordinary statesman at the head of so turbulent a combination of irascible individuals as the Democratic party of the United States, were all condoned by those minor leaders of faction who, yielding to the magic persuasiveness of his pen, assured their followers that the great man could do no wrong. Read in connection with the events of his time, Jefferson's writings must be considered of permanent value and interest. As a political leader he was literally a man of letters; and his letters are masterpieces, if viewed as illustrations of the arts by which political leadership may be attained. In his private correspondence he was a model of urbanity and geniality. The whole impression derived from his works is that he was a better man than his enemies would admit him to be, and not so great a man as his partisans declared him to be. Few public men who have been assailed with equal fury have exhibited a more philosophical temper in noticing assailants. Though occasionally spiteful in his references to rivals, his leading fault, as a political leader, was not so much in being himself a libeler as in the protection he extended to libelers who lampooned men obnoxious to him. His own mind seems to have been singularly temperate; but he had a marvelous toleration for the intemperance of the rancorous defamers of Washington, Hamilton, and Adams. The Federalists hated him with such a mortal hatred, and showered on him such an amount of horrible invective, that he may have witnessed with a sarcastic smile the still coarser and fiercer calumnies which the band of assassins of character in his interest showered on the leading Federalists. Jefferson in this contest proved himself capable of malice as well as insincerity; but in a scrutiny of his works it will be found that individually he had more amenity of temper than his opponents, for it must be remembered that in his political career he was stigmatized not only as the most wicked and foolish of politicians, but as the sultan of a negro harem, and that every circumstance of his private life was malignantly misrepresented. Many eminent New England divines regarded him as an atheist as well as an anarchist, and thundered at him from their pulpits as though he was a new incarnation of the evil principle. Jefferson's comparative moderation, in view of the savage fierceness of the attacks on his personal, political, and moral character, must, on the whole, be commended; but still his moderation covered a large amount of private intrigue, and a readiness to use underhand means to compass what he may have deemed beneficent ends.

The names of Hamilton, Madison, and Jay are inseparably associated as the authors of the *Federalist*, the political classic of the United States. Of the essays it contains, Hamilton wrote fifty-one, Madison twenty-nine, and Jay five. It is generally considered that Hamilton's are the best. Indeed, Alexander Hamilton was, next to Franklin, the most consummate statesman among the band of eminent men who had been active in the Revolution, and who afterward labored to convert a loose confederation of States into a national government. His mind was as plastic as it was vigorous and profound. It was the appropriate intellectual expression of a poised nature whose power was rarely obtrusive, because it was half concealed by the harmonious adjustment of its various faculties. It was a mind deep enough to grasp principles, and broad enough to regard relations, and fertile enough to devise measures. Indeed, the most practical of our early statesmen was also the most inventive. He was as ready with new expedients to meet unexpected emergencies as he was wise in subordinating all expedients to clearly defined principles. In intellect he was probably the most creative of our early statesmen, as in sentiment Jefferson was the most widely influential. And Hamilton was so bent on practical ends that he was indifferent to the reputation which might have resulted from a parade of originality in the means he devised for their accomplishment. There never was a statesman less egotistic, less desirous of labeling a policy as "my" policy; and one of the sources of his influence was the subtle way in which he insinuated into other minds ideas which they appeared to originate. His moderation, his self-command, the exquisite courtesy of his manners, the persuasiveness of his ordinary speech, the fascination of his extraordinary speeches, and the mingled dignity and ease with which he met men of all degrees of intellect and character, resulted in making his political partisans look up to him as almost an object of political adoration. It is difficult to say what this accomplished man might have done as a leader of the Federal opposition to the Democratic administrations of Jefferson and Madison, had he not, in the maturity of his years and in the full vigor of his faculties, been murdered by Aaron Burr. Nothing can better illustrate the folly of the practice of dueling than the fact that, by a weak compliance with its maxims, the most eminent of American statesmen died by the hand of the most infamous of American demagogues. Certainly Hamilton had no need to accept a challenge in order to vindicate his claim to courage. That had been abundantly shown in the field, at the bar, in the cabinet, before the people. There was hardly any form of courage, military, civic, or moral, in which he had not proved that he was insensible to every kind of fear. The most touching expression of it was, perhaps, the confession he publicly made that he had been entrapped into a guilty intrigue with a wily woman. The confession was necessary to vindicate his integrity as a statesman, assailed by rancorous enemies. In reading it one is impressed with the innate dignity of character which such a mortifying disclosure of criminal weakness could not essentially degrade; and the allusion to his noble wife can hardly even now be read without tears. "This confession," he nobly says, "is not made without a blush. I can not be the apologist of any vice because the ardor of passion may have made it mine. I can never cease to condemn myself for the pang which it may inflict on a bosom eminently entitled to all my gratitude, fidelity, and love; but that bosom will approve that, even at so great an expense, I should effectually wipe away a more serious stain from a name which it cherishes with no less elevation than tenderness. The public, too, I trust, will excuse the confession. The necessity of it to my defense against a more heinous charge could alone have extorted from me so painful an indecorum."

John Jay, another of the wise statesmen of the Revolution, who survived to perform services of inestimable value to the new constitutional government, was a man whose character needs no apologists. Webster finely said that "the spotless ermine of the judicial robe, when it fell on the shoulders of John Jay, touched nothing not as spotless as itself." His integrity ran down into the very roots of his moral being, and honesty was in him a passion as well as a principle. A great publicist as well as an incorruptible patriot, with pronounced opinions which exposed him to all the shafts of faction, his most low-minded and venomous adversaries felt that both his private and public character were unassailable. The celebrated "treaty" with Great Britain which he negotiated as the minister of the United States occasioned an outburst of Democratic wrath such as few American diplomatists have ever been called upon to face; but in all the fury of the opposition to it, few opponents were foolish enough to assail his integrity in assailing his judgment and general views of public policy.

Judge Story once said that to James Madison and Alexander Hamilton we were mainly indebted for the Constitution of the United States. It is curious that to Madison we are also mainly indebted for those Virginia "Resolutions of '98," which have been used to justify nullification and secession. With all his mental ability, Madison had not much original force of nature. He leaned now to Hamilton, now to Jefferson, and at last fell permanently under the influence of the genius of the latter. He was lacking in that grand moral and intellectual impulse, underlying mere knowledge and logic, which distinguishes the man who reasons from the mere reasoner. His character was not on a level with his talents and acquirements; his much-vaunted moderation came from the absence rather than from the control of passion; and his understanding, though broad, was somewhat mechanical in its operations, and had no foundation in a corresponding breadth of nature. The "Resolutions of '98," which Southern Democrats came gradually to consider as of equal authority with the Constitution, were originally devised for a transient party purpose. The passage of the Alien and Sedition Laws, during the administration of John Adams, provoked Jefferson into writing a new "Declaration of Independence"—in this case directed not against Great Britain, but against the United States. He drew up a series of resolutions, which he sent to one of his subagents, George Nicholas, of Kentucky, to be adopted by the Legislature of that State. They were, with some omissions, passed. These resolutions substantially declared that the Federal Constitution was a compact between sovereign States, and that in case of a supposed violation of the compact, each party to it, as in other cases of parties having no common judge, had "an equal right to judge for itself, as well of infractions as of the mode and measure of redress." In a somewhat modified form, but still implicitly containing the poison of nullification, similar resolutions, drafted by Madison, were passed by the Legislature of Virginia. The object evidently was to frighten the general government by a threat of State resistance to its authority, without any settled purpose of nullification or rebellion. When Jefferson and Madison became successively Presidents of the United States, they seemed to have forgotten their "resolutions," except to express their horror when, seventeen years afterward, a few mild Federal gentlemen, meeting at Hartford, appeared to show some vague intention of availing themselves of the precious constitutional doctrines which Jefferson and Madison had so boldly announced. The "Resolutions of '98" must be considered an important portion of our national literature, for they were exultingly adduced as the logical justification of the gigantic rebellion of 1861. It is rare, even in the history of political factions, that a string of cunningly written resolves, designed to meet a mere party emergency, should thus cost a nation thousands of millions of treasure and hundreds of thousands of lives.

When an armed ship has her upper deck cut down, and is thus reduced to an inferior class, it is said that she is "razeed." Fisher Ames may be called, on this principle, a razeed Burke. Of all the Federal writers and speakers of his time, he bears away the palm of eloquence. He has something of Burke's affluence of imagination, something of Burke's power of condensing political wisdom into epigrammatic apothegms, and more than Burke's hatred of "French principles;" but he lacks the immense moral force of Burke's individuality, the large scope of his reason, the overwhelming intensity of his passion. Still, his merits as a writer, when compared with those of most of his contemporaries, are so striking that his countrymen seem unjust in allowing such an author to drop out of the memory of the nation. He was the despairing champion of a dying cause; he decorated the grave of Federalism with some of the choicest flowers of rhetoric; but the flowers are now withered, and the tomb itself hardly receives its due meed of honor.

The most eminent writers of the period which extends from 1776 to the first decade of the nineteenth century were either statesmen or theologians. Between these the poets, essayists, and romancers occupy a comparatively subordinate place; for we estimate the value of a literature, not so much by the character of the subjects with which it deals, as by the power of mind it evinces in dealing with them. As it regards our scholars and men of letters of that time, it must be remembered that the colonies were colonies of intellectual as well as of political Britain, and that their ideals of intellectual excellence were formed on English models. Our poets could only give a local color to a diction which was essentially that of Milton, or Dryden, or Pope, or Goldsmith, or Gray. They imitated these poets in a vain attempt to attain their elevation, simplicity, or compactness of style; but in doing this they merely did what contemporary versifiers in London or Edinburgh were intent on doing. Their verse has not survived, but it is not more completely forgotten than the verse of Mason, and Hayley, and Henry James Pye. They could write heroic verse as well as most of the English imitators of Pope, and Pindaric odes as well as most of the English imitators of Gray. Indeed, the verses with which our forefathers afflicted the world are generally not so bad as the verses of the poet laureates of England, from the period when Dryden was deprived of the laurel, to the period when Southey reluctantly accepted it. Timothy Dwight, an eminent patriot and theologian, was early smitten with the ambition to be a poet. He wrote "America," "The Conquest of Canaan" (an epic), "Greenfield Hill," and "The Triumph of Infidelity." These poems are not properly subjects of criticism, because they are hopelessly forgotten, and no critical resurrectionist can give them that slight appearance of vitality which would justify an examination of their merits and demerits.

Yet they are reasonably good of their kind, and "Greenfield Hill," especially, contains some descriptions which are almost worthy to be called charming. Dwight, as a Latin scholar, occasionally felt called upon to show his learning in his rhymes. Thus in one of his poems he characterizes one of the most delightful of Roman lyrists as "desipient" Horace. After a diligent exploration of the dictionary, the reader finds that desipient comes from a Latin word signifying "to be wise," and that its English meaning is "trifling, foolish, playful." It might be supposed that in the whole range of English poetry there was no descriptive epithet so ludicrously pedantic; but, fortunately for our patriotism, we can convict Dryden of a still greater sin against good taste. In Dryden's first ode (1687) for St. Cecilia's Day we find the following lines:

"Orpheus could lead the savage race,
And trees uprooted left their place,
Sequacious of the lyre."

It can not be doubted that Timothy Dwight's "desipient" is as poetically justifiable as John Dryden's "sequacious."

Perhaps the most versatile of our early writers of verse was Philip Freneau (1752–1832), a man of French extraction, possessing the talents of a ready writer, and endowed with that brightness and elasticity of mind which makes even shallowness of thought and emotion pleasing. He composed patriotic songs and ballads, satirized Tories, enjoyed the friendship of Franklin, Adams, Jefferson, Madison, and Monroe, and was in his day quite a literary power. Most of his writings, whether in verse or prose, were "occasional," and they died with the occasions which called them forth.

Perhaps a higher rank should be assigned to John Trumbull (1750–1831), who at the breaking out of the Revolution wrote the first canto of "McFingal," and published the third in 1782. This poem, written in Hudibrastic verse, is so full of original wit and humor that we hardly think of it as an imitation of Butler's immortal doggerel until we are reminded that many of the pithy couplets of "McFingal" are still quoted as felicitous hits of the ingenious mind of the author of "Hudibras." The immense popularity of the poem is unprecedented in American literary history. The first canto rapidly ran through thirty editions. Longfellow's "Evangeline" attained about the same circulation when the population of the country was thirty millions. "McFingal" was published when our population was only three millions. The poem, indeed, is to be considered as one of the forces of the Revolution, because, as a satire on the Tories, it penetrated into every farm-house, and sent the rustic volunteers laughing into the ranks of Washington and Greene. The vigor of mind and feeling displayed throughout the poem gives an impetus to its incidents which "Hudibras," with all its wonderful flashes of wit, comparatively lacks.

Francis Hopkinson (1737–91) was another of the writers who served the popular cause by seizing every occasion to make the British pretensions to rule ridiculous as well as hateful. His "Battle of the Kegs" probably laughed a thousand men into the republican ranks. His son, Francis Hopkinson, wrote the most popular of American lyrics, "Hail, Columbia." It is curious that this ode has no poetic merit whatever. There is not a line, not an epithet, in the whole composition which distinguishes it from the baldest prose.

Robert Treat Paine, Jun., was originally named by his father Thomas; but being a zealous Federalist, he induced the Legislature of Massachusetts to change his cognomen into Robert Treat, because, detesting the theological iconoclast who was both a Democrat and an infidel, he desired, he said, to have a *Christian* name. His song of "Adams and Liberty" is far above Hopkinson's "Hail, Columbia" in emphasis of phrase, richness of illustration, and resounding harmony of versification. Even now it kindles enthusiasm, like the lyrics of Campbell, though it is, of course, more mechanical in structure and more rhetorical in tone than the "Battle of the Baltic" and the "Mariners of England." At the time, however, it roused a similar enthusiasm.

But all the poets of the United States were threatened with extinction or subordination when Joel Barlow (1755–1812) appeared. He was, according to all accounts, an estimable man, cursed with the idea not only that he was a poet, but the greatest of American poets; and in 1808 he published, in a superb quarto volume, "The Columbiad."

It was also published in Paris and London. The London *Monthly Magazine* tried to prove not only that it was an epic poem, but that it was surpassed only by the Iliad, the Æneid, and "Paradise Lost." Joel Barlow is fairly entitled to the praise of raising mediocrity to dimensions almost colossal. Columbia is, thank Heaven, still alive; "The Columbiad" is, thank Heaven, hopelessly dead. There are some elderly gentlemen still living who declare that they have read "The Columbiad," and have derived much satisfaction from the perusal of the same; but their evidence can not stand the test of cross-examination. They can not tell what the poem is, what it teaches, and what it means. No critic within the last fifty years has read more than a hundred lines of it, and even this effort of attention has been a deadly fight with those merciful tendencies in the human organization which softly wrap the overworked mind in the blessedness of sleep. It is the impossibility of reading "The Columbiad" which prevents any critical estimate of its numberless demerits.

It is to be noted that, admitting all the poetic talent that our versifiers from 1776 to 1810 can claim, they are exceeded in all the requisites of poetry by contemporary prose writers. Fisher Ames, in a political article contributed to a newspaper, often displayed a richness of imagery, a harmony of diction, and an intensity of sentiment and passion which would have more than supplied our rhymers with materials for a canto. John Jay was not, like Fisher Ames, a man who thought in images, yet in one instance his fervid honesty enabled him to outleap every versifier of his time in the exercise of impassioned imagination. In a letter addressed to the States of the Confederation he showed the horrible injustice wrought by the depreciated currency of the country. "Humanity," he said, "as well as justice, makes this demand upon you; the complaints of ruined widows and the cries of fatherless children, whose whole support has been placed in your hands and melted away, have doubtless reached you; *take care that they ascend no higher*." And, if we consider poetry in its inmost essence, what can exceed in sentiment and imagination the statement in prose of the perfections of the maiden whom Jonathan Edwards, the austere theologian, was so fortunate as to win for his wife? To be sure, the description runs back to the year 1723, when Edwards was only twenty years old. "They say," he writes, "there is a young lady in New Haven who is beloved of that Great Being who made and rules the world, and that there are certain seasons in which this Great Being, in some way or other invisible, comes to her and fills her mind with exceeding sweet delight, and that she hardly cares for any thing except to meditate on Him, that she expects, after a while, to be received up where He is, to be raised up out of the world and caught up into heaven, being assured that He loves her too well to let her remain at a distance from Him always. There she is to dwell with Him, and to be ravished with His love and delight forever. Therefore, if you present all the world before her, with the richest of its treasures, she disregards it and cares not for it, and is unmindful of any pain or affliction. She has a strange sweetness in her mind, and singular purity in her affections; is most just and conscientious in all her conduct; and you could not persuade her to do any thing wrong or sinful if you would give her all the world, lest she should offend this Great Being. She is of a wonderful sweetness, calmness, and universal benevolence of mind, especially after this Great God has manifested Himself to her mind. She will sometimes go about from place to place singing sweetly, and seems to be always full of joy and pleasure, *and no one knows for what*. She loves to be alone, walking in the fields and groves, and seems to have some one invisible always conversing with her." The "sage and serious" Spenser, in all his lovely characterizations of feminine excellence, never succeeded in depicting a soul more exquisitely beautiful than this of Sarah Pierrepont as viewed through the consecrating imagination of Jonathan Edwards.

The leading writers of fiction during the period immediately succeeding the Revolution were Susanna Rowson, Hugh Henry Brackenridge, and Charles Brockden Brown. Mrs. Rowson's novel of *Charlotte Temple* attained the unprecedented circulation of 25,000 copies, not so much for its literary merits as on account of its foundation in a mysterious domestic scandal which affected the reputation of a number of prominent American families. Brackenridge was a Democrat of a peculiar kind, generally supporting his party, but reserving to himself the right of criticising and satirizing it. At the time the antislavery section of the Democratic party in the State of New York was called by the nickname of "Barnburners," Mr. J. G. Saxe, the poet, was asked to define his position. "I am," he replied, "a Democrat with a proclivity to arson." Brackenridge at an earlier period showed a similar restlessness in his dissent from the policy of a party whose principles he generally advocated. His principal work is *Modern Chivalry; or, the Adventures of Captain Farrago and Teague O'Regan, his Servant.* The author had a vague idea of Americanizing Don Quixote and Sancho Panza. The adventures are somewhat coarsely and clumsily portrayed, but it gave Brackenridge an opportunity to satirize the practical workings of Democracy, and he did it with pitiless severity. Teague is represented as a creature only a little raised above the condition of a beast, ignorant, credulous, greedy, and brutal, lacking both common-sense and moral sense, but still ambitious to attain political office, and willing to put himself forward as a candidate for posts the duties of which he could not by any possibility perform. The exaggeration is heightened at times into the most farcical caricature, but the book can be read even now with profit by the champions of civil service reform. There are also in the course of the narrative some deadly shafts launched, in a humorous way, against the institution of slavery. Charles Brockden Brown (1771–1810) was our first novelist by profession. At the time he wrote *Arthur Mervyn, Edgar Huntley, Clara Howard,* and *Wieland* the remuneration of the novelist was so small that he could only make what is called "a living" by sacrificing every grace and felicity of style to the inexorable need of writing rapidly, and therefore inaccurately. Brown, in his depth of insight into the morbid phenomena of the human mind, really anticipated Hawthorne; but hurried as he was by that most malignant of literary devils, the printer's, he produced no such masterpieces of literary art as *The Scarlet Letter, The Blithedale Romance,* and *The Marble Faun.* Brown is one of the most melancholy instances of a genius arrested in its orderly development by the pressure of circumstances. In mere power his forgotten novels rank very high among the products of the American imagination. And it should be added that though he is unread, he is by no means unreadable. *Wieland; or, the Transformation,* has much of the thrilling interest which fastens our attention as we read Godwin's *Caleb Williams,* or Hawthorne's *Scarlet Letter.* With all his faults, Brown does not deserve to be the victim of the bitterest irony of criticism, that, namely, of not being considered worth the trouble of a critical examination. His writings are contemptuously classed among dead books, interesting to the antiquary alone. Still, they have that vitality which comes from the presence of genius, and a little stirring of the ashes under which they are buried would reveal sparks of genuine fire.

The progress of theology during the thirty years which followed the Revolution is illustrated by the works of many men of mark in their profession, and by two men of original though somewhat crotchety religious genius, Samuel Hopkins and Nathaniel Emmons. It is the rightful boast of Calvinism, that whatever judgment may be passed on the validity of its dogmas, nobody can question its power to give strength to character, to educate men into strict habits of deductive reasoning, and to comfort regenerated and elected souls with the blissful feeling that they are in direct communication with the Divine mind. But even before the Revolution broke out there was a widely diffused though somewhat lazy mental insurrection against its doctrines by men who were formally connected with its churches; and Jonathan Edwards, the greatest successor of Calvin, was dismissed from his pastoral charge in Northampton because he had attempted to refuse Christian fellowship to those members of the church who, though they assented to Calvinistic opinions, had given "no evidence of saving grace" in their hearts. The devil, Edwards said, was very orthodox in faith, and his speculative knowledge in divinity exceeded that of "a hundred saints of ordinary education." It was but natural that the unconverted members of orthodox churches, who were distinguished more by their social position, wealth, and good moral character than by their capacity to stand Edwards's test of vital piety, should end in doubting the truth of the doctrines by the relentless application of which they were proscribed as non-Christian. The Revolution brought into the country not merely French soldiers, but the skeptical philosophy of the great French writers of the eighteenth century. The French officers were practically missionaries of unbelief. The light but stinging mockery of Voltaire had educated the intelligent French mind into a shallow contempt for all the mysteries of the Christian religion; and in fighting for our liberties, these gay, bright Frenchmen fought also against our accredited theological faith. There is something ludicrous in this contact of the French with the Yankee mind. Men like Franklin, Jefferson, John Adams, and others, had already adopted opinions which were opposed to Calvinism, but they had no strong impulse to announce their religious convictions. The general drift of the popular mind set in such an opposite direction, that they hesitated to peril their political aims in a vain attempt to enforce their somewhat languid theological views. Unitarianism, or Liberal Christianity, so called, had not yet arisen; and the protest against Calvinism first took the form of an open denial of the Christian faith. Thus Ethan Allen published, in 1784, a work which he called *Reason the Only Oracle of Man.* He summoned the fort of Ticonderoga to surrender in "the name of the Great Jehovah, and of the Continental Congress;" he afterward demanded that the impregnable fortress of Christianity should surrender in the name of Ethan Allen. Christianity declined to obey the summons of this stalwart Vermont soldier—doubtless much to his surprise.

But the man who was the most influential assailant of the orthodox faith was Thomas Paine. He was the arch-infidel, the infidel *par éminence,* whom our early and later theologians have united in holding up as a monster of iniquity and unbelief. The truth is that Paine was a dogmatic, well-meaning iconoclast, who attacked religion without having any religious experience or any imaginative perception of the vital spiritual phenomena on which religious faith is based. Nobody can read his *Age of Reason,* after having had some preparatory knowledge derived from the study of the history of religions, without wondering at its shallowness. Paine is, in a spiritual application of the phrase, color-blind. He does not seem to know what religion is. The reputation he enjoyed was due not more to his masterly command of all the avenues to the average popular mind than to the importance to which he was lifted by his horrified theological adversaries. His merit as a writer against religion consisted in his hard, almost animal, common-sense, to whose tests he subjected the current theological dogmas. He was a kind of vulgarized Voltaire. His eminent services to the country during the Revolutionary war were generally known—indeed, were acknowledged by the leading statesmen of the United States. His memorable pamphlet entitled *Common-Sense* reached a circulation of a hundred thousand copies. It was followed up by a series of tracts, under the general name of "The Crisis," which were almost as efficient as their predecessor in rousing, sustaining, and justifying the patriotism of the nation. He was the author of the now familiar maxim that "these are the times that try men's souls." His after-career in England and France resulted in his pamphlet on *The Rights of Man,* directed against Burke's assault on the principles and methods of the French Revolutionists of 1789. It was unmistakably the ablest answer that any of the democrats of France, England, and the United States had made to Burke's eloquent and philosophic impeachment of the motives and conduct of the actors in that great convulsion. One passage still survives, because it almost rivals Burke himself in the power of making a thought tell on the general mind by aptness of imagery. "Nature," says Paine, "has been kinder to Mr. Burke than he is to her. He is not affected by the realities of distress touching his heart, but by the showy resemblance of it striking his imagination. *He pities the plumage, but forgets the dying bird.*" A writer thus known to the American people not only as the champion of their individual rights, but of the rights of all mankind, could not fail to exert much influence when he brought his peculiar power of simple, forcible, and sarcastic statement to an assault on the religion of the country whose nationality he had done so much to establish. He never touched the inmost sanctuaries of Calvinism, though he seriously damaged some of its outworks; and the fault of the eminent divines who opposed him was in throwing all their strength in defending what was proved in the end to be indefensible.

Indeed, it is pitiable to witness the obstructions which strong minds and religious hearts raised against an inevitable tendency of human thought. While infidelity was slowly undermining the system of theology on which they based the sentiment and the substance of religious belief, these theologians exerted their powers of reasoning in controversies, waged against each other, relating to the question whether deductive arguments from adroitly detached Scriptural texts could fix the time when original sin made infants liable to eternal damnation. Some argued that the spiritual disease was communicated in the moment of conception; others, a little more humane, contended that the child must be born before it could righteously be damned; others insisted that a certain time after birth, left somewhat undetermined, but generally assigned to the period when the child attains to moral consciousness, should elapse before it was brought under the penalties of the universal curse. The current theology of his time could not sustain the attacks of such a hard, vulgar reasoner as Paine, except by withdrawing into its vital and unassailable position, namely, its power of converting depraved souls into loving disciples of the Lord. The thinking of the dominant theologians of that period has been quietly repudiated by their successors, and it has failed to establish any place in literature because it was exerted on themes which the human mind and human heart have gradually ignored. Still, the practical effects of the teaching of the great body of orthodox clergymen have been immense. It would be unjust to measure their influence by the success or failure of theories devised by the speculative ingenuity of their representative divines. It is impossible to estimate too highly the services of the clergymen of the country in the formation of the national character. Their sermons have not passed into literature. A band of "ministers," contented with small salaries, on which they almost starved, and with no reputation beyond their little parishes, labored year after year in the obscure work of purifying, elevating, and regenerating the individuals committed to their pastoral charge; and when they died, in all the grandeur with which piety invests poverty, they were swiftly succeeded by men who valiantly trod the same narrow path, leading to no success recognized on earth as brilliant or self-satisfying.

The period of our literary history between 1810 and 1840 witnessed the rise and growth of a literature which was influenced by the new "revival of letters" in England during the early part of the present century, represented by Wordsworth, Coleridge, Southey, Scott, Campbell, Byron, Shelley, Keats, and Moore. Most of these eminent men were not only writers but powers; they communicated spiritual life to the soul, as well as beautiful images and novel ideas to the mind; and touching, as they did, the profoundest sources of imagination, reason, and emotion, they quickened latent individual genius into original activity by the magnetism they exerted on sympathetic souls, and thus stimulated emulation rather than imitation. The wave of Wordsworthianism swept gently over New England, and here and there found a mind which was mentally and morally refreshed by drinking deeply of this new water of life. But Pope was still for a long time the pontiff of poetry, recognized by the cultivated men of Boston no less than by the cultivated men of London and Edinburgh. Probably there occurred no greater and more sudden change from the old school to the new than in the case of a precocious lad who bore the name of William Cullen Bryant. At the age of fourteen, in the year 1808, he produced a versified satire on Jefferson's administration called "The Embargo." It was just as good and just as bad as most American imitations of Pope; but the boy indicated a facility in using the accredited verse of the time which excited the wonder and admiration of his elders. Vigor, compactness, ringing emphasis in the constantly recurring rhymes, all seemed to show that a new Pope had been born in Massachusetts. The genius of the lad, however, was destined to take a different road to fame than that which was marked out by his admirers. He read the lyrical ballads of Wordsworth; and his friend, R. H. Dana, informs us that Bryant confessed to him that on reading that volume "a thousand springs seemed to gush up at once into his heart, and the face of nature of a sudden changed into a strange freshness and life." Accordingly his next poem of any importance was "Thanatopsis." We are told that it was written when he was only eighteen. It was published in the *North American Review* for 1816, when he was twenty-two. The difference of four years makes little difference in the remarkable fact that the poem indicates no sign of youth whatever. The perfection of its rhythm, the majesty and dignity of the tone of matured reflection which breathes through it, the solemnity of its underlying sentiment, and the austere unity of the pervading thought, would deceive almost any critic into affirming it to be the product of an imaginative thinker to whom "years had brought the philosophic mind." Still it must be remembered that the poets in whom meditation and imagination have been most harmoniously blended have produced some of their best works when they were comparatively young. This is specially the case as regards Wordsworth. His poem on revisiting Tintern Abbey, written when he was twenty-eight, introduced an absolutely new element into English poetry, and was specially characterized by that quality of calm, deep, solid reflection which is commonly considered to be the peculiarity of genius when it has attained the maturity which age and experience alone can give. The wonderful "Ode on the Intimations of Immortality from Recollections of Early Childhood," written about four years later, indicates the highest point which the poetic insight and the philosophic wisdom of Wordsworth ever reached; and it ought, on ordinary principles of criticism, to have been written thirty years later than the date which marks its birth. Nothing which Wordsworth afterward wrote, though precious in itself, displayed any thing equal to these poems in maturity of thought and imagination. It is doubtful if Bryant's "Thanatopsis" has been excelled by the many deep and beautiful poems which he has written since. In his case, as in that of Wordsworth, we are puzzled by the old head suddenly erected on young shoulders. They leap over the age of passion by a single bound, and become poetic philosophers at an age when other poets are in the sensuous stage of imaginative development. In estimating the claim of Bryant to be ranked as the foremost of American poets, it may be said that he opened a rich and deep, if somewhat narrow, vein, which he has worked with marvelous skill, and that he has obtained more pure gold from his mine than many others who have sunk shafts here and there into more promising deposits of the precious metal. He is, perhaps, unequaled among our American poets in his grasp of the elemental life of nature. His descriptions of natural scenery always imply that nature, in every aspect it turns to the poetic eye, is thoroughly *alive*. Nobody can read his poems called "The Evening Wind," "Green River," "The Death of the Flowers," the invocation "To a Water-Fowl," "An Evening Reverie," "To the Fringed Gentian," not to mention others, without feeling that this poet has explored the inmost secrets of nature, and has shown how natural objects can be wedded to the human mind in "love and holy passion." In the abstract imagination which celebrates the fundamental idea and ideal of our American life, what can excel his noble verses on "The Antiquity of Freedom?" "The Land of Dreams" is perhaps the most exquisite of Bryant's poems, as in it thought, sentiment, and imagination are more completely dissolved in melody than in any other of his poems. In a criticism of the range of Bryant's mind it must be remembered that his poetry is only one expression of it. His life has been generally passed in political struggles which have called forth all his powers of statement and reasoning, based on a patient study of the phenomena presented by our social and political life. As the editor of the New York *Evening Post*, he has shown himself an able publicist, an intelligent economist, and a resolute party champion. And at a period of life when most men are justified in resting from their labors, he undertook the gigantic task of translating into blank verse such as few but he can give, the whole of the Iliad and the Odyssey.

Another eminent writer of the period, and one who also happily survives, at the advanced age of eighty-eight, an object of the deserved respect and admiration of his countrymen, was Richard Henry Dana. His articles in the *North American Review*, from 1817 to 1819, were remarkable compositions for the time. The long paper on the English poets, published in 1819, surveys the whole domain of English poetry from Chaucer to Wordsworth. It exhibits a comprehensiveness of taste, a depth and delicacy of critical perception, and a grasp of the spiritual elements which enter into the highest efforts of creative minds, unexampled in any previous American contribution to the philosophy of criticism. His discernment of the relative rank and worth of British poets is specially noticeable. He interpreted before he judged; and in interpreting he showed, in old George Chapman's phrase, that he possessed the "fit key," that is, the "deep and treasurous heart,"

"With poesy to open poesy."

Even among the cultivated readers of the *North American*, there were few who could appreciate Dana's profound analysis of the genius of Wordsworth and Coleridge. In 1821 he began *The Idle Man*, of which six numbers were published. In this appeared his celebrated paper on Edmund Kean, the best piece of theatrical criticism in American literature; two novels, *Tom Thornton* and *Paul Felton*, dealing with the darker passions of our nature in a style so abrupt, a feeling so intense, and a moral purpose so inexorable that they rather terrified than pleased the "idle men" who read novels; and several of those beautiful meditations on nature and human life, in which the author exhibits himself as

"A being breathing thoughtful breath,
A traveler betwixt life and death."

The Idle Man did not succeed. In 1827 he published a thin volume entitled *The Buccaneer, and Other Poems*. These are sufficient to give him a high rank among American poets, though they have obtained but little hold on popular sympathy. "The Buccaneer" is remarkable for its representation, equally clear, of external objects and internal moods of thought and passion. In one sense it is the most "objective" of poems; in another, the most "subjective." The truth would seem to be that Dana's overpowering conception of the terrible reality of sin—a conception almost as strong as that which was fixed in the imagination of Jonathan Edwards—interferes with the artistic disposition of his imagined scenes and characters, and touches even some of his most enchanting pictures with a certain baleful light. An uneasy spiritual discontent, a moral despondency, is evident in his verse as well as in his prose, and his large powers of reason and imagination seem never to have been harmoniously blended in his artistic creations. Still, he remains one of the prominences of our literature, whether considered as poet, novelist, critic, or general thinker.

Washington Allston, the greatest of American painters, was also a graceful poet. "His mind," says Mr. Dana, "seems to have in it the glad but gentle brightness of a star, as you look up to it, sending pure influences into your heart, and making it kind and cheerful." As a poet, however, he is now but little known. As a prose writer, his lectures on Art, and especially his romance of *Monaldi*, show that he could paint with the pen as well as with the brush. It is difficult to understand why *Monaldi* has not obtained a permanent place in our literature. There is in it one description of a picture representing the visible struggle of a soul in the toils of sin which, in intensity of conception and passion, exceeds any picture he ever painted. The full richness of Allston's mind was probably only revealed to those who for years enjoyed the inestimable privilege of hearing him converse. It is to be regretted that no copious notes were taken of his conversations. Mrs. Jameson, in her visit to the United States, was so surprised to witness such opulence of thought conveyed in such seemingly careless talk, that she took a few notes of his deep and beautiful sayings. It would have been well if Dana and others who from day to day and year to year saw the clear stream of conversation flow ever on from the same inexhaustible mind, had made the world partakers of the wealth with which they were enriched. Allston, indeed, was one of those men whose works are hardly the measure of their powers—who can talk better than they can write, and conceive more vividly than they can execute.

The "revival" of American literature in New York differed much in character from its revival in New England. In New York it was purely human in tone; in New England it was a little superhuman in tone. In New England they feared the devil; in New York they dared the devil; and the greatest and most original literary daredevil in New York was a young gentleman of good family, whose "schooling" ended with his sixteenth year, who had rambled much about the island of Manhattan, who had in his saunterings gleaned and brooded over many Dutch legends of an elder time, who had read much but had studied little, who possessed fine observation, quick intelligence, a genial disposition, and an indolently original genius in detecting the ludicrous side of things, and whose name was Washington Irving. After some preliminary essays in humorous literature, his genius arrived at the age of *in*discretion, and he produced, at the age of twenty-six, the most deliciously audacious work of humor in our literature, namely, *The History of New York, by Diedrich Knickerbocker*. It is said of some reformers that they have not only opinions, but the courage of their opinions. It may be said of Irving that he not only caricatured, but had the courage of his caricatures. The persons whom he covered with ridicule were the ancestors of the leading families of New York, and these families prided themselves on their descent. After the publication of such a book he could hardly enter the "best society" of New York, to which he naturally belonged, without running the risk of being insulted, especially by the elderly women of fashion; but he conquered their prejudices by the same grace and geniality of manner, by the same unmistakable tokens that he was an inborn gentleman, through which he afterward won his way into the first society of England, France, Germany, Italy, and Spain. Still, the promise of Knickerbocker was not fulfilled. That book, if considered as an imitation at all, was an imitation of Rabelais, or Swift, or of any author in any language who had shown an independence of all convention, who did not hesitate to commit indecorums, and who laughed at all the regalities of the world. The author lived long enough to be called a timid imitator of Addison and Goldsmith. In fact, he imitated nobody. His genius, at first riotous and unrestrained, became tamed and regulated by a larger intercourse with the world, by the saddening experience of life, and by the gradual development of some deep sentiments which held in check the audacities of his wit and humor. But even in the portions of *The Sketch-Book* relating to England it will be seen that his favorite authors belonged rather to the age of Elizabeth than to the age of Anne. In *Bracebridge Hall* there is one chapter called "The Rookery," which in exquisitely poetic humor is hardly equaled by the best productions of the authors he is said to have made his models. That he possessed essential humor and pathos, is proved by the warm admiration he excited in such masters of humor and pathos as Scott and Dickens; and style is but a secondary consideration when it expresses vital qualities of genius. If he subordinated energy to elegance, he did it, not because he had the ignoble ambition to be ranked as "a fine writer," but because he was free from the ambition, equally ignoble, of simulating a passion which he did not feel. The period which elapsed between the publication of Knickerbocker's history and *The Sketch-Book* was ten years. During this time his mind acquired the habit of tranquilly contemplating the objects which filled his imagination, and what it lost in spontaneous vigor it gained in sureness of insight and completeness of representation. *Rip Van Winkle* and *The Legend of Sleepy Hollow* have not the humorous inspiration of some passages in Knickerbocker, but perhaps they give more permanent delight, for the scenes and characters are so harmonized that they have the effect of a picture, in which all the parts combine to produce one charming whole. Besides, Irving is one of those exceptional authors who are regarded by their readers as personal friends, and the felicity of nature by which he obtained this distinction was expressed in that amenity, that amiability of tone, which some of his austere critics have called elegant feebleness. As a biographer and historian, his *Life of Columbus* and his *Life of Washington* have indissolubly connected his name with the discoverer of the American continent and the champion of the liberties of his country. In *The Chronicle of the Conquest of Granada* and *The Alhambra* he occupies a unique position among those writers of fiction who have based fiction on a laborious investigation into the facts of history. His reputation is not local, but is recognized by all cultivated people who speak the English language. If Great Britain established an English intellectual colony in the United States, such men as Irving and Cooper may be said to have retorted by establishing an American intellectual colony in England.

James Fenimore Cooper was substantially a New Yorker, though accidentally born (in 1789) in New Jersey. He entered Yale College in 1802, and, three years after, left it without graduating, having obtained a midshipman's warrant in the United States navy. He remained in the naval service for six years. In 1811 he married, and in 1821 began a somewhat memorable literary career by the publication of a novel of English life, called *Precaution*, which failed to attract much attention. In the same year, however, he published another novel, relating to the Revolutionary period of our history, called *The Spy*, and rose at once to the position of a power of the first class in our literature. The novels which immediately followed did, on the whole, increase his reputation; and after the publication of *The Red Rover*, in 1827, his works were not only eagerly welcomed by his countrymen, but were translated into almost all the languages of Europe. Indeed, it seemed at one time that Cooper's fame was co-extensive with American commerce. The novels were intensely American in spirit, and intensely American in scenery and characters; but they were also found to contain in them something which appealed to human nature every where. Much of their popularity was doubtless due to Cooper's vivid presentation of the wildest aspects of nature in a comparatively new country, and his creation of characters corresponding to their physical environment; but the essential influence he exerted is to be referred to the pleasure all men experience in the kindling exhibition of man as an active being. No Hamlets, or Werthers, or Renés, or Childe Harolds were allowed to tenant his woods or appear on his quarter-decks. Will, and the trained sagacity and experience directing will, were the invigorating elements of character which he selected for romantic treatment. Whether the scene be laid in the primitive forest or on the ocean, his men are always struggling with each other or with the forces of nature. This primal quality of robust manhood all men understand, and it shines triumphantly through the interposing fogs of French, German, Italian, and Russian translations. A physician of the mind could hardly prescribe a more efficient tonic for weak and sentimental natures than a daily diet made up of the most bracing passages in the novels of Cooper.

Another characteristic of Cooper, which makes him universally acceptable, is his closeness to nature. He agrees with Wordsworth in this, that in all his descriptions of natural objects he indicates that he and nature are familiar acquaintances, and, as Dana says, have "talked together." He takes nothing at second-hand. If brought before a justice of the peace, he could solemnly swear to the exact truth of his representations without running any risk of being prosecuted for perjury. Cooper as well as Wordsworth took nature, as it were, at first-hand, the perceiving mind coming into direct contact with the thing perceived; but Wordsworth primarily contemplated nature as the divinely appointed food for the nourishment of the spirit that meditates, while Cooper felt its power as a stimulus to the spirit that acts. No two minds could, in many respects, be more different, yet both agree in the instinctive sagacity which detects the heroic under the guise of the homely. The greatest creation of Cooper is the hunter and trapper, Leatherstocking, who appears in five of his best novels, namely, *The Pioneers*, *The Last of the Mohicans*, *The Prairie*, *The Pathfinder*, and *The Deerslayer*, and who is unmistakably the life of each. The simplicity, sagacity, and intrepidity of this man of the woods, his quaint sylvan piety and humane feeling, the perfect harmony established between his will and reason, his effectiveness equal to all occasions, and his determination to dwell on those vanishing points of civilization which faintly mark the domain of the settler from that of the savage, altogether combine to make up a character which is admired equally in log-cabins and palaces. Wordsworth, in one of the most exquisite of his minor poems — "Three Years She grew in Sun and Shower"—has traced the process of nature in making "a lady of her own." Certainly Leatherstocking might be quoted as a successful attempt of the same austere goddess to make, out of ruder materials, a man of "her own."

Cooper lived to write thirty-four novels, the merits of which are so unequal that at times we are puzzled to conceive of them as the products of one mind. His failures are not to be referred to that decline of power which accompanies increasing age, for *The Deerslayer*, one of his best novels, was written six years after his worst novel, *The Monikins*. He often failed, early as well as late in his career, not because his faculties were impaired, but because they were misdirected. One of the secrets of his fascination was also one of the causes of his frequent dullness. He equaled De Foe in the art of giving reality to romance by the dextrous accumulation and management of details. In his two great sea novels, *The Pilot* and *The Red Rover*, the important events are preceded by a large number of minor incidents, each of which promises to be an event. The rocks which the vessel by cunning seamanship escapes are described as minutely as the rocks on which she is finally wrecked. It is difficult for the reader to conceive that he is not reading an account of an actual occurrence. He unconsciously transports himself to the deck of the ship, participates in all the hopes and fears of the crew, thanks God when the keel just grazes a ledge without being seriously injured, and finally goes down into the "hell of waters" in company with his imagined associates. In such scenes the imagination of the reader is so excited that he has no notion whether the writer's style is good or bad. He is made by some magic of words to see, feel, realize, the situation; the verbal method by which the miracle is wrought he entirely ignores or overlooks. But then the preliminaries to these grand scenes which exhibit intelligent man in a life-and-death contest with the unintelligent forces of nature—how tiresome they often are! The early chapters of *The Red Rover*, for example, are dull beyond expression. The author's fondness for detail trespasses on all the reserved fund of human patience. It is only because "expectation sits i' the air" that we tolerate his tediousness. If we desire to witness the conduct of the man-of-war in the tempest and the battle, we must first submit to follow all the cumbersome details by which she is slowly detached from the dock and laboriously piloted into the open sea. There is more "padding" in Cooper's novels than in those of any author who can make any pretensions to rival him. His representative sailors, Long Tom Coffin, Tom Tiller, Nightingale, Bolthrope, Trysail, Bob Yarn, not to mention others, are admirable as characters, but they are allowed to inflict too much of their practical wisdom on the reader. In fact, it is a great misfortune, as it regards the permanent fame of Cooper, that he wrote one-third, at least, of his novels at all, and that he did not condense the other two-thirds into a third of their present length.

Cooper, on his return from Europe in 1833 or 1834, published a series of novels satirizing what he considered the faults and vices of his countrymen. The novels have little literary merit, but they afforded an excellent opportunity to exhibit the independence, intrepidity, and integrity of the author's character. It is a pity he ever wrote them; still, they proved that he became a bad novelist in order to perform what he deemed to be the duties of a good citizen. Indeed, as a brave, high-spirited, noble-minded man, somewhat too proud and dogmatic, but thoroughly honest, he was ever on a level with the best characters in his best works.

The names of Joseph Rodman Drake and Fitz-Greene Halleck are connected, not merely by personal friendship, but by partnership in poetry. Both were born in the same year (1795), but Drake died in 1820, while Halleck survived to 1867. Halleck, in strength of constitution as well as in power of mind, was much superior to his fragile companion; but Drake had a real enthusiasm for poetry, which Halleck, though a poet, did not possess. Drake's "Culprit Fay" is an original American poem, formed out of materials collected from the scenery and traditions of the classical American river, the Hudson, but it was too hastily written to do justice to the fancy by which it was conceived. His "Ode on the American Flag" derives its chief strength from the resounding quatrain by which it is closed, and these four lines were contributed by Halleck. Indeed, Drake is, on the whole, less remembered by his own poems than by the beautiful tribute which Halleck made to his memory. They were coadjutors in the composition of the "Croaker Papers," originally contributed to the New York *Evening Post;* but the superiority of Halleck to his friend is manifest at the first glance. One of the puzzles which arrest the attention of a historian of American literature is to account for the strange indifference of Halleck to exercise often the faculty which on occasions he showed he possessed in superabundance. All the subjects he attempted —the "Croaker Papers," "Fanny," "Burns," "Red Jacket," "Alnwick Castle," "Connecticut," the magnificent heroic ode, "Marco Bozzaris"—show a complete artistic mastery of the resources of poetic expression, whether his theme be gay or grave, or compounded of the two. His extravagant admiration of Campbell was founded on Campbell's admirable power of compression. Halleck thought that Byron was a mere rhetorician in comparison with his favorite poet. Yet it is evident to a critical reader that a good deal of Campbell's compactness is due to a studied artifice of rhythm and rhyme, while Halleck seemingly writes in verse as if he were not trammeled by its laws; and his rhymes naturally recur without suggesting to the reader that his condensation of thought and feeling is at all affected by the necessity of rhyming. Prose has rarely been written with more careless ease and more melodious compactness than Halleck has shown in writing verse. The wonder is that with this conscious command of bending verse into the brief expression of all the moods of his mind, he should have written so little. The only explanation is to be found in his skepticism as to the vital reality of those profound states of consciousness which inspire poets of less imaginative faculty than he possessed to incessant activity. He was among poets what Thackeray is among novelists. Being the well-paid clerk and man of business of a millionaire, his grand talent was not stung into exertion by necessity. Though he lived to the age of seventy-two, he allowed year after year to pass without any exercise of his genius. "What's the use?"—that was the deadening maxim which struck his poetic faculties with paralysis. Yet what he has written, though very small in amount, belongs to the most precious treasures of our poetical literature. What he might have written, had he so chosen, would have raised him to a rank among our first men of letters, which he does not at present hold.

James K. Paulding (1778–1860) completes this peculiar group of New York authors. He was connected with Irving in the production of the "Salmagundi" essays, and was at one time prominent as a satirist, humorist, and novelist. Most of his writings are now forgotten, though they evinced a somewhat strong though coarse vein of humor, which was not without its effect at the period when its local and political allusions and personalities were understood. A scene in one of his novels indicates the kind of comicality in which he excelled. The house of an old reprobate situated on the bank of a river is carried away by a freshet. In the agony of his fear he strives to recall some prayer which he learned when a child; but as he rushes distractedly up and down the stairs of his floating mansion, he can only remember the first line of the baby's hymn, "Now I lay me down to sleep," which he incessantly repeats as he runs.

While these New York essayists, humorists, and novelists were laughing at the New Englander as a Puritan and satirizing him as a Yankee, there was a peculiar revival of spiritual sentiment in New England, which made its mark in general as well as in theological literature. In the very home of Puritanism there was going on a reaction against the fundamental doctrines of Calvinism and the inexorable faith of the Pilgrim Fathers. This reaction began before the Revolutionary war, and continued after it. Jonathan Mayhew, the pastor of the West Church, of Boston, was not only a flaming defender of the political rights of the colonies, but his sermons also teemed with theological heresies. He rebelled against King Calvin as well as against King George. Probably Paine's *Age of Reason* had afterward some effect in inducing prominent Boston clergymen, reputed orthodox, to silently drop from their preaching the leading dogmas of the accredited creed. With such accomplished ministers as Freeman, Buckminster, Thacher, and their followers, sermonizing became more and more a form of moralizing, and the "scheme of salvation" was ignored or overlooked in the emphasis laid on the performance of practical duties. What would now be called rationalism, either expressed or implied, seemed to threaten the old orthodox faith with destruction by the subtle process of sapping and undermining without directly assailing it. The sturdy Calvinists were at first puzzled what to do, as the new heresiarchs did not so much offend by what they preached as by what they omitted to preach; but they at last forced those who were Unitarians in opinion to become Unitarians in profession, and thus what was intended as a peaceful evolution of religious faith was compelled to assume the character of a revolutionary protest against the generally received dogmas of the Christian churches. The two men prominent in this insurrection against ancestral orthodoxy were William Ellery Channing and Andrews Norton. Channing was a pious humanitarian; Norton was an accomplished Biblical scholar. Channing assailed Calvinism because, in his opinion, it falsified all right notions of God; Norton, because it falsified the true interpretation of the Word of God. Channing's soul was filled with the idea of the dignity of human nature, which, he thought, Calvinism degraded; Norton's mind resented what he considered the illogical combination of Scripture texts to sustain an intolerable theological theory. Channing delighted to portray the felicities of a heavenly frame of mind; Norton delighted to exhibit the felicities of accurate exegesis. Both were masters of style; but Channing used his rhetoric to prove that the doctrines of Calvinism were abhorrent to the God-given moral nature of man; Norton employed his somewhat dry and bleak but singularly lucid powers of statement, exposition, and logic to show that his opponents were deficient in scholarship and sophistical in argumentation. Channing's literary reputation, which overleaped all the boundaries of his sect, was primarily due to his essay on Milton; but Norton could not endure the theological system on which "Paradise Lost" was based, and therefore laughed at the poem. Norton had little of that imaginative sympathy with the mass of mankind for which Channing was pre-eminently distinguished. Any body who has mingled much with Unitarian divines must have heard their esoteric pleasantry as to what these two redoubtable champions of the Unitarian faith would say when they were transferred from earth to heaven. Channing, as he looks upon the bright rows of the celestial society, rapturously declares, "This gives me a new idea of the dignity of human nature;" Norton, with a certain patrician exclusiveness born of scholarly tastes, folds his hands, and quietly says to St. Peter or St. Paul, "Rather a miscellaneous assemblage." But on earth they worked together, each after his gifts, to draw out all the resources of sentiment, scholarship, and reasoning possessed by such able opponents as they found in Stuart, Woods, and Park. There can be no doubt that Calvinism, in its modified Hopkinsian form, gained increased power by the wholesome shaking which Unitarianism gave it; for this shaking kindled the zeal, sharpened the intellects, stimulated the mental activity of every professor of the evangelical faith. Neither Channing nor Norton, in assailing the statements in which the Calvinistic creed was mechanically expressed, exhibited an interior view of the creed as it vitally existed in the souls of Calvinists. Channing, however, was still the legitimate spiritual successor of Jonathan Edwards in affirming, with new emphasis, the fundamental doctrine of Christianity, that God is in direct communication with the souls of His creatures. The difference is that Edwards holds the doors of communication so nearly closed that only the elect can pass in; Channing throws them wide open, and invites every body to be illumined in thought and vitalized in will by the ever-fresh outpourings of celestial light and warmth. But Channing wrote on human nature as though the world was tenanted by actual or possible Channings, who possessed his exceptional delicacy of spiritual perception, and his exceptional exemption from the temptations of practical life. He was, as far as a constant contemplation of the Divine perfections was concerned, a meditative saint, and had he belonged to the Roman Catholic Church, he probably would, on the ground of his spiritual gifts, have been eventually canonized. Still, the seductive subjectivity of his holy outlook on nature and human life tended to make the individual consciousness of what was just and good the measure of Divine justice and goodness; and in some mediocre minds, which his religious genius magnetized, this tendency brought forth distressing specimens of spiritual sentimentality and pious pertness. The most curious result, however, of Channing's teachings was the swift way in which his disciples overleaped the limitations set by their master. In the course of a single generation some of the most vigorous minds among the Unitarians, practicing the freedom of thought which he inculcated as a duty, indulged in theological audacities of which he never dreamed. He was the intellectual father of Theodore Parker, and the intellectual grandfather of Octavius B. Frothingham. Parker and Frothingham, both humanitarians, but students also of the advanced school of critical theologians, soon made Channing's heresies tame when compared with the heresies they promulgated. The Free Religionists are the legitimate progeny of Channing.

But, in the interim, the theologian and preacher who came nearest to Channing in the geniality and largeness of his nature, and the persuasiveness with which he enforced what may be called the conservative tenets of Unitarianism, was Orville Dewey, a man whose mind was fertile, whose religious experience was deep, and who brought from the Calvinism in which he had been trained an interior knowledge of the system which he early rejected. He had a profound sense not only of the dignity of human nature, but of the dignity of human life. In idealizing human life he must still be considered as giving some fresh and new interpretations of it, and his discourses form, like Channing's, an addition to American literature, as well as a contribution to the theology of Unitarianism. He defended men from the assaults of Calvinists, as Channing had defended Man. Carlyle speaks somewhere of "this dog-hole of a world;" Dewey considered it, with all its errors and horrors, as a good world on the whole, and as worthy of the Divine beneficence.

The work which may be said to have bridged over the space which separated Channing from Theodore Parker was *Academical Lectures on the Jewish Scriptures and Antiquities*, by Dr. John G. Palfrey, Professor of Biblical Literature in the University of Cambridge, published in 1838, but which had doubtless influenced the students who had listened to them many years before their publication. This book is noticeable for the scholarly method by which most of the miracles recorded in the Old Testament are explained on natural principles, and the calm, almost prim and polite, exclusion of miracle from the Hebrew Scriptures. Accepting miracle when he considered it necessary, Dr. Palfrey broke the spell and charm, at least among Unitarian students of theology, which separated the Hebrew Bible from other great works which expressed the religious mind of the human race; and his *Academical Lectures* remain as a palpable landmark in the progress of American rationalism.

But probably the greatest literary result of the Unitarian revolt was the appearance in our literature of such a phenomenon as Ralph Waldo Emerson. He came from a race of clergymen; doubtless much of his elevation of character and austere sense of the grandeur of the moral sentiment is his by inheritance; but after entering the ministry he soon found that even Unitarianism was a limitation of his intellectual independence to which he could not submit; and, in the homely New England phrase, "he set up on his account," responsible *for* nobody, and not responsible *to* any body. His radicalism penetrated to the very root of dissent, for it was founded on the idea that in all organizations, social, political, and religious, there must be an element which checks the free exercise of individual thought; and the free exercise of his individual thinking he determined should be controlled by nothing instituted and authoritative on the planet. Descartes himself did not begin his philosophizing with a more complete self-emancipation from all the opinions generally accepted by mankind. But Descartes was a reasoner; Emerson is a seer and a poet; and he was the last man to attempt to overthrow accredited systems in order to substitute for them a dogmatic system of his own. In his view of the duty of "man thinking," this course would have been to violate his fundamental principle, which was that nobody "could lay copyright on the world;" that no theory could include nature; that the greatest thinker and discoverer could only add a few items of information to what the human mind had previously won from "the vast and formless infinite;" and that the true work of a scholar was not to inclose the field of matter and mind by a system which encircled it, but to extend our knowledge in straight lines, leading from the vanishing points of positive knowledge into the illimitable unknown spaces beyond. Emerson's peculiar sphere was psychology. By a certain felicity of his nature he was a non-combatant; indifferent to logic, he suppressed all the processes of his thinking, and announced its results in affirmations; and none of the asperities which commonly afflict the apostles of dissent ever ruffled the serene spirit of this universal dissenter. He could never be seduced into controversy. He was assailed both as an atheist and as a pantheist; as a writer so obscure that nobody could understand what he meant, and also as a mere verbal trickster, whose only talent consisted in vivifying commonplaces, or in converting, by inversion, stale truisms into brilliant paradoxes; and all these varying charges had only the effect of lighting up his face with that queer, quizzical, inscrutable smile, that amused surprise at the misconceptions of the people who attacked him, which is noticeable in all portraits and photographs of his somewhat enigmatical countenance. His method was very simple and very hard. It consisted in growing up to a level with the spiritual objects he perceived, and his elevation of thought was thus the sign and accompaniment of a corresponding elevation of character. In his case, as in the case of Channing, there was an unconscious return to Jonathan Edwards, and to all the great divines whose "souls had sight" of eternal verities. What the orthodox saints called the Holy Ghost, he, without endowing it with personality, called the Over Soul. He believed with them that in God we live and move and have our being; that only by communicating with this Being can we have any vital individuality; and that the record of a communication with Him or It was the most valuable of all contributions to literature, whether theological or human. The noblest passages in his writings are those in which he celebrates this august and gracious communion of the Spirit of God with the soul of man; and they are the most serious, solemn, and uplifting passages which can perhaps be found in our literature. Here was a man who had earned the right to utter these noble truths by patient meditation and clear insight. Carlyle exclaimed, in a preface to an English edition of one of Emerson's later volumes: "Here comes our brave Emerson, with *news* from the empyrean!" That phrase exactly hits Emerson as a transcendental thinker. His insights were, in some sense, revelations; he could "gossip on the eternal politics;" and just at the time when science, relieved from the pressure of theology, announced materialistic hypotheses with more than the confidence with which the bigots of theological creeds had heretofore announced their dogmas, this serene American thinker had won his way into all the centres of European intelligence, and delivered his quiet protest against every hypothesis which put in peril the spiritual interests of humanity. It is curious to witness the process by which this heresiarch has ended in giving his evidence, or rather his experience, that God is not the Unknowable of Herbert Spencer, but that, however infinitely distant He may be from the human understanding, He is still intimately near to the human soul. And Emerson knows by experience what the word soul really means!

"Were she a body, how could she remain
Within the body, which is less than she?
Or how could she the world's great shape contain,
And in our narrow breasts containèd be?

"All bodies are confined within some place,
But she all place within herself confines;
All bodies have their measure and their space,
But who can draw the soul's dimensive lines?"

In an unpublished speech at a celebration of Shakspeare's birthday, he spoke of Shakspeare as proving to us that "the soul of man is deeper, wider, higher than the spaces of astronomy;" and in another connection he says that "a man of thought must feel that thought is the parent of the universe," that "the world is *saturated* with deity and with law."

It is this depth of spiritual experience and subtilty of spiritual insight which distinguish Emerson from all other American authors, and make him an elementary power as well as an elementary thinker. The singular attractiveness, however, of his writings comes from his intense perception of Beauty, both in its abstract quality as the "awful loveliness" which such poets as Shelley celebrated, and in the more concrete expression by which it fascinates ordinary minds. His imaginative faculty, both in the conception and creation of beauty, is uncorrupted by any morbid sentiment. His vision reaches to the very sources of beauty—the beauty that cheers. The great majority even of eminent poets are "saddest when they sing." They contrast life with the beautiful possibilities of life which their imaginations suggest, and though their discontent with the actual may inspire by the energy of its utterance, it tends also to depress by emphasizing the impossibility of realizing the ideals it depicts. But the perception of beauty in nature or in human nature, whether it be the beauty of a flower or of a soul, makes Emerson joyous and glad; he exults in celebrating it, and he communicates to his readers his own ecstatic mood. He has been a diligent student of many literatures and many religions; but all his quotations from them show that he rejects every thing in his manifold readings which does not tend to cheer, invigorate, and elevate, which is not nutritious food for the healthy human soul. If he is morbid in any thing, it is in his comical hatred of all forms of physical, mental, and moral disease. He agrees with Dr. Johnson in declaring that "every man is a rascal as soon as he is sick." "I once asked," he says, "a clergyman in a retired town who were his companions—what men of ability he saw. He replied that he spent his time with the sick and the dying. I said he seemed to me to need quite other company, and all the more that he had this; for if people were sick and dying to any purpose, we should leave all and go to them, but, as far as I had observed, they were as frivolous as the rest, and sometimes much more frivolous." Indeed, Emerson, glorying in his own grand physical and moral health, and fundamentally brave, is impatient of all the weaknesses of humanity, especially those of men of genius. He never could be made to recognize the genius of Shelley, except in a few poems, because he was disgusted with the wail that persistently runs through Shelley's wonderfully imaginative poetry. In his taste, as in his own practice as a writer, he is a stout believer in the desirableness and efficacy of mental tonics, and a severe critic of the literature of discontent and desperation. He looks curiously on while a poet rages against destiny and his own miseries, and puts the ironical query, "Why so hot, my little man?" His ideal of manhood was originally derived from the consciousness of his own somewhat haughty individuality, and it has been fed by his study of the poetic and historic records of persons who have dared to do heroic acts and dared to utter heroic thoughts. Beauty is never absent from his celebration of these, but it is a beauty that never enfeebles, but always braces and cheers.

Take the six or eight volumes in which Emerson's genius and character are embodied—that is, in which he has converted truth into life, and life into more truth—and you are dazzled on every page by his superabundance of compactly expressed reflection and his marvelous command of all the resources of imaginative illustration. Every paragraph is literally "rammed with life." A fortnight's meditation is sometimes condensed in a sentence of a couple of lines. Almost every word bears the mark of deliberate thought in its selection. The most evanescent and elusive spiritual phenomena, which occasionally flit before the steady gaze of the inner eye of the mind, are fixed in expressions which have the solidity of marble. The collection of these separate insights into nature and human life he ironically calls an essay; and much criticism has been wasted in showing that the aphoristic and axiomatic sentences are often connected by mere juxtaposition on the page, and not by logical relation with each other, and that at the end we have no perception of a series of thoughts leading up to a clear idea of the general theme. This criticism is just; but in reading Emerson we have not to do with such economists of thought as Addison, Johnson, and Goldsmith—with the writers of the *Spectator*, the *Rambler*, and the *Citizen of the World*. Emerson's so-called essay sparkles with sentences which might be made the texts for numerous ordinary essays; and his general title, it may be added, is apt to be misleading. He is fragmentary in composition because he is a fanatic for compactness; and every paragraph, sometimes every sentence, is a record of an insight. Hence comes the impression that his sentences are huddled together rather than artistically disposed. Still, with all this lack of logical order, he has the immense advantage of suggesting something new to the diligent reader after he has read him for the fiftieth time.

It is also to be said of Emerson that he is one of the wittiest and most practical as well as one of the profoundest of American writers, that his wit, exercised on the ordinary affairs of life, is the very embodiment of brilliant good sense, that he sometimes rivals Franklin in humorous insight, and that both his wit and humor obey that law of beauty which governs every other exercise of his peculiar mind. He has many defects and eccentricities exasperating to the critic who demands symmetry in the mental constitution of the author whose peculiar merits he is eager to acknowledge. He occasionally indulges, too, in some strange freaks of intellectual and moral caprice which his own mature judgment should condemn—the same pen by which they were recorded being used to blot them out of existence. They are audacities, but how unlike his grand audacities! In short, they are somewhat small audacities, unworthy of him and of the subjects with which he deals—escapades of epigram on topics which should have exacted the austerest exercise of his exceptional faculty of spiritual insight. Nothing, however, which can be said against him touches his essential quality of manliness, or lowers him from that rank of thinkers in whom the seer and the poet combine to give the deepest results of meditation in the most exquisite forms of vital beauty. And then how superb and animating is his lofty intellectual courage! "The soul," he says, "is in her native realm, and it is wider than space, older than time, wide as hope, rich as love. Pusillanimity and fear she refuses with a beautiful scorn. They are not for her who putteth on her coronation robes, and goes through universal love to universal power."

Emerson, though in some respects connected with the Unitarian movement as having been a minister of the denomination, soon cut himself free from it, and was as independent of that form of Christian faith as he was of other forms. He drew from all quarters, and whatever fed his religious sense of mystery, of might, of beauty, and of Deity was ever welcome to his soul. As he was outside of all religious organizations, and never condescended to enter into any argument with his opponents, he was soon allowed silently to drop out of theological controversy. But a fiercer and more combative spirit now appeared to trouble the Unitarian clergymen—a man who considered himself a Unitarian minister, who had for Calvinism a stronger repulsion than Channing or Norton ever felt, and who attempted to drag on his denomination to conclusions at which most of its members stood aghast.

This man was Theodore Parker, a born controversialist, who had the challenging chip always on his shoulder, which he invited both his Unitarian and his orthodox brethren to knock off. There never was a man who more gloried in a fight. If any theologians desired to get into a controversy with him as to the validity of their opposing beliefs, he was eager to give them as much of it as they desired. The persecution he most keenly felt was the persecution of inattention and silence. He was the Luther of radical Unitarianism. When the Unitarian societies refused fellowship with his society, he organized a church of his own, and made it one of the most powerful in New England. There was nothing but disease which could check and nothing but death which could close his controversial activity. He became the champion of radical as against conservative Unitarianism, and the persistent adversary even of the most moderate Calvinism. Besides his work in these fields of intellectual effort, he threw himself literally head-foremost — and his head was large and well stored—into every unpopular reform which he could aid by his will, his reason, his learning, and his moral power. He was among the leaders in the attempt to apply the rigid maxims of Christianity to practical life; and many orthodox clergymen, who combined with him in his assaults on intemperance, slavery, and other hideous evils of our civilization, almost condoned his theological heresies in their admiration of his fearlessness in practical reforms. He was an enormous reader and diligent student, as well as a resolute man of affairs. He also had great depth and fervency of piety. His favorite hymn was "Nearer, my God, to Thee." While assailing what the great body of New England people believed to be the foundations of religion, he startled vigorous orthodox reasoners by his confident teaching that every individual soul had a consciousness of its immortality independent of revelation, and superior to the results of all the modern physical researches which seemed to place it in doubt. Indeed, his own incessant activity was an argument for the soul's immortality. In spite of all the outside calls on his energies, he found time to attend strictly to his ministerial duties, to make himself one of the most accomplished theological and general scholars in New England, and to write and translate books which required deep study and patient thought. The physical frame, stout as it was, at last broke down—his mind still busy in meditating new works which were never to be written. Probably no other clergyman of his time, not even Mr. Beecher, drew his society so closely to himself, and became the object of so much warm personal attachment and passionate devotion. Grim as he appeared when, arrayed in his theological armor, he went forth to battle, he was, in private intercourse, the gentlest, most genial, and most affectionate of men. And it is to be added that few orthodox clergymen had a more intense religious faith in the saving power of their doctrines than Theodore Parker had in the regenerating efficacy of his rationalistic convictions. When Luther was dying, Dr. Jonas said to him, "Reverend father, do you die in implicit reliance on the faith you have taught?" And from those lips, just closing in death, came the steady answering "Yes." Theodore Parker's answer to such a question, put to him on his death-bed, would have been the same.

The theological protest against Unitarianism was made by some of the most powerful minds and learned scholars in the country—by Stuart, Park, Edwards, Barnes, Robinson, Lyman Beecher, the whole family of the Alexanders, of which Addison Alexander was the greatest, not to mention fifty others. The thought of these men still controls the theological opinion of the country, and their works are much more extensively circulated, and exert a greater practical influence, than the writings of such men as Channing, Norton, Dewey, Emerson, and Parker; but still they have not affected in a like degree the literature which springs from the heart, the imagination, and the spiritual sentiment. Unitarianism, through its lofty views of the dignity of human nature, naturally allied itself with the sentiment of philanthropy. While it has not been more practically conspicuous than other denominations for the love of man, as expressed in works to ameliorate his condition, it has succeeded better in domesticating philanthropy in literature, especially in poetry. Witness Bryant, Longfellow, Whittier, Holmes, Lowell, and Mrs. Howe.

Longfellow is probably the most popular poet of the country. The breadth of his sympathy, the variety of his acquisitions, the plasticity of his imagination, the sonorousness and weight of his verse, the vividness of his imagery, the equality, the beauty, the beneficence of his disposition, make him universally attractive and universally intelligible. Each of his minor poems is pervaded by one thought, and has that artistic unity which comes from the economic use of rich material. There is a solidity in them in which many occasional poems are wanting, though they may exhibit more fertility of thought and imagery; this fertility is less directed to produce one impressive effect. Take the "Hymn to the Night," "A Psalm of Life," "Footsteps of Angels,"

"The Skeleton in Armor," "The Wreck of the Hesperus," "The Village Blacksmith," "Excelsior," "The Arsenal at Springfield," "Sea-Weed," "Resignation," and other of his minor poems have found a lodgment in the memory of every body, and it will be found that their charm consists in their unity as well as in their beauty, that they are as much poems, complete in themselves, as "Evangeline" or "Hiawatha." In "Maidenhood" and "Endymion," especially in the latter, the poet is revealed in all the exquisiteness, the delicacy, the refinement, of his imaginative faculty; but they are less popular than the poems previously mentioned, because they embody more subtile moods of the poetic mind. Longfellow's power of picturing to the eye and the soul a scene, a place, an event, a person, is almost unrivaled. His command of many metres, each adapted to his special subject, shows also how artistically he uses sound to re-enforce vision, and satisfy the ear while pleasing the eye.

> "When descends on the Atlantic
> The gigantic
> Storm-wind of the equinox,
> Landward in his wrath he scourges
> The toiling surges,
> Laden with sea-weed from the rocks."

The ear least skilled to detect the harmonies of verse feels the obvious effect of lines like these. In his long poems, such as "Evangeline," "The Golden Legend," "Hiawatha," "The Courtship of Miles Standish," "The New England Tragedies," Longfellow never repeats himself. He occupies a new domain of poetry with each successive poem, and always gives the public the delightful shock of a new surprise. In his prose works, *Outre-Mer*, *Hyperion*, and *Kavanagh*, he is the same man as in his verse—ever sweet, tender, thoughtful, weighty, vigorous, imaginative, and humane. His great translation of Dante is not the least of his claims to the gratitude of his countrymen, for it is a new illustration of his life-long devotion—rare in an American—to the service of literature, considered as one of the highest exercises of patriotism.

Longfellow has enjoyed every advantage that culture can give, and his knowledge of many nations and many languages undoubtedly has given breadth to his mind, and opened to him ever new sources of poetic interest; but John Greenleaf Whittier, who contests with him the palm of popularity as a poet, was one of those God-made men who are in a sense self-made poets. A musing farmer's boy, working in the fields, and ignorant of books, he early felt the poetic instinct moving in his soul, but thought his surroundings were essentially prosaic, and could never be sung. At last one afternoon, while he was gathering in the hay, a peddler dropped a copy of Burns into his hands. Instantly his eyes were unscaled. There in the neighboring field was "Highland Mary;" "The Cotter's Saturday Night" occurred in his own father's pious New England home; and the birds which caroled over his head, the flowers which grew under his feet, were as poetic as those to which the Scottish plowman had given perennial interest. Burns taught him to detect the beautiful in the common, but Burns could not corrupt the singularly pure soul of the lad by his enticing suggestions of idealized physical enjoyment and unregulated passion. The boy grew into a man, cultivating assiduously his gift of song, though shy of showing it. The antislavery storm swept over the land, awakening consciences as well as stimulating intellects. Whittier had always lived in a region of moral ideas, and this antislavery inspiration inflamed his moral ideas into moral passion and moral wrath. If Garrison may be considered the prophet of antislavery, and Phillips its orator, and Mrs. Stowe its novelist, and Sumner its statesman, there can be no doubt that Whittier was its poet. Quaker as he was, his martial lyrics had something of the energy of a primitive bard urging on hosts to battle. Every word was a blow, as uttered by this newly enrolled soldier of the Lord. "The silent, shy, peace-loving man" became a "fiery partisan," and held his intrepid way

> "against the public frown,
> The ban of church and state, the fierce mob's hounding down."

It is impossible even now to read his kindling lyrics of that shameful period in our history without feeling the blood boil in the veins, and experiencing the hot impulse to instant battle. They had a vast effect in rousing, condensing, and elevating the public sentiment against slavery. The poetry was as genuine as the wrath was terrific, and many a political time-server, who was proof against Garrison's hottest denunciations and Phillips's most stinging invectives, quailed before Whittier's smiting rhymes. Yet he tells us he was essentially a poetic dreamer, unfit "to ride the winged hippogriff Reform."

"For while he wrought with strenuous will
The work his hands had found to do,
He heard the fitful music still
Of winds that out of dream-land blew.

* * * * * * *

"The common air was thick with dreams—
He told them to the toiling crowd;
Such music as the woods and streams
Sang in his ear he sang aloud.

"In still, shut bays, on windy capes,
He heard the call of beckoning shapes,
And, as the gray old shadows prompted him,
To homely moulds of rhyme he shaped their legends grim."

In these lines he refers to two kinds of poetry in which he has obtained almost equal eminence—his intensely imaginative and meditative poems, and his ringing, legendary ballads, the material of the latter having been gathered, in his wanderings, from the lips of sailors, farmers, and that class of aged women who connect each event they relate with the superstitions originally ingrafted upon it. It is needless to add that during the war of the rebellion, and the political contests accompanying reconstruction, the voice of Whittier rang through the land to cheer, to animate, to uplift, and also to warn and denounce. All sorts of cowardice, physical, mental, political, moral, felt mean and abashed when detected and smitten by one of his heroic lyrics. In all his poetry, whether descriptive, meditative, narrative, or impassioned, the power, in the last analysis, is found to reside in the soul of the poet rather than in his exceptional gifts of sensibility, understanding, and imaginative vision and faculty. This soul touched what remains of soul existed in the most selfish and malignant natures; for it was a soul that drew its force from the Soul of souls, and ever reverently listened to the slightest whisper of command, of monition, of consolation, of cheer, coming to it from the Divine Being it recognized as Master, Inspirer, and Friend. Whittier, indeed, though creedless, is one of the most religious of our poets. In these days of skepticism as to the possibility of the communication of the Divine Mind with the human, it is consolatory to read his poem on "The Eternal Goodness"—especially this stanza:

"I know not where His islands lift
Their fronded palms in air:
I only know I can not drift
Beyond His love and care."

It is curious that Whittier, whose general style is so clear that every body can understand it, should, in this beautiful declaration of his abiding faith—a faith full of the "magnanimous might of meekness"—have used a technical epithet, drawn from the science of botany, like "fronded."

Oliver Wendell Holmes—wit, satirist, humorist, novelist, scholar, scientist—is, above every thing, a poet, for the qualities of the poet pervade all the operations of his variously gifted mind. His sense of the ludicrous is not keener than his sense of the beautiful; his wit and humor are but the sportive exercise of a fancy and imagination which he has abundantly exercised on serious topics; and the extensive learning and acute logic of the man of science are none the less solid in substance because in expression they are accompanied by a throng of images and illustrations which endow erudition with life, and give a charm to the most closely linked chain of reasoning. The first thing which strikes a reader of Holmes is the vigor and elasticity of his nature. He is incapable of weakness. He is fresh and manly even when he securely treads the scarcely marked line which separates sentiment from sentimentality. This prevailing vigor proceeds from a strength of individuality which is often pushed to dogmatic self-assertion. It is felt as much in his airy, fleering mockeries of folly and pretension, as in his almost Juvenalian invectives against baseness and fraud—in the pleasant way in which he stretches a coxcomb on the rack of wit, as in the energy with which he grapples an opponent in the tussle of argumentation. He never seems to imagine that he can be inferior to the thinker whose position he assails, any more than to the noodle whose nonsense he jeers at. In argument he is sometimes the victor, in virtue of scornfully excluding what another reasoner would include, and thus seems to make his own intellect the measure of the whole subject in discussion. When in his Autocrat, or his Professor, or his Poet, at the Breakfast Table, he touches theological themes, he is peculiarly exasperating to theological opponents, not only for the effectiveness of his direct hits, but for the easy way in which he gayly overlooks considerations which their whole culture has induced them to deem of vital moment. The truth is that Holmes's dogmatism comes rather from the vividness and rapidity of his perceptions than from the arrogance of his personality. "This," he seems to say, "is not my opinion; it is a demonstrated law which you willfully ignore while pretending to be scholars." The indomitable courage of the man carries him through all the exciting controversies he scornfully invites; and it has been found that to attack him by argument pointed with wit is as futile as attacking a porcupine armed on all sides with his quills. Holmes, for the last forty years, has been expressing this inexhaustible vitality of nature in various ways, and to-day he appears as vigorous as he was in his prime, and more vigorous than he was in his youth. Indeed, he has rather grown younger in sentiment as he has grown older in years. His early poems sparkled with thought and abounded in energy; but still they can not be compared in wit, in humor, in depth of sentiment, in beauty of diction, in thoughtfulness, in lyrical force, with the poems of the past twenty-five years of his life. It is needless to give even the titles of the many pieces which are fixed in the memory of all cultivated readers among his countrymen. His novels, *Elsie Venner* and *The Guardian Angel*, rank high among original American contributions to the domain of romance. In prose, as in verse, his fecundity and vigor of thought have found adequate expression in a corresponding point and compactness of style.

James Russell Lowell is now in the prime of his genius and at the height of his reputation. His earlier poems, pervaded by the transcendental tone of thought current in New England at the time they were written, were full of promise, but gave little evidence of the wide variety of power he has since displayed. The spirituality of his thinking has deepened with advancing years. Nothing in his first volume, *A Year's Life*, suggests the depth of moral beauty he afterward embodied in "The Vision of Sir Launfal," the throng of subtle thoughts and images which almost confuse us by their multiplicity in "The Cathedral," and the grandeur of "The Commemoration Ode." Still less could it have been supposed that the youthful poetical enthusiast, singing of sirens and such questionable folks, should have suppressed that side of his richly endowed nature, by which he has since obtained a prominent rank among the greatest wits, satirists, and humorists of the century. *The Biglow Papers* are unique in our literature. Lowell adds to his other merits that of being an accomplished philologist; but granting his scholarship as an investigator of the popular idioms of foreign speech, he must be principally esteemed for his knowledge of the Yankee dialect. Hosea Biglow is almost the only writer who uses the dialect properly, and most other pretenders to a knowledge of it must be considered caricaturists as compared with him; for Biglow, like Burns, makes the dialect he employs flexible to every mood of thought and passion, from good sense as solid as granite to the most bewitching descriptions of nature and the loftiest affirmations of conscience. Lowell has been doubly doctored by the English universities of Oxford and Cambridge, but it is understood that this exceptional distinction was not so much due to the range of his scholarship and the beauty and power of his English prose and verse as to the new vein of sense, sentiment, and imagination he opened in *The Biglow Papers*—some of which, by-the-way, are the sharpest satires on England ever written, especially in commenting on her conduct to this country during the storm and stress of the Southern rebellion. As a prose writer, Lowell is quite as eminent as he is as a poet. His essays, where nature is his theme, are brimful of delicious descriptions, and his critical papers on Chaucer, Shakspeare, Spenser, Dryden, Pope, and Rousseau, not to mention others, are masterpieces of their kind. His defect, both as poet and prose writer, comes from the too lavish use of his seemingly inexhaustible powers of wit, fancy, and imagination. He is apt to sacrifice unity of general effect by overloading his paragraphs with suggestive meaning. The mind is sometimes dazzled away from the general subject by the wit and beauty of the separate illustrations and images which are intended to enforce it. A line or a sentence contains something so charming in itself that we forget the end in the means. That wise reserve of expression to which Longfellow owes so much of his reputation, that subordination of minor thoughts to the leading thought of the poem or essay, are frequently disregarded by Lowell. His mind is too rich to submit even to artistic checks on its fertility.

Julia Ward Howe, one of the most accomplished women in the United States, a scholar, a reasoner, an excellent prose writer, a poet with the power to uplift as well as to please, is also generally known as a champion of the right of women to vote. In the facts, arguments, and appeals which she brings to bear on this debated question, and the felicity of the occasional sarcastic strokes with which she smites an opponent who has offended her reason as well as vexed her patience, we find a woman fully equipped to do battle for the cause of woman; and certainly that man must be exceptionally endowed with brains who can afford to indulge in the luxury of despising her intellect. Loftiness of sentiment and force of mind are her prevailing characteristics; but she also possesses a certain demure humor which is all the more effective from its seeming innocence of humorous intent. It was she who said, when she saw a sign on which in large letters was printed, "Boston Charitable Eye and Ear Infirmary," that she did not know till then that there were any charitable eyes and ears in Boston. As a poet she is comparatively little appreciated as regards the depth and subtilty of thought and imagination which are discernible to the critical eye in her volume of *Later Lyrics*. That volume, to be sure, includes the poems which have made her reputation; but they are known to the public through newspapers rather than from the possession of the volume, of which they form but a small portion. The thrilling "Battle Hymn of the Republic" is an artistic variation on the John Brown song. The original is incomparable of its kind. No poet could have written it. Such rudeness and wildness are beyond the conception even of Walt Whitman and the author of "Festus." One would say that it was written by the common soldiers who sang it as they advanced to battle; that it was an elemental tune, suited to the rugged natures that shouted its refrain as they resolutely faced death, with the confident assurance of immortality. The words are verbal equivalents of rifle-bullets and cannon-balls; the tune is a noise, like the shriek of the shell as it ascends to the exact point whence it can most surely descend to blast and kill. Mrs. Howe's hymn has not this elemental character, but it is still wonderfully animating and invigorating; and the constant use of Scripture phrases shows the high level of thought and sentiment to which her soul had mounted, and from which she poured forth her exulting strains. "Our Country," "The Flag," "Our Orders," are also thoughtful or impassioned outbreaks of the same spiritual feeling which gives vitality to the "Battle Hymn."

The authors thus grouped together, differing so widely as they do in the individuality impressed on their genius, are still connected by that peculiar impulse given to American literature by Channing's revolt against the Calvinistic view of human nature, and by the emphasis they all lay on the ethical sentiment, not merely in its practical application to the concerns of actual life, but as highly idealized in its application to that life which is called divine. In all the serious efforts of these men and women of genius human nature is glorified through its receptivity of influences which transcend the sphere of ordinary moral maxims, and touch whatever is aspiring, heroic, and holy in the human soul; and though theology at first interposed objections, it has, on the whole, accepted the contributions made to its spiritual wealth by authors it was still compelled to consider as somewhat unauthorized explorers of its special domain. There still remained a class of writers whom it could accept as men of letters, and whom it could not assail as impertinent intruders into its province. Charles Sprague was the earliest and most eminent of these. The new poetical metaphysics and theology had not touched the mind of this upholder of the school of Dryden, of Pope, of Goldsmith, of Gray, of Cowper, of Burns. His poem of

"Curiosity," delivered in 1829 before the Phi Beta Society of Harvard College, is so excellent in description, in the various pictures it gives of human life, in the pungency of its wit and satire, that it deserves a place among the best productions of the school of Pope and Goldsmith. His odes are more open to criticism, though they contain many thoughtful, impassioned, and resounding lines. His "Shakspeare" ode is the best of these; and he concludes it with a very felicitous image, contrasting the success of the great poet of England in doing that which her statesmen and soldiers could not perform:

> "Our Roman-hearted fathers broke
> Thy parent empire's galling yoke;
> But thou, harmonious monarch of the mind,
> Around their sons a gentler chain shall bind.
> Still o'er our land shall Albion's sceptre wave,
> And what her mighty lion lost her mightier swan shall save."

A more homely illustration of the fact that Shakspeare binds the English race together whithersoever it wanders, is afforded by the remark of a sturdy New England farmer when he heard the rumor that England intended to make the Mason and Slidell affair an occasion for war with the United States, and thus insure success to the Confederates. The farmer paused, reflected, sought out in his mind something which would indicate his complete severance not only from the people of England, but from the English mind, and at last condensed all his wrath in this intense remark, "Well, if that report is true, all I can say is that Lord Lyons is welcome to my copy of Shakspeare."

Perhaps Sprague's most original poems are those in which he consecrated his domestic affections. Wordsworth himself would have hailed these with delight. Any body who can read with unwet eyes "I See Still," "The Family Meeting," "The Brothers," and "Lines on the Death of M. S. C." is a critic who has as little perception of the language of natural emotion as of the reserves and refinements of poetic art.

Sprague had the good fortune, as the cashier of a leading Boston bank, to be independent of his poetic gifts, considered as means of subsistence. But Nathaniel Parker Willis was, perhaps, the first of our poets to prove that literature could be relied upon as a good business. He certainly enjoyed all those advantages which accompany competence, and the only bank he could draw upon was his brain. He thoroughly understood the art of producing what people desired to read, and for which publishers were willing to pay. His early Scripture sketches, written when he was a student of Yale, gave him the reputation of a promising genius, and though the genius did not afterward take the direction to which its first successes pointed, it gained in strength and breadth with the writer's advancing years. In his best poems he displayed energy both of thought and imagination; but his predominant characteristics were keenness of observation, fertility of fancy, quickness of wit, shrewdness of understanding, a fine perception of beauty, a remarkable felicity in the choice of words, and a subtle sense of harmony in their arrangement, whether his purpose was to produce melodious verse or musical prose. But he doubtless squandered his powers in the attempt to turn them into commodities. To this he was driven by his necessities, and he always frankly acknowledged that he could have done better with his brain had he possessed an income corresponding to that of other eminent American men of letters, who could select their topics without regard to the immediate market value of what they wrote. He became the favorite poet, satirist, and "organ" of the fashionable world. He wrote editorials, letters, essays, novels, which were full of evidences of his rare talent without doing justice to it. He idealized trivialities; he gave a kind of reality to the unreal; and week after week he lifted into importance the unsubstantial matters which for the time occupied the attention of "good society." Some of his phrases, such as "the upper ten thousand," "Fifth-Ave-nudity," are still remembered. The paper which Willis edited, the *Home Journal*, exerted a great deal of influence. However slight might be the subjects, there can be no question that the editor worked hard in bringing the resources of his knowledge, observation, wit, and fancy to place them in their most attractive lights. The trouble was not in the vigor of the faculties, but in the thinness of much of the matter. As an editor, however, Willis had an opportunity to display his grand generosity of heart, and the peculiar power he had of detecting the slightest trace of genius in writers who were the objects of his appreciative eulogy. In the whole history of American literature there is no other example of a prominent man of letters who showed, like Willis, such a passionate desire to make his natural influence effective in dragging into prominence writers who either had no reputation at all, or whose reputation was notoriously less than his. Authors who have obtained reputation are commonly so much occupied in keeping or adding to it that they are not wont to take an active part in celebrating the merits of aspirants for renown. There must be scores of persons still living who remember with love and gratitude Willis's generous recognition of their first immature efforts, and all the more because at the time Willis's cordial praise, unlike that of an ordinary notice in a newspaper or magazine, arrested public attention to their merits. As a poet, Willis still survives as the author of some of the most beautiful and graceful poems in our literature; as a prose writer, he deserves a higher position than he now occupies, because nobody has yet attempted to separate the wheat from the chaff in his prose works; as an interpretive critic, he is much underrated, not only because it is difficult to estimate how much impulse he communicated to other minds by his genial estimate of their early promise, but because it is the fashion now to crush budding talent rather than to encourage it. Many of our present critics are inspired not so much by taste as by distaste. Like Indian chiefs on the war-path, they glory in the number of scalps they have deftly detached from the heads of their victims. Perhaps it would be sentimental to bemoan the coarse masculine locks which cling to most of the scalps these gentlemen ostentatiously display as evidence of their skill; but one thinks admiringly of the chivalry of Willis when he sees the fine hair of women triumphantly flourished in his eyes as an indication that, in invading the literary household, these critical "braves" are as regardless of sex as of age, and scalp maidens, wives, and mothers with the same impartial ferocity which leads them to scalp brothers, husbands, and fathers.

James G. Percival had not Willis's happy disposition and adaptive talent. Though recognized by friends as a poet of the first (American) class, he never succeeded in interesting the great body of his intelligent countrymen in any but a few of his minor poems. He ranks among the great sorrowing class of neglected geniuses. A man of large though somewhat undigested erudition, knowing many languages and many sciences, he was seemingly ignorant of the art of marrying his knowledge to his imagination. When he wrote in prose, he was full of matter; when he wrote in verse, he was full of glow and aspiration and fancy, but wanting in matter. Allston's imagined painter grinds up every thing he feels and knows "into paint;" Tennyson and Longfellow, as poets, do the same; but Percival seems to have had no power of so melting and fusing his learning as to make it the auxiliary of his fancy, and thus give substance to his poetic dreams. At least his best poems, however much they may charm the ear by their melody, and the eye by their flashing pictures of bits of natural scenery, are deficient in thought and in those burning or suggestive epithets which awake a whole train of associations in cultivated minds, and "make the burial-places of memory give up their dead." Hence the vagueness of the impression he leaves on the reader. It is sad, however, to think that neither his erudition nor his inspiration gave him a decent livelihood. Some infirmities of character, not vicious, may have led to this result. The period in which he lived was one in which no man of letters could, without shrewd management, be maintained by his writings alone. His failure as a poet is primarily due to the deliberate disunion between what he knew and what he sang. At present, the poet is required to supply nutriment as well as stimulant. Tennyson's immense popularity, which makes every new poem from his pen a literary event, is to be referred not merely to his imaginative power, but to his keeping himself on a level with the science and scholarship of his age. "In Memoriam" would not have attracted so much attention had it not been felt that the poet who celebrates a dead friend was, at the same time, all alive to the importance of problems, now vehemently discussed by theologians and scientists, which relate to the question of the reality and immortality of the human soul. Even the poet's affirmations are at present hesitatingly received if they do not imply a knowledge of the physiological science which seems to cast doubt on their validity. Emerson, also, is not more noted for his grand reliance on the soul than for his acquaintance with the scientific facts and theories which appear to deny its existence.

Edgar Allan Poe, like Willis and Percival, adopted, or was forced into, literature as a profession. He was a man of rare original capacity, cursed by an incurable perversity of character. It can not be said he failed of success. The immediate recognition as positive additions to our literature of such poems as "The Raven," "Annabel Lee," and "The Bells," and of such prose stories as "The Gold Bug," "The Purloined Letter," "The Murders of Rue Morgue," and "The Fall of the House of Usher," indicates that the public was not responsible for the misfortunes of his life. He also assumed the position of general censor and supervisor of American letters, and in this he also measurably succeeded; for his critical power, when not biased by his caprices, was extraordinarily acute, and during the period of his domination no critic's praise was more coveted than his, and no critic's blame more dreaded. In most of his literary work he displayed that rare combination of reason and imagination to which may be given the name of imaginative analysis. He was so proud of this power that he was never weary of unfolding, even to a chance acquaintance, the genesis of his poems and stories, accounting, on reasonable grounds, for every melodious variation in the verse, every little incident touched upon in the narrative, as steps in a deductive argument from assumed premises. One of two things was necessary to quicken his mind into full activity. The first was animosity against an individual; the second was some chance suggestion which awakened and tasked all the resources of his intellectual ingenuity. The wild, weird, unearthly, *under*-natural, as distinguished from supernatural, element in his most popular poems and stories is always accompanied by an imagination which not only spiritually discerns but relentlessly dissects. The morbid element, directing his powers, came from his character; the perfection of his analysis came from an intellect as fertile as it was calm, and as delicate in selecting every minute thread of thought as in seizing every evanescent shade of feeling. Poe, as a writer, though admired by his own countrymen, is more highly appreciated in London and Paris than in New York and Philadelphia. He should have been a naturalized Frenchman, the associate of Merimée, De Musset, Gautier, and Baudileire, and been allowed to develop the unmoral but artistic character of his genius in a free way. In France his peculiar theory of practical as distinguished from intellectual life would have been understood. In conduct he justified all his escapes from moral rules by his theory of poetic ecstasy; and he was irritated when any of his friends suggested that ecstasy, though laudable in the realm of imagination, was of doubtful authority in the concerns of daily life. In Paris his adherence to a certain artistic mechanism in verse and prose would have condoned any improprieties he might have committed in carrying the fine frenzy, the bold promptings of the poetic instinct—the poetic ecstasy, in short—into such an insignificant matter as private conduct. And it is also to be remembered that Poe's escapades were only occasional. The worst thing in him was his perversity, which made many of the sincerest admirers of his genius unable to benefit him. The fact that he often needed assistance vexed him against those who were ready to afford it. To do him a favor was to run the risk of incurring his enmity.

Bayard Taylor is justly esteemed as one of the most eminent of American men of letters. He is not a "self-made" man, for his books give evidence that the Lord had some share at least in making him; but he is one of our best specimens of a self-educated man. A graduate of no university, he has mastered many languages; born in a Pennsylvania village, he may be said to have been every where and to have seen every body; and all that he has achieved is due to his own persistent energy and tranquil self-reliance. Journalist, traveler, essayist, critic, novelist, scholar, and poet, he has ever preserved the simplicity of nature which marked his first book of travels, and the simplicity of style which the knowledge of many lands and many tongues has never tempted him to abandon. His books of voyages and travels are charming, but their charm consists in the austere closeness of the words he uses to the facts he records, the scenery he depicts, and the adventures he narrates. The same simplicity of style characterizes his poems, his few novels, and numerous stories. The richness of his vocabulary never impels him to sacrifice truth of representation to the transient effectiveness which is readily secured by indulgence in declamation. One sometimes wonders that the master of so many languages should be content to express himself with such rigid economy of word and phrase in the one he learned at his mother's knee. As a poet, though kindling with his theme, and with all the dictionaries at his beck, he ever discriminates between inspiration and aspiration. He ascends easily to that peak of imaginative contemplation or rapture which he has earned the right to occupy by experience and character, and he would think it ridiculous to attempt to carry higher elevations, not by force of genius, but by dint of spasmodic ejaculations and a parade of resounding adjectives. Among Taylor's minor poems, it is difficult to select those which exhibit his genius at its topmost point. Perhaps "Camadeva" may be instanced as best showing his power of blending exquisite melody with serene, satisfying, uplifting thought. The song which begins with the invocation, "Daughter of Egypt, veil thine eyes!" is as good as could be selected from his many pieces to indicate the energy and healthiness of his lyric impulse. His longer poems would reward a careful criticism. The best of them is "The Masque of the Gods"—a poem comprehensive in conception, noble in purpose, and admirable in style. Taylor has also done a great work in translating, or rather transfusing, the two parts of Goethe's "Faust" into various English metres corresponding to the original German verse, literal not only in reproducing ideas, but in reproducing melodies. This long labor could only have been undertaken by an American man of letters whose love of lucre was entirely subordinate to his love of literature. A few weeks devoted to lecturing before lyceums would have given him more visible returns in money than he could hope to obtain by the sale of this translation during the next twenty years. Longfellow and Bryant, men of property, could afford to translate Dante and Homer; but Bayard Taylor devoted the leisure of ten years, generally passed in what is called "getting a living," in giving *English* life to the greatest work of German genius. He is now engaged in a *Life of Goethe* which promises to be the best biography of the serene autocrat of German literature that has appeared either in German or English. Such unremunerated labors deliberately entered upon by a man who has depended upon his pen for his subsistence, who has never degraded his profession by pandering to any thing mean or base, and who has become popular only by means which do him honor, are worthy of a cordial recognition by every well-wisher of American letters.

Another American writer who has made literature a profession is George William Curtis. Mr. Curtis opened a new vein of satiric fiction in *The Potiphar Papers*, *Prue and I*, and *Trumps;* but probably the great extent of his popularity is due to his papers in *Harper's Magazine*, under the general title of the Editor's Easy Chair. In these he has developed every faculty of his mind and every felicity of his disposition; the large variety of the topics he has treated would alone be sufficient to prove the generous breadth of his culture; but it is in the treatment of his topics that his peculiarly attractive genius is displayed in all its abundant resources of sense, knowledge, wit, fancy, reason, and sentiment. His tone is not only manly, but gentlemanly; his persuasiveness is an important element of his influence; and no reformer has equaled him in the art of insinuating sound principles into prejudiced intellects by putting them in the guise of pleasantries. He can on occasion send forth sentences of ringing invective; but in the Easy Chair he generally prefers the attitude of urbanity which the title of his department suggests. His style, in addition to its other merits, is rhythmical; so that his thoughts slide, as it were, into the reader's mind in a strain of music.

Not the least remarkable of his characteristics is the undiminished vigor and elasticity of his intelligence, in spite of the incessant draughts he has for years been making upon it.

In the domain of history and biography, American literature, during the past fifty years, can boast of works of standard value. The most indefatigable of all explorers into the unpublished letters and documents illustrating the history of the United States was Jared Sparks. His voluminous editions of *The Life and Writings of Washington and Franklin*, his *Diplomatic Correspondence of the Revolution*, and other books devoted to the task of adding to the authentic materials of American history, are mines of information to the students of history; but Mr. Sparks, though a clear and forcible writer, had not thé gift of attractiveness; and the results of his investigations have been more popularly presented by Irving, in his *Life of Washington*, and Parton, in his *Life of Franklin*, than by his own biographies of those eminent men, based on the results of tireless original research extending through many years, and of which both Irving and Parton, with the usual polite display of gratitude to the drudge who had saved them from so much disgusting toil, gladly availed themselves in writing their more captivating biographies.

In the political history of the country there only remain two "families," in the English sense of the term. These are the Adamses and the Hamiltons. Charles F. Adams has published a collection of his grandfather's works, in ten volumes, introduced by a life of John Adams, which is one of the most delightful of American biographies, and, at the same time, a positive addition to the early history of the United States under our first two Presidents. An edition of Hamilton's works has also been published; and one of Hamilton's sons has written a *History of the Republic of the United States*, "as traced in the writings of Alexander Hamilton and of his contemporaries." It is needless to say that the controversies between the two families have added new matter of great value to the mass of documents which shed light on our early history as a united nation.

It would be tedious to enumerate other works, which are valuable contributions to our annals; but, in 1834, George Bancroft appeared as *the* historian of the United States, or rather the historian of the process by which the States became united. He professed to have seized on the underlying Idea which shaped the destinies of the country; in later volumes he indicated his initiation in the councils of Providence; and though his last volume (the tenth), published in 1874, only brings the history down to the conclusion of the Revolutionary war, his labor of forty years has confirmed him in his historical philosophy. Bancroft has been prominent in American politics during all this period; he has been successively Collector of the port of Boston, Secretary of the Navy, American minister in London and Berlin, and has thus enjoyed every possible advantage of correcting his declamation by his experience; but his tendency to rhapsody has not diminished with the increase of his knowledge and his years. He has, to be sure, availed himself of every opportunity to add to the materials which enter into the composition of American history, and has been as indefatigable in research as confident in theorizing. The different volumes of his work are of various literary merit, but they are all stamped by the unmistakable impress of the historian's individuality. There is no dogmatism more exclusive than that of fixed ideas and ideals, and this dogmatism Mr. Bancroft exhibits throughout his history both in its declamatory and speculative form. Indeed, there are chapters in each of his volumes which, considered apart, might lead one to suppose that the work was misnamed, and that it should be entitled, "The Psychological Autobiography of George Bancroft, as Illustrated by Incidents and Characters in the Annals of the United States." Generally, however, his fault is not in suppressing or overlooking facts, but in disturbing the relations of facts —substituting their relation to the peculiar intellectual and moral organization of the historian to their natural relations with each other. Other eminent historians might be quoted as too apt to disturb the natural relations of things by the intrusion of their individual point of view; but they so contrive to diffuse their prepossessions through every part of the narrative that the conclusions they reach seem to be the inevitable result of their presentation of the facts. Mr. Bancroft begins with an emphatic statement of lofty abstractions, which his narrative by no means sustains. There is a palpable gulf between his theories and the realities he brings in to support his theories. This inartistic separation of thoughts from things deprives his history of the unity which we feel in reading such historians as Gibbon, Grote, and Macaulay. He is also accused of doing gross injustice to certain prominent Americans, and of refusing to correct his demonstrated mistakes. His patriotism, likewise, is sometimes of that kind which looks not so much to the glory of his country as to its glorification. Admitting, however, all the charges against him, it must still be said that he has written the most popular history of the United States (up to 1782) which has yet appeared, and that he has made a very large addition to the materials on which it rests. Perhaps he would not have been so tireless in research had he not been so passionately earnest in speculation.

The necessarily slow progress of Mr. Bancroft's history, and the various protests against his theories and his judgments, impelled Richard Hildreth, a bold, blunt, hard-headed, and resolute man, caustic in temper, keen in intellect, indefatigable in industry, and blessed with an honest horror of shams, to write a history of the United States, in which our fathers should be presented exactly as they were, "unbedaubed with patriotic rouge." The first volume was published in 1849, the sixth in 1852. The whole work included the events between the discovery and colonization of the continent and the year 1821. As a book of reference, this history still remains as the best in our catalogues of works on American history. The style is concise, the facts happily combined, the judgments generally good; and while justice is done to our great men, there is every where observable an almost vindictive contempt of persons who have made themselves "great" by the arts of the demagogue. Hildreth studied carefully all the means of information within his reach; but his plan did not contemplate original research on the large scale in which it was prosecuted by Bancroft.

The *History of New England*, by John G. Palfrey, is distinguished by thoroughness of investigation, fairness of judgment, and clearness and temperance of style. It is one of the ablest contributions as yet made to our colonial history. The various histories of Francis Parkman, *The Conspiracy of Pontiac*, *The Pioneers of France in the New World*, *The Jesuits in North America*, *The Discovery of the Great West*, exhibit a singular combination of the talents of the historian with those of the novelist. The materials he has laboriously gathered are disposed in their just relations by a sound understanding, while they are vivified by a realizing mind. The result is a series of narratives in which accuracy in the slightest details is found compatible with the most glowing exercise of historical imagination, and the use of a style singularly rapid, energetic, and picturesque.

William H. Prescott had one of those happily constituted natures in which intellectual conscientiousness is in perfect harmony with the moral quality which commonly monopolizes the name of conscience. He was as incapable of lies of the brain as of lies of the heart. When he undertook to write histories, he employed an ample fortune to obtain new materials, sifted them with the utmost care, weighed opposing statements in an understanding which was unbiased by prejudice, and, suppressing the laborious processes by which he had arrived at definite conclusions, presented the results of his toil in a narrative so easy, limpid, vivid, and picturesque that his delighted readers hardly realized that what was so pleasing and instructive to them could have cost much pain and labor to him. Echoes beyond the Atlantic, coming from England, France, Germany, Italy, and Spain, gradually forced the conviction into the ordinary American mind that the historian of Ferdinand and Isabella, of the conquerors of Mexico and Peru, of Philip the Second, had in his quiet Boston home made large additions to the history of Europe in one of its most important epochs. Humboldt was specially emphatic in his praise. Prescott was enrolled among the members of many foreign academies, whose doors were commonly shut to all who could not show that they had made contributions to human knowledge as well as to human entertainment. Much of his foreign reputation was doubtless due to his lavish expenditure of money to obtain rare books and copies of rare MSS. which contained novel and important facts; but his wide popularity is to be referred to his possession of the faculty of historical imagination; that is, his power of realizing and reproducing the events and characters of past ages, and of becoming mentally a contemporary of the persons whose actions he narrated. His partial blindness, which compelled him to listen rather than to read, and to employ a cunningly contrived apparatus in order to write, was in his case an advantage. He had the eyes of friends and faithful secretaries eager to serve him. What passed into his ear became an image in his mind, and his bodily infirmity quickened his mental sight. His judgment and imagination brooded over the throng of details to which he listened; he formed a mental picture out of the dry facts; and by assiduous thinking he disposed the facts in their right relations without losing his hold on their vitality as pictures of a past age. People who passed him in his daily afternoon walks around Boston Common knew that his thoughts were busy on Ferdinand, or Cortez, or Pizarro, or Philip, and not on the news of the day; and his rapid pace and the peculiar swing of his cane as he trudged on indicated that he was looking not on what was imperfectly present to his bodily eye, but on objects to which physical exercise had given new life and significance as surveyed by the eye of his mind. His intense absorption in the subject-matter of his various histories gave to them a peculiar attractiveness which few novels possess. Any body who, after reading Lew Wallace's recent romance of *The Fair God*, or Dr. Bird's *Calavar*, will then turn to Prescott's *History of the Conquest of Mexico*, can not fail to be impressed with the historian's superiority to the romancer in the mere point of romantic interest.

Another American historian, John Lothrop Motley, the author of *The Rise of the Dutch Republic*, *The History of the United Netherlands*, *The History of John of Barneveld*, and, it is to be hoped, of the great Thirty Years' War, has been, like Prescott, untiring in research, has made large additions to the facts of European history, has decisively settled many debatable questions which have tried the sagacity of French and German historians of the sixteenth century, and has poured forth the results of his researches in a series of impassioned narratives, which warm the blood and kindle the imagination as well as inform the understanding. His histories are, in some degree, epics. As he frequently crosses Prescott's path in his presentation of the ideas, passions, and persons of the sixteenth century, it is curious to note the serenity of Prescott's narrative as contrasted with the swift, chivalric impatience of wrong which animates almost every page of Motley. Both imaginatively reproduce what they have investigated; both have the eye to see and the reason to discriminate; both substantially agree in their judgment as to events and characters; but Prescott quietly allows his readers, as a jury, to render their verdict on the statement of the facts, while Motley somewhat fiercely pushes forward to anticipate it. Prescott calmly represents; Motley intensely feels. Prescott is on a watch-tower surveying the battle; Motley plunges into the thickest of the fight. In temperament no two historians could be more apart; in judgment they are identical. As both historians are equally incapable of lying, Motley finds it necessary to overload his narrative with details which justify his vehemence, while Prescott can afford to omit them, on account of his reputation for a benign impartiality between the opposing parties. A Roman Catholic disputant would find it hard to fasten a quarrel on Prescott; but with Motley he could easily detect an occasion for a duel to the death. It is to be said that Motley's warmth of feeling never betrays him into intentional injustice to any human being; his histories rest on a basis of facts which no critic has shaken; and to the merit of being a historian of wide repute, it is to be added that he has ever been a stanch friend, in the emergencies of the politics of the country, to every cause based on truth, honor, reason, freedom, and justice. The same high chivalrous tone which rings through his histories has been heard in every crisis of his public career.

The European histories of Prescott and Motley required an introduction, and this was furnished by John Foster Kirk, in his *History of Charles the Bold*, Duke of Burgundy. The breaking up of the feudal system of Europe, and the gradual establishment of monarchies and states after the modern fashion, were the slow results of time. Prescott seized on an important point of this process in his *History of Ferdinand and Isabella*, as Robertson had in his *History of Charles the Fifth*. There remained for a historian sufficiently robust in research and quick in intellect a domain of history still imperfectly investigated, namely, that of the struggles between Charles of Burgundy and Louis XI. of France, the latter monarch being unquestionably the great disintegrating force which was brought to bear on the old feudal system. Mr. Kirk was one of the ablest, most scholarly, and most enthusiastic of Prescott's secretaries. He had the sagacity to perceive the importance of the period of which he proposed to write the history, and the perseverance to execute the difficult task. Charles and Louis were known to all people who spoke the English tongue by Scott's famous novel of *Quentin Durward*, and his feebler concluding romance of *Anne of Geierstein;* and Mr. Kirk had a right to suppose that an account of an important era of European history would lose none of its attractiveness by being rigidly conformed to historical facts. As to his research, it is sufficient to say that in his investigations in the archives of Switzerland alone he was probably the first man to disturb the dust which nearly four centuries had heaped on precious manuscript documents. As a thinker he is always ingenious, and as generally sound as he is original. In narrative, the richness of his materials, as in the case of Motley, tempts him sometimes into seemingly needless minuteness of detail. All our modern historians are open to this charge. It is hard, when a writer has devoted a week or a month to the discovery or verification of a fact, that he should be refused the gratification of devoting a sentence or a paragraph to its statement. The *History of Charles the Bold* is redundant in matter; its three volumes might be judiciously condensed into two; but whether compression would add to its mere interest may be doubted.

Among other works which do credit to the historical literature of the country may be named *The Life and Correspondence of Nathaniel Greene*, from original materials, by George W. Greene—a work which, of its kind, is of the first class. The same writer's *Historical View of the American Revolution* is an excellent compend drawn from original sources. The various volumes of Richard Frothingham are admirable for accuracy and research. On the general subject of history, the elaborate work of Dr. John W. Draper, *The History of the Intellectual Development of Europe*, is comprehensive in scope, brilliant in style, and bold in speculation. The first volume of *The History of France*, by Parke Godwin, is so good that it is to be regretted the author has not continued his task. The various biographies written by James Parton—namely, the lives of Burr, Jackson, Franklin, and Jefferson—have the great merit of being entertaining, while they rest on a solid basis of facts which the writer has diligently explored. His love of paradox, though a fault, certainly gives piquancy to his lucid narrative. He starts commonly with a peculiar theory, and if sometimes unjust, the injustice comes from his surveying the subject from an eccentric point of view, and not from any deliberate intention to misstate facts or disturb their relations. *The Life of Josiah Quincy*, by his son, Edmund Quincy, is an admirably executed portrait of one of the stoutest specimens of political manhood in American history. Like Parton, Quincy interests by reproducing the period of which he writes, and, like him, is a painter of "interiors." *The Rise and Fall of the Slave Power in America*, by Henry Wilson, is the work of a man who as Senator of the United States was long in the thick of the fight against slavery, who knew by experience the thoughts, passions, and policies of the parties in the contest, and who wrote the history of the contest with simplicity, earnestness, and impartiality. *The Life of Madison*, by William C. Rives, is a work of interest and value. Among the antiquarians and anecdotists who have illustrated American history, the highest reputation belongs to Benson J. Lossing and the family of the Drakes.

In military history and biography, the most notable work the country has produced is *Memoirs of General W. T. Sherman, Written by Himself*—or, as it might be called,

"My Deeds in My Words." The sharpness, conciseness, and arbitrariness of the autobiographer's style are characteristic of the man. He is intensely conscious of his superiority. The word of command is heard ringing in every page of his two octavos. No man could, without being laughed at, have written what he has written unless he had done what he has done. Throughout his autobiography he appears self-centred, self-referring, self-absorbed, and, when opposed, prouder than a score of Spanish hidalgoes. Like George Eliot's innkeeper, he divides human thought into two parts, namely, "my idee," and "humbug;" there is no middle point; but then his intelligence is as solid, quick, broad, and full of resource as his will is defiantly self-reliant. Though there is something bare, bleak, harsh, abrupt, in his style, his blunt egotism every now and then runs into a rude humor. He pats on the back men as brave if not as skillful as himself, and looks down upon them with good-natured toleration as long as they look up to him; but when they do not, disbelief in Sherman denotes incompetency or malignity in the critic. His enmities are hearted, and sometimes vindictive. The grave has closed over a man who in his sphere did at least as much as Sherman to overturn the rebellion, and yet Sherman spares not Secretary Stanton dead any more than he spared Stanton living. Still, the book is thoroughly a soldier's book, and must take a rank among the most instructive and entertaining military memoirs ever written.

In that department of history which describes the rise and growth of literatures, the most important work which has been produced by an American scholar is *The History of Spanish Literature*, by George Ticknor. As far as solid and accurate learning is concerned, it is incomparably the best history of Spanish literature in existence, and is so acknowledged in Spain. The author, in his travels in Europe, sought out every book which shed the slightest light on his great subject. The materials of his work are a carefully selected Spanish library, purchased by himself. He deliberately took up the subject as a task which would pleasingly occupy a lifetime. The latest edition, published shortly after his death, showed that the volumes always were on his desk for supervision, revision, and the introduction of new facts, and that he continued pruning and enlarging his work to the day when the pen dropped from his hand. In research he was as indefatigable as he was conscientious, and possessing ample leisure and fortune, he tranquilly exerted the powers of his strong understanding and the refinements of his cultivated taste in forming critical judgments, which, if somewhat positive, had the positiveness of knowledge and reflection. Besides, his culture was cosmopolitan; he had enjoyed as wide opportunities for conversing with men as with books, and there was hardly an illustrious European scholar or man of letters of his time with whom he had not been on terms of intimacy; but erudition can not confer insight, nor can genius be communicated by mere companionship with it. Mr. Ticknor's defect was a lack of sympathy and imagination, and, to the historian of literature, nothing can compensate for a deficiency in these. He could not mentally transform himself into a Spaniard, and therefore could not penetrate into the secret of the genius of Spain. He studied its great writers, but he did not look into and behold their souls. There was something cold, hard, resisting, and repellent in his mind. His criticism, therefore, externally judicious, had not for its basis mental facts vividly conceived and vitally interpreted. He never seemed to have made himself, in imagination, an inhabitant of Spain; to have felt the fine intoxication of its poetic and romantic literature; to have reproduced by sympathy the ecstasy of imaginative creation; to have hospitably taken into his mind all the strange moods of Spanish thought and emotion; to have been genially receptive, in short, of impressions absolutely new to his own consciousness. With all his immense acquisitions, he used his knowledge somewhat legally. The external evidence was drawn from Spanish books; the judicial decisions bore unmistakable marks of having been delivered from his residence on Beacon Hill, Boston. Had Mr. Ticknor possessed the realizing imagination of his friend Prescott—who was never in Spain—he would have made what is now a valuable work, also a work of fascinating interest and extensive popularity.

In the department of history may be included works on the origin, progress, organization, comparison, and criticism of the religious ideas of various nations. Three works of this kind have been produced in the United States during the past twenty years, each of which indicates a "liberal" bias. The first is *The History of the Doctrine of a Future Life*, by William R. Alger. This is a mine of generalized information, obtained by great labor, and sifted, analyzed, and classified with care and skill. Indeed, it is said that some of the author's acquaintances, knowing the comprehensiveness of the plan, and seeing year after year pass by without any signs of approaching publication, gently hinted to him that the book, as he was writing it, would only be finished in that state of existence which it took for its theme. The second is *Oriental Religions*, by Samuel Johnson, the product of a learned, intelligent, and intrepid "Free Religionist." The third is *Ten Great Religions*, by James Freeman Clarke. The boldness of the thinking in these works is as noticeable as the abundance of the knowledge.

The number of American statesmen who since 1810 have combined literary with political talent is numerous—so numerous, indeed, that, in despair of doing justice to all, we are forced to select three representative men as indicating three separate tendencies in our national life. These are John C. Calhoun, Daniel Webster, and Charles Sumner. Calhoun specially followed the Jefferson who prompted the Resolutions of '98; Sumner, the Jefferson who wrote the Declaration of Independence; Webster, the men who drew up and carried into effect the Constitution of the United States. Calhoun was in politics what Calvin was in theology—a great deductive reasoner from premises assumed. The austerity of his character found a natural outlet in the rigor of his logic. He had the grand audacity of the intellectual athlete, pushed his argumentation to its most extreme results, was willing to peril life and fortune on an inference ten times removed from his original starting-point, and was always a reasoning being in matters where he seemed to be, on practical grounds, an unreasonable one. Despising rhetoric, he became a rhetorician of a high class by pure force of logical statement. Every word he used meant something, and he never indulged in an image or illustration except to condense or enforce a thought. In the discussions in the Senate of the United States regarding the very foundations of the government, raised by what is called "Foote's Resolution," Webster, in 1830, made his celebrated speech in reply to Hayne. In all the resources of the orator—statement, reasoning, wit, humor, imagination, passion—this speech has, like one of the masterpieces of Burke, acquired reputation as a literary work, as well as by its lucid exposition of constitutional law. Webster was so completely victorious over his antagonist in argument as well as eloquence, that only when the question of nullification came up was his triumph seriously questioned. Calhoun, who thought that Hayne had not made the most of the argument for State rights, introduced, in January, 1833, a series of resolutions into the Senate, carefully modeled on the Resolutions of '98, and afterward based an argument upon them as though they were of a validity equal to that of the Constitution itself. The speech was one of the most remarkable efforts of his ingenious, penetrating, and logical mind, and can now be studied with admiration by every body who enjoys following the processes of impassioned deductive reasoning on a question affecting the life of individuals and of States.

Webster's reply, called "The Constitution not a Compact between Sovereign States," was his greatest intellectual effort in the sphere of pure argumentation. Calhoun, a greater reasoner than Jefferson or Madison, had deduced from their propositions—originally thrown out to serve as a convenient cover for a somewhat factious opposition to the administration of John Adams—a theory of the government of the United States for all time to come. Webster resolutely attacked the premises of Calhoun's speech, and paid little attention to his opponent's deductive reasoning from the premises. Calhoun retorted in a speech in which he complained that Webster had not answered his argument. It was not Webster's policy to discredit Madison, and he simply declared that Madison, in his old age, had repudiated such inferences as Calhoun had drawn from the Resolutions of '98. On constitutional grounds Webster was as triumphant in his contest with Calhoun as he had been in his previous contest with Hayne; but arguments are of small account against interests and passions, and it required the bloodiest and most expensive of civil wars to prove that strictly logical deductions from the Resolutions of '98 did not express the meaning of the Constitution of the United States. The victory intellectually won was eventually decided by "blood and iron." In addition to Webster's extraordinary power of lucid statement, on which he based the successive steps and wide sweep of his argumentation, he was master of an eloquence unrivaled of its kind, because it represented the kindling into unity of all the faculties and emotions of a strong, deep, and broad individual nature. Generally, understanding was his predominant quality; in statement and argument he seemed to be specially desirous to unite thought with facts; he distrusted all rhetoric which disturbed the relations of things; but in the heat of controversy he occasionally mounted to the real elevation of his character, and threw off flashes and sparks of impassioned imagination which had the electric, the smiting, effect of a completely roused nature. It is curious that he never exhibited the higher qualities of imagination in his speeches until the suppressed power flamed unexpectedly out after all his other faculties had been thoroughly kindled, and then it came with formidable effect. That Webster is one of the most eminent of our prose writers is acknowledged both at the North and the South. He was also a magnificent specimen of physical manhood; his mere presence in an assembly was eloquence; and when he spoke, voice and gesture added immensely to the effect of his majestic port and bearing. Fox said of Lord Chancellor Thurlow that he must be an impostor, for no man could be as wise as he looked. Webster was wiser in look than even Thurlow, but his works show that he was no impostor in the matter of political wisdom, laughable as are some of the epithets by which his admirers exaggerated his claims to reverence, as though he had clapped copyright on political thought. In the heathenism of partisan feeling, however, few deities of party were more worthy of apotheosis than "the godlike Dan!"

Up to 1850, when he made his memorable "7th of March speech" in the Senate, Webster was considered the leading champion of the non-extension of slavery; but in that speech he waived the application of the principle to the Territories acquired by the Mexican war, though he contended that he still adhered to the principle itself. He lost, by this concession, his hold on the minds and consciences of the political antislavery men, and the position he vacated was eventually occupied by Charles Sumner, though Sumner had numerous competitors for that station of glory and difficulty. Webster must have foreseen the inevitable conflict between the Slave and Free States, but he labored to postpone a catastrophe he was powerless to prevent, thinking that judicious compromise might soften the shock when the collision of irreconcilable principles and persons could no longer be avoided. Sumner in heart was as earnest an abolitionist as Garrison or Phillips; his soul was on fire with moral enthusiasm; but he also had a vigorous understanding, and a memory stored with a vast amount of historical and legal knowledge. He never forgot any thing he had read, and he passed not a day without reading. Accordingly, when he entered the Senate of the United States, this philanthropic student-statesman was as ready in citing the precedents as he was fiery in declaring the principles of freedom. During the years preceding the civil war the dominant party in the government was bent on establishing a slave power, which, had it succeeded, would have disgraced the country forever. Law, logic, philosophy, even theology, were in the South all subordinated to the permanence and extension of negro slavery, and hundreds of sermons south of Mason and Dixon's line inculcated the refreshing doctrine that if Christ came primarily on earth to save sinners, his secondary, though not less important, object was to enslave "niggers." It is easy to say that it requires no parade of authorities to settle the proposition that two and two make four, but ethically and politically this was the proposition that Charles Sumner had to sustain by quotations from Vico and Leibnitz, from Coke, Mansfield, Camden, and Eldon, from Adams, Jefferson, Madison, Marshall, Story, and Webster. Those who were foiled in their purposes by these quotations from authorities they could not but respect, called him a pedant; but what really vexed them was that in no case in which this pedant encountered an opponent did he fail to justify his course by the extent of his knowledge, as well as by the keenness of his intellect and the warmth of his sentiments. When the civil war broke out, he saw that negro slavery was doomed. In his endeavors to hasten emancipation he always contrived to make himself unacceptable to the more prudent statesmen of his own party, by inaugurating measures which the course of events eventually compelled them to adopt; and after the war he dragged the Republican party up to his own policy of reconstruction, being in most cases only some six or twelve months ahead of what sober and judicious Republicans found at length to be the wisest course. Throughout his career Sumner was felt as a force as well as an intelligence, and probably the future historian will rank him high among the select class of American public men who have the right to be called creative statesmen. He always courted obloquy, not only when his party was depressed, but when it was triumphant. "Forward!" was ever his motto. When his political friends thought they had at last found a resting-place, his voice was heard crying loudly for a new advance. Many of his addresses belong to that class of speeches which are events. His collected works, carefully revised by himself, have now become a portion of American literature. They quicken the conscience of the reader, but they also teach him the lesson that moral sentiment is of comparatively small account unless it hardens into moral character, and is also accompanied by that thirst for knowledge by which intellect is broadened and enriched, and is trained to the task of supporting by facts and arguments what the insight of moral manliness intuitively discerns. Probably no statesman that the country has produced has exceeded Sumner in his passion for rectitude. In every matter that came up for discussion he vehemently put the question, "Which of the two sides is Right?" He so persistently capitalized this tremendous monosyllable, and poured into its utterance such an amount of moral fervor or moral wrath, that the modest word, which every body used without much regard to its meaning, blazed out in his rhetoric, not as a feeble and faded truism, but as a dazzling and smiting truth. It is in discovering the hidden meaning of simple words that great men have often exhibited the full force of their genius. In the political history of the country nobody has excelled Sumner in restoring to its original majestic significance the much-abused term of "Right."

A word may be said here of two public men, one of whom belongs to literature by cultivation and of set purpose, the other accidentally and in the ordinary discharge of his public duties. Edward Everett was one of the most variously accomplished of the American scholars who have been drawn into public life by ambition and patriotism. Though he attained high positions, his nature was too sensitive and fastidious for the rough contentions of party, and he could not steel himself to bear calumny without wincing. He suffered exquisite mortification and pain at unjust attacks on his principles and character, whereas such attacks awakened in Sumner a kind of exultation, as they proved that his own blows were beginning to tell. As an orator, Everett's special gift was persuasion, not invective. The four volumes of his collected works are, in elegance and energy of style, wealth of information, and fertility of thought, important contributions to American literature; but being mostly in the form of speeches and addresses, they have not produced the impression which less learning, talent, and eloquence, concentrated on a few subjects, would assuredly have made. A very different man was Abraham Lincoln. He was a great rhetorician without knowing it. The statesman was doubtless astonished that messages and letters, written for purely practical purposes, should be hailed by fastidious critics as remarkable specimens of style. The truth was that Lincoln was deficient in fluency; he was compelled to wring his expression out of the very substance of his nature and the inmost life of the matter he had in hand; and the result was seen in sinewy sentences, in which thoughts were close to things, and words were close to thoughts. And finally, in November, 1863, his soul devoutly impressed with the solemnity and grandeur of his theme, he delivered at Gettysburg an address of about twenty lines, which is considered the top and crown of American eloquence.

There are certain writers in American literature who charm by their eccentricity as well as by their genius, who are both original and originals. The most eminent, perhaps, of these was Henry D. Thoreau—a man who may be said to have penetrated nearer to the physical heart of nature than any other American author. Indeed, he "experienced" nature as others are said to experience religion. Lowell says that in reading him it seems as "if all out-doors had kept a diary, and become its own Montaigne." He was so completely a naturalist that the inhabitants of the woods in which he sojourned forgot their well-founded distrust of man, and voted him the freedom of their city. His descriptions excel even those of Wilson, Audubon, and Wilson Flagg, admirable as these are, for he was in closer relations with the birds than they, and carried no gun in his hand. In respect to human society, he pushed his individuality to individualism; he was never happier than when absent from the abodes of civilization; and the toleration he would not extend to a Webster or a Calhoun, he extended freely to a robin or a woodchuck. With all this peculiarity, he was a poet, a scholar, a humorist; also, in his way, a philosopher and philanthropist; and those who knew him best, and entered most thoroughly into the spirit of his character and writings, are the warmest of all the admirers of his genius. Another Concord hermit is W. E. Channing, who has adopted solitude as a profession, and seclusion from his kind as the condition of independent perception of nature. The thin volume of poems in which he has embodied his insights and experiences contains lines and verses which are remarkable both for their novelty and depth. A serener eccentric, A. Bronson Alcott, is eccentric only in this, that he thinks the object of life is spiritual meditation; that all action leads up to this in the end; and he has spent his life in tranquilly exploring those hidden or elusive facts of the higher consciousness which practical thinkers overlook or ignore. He is a Yankee seer who has suppressed every tendency in his Yankee nature toward "argufying" a point. Very different from all these is Walt Whitman, who originally burst upon the literary world as "one of the roughs," and whose "barbaric yawp" was considered by a particular class of English critics as the first original note which had been struck in American poetry, and as good as an Indian war-whoop. Wordsworth speaks of Chatterton as "the marvelous boy;" Walt Whitman, in his first *Leaves of Grass*, might have been styled the marvelous "b'hoy." Walt protested against all convention, even all forms of conventional verse; he seemed to start up from the ground, an earth-born son of the soil, and put to all cultivated people the startling question, "What do you think of Me?" They generally thought highly of him as an original. Nothing is more acceptable to minds jaded with reading works of culture than the sudden appearance of a strong, rough book, expressing the habits, ideas, and ideals of the uncultivated; but unfortunately Whitman declined to listen to the suggestion that his daring disregard of convention should have one exception, and that he must modify his frank expression of the relations of the sexes. The author refused, and the completed edition of the *Leaves of Grass* fell dead from the press. Since that period he has undergone new experiences; his latest books are not open to objections urged against his earliest; but still the *Leaves of Grass*, if thoroughly cleaned, would even now be considered his ablest and most original work. But when the first astonishment subsides of such an innovation as Walt Whitman's, the innovator pays the penalty of undue admiration by unjust neglect. This is true also of Joaquin Miller, whose first poems seemed to threaten all our established reputations. Each succeeding volume was more coldly received; and though the energy and glow of his verse were the same, the public, in its calmer mood, found that the richness of the matter was not up to the rush of the inspiration.

This eccentric deviation from accredited models is perhaps best indicated in American humorists, whose characteristic is ludicrous absurdity. George H. Derby (or John Phœnix) was perhaps the first who carried the hyperboles of humor to the height of humoristic extravaganzas. There are few men who have roused a greater number of irresistible bursts of laughter from so limited a number of humorous sketches. Indeed, many of his readers have his whole works by heart, and never recur to them without honoring his memory by a fresh outbreak of merriment. The peculiarity of the whole school is to revel in the most fantastic absurdities of an ingenious fancy. There is a Western story told of a man who was so strong that his shadow once falling on a child instantly killed it. This is the kind of humor in which Americans excel. Charles F. Browne (Artemus Ward), indulging at his will in the oddest and wildest caricatures, still contrived to make his showman an original character, and to stamp on the popular imagination an image of the man, as well as to tickle the risibilities of the public by his sayings and doings. Perhaps the most delicious among his many delicious absurdities was his grave statement that it had been better than ten dollars in Jeff Davis's pocket "if he'd never been born." S. L. Clemens (Mark Twain), the most widely popular of this class of humorists, is a man of wide experience, keen intellect, and literary culture. The serious portions of his writings indicate that he could win a reputation in literature even if he had not been blessed with a humorous fancy inexhaustible in resource. He strikes his most effective satirical blows by an assumption of helpless innocence and bewildered forlornness of mind. The reader or the audience is in convulsions of laughter, while he preserves an imperturbable serenity of countenance, as if wondering why his statement is not received as an important contribution to human knowledge. Occasionally he indulges in a sly and subtle stroke of humor, worthy of the great masters, and indicating that his extravagancies are not the limit of his humorous faculty. D. R. Locke (Petroleum V. Nasby) is not only a humorist, but he was a great force in carrying the reconstruction measures of the Republican party, after the war, by his laughable but coarse, broad, and merciless pictures of the lowest elements in the Western States that had been opposed to the policy of equal justice. The *Nasby Papers* are exceedingly amusing; they are also evidently the work of a man of clear intelligence, and to the future historian they will doubtless be considered as exerting an influence on the popular mind much greater than that exerted by the speeches of many eminent legislators. Though they seem to be extravagant caricatures, the author is understood to insist on their substantial truth to fact. His latest satire is on paper money; its greatest hit is Mr. Nasby's statement that he did not issue fractional currency, because it was as easy to print a hundred-dollar bill as one for fifty cents. H. W. Shaw (Josh Billings) is a humorist of such bright glimpses of practical perception and insight that one wonders why he strives to vulgarize his sagacity by bad spelling. Charles G. Leland, an accomplished man of letters, the best translator of the most difficult pieces of Heine, has won a large reputation by his *Hans Breitmann Ballads*, Hans being a lyrist who sings seemingly from the accumulated inspiration drawn from tuns of lager-beer. B. P. Shillaber, not so prominent as others we have named, has given a new life to Mrs. Partington, and has added Ike to the family. While he participates in the extravagance of the popular American humorists, he has a demure humane humor of his own which is quite charming. It would be impossible in our brief space to note all the writers who have followed, with more or less ingenuity of intellect, in what seems to be the most direct road to American renown.

Among those authors who combine humor with a variety of other gifts, the most conspicuous is F. Bret Harte. His subtilty of ethical insight, his depth of sentiment, his power of solid characterization, and his pathetic and tragic force are as evident as his broad perception of the ludicrous side of things. In his California stories, as in some of his poems, he detects "the soul of goodness in things evil," and represents the exact circumstances in which ruffians and profligates are compelled to feel that they have human hearts and spiritual natures. He is original not only in the ordinary sense of the word, but in the sense of discovering a new domain of literature, and of colonizing it by the creations of his own brain. Perhaps the immense popularity of some of his humorous poems, such as "The Heathen Chinee," has not been favorable to a full recognition of his graver qualities of heart and imagination.

John Hay is, like Bret Harte, a humorist, and his contributions, in *Pike County Ballads*, to what may be called the poetry of ruffianism, if less subtile in sentiment and characterization than those of his model, have a rough raciness and genuine manliness peculiarly his own. His delightful volume called *Castilian Days*, displaying all the graces of style of an accomplished man of letters, shows that it was by a strong effort of imagination that he became for a time a mental denizen of Pike County, and made the acquaintance of Jim Bludso, and other worthies of that kind.

The writings of William D. Howells are masterpieces of literary workmanship, resembling the products of those cunning artificers who add one or two thousand per cent. to the value of their raw material by their incomparable way of working it up. What they are as artisans, he is as artist. His faculties and emotions are in exquisite harmony with each other, and unite to produce one effect of beauty and grace in the singular felicity of his style. He has humor in abundance, but it is so thoroughly blended with his observation, fancy, imagination, taste, and good sense, that it seems to escape from him in light, demure, evanescent flashes rather than in deliberate efforts to be funny. He has revived in some degree the lost art of Addison, Goldsmith, and Irving. Nobody ever "roared" with laughter in reading any thing he ever wrote; but few of our American humorists have excelled him in the power to unseal, as by a magic touch, those secret interior springs of merriment which generally solace the soul without betraying the happiness of the mood they create by any exterior bursts of laughter. His *Venetian Life, Italian Journeys, Suburban Sketches*—his novels, entitled *Our Wedding Journey, A Chance Acquaintance,* and *A Foregone Conclusion*—all indicate the presence of this delicious humorous element, penetrating his picturesque descriptions of scenery, as well as his refined perceptions of character and pleasing narratives of incidents. His prose style, with its "polished want of polish," and elaborate, deliberate simplicity, is marked not only by felicities of diction, but by the continual oversight of an exacting taste. Indeed, the story goes that when, as editor of *The Atlantic Monthly*, he incurred the ire of a rejected contributor, the latter was consoled by the remark of Howells that he frequently rejected his own contributions when he found that they did not satisfy his austere editorial judgment.

Charles Dudley Warner, like Howells, is an author whose humor is intermixed with his sentiment, understanding, and fancy. In *My Summer in a Garden, Back-log Studies*, and other volumes he exhibits a reflective intellect under the guise of a comically sedate humor. Trifles are exalted into importance by the incessant play of his meditative facetiousness.

Thomas Bailey Aldrich first won his reputation as a poet. In the exquisite ballad of "Babie Bell," and in other poems, he has, as it were, so dissolved thought and feeling in melody that rhyme and rhythm seem to be necessary and not selected forms of expression. As a prose writer he combines pungency with elegance of style, and in his stories has exhibited a sly original vein of humor, which, while it steals out in separate sentences, is most effectively manifested in the ludicrous shock of surprise which the reader experiences when he comes to the catastrophe of the plot. In this respect *Marjorie Daw* is one of the best prose tales in our literature. Aldrich has written many others constructed on a similar plan, and almost equally attractive. His *Story of a Bad Boy* belongs to the class of juvenile works, and it is a charming satire on the "do-me-good" narratives which are so copiously supplied for the improvement and delectation of American lads.

Among the American novelists who have risen into prominence during the past thirty years, the greatest, though not the most popular, is Nathaniel Hawthorne. His first romance, *The Scarlet Letter*, did not appear until the year 1850, but previously he had published collections of short stories under the titles of *Twice-told Tales* and *Mosses from an Old Manse.* These were recognized by judicious readers all over the country as masterpieces of literary art, but their circulation was ludicrously disproportioned to their merit. For years one of the greatest modern masters of English prose was valued at his true worth only by those who had found by experience in composition how hard it is to be clear and simple in style, and at the same time to be profound in sentiment, exact in thought, and fertile in imagination. Most of these short stories contain the germs of romances, and a literary economist of his materials, like Scott or Dickens, would have expanded Hawthorne's hints of passion and character into thrilling novels. *The Scarlet Letter*, the romance by which Hawthorne first forced himself on the popular mind as a genius of the first class, was but the expansion of an idea expressed in three sentences, written twenty years before its appearance, in the little sketch of "Endicott and the Cross," which is included in the collection of *Twice-told Tales*. But *The Scarlet Letter* exhibited in startling distinctness all the resources of his peculiar mind, and even more than Scott's *Bride of Lammermoor* it touches the lowest depths of tragic woe and passion—so deep, indeed, that the representation becomes at times almost ghastly. If Jonathan Edwards, turned romancer, had dramatized his sermon on "Sinners in the Hand of an Angry God," he could not have written a more terrific story of guilt and retribution than *The Scarlet Letter*. The pitiless intellectual analysis of the emotions of guilty souls is pushed so far that the reader, after being compelled to sympathize with the Puritanic notion of Law, sighs for some appearance of the consoling Puritanic doctrine of Grace. Hawthorne, in fact, was a patient observer of the operation of spiritual laws, and relentless in recording the results of his observations. Most readers of romances are ravenous for external events; they demand that the heroes and heroines shall be swift in thought, confident in decision, rapid in act. In Hawthorne's novels the events occur in the hearts and minds of his characters, and our attention is fastened on the ecstasies or agonies of individual souls rather than on outward acts and incidents; at least, the latter appear trivial in comparison with the inward mental states they imperfectly express. Carlyle says that real genius in characterization consists in developing character from "within outward." Hawthorne's mental sight in discerning souls is marvelously penetrating and accurate, but he finds it so difficult to give them an adequate physical embodiment that their very flesh is spiritualized, and appears to be brought into the representation only to give a kind of phantasmal form to purely mental conceptions. These souls, while intensely realized as individuals, are, however, mere puppets in the play of the spiritual forces and laws behind them, and while seemingly gifted with will, even to the extent of indulging in all the caprices of willfulness, they drift to their doom with the certainty of fate. In this twofold power of insight into souls, and of the spiritual laws which regulate both the natural action and morbid aberrations of souls, Hawthorne is so incomparably great that in comparison with him all other romancers of the century, whether German, French, English, or American, seem to be superficial. The defect of his method was that he penetrated to such a depth into the human heart, and recorded so mercilessly its realities and possibilities of sin and selfishness as they appeared to his piercing, passionless vision of the movements of passion, that he rather frightened than pleased the ordinary novel-reader. The old woman who sagely concluded that she must be sick, because in reading the daily newspaper she did not, as was her wont, "enjoy her murders," unconsciously hit on the distinction which separates artistic representations of human life which include crime and misery from those representations in which the prominence of crime and misery is so marked as to become unpalatable. Hawthorne did not succeed in making his psychological pictures of sin and woe "enjoyable." The intensity of impassioned imagination which flames through every page of *The Scarlet Letter* was unrelieved by those milder accompaniments which should have been brought in to soften the effect of a tragedy so awful in itself. Little Pearl, one of the most exquisite creations of imaginative genius, is introduced not to console her parents, but, in her wild, innocent willfulness, to symbolize their sin, and add new torments to the slow-consuming agonies of remorse. *The Scarlet Letter* is incidentally the strongest of all arguments against the heresy of "free love." In *The House of the Seven Gables*, *The Blithedale Ro-*

mance, and *The Marble Faun*, Hawthorne deepened the impression made by his previous writings that he did not possess his genius, but was possessed *by* it. The most powerful of his creations of character were inspired not by his sympathies, but his antipathies. Personally he was the most gentle and genial and humane of men. He detested many of the characters in whose delineation he exerted the full force of his intellect and imagination; but he was so mentally conscientious that he never exercised the right of the novelist to kill the personages who displeased him at his own will and pleasure. So intensely did he realize his characters that to run his pen through them, and thus blot them out of existence, would have seemed to him like the commission of willful murder. He watched and noted the operation of spiritual laws on the malignant or feeble souls he portrayed, but never interfered personally to divert their fatal course. In thus emphasizing the tragic element in Hawthorne's genius, we may have too much overlooked his deep and delicate humor, his ingenuity of playful fancy, his felicity in making a landscape visible to the soul as well as the eye by his charming power of description, and the throng of thoughts which accompany every step in the progress of his narrative. Not the least remarkable characteristic of this remarkable man was the prevailing simplicity, clearness, sweetness, purity, and vigor of his style, even when his subjects might have justified him in deviating into some form of *Carlylese*.

The most widely circulated novel ever published in this country, or perhaps in any other, is *Uncle Tom's Cabin*, by Mrs. Harriet Beecher Stowe. The book has in the United States attained a sale of over 350,000 copies, and after the lapse of twenty-four years the demand for it still continues. It has been translated into almost every known language. Inspired by the insurrection of the public conscience against the Fugitive Slave Law, its popularity has survived the extinction of slavery itself. Its original publication, in 1852, was an important political event. It practically overturned the arguments of statesmen and decisions of jurists by an irresistible appeal to the heart and imagination of the American people. It was one of the most powerful agencies in building up the Republican party, in electing Abraham Lincoln to the Presidency, and in raising earnest volunteers for the great crusade against slavery. This effect was produced not by explosions of moral wrath against the iniquity it assailed, not by righteous vituperation of the liberticides who meanly lent themselves to the support of the slave power, but by a vivid dramatic presentation of the facts of the case, in which complete justice was done equally to the slave-holder and the slave. And the humor, the pathos, the keen observation, the power of characterization, displayed in the novel were all penetrated by an imagination quickened into activity by a deep and humane religious sentiment. Next to *Uncle Tom*, *The Minister's Wooing* is the best of Mrs. Stowe's novels. Her *Oldtown Folks* and *Sam Lawson's Stories* are full of delightful Yankee humor.

It is impossible for us to spare the space for even an inadequate notice of all the novelists of the United States. At the time (1827) Miss Catharine M. Sedgwick published *Hope Leslie* she easily took a prominent position in our literature, in virtue not only of her own merits, but of the comparative absence of competitors. Since then there has appeared a throng of writers of romantic narratives, and the number is constantly increasing. We are compelled to confine our remarks to a few of the representative novelists. William Ware gained a just reputation by his *Letters from Palmyra* (1836). The style is elegant, the story attractive, and the pictures of the court of Zenobia are represented through a visionary medium which gives to the representation a certain charming poetic remoteness. Charles Fenno Hoffman, a poet as well as prose writer, whose song of "Sparkling and Bright" has probably rung over the emptying of a million of Champagne bottles, was a man who delighted in "wild scenes in forest and prairie," and whose *Greyslaer* shows the energy of his nature, as well as the brilliancy of his intellect. R. B. Kimball is noted for his business novels, and his heart-breaks come not from failures in love, but from failures in traffic. Donald G. Mitchell, in his *Reveries of a Bachelor*, originated a new style, in which a certain delightful daintiness of sentiment was combined with a fertile fancy and touches of humorous good sense. Sylvester Judd, a Unitarian clergyman, went into the great lumber region of Maine, and came out of it to record his observations, experiences, and insights in the novel of *Margaret*, which Lowell once affirmed to be the most intensely *American* book ever written. Thomas W. Higginson, distinguished in many departments of literature for the thoroughness of his culture and the classic simplicity and elegance of his style, is the author of a novel called *Malbone*, quite notable for beauty of description, ingenuity of plot, and subtilty of characterization. Herman Melville, after astonishing the public with a rapid succession of original novels, the scene of which was placed in the islands of the Pacific, suddenly dropped his pen, as if in disgust of his vocation. Mrs. Harriet Prescott Spofford is the author of many thrilling stories, written in a style of perhaps exaggerated splendor, but in which prose is flushed with all the hues of poetry. Maria S. Cummins published in 1854 a novel called *The Lamplighter*, which attained an extraordinary popularity, owing to the simplicity, tenderness, pathos, and naturalness of the first hundred pages. Seventy thousand copies were sold in a year. Miss E. S. Phelps, in her *Gates Ajar*, *Hedged In*, and in a variety of minor tales, has exhibited a power of intense pathos which almost pains the reader it melts. Henry James, Jun.—long may it be before the "Jun." is detached from his name!—has a deep and delicate perception of the internal states of exceptional individuals, and a quiet mastery of the resources of style, which make his stories studies in psychology as well as models of narrative art. J. W. De Forest, the author of *Kate Beaumont* and other novels, is a thorough realist, whose characterization, animated narrative, well-contrived plots, and pitiless satire only want the relief of ideal sentiment to make them as pleasing as they are powerful. Edward Everett Hale, the author of *The Man without a Country, My Double, and How he Undid Me*, and *Sybaris and Other Homes*, is fantastically ingenious in the plan and form of his narratives, but he uses his ingenuity in the service of good sense and sound feeling, while he inspires it with the impulses of a hopeful, vigorous, and elastic spirit. Miss Louisa M. Alcott, in her *Little Women* and *Little Men*, has almost revolutionized juvenile literature by the audacity of her innovations. She thoroughly understands that peculiar element in practical youthful character which makes romps of so many girls and "roughs" of so many boys. Real little women and real little men look into her stories as into mirrors in order to get an accurate reflection of their inward selves. She has also a tart, quaint, racy, witty good sense, which acts on the mind like a tonic. Her success has been as great as her rejection of conventionality in depicting lads and lasses deserved. Mrs. A. D. T. Whitney has more sentiment and a softer manner of representation than Miss Alcott; but she has originality, though of a different kind; and her books, like those of Miss Alcott, have penetrated into households in every part of the country, and their characters have been domesticated at thousands of firesides. Faith Gartney especially is a real friend and acquaintance to many a girl who has no other. William G. Simms, the most prolific of American historical novelists, and in tireless intellectual energy worthy of all respect, failed to keep his hold on the popular mind by the absence in his vividly described scenes of adventure of that peculiar something which gives to such scenes a permanent charm. Theodore Winthrop, the author of *Cecil Dreeme*, *John Brent*, and other striking and admirable tales, rose suddenly into popularity, and as suddenly declined—a conspicuous instance of the instability of the romancer's reputation. J. G. Holland has succeeded in every thing he has undertaken, whether as a sort of lay preacher to the young, as an essayist, as a novelist, or as a poet. It is hardly possible to take up any late edition of any one of his numerous volumes without finding "fortieth thousand" or "sixtieth thousand" smiling complacently and benignly upon you from the title-page. Both in verse and prose he has addressed the *bourgeoisie* of readers, disdaining to court the *proletariat*, and disregarding the fleers of the patricians. Mrs. Mary J. Holmes, the author of *Lena Rivers*, Mrs. Terhune (Marian Harland), the author of *Hidden Path*, Mrs. Augusta Evans Wilson, the author of *St. Elmo*, are novelists very different from Dr. Holland, yet whose works have obtained a circulation corresponding in extent. We pause here in reading the list, not for want of subjects, but for want of space, and also, it must be confessed, for want of epithets.

It is a great misfortune that the temptation which besets clever people to write mediocre verses, and afterward to collect them in a volume, is irresistible. Time, and short time at that, proves the truth of Mr. Jonathan Oldbuck's remark, that "your fugitive poetry is apt to become stationary with the publisher." Even when a little momentary reputation is acquired, the writers are soon compelled to repeat mournfully the refrain of Pierpont's beautiful and pathetic poem, "Passing away! passing away!" It is not one of the least mysteries of this mismanagement of talent that the want of public recognition does not appease the desire to attain it. As a general rule, books of verses, even good verses, are the most unsalable of human products. There are numerous cases where genuine poetic faculty and inspiration fail to make the slightest impression on the public imagination. The most remarkable instance of this kind in our literature is found in the case of Mrs. Maria Brooks (Maria del Occidente), who printed, some forty years ago, a poem called "Zophiel, or the Bride of Seven," which Southey warmly praised, which was honored with a notice in the *London Quarterly Review*, which deserved most of the eulogy it received, which fell dead from the press, and which not ten living Americans have ever read. Again, some of the most popular and most quoted poems in our literature are purely accidental hits, and their authors are rather nettled than pleased that their other productions should be neglected while such prominence is given to one. Thus it might be somewhat dangerous now to compliment T. W. Parsons for his "Lines on a Bust of Dante," because he has become sick of praise confined to that piece, while the delicate beauty of scores of his other poems, and his noble rhymed translation of "Dante's Inferno," find few readers. Miss Lucy Larcom, when she pictured "Hannah Binding Shoes," did not dream that Hannah was to draw away attention from her other heroines, and concentrate it upon herself. Freneau's "Indian Burying-Ground" is the only piece of that poet which survives. "The Gray Forest Eagle" of A. B. Street has screamed away attention from his "rippling of waters and waving of trees"—from his hundreds of pages of descriptive verse which are almost photographs of natural scenery. People quote the "Summer in the Heart" and "A Life on the Ocean Wave" of Epes Sargent, and overlook many better specimens of his melody and his imagination. There are some poems which almost every body has read, which are commonly considered the only poems of the writers. Such are "The Star-spangled Banner," by F. S. Key; "Woodman, Spare that Tree" (very insipid, by-the-way), by George P. Morris; "A Hymn," by Joseph H. Clinch; "The Baron's Last Banquet" and "Old Grimes is Dead," by A. G. Greene; "My Life is like the Summer Rose," by R. H. Wilde; "Sweet Home," by John Howard Payne; "The Christmas Hymn," by E. H. Sears; "The Old Oaken Bucket," by Samuel Woodworth; "Milton's Prayer of Patience," by Elizabeth Lloyd Howell; "The Relief of Lucknow," by Robert Lowell; "The Old Sergeant," by Forceythe Wilson; "The Vagabonds," by J. T. Trowbridge; and "Gnosis," by C. P. Cranch. There are other pieces, like the "Count Paul," and especially the "Theodora," of Mrs. Drinker (Edith May), which seem to be more deserving of success than some of those which have attained it. But little justice has been done to the poetic and dramatic talent of George H. Boker. "The King's Bell," exquisite for the limpid flow of its verse and the sweetly melancholy tone of its thought, together with other poems by Richard Henry Stoddard, have not received their due meed of praise. T. Buchanan Read wrote volumes of rich descriptive poetry, but the popularity of "Sheridan's Ride" is not sufficient to attract attention to them.

In thus commenting on the instability and uncertainty of the public taste in respect to poets, we have unconsciously indicated quite an excellent body of American poetry, and we may proceed with the enumeration.

W. W. Story, famous as a sculptor, is also a poet, who throws into verse the same energy of inspiration which is so obvious in his statues. Mrs. Frances S. Osgood had a singularly musical nature, and her poems sing of themselves. She did not appear to feel the fetters of rhyme; she danced in them. Her poems, however, have the thinness of substance which often accompanies quickness of sensibility and activity of fancy. As it is, the reader rises from the perusal of her poems with a delicious melody in his ears, a charming feeling in his heart, and with but few thoughts in his head. Mrs. M. J. Preston has a more robust intellect, greater intensity of feeling, and more force of imagination than Mrs. Osgood, though lacking her lovely grace and bewitching melodiousness; but Mrs. Osgood could not have written a poem so deeply pathetic as "Keeping his Word." Henry Timrod and Paul H. Hayne are, with Mrs. Preston, the most distinguished poets of the South. Timrod's ode sung on the occasion of decorating the graves of the Confederate dead is, in its simple grandeur, the noblest poem ever written by a Southern poet. Hayne exhibits in all his pieces a rich sensuousness of nature, a seemingly exhaustless fertility of fancy, an uncommon felicity of poetic description, and an easy command of the harmonies of verse. John G. Saxe owes his wide acceptance with the public not merely to the elasticity of his verse, the sparkle of his wit, and the familiarity of his topics, but to his power of diffusing the spirit of his own good humor. The unctuous satisfaction he feels in putting his mood of merriment into rhyme is communicated to his reader, so that, as it were, they laugh joyously together. Edmund Clarence Stedman, in addition to his merits as a critic of poetry, has written poems which stir the blood as well as quicken the imagination. Such, among others, are "John Brown of Osawatomie" and "Kearney at Seven Pines." Perhaps the finest recent examples of exquisitely subtile imagination working under the impulse of profound sentiment are to be found in the little volume entitled "Poems by H. H." (Mrs. Helen Hunt).

We have space only to mention the names of Jones Very, Celia Thaxter, Mrs. Lippincott (Grace Greenwood), H. H. Brownell, Will Carleton (author of *Farm Ballads*), Alice and Phœbe Cary, and Mrs. L. C. Moulton, though each would justify a detailed criticism.

The limits of this essay do not admit the mention of every author who is worthy of notice. The reader must be referred for details to the various volumes of Dr. R. W. Griswold, to the *Cyclopedia of American Literature*, by E. A. and G. L. Duyckinck, to the useful *Manual of American Literature*, by Dr. John S. Hart, and the excellent *Hand-Book of American Literature*, by F. H. Underwood. Still, before concluding, it may be well to mention some names without which even so limited a view of American literature as the present would be incomplete. And, first, honor is due to Henry T. Tuckerman, who for nearly forty years was the associate of American authors, and who labored, year after year, to diffuse a taste for literature by his articles in reviews and magazines. He belonged to the class of appreciative critics, and was never more pleased than when he exercised the resources of a cultivated mind to analyze, explain, and celebrate the merits of others. Richard Grant White, a critic of an austerer order, has for some time been engaged literally in a war of words. In the *minutiæ* of English philology he has rarely met an antagonist he has not overthrown. In these encounters he has displayed wit, learning, logic, a perfect command of his subject, an imperfect command of his temper. The positiveness of his statements, however, seems always to come from the certainty of his knowledge. In his admirable edition of Shakspeare, and in his *Life and Genius of Shakspeare*, he has exhibited his rare critical faculty at its best. Henry N. Hudson, also an editor, biographer, and critic of Shakspeare, has specially shown his masterly power of analysis in commenting on the characters of the dramatist. Henry Giles, in two or three volumes of biography and criticism, has proved that clear perceptions, nice distinctions, and sound sense can be united with a rush of eloquence which seems too rapid for the pausing doubt of discriminating judgment. S. A. Allibone's *Dictionary of Authors*, with its 46,000 names, is one of those prodigies of labor which excite not only admiration, but astonishment. George P. Marsh, one of the most widely accomplished of American scholars, is principally known as the author of *Lectures on the English Language* and of *The English Language and Early English Literature*, both critical works of a high class. The greatest comparative philologist the country has produced, William D. Whitney, has, like Max Müller, in England, popularized some of the results of his investigations in an admirable volume on *Language, and the Study of Language.*

The theological literature of the United States covers so wide a field that it would be wild to attempt to characterize here even its eminent representatives. We can give only a few names. Henry Ward Beecher, the most widely renowned pulpit and platform orator of the country, is more remarkable for the general largeness and opulence of his nature than for the possession of any exceptional power of mind or extent of acquisition. As a theological scholar, or, indeed, as a trained and accurate writer, nobody would think of comparing him with Francis Wayland, or Leonard Bacon, or Edwards A. Park, or Frederick H. Hedge. In depth of spiritual insight, though not in depth of spiritual emotion, he is inferior to Horace Bushnell, Cyrus A. Bartol, and many other American divines. He feels spiritual facts intensely; he beholds them with wavering vision. But his distinction is that he is a formidable, almost irresistible, moral force. His influence comes from the conjoint and harmonious action of his whole blood and brain and will and soul, and his magnetism being thus both physical and mental, he communicates his individuality in the act of radiating his thoughts, and thus *Beecherizes* his readers as he *Beecherizes* his audiences. He overpowers where he fails to convince. The reader, but especially the listener, is brought into direct contact or collision not only with a thinker and a stirrer up of the emotions, but with a strong, resolute, intrepid man. As Emerson would say, he could mob a mob, and compel it to submit. This continual sense of conscious power impels him into many imprudences and indiscretions, and stamps on what he says, and what he writes, and what he does, a character of haste and extemporaneousness. No man could throw off such an amount of intellectual work as he performs, who thought comprehensively or who thought deeply; for the comprehensive thinker hesitates, the deep thinker doubts; but hesitation and doubt are foreign to Mr. Beecher's intellectual constitution, and only intrude into his consciousness in those occasional reactions caused by the moral fatigue resulting now and then from his hurried, headlong intellectual movement. Observation, sense, wit, humor, fancy, sentiment, moral perception, moral might, are all included and fused in the large individuality whose mode of action we have ventured to sketch.

There are some books which it is difficult to class. Thus, Richard H. Dana, Jun., published some thirty years ago a volume called *Two Years Before the Mast,* which became instantly popular, is popular now, and promises to be popular for many years to come. In reading it any body can see that it is more than an ordinary record of a voyage, for there runs through the simple and lucid narrative an element of beauty and power which gives it the artistic charm of romance. Again, *Six Months in Italy,* by George S. Hillard, and *Notes of Travel and Study in Italy,* by Charles E. Norton, would be superficially classed among books of travel, but they are essentially works of literature, and their chief worth consists in descriptions of natural scenery, in pointed reflection, in delicate criticism of works of art. The volume entitled *White Hills,* by Thomas Starr King, apparently intended merely to describe the mountain region of New Hampshire, is all aglow with a glad inspiration drawn from the ardent soul and teeming mind of the writer. Charles T. Brooks would generally be classed as a translator, but being a poet, he has so translated the novels of Richter that he has domesticated them in our language. Such translations are greater efforts of intelligence and imagination than many original works. Horace Mann's reports as secretary of the Massachusetts Board of Education rank with legislative documents, yet they are really eloquent treatises, full of matter, but of matter burning with passion and blazing with imagery. *Substance and Shadow,* by Henry James, might be classed either with theological or metaphysical works, were it not that the writer, while treating on the deepest questions which engage the attention of theologians and metaphysicians, stretches both theologians and metaphysicians on the rack of his pitiless analysis, and showers upon them all the boundless stores of his ridicule. Miss Mary A. Dodge (Gail Hamilton) might be styled an essayist, but that would be but a vague term to denote a writer who takes up all classes of subjects, is tart, tender, shrewish, pathetic, monitory, objurgatory, tolerant, prejudiced, didactic, and dramatic by turns, but always writing with so much point, vigor, and freshness that we can only classify her among "readable" authors. Margaret Fuller Ossoli, scholar, critic, teacher, translator, metaphysician, philanthropist, revolutionist, a pythoness in a transcendental coterie, a nurse in a soldiers' hospital, a martyr heroine on board a wrecked ship—we can only say of her that she was a woman. There is a delightful book entitled *Yesterdays with Authors*, by James T. Fields—a combination of gossip, biography, and criticism, but refusing to be ranked with either, and depending for its interest on the life-like pictures it presents of such men as Hawthorne, Dickens, and Thackeray in their hours of familiar talk and correspondence. There is also one work of such pretension that it should not be omitted here, namely, *Outlines of Cosmic Philosophy, based on the Doctrine of Evolution*, by John Fiske. It is mainly a lucid exposition of the philosophy of Herbert Spencer, with the addition of original and critical matter. The breadth and strength of understanding, the fullness of information, the command of expression, in this book are worthy of all commendation. The curious thing in it is that the author thinks that a new religion is to be established on the co-ordination of the sciences, and of this religion, whose God is the "Unknowable," he is a pious believer.

In conclusion, we can only allude to the intellectual force, the various talents and accomplishments, employed in the leading newspapers of the country. During the past thirty years these journals have swarmed with all kinds of anonymous ability. Though the articles appeared to die with the day or week on which they were printed, they really passed, for good or evil, into the general mind as vital influences, shaping public opinion and forming public taste. It would be difficult, for example, to estimate the beneficent action on our literature of such a critic and scholar as George Ripley, who for many years directed the literary department of a widely circulated newspaper. The range of his learning was equal to every demand upon its resources; the candor of his judgment answered to the comprehensiveness of his taste; the catholicity of his literary sympathies led him to encourage every kind of literary talent on its first appearance; and he was pure from the stain of that meanest form of egotism which grudges the recognition of merit in others, as if such a recognition was a diminution of its own importance. The great development, during a comparatively recent period, of the magazine literature of the country has had an important effect in stimulating and bringing forward new writers, some of whom promise to more than fill the places which their elders will soon leave vacant. It would be presumptuous to anticipate the verdict of the next generation as to which of these will fulfill the expectations raised by their early efforts. That pleasant duty must be left to the fortunate person who shall note the Centennial Progress of American Literature in 1976.

XIII.

PROGRESS OF THE FINE ARTS.

PAUL REVERE.—[1735-1818.]

THE growth of the arts of design in this country has been of necessity much slower than the national development in other directions. The early colonists had neither time nor inclination for the culture of art. They distrusted and restrained the imaginative faculty, which is the soul of art, and applied all their energies to the great practical tasks which confronted them on their arrival on the shores of the New World. They had the vast wilderness to subdue, houses to build for themselves and their children, to found commonwealths on the broad basis of liberty and justice, and for many generations were compelled to maintain fierce warfare with crafty and cruel foes allied with the civilized enemies of the religious freedom which they had fled hither to establish. If the early New England colonists gave any thought to art, they probably regarded it as one of the forms of luxurious vanity and license belonging to a state of society which they held in abhorrence, and from which they were resolved to keep their land of refuge free. Allowance must also be made for the force of circumstances. The struggle for mere subsistence was too severe for the indulgence of the imagination. The only graces known to the early colonists were the austere virtues of their rigid theology. To adorn the home or the person was in their eyes a sinful waste of time, which could be well employed only in the practical duties of the present life and in preparing for the next. The influence of this stern training was of long duration ; it still exists, indeed, in the prejudice to be found in many communities against the presence of pictures or sculpture in houses of worship, although this may be partially ascribed to the old Puritan revolt against Romish practices.

With the physical development of the country, and the consequent freedom from the harassing cares which had kept the thoughts of the early colonists on the arts of necessity, one form of luxury after another crept in upon the homely life of our ancestors. Pictures began to find their way here from the Old World, and artists began to visit the colonies. It is probable that they met with many discouragements and but scanty patronage, for few authentic traces have been preserved of those early pioneers of art. Cotton Mather, in his *Magnolia,* refers to a "limner," but he gives us no name. One of the first of whom we have other than vague traditions was a native of Scotland, John Watson by name, who came to the colonies in 1715, and established himself as a portrait painter at Perth Amboy, then a flourishing commercial rival of New York. In a building adjoining his dwelling-house he established the first picture-gallery in America. The collection was probably of little value. Watson, who combined the art of portrait painting with the business of a money-lender, amassed a considerable fortune. He never married, and dying in 1768, at the age of eighty-three,

JOHN SINGLETON COPLEY.—[1737-1815.]

left his wealth and his pictures to a nephew. Taking sides with the loyalists in 1776, the nephew was compelled to flee the country. The deserted picture-gallery, left to the mercies of the undisciplined militia, was broken up, and the collection of paintings was so effectually scattered that all trace of them was lost. None of the portraits executed by Watson are known to be in existence, and he is remembered only as an obscure pioneer in the culture and development of a taste for the fine arts in this country.

To John Smybert, also a Scotchman, American art is more largely indebted. He came to this country in 1728 with Dean Berkeley, afterward Bishop of Cloyne, whose fellow-traveler he had been in Italy. The failure of the dean's grand scheme for the establishment of a "universal college of science and arts for the instruction of heathen children in Christian duties and civil knowledge" left Smybert to the free exercise of his profession. In early youth he had served his time, says Horace Walpole, "with a common house painter; but eager to handle a pencil in a more elevated style, he came to London, where, however, for a subsistence he was compelled to content himself at first with working for coach painters. It was a little rise to be employed in copying for dealers, and from thence he obtained admittance into the Academy. His efforts and ardor at last carried him to Italy, where he spent three years in copying Raphael, Titian, Vandyck, and Rubens, and improved enough to meet with much business at his return." Thus accomplished, Smybert was well fitted for a career in the New World, which presented no rival in culture and experience. His talents appear to have been in great demand, and they were certainly used to good purpose. To his pencil we owe many excellent portraits of eminent divines and magistrates of his time, and the only authentic portrait of Jonathan Edwards. His picture of the Berkeley household, now in the Yale College Gallery, is said to have been the first containing more than one figure ever painted in this country. He may be said to have been the first teacher of art in America, as it was from his copy of a painting by Vandyck that Allston, Copley, and Trumbull received their earliest inspiration and their first impressions of color and drawing.

It was long before art received popular encouragement and support in this country. True, Benjamin Franklin, in a letter to Charles Wilson Peale, dated London, July 4, 1771, prophesied the future prosperity of art among his countrymen. "The arts," he says, "have always traveled westward; and there is no doubt of their flourishing hereafter on our side of the Atlantic, as the number of wealthy inhabitants shall increase who may be able and willing suitably to reward them, since, from several instances, it appears that our people are not deficient in genius." But Trumbull, who spoke from experience, bluntly told a young aspirant for fame that he "had better learn to make shoes or dig potatoes than become a painter in this country." Year by year, however, partly through the influence of art associations, and partly through the influx of the works of foreign artists, the love of art became diffused among our people, and it is many years since American painters and sculptors could justly complain of the want of popular appreciation.

One cause of the slow growth of art sentiment and art knowledge among Americans was the absence, even in the larger cities, of public and private galleries of paintings like those to which the people of every European

BENJAMIN WEST.—[1738-1820.]

city have constant access, and where they may become familiar with the works of the great masters of almost every age and country. Of late years these opportunities have notably increased among us. Wealthy citizens of New York, Philadelphia, Boston, Washington, Cincinnati, and other cities have accumulated extensive and valuable private galleries of the best works of native and foreign artists, and have evinced commendable liberality in opening their doors to the public. There are also fine galleries of paintings and statuary belonging to societies, like the Boston Athenæum and our own Historical Society; but to most of these the general public can not claim admission, and their usefulness as a means of art culture is, therefore, comparatively restricted. There should be in every large city a public gallery of art, as in Paris, Berlin, Munich, London, Dresden, Florence, and other European cities, to which, on certain days of the week, access should be free to all. The influence of such institutions would be immense. There is many a working-man in Paris who knows more about pictures and statues than the majority of cultivated people in this country. He visits freely the magnificent galleries of the Louvre, hears artists and connoisseurs converse, and if he is a man of ordinary intelligence and perception, he acquires a knowledge of pictures and artists which can not be attained in a country where such opportunities are rare, or only to be enjoyed either by paying for them or by the favor of some private collector. True, the want of public art galleries has been in a measure supplied, in most of our large cities, by the collections of art dealers like Schaus and Goupil, who of late years have imported many of the finest specimens of the works of foreign artists, and who admit the public to their exhibition rooms without fee. But this privilege is, for the most part, confined to the educated and the wealthy. Rarely is a working-man or working-woman seen in these rooms, although no respectable and well-behaved person would be denied admission. Enter the galleries of Paris, of Munich, or Dresden, on a holiday, and you will find hundreds of people belonging to the working classes, men, women, and children, feasting their eyes on the treasures of art, and filling their minds with love for the beautiful. The refining influence of such an education can not be overvalued. It may not be quite as useful as the practical instruction of our common schools; but while we can not subscribe to Ruskin's opinion that it is more important that a child should learn to draw than that he should learn to write, there can be no question as to the ennobling and refining influence of art upon personal character and upon the community. The lack of this culture among

GILBERT STUART.—[1754-1828.]

our people only a few years ago was manifested by the commotion which Powers's "Greek Slave" made on its arrival in this country. Many persons questioned the propriety of exhibiting a nude statue. A delegation of distinguished clergymen was sent to view it, when it was at Cincinnati, for the purpose of deciding whether it should be "countenanced by religious people." Not many years ago a well-educated country lady, visiting Boston for the first time in her life, was shocked to find a pretty and modest-looking young woman seated at the ticket table in the statue gallery of the Athenæum. The young woman was engaged in sewing-work. "She ought to employ her time in making aprons for these horrid, shameful statues," remarked the indignant visitor, as she left the room. Prejudices like these, the fruit of ignorance, are happily dying out, and few traces of them will be found in the next generation.

The American Art Union, founded in 1839, in imitation of the French *Société des Amis des Arts*, exerted an important influence upon American art culture. For upward of ten years it distributed annually from five hundred to more than a thousand works of art. Its yearly subscriptions reached the sum of one hundred thousand dollars. It issued a series of fine engravings from the works of American artists, and for several years published a bulletin embracing a complete record of the progress of art in this country, together with much valuable and interesting information regarding the arts and artists of Europe. Through the agency of its commissions several American artists, who have since attained high rank in their profession, were first brought to public notice. The institution was broken up about ten years after its organization on account of the violation, by its method of distributing prizes, of the State laws against lotteries. But during the period of its existence it accomplished much toward awakening a love of art throughout the country, and it deserves to be gratefully remembered for its services in this direction.

In one respect, however, the Art Union was the indirect means of temporary harm. Through its activity America was revealed to the proprietors of the great picture manufactories of Italy and Belgium as a new and promising field for the sale of their wretched copies and imitations. Thousands of these vile productions were palmed off upon innocent persons in this country as genuine works by old or modern masters of note. The writer was once present at an auction sale of such a collection in a flourishing city in the western part of this State. There was great excitement over it. Here were "old masters" by the dozen, their genuineness attested by printed labels on the back of the frames giving names and dates, while the catalogue, filled with glowing praises of the artists and their works, made no mention of copies. The pictures were marvelously cheap. A Madonna by Raphael sold for thirty dollars, frame and all; a large picture by Rubens for about the same price; and landscapes by Claude, Ruysdael, and others brought from ten to twenty dollars each, according to the expensiveness of the frames. This was about twenty-five years ago. Thanks to the general advance of culture and knowledge, there is now probably hardly a village, and certainly not a city, in the country where such an imposition could be attempted without detection. Most of the "old masters" purchased at these sales have long since found their appropriate resting-place in the lumber-room.

The National Academy of Design, in this city, has unquestionably exerted a most important influence on the culture of art in America, and in the diffusion of the knowledge and love of art among the people. The present organization was preceded by an association of artists formed in 1801 under the name of the New York Academy of Fine Arts. Seven years later it received the act of incorporation, under the name of the American Academy of Fine Arts, and Chancellor Livingston was chosen president; Colonel John Trumbull, vice-president; De Witt Clinton, David Hosack, John R. Murray, William Cutting, and Charles Wilkes, directors. Through the instrumentality of the American minister at Paris, the Emperor Napoleon presented to the institution many valuable busts, antique statues, and rare prints. There was still, however, so little general support afforded by the community, and picture buyers were so few, that the enterprise languished from the first, and it was saved from total dissolution only by the temporary accession of Vanderlyn's celebrated "Ariadne," afterward so admirably engraved by Durand, and certain pictures of West, in 1816. These important additions to its collection enabled the institution for a time to tide over the danger which threatened its existence. A school of instruction, with models and art lectures, was also organized, in the hope of reviving popular interest in the Academy, but want of means to carry out the plan on a broad and liberal foundation interfered with the working of the project; and a fire, which destroyed a great part of its models and drawings, in 1828, gave the *coup de grâce* to an institution which had been dying by slow degrees.

The American Academy of Fine Arts having given up the ghost, another institution was formed to take its place and carry on the work it had begun—the National Academy of Design, of which the first president was Professor Morse, whose invention of the electric telegraph, some years later, cast his artistic career wholly in the shade. Founded on a broader basis than its predecessor, and meeting more fully the wishes and aims of the artists, the new institution speedily acquired strength and popularity, and it is to-day the most important and most influential art society in the United States. The most eminent painters and sculptors of America are enrolled among its members. Its management has frequently subjected the Academy to sharp animadversion, sometimes not undeserved, from those who deemed it too conservative, not to say illiberal, for the progressive tendency of the age; but none can be so unjust as to deny that its general course has tended to the elevation of American art and the popular diffusion of art culture. Nor should fault be too rashly found with its acknowledged conservatism. The best and most enduring reforms are those which come slowly, in obedience to the demands of long experience and mature consideration, while nothing can be worse, in a society as well as in the state, than capricious and hasty changes, which frequently introduce abuses more objectionable than the old.

For more than a third of a century the National Academy, to use the words of Bryant's address on laying the corner-stone of the Academy building, "had a nomadic existence, pitching its tent now here, now there, as convenience might dictate, but never possessing a permanent seat." At length the munificence of art-loving citizens of New York enabled the society to erect a building well suited to its purposes and worthy of the great city in which it stands. The corner-stone was laid October 19, 1863, and the first exhibition was held in the completed building in the spring of 1865. The Academy building, on the corner of Twenty-third Street and Fourth Avenue, is a handsome structure in the style of the celebrated Doge's palace at Venice. It is built of marble, banded with graywacke, with simple

COLONEL JOHN TRUMBULL.—[1756-1843.]

and appropriate decorations. The cost of the ground and building was about two hundred thousand dollars, a large part of which was contributed by citizens of New York. There are six exhibition galleries, including the corridor, which for the present afford all the space required for the Academy and water-color exhibitions; but an enlargement will be necessary in the near future to meet the increasing demands for room.

Philadelphia was not far behind New York in establishing an Academy of Art. In December, 1805, a meeting of seventy gentlemen of that city, most of them members of the bar, was held in Independence Hall for the purpose of considering the project. Their deliberations resulted in the

ALEXANDER ANDERSON.—[1775-1870.]

signing of articles of agreement, the original of which is still preserved, providing for the creation of an Art Academy, which was pledged "to promote the cultivation of the Fine Arts in the United States of America, by introducing correct and elegant copies from works of the first masters in Sculpture and Painting." George Clymer, a signer of the Declaration of Independence, was elected first president of the association; of the twelve directors only two were professional artists—William Rush and Charles Wilson Peale. Benjamin West, as the most distinguished son of Pennsylvania in the ranks of art, was elected an honorary member of the Academy. He was then under a cloud in his adopted country. His royal patron had become insane, and the Prince Regent had withdrawn the commission for the decoration of Windsor Chapel with a series of large pictures on the progress of Revealed Religion. He was sixty-seven years old, and this recognition from his native State, coming at a time when he was smarting under a sharp disappointment, deeply touched the venerable painter's heart. "Be assured, gentlemen," he wrote in reply, "that that election I shall ever retain as an honor from a relative." Robert Fulton, artist and inventor, and Bushrod Washington were the next honorary members after West.

Unlike its New York rival, the Philadelphia Academy made haste to provide for itself a permanent home. The society's charter, procured in the spring of 1806, makes mention of a building then near completion. It was of simple design and well proportioned. Its main feature was the "Rotunda"—a handsome circular room with a domed ceiling. The first exhibition was held in March, 1806. The collection of works of art contained over fifty casts of antique statues from the Louvre, two Shakspearean paintings by West, and a few other pictures by European artists. The ladies of Philadelphia appear to have been peculiarly sensitive on the subject of nude statuary, and one day in the week the Academy was thrown open for their exclusive benefit. Gradually the Academy acquired a large and valuable collection of paintings and casts, many of them bequests from wealthy citizens. In 1811, in conjunction with the Society of Artists, it gave its first annual exhibition. The second, in 1812, was marked by the presence of several important works by American artists, evincing the progress made by native talent. In 1816 the Academy collection was enriched with a noble painting by Allston, "The dead Man revived by touching the Relics of Elisha," and also by Leslie's "Clifford"—a fine composition, taken from the scene in *Henry VI.* where Clifford murders the young Plantagenet, Rutland.

The collection gradually increased in value by gifts and judicious purchases, and at the time of the destruction of the building by fire, in 1845, it was without a rival in America. A valuable Murillo, a representation of the "Carità Romana," or Roman Daughter, bought in Spain from the collection of Joseph Bonaparte, perished in the flames, with many other paintings, casts, and statues in marble. The Academy soon recovered from this disaster. It now possesses a valuable gallery of statuary, comprising modern works in marble and casts from the antique, a permanent gallery of paintings, consisting of about a hundred and fifty works by native and foreign artists, and an excellent library. Its new building, the opening of which will be one of the most interesting features of the Centennial celebration, is a noble structure, admirably suited to the purposes for which it is designed.

It is only within a recent period that the

beautiful art of painting in water-color, long since carried to perfection in England, became popular in this country. It had many stubborn prejudices to contend with. Works in water-color looked slight and unsubstantial compared with those in oil, and a taste for them had to be created and fostered. In the Academy exhibitions a corner was usually set apart for them, but they were generally few in number and of trifling value. The first organized movement in the direction of a water-color society in this country was made in 1850, when a class was started in New York for study from life, the sketches being made in water-color. The members were for the most part well-known designers or engravers. They held their meetings every fortnight. In December, 1850, this "class" adopted a constitution, and thus formed the first Society of Painters in Water-Colors in the United States. There are records of meetings held from time to time until the opening of the Crystal Palace in this city in 1853. Then each member of the society contributed a specimen of his work. The collection was hung by itself on a screen, and was specified in the catalogue of the exhibition as "Water-color Paintings by Members of the New York Water-color Society." This was a dying effort. Nothing was ever heard of the society again.

REMBRANDT PEALE.—[1778-1860.]

WASHINGTON ALLSTON.—[1779-1843.]

With the exception of one or two foreign collections, nothing more was seen of water-color paintings in this country until the autumn of 1866, when the Artists' Fund Society, in its annual exhibition held in the National Academy of Design, made a feature of this branch of art. Mainly through the efforts of Mr. John M. Falconer, an enthusiast in water-colors, the society was able to fill the East Gallery and part of the corridor with a fine collection of works by native and foreign artists. Encouraged by the pleasure manifested by the art-loving public, which then for the first time had the opportunity to judge of the real capabilities of water-color painting, a number of artists at once started a project for the organization of a water-color society which might popularize this beautiful art on this side of the Atlantic. A call signed by Samuel Colman, William Hart, Gilbert Burling, and William Craig was sent out to all the professional and amateur artists who were known to be interested in the movement. The result was the organization, in December, 1866, of the present flourishing institution of "The American Society of Painters in Water-Colors."

The first exhibition of the new society was held in the galleries of the National Academy of Design, under Academy management, in connection with the fall and winter exhibition of oil-paintings. It was in many respects a successful experiment. The collection contained nearly three hundred works, among which were many crude and insipid compositions side by side with works of great value and still greater promise. The public was pleased with the novelty; the water-color galleries were crowded day and evening with admiring spectators. But the sales were few. The public admired, but did not buy. But the water-colorists were not discouraged. They clung to their work, firm in the faith that as knowledge ripened, their reward would come. Each year witnessed a marked improvement in their exhibition, both in the number and quality of the works exposed to view. The exhibition of 1874 filled all the Academy galleries except one, which is considered unfavorable to the proper display of water-colors, and the hanging committee was obliged, for want of room and other reasons, to return almost as many pictures as were exhibited in 1867. The popular prejudice against water-colors gave way to a just appreciation. During the first four exhibitions the number of sales could almost be counted upon one's fingers; but during the six weeks of the exhibition of 1874 the sales of water-colors on the walls amounted to $20,000, a success unprecedented in this country. Now that it pays to paint in water-colors, the permanent success of the society depends only upon the members and the exercise of good judgment in the conduct of its affairs. Its exhibitions, although held in the Academy building, are no longer under the management of the National Academy, nor in connection with its exhibitions. The water-color society has an active membership of fifty-four artists. Its financial affairs are in a flourishing condition, and there is every reason to predict for it a brilliant future. Plans have already been perfected which will secure for the society a creditable display at the Centennial Exhibition at Philadelphia, when the country will have an opportunity to see what our artists have been able to do toward rivaling those of England in this important branch of painting.

Turning from these societies, the most important art associations in the United States, to special departments of art, we come first to the consideration of portraiture, which was pursued with more success than any other branch before and immediately after the Revolution. Benjamin West, whose career, like that of John Singleton Copley, belongs mainly to England, began portrait painting in 1753, and had he not forsaken it for historical and religious painting, his fame would probably have been more enduring. Of the immense number of paintings executed by him during his long career, estimated at upward of three thousand, only one—"The Death of Wolfe"—rises appreciably above the dead level of Academical mediocrity. His mind, hopelessly devoid of imagination, constantly aspired to the treatment of themes which might well appall the most daring genius—such, for example, as "Moses receiving the Law on Mount Sinai," "The Opening of the Seventh Seal in the Revelations," "The Mighty Angel with one Foot on the Sea and the other on the Earth," etc. A pretty story is told of his first attempts at painting. Inspired at the age of nine by the sight of some engravings and the gift of a paint-box, he used to play truant from school, "and as soon as he got out of sight of his father and mother, he would steal up to his garret, and there pass the hours in a world of his own. At last, after he had been absent from school some days, the master called at his father's house to inquire what had become of him. This led to the discovery of his secret occupation. His mother, proceeding to the garret, found the truant; but so much was she astonished and delighted by the creations of his pencil, which also met her view when she entered the apartment, that, instead of rebuking him, she could only take him in her arms and kiss him with transports of affection." Doubtless many other soft-hearted mothers have thus greeted what they fondly imagined to be the dawning of genius in their offspring, but with consequences less appalling. The young artist went early to Rome, where his appearance, coming from the far Western world, excited curious interest and attention. Crowds followed him to observe the impressions created by the marvels he encountered. On the completion of his studies, which he pursued with assiduity, he went to England, there soon afterward married, and there remained until his death, at the age of seventy-nine. But a very small number of his works are owned in this country. His

"Christ healing the Sick," presented by the artist to the Pennsylvania Hospital, is still in the possession of that institution. It was once greatly admired. The Philadelphia Academy of Fine Arts owns his "Death on the Pale Horse;" his "Christ Rejected" and his "Cupid" are also owned in that city. His "Lear" may be seen in the gallery of the Boston Athenæum. Two of his pictures, illustrating scenes from the Iliad, belong to the collection of the New York Historical Society. It must be remembered to his honor that he was the first historical painter to break through the absurd Academical traditions which required modern subjects to be painted in the so-called classic style. When his "Death of Wolfe" was exhibited at the Royal Academy of London, the adherents of the old style "complained of the barbarism of boots, buttons, and blunderbusses, and cried out for naked warriors with bows, bucklers, and battering-rams." Reynolds and the Archbishop of York remonstrated with West against his daring innovation. The artist calmly replied that "the event to be commemorated happened in the year 1758, in a region of the world unknown to the Greeks and Romans, and at a period when no warrior who wore classic costume existed. The same rule which gave law to the historian should govern the painter." Reynolds was at length compelled to acknowledge the justice of the popular verdict in favor of the new style, and to declare that "West has conquered. I foresee that this picture will not only become one of the most popular, but will occasion a revolution in art." West was a sensible, kindly man, of pure life and lofty aims. His ambition, unhappily, was far beyond his capacity as an artist, and his fame has steadily declined since his death. His highest distinction as an artist was his elevation to the presidency of the Royal Academy.

Copley's American career closed with the beginning of the Revolution. He was born in Boston on the 3d of July, 1737, and died in London on the 25th of September, 1815. He was the only native painter of real genius and culture of whom the New World could boast prior to the Declaration of Independence; and the skill and assiduity with which he pursued his profession are attested by the number of portraits from

THOMAS SULLY.—[1783-1872.]

his pencil which still exist in the possession of old families in New England, and occasionally in the Southern States. It has been said that the possession of one of these ancestral portraits is an American's best title of nobility. Chiefly celebrated for his portraits, Copley also attempted historical compositions, a department of art in which he received but little encouragement, although the "Death of Chatham," and "The Death of Major Pierson," the latter being regarded as his greatest work, evinced considerable power of composition and color.

Dunlap, in his scrappy but entertaining history of the arts of design in America, gives the names of a large number of portrait painters, native and foreign, who flourished during colonial and Revolutionary times in this country. Most of them have been long forgotten, and but few merit attention at the present day. There was Wollaston, who painted several portraits in Philadelphia in 1758, and afterward in Maryland. His portrait of Mrs. Washington was engraved for Sparks's biography of our first President. Judge Hopkinson paid him a tribute in commonplace verse in the *American Magazine* for September, 1758. In many of the older dwellings in Maryland may be found portraits from the pencil of Hesselius, an English painter of respectable capacity, settled in Annapolis in 1763. Cosmo Alexander, who came to this country in 1770 and remained a year, was Stuart's first instructor in art. His best-known work is a portrait of the Hon. John Ross, a prominent member of the Philadelphia bar. Blackburn, an Englishman, a contemporary of Smybert, painted several excellent portraits during a brief visit to this country, which are still held in high esteem. The name of Robert E. Pine is chiefly remembered for his portrait of Washington. This artist brought to America the earliest cast of the Venus de' Medici, "which was privately exhibited to the select few—the manners and morals of the Quaker City forbidding its exposure to the

PROFESSOR MORSE.—[1791-1872.]

common eye." Pine sympathized with the American cause, and projected a grand series of historical paintings to illustrate the events of the Revolutionary war. His plan also comprehended the portraits of leading generals and statesmen. Invited to Mount Vernon in 1785, he passed three weeks at that place, and produced a portrait of Washington which is believed by many to be a more correct and characteristic likeness of the man than the later and better-known portrait by Stuart.

Passing over several names on which it would be pleasant to dwell if space permitted, we come to Charles Wilson Peale, the first painter of Washington. He was born in Chestertown, Maryland, in 1741. Determining at an early age on the profession of portrait painting, he first sought instruction in Philadelphia, and afterward in Boston, where he studied Copley's pictures. In 1770 he went to England, and there studied with West, who, with his usual kindness, opened his heart and purse to the poor and struggling artist. Peale returned home after a residence of about four years abroad, and became an officer in the Revolutionary army. "He did not," says Tuckerman, "forget the artist in the soldier, but sedulously improved his leisure in camp by sketching from nature, and......by transferring to his portfolio many heads which afterward he elaborated for his gallery of national portraits." His portrait of Washington as a Virginia colonel, well known through the art of engraving, possesses a historical value as great as its artistic merit. It was painted in 1772, and is the earliest authentic likeness of Washington in existence. A subsequent portrait was executed by Peale in compliance with a resolution of Congress, passed before the occupation of Philadelphia. "Its progress," writes Titian R. Peale to a friend, "marks the vicissitudes of the Revolutionary struggle. Commenced in the gloomy winter and half-famished encampment at Valley Forge in 1778, the battles of Trenton, Princeton, and Monmouth intervened before its completion. At the last place Washington suggested that the view from the window of the farm-house opposite to which he was sitting would form a desirable background. Peale adopted the idea, and represented Monmouth Court-house, and a party of Hessians under guard marching out of it." Congress adjourned without making an appropriation for the payment of the artist, and the portrait remained on his hands. The testimony of contemporaries stamps this picture as a most faithful likeness of Washington in the prime of life. Peale painted fourteen portraits of Washington, of which the two we have mentioned are the most important. His career was long and honorable. His talent as a portrait painter in oil and miniature was in constant demand far and wide, not only in this country, but by sitters from Canada and the West Indies. He died, revered and regretted, at the age of eighty-four, in 1826. His son, Rembrandt Peale, at the age of eighteen, made a pencil sketch of Washington, and long afterward painted a portrait of him from memory, assisted by Houdin's bust.

We must pass with only brief mention the names of William Dunlap, chiefly known for his history of the arts of design; Robert Fulton, more celebrated as an inventor than as an artist; John Wesley Jarvis, genial, gifted, and erratic; Malbone, like Jarvis, celebrated for his success in miniature painting; Chester Harding, once the rival of Stuart in portraiture; Gilbert Stuart Newton, whose memory is affectionately honored in Leslie's autobiography; C. C. Ingham, one of the last of the old generation of portrait painters; and Morse, who early forsook painting, and whose name is connected with the most important invention of this century, the electric telegraph. Contemporary with these artists were many who achieved high reputation in their day, but whose names are now known only through the annals of art societies.

One of the greatest portrait painters of America, Gilbert Charles Stuart, was also one of the earliest. He was born in Narraganset, Rhode Island, in 1754, according to an anecdote of his own, quoted by Dunlap, in a snuff mill, the first in New England, erected by his father. In after-years he dropped his middle name, which had been

HENRY INMAN.—[1801-1846.]

THOMAS COLE.—[1801-1848.]

given to him at his baptism to signify his father's fidelity to the royal house of Stuart. He commenced portrait painting at Newport, Rhode Island; was taken to Edinburgh at the age of eighteen; resided several years in London, where his success was marked, and passed some time in Dublin and Paris. In 1793 Stuart returned to this country, and from that time till his death, at Boston, in 1828, pursued a career of remarkable industry and ability. Many of the most famous statesmen of America sat to him, and his portraits of Washington, John Adams, Jefferson, Monroe, and other distinguished men are well known through engravings. Our ideas of Washington's personal appearance are derived from Stuart rather than from Pine or Peale. He also painted an immense number of society portraits. His works are widely scattered on both sides of the Atlantic. In power of drawing and expression, and in truth and purity of color, his portraits stand almost without rival in American or European art. He was great in the portrayal of individual character. Allston declared that he "seemed to dive into the thoughts of men, for they were made to live and speak on the surface." The same admirable artist has also well said that Stuart "was, in its widest sense, a philosopher in his art. He thoroughly understood its principles, as his works bear witness, whether as to harmony of colors or of lines, or of light and shadow, showing that exquisite sense

HORATIO GREENOUGH.—[1805-1852.]

of a whole which only a man of genius can realize and embody. Of this not the least admirable instance is his portrait of John Adams, whose bodily tenement at the time seemed rather to present the image of a dilapidated castle than the habitation of the unbroken mind. But not such is the picture. Called forth from its crumbling recesses, the living tenant is there, still ennobling the ruin, and upholding it, as it were, by the strength of his inner life." Stuart painted but three portraits of Washington from life, but made twenty-six copies of these originals. There is a certain weakness about the mouth, Washington having lost his teeth when the originals were painted, but the general bearing is noble and dignified; and we may congratulate ourselves, with Leslie, "that a painter existed in the time of Washington who could hand him down looking like a gentleman."

To sketch even in outline the career of every American artist who has achieved celebrity in portraiture or any other branch of art would extend this article into a good-sized volume. Among those artists who belonged partly to the last and partly to the present century, and whose genius has left a deep impression upon American art, may be mentioned John Vanderlyn, whose "Ariadne" and "Marius" are justly celebrated, and who has given us the best portraits extant of Madison, Monroe, Randolph, Clinton, Calhoun, and other eminent Americans; and Thomas Sully, a native of England, but whose career belongs to America, and whose portraits are distinguished by exquisite grace and refinement. To the present century belong many eminent names, such as Henry Inman, happiest in portraiture, but also charming in landscape, and the first American artist who attempted *genre* painting with success; William Page, who emulates Titian and Veronese as a colorist, whose portraits rank among the noblest of modern times, and whose Venetian reproductions have excited the highest admiration as well as the severest criticism; Charles Loring Elliot, whose portraits are distinguished by richness of color, a manly simplicity and force of execution, combined with a subtile grasp of individuality which no other American portrait painter has evinced in an equal degree; Daniel Huntington, whose versatile pencil, not confined to any single branch of art, is equally happy in portraiture, landscape, *genre*, and historical painting; Oliver Stone, recently deceased, whose portraits of women and children, in which he chiefly excelled, are characterized by a peculiar grace and refinement; Thomas Le Clear; Richard M. Staigg, who, besides the exquisite ivory miniatures by which he is chiefly known, has shown a happy talent in *genre* painting; George A. Baker, whose portraits of women and children are of rare beauty and refinement. Other names might be mentioned did not want of space forbid.

Historical painting has not found in America the encouragement accorded to other branches of art, partly, perhaps, because we have never had a really great historical painter, and partly because the genius of the age does not favor it. Colonel John Trumbull attempted to depict the events of the Revolution in a series of large historical *tableaux*, which are now chiefly valued for the faithful portraits they contain of the soldiers and statesmen of that time. His sketches and studies for these works show a vigor and grasp which are wanting in the larger canvases. His "Death of Montgomery," the "Signing of the Declaration of Independence," and the "Battle of Bunker Hill," and others of his important works, exhibit considerable skill in grouping and composition, but it would have been better for his fame had nothing remained but the original sketches and portraits. His talent is displayed to greater advantage in the "Trumbull Gallery" at New Haven than in the national Capitol. As aid-de-camp to General Washington in the early part of the Revolution, Colonel Trumbull enjoyed peculiar facilities for studying his character and features under the most varied circumstances, and his portrait of him now in the gallery at New Haven is full of soldierly spirit. By contemporaries, to whom it recalled the leader of the American armies, it was preferred to Stuart's.

Pre-eminent among American historical painters stands the honored name of Washington Allston; yet even of him it must be said that performance lagged far behind design, and that his fame is in great part the legacy of contemporary admiration. The quality of his genius was akin to that of the old masters of religious art. It might be said of him that he painted for antiquity. His mind, even in youth inclined to serious contemplation, was moulded by early study of the old masters, and the results of this training may be traced in all his works. It was to him that Fuseli bluntly said, "You have come a great way to starve," when the young American, on his first visit to London, announced his purpose to devote himself to historical painting. Nothing daunted, Allston pursued his studies in England, France, and Italy with unflagging diligence, and with the grand goal of his ambition constantly in view. His earliest large picture, "The Dead Man Revived," obtained the prize of two hundred guineas from the British Institution, and was soon after purchased by the Philadelphia Academy of Fine Arts. This was followed by a long list of important works, many of which are owned in England, where Allston enjoys even greater repute than in his own country. He suffered much from feeble health and from pecuniary embarrassment, and one of his most important works, "Belshazzar's Feast," remained, in consequence, unfinished at his death. His first studies for this painting were made in London in 1817. At intervals he worked upon it for nearly thirty years, and was engaged upon it on the last day of his life. Even in its unfinished state it attests the grandeur of the artist's conception, but it also reveals in a striking degree the limitations of his genius, chiefly the vacillation of thought, the wavering choice, displayed in changes of plan and apparent dissatisfaction with parts of the work as it proceeded. Allston himself regarded this picture as his greatest composition; to finish it worthily was the desire of his heart; but his genius found its best expression in some of his less ambitious paintings, in which his refined sense of the beautiful, his love of the graceful, and his intimate knowledge of form are allowed free play, untrammeled by the struggle to paint in the "grand style."

Historical painting in America has been mainly, thus far at least, the reflex of European schools of art. Trumbull's style was formed in London under the tuition of Benjamin West, Allston's by long and conscientious study of the great masters of the Venetian schools, and Emanuel Leutze, our most vigorous and prolific historical painter in recent times, the engraving from whose picture of "Washington crossing the Delaware" has carried his name into every American household, was the disciple of Lessing, with whom he studied at Düsseldorf. The conditions of American society are not, indeed, favorable to the development of this branch of art, which can not flourish without a patronage which does not exist in this country. Our government patronage has been a positive detriment to art. With few exceptions, the national commissions have been award-

HIRAM POWERS.—[1805-1873.]

ed to artists of inferior merit, whose success was often due to lobby influence. The consequence is that the national paintings at Washington are, with a few worthy exceptions, a national disgrace. A blank white wall would be less displeasing to the cultivated eye. It is, perhaps, vain to hope for a remedy. In the scramble for government art patronage, charlatans alone enter the course; men of genius, whose productions would do the nation honor, will never descend to an unseemly scrub race with "artists" who could hardly paint a respectable sign for a village tavern. Hence it is that while we occasionally see an American historical painting of high merit, the branches of art which most flourish in this country, and which have reached a degree of excellence unsurpassed in Europe, are portraiture, landscape, and *genre* painting. For correct drawing, truth of color, and a fidelity to expression as nearly absolute as the art can be carried, American portrait painters, as a class, stand in advance of their European brethren. There are no portraits in the world, if we except those of the old Venetian masters, superior in the highest qualities of art to those of Stuart, Elliot, Page, Huntington, Le Clear, Stone, Baker, and others who have devoted their genius to this branch of art. American portraiture may not display so much Academical "effect" as the French, but effect is not in itself an essential quality of high art. It is often an artistic trick to catch the uncultivated eye and hide defects of drawing.

In landscape painting, as in portraiture, America very early declared her independence of European schools. Our artists have gone directly to nature for inspiration, and each, following the tendency of his own genius, has found in her varied aspects of loveliness and grandeur what no Academical training could have taught. Fidelity to nature is a characteristic trait of American landscape art; a fidelity not servile, but conscientious and loving, with none of the conventional trickery and Academical effects characteristic of every European school of landscape except the English; a fidelity not inconsistent with the widest display of imagination and fancy, nor with freedom of individual expression. If characteristic specimens of the art of each of our landscape painters, from the venerable Durand, whose hand has not yet forgot its cunning, to the youngest aspirant for a place on the walls of the Academy, could be gathered into one gallery, they would form an exhibition unrivaled in the world in all the higher qualities of art, in individuality, and in truth to nature. Such a collection—a nucleus already exists in our Metropolitan Museum of Art—ought to find a place in New York. How interesting to the student would it be to trace the development of landscape art in the pictures of Durand, Cole, Huntington, Inness, Church, Bierstadt, Gifford, Kensett, Whittredge, M'Entee, Colman, Hubbard, and a host of others who have won deserved honors by their faithful delineations of nature! The limits of this sketch preclude extended personal characterizations where so many deserve special notice; and equally out of the question is even the briefest account of what the most eminent have accomplished toward bringing American landscape art to its present high position.

In more senses than one such an exhibition would be essentially American; for although many of our foremost landscape painters have gone abroad for study or in search of special aspects of nature, they have found in the grandeur and in the beauty of our own country the highest inspiration. Gifford brings nothing from Venice or the East superior to his magnificent transcripts of the scenery of the Hudson and the sea-coast, although that element of the picturesque afforded by the architecture of the Old World is wanting in the New; nor did Church find in the Andes inspiration for a nobler picture than his "Niagara." Bierstadt's splendid delineations of the sublime scenery of California and the Rocky Mountains far surpass his "Vesuvius." Thomas Cole found in the Catskills the material for his most beautiful pictures; and where but in America could M'Entee have become the interpreter of those autumnal effects which he renders with such beauty and fidelity? The happiest efforts of Kensett were inspired by years of patient study among the mountains of New England and New York, the lakes and rivers of the Middle States, and along the Eastern sea-coast. Whittredge's magnificent pictures of Western scenery cast into the shade his earlier though beautiful views on the Rhine. But the list is almost inexhaustible; it would include nearly every eminent landscape painter in America.

Several of our most eminent landscapists are known also as successful marine painters. Colman began his artistic career by painting shipping and sea views. Many of the finest pictures of Kensett and Gifford represent various aspects of the sea in connection with views of the coast. One of Church's most important compositions is his picture of a gigantic iceberg floating majestically in a tranquil expanse of ocean. William Bradford has devoted himself almost exclusively to the delineation of the arctic seas, with their rugged glacier-riven coasts, their icebergs, and their terrible ice-plains, the scene of adventure and disaster. Among our most noteworthy marine painters may be mentioned F. H. De Haas, a native of Rotterdam, but for many years a resident of this country. His pictures of sea storms are strong and effective; and he has also painted many beautiful coast scenes. Charles Temple Dix, had his life been spared, would have achieved great success in this branch of painting.

In figure and *genre* painting we have the names of many gifted and accomplished artists, such as Eastman Johnson, Edwin White, E. W. Perry, Matteson, S. Mount, J. Wood, J. G. Brown, John W. Ehninger, Elihu Vedder, George H. Boughton, W. J. Hennessy, R. C. Woodville, and others. Mr. White is also a careful and admired portrait painter, and has essayed historical composition with marked success. Mr. Johnson stands at the head of American *genre* painters. He was among the first to recognize in American life the picturesque and characteristic traits which our artists were once fain to seek abroad. Thanks to his intuition and to the example of his admirable achievements, American *genre* painting now rivals that of any European nation in variety and excellence, and gives promise of greater triumphs in the future.

The best animal painter in America is W. H. Beard, whose half-humorous, half-serious compositions have not been excelled by any other artist at home or abroad. He has a special *penchant* for bears, and has made them the medium of caustic satire on hu-

THOMAS CRAWFORD.—[1813–1857.]

manity, as in his "Bears on a Bender"—a picture which established his name, and the great success of which influenced his career. His brother, James H. Beard, also an animal painter of merit, employs his pencil almost exclusively in the delineation of domestic animals. The late William Hays painted many admirable animal pictures, of which the most important are "The Stampede" and "The Herd on the Move." The names of Tait and Bispham must also be included in the list of painters who have made special study of animal life, and have been successful in the delineation of it.

The list of American sculptors embraces a number of eminent names, beginning with that of Horatio Greenough, from whose hand came the first marble group executed by an American. Sculpture, as is well known, was not popular in this country for some years after the Revolution. Nude statuary was especially an abomination not to be tolerated; and Greenough, Crawford, and Powers waited many years and endured keen disappointments before they received popular recognition. Their residence abroad, rendered necessary by the absence of the proper facilities for the prosecution of their art at home, removed them in a great measure from popular sympathy, and their achievements, except by report, were known to a comparatively small number of people. But travel, culture, familiarity with foreign galleries, and the more general distribution of casts and statuary throughout the country have produced a marked change in popular ideas. Statuary forms a more or less important part of every Academy exhibition, and it is no longer necessary to set apart a day exclusively for the admission of ladies. Nor is it longer essential that an American sculptor should reside in Italy, or go abroad at all, except for the purpose of study among the masterpieces of antique art. Several of our most eminent sculptors pursue their art at home, and retain an individuality which might be endangered, in some degree at least, by a foreign residence. Our foremost living sculptor, J. Q. A. Ward, achieved several signal triumphs in his art, without the advantages supposed to be only attainable abroad. His "Indian Hunter," his "Freedman," his statue of Shakspeare, now in Central Park, and his numerous portrait busts, all attest the vigor and originality of his genius. Ward is the most thoroughly American of all our sculptors. Greenough, Crawford, Powers, Story, went early to the studios of Florence or Rome, and in the contemplation of ancient art they lost the inspiration of the New World, and became European artists, not to be distinguished, by any characteristic of their work, from the English, French, German, and Italian sculptors surrounding them. Palmer, like Ward, never studied abroad, and yet, despite certain peculiar theories in regard to his art, he has produced some admirable work. Besides the artists already named, among those who have acquired distinction as American sculptors may be named Thomas Ball, Henry Kirke Brown, Randolph Rogers; Joel T. Hart, of Kentucky; and Launt Thompson, who, though born in Ireland, has become thoroughly Americanized. He acquired his art with Palmer, in whose studio he remained about nine years. Thompson has executed some very characteristic portrait busts and several statues of great merit, the most important being that of General Sedgwick. The varied *genre* groups of John Rogers, chiefly representing scenes and episodes of the late war, entitle this artist to a permanent, if not very lofty, place among American sculptors. Several American women, among them Miss Harriet Hosmer, Miss Margaret Foley, and Miss Emma Stebbins, have also attained high repute as sculptors.

JOHN F. KENSETT.—[1818-1872.]

The art of engraving has reached a high degree of excellence in America during the hundred years which have elapsed since Paul Revere, the hero of the memorable ride celebrated in Longfellow's verse, engraved caricatures and historical subjects in Boston. Revere worked on copper, an art which, like lithography, has been almost driven out of existence by wood-engraving. The first wood-engraver in America was Dr. Anderson, who died a few years since at the age of ninety-five, having, in the course of his long career, seen the art advance from a rude state to the finish and refinement it has attained in the hands of such men as Linton and Anthony, and of men who are second to these masters only. Wood-engraving has been a powerful agent in the dissemination of a knowledge and love of art throughout the country, not only by the reproduction of the works of eminent masters of Europe and America, but by spreading broadcast through illustrated books, magazines, and journals the artistic creations of Darley, Hoppin, Fredricks, Nast, Moran, Sol Eytinge, and a hundred others who have devoted their talents to illustration.

The history of caricature in the United States has been so recently and so amply given by Mr. Parton in the pages of *Harper's Magazine* that it is only necessary here to note some of the leading names in this department of art. Among political caricaturists Thomas Nast stands without a rival in the vigor and sharpness of his satire and in versatility of invention. In social caricature we have Sol Eytinge, whose inimitable delineations of the humorous side of negro character excite genial amusement, but never derisive laughter; Bellew, Woolf, Reinhart, Frost, Wust, Thomas Worth, Hopkins, and many others, whose names would fill a large catalogue.

Looking back through the hundred years of our existence as an independent nation, we see a steady and healthful growth of art in all sections of the country. Year by year the number of American artists has increased with the diffusion of culture among the people; art societies are springing up in all parts of the country; exhibitions worthy of the Old World are held in cities where fifty years ago there was scarcely a break in the primeval forest. Europe sends us yearly an accession of artists, who become American, as West, Copley, and Leslie became English painters. Schools of art spread culture and knowledge all over the land. Massachusetts has made drawing a part of her system of common-school education with admirable results. The art school connected with the Cooper Union in this city has also done great service in the way of elementary training in drawing, painting, wood-engraving, etc. The work begun by the American Institute of Architects awakens the hope that another generation will see a vast improvement in the architecture of our public and private buildings. As wealth and culture increase, the fine arts will find increasing support, and the coming century will witness a development in the sculpture, painting, and architecture of this country as marvelous as its progress has been in the mechanical and industrial arts.

XIV.

MEDICAL AND SANITARY PROGRESS.

WHAT has been done in these United States of America since the declaration of their independence in the way of medical and sanitary progress? To answer this question fully it would be necessary to write the history of American medicine, for which at least a volume would be required. In undertaking to review the past centennial period, with reference to this question, within the limits of a few pages, I must be content with a large outline and certain representative facts.

Evidence of progress is to be sought for in educational institutions. At the close of the colonial government there were two American medical colleges, one in Philadelphia, the other in New York; the former established in 1765, and the latter in 1768. The operations of both were suspended during the Revolutionary war. Up to that time they had conferred medical degrees upon less than fifty candidates. The great majority of the physicians and surgeons in the colonies had obtained what education they possessed in commencing practice by having served for a period of from three to seven years as apprentices to medical practitioners, the duties of apprenticeship embracing certain menial offices as well as study and the compounding of medicines. A favored few were able to resort to the celebrated schools of London, Edinburgh, and Leyden. At the close of the war the two American colleges resumed operations, and three others came into existence before the end of the eighteenth century, namely, the medical department of Harvard University, of Dartmouth College, and of Rutgers College, of New Jersey. The number of graduates from all these institutions at the beginning of the nineteenth century had not much exceeded two hundred. During the first half of the present century medical colleges were multiplied nearly at the rate of a new college annually, distributed among the different States, and many of them established in small villages. This multiplication and distribution met the requirements of medical education at that time, in view of the rapid settlement of distant parts of our vast country, stage-coaches being the only public mode of traveling by land, and the great majority of students and practitioners in medicine having limited pecuniary resources. After the extension of railway communications and the development of the material resources of newly settled States and Territories, the increase in the number of colleges was less, and for the most part it has been confined to metropolitan or large towns, many of those in villages having been discontinued. At the present time about seven thousand medical students attend annually the various colleges, and the annual number of graduates exceeds two thousand.[1] During the last quarter of a century there has been progressive improvement in collegiate and extra-collegiate instruction by means of extension of the terms of lectures, subdivisions of the different departments, the institution of special courses, combining more and more illustrations with didactic teaching, the systematic regulation of study with recitations, and private lectures or demonstrations in various branches. Without presumption, it may be claimed in behalf of the leading American medical schools that especially, although not exclusively, as regards practical instruction, they compare favorably with the long-distinguished schools in Great Britain, France, and Germany.

In connection with this sketch of educational institutions it is but just to the medical profession of this country to present certain facts. To this profession belongs chiefly whatever credit may pertain to the rise and progress of these institutions now and in the past. Our State Legislatures incorporate medical colleges, and generally charters are obtained without difficulty. Legislative aid in the way of money is the

---

[1] Vide *Toner's Annals of Medical Progress* for these and other statistics. For the dates of the establishment of different schools and other details, vide *History of Medical Education*, etc., by N. S. Davis, M.D.

exception, not the rule, albeit it is very evident that well-educated physicians and surgeons are literally of *vital* importance to the public weal. As a rule, with some notable exceptions, the pecuniary means for the establishment of a medical school are not largely furnished either by municipal appropriations or private contributions from other than members of the medical profession. After having been established, the revenue of the colleges is derived commonly from the fees of students: few colleges have any endowment. A certain measure of success in a medical school, as regards the size of its classes, is therefore essential to its continuance, and its prosperity depends on the number of students attracted to it. The primary organization and the management in all respects, including the appointment of professors, are usually, either directly or indirectly, under the control of the faculties of the schools. These facts involve some objections which are plausible, and in a measure veritable, namely, a medical college can not, without risk of its prosperity, require a higher grade of preliminary education or of the qualifications for a degree than those institutions with which it is in immediate competition, and professional positions are exposed to insecurity from the action of colleagues. On the other hand, there are advantages which more than outweigh these objections. An active, honorable competition enforces the best exertions, the selection of the ablest teachers, and the largest available facilities for instruction.

Another fact, in justice to the profession, should be presented, namely, there are practically no legal restrictions on the practice of medicine in most of the States of the Union. Not only are licenses to practice easily obtained, but rarely, if ever, are legal penalties, if they exist, enforced for practicing without a diploma or a license. The desire for instruction is therefore the leading motive impelling medical students to resort to medical schools. Moreover, the classes, especially in metropolitan medical schools, consist in part of licentiates or graduates who have been for a greater or less period engaged in practice. Again, in the schools which are considered as offering the largest advantages the classes preponderate greatly in numbers over those in other schools. At the present time more than a thousand students and practitioners are in attendance at the schools in the city of New York during the winter, and the winter classes in Philadelphia are not much smaller. A considerable proportion of the members of the classes in these two cities is from distant parts of our country, the fees are considerably higher than in provincial schools, and the expenses incident to city life and long journeys are not small. Herein is exemplified the strength of the impelling motive, namely, the desire for instruction; and these facts certainly denote a spirit of progress among those who are already, and those who are about to become, members of the medical profession.

We are to look for evidence of progress in the number and character of associations for the promotion and diffusion of medical knowledge. Prior to the Revolutionary war there was but one State medical society. This was formed in New Jersey in 1766, but not regularly incorporated until 1790. Shortly before the war closed, the Massachusetts Medical Society was incorporated. After the national independence was achieved, associations were speedily organized in several of the States. At the beginning of the present century they existed in Pennsylvania, Delaware, New Hampshire, South Carolina, Connecticut, and Maryland. Following these were local associations in different counties and large towns. At the present time probably every State in the Union has its society, and there are few situations so remote or isolated as not to be embraced within the area of some local association. In 1846 a convention of representatives of medical societies, hospitals, and colleges throughout the United States was held in the city of New York, and the result was the establishment, in 1847, of the American Medical Association, which, excepting during the late war of the rebellion, has ever since held annual meetings in different parts of the Union. Quite recently (1872) an association has been formed for the promotion and diffusion of knowledge relating to the prevention of disease. This, entitled the Public Health Association, gives promise of much usefulness. National societies within late years have been formed for the promotion and diffusion of knowledge relating to special departments of medicine—for example, insanity, and diseases of the eye and ear—and local societies of this character exist in most of the larger cities. All of the numerous associations originated with medical men, and have been kept up by their efforts. Many publish Transactions at stated intervals. The American Medical Association has published twenty-five large volumes, and the New York State Medical Society nearly or quite as many. Collectively, the Transactions of the societies in various States constitute not an inconsiderable portion of our periodical medical literature. The associations are all voluntary; membership is not rendered obligatory by legal requirement, but in many, if not in most, parts of the country it is considered essential to an unequivocal professional status to become a member of some regularly organized association. This arises from the fact that in certain associations are vested, by general agreement, the right to take cognizance of violations of medical ethics by any of their members, and to reprimand, suspend, or expel for unprofessional conduct. Passing by further details, it may be said of our medical associations that in number and character they denote a general and active co-operation of the practitioners of medicine for the promotion and diffusion of knowledge, to which may be added the maintenance and elevation of the honor and usefulness of the profession. The associations thus furnish evidence, while they are also important means, of medical sanitary progress.

The literature of a particular province of science and art, for a given period, offers a good criterion of the progress made during that period. This statement is as applicable to medicine as to any department of knowledge. Comparing the present with the past, in this aspect, as in other points of contrast, due consideration is to be given to the difference in population, which at the time independence was declared was not much over 3,000,000, while at the present time it is estimated to be about 40,000,000.[1]

During the colonial government there was not entire absence of an American medical literature. Davis gives a list of twenty-eight publications, most of which were works of small or moderate size, but several of them possessing much merit on the score of originality and ability. There was no American medical periodical during this period, the first being the *Medical Repository*, the publication of which was commenced in the city of New York in 1797. This was a quarterly of about 150 pages, ably conducted, and its publication ceased with the twenty-third volume. In 1804 the publication of two medical journals was commenced in Philadelphia. The subsequent multiplication of medical periodicals and their publication in different parts of the Union constitute striking evidence of progress. At the present time there are between thirty and forty medical journals published in the United States, not including the Transactions of societies, hospital reports, and other publications properly belonging to periodical literature. The history of medical journalism in this country during the last half century would show many changes, but it is noteworthy that a quarterly journal, *The American Journal of Medical Sciences*, established in 1827, succeeding the Philadelphia *Journal of the Medical and Physical Sciences*, established in 1820, still lives, the arrangement of contents never having been changed, the present publisher the successor of the house which from the first issued this, as also the preceding work, and conducted now by the same able editor as over forty years ago. The Boston *Medical and Surgical Journal*, with divers changes, has been in existence for about the same length of time.

The bibliography of the first quarter of the present century embraces not a few able works, among which the voluminous writings of Rush are prominent. The standard works and text-books, however, were chiefly of foreign authorship. During the second quarter the number of works by American authors had largely increased, the list embracing acceptable text-books in anatomy, physiology, surgery, midwifery, the practice of medicine, and the *materia medica*. Then, as now, the absence of any international copyright restrictions favored the republication of works by British in preference to those by native authors, the former having the advantage of a success already acquired,

[1] Toner, op. cit.

and the reprint requiring no royalty. Here is an obstacle in the way of the development and progress of a national literature which, in justice to American authors, should be borne in mind. Notwithstanding this obstacle, and a prevailing sentiment that exotics transplanted from the older countries, as a matter of course, are superior to native productions, the increase of original books has been progressive during the last twenty-five years. At this moment the majority of the works recognized by medical schools and the profession as text-books in the different departments of medical education are by American authors, and there are few topics within the range of the science and art of medicine which are not creditably represented in our own literature. At the same time, foreign books and periodical publications now, as heretofore, have a large circulation in this country. Our native productions do not displace exotics, but both flourish together, competing with a fair rivalry.

Medical progress, as evidenced in the literature of medicine, is more especially marked in works of a practical character. This is owing to the fact that the vast majority of those who pursue medical studies in this country have chiefly in view the duties and responsibilities of the practitioner. The prosecution of researches of a purely scientific character, having no immediate practical bearing, is comparatively rare. It is easy to explain the lack of progress in this direction, as shown by comparison with other countries. The rapid increase of our population and its extension over new territory have involved a large demand for practitioners, a large proportion of whom are, to a greater or less extent, isolated as regards much intercourse with each other, and therefore obliged to depend greatly on their own resources in medical and surgical practice. Hence a predominant desire for knowledge which is plainly and directly practical. Another and more potential reason is the absence of inducements or even encouragement for purely scientific researches beyond their intrinsic attractions. Our collegiate institutions, from want of endowment, are unable to make adequate provisions for investigations which have no appreciable relations to practical teaching; the policy of our State governments, already referred to, is to leave the cultivation of all the departments of medicine in the hands of the medical profession, without offering incitements or rewards, and the spirit of emulation is not what it would be were there a larger number in the field of original scientific investigations. These are the reasons for the fact that the medical literature of this country up to the present time, as compared with that of other countries, is deficient in what may be distinguished as scientific in contrast with practical medicine. A list of American publications relating to medicine and sanitary science during the last hundred years would show a steadily increasing progress in this direction, and such a list would include not an inconsiderable number of works of a purely scientific character. The reader who may desire information concerning the medical bibliography of our country is referred to a late publication, entitled *History of American Medical Literature from* 1776 *to the Present Time,* by Professor S. D. Gross, of Philadelphia.

Within the past few years subjects relating to sanitary knowledge have entered into our literature more largely than heretofore. The publications by Health Boards have been of much interest and value. These subjects have also occupied a considerable share of medical journals and the Transactions of medical associations, and at the present time there is at least one journal devoted specially to this department of knowledge. It is fair to acknowledge that the recent activity in this direction is in a great measure due to the labors prosecuted under governmental co-operation and support in Great Britain and other countries. The attention now given to what has been called "preventive medicine" may be especially referred to as evidence of progress. To promote public health by removing or lessening the causes of disease, to forestall epidemics and endemics or arrest their course, are objects of medical science higher in importance than therapeutics. The truth of this statement is recognized by the philosophic and philanthropic physician; and there is ground for the belief that already the study of sanitary science has led to the saving of much life. Were it consistent with the limits of this article, I might cite the facts in the history of epidemic cholera in the city of New York in 1866 and 1867 as proof that by prompt and efficient preventive measures this disease may be effectually "stamped out."[1] Sanitary science and medical science are to a great extent convertible terms, as implied in the name, preventive medicine. The prevention of diseases is the practical result of our knowledge of their character and causes. Our knowledge of the causes of diseases, more especially of the special causes which give rise to epidemics and endemics, is confessedly defective; thus far in the history of medical and sanitary progress we have been obliged to content ourselves with the investigation of their laws without being able to determine with positiveness their essential nature and mode of production. Conceding this, it is, perhaps, not an extravagant assertion to say that, with our present knowledge and experience, by means of the skillful employment of disinfecting agents, together with other sanitary measures, the prevalence of certain diseases—epidemic cholera and yellow fever—is within the power of scientific control. In this direction of progress there is reason to hope that much will be accomplished by continued investigations. For carrying on these investigations and enforcing sanitary measures the co-operation of the public and legal powers is essential; hence the importance of awakening public interest on the subject, and diffusing as far as practicable popular information.

In this connection may be mentioned improvement in quarantine regulations. The problem in the department of sanitary science relating to quarantine is to provide to the utmost extent for the public health, with the least interference with personal freedom and the interests of commerce. A review of the history of quarantine laws would show how great has been the progress toward the solution of this problem, as a result of the increase of knowledge of the causes of disease and of preventive measures. From the necessity of resisting a temptation to enter into details, I must be content with the general statement that the quarantine regulations of our large commercial cities at the present time exemplify the progress made within late years in this most important matter.[1]

Medical and sanitary progress, as evidenced by important discoveries or improvements, next claims attention. Of course those originating in this country are more especially characteristic of American progress, yet the ready adoption of discoveries and improvements which have originated in other countries is significant of a progressive spirit.

The greatest event in the medical history of the last centennial period, the whole world included, was the announcement of the discovery of vaccination. Jenner announced his discovery in a paper "printed for the author" in 1798. He had desired that the paper should appear under the auspices of the Royal Society of London, but it was declined by that learned body on the ground that its publication would damage the reputation which the author had already acquired by some observations on the cuckoo! If we recognize as a criterion of the importance of a discovery the saving of human life, that of Jenner far transcends any other in the history of the world. A medical writer in 1849 represents the number of lives saved as follows: "In England alone the absolute mortality from small-pox is less by 20,000 a year than it was half a century ago. If a similar rate of reduction in the number of deaths from small-pox holds good, as we have every reason to believe is the case, in the other kingdoms of Europe, then, out of the 220,000,000 of people that inhabit this quarter of the globe, 400,000 or 500,000 fewer now die of small-pox than, with a similar population, would have died from this malady fifty years ago. ......During the long European wars connected with and following the French Revolution it has been calculated that five or six millions of human lives were lost. In Europe vaccination has already preserved from death a greater number of human be-

[1] Vide reports of the Metropolitan Board of Health, New York, for these years.

[1] The reader interested in this matter is referred to a paper entitled *Quarantine: General Principles affecting its Organization*, by S. Oakley Vanderpoel, M.D., Health Officer of the port of New York, etc., 1875.

ings than were sacrificed during the course of these wars. The lancet of Jenner has saved far more human lives than the sword of Napoleon destroyed."[1]

The introduction of vaccination met with virulent opposition in England. It was scouted by many as entailing on man diseases of inferior animals, as likely to cause a physical and mental deterioration of the human race, and as an impious attempt at interference with the ordinances of Providence, so that many years elapsed before the importance of the discovery was practically recognized in the country so much honored by the nativity of the discoverer. We have a right to take credit for the promptness with which vaccination was adopted in this country, and for its being popularized with comparatively small opposition. In 1799 Professor Benjamin Waterhouse, in Boston, having obtained the virus from Jenner, vaccinated four of his own children. In 1801 Dr. Valentine Seaman procured virus from the arm of a patient who had been vaccinated by Dr. Waterhouse, and performed the first vaccination in the city of New York; and in 1802 an institution was established in New York for the purpose of vaccinating the poor gratuitously and keeping up a supply of the virus. Not going into further details, may not the introduction of vaccination in this country be cited as indicating at that day a spirit of medical and sanitary progress?

Numerous examples of the ready adoption in this country of discoveries and improvements of lesser magnitude than the discovery of vaccination might be cited in illustration of a spirit of progress. I will mention but two of these, namely, the discovery of auscultation, and the employment of the thermometer in the study of diseases. Laennec's discovery of auscultation was an event of great importance in the history of medicine. By means of the physical signs determined by listening to sounds within the chest, the different affections of the lungs and heart are now readily distinguished from each other, and our knowledge of the symptoms and laws of these affections has been brought to great perfection. The great work by Laennec on auscultation was published in Paris in 1819. It was translated into English by Dr. Forbes, of London, in 1821. The importance of this new method of examination was not at once appreciated either in France or other countries in Europe. It met with indifference, skepticism, and ridicule. At that time crossing the Atlantic for medical improvement was a great undertaking. Nevertheless, not a few of the young medical men of this country resorted to Paris, London, and Edinburgh with that purpose. The stethoscope of Laennec, through their agency, was speedily in use on this side of the Atlantic. The writer can testify that, as far back as 1832, the facts of auscultation entered largely into medical teaching. At this time an important physical sign had been discovered by a most promising American physician, who died as he was just entering upon an active professional life.[1] In 1836 a prize was offered for competitive dissertations on this together with other methods of exploration, the successful competitor being Oliver Wendell Holmes, whose early labors in medicine were of a character to occasion in the minds of those devoted to this department of knowledge a feeling of regret that his talents have been diverted to the pursuits of literature, in which he has achieved such great distinction.

The employment of the thermometer in practical medicine is of recent date. Although advocated and to some extent exemplified by previous medical observers, it is chiefly owing to the labors of Wunderlich, in Germany, that this instrument is now in common use in the practice of medicine. Simple as seems the proposition to determine the heat of the body in diseases by exact measurement, in place of the fallacious evidence afforded by the sensations of the patient or the physician's touch, its importance has only been appreciated within the last ten or fifteen years. Wunderlich's labors have established certain thermometric laws in disease which are now considered as of great value in estimating danger and in discriminating diseases from each other. The promptness with which medical thermometry was adopted in this country, and the very general use of

[1] Sir James Simpson on anæsthesia, etc., 1849.

[1] James Jackson, Jun., of Boston.

the thermometer, may be mentioned as evidence of a spirit of progress.[1]

Passing now to discoveries and improvements originated in this country, I must restrict myself to certain of those which are prominent, overlooking much that it would be culpable to omit in a history of American medicine. Adopting a chronological arrangement, the formidable surgical operation known as ovariotomy is the first in the series.

This operation was performed for the first time by Ephraim M'Dowell, of Danville, Kentucky, in 1809. After having performed it in two other instances, he reported very briefly the three cases in the *Eclectic Repertory and Analytical Review*, in 1816. The operation was successful in each of the three cases. He subsequently performed it ten times, making the whole number of cases thirteen, of which eight, at least, were successful. Although never before performed, the possibility and propriety of the operation had been advocated, especially by John Bell, a distinguished teacher of anatomy and surgery in Edinburgh. M'Dowell was a private pupil of Bell in 1793 and 1794, and it is probable that the determination was then formed to undertake the operation whenever the opportunity offered.

M'Dowell's report of cases was received with incredulity, and the operation was not repeated by any other surgeon until the year 1821, when it was performed by Nathan Smith, Professor of Surgery in Yale College. It was performed by the latter surgeon without the knowledge of M'Dowell's previous operations. For more than twenty years it was practically almost ignored in this country, and during the next twenty years it encountered much opposition from members of the medical profession. Within the last fifteen years this opposition has in a great measure ceased, and the number of operations has progressively increased, so that in 1871 the number of reported cases amounted to 739, an analysis of 660 of the cases giving a success of sixty-eight per cent.[2]

M'Dowell's report of his first three cases was published in Great Britain in 1824. Here too it was received with incredulity. The editor of the most influential of the English medical journals at that time, the *Medical and Chirurgical Review*, applied the quotation, *Credat Judœus, non ego.* Subsequently he used this language: "In despite of all that has been written respecting this cruel operation, we entirely disbelieve that it has ever been performed with success, nor do we think it ever will." Having quoted this extract, another should be added, taken from the same journal of the following year (1826): "A back settlement of America—Kentucky—has beaten the mother country, nay, Europe itself, with all the boasted surgeons thereof, in the fearful and formidable operation of gastrotomy with extraction of diseased ovaries. In the second volume of this series we adverted to the cases of Dr. M'Dowell, of Kentucky, published by Mr. Lizars, of Edinburgh, and expressed ourselves as skeptical respecting their authenticity. Dr. Coates, however, has now given us much more cause for wonder at the success of Dr. M'Dowell; for it appears that out of five cases operated on in Kentucky by Dr. M'Dowell, four recovered after the operation, and only one died. There were circumstances in the narratives of the first three cases that caused misgivings in our minds, for which uncharitableness we ask pardon of God and Dr. M'Dowell of Danville." The first cases in Scotland proving unsuccessful, the operation was not repeated for twenty years. In England it was first successfully performed in 1836. Here, as in America, under considerable violent opposition, operations within the last twenty years have multiplied rapidly, so that in 1863, 377 cases had been reported, sixty per cent. of which had been successful. In 1870 the number of operations performed in England had increased to 1000 or 1100, more than 300 having been performed by one surgeon. In France ovariotomy was first performed in 1844, and was successful. The operation was here denounced by distinguished surgeons. In 1870 there had been reports of 190 operations, all but seven after 1862, the percentage of success being less than in England and America. In Germany in 1870 there had been 180 operations, with

---

[1] The remarks in relation to the thermometer are equally applicable to two still more recent improvements in the means of investigating the phenomena of disease, namely, the ophthalmoscope and the laryngoscope.

[2] Peaslee on ovarian tumors, 1872.

a percentage of only forty-one per cent. of recoveries.[1]

I have cited the foregoing historical facts in order that the non-medical reader may to some extent appreciate the importance of this operation. That it has saved many lives can not be doubted; and if in some instances life might not have been destroyed by the disease, the successful performance of the operation has relieved patients from a distressing burden and deformity. Its origination, therefore, is one of the prominent events illustrative of American medical progress. When the large size of the ovarian tumors is considered, together with the nature of the operation—opening the abdomen by a long incision, and exposing the contained viscera—one can not but admire the boldness, self-confidence, and philanthropy which led to this great surgical achievement.

Other important surgical operations were performed in this country for the first time not long after the operations of M'Dowell. Early in the past centennial period the great John Hunter introduced a new operation for the cure of popliteal aneurism. Previously the operation had been opening the aneurismal sac, removal of the fibrinous or bloody clots contained within it, and tying the artery above and below it—an operation attended with not a little risk of life from loss of blood and subsequent dangers, rendering it often unsuccessful. The Hunterian operation, as it was termed, consisted in tying the femoral artery at a distance from the tumor, leaving the latter to diminish or disappear from the gradual absorption of its contents. An account of this great improvement in surgery was first published in 1787.

Hunter's operation opened up a new field in practical surgery, namely, the ligation of arteries of a still larger size, not only in cases of aneurism, but to arrest hemorrhages, and for the relief or cure of certain local affections. Successive operations in this new field are among the most striking of the events denoting progress during the next thirty years. American surgeons took a prominent part in these operations. Abernethy tied the external iliac artery, in the groin, for aneurism in 1802. Stevens in Santa Cruz and Atkinson in England had tied the internal iliac artery, the former with and the latter without success, when the operation was successfully performed by S. Pomeroy White, of Hudson, New York, in 1827. In the same year Valentine Mott successfully tied the common iliac artery in a case of aneurism. This artery had been tied but once previously, and in that instance the operator was an American surgeon, Gibson, then of Maryland, afterward of Philadelphia. In the latter case the operation was to arrest hemorrhage after a wound in the abdomen. The carotid artery on one side was first tied by Sir Astley Cooper in 1808. At that time probably no surgeon would have ventured to tie the common carotid artery on both sides. This was done in 1829, by Mussey, an American surgeon, twelve days intervening between the two operations. The disease was aneurism by anastomosis; the aneurismal tumor was afterward removed, and the patient recovered.

Tying the subclavian artery above the collar-bone had been attempted by Sir Astley Cooper, and the operation abandoned, in 1809. Subsequently the operation had been performed in Great Britain four times, but in each case without success, when it was for the first time successfully performed by Wright Post, of New York, in 1817. In 1818 Valentine Mott performed the difficult and bold operation of tying the innominate artery. This operation, in the language of his biographer, Professor Gross, "gave him a world-wide reputation, and placed him in the very foremost rank of the illustrious surgeons of his day." To appreciate the operation, some knowledge of anatomy and physiology is requisite. Suffice it to say that the innominate artery, situated in "fearful proximity to the heart," is the vessel which distributes the blood to the right side of the head and the right upper extremity. Cutting off suddenly with a ligature the flow of blood through this vessel, the reliance for the circulation of blood in the parts just mentioned is upon the communications between its branches and those of other arteries. Appreciating the sense of responsibility which the surgeon must have felt in venturing on such an operation

[1] For further details vide Peaslee, op. cit.

for the first time, we can sympathize in the intense anxiety as thus described by his biographer: "Doubtful whether so large a quantity of blood could suddenly be intercepted so near the heart without very serious effects upon the brain, he drew the cord very gradually, with his eyes intently fixed upon the patient's countenance, determined to withdraw it instantly if any alarming symptoms should arise. His feelings had been wrought to the highest pitch, and we may therefore easily imagine the relief he experienced when he perceived, to use his own language, 'no change of feature or agitation of body.'" The operation was not successful, the patient dying from secondary hemorrhage twenty-two days after its performance; the fact, however, that so large a vessel may be tied with impunity was demonstrated. The operation was afterward repeatedly performed, without success, owing to the occurrence of hemorrhage. It was reserved for an American surgeon at length to perform it with complete success. In 1864 this artery was tied by A. W. Smyth, of New Orleans. Repeated hemorrhages having taken place, as in the other cases, Smyth, fifty-four days after the operation, tied another of the arteries carrying blood to the brain—the vertebral artery—and by this second operation the loss of blood was controlled. The patient recovered.

I have referred to the tying of large arteries with some detail, because these successive operations represent important discoveries and improvements. It has been seen that with these operations the surgeons of this country were in no small measure identified. I do not refer to other great surgical operations performed by Mott and others, showing knowledge, skill, and boldness in the operations. It would be an injustice to distinguished members of the profession to omit doing this were I writing a history of American medicine; but the object of this sketch, it is to be borne in mind, is not to do honor to the individuals by whose attainments and labors the profession has been honored, but to cite representative facts as illustrative of progress.

The next important event belonging in this series pertains to physiology, namely, the remarkable observations of Beaumont in relation to digestion. A Canadian boatman, named Alexis San Martin, from an accidental discharge of a musket loaded with buckshot, was wounded in the abdomen, and recovered with a permanent opening into the stomach. He was under the care of Beaumont, a surgeon of the United States army, who at once recognized the opportunity of making important observations and experiments, the opening enabling him to withdraw the contents of the stomach at will without any injury to the patient. Prior to this time it had been ascertained that the processes of digestion in the stomach were dependent on the presence of a secreted liquid—the gastric juice. This liquid, however, had never been obtained in so large quantity and in such a state of purity as was now practicable. Beaumont, securing the co-operation of the patient, and keeping him daily under observation from the year 1825 to 1832, studied with great patience and ability the character of this liquid when withdrawn from the stomach, and the successive changes taking place in the aliment during digestion. The effects of the gastric juice upon different kinds of nutriment out of the body were carefully observed; the relative digestibility of the various articles of food within the stomach was accurately determined, and the effects of disturbing extrinsic influences were noted. Beaumont published an account of his experiments and observations in 1834. This event was one of great importance in the progress of physiology. The facts contained in his publication at this day are to be found in the physiological text-books of all countries. Within late years experimental physiologists have been accustomed to produce, in inferior animals, especially in the dog, an artificial communication with the interior of the stomach such as was occasioned by accident in the case of the Canadian boatman, in order to obtain the gastric juice, and to demonstrate its effect upon food both within and without the organ. It is obvious, however, that the results of these experiments and observations could not be considered as representing, in all regards, facts pertaining to digestion in man, and hence, as furnishing a standard for comparison, those made by Beaumont are invaluable.

I come now to the crowning event in the

history of American medical and sanitary progress during the last centennial period. If it be admitted that every thing pertaining to the physical universe and to living beings is in conformity with an infinitely intelligent and wise government, diseases exist for certain purposes, and the means of preventing, controlling, and ameliorating them acquired by human knowledge are not left to chance. The history of medical and sanitary progress in the past shows that epochs characterized by great discoveries do not occur in rapid succession. Jenner's discovery at the end of the last century constituted a great epoch. The discovery of the useful application of anæsthetics may be considered as constituting the second great epoch within the last centennial period. Had it been announced a century ago that ere long surgical operations were to be divested of suffering, that the law of distress in child-birth imposed upon woman in the primeval curse was to be abrogated, and that pain need no longer be an element in many diseases, would not such an announcement have seemed as marvelous, to say the least, as that, by means of steam, the Atlantic Ocean might be traversed in less than ten days, the American continent in a still less number of days, and that, through the agency of the electrical current, a communication could be sent around the globe in the space of a few minutes?

The successful application of anæsthesia by the inhalation of ether, or etherization in surgery, was first demonstrated in Boston, in 1846. The first application in operative midwifery was also made in Boston, in 1847. Chloroform, which was speedily to a considerable extent substituted for sulphuric ether as the anæsthetic agent, was introduced by Simpson, of Edinburgh, shortly after the discovery of etherization. It is needless to dilate on the inestimable boon which anæsthesia, in its various useful applications, has conferred on mankind. The annihilation of pain was so obviously such a great blessing that almost the only questions ever raised in opposition have related to the impossibility of absolute security against the occasional loss of life from the anæsthetic agent. Of the two anæsthetic agents, ether and chloroform, the latter has been generally employed in Europe, and also to a considerable extent in this country. A combination of the two agents is sometimes employed. The danger to life is undoubtedly greater from chloroform than from ether, but the administration of the latter is more difficult, and the inhalation is often disagreeable: these are the reasons for the preference given so largely to the former. The danger from ether is almost *nil*, and that from chloroform is exceedingly small. Thus, at Guy's Hospital, London, chloroform had been used in more than 12,000 cases before any serious accident occurred, and in the Crimean war it was administered more than 25,000 times without a single death.[1]

It is difficult to appreciate blessings without taking as a stand-point a period when they were not enjoyed. Events with which we become familiar cease after a time to excite wonder or admiration; and when the mind becomes accustomed to extraordinary acquisitions, they seem to have come as a matter of course. If we go back to the time when severe, tedious surgical operations were performed without anæsthesia, recalling the prolonged agony of the sufferer, the strongest endurance tasked to the utmost, the patient sometimes requiring to be forcibly restrained by powerful assistants, or confined by straps to the operating table, one can form an adequate estimate of the precious discovery of a prompt, efficient, and safe method of annihilating pain. Contrast with the picture just presented the severest of operations at the present day, the patient falling easily and quickly into a quiet sleep, and awakening to find, to his astonishment, that all is over! This contrast might be extended to cases of severe, protracted confinements, and also to certain diseases characterized by intense suffering. But the advantages of anæsthesia are not limited to the relief of suffering. The annihilation of pain often contributes to recovery; for the shock and exhaustion caused by pain may do much toward an unfavorable termination after surgical operations, or in cases of confinement and disease, and may even be the immediate cause of death. Anæsthesia thus has been the means of the saving of human life. Moreover, it

---

[1] Gross's *System of Surgery*.

has had this effect in another mode. Patients heretofore sometimes preferred death to the terrible trial of painful operations which now have no terrors. There is still another application in which anæsthesia is of incalculable benefit. It enables the surgeon or physician to make careful and thorough examinations after injuries, and to explore by appropriate means internal parts, the requisite manipulations heretofore causing so much suffering that they were thereby impracticable or hazardous.

It would be pleasant to connect the discovery of the useful applications of anæsthesia with the name of a discoverer holding a position as a benefactor of mankind like that of Jenner. While we claim for our country the honor of the discovery, the circumstances connected with it are not in all respects agreeable or creditable. The merit of the discovery seems due to the late Horace Wells, a practicing dentist in Hartford, Connecticut. He first made the application to himself, inhaling the nitrous oxide gas, and having a tooth extracted while insensible from this anæsthetic. Afterward he employed this agent for the same purpose in several instances. He attempted to bring the matter before the profession by a public demonstration at the medical college in Boston, but his experiments not proving successful on that occasion, he met with ridicule instead of encouragement. Driven to despondency and insanity, he subsequently committed suicide. His successful applications of the nitrous oxide gas were made in 1844. Morton, a dentist in Boston, who had been a pupil of Wells, subsequently made experiments upon himself and others, using as the anæsthetic agent sulphuric ether. In the selection of this agent and in the manner of using it he was guided by C. T. Jackson, a distinguished chemist in Boston. It was by Morton's solicitation that John C. Warren was induced to perform, at the Massachusetts General Hospital, an operation for the removal of a tumor of the neck on a patient rendered insensible by the inhalation of ether. The anæsthesia in this instance was not complete, but the suffering from the operation was evidently diminished. On the following day an operation was performed by George Hayward on a patient etherized by Morton and rendered entirely insensible. This was the first completely successful application to a surgical operation, exclusive of the previous experiments for the extraction of teeth. From that date the employment of anæsthesia rapidly extended. To Morton is due the credit of accomplishing the practical application of anæsthesia to surgical operations, but he probably derived the idea from his preceptor, Wells. Jackson suggested ether in place of the nitrous oxide gas, and aided Morton by his chemical knowledge. Unhappily Morton and Jackson were led to declare the anæsthetic agent a compound which they kept a secret, calling it *letheon*, and obtaining a patent for it as a joint discovery. Such a procedure is in violation of medical ethics, and was in no wise creditable. Afterward each claimed to be the discoverer. These circumstances, together with the conflicting statements and acrimonious discussions which followed, are painful to think of in connection with a discovery which has rendered such great service to mankind.

In referring to the extraction of teeth in connection with anæsthesia, I have not considered this in the light of a surgical operation, but inasmuch as most persons have had more or less practical acquaintance with it, to describe the painfulness of the process were superfluous. It is worthy of note that the inhalation of the nitrous oxide gas, the anæsthetic agent with which Wells experimented, is now largely used to render painless the extraction of teeth. The anæsthesia induced thereby is not sufficiently lasting for most surgical operations, but it answers for this purpose; and thus far, having been administered many thousand times, it has not been followed by any serious consequences. In this regard the dentist's chair is now deprived of all its terrors: after a moment of pleasant dreams, its occupants awaken to find the offending members gone.

Passing from the foregoing brief account of the more notable of the discoveries and improvements exemplifying medical and sanitary progress, I must be satisfied with a cursory notice of some of those of lesser importance, belonging, for the most part, to the history of the last forty years. I desire to premise distinctly that I by no means undertake to include in the following list all, or even the greater part, of the minor contributions which have been made during this period to the science and art of medicine—using the term medicine here, as hitherto, in its comprehensive sense, which embraces every thing relating directly or indirectly to surgery and obstetrics, as well as to the study of the human organism in health and in disease. My object is simply, as already noted, to cite illustrations of the co-operation of our country in medical progress, and the facts cited are those which suggest themselves in my own retrospection.

The substitution of simple manual efforts for pulleys and other mechanical appliances in the reduction of dislocations of the hip joint is an American improvement. It had been taught by Nathan Smitt and practiced by Physic, but for its complete exposition and popularization the profession is indebted to the late W. W. Reid, of Rochester, New York. By means of the improvement, quoting the words of an eminent surgeon, "the reduction of this dislocation is no longer, as it once was, the dread of the surgeon and the terror of the patient." Reid published his experiments and observations in 1851.

In 1848 Gurdon Buck reported a series of cases in which the rare and fatal affection known as œdema of the glottis had been successfully treated by scarifications of the glottis and epiglottis. This affection in some instances destroys life very suddenly, and the only resource is in prompt surgical interference. Buck's simple operation was a substitute for opening the larynx, or laryngotomy. The operation was original with him, although it was afterward ascertained that it had been performed by Lisfranc, of Paris, but without having attracted attention.

In 1850 H. I. Bowditch resorted to puncture with a small-sized instrument and the employment of suction for the purpose of withdrawing morbid liquids from the chest. He subsequently employed this method in cases of pleurisy in a very large number of cases, and also applied it to the removal of purulent liquid in other situations. The method has been since employed by others in this country and in Europe with great success. Latterly, under the name of aspiration, it has become popularized, and it is one of the most important of the improvements in practical medicine within the last quarter of a century.

In 1846 Horace Green published a work on diseases of the air passages, in which he asserted that it was practicable to introduce an instrument through the mouth into the larynx, and in this way to make topical applications in the treatment of diseases here seated. The assertion was at first received with much incredulity and distrust, the feasibility of the operation being by many denied. On this point, however, at the present time few, if any, are skeptical.

In 1848 Jonathan Knight, of New Haven, Connecticut, reported the first successful case in which recovery from aneurism was effected by means of digital compression—a method of treatment which has since been resorted to successfully in a considerable number of cases.

Of American surgeons now living or recently deceased a considerable number have rendered valuable service by either originating or modifying operations, and by contributions to surgical literature. In this list are Gross, who most appropriately heads it, and whose voluminous writings are held in the highest estimation not only in this country but abroad; Hamilton, whose treatise on fractures and dislocations is recognized as a standard work in all countries; Sayre, whose original operations on diseases of joints and ingenious improvements in orthopædic surgery have secured for him transatlantic honors; Brainard, John C. Warren, his son, J. Mason Warren, George Hayward, Henry I. Bigelow, James R. Wood, Van Buren, Parker, Markoe, Eve, Moore, and many others whose names would not be omitted in a full history of the progress of American surgery. To all justice will doubtless be done in papers to be presented at the Centennial International Medical Congress to be held in Philadelphia in September next.

Important improvements in certain operations for the treatment of the accidents incident to confinement and the diseases of women have been contributed within the last quarter of a century by J. Marion Sims, James P. White, T. G. Thomas, Emmet, Peaslee, Barker, and others whose names are identified with the literature of this department of medicine. To notice these contributions more specifically would in this article be out of place.

The foregoing improvements relate to practical surgery, and, for obvious reasons, they are more easily characterized than those relating to the remedial or other measures of treatment in cases of disease. An improvement pertaining to the physical diagnosis of the diseases of the chest may be mentioned, namely, the binaural stethoscope invented by Canmann in 1854. The advantages of this acoustic instrument in the practice of auscultation are such that, unless it be superseded by further improvements, it must take the place of the various stethoscopes devised since the time of Laennec.

Let it not be inferred, from the omission to specify original views and improvements relating to the treatment of diseases, that progress in the latter within late years has been less marked than in surgery. The writings and oral teachings of such men as James Jackson, John Ware, Bowditch, and Shattuck, of Boston; George B. Wood, Dickson, Stillé, J. R. Mitchell, Da Costa, and La Roche, of Philadelphia; Davis and Allen, of Chicago; Elisha Bartlett, Swett, and Alonzo Clark, of New York; and Daniel Drake, of Ohio, have rendered the science and art of medicine in this country steadily progressive. In this connection reference should be made to a discourse, published in 1835, "on self-limited diseases," by Jacob Bigelow, of Boston, which led physicians in this country to recognize more fully than before the important fact that many diseases tend intrinsically to recovery, and to appreciate the importance of the study of the natural history of diseases.

Important contributions to the *materia medica* have not been wanting. As long ago as 1807 the remedy known as ergot was brought to the notice of the profession by Dr. Stearns, and named by him *pulvis parturiens*, a term expressive of its peculiar operation in cases of confinement. Its potency in the application denoted by this term has since been every where recognized, and of late it has been found to have a much wider range of usefulness, being now regarded by many as possessing much efficiency in arresting hemorrhages in different situations. The veratrum viride was employed as a medicine by Tully, Osgood, and other physicians in New England as far back as 1835; but it was brought forward more recently (1850) as a remedy of great power in producing a sedative operation on the heart, by Norwood, of South Carolina. The lobelia, or Indian tobacco, is also an American remedy, introduced to the notice of the profession by the Rev. Dr. Cutter, of Massachusetts, for the relief of asthma, and afterward much used as a palliative in that disease both here and abroad. The use of the anthelmintic remedy, chenopodium or worm-seed, originated in Virginia in the early part of the present century. The anæsthetic agent, chloroform, so extensively used since its employment by Simpson in 1848, was discovered by Guthrie, of Sackett's Harbor, New York, at about the same time that it was also discovered by Soubeiran, at Paris, in 1831.

The medical history of our country within the last quarter of a century is not altogether barren in contributions to anatomy and physiology, albeit the tendency to studies having a direct and obvious practical bearing is predominant. The researches of Isaacs in relation to the structure of the kidneys were characterized by great minuteness, completeness, and accuracy. They have been so considered and adopted in Europe as well as in America. Brown-Séquard, although not a native of this country, is of American paternity, his father having been born in Philadelphia. Moreover, a considerable part of his anatomical, physiological, and pathological labors have been prosecuted and the results originally published here. He has contributed largely toward our knowledge of the structure, functions, and morbid conditions of the nervous system; also important facts relating to other organs and functions of the body. Bennett Douler, of New Orleans, had made valuable contributions to our knowledge of the temperature of the body in anticipation of recent researches in that direction, and he has also made interesting contributions to the study of the nervous system. John C. Dalton has published original and valuable observations relating to the nervous system, digestion, the functions of glands, and other physiological subjects. To him is due the credit of the introduction of vivisections into physiological teaching, which important mode of illustration is probably practiced in certain of our medical schools more largely than in those of Europe. S. Weir Mitchell has developed important facts in relation to the nervous system. Austin Flint, Jun., has contributed new views respecting circulation and respiration, together with experimental researches relating to a new function of the liver. The latter received honorable mention by the French Academy of Sciences, with a recompense of 1500 francs. Brown-Séquard, Dalton, and Flint junior have contributed largely to physiological literature.

It remains to consider briefly medical and sanitary progress as exemplified by mutations in the practice of medicine. It is a curious fact that, according to a wide-spread popular belief, physicians of the present day hold strictly to doctrines handed down by Hippocrates, Galen, and others of the early fathers in medicine. These ancient doctrines, it is by many supposed, have with the medical profession somewhat of the force exerted by theological dogmas on their adherents. The practice of medicine is thought to embrace a binding creed, from which physicians are expected not to swerve under the penalty of being repudiated by their brethren. Hence it is common to speak of a medical man as belonging to the "old school." I say this is a curious fact, for quite the reverse is the truth. The past history of medicine shows a series of mutations in its principles and practice. It is far more open to attack on the score of successive changes than of fixedness. The illegitimate systems which from time to time have sprung up are distinguished by being based on particular dogmas. Their followers are truly sectarians. There is no other standard for medical orthodoxy than the opinions held by the reputable physicians and inculcated in the accredited works. As regards individual opinions and modes of practice, so long as they are not maintained in a sectarian spirit nor adopted for unworthy ends, there are no restrictions in the way of professional fellowship. The views of a physician, theoretical or practical, may be never so eccentric or absurd without interference with his fraternal relations, provided he conforms to the established principles of medical ethics, and does not place himself in an attitude of antagonism toward the honor and dignity of the profession.

A comparison of the early and latter part of the last centennial period furnishes many striking points of contrast. Of course it can not be expected in this paper to go into details; I must confine myself to leading characteristics. A very marked contrast relates to the use of certain potential measures of treatment, such as blood-letting, cathartics, emetics, blisters, or other methods of counter-irritation, the use of mercurial remedies, etc. Comparatively these are but little employed at the present time. This therapeutical change is by no means proof that these measures are not useful. Their usefulness has heretofore undoubtedly in many instances been overestimated, and it is not improbable that further progress in medical experience will show that they are now underestimated. One reason for their being used with more circumspection and reserve is, the ends for which they were employed, owing to improvements in *materia medica* and pharmacy, are now accomplished by remedies which involve less repugnance on the part of the patient, and which are less liable to do harm if injudiciously employed. In this point of view, therefore, the change denotes progress in knowledge. Perhaps nowhere more than in this country is the practice of medicine characterized by the change just adverted to.

Potential drugs of all kinds are less used now than heretofore. This is due in a measure to a better knowledge than formerly of their operation, acquired by accumulated clinical experience and experiments on the lower animals. But it is in a great measure attributable to the results of the study within late years of the natural history of diseases. This term embraces the laws regulating the termination, the duration, the phenomena, and the complications of diseases, irrespective of the operation of active measures of treatment. The importance of this study has been for the past half century more appreciated than formerly. As opportunities have offered, it has been prosecuted with much zeal and patience. Physicians in this country have taken not an insignificant part in the prosecution of this study. The results have shown that many diseases are self-limited in duration, and pursue a favorable course without active medicinal interference, and, as a consequence, there is a greater reserve now than heretofore in the use of potential drugs. And in proportion to this reserve a greater importance has been attached to what may be distinguished as sanitary measures of treatment, such as ventilation, regulation of temperature, etc. It is undoubtedly true that many diseases are more successfully managed on account of these changes. In the dietetic management of the sick there has been great improvement. The recognition of the importance of supporting the powers of life by an adequate alimentation, together with the judicious use of alcoholic stimulants, is one of the striking characteristics of progress in the practice of medicine during the last half century. In all these mutations indicative of progress, it may be claimed, in behalf of the medical profession of this country, that they have not been backward in conforming to them nor in promoting them. The American medical mind may be said to be eminently cosmopolitan and eclectic. With perhaps some undue readiness in accepting opinions emanating from abroad, the prevailing disposition is to seek every where for new developments of knowledge, especially in the practical departments of medicine. In this country, as elsewhere, one point of contrast between the present and the past is the diminished power of individual authority in medical doctrines. At this day, much less than in former times, is the phrase, *Jurare in verba magistri*, applicable to the medical profession.

In the preparation of remedies there is a notable contrast between the earlier and later portions of the last centennial period. The improvements in pharmacy have been very great. Concentrated forms of medicine have largely supplanted infusions or decoctions and bulky medicinal substances. The discovery of the alkaloid quinia was in 1820. Previously malarial fevers were treated with the powdered cinchona bark, the quantity requisite for a cure being so large that, on this account, the treatment was very often unsuccessful. Let it be considered that pounds of the bark are represented by a few grains of the alkaloid. Quinia was speedily after its discovery in use in America, where malarial fevers were a great obstacle in the way of the settlement of our vast national domain. As early as 1841 it had been employed in doses which had not been ventured upon in Europe, but which since that time have been found essential to secure its full remedial power, not only in malarial fevers, but in other diseases. The experience in our country did much toward developing knowledge respecting the curative power of this great antiperiodic remedy.

In the manufacture and employment of other isolated medicinal principles from vegetable remedies, and of extracts, the pharmaceutists and physicians in this country have not been far behind those of Europe. To appreciate the progress in this regard, from the stand-point of the patient, one must be able to recall the time when the nauseousness of physic could not fail to tempt many to throw it to the dogs. Thanks to pharmaceutical improvements, doses of medicine are now rarely disagreeable, and not unfrequently they are even rendered palatable.

Passing from this brief reference to mutations in practice to the character of the medical profession, as represented by the average of the professional attainments, together with the intellectual and moral qualifications of its members, it is needless to say that the progress has been marked. In these respects the medical profession in the United States to-day will compare favorably with the profession in any part of the world. This may be asserted without presumption. It would be easy to cite the testimony to that effect of competent observers from abroad who have been among us. Nowhere in civilized countries do medical men hold a higher social position than here. Nowhere, as a class, do they exert a stronger influence upon other members of society. In our democratic form of government no body of men are more influential. Were the physicians of any of the States in the Union to combine together to form a political party, their power would be irresistible. With such a combination, the election of officers and law-makers would be under their control. Fortunately, or unfortunately, this is not likely to happen, for, as a rule, physicians are not inclined to take an active part in politics. By those who might deprecate a political party composed of doctors it will doubtless be said, such a union is rendered impossible by their proverbial tendency to disagree. The disagreement of doctors has long been a proverb. They are considered fair game for jests in this regard. Were the charge made in earnest, it would be out of place in this article to undertake to refute it. Of the three professions, the imputation, even in jest, would hardly come with a good grace from the clergy. Our legal friends are sometimes fond of comparing, in this point of view, the medical profession with their own. If any of these should honor this article by a perusal, I am sure they will not take offense if I introduce an anecdote which, as I hope, will not be considered frivolous or out of taste in treating of so sober a subject as medical and sanitary progress. The anecdote was told by an eminent member of the bar in Connecticut, who was a party in the colloquy, and who related it, by-the-way, as evidence that a talent for humor which formerly was possessed by not a few physicians had nearly become extinct, the profession in this respect having retrograded rather than advanced. This distinguished lawyer, meeting one day an old physician of the humoristical school, in order to elicit a witty rejoinder attacked him on the score of the disagreement of doctors, referring, in contrast, to the habitual agreement of lawyers, no matter how violently they opposed each other in their professional antagonism. He asked his friend the doctor to explain this contrast. "Oh," said the doctor, "Milton has given the explanation of the difference between us in this respect in the following quotation:

> "'Devils with devils damn'd firm concord hold;
> Men only disagree.'"

The proper scope of this article takes in only the past; but anticipations naturally follow retrospections. After a review of the progress made during the last hundred years, one can hardly forbear to ask, what will have taken place at the end of the next centennial period? A few thoughts suggested by this question may be permitted in concluding the article. It is quite certain that medical and sanitary progress will continue. This is a fair inference from the continued progress hitherto up to this time. It is also a logical conclusion, from the facts in the past history of medicine, that future progress in this direction will be by slow advances. As it has been heretofore, so it will be hereafter: great discoveries or improvements will not follow in rapid succession. The great event in the seventeenth century was the discovery of the circulation of the blood, in the eighteenth century the discovery of vaccination, and in the present century the discovery of anæsthesia. Events like these are not to be expected to recur at much shorter intervals. What is to be the next great event? It would, of course, be absurd to attempt to answer this inquiry. Sometimes, however, preliminary circumstances, as we can see afterward, have pointed distinctly to the direction in which a great discovery was to be looked for. If I were to indulge a prophetic fancy, it would lead me to predict that, ere long, the nature of what are called the special or specific causes of disease will be demonstrated. By special causes I mean those which produce certain diseases, such as the continued, the periodical, and the eruptive fevers. That these and some other diseases have each its own special cause, never occurring without the action of its own cause, and the latter producing only that particular disease, is rationally almost certain. We are acquainted with many of the conditions under which these causes are developed, and we know many of the laws of their operation; but their nature has not been ascertained. It is easy to imagine that were these causes fully known, a great impetus would be given to the progress of medicine. The discovery of the nature of one special cause would probably lead, by analogy, to a similar knowledge of the other causes. It may reasonably be supposed that the knowledge of their essential nature would lead to the means of destroying them, or of neutralizing their morbific operation, and in this way the most destructive to human life of the acute diseases would be prevented or arrested. Many circumstances combine to render it probable that these special causes are either vegetable or animal organisms. On these circumstances are based the "germ theory" of disease. It is, indeed, claimed by some that the causation of certain diseases by specific organisms of microscopical minuteness has been demonstrated; by the majority of medical thinkers, however, the demonstrative evidence is not considered as complete. It is an interesting fact that a quarter of a century ago the cryptogamic origin of many diseases was advocated with cogent evidence and argument by a distinguished medical teacher in this country—the late J. R. Mitchell.

Judging from the past, the future progress of medicine will involve improvements of and additions to the means of investigating the body in health and disease. Within the present century the different organs were resolved into their component tissues by differences mainly in sensible properties. In this way Bichat created the department of general anatomy, that is, the description of the elementary tissues into which the organs are resolvable. Next came the application of analytical chemistry to the study of the solids and fluids, by means of which the department of general anatomy was extended. Then followed the employment of the microscope, giving rise to a new province in anatomy and pathology, namely, histology. Meanwhile the investigation of the heart and lungs by means of the conduction of sounds engaged attention, and auscultation became a branch of medicine. Still later the exploration of the interior of the eye and of the air passages by means of optical instruments has given rise to ophthalmoscopy and laryngoscopy. To these might be added numerous improved methods of examining internal parts by manual instruments.

The improved and added means of investigation which are in the future can not be foreseen, but it may be hoped that thereby, before the lapse of another hundred years, will be gained an insight into the molecular processes involved in nutrition, secretion, and excretion. At present our knowledge of these processes is limited to the conditions under which they take place, with certain of their laws and their effects. In proportion as they are more fully understood, the processes involved in inflammation, the various morbid alterations of structure, and the disorders of glandular organs may be expected to be better comprehended, contributing, moreover, to the progress of therapeutics as well as of pathology, and changing materially the principles and practice of medicine.

If, as regards new remedies and improvements in pharmacy, progress continue as it has taken place in the past, the present may very imperfectly represent the future treatment of diseases. It is but a little over half a century since the great antiperiodic remedy, quinia, was discovered. It is not improbable that before the end of another half century a remedy, or remedies, may be discovered which will arrest other fevers or acute inflammatory affections as quinia arrests malarial diseases. If such an event take place, how great will be the change in practical medicine! New modes of introducing remedies into the system may be ascertained more effective than the recently employed method of injecting medicated solutions beneath the skin.

The extent to which abnormal conditions of the mind are dependent on morbid states of the body is hardly yet fully recognized, though it has been the subject of much thought. Mental disorders falling short of insanity have hitherto entered too little into pathological study. The time may come when, with a better knowledge of the mutual relations of the mental and vital functions, disorders of the former, now in a great measure left for "the patient to minister to himself," will be prevented or successfully treated, and the development of insanity thereby often forestalled. With future progress in this direction, it may be that not a little of the abnormities and enormities which the law considers and punishes as crimes will be recognized as more properly belonging to pathology, claiming the judicious management of the physician rather than judicial treatment.

Finally, the spirit of imaginary foresight which has led to the few foregoing thoughts suggests the question, how will the coming physician differ from the physician of to-day? The question gives rise to a train of speculation which it would be pleasant enough on the part of the writer to pursue; but this I must forego. Suffice it to say that the coming physician will not be regarded even as much as now in the light of a mere prescriber of drugs. I would by no means be thought to underrate the importance of this function. Diseases will always claim medicinal treatment, and doubtless medicines will be prescribed a hundred years hence with more efficacy than in the present stage of medical progress. But the coming physician will be regarded in a higher point of view, as one on whose judgment people will be content to rely in the interdiction as well as in the prescribing of drugs. It will be more and more considered that one of the most important of his professional functions is to determine, by skilled interrogation of the different organs of the body, their freedom from disease, as well as, on the other hand, to detect accurately and early deviations from health. He will himself appreciate more and more the fact that prophylaxis—the prevention of disease—is a higher and more useful branch of medicine than therapeutics. The prevention of crime and the proper treatment of criminals will be recognized as embraced within the scope of medical knowledge and practice. His offices as a hygienic adviser in matters pertaining to mind and body will become equal, if not superior, to his duties as a therapeutist; and the future enlightened lawgiver, with "others in authority," will co-operate in devising and carrying out measures for medical education, the promotion of medical knowledge, and those having reference to public health.

XV.

AMERICAN JURISPRUDENCE.

THE story is told that a company of settlers in a New England colony initiated their acts of organized legislation by passing the resolve, "That this colony be governed by the laws of God in the Old Testament until we have time to prepare better."

In this we discern four tones: key-note—a reverent recognition of Divine authority underlying human law; third—a conservative willingness to obey for the present the existing law; fifth—a progressive confidence in ability to improve the forms and modes of law as the growth of affairs requires; octave—a resolute purpose to make that improvement in due season. These four tones have formed the common chord of American jurisprudence. In the brief, faint echo which this article will bring to the ear of 1876, one may perceive that this harmony constantly recurs.

THE AMERICAN LIBRARY OF LAW.

To indicate the impossibility of stating details in this article, let us take at the outset a topic which otherwise might well stand for the close—the collection of books embodying the law. A glance at these, in their number and complexity, will show the magnitude and elaboration of the field of thought which they include. Jurisprudence even within a single jurisdiction is too minute in its distinctions, its lines are too unyielding, its angles are too sharp, and its growth is too wayward, to admit of reproducing its history in an epitome which shall be both brief and accurate. In our country such difficulty is increased by the consideration that the law in all its details differs exceedingly in the different States. A history of the rights of married women in New York could have no application to Tennessee. A sketch, even very general, of modes of judicial procedure in Illinois would be altogether untrue for Indiana. The legal history and policy of Louisiana differ essentially from those of Massachusetts. Hence in matters of law it is not possible to give concise, simple answers, which shall be accurate, to even the simplest questions. *What is the lawful rate of interest?* One must give a dozen different rules to represent the different States. "Six per cent. in such and such States, seven in others, again ten, and elsewhere it is left to private contract." *What is murder, and how is it punished?* An essay giving the pith of the statutes on this topic, and the rules and distinctions established by the courts, necessary to a correct answer for the different States, though it excluded all legal verbiage and narratives of particular trials, would overrun the reasonable length of an article.

Was there once a photographer who endeavored to take the surface of the whole United States in one picture? or a composer who tried to bring all varieties of music within one orchestral piece? Did they succeed? No. Then this writer will not attempt to portray details in this sketch of the development of jurisprudence.

Imagine, then, that we see arranged before us the printed books which comprise the law as it has grown throughout the United States during the century, being such a collection as many societies and some few individual lawyers have really made; only these actual libraries include numerous English and some Continental works, while our imaginary shelves hold works of American origin alone.

These books, by-the-way, are, as a mass, the product of this century. There exist a few volumes of decisions rendered previous to the Revolution; but as to most of these, the books were published since, though the decisions were rendered before. There are rare old volumes of colonial statutes, published in colonial days; but they have become reduced almost to the rank of curiosities or paper-stock by repeals or revisions of the laws. With trivial exceptions, the American library of law is the growth and fruit of this last one hundred years.

First in practical importance come the "Reports." These contain the official accounts of what the various courts have decided; not, as a general rule, the trials which one sees reported in the public journals, nor the extended testimony of witnesses and speeches of lawyers, but a concise statement of the facts involved in particular questions of law, a brief memorandum of the positions assumed and authorities cited by the respective counsel, and the deliberate opinion of the court. These reports now number, excluding mere curiosities and trivialities, second editions, magazines, and the like, about 2500 volumes. Of these the United States courts have contributed about 216. There is a great disparity in the number in the different States. Thus, among the older States, New York and Pennsylvania have produced 392 and 184 volumes respectively; New Jersey, sixty-two; and Delaware and Rhode Island, eight and ten. Among the States most recently organized, California exhibits forty-eight volumes; Minnesota, twenty; Kansas, thirteen; Nevada, nine; and Nebraska, three.

Next in order are the books of "Statutes." These contain the enactments of new laws, the acts of Congress or of the State Legislatures; not the bills and amendments considered, nor the debates and votes, but only the laws finally passed. The publication of these follows the adjournment of each legislative session. The number of volumes does not admit of any precise statement, for several reasons; one, because in many instances the work of separate sessions of law-makers is given in small pamphlets; another, because the same law is often produced again and again in successive revisions and re-enactments. These books of reports and statutes are the original sources and authorities from which the law is to be learned, but the difficulty of grappling with so many has given rise to the production of many Digests, Indexes, and Treatises, each devoted to a certain subject, sphere, or field, and designed to give to the lawyer, in brief, convenient form, the rules derivable from the reports and statutes. And there are about twenty-five periodicals which may fairly be deemed devoted to jurisprudence as their specialty. Among these the Albany *Law Journal*, *American Law Review*, *American Law Register*, *Central Law Journal*, Chicago *Legal News*, *Legal Intelligencer*, *Pacific Law Monthly*, and *Western Jurist* have attained celebrity and influence.

The preparation of treatises has enlisted the best efforts of some of the ablest and most experienced of American lawyers and judges. And some American treatises—Greenleaf on Evidence, Kent's Commentaries on American Law, several of Judge Story's volumes, the Law Dictionary and the Institutes of Bouvier, Wheaton's famous treatise on International Law, and works of Angell, George T. Curtis, Dr. Lieber, Judge Redfield, Theodore Sedgwick, Francis Wharton—have been approved and accepted abroad, some of them having received the honor of republication, and even of translation.

Five hundred volumes is a moderate allowance for the statutes, treatises, digests, and periodicals; hence the American library of law, developed through our century, now exceeds three thousand volumes.

The occasions for consulting these books do not, upon the whole, diminish. True it is, upon the one hand, that there is, at the present day, less subordination to precedents, merely as such, than in early years. Courts are not as much swayed by a sense that they must obey any and every decided case. But, on the other hand, the extent, variety, and complexity of the questions brought before the courts increase faster than the learning, mental power, and vigor of judicial will among judges; hence there is growing inclination to be advised by past decisions; enlarged necessity for the judge to take time for learning all that is known affecting the cause before him; more hesitation to decide a question until what has been adjudicated upon it has been reviewed. No expedients seem to dispense with the labor of research among the reports and statutes. Authors and publishers, indeed, have proffered compilations of various kinds as substitutes for the original books; but the working lawyers have generally preferred to employ them as means by which they might prosecute research among the reports and statutes themselves more rapidly, and carry it further, and have valued each compilation in proportion as it fulfilled this end. Codes have been enacted in the hope of superseding by concise, authoritative rules the undigested discussions of the reports. Codes are useful; but immediately relieving the lawyer of his library has not been their strong point. The books found necessary to explain the code sometimes seem to outnumber those which the code assumes to consolidate, besides arousing a new zeal for research in older books to find the origin and materials of the new enactment. Lapse of time does not assist, for the books which grow obsolete with the advance of civilization are not as many as those to which each new year gives birth. The necessity, real or imaginary, of "consulting the books" is a large and growing element in the professional labor of the industrious, painstaking lawyer. He must—or thinks he must—examine, read in, perhaps quote from, two or three hundred of the three thousand volumes in the collection before him, to prepare himself for a single argument; and this adds a serious and wearying physical task to the mental duty. In the morning, when strength is fresh and interest awake, the books come down easily and pleasantly enough. But at night, when the brief is written, and a hundred or so of volumes are strewed upon the tables and chairs, then one does wish that book covers were fitted with springs and muscles like wings of birds, and that one could clap his hands and frighten the whole bevy to fly up to their perches on the lofty shelves. A Hint to Inventors!

JURISPRUDENCE IN COLONIAL TIMES.

Most persons will recall reminiscences of general reading touching the status of jurisprudence at the close of colonial history, which will indicate that the great fundamental principles underlying both the rules and the methods of the science were recognized and obeyed then substantially as they are now. The changes have been modifications and expansions of old principles, improvements of ancestral instruments and methods, rather than discoveries that can be called new. There has been a great advance, but it has consisted in the steady, progressive application of the Law to the new rights and relations, the new ideas and possessions, which the growth of the country has developed.

Throughout colonial times it was understood that the administration of justice in the colonies was guided by the general laws and usages of England. Parliament claimed an authority over the colonies, which they repudiated, but it was never understood, even by advocates of Parliamentary authority, that every act of Parliament of general operation throughout England was necessarily of force in the colonies. At the outset the existing laws and the established decisions in England formed a body of law which obtained authority by adoption in the English colonies, except so far as provisions of the charter or peculiar circumstances of the provincial situation prevented. This body of law was somewhat modified during colonial history by provincial laws; also by changes introduced by or adopted from new laws in England. The various colonies of English origin, therefore, possessed a common law composed of the English common law and statutes, and deducible from the reported decisions and authoritative text-books of English law, but varied in many of its applications to suit the circumstances or views of the American people. This has continued the basis of the jurisprudence of these communities since they have ripened into States. The Revolution, which repudiated the crown and Parliament as the source of sovereign authority in the state, and accorded all allegiance to the *People* as the ultimate authors of civil government, did not repudiate or materially change the rules and methods of the law as then existing.

But while jurisprudence remains in nature and essential principles substantially unchanged, there is great contrast between the early and the closing years of our century in respect to many of its applications. In so far as family and domestic relationships remain in fact unchanged, they have the same protection of law now as then. But views and usages of the authority of a parent over his child, of a husband over his wife, of a master over his apprentice, have advanced among our people, and the law has followed, though at a respectful distance, the alteration in customs. Corporations were known to the law in their nature, and in a few of the many uses for which, nowadays, they are constituted; but that multitude of incorporated companies with which our whole country is now populous were, in 1775, unborn. Land was recognized as property, and as fast as the wilderness was reclaimed, our ancestors—except for the repudiation of the feudal idea that land was allotted to its possessor as a reward for his military services to his sovereign, and should therefore at his death descend undivided to his eldest son—employed the leading rules of the law of England to protect the possession of real property and regulate its transfer. But how limited must have been the scope of this branch of jurisprudence before immigration had rendered land valuable, before surveyors had mapped the general surface to render it divisible, and while only a few sea-board cities, inland towns, and limited agricultural regions spotted what otherwise was, so far as practical possession and enjoyment were involved, a wilderness! Contracts were enforced and personal wrongs redressed by courts of justice upon substantially the same general principles of what is right between man and man as now obtain; but how few were the occasions for judicial interference compared with what we now witness! How could there be any law of railway traffic, or of express or telegraph business, when there were no railroads, expresses, or telegraphs? or many libel suits, when there were so few newspapers?

What may be said as to the law of *Crimes?* The English law, as in force throughout the colonies generally, recognized and punished as crimes some things which have now ceased to be so regarded. Absence from church, apostasy, and heresy were punishable. Witchcraft, prophesying, divination, and sorcery in various forms were dealt with as crimes, upon the theory, now obsolete among jurists, that it was possible truth could be ascertained or real effects produced by human employment of supernatural or necromantic means; and so of "multiplying the precious metals." English laws, presumably in force in some of the colonies, punished some practices as being infringements of sound honest trading which now pass unchallenged by any legal penalties—such as "engrossing," or the buying quantities of provisions by a speculator to enhance the market price; "forestalling," or hindering merchandise upon its way to market; and "regrating," or buying provisions within a market with intent to sell them within the same. So of exercising a trade without having served due apprenticeship. Assembling in numbers to petition Parliament was deemed in England to deserve criminal penalty; and a great variety of acts indirectly prejudicial to the stability of government were construed to come within the offense of treason. And besides matters which old English law may have made criminal, many semi-religious regulations were prescribed by provincial laws, founded upon a theory that civil government should punish disobedience to the laws of Moses.

The administration of the criminal law was severe in those days as compared with ours. Punishments were graver, the punishment of death being imposed for almost any of the principal offenses, instead of being reserved for two or three, the most heinous. The attitude of government toward those accused of crime was arbitrary and positive. The proceedings in criminal cases were strict, and the accused, if convicted, had no appeal. The custody of prisoners was little regulated for their comfort or welfare. But accused persons enjoyed, by adoption from England, the privileges of the writ of *habeas corpus* as a protection against unauthorized or pretended imprisonments, and of trial by jury as a preventive of oppressive or forced convictions of crime. Some of the colonies also possessed important assurances of individual rights in a "Bill of Rights," embodying a distinct declaration of principles of liberty obligatory on government in every prosecution of an individual. The principles and means which were to operate toward an amelioration of the criminal law were in existence at the era of the Revolution. And the amelioration which has been accomplished is by no means confined to American communities or attributable to American ideas. It has been as clear and steady in England as among us.

WRITTEN CONSTITUTIONS.

The art of administering government according to the directions of a written constitution may fairly be named among the products of American thought and effort during our century. The adoption of written constitutions by Virginia and Pennsylvania in 1776, and by other States not long afterward, upon recommendation of the Continental Congress, initiated the system which has become fundamental to our security, prosperity, and progress.

It is true there were written resolutions adopted by the people for the guidance of government before the era of the Revolution, and there have been such abroad as well as among us. They were, however, very limited in scope as compared with the constitutions of our day. Most of them, the more ancient ones, like Magna Charta, for example, instead of embodying an attempt to create and organize a government, assumed a government already existing by hereditary right, and only sought to impose some special restrictions upon its action. Now a "constitution," as we in America understand the term, is something far deeper and more fundamental than any of the state papers of past centuries. Our idea is that there is no hereditary right, but that all the powers of government, all the authority which society can rightly exercise toward individuals, are originally vested in the masses of the people; that the people meet together (by their delegates) to organize a government, and freely decide what officers they will have to act for them in making and administering laws, and what the powers of these officers shall be. These written directions of the people, declaring what their officers may do and what they may not, form the constitution. The idea, in its practical development, is American.

The course of jurisprudence through our century has shown that it is possible, and, with the short though severe exception of the civil war, that it is not difficult, for an intelligent, conscientious, self-controlled community, who realize that the will of the people is the source of power, to create and administer government by and under these written constitutions. It has been practicable to have these writings framed. The thirteen colonies, in obedience to the suggestion of their Congress, and notwithstanding the embarrassments and discord of the period, severally adopted constitutions at a very early day, and from time to time since, as new communities in the Territories have grown to sufficient numbers, they have been prompt to ask an enabling act from Congress, and have readily given the time and attention needed for assembling a convention of delegates to prepare a constitution, and for holding a popular election to enact it. It has been practicable to have these writings expounded. The judiciary created by a constitution sits clothed with power to explain whatever doubtful provisions may be found therein, and to test the acts of the Legislature by the constitutional standard; and these decisions have been readily accepted. It has been practicable to secure obedience. Throughout the land a constant succession of elections has been held, pursuant to the directions of the constitution; the defeated candidates have retired cheerfully; the successful ones have assumed the powers, privileges, and duties prescribed by the written charter, have administered them through the defined term, and have obediently relinquished them at its close to constitutionally elected successors. It has been practicable to have these constitutions amended. They do not become rigid, iron-bound shrouds, stifling the growth of the people, but contain within themselves due provision for alteration as time may require. Thus the people of New York, who formed their original constitution in 1777, formed new ones in 1822 and in 1846; and in 1869, in a popular election, weighed a new constitution against three amendments to the old one, and accepted one of the amendments, while rejecting all other changes. The people of Massachusetts, who framed a constitution in 1780, have several times adopted amendments, and in 1853 employed delegates four months in drawing a new one, deliberately considered the draft, and rejected it at the polls. In Louisiana, where the original constitution was framed in 1812, new ones were adopted in 1845 and 1853. In 1864 a fourth was adopted, but disallowed by Congress, whereupon a fifth, under the reconstruction laws, was prepared and adopted. The history of other States is similar.

THE TWOFOLD SYSTEM OF COURTS.

The character of the somewhat complicated system of government which has become established in our country has been the subject of much discussion among political writers and theorists. For while the duties of the various members and officers of government are pretty distinctly described in the authoritative constitutions, those instruments give little or no theoretic explanation of the nature of the union intended to be formed. Many theories have been propounded.

At one extreme stands what has been called the "State Rights" theory, which presents the Constitution as a species of treaty or compact between the States. According to this view, the colonies, upon declaring and establishing their independence, became independent State governments. Desiring to organize some mode of securing their common interests, they formed an alliance or compact for that purpose, which was the old confederation; and this was the agreement of the States, not of the people. Finding this compact insufficient for the purpose, the States rescinded it, and framed another, more intimate and efficient, which is the Constitution, and which is likewise a compact of the States, and to which States subsequently springing into existence by political acts of the people of new Territories have given a voluntary adhesion.

At the other extreme stands a theory that the Union is the original government, and the State governments derive their existence from it or by its authority. Upon this view, the colonies, desirous before they had existence as States to achieve independence, formed a union under the Continental Congress, which, indeed, was not very formally organized, and was incomplete and inefficient as to many subjects, but was yet a real national government, by the military operations of which the colonies were set free from foreign control, and by the permission of which, after they were free, State governments were organized for the exercise of such powers as were not vested in the Union. These governments, at the demand of the Union, conceded a more explicit statement of the powers and authority of the latter in the old Articles of Confederation; and still later, by the Constitution, surrendered to the national government all those broad powers which it now wields. The Union, having at the outset given liberty and political existence to the thirteen States, and having acquired extensive territory and national jurisdiction beyond their limits, has authorized the settlement of that territory, and has from time to time organized the settlements into States created by the Union, and subject to its proper national authority.

A medium view may be stated thus: that the colonial governments were in no proper sense even the germs which have ripened into the governments which now exist, but were creations of foreign authority, and perished with the sundering of the political ties which united our ancestors to the land of their origin; that when, not the colonial governments, but the people of the colonies, became weary of foreign rule and declared themselves independent, this, whether manifested by means of the forms and officers in use in colonial government or by other modes, was a revolutionary and popular act, and not an act of the governments then existing; and the independence which they established was rather the independence of the People from any government, colonial or other, of British origin, than the independence of the colonial governments; and they, the people, then became the true and ultimate source of all political power, though whether the day when they declared this right or the day when the adversary acquiesced in it should be taken as the birthday of the principle is a question of some nicety. The people within what were formerly the thirteen colonies did, by adoption of State constitutions and other less formal and distinct but really popular acts, establish State governments; and these State governments allied themselves for mutual defense and other public purposes, under the old Articles of Confederation. This attempt of the States to provide for the general welfare proved inefficient; upon which the people did, by a new, original act, revolutionary though peaceful, and popular though in part performed by the use of State governmental instrumentalities, withdraw from the States a portion of their powers, and vest them, as expressed in the Constitution, in a new and national government. Since that time new communities of people coming into existence in newly settled Territories have formed new State governments, and have also, upon the consent of the nation, united in the general government. As the general result, the American people have established a duplex political system—a national government for national purposes, for duties of common concern to all their communities; and a government by States for objects local or peculiar, or colored by the differing situations, circumstances, and desires of the different communities.

Very consonant to the last-described theory is the appearance of the judicial system as it exists in our day. An important achievement of our people during the century has been the actual organization of a duplex system of tribunals, adapted to preserve and enforce the administration of the powers vested in the two fundamental organizations respectively. By the constitutions and laws of the States the people have created courts adequate to the administration of justice in all matters intrusted to the States. By the national Constitution they have created a Supreme Court of the United States, clothed with power to try originally certain controversies of high political importance, and also, what is of more general interest, to review and correct the decisions of subordinate courts. By acts of Congress they have created, for the ordinary administration of justice throughout the States in controversies coming within the national jurisdiction, a system of district and circuit courts.

The controversies intrusted to the national tribunals, omitting to mention some of rare occurrence, are of three kinds: cases arising under any law of the United States; cases of admiralty jurisdiction, that is, arising at sea, or immediately connected with maritime matters; and cases between citizens of different States. It was appropriate and highly consistent with the general plan to confide to the States all local and separate concerns; to the Union all general and national affairs. A controversy depending on the laws of the Union or upon the general maritime law of the commercial world should be referred to the courts of the Union, for they might be expected to determine such cases more wisely and more uniformly and consistently than would be done by twenty or thirty independent State courts. Controversies between citizens of different States are referred to national tribunals for other reasons: largely to secure protection against any favor or partiality which courts of one State might bestow upon its own citizens as compared with citizens of another.

To carry this system into practical effect the States have been divided by Congress into judicial districts, of which there are now fifty-seven in all; twenty of these districts are co-extensive each with one State; fourteen States are divided each into two districts; Alabama, New York, and Tennessee are each divided into three. For each district there is a district judge. The districts have also been allotted in circuits, of which there are nine, and for each circuit there is a circuit judge. These judges hold United States circuit and district courts at designated places throughout the States, systematic provision having been made for court-rooms, clerks, marshals, and records, wholly independent of State legislation or control; so that every where individuals concerned in controversies depending on national laws, or arising upon matters of maritime origin, or in which citizens of one State are pitted against those of another, may seek justice in a court of the Union, free, by its creation and surroundings and by all its precedents and traditions, from any undue influence or bias arising from differences among the States. To complete this statement of the national courts, it should be added that appropriate courts have been organized for the general administration of justice in the Territories and the District of Columbia, throughout which the States can not act; and a "Court of Claims" has been established for the determination of claims by citizens against the government of the Union.

The organization of an appropriate system of tribunals in the various States is no less complete and thorough, though less easy to be described in brief. As to almost every State it may be said that there is a Supreme Court, the judges of which separately visit various county seats at stated times to hold jury trials, and afterward meet and hold court together to review and correct the decisions made by each other upon their circuits. In New York decisions of the Supreme Court may be reviewed in the Court of Appeals; but throughout the country generally the Supreme Court of each State is the highest court, and the decisions of the full bench of judges settle the law for that State upon all questions falling within the sphere of State government. If the authority and powers of the national government are involved in the case, there is a mode by which it may be carried to the Supreme Court of the United States for final decision.

For each of the counties into which the States are divided there is, as a general rule, a court for the trial of suits, known as the Court of Common Pleas, the County Court, the Circuit Court for the county, or some similar name; also a court for the care of estates of deceased persons and superintendence of children and lunatics, and for other matters involving legal care of property without active lawsuits, which is differently styled Court of Probate, Orphans' Court, Surrogate's Court, and the like, in different States. One town in each county is designated by law as the county seat, where these county courts shall be held, and where all the judicial and public records of the law business arising in the county shall be preserved.

The counties, again, are, except in some unsettled regions, divided into townships, and throughout these are justices of the peace, who have authority to try lawsuits involving small amounts or founded upon minor wrongs.

In many of the larger cities, where it has been found that the general system of justices of the peace and a county court is not adequate to the judicial business of the place, additional courts for the city are established. Thus in New York, in Buffalo, in Cincinnati, in Indianapolis, there is a "Superior Court;" in Brooklyn there is a "City Court." And for similar reasons the justices of the peace are in some cities organized into quite a formal system of courts.

For the trial of crimes there is, as a general rule, a similar arrangement. Petty offenses may be tried before a justice of the peace. For offenses of a higher but medium grade there is very often a Court of Sessions, or a criminal jurisdiction in the court of the county; or they are tried in a branch of the Supreme Court, sometimes bearing the old-fashioned name "Oyer and Terminer."

We are so accustomed to hear allusions to these tribunals that their existence seems a matter of course. But in truth a great deal of organizing power and judicial and business ability have been required and displayed in establishing over so large a country so varied a scheme of courts, cooperating in harmony to secure the administration of justice.

OUR ADMIRALTY JURISDICTION.

Every reader upon legal topics understands that all commercial nations have acknowledged a general system of "maritime law," and have employed courts of "admiralty jurisdiction" to administer it; that this law and these courts deal with controversies arising out of the management of *ships*, the carriage and delivery of *cargoes*, the employment and treatment of *seamen*, the award of damages for *collisions* between vessels, or of compensation for *salvage* of vessels in peril of wreck, the condemnation and sale of ships captured as *prize* of war, and the punishment of *crimes on board ship*. All jurisdiction of this nature was by our Constitution reserved from the States, and vested, by very general language, in the courts of the Union. The manner in which the scope of this jurisdiction has grown to meet the wants of growing American commerce forms a good illustration of the expansibility of our jurisprudence, and shows that if the law is administered in the future in the same spirit as has prevailed in the past, traditions and precedents may guide and advise, but can not restrict, progress.

Admiralty, as has just been said, deals with matters arising "at sea." But what constitutes the sea, and what are its limits and bounds? Is the mouth of the Hudson or of the Mississippi a part of the sea? If so, how far up stream is "sea?" if not, how far out into the blue waters is "river?" Goods are laden on board ship in a foreign land to come to an American port, and they are to be protected for their owner by the Admiralty (or district) court while they are at sea, and by the Common-law (or State) court after they are brought ashore. But when do they cease to be "at sea?" Is it when the vessel enters the pilotage grounds of the port? or when she is fairly within the sheltered harbor? or when she is fast moored? or not until the goods are piled upon the solid wharf or pier?

The leading test for determining these questions in early English times was the ebb and flow of the tide. There was a long-continued and deep prejudice against the admiralty, and as England had no important interior commerce, and the tidal line corresponded quite nearly with the actual wants and use of her people in commercial matters, that line (with the modification that admiralty should not interfere, tide or no tide, with matters occurring within the legal bounds of an English county) was easily made the dividing line between the rival courts. There is an antique caricature representing the petty disputes that in old times engrossed English tribunals on this subject, by exhibiting a common-law lawyer, armed with a mace, running back and forth along the sea-side, defending his jurisdiction from the incursions of an admiralty lawyer, who floats in a tub upon the water, brandishing a trident. One can easily imagine that, as the tide rises, the tub is borne in to high-water mark, and the jurisdiction of the admiralty lawyer is in the ascendant. As it falls, the common-law practitioner can push his competitor backward with the receding waves, until he can flourish the mace over the entire moist beach above low water.

For two-thirds of the century our courts followed, without much question, the view of admiralty which obtained in England, and treated the word "admiralty" in the Constitution as meaning only that jurisdiction, limited to tide-waters, which was implied by it in old English law. There were no early reasons of importance impressing a different view. But in later years the increase of navigation and all allied interests upon the Great Lakes and the rivers at points above the rise of the tide, together with the advance and development of all forms of commerce upon the various waters connecting the States, have demanded and obtained an entire reconsideration of the subject. The year 1845 may be deemed the salient era of the change. An act of Congress passed in that year asserting admiralty jurisdiction over the lakes and navigable waters connecting them, and a decision of the Supreme Court announced in 1846, but founded on facts occurring earlier, introduced the view that our admiralty jurisdiction is not necessarily that recognized in England when our Constitution was framed, but the broader one known in commercial countries elsewhere; and this idea has been developed by subsequent adjudications, until it is now understood that (except as to matters arising within the internal commerce of a single State) the question whether any particular waters are within the American admiralty jurisdiction or not depends upon whether they are *navigable*, not upon their susceptibility to the tide; the jurisdiction may extend, as has been happily said, "wherever vessels float and navigation successfully aids commerce." The result of the advanced opinion is, that while commerce within a single State—such as the management of a ferry-boat between New York and Brooklyn, a claim for wages earned in running a boat on a merely local canal—is reserved to the State courts, controversies connected with vessels in general commerce upon our lakes and great rivers, upon canals connecting them, upon streams which, though originally unnavigable, have been practically opened to navigation by engineering skill and artificial improvements, and upon waters fit for general navigation, are subject to one uniform rule of law, course of procedure, and line of decisions in the national courts.

There is a parallel question relative to the rights of land-owners upon shores of streams. By a long-ago adopted rule of English law, the proprietors of land upon the banks of petty streams are understood to own the land under the water, each to the middle—to an imaginary thread running up and down the stream half-way between its banks. But if the stream is navigable, the property of the land-owner terminates at the water-line; the bed of the stream, with the waters, is public. In England, as with reference to admiralty jurisdiction, so with reference to land titles, a stream was deemed navigable and public as far up as the tide ebbed and flowed. Beyond this point, or if there was no tide, it was deemed private. Now this is a question which in America each State settles for itself, and not one which, like admiralty jurisdiction, can be determined for the whole country by the United States Supreme Court. And the

States are not agreed. The courts of most of the New England States, and of Mississippi and Virginia, have been contented to follow the old rule. New York, Pennsylvania, and several of the Southern States have, however, adopted the rule that if the river is actually navigable for purposes of commerce, it must be treated as public, whether tidal or not. The West is divided on the question. Some States have had no occasion yet to consider it. But the probability is that ultimately, in all the States where there are any important navigable streams which are not tidal, the tides will be discarded and actual navigability substituted as the test of the extent of the shore-owner's right.

PATENTS—COPYRIGHTS.

The framers of the national Constitution foresaw the advantage of general and uniform laws to secure patents for inventions and copyrights for writings; and the power to legislate upon these subjects was conferred upon Congress. There were early laws of these kinds; a system of patent law was established by an act of 1793, and of copyright law by acts of 1790 and 1802, which, as amended by some later laws, continued in operation for many years. In 1831 as to copyrights, and 1836 as to patents, substantially new systems of law were established; and these, while they have been altered in details, continued in force quite down to our own time. In 1870 these laws were thoroughly re-examined, a new system of provisions covering the entire field, with the addition of trade-marks, was enacted, all the old laws being repealed; and this act, as re-enacted, with some changes of arrangement and expression, in the United States Revised Statutes, forms the present law for the whole country.

Authors frequently contend, and inventors probably agree with them, that the composer of a new writing or the contriver of a new machine has a natural and inherent right of property in his ideas, extending to all the copies or reproductions of them. Compositions and inventions, they urge, are just as much the property of those who by talent, time, and labor have wrought them to perfection as are crops, manufactures, or merchandise the property of those whose capital and labor have brought them into being; and the law ought, they urge, to protect the author in his books (and, by a like reasoning, the inventor in his machine), no matter where he lives, nor how long he has enjoyed them. In particular it is said to be a groundless injustice to deny to a foreign author the same protection as is accorded to a citizen. But this theory of an unqualified natural property in all the reproductions of an idea, whether philosophically correct or not, is not accepted as the basis of our jurisprudence. Our law of copyright, for instance, rests upon the theory that when an author has by his labor and skill embodied ideas in a manuscript, he has a natural property in his work, but it is limited to the identical work he has done, the manuscript he has prepared. In this property he will be protected, just as is the owner of any other article: it shall not be used by another without his consent; if it is borrowed, the law will compel its return; if it is stolen from him, the thief may be punished. But his natural property does not preclude him from giving his ideas away to the public; and if he does this, no rule of jurisprudence warrants him in reclaiming them, or in exacting compensation from those who adopt and use them.

But the practical value of a literary work or an invention to the original proprietor does not consist in his own sole use, but in some means of disposing of reproductions. Hence public policy advises that, as an encouragement, some control over the reproduction of the fruits of mental labor should be assured to the originators of ideas, in addition to the natural right of property, by authority of which they might, if they chose, keep what they produce themselves instead of disseminating it. Whatever of monopoly is given is proffered by the government not as a limited concession to a natural right which the law recognizes while unwilling or unable to protect it, but as a gift, by way of reward or stimulus, additional to native right. Such, at least, has been the foundation of our copyright and patent laws—that it is wholesome and for the general good not to leave authors and inventors to starve upon the mere property in what they produce, but to encourage their beneficent labors by assuring to them a control over all reproductions of the results. How much control to give them, and for how long, is, upon the theory of our jurisprudence, purely a question of government policy.

Under the patent laws, particularly, an immense number of inventions have been developed, and many of the patents issued have proved very remunerative. The pecuniary interests secured under these laws have become of great importance. The general features of the manner in which they are protected by jurisprudence, by means of injunctions to prevent continuing an infringement, or actions for damages for an infringement already committed, are familiarly known.

EXTRADITION OF CRIMINALS.

When a Tweed absconds, a misty question arises over the community, "Can we find him?" And there is a second question, "Can we fetch him back?" Or must we content ourselves with a new application of the words, "We may go to him, but he will not return to us?" The first of these questions is for the detective force; the second is answered by extradition treaties.

The plan of a government combining independent states within a homogeneous national organization involves a necessity for a duplex provision for returning fugitive criminals. The national territory, as a whole, is naturally a retreat for criminals from foreign lands, and offenders against the laws of one State will constantly seek to escape punishment in their home courts by passing into the territory of another. Provision has been needed, and has been made, for both classes.

The matter of returning criminals who escape hither from foreign countries lies between the foreign nations and our national government. The Governor of a State is not warranted, according to the prevailing opinion, in sending an escaped criminal from a foreign country home again for trial; but it is a matter for the President and Secretary of State at Washington, and for the United States courts. Even the national government does not hold itself bound by any absolute or natural obligation to return an offender. As a rule, he is returned only under some treaty stipulation. But the United States, mindful of the public necessity of reciprocal efforts between different nations to promote each other's administration of criminal justice, has from time to time formed treaties upon this subject with different governments abroad, until at length an extensive though somewhat complex system has become established, and is in full operation under the provisions of a systematic act of Congress prescribing the mode of proceeding.

These treaties have some features in common. They are usually limited to crimes involving grave moral guilt, so that merely political offenders and refugees can not be reclaimed; for the United States has never lent its aid to any disposition in monarchical governments to repress by criminal punishments the exercise of what are deemed in this country the individual rights of the citizen. The treaties do not require absolute proof of the guilt of an alleged offender; but, as a rule, he can be sent home only upon evidence which would be deemed sufficient by our law to warrant holding him for trial if he were charged with committing the crime in this country. Whether he may be tried here upon any other charge than that on which he was sent home is a vexed question. And the treaties are reciprocal; that is, it is the policy of this country to return only offenders of the same class as those whom we are allowed to reclaim. This last principle has led to a great variety in the provisions of the different treaties governing extradition.

Thus our treaty with Great Britain of August 9, 1842, provides that the United States and Great Britain shall, upon mutual requisitions by their authorities, deliver up to justice all persons who, being charged with the crime of murder, or assault with intent to commit murder, or piracy, or arson, or robbery, or forgery, or the utterance of forged paper, committed within the jurisdiction of either, shall seek an asylum or be found within the territories of the other. And our treaty with the Hawaiian Islands of December 20, 1849, contains provisions corresponding with these.

We have three treaties with France providing for returning from either country to the other persons accused of murder or attempt to commit murder; or with rape, forgery, arson, robbery, burglary; or with embezzlement by public officers or private employés, or forging, or circulating counterfeit coin or false notes, when such offense is subject to infamous punishment. With the Orange Free State we have a treaty of December 22, 1871, covering these crimes, with the addition of piracy.

Our treaty with Sweden of March 21, 1860, includes murder or attempt to commit murder, rape, piracy (including aggravated mutinies of seamen), arson, robbery and burglary, forgery, and the fabrication of counterfeit coin or paper money, and embezzlement by public officers. The treaty of July 3, 1856, with Austria, and that with San Salvador of June 28, 1872, are to the same effect. So are the treaties with Nicaragua, June 25, 1870, and with Equador of June 28, 1872, except that these omit attempts to murder. So is that with Venezuela of August 27, 1860, that with the Dominican Republic of February 8, 1867, that with Italy of March 23, 1868, and that with Belgium of March 19, 1874, except that each of these extends to the embezzlement of private funds. To the same effect is the treaty with Switzerland of November 25, 1850, except that counterfeiting is omitted, and the embezzlement of private funds embraced.

Our treaty with Prussia of June 16, 1852, includes murder or assaults with intent to commit murder, piracy, arson, robbery, forgery, or utterance of forged papers, or fabrication of counterfeit coin or paper money, and embezzlement of public funds. By a subsequent treaty this engagement is extended to all the states of the North German Confederation. And the same enumeration of crimes is found in the treaty with Bavaria of September 12, 1853.

Our treaty with Mexico of December 11, 1861, embraces murder, assault with intent to commit murder, mutilation, piracy, arson, rape, kidnaping (whether by force or deception), forgery and counterfeiting, or circulating forged or counterfeit coin or paper money, embezzlement of public moneys, robbery or burglary, and larceny of property above twenty-five dollars in value, committed within the frontier States and Territories of the contracting parties.

Our treaty with Peru of September 12, 1870, provides for murder; for rape and abduction by force; bigamy and arson; kidnaping, by force or deception; robbery, larceny, burglary; counterfeiting; forgery —broadly defined, and extended to public securities, judicial acts and records, postage and revenue stamps, public and authentic deeds and documents; embezzlement of public or private funds; fraudulent bankruptcy; fraudulent barratry; mutiny, when the crew have taken forcible possession of the ship, or have transferred it to pirates; severe injuries intentionally caused on railroads, to telegraph lines, or to persons by means of explosions of mines or steam-boilers; and piracy.

So much for the right or duty of our nation to claim or to make return of a fugitive when the question arises between ours and a foreign country. Quite as often, perhaps, it arises where a criminal escapes from one State into another. With these cases the general government has no concern, except that Congress has prescribed the mode of proceeding. The right and the duty lie between the two States. The President and Secretary of State at Washington have no part in the extradition. The Governor of the one State makes a requisition upon the Governor of the other, demanding the return of the offender; and upon this demand, accompanied by certain formal proofs, being laid before the Governor of the other, it is his duty to direct the fugitive, if found within his State, to be arrested and sent home for trial.

But if a Governor should refuse performance of this duty, there does not appear to be any way by which it can be compelled. The national courts can not oblige him to act. The Constitution simply says that such a fugitive "shall be delivered up," but leaves the performance of the duty to the several States.

BANKRUPTCY.

Independent of something like a bankrupt law, a merchant who fails in business is liable to be harassed to an extreme by the pressing demands and suits of rival creditors, and to be for long years excluded from resuming industry or seeking new prosperity by the peril that any acquisitions he may make will be seized by those who hold old claims—a peril which both disheartens him in exertion and discourages those who might be willing to give him assistance and credit. The creditors being independent in proceedings to collect their dues, each endeavors to anticipate the others, and numerous anecdotes are current of ingenious devices of attorneys to outstrip one another in the race of diligence. There is the story of one who "attached" the water-wheel of a factory whose proprietors would not pay his demand. In another anecdote four attorneys, in pursuit of the same debtor, reached the railroad terminus late at night, and three, by concert to exclude the other, hired the only cab in sight, meaning to belate the fourth by compelling him to walk; but he jumped on the box, bought cab and horse from the driver, drove to a choice spot, and upset the cab with the door back against a stone wall, then ran forward and served his writ while his competitors were struggling among the cushions and the broken glass. So an absconding debtor, who undertook to escape across a lake on skates, bearing the proceeds of his fraudulent sales in a fat pocket-book, was followed and overtaken by a collecting agent, also upon skates; and when the unlucky fugitive broke through the ice, the collector insisted on his throwing out the pocket-book to pay demands in full before he would help him ashore.

Upon the other hand, the pressure of creditors often impels debtors to schemes of fraud or of unjust preference in paying rival claimants.

In view of these tendencies of the ordinary laws for collection of debts, the Constitution has authorized Congress to establish uniform laws upon the subject of bankruptcies. Precisely what is "a bankrupt law" has been the subject of some conflicting discussion. But practically it is understood to be a law which ascertains what persons have become, from want of means, unable to pay their debts in ordinary course of business, which takes their remaining property into legal custody, and distributes it equitably among the persons who are proved to have just demands, and which gives the debtor, except in such few cases as are excluded from the benefit, a discharge from his past debts, assuring him of immunity from further lawsuits to collect them.

In 1800, and again in 1841, laws of this description were enacted under stress of general commercial trouble then existing; but each was, within two or three years, repealed. In 1867 a comprehensive and well-considered bankrupt law was passed. Proposals for its repeal have been warmly urged and earnestly discussed, but have thus far resulted only in some comprehensive amendments, indicating that it may probably long continue a feature of the jurisprudence of the country.

Under this law the petition of a debtor to be discharged as a bankrupt, or of his creditors that a surrender of his estate may be compelled, brings up, in the first instance, the question whether the debtor is really a bankrupt and within the provisions of the law. If the debtor is the petitioner, there is not much opportunity for question upon this point; but when creditors make the application, they must prove that the debtor has committed some "act of bankruptcy:" that he has absconded or concealed himself, or has concealed or disposed of or assigned his property to defraud his creditors; or has been arrested or imprisoned for debt for at least a week; or has allowed one creditor in preference to others to get judgment against him or to seize his property; or has suspended payment of ordinary business paper for a fortnight. Such acts as these expose a person to be thrown into bankruptcy by a creditor.

After an adjudication that the debtor is a bankrupt, an assignee is appointed, generally upon a choice by the creditors, to take and dispose of the debtor's estate. The debtor is required to furnish schedules or lists of all his property, also of all his debts, and may be strictly examined upon oath as to all the facts. The assignee takes possession of the property, sells it, defrays any specific charges or liens that ought to be paid in full, and collects the proceeds to be distributed among the creditors. To enable him to do this, very full powers are given him to take the place of the bankrupt in all matters connected with his property, and to prosecute any suits which the bankrupt might have done if the surrender had not been made.

Meantime an opportunity is accorded to the creditors to make proof of their demands. Each one must file a statement and make oath, and if his claim is disputed, must adduce proof that it is lawful. The questions, how much is due, at what date, what interest is to be allowed, what offsets should be made, and the like, are all determined. The money realized by the assignee is then paid over by him to the creditors. The general rule is to distribute the fund among the creditors in proportion to their demands proved. But the expenses of the proceedings, and some demands, such as debts to the United States or to the State in which the proceedings are held, taxes, and wages recently earned to the amount of $50, are allowed to be paid in full before ordinary debts.

The ultimate step in the proceedings is to grant the debtor a discharge. This may be refused him if he has been guilty of misconduct, such as giving false testimony, withholding his property from the assignee, falsifying his accounts, or giving portions of his estate to particular creditors to buy their consent to a discharge. And there are some restrictions applicable where a debtor's property fails to pay more than a specified portion of his debts. The discharge does not extend to debts incurred by embezzlement, or positive fraud, or breach of trust. But, with exceptions like these, one main purpose of the law is to set the bankrupt free from indebtedness, that he may commence business life anew.

THE CALIFORNIA LAND CLAIMS.

Between the California of Dana's *Two Years Before the Mast* and that of Nordhoff's recent volumes, how great is the difference! A third part of a century has seen an immense wilderness become a flourishing and influential State. The course of this transformation threw upon the United States judiciary the burden of determining a conglomeration of controversies fully as complex, novel, and pressing as any which the history of jurisprudence discloses—the "private land claims."

About a month after our declaration of independence, by a royal order of the government of Spain, provinces of Mexico which included California were organized as "the Internal Provinces of New Spain." From that time until 1847—the date of the transfer of California to the United States, upon the close of our war with Mexico, closely followed in 1848 by the discovery of gold—the province was under a succession of Spanish and Mexican governments, whose policy was to make liberal grants of land to persons who would engage to settle upon and cultivate the tracts given them. This was done for the purpose of attracting immigrants. Immense quantities—eleven square leagues being a usual limit—were granted without exacting any payment, upon simple conditions that the settler should occupy, build upon, and cultivate his acquisition.

By the treaty which transferred California from Mexico to the United States our government engaged to recognize and protect the rights of these settlers; not only of those who had fully performed all conditions and had received full papers of title to their lands, but also those who, by any circumstances, ought to be allowed to continue incomplete or delayed improvements, and to acquire lands which had been promised them therefor.

At the time of the treaty an immense number of these claims existed. In some cases the settler had died, and there were claims of his heirs to be considered; in others, he had sold his claim, and the purchaser demanded to fulfill the conditions and take the title in his place; or he had commenced building and cultivation, but had delayed completing what was prescribed; or he had been prevented from so doing, notwithstanding his best efforts; or he had neglected and abandoned his grant altogether; or he had lost his papers. The claims involved questions of all sorts; but the United States agreed to take the place of Mexico in regard to the lands, to recognize and respect such equitable claims as had their origin in the action of the Mexican government, but were yet inchoate and imperfect, and to take such steps as were needed to perfect them, just as if the sovereignty of the country had continued unchanged.

The ink of this treaty was hardly dry when the discovery of gold aroused intense interest in these wild lands. Claims that had been neglected were revived; settlements that had been abandoned were renewed. All kinds of reasons were brought forward to excuse the delays of grantees in taking possession and cultivating as they had engaged. False claims were advanced, and spurious records and papers were prepared to support them. There arose very rapidly a large mass of claims very novel, complex, and extensive, and pressed with the utmost zeal.

Under these circumstances Congress in 1851 created a board of commissioners, who should, under review by the United States courts, try and determine these claims; and this complicated and difficult task has been, during the past quarter of a century, quietly and successfully accomplished. The extent and scope of the Governors' powers, under the old laws of Spain and Mexico, to make these grants have been ascertained, and the date when their power ceased has been determined. Of course all grants made in excess of their authority, or after it expired, have been adjudged valueless. The validity of each grant has been examined—whether the papers were genuine, whether they were regular in form and duly signed. The conditions imposed upon the grantee have received attention, and the claimant has been required to show by some proper proof that the grantee took possession, that he built and cultivated as was required, or to show some excuse. Claims which could not be substantiated have been forever annulled, while all which would bear a judicial investigation have been formally confirmed, and complete and final evidences of title have been issued to the claimants.

In this affair the number and variety of the claims the extent of the tracts of land involved, their remoteness from the seat of government and settled portions of our country, the difficulty of obtaining evidence in that wilderness, the novelty and obscurity of the questions involved, and the value placed upon the lands since their sudden appreciation, have combined to render the task of judicial determination one of unusual difficulty and magnitude.

And it is worth noting that during earlier years of the century numerous land claims of similar nature, though less extended in respect of territory, less sudden in their rise, and less romantic in the attendant circumstances, involving lands in Alabama, Arkansas, Florida, Louisiana, Mississippi, and Missouri, have been determined by our judiciary upon similar principles and with like success.

RIGHTS OF MARRIED WOMEN.

By the English law, as enforced through early years in this country except in Louisiana, the legal existence and rights of a wife were for the most part deemed merged in those of her husband. She continued, indeed, the owner of her lands, but he controlled them and their income. Money or personal property coming to her, vested at once in him, and so did the fruits or proceeds of any demand or right of action, if he would take the trouble to assert his marital rights. Her services also belonged to him. She was disabled from making any contracts. In almost all judicial proceedings affecting her he either took her place or stood by her side, with a practical control of the affair. As to any criminal acts done in his presence, she was irresponsible, and he alone was legally to blame.

Throughout the recent third of the century in many of the States there has been a steady change introduced by legislation, and carried into effect by the courts in the whole jurisprudence of this subject. The change has been of slow growth. The increased rights and privileges have been accorded piecemeal. Take Connecticut, for example. Full and complete protection to married women in their rights of property, against creditors of the husband, is now the established policy of the State. But this result has been attained gradually and with difficulty. The first act was passed in 1845; it protected the interest of the husband in the real estate of the wife which was hers at the time of the marriage, or accrued to her by devise or inheritance during coverture. The second, in 1849, protected the personal estate which should thereafter accrue to her during her married life by bequest or distribution, by vesting it in him as trustee for her. The third, in 1850, protected real estate conveyed to her in consideration of money or property acquired by her personal services. The fourth, also in 1850, protected re-investments of the avails of her real estate when sold. The fifth, in 1853, vested in her for her sole use all her property, real and personal, when abandoned. The sixth, in 1855, extended the provisions of the act of 1849 to personal property owned by her at time of marriage. The seventh, in 1856, extended the provisions of the act of 1849 to patent-rights, copyrights, pensions, and grants and allowances by government; and an eighth, in 1857, further extended it to property acquired by gift. The ninth, in 1860, extended the act of 1850 respecting property acquired by personal services to re-investments of the same. The tenth, in 1865, extended the provisions of the act of 1845 to real estate acquired by gift or purchase; and by the eleventh, in 1866, that of 1849 was extended and applied to all personal property, whether acquired before or after marriage. But while the method of the reform has been irregular, the results have been extensive and thorough; and the rules that the real and personal property of a wife, coming to her before or after marriage, continues hers, to be used, enjoyed, and disposed of, except as to manner and form of conveyance, as if she were single, may be said to be substantially true in the majority of the States.

An independent capacity to sue and be sued alone has been conferred in many; and in not a few of the States wide powers to make contracts and to carry on general business, even to the extent of employing the husband as a managing agent of a large farm or manufacturing establishment, have been conferred.

HOMESTEAD AND EXEMPTION LAWS.

Books tell us of ancient laws by which a debtor who could not pay his debts might, upon demand of his creditors, be cut in pieces and divided bodily among them. Rigor like this had become obsolete long before the commencement of our century, but the law for the collection of debts was still rigid in exacting all property that could be obtained from a debtor for the satisfaction of his creditors. In modern years the view has obtained that creditors shall not have every thing; some reservation of property shall be allowed, to provide for the instant wants of an insolvent, and to relieve his family from absolute destitution. This privilege is given by laws of the various States allowing a head of a family to designate by public record a house and lot as his "homestead," which shall not thereafter be taken for his general debts, and by laws prescribing certain kinds and amounts of personal property which shall be "exempt from sale on execution." The principle of allowing a debtor to retain some little property for himself, and still more for his family, if he has one, is now recognized throughout the country. The extent of the privilege granted differs in the different States. Probably every State accords some privilege of exemption of personal property —clothing, a little live stock, and necessary tools for the debtor's farm, a limited number of articles of furniture for the house, wages just earned, and the like; but the different statutes upon the subject run into an immense number of petty details.

Homestead exemptions are not allowed in all the States. Down to 1875, Connecticut, Delaware, Indiana, Maryland, Oregon, Pennsylvania, and Rhode Island, also the District of Columbia, appear not to have passed laws of this kind. Through the other States there are laws by which a head of a family may designate a homestead, and protect it from being sold for his debts, except for the price of it, or for a mortgage upon it, or other special indebtedness. If the property is a farm, the privilege is limited in about half the States by number of acres; forty, eighty, or one hundred and sixty is a common limit. In others the restriction is by value, such as $5000, $2000, or in some of the States less. In Texas two hundred acres may be exempt. If the property is a town or city lot, the exemption is generally limited by a value corresponding to the value allowed for farms, or the quantity is closely restricted—as to a quarter or half an acre. The homestead laws usually give the wife of the proprietor some control over any sale or mortgage of the property.

MECHANICS' LIEN LAWS.

When an owner of land desires to erect a building, he does not usually himself buy the wood, the brick, and the iron-mongery needed, nor personally hire and pay the workmen employed. By custom he makes a contract with a builder for the erection, and the builder makes the purchases and employs the workmen. It has long been found that this system is prolific of frauds or losses to those who sell the materials or do the labor. The builder may collect the contract price of the house from the owner, and refuse to pay his subordinates, and the latter may lose their remedy against the builder for want of his having any tangible property which they can reach, and against the owner because he made no contract with them, while they can not reclaim each what he contributed toward the work, because, whatever it is, it has become inextricably involved in the building.

To prevent or redress such frauds, laws have gradually been framed in the various States to give the subordinate mechanics a lien upon the property which they assist to improve. Under these laws, "material men," as those who sell materials for a building may be called, or laborers, may file a notice in a designated public office, setting forth what they have done toward a building, and what is due to them for the same. By doing this they gain a right to be paid out of the value of the property. If the contractor pays them, as he should do, very well. If he does not, the owner may pay them and deduct from the money due the contractor. If neither will pay, the property may be sold, and the demands paid from the proceeds.

Laws of this description exist in nearly all the States, though they vary greatly in details, and within any one State the law may differ in different counties. In Louisiana and Florida a lien is allowed for advances made or work done in carrying on a plantation or farm.

PROTECTION OF ANIMALS.

The notable and successful efforts which have been made for the protection of animals involve a new thought. In the administration of the law in old times there is very little trace of any recognition of animals as entitled in themselves to any legal care or protection. Animals have very long been esteemed property, and ill treatment of one which rendered it less valuable to the owner has been recognized as a wrong which the law would redress. Inhuman and barbarous treatment may also be committed under circumstances rendering it demoralizing to those who witness it; on this ground it has long been punishable. But the additional view that sentient life should be, for its own sake, sheltered and guarded by the law, has only lately been developed with any distinctness and efficiency. Founded upon this sentiment, laws and efficient societies for the prevention of cruelty to animals have been established in thirty-seven of the States and Territories. Throughout the world there are no less than 229 of these societies, the movement having been initiated by the New York society.

REFORMED PROCEDURE.

The English law of civil rights and remedies, as administered throughout our country at the era of our Revolution, and for more than half a century afterward, abounded in strict rules and exact forms, which were designed, and, if skillfully followed, were in many respects adapted, to shorten and perhaps to simplify legal proceedings, but, as actually pursued, were often the means of doing injustice in the name of the Law. The proceedings in the law courts were also subject to interference in large classes of cases from courts of equity, whose mode of proceeding and principles of deciding causes were very different from those of the law courts. Thus it might happen that a man who had an unquestionable right to recover in a suit lost his case because his lawyers brought the suit in the wrong court, or because, bringing it in the right court, they drew the papers in the wrong form of action. The double and technical system which prevailed gave rise to great inconvenience, and the fictions constantly employed strengthened the distrust which other causes created. Attempts have often been made to justify the obnoxious features of the system upon the ground of accuracy, simplicity, brevity, and the like; but, in truth, the reasons were historic, not logical or practical. The practice was as it had grown to be, not as it ought to be.

The Reformed practice is now just above a quarter of a century old. It was initiated by a Code of Procedure adopted in New York in 1848, and amended and re-enacted in 1849. More than half the States have since adopted its essential principles and leading provisions, and they underlie a very important measure of law reform which has recently gone into operation in England.

The important features of these codes of reformed procedure are four. 1. The distinction between courts of law and equity is abrogated; the same court has power to apply the rules of law or principles of equity to the controversy before it as circumstances may require. 2. Forms of action, particularly the technical differences between what used to be called actions of assumpsit and debt, of case and trespass, of trover and replevin, are abolished; John Doe and Richard Roe are dead and buried. 3. They recognize the assignee of all assignable demands; and allow the real owner of the cause of action to sue, instead of requiring the action to be brought, by fiction of law, in the name of the original party, as was formerly the case. 4. They discard the strict technical nicety of pleading and practice which was required by the common-law system; and seek to elicit and try the real merits of the controversy, permitting liberal amendments, and disregarding errors and variances, unless such as to cause real injustice.

CODES AND REVISED STATUTES.

The readiness of American Legislatures to codify or revise the laws is a noticeable feature. By a code, in strict usage, is understood a concise, comprehensive, systematic re-enactment of the law, deduced from both sources—the pre-existing statutes and the adjudications of courts. A revision of the statutes is a less extensive undertaking; it aims only to exhibit, in brief compass and with proper corrections and improvements, the statutes which have been for a period accumulating in annual volumes. A code, if perfect and unambiguous, would be at its first enactment a substitute both for statutes and reports previously in use. A revision, however complete, would supersede only previous acts of the Legislature. But this distinction is not very nicely regarded in the nomenclature of our books of legislation. There are, at the present time, about ten "Codes," so called, and partaking largely of the nature of a true code; about fifteen systems of "Revised Statutes;" and about twelve compilations, which are in substance revisions, but are named "General Statutes," "Compiled Statutes," and the like. Some works of this class are merely private compilations. But nearly every State has either authorized and adopted as official a compilation of its laws by lawyers of ability and reputation, or has employed commissioners to draft its laws into a system, and has re-enacted them as compiled. In many of the States one or other of these things has been done several times. There does not appear to be any State, with perhaps the exception of Pennsylvania and Tennessee, which does not possess a codification or revision of the laws made since the commencement of 1860; and in the great majority there are such dating within the past ten years.

Some of these works involve important and extended reforms of the pre-existing law; others do not. The New York Revised Statutes, adopted in 1828 and 1830, and the Massachusetts General Statutes of 1860, are notable examples of revisions embodying many improvements. The United States Revised Statutes (1873) is an instance of a simple consolidation. The statutes, as annually published, were rapidly accumulating, and had become not only inconveniently bulky, but inconsistent and obscure. The revision aims to present, in a single volume, the general and permanent laws, previously running through seventeen volumes, accurately condensed, but unchanged in substance.

A BRIEF RETROSPECT.

This paper draws toward a close, but not for want of further examples of the progress of our law. The brief illustrations which have been given might easily be doubled in number. Each one suggests auxiliary topics. Jurisprudence has not only made exposition of the law in three thousand published volumes, and declared its rules anew in half a hundred distinct codes or revisions, but has dotted the States with *Law Schools* well equipped for the systematic instruction of her disciples. She has not only developed written constitutions and wrought out a twofold system of courts, but has erected State and national *Capitals*, and organized county seats supplied with buildings, extensive record books and files, and libraries appropriate for judicial labor. She has not only devised a new and homogeneous mode of pleading and practice in courts of justice, but has extensively relaxed the old technical rules excluding *Witnesses* who might be interested in a suit, even to the extent in several jurisdictions of allowing one upon trial for a crime to testify in his own behalf.

She has not only established the law of the sea over our inland waters, but has also brought the employment and treatment of *Merchant Seamen* under one uniform and national system of regulations. Upon the land she has not only adjusted the private land claims arising against former governments, she has also administered systems of laws governing the survey and disposal of the *Public Lands*, under which the territory owned by the nation or by the various States has been subdivided and opened to a peaceful settlement and cultivation as fast as has been desired. She has promoted such settlement by a hospitable *Naturalization Law;* by large modifications of the ancient *Land Titles*, discarding primogeniture and complicated entails and trusts, and promoting subdivision and ready sale of estates; by prescribing modes in which lands needed for public uses may be freely taken in right of *Eminent Domain*, but strictly requiring compensation to the land-owner; and by devising in the rich mineral Territories of the far West appropriate rules for the development of *Mines* and the protection of mining claims. Witnessing, without power to prevent them, the evils of a gigantic system of *Slavery* and the horrors of a *Civil War*, she did something while they lasted to control and restrain them, and is doing much in superintending the reconstruction of the shattered social fabric, in harmonizing the individual controversies of which the war was so fruitful, and has fairly entered upon the newly assigned duty of elevating four millions of a lately enslaved and still depressed and ignorant race to enjoyment of equal *Civil Rights*. She has encouraged *Corporations*, has added to the old method of incorporation by charter a free system of general laws for their formation, management, and dissolution, and to the old remedies against corporate property a principle of individual liability, so that incorporation has become a familiar, convenient, and approved mode of uniting many men and aggregating large capital in the pursuit of almost every species of enterprise or purpose, of very many purposes to which in old times it never was, and in old countries even now it scarcely is, applied. She has rescued *Banking* from the uncertain basis of private capital and responsibility, and has established it upon a foundation of securities lodged with government—that of the State or nation, as you please—for the bill-holder's protection. She has liberalized the ancient law of *Carriers*, giving them leave to restrict their liability by a special contract, and thus has promoted that expansion of our facilities for commerce which has been accomplished by adding to the ships, stage-coaches, and baggage-wagons of old times our immense net-work of canals, steamboats, and railway routes, express and telegraph lines. She has fostered the principle of education of the common people at the charge of the State, and superintends a comprehensive and efficient system of *Public Schools*. She has liberalized the *Criminal Law* and ameliorated *Prison Discipline* (until the element of humanity sometimes seems to verge upon laxity), has restricted the old views of *Sedition* and *Treason* to conform to the principles of a popular government, and has given increased efficiency to the writ of *Habeas Corpus;* but has by *Liquor Laws*, embodying even the endeavor to prohibit the traffic in intoxicating drink entirely, or to compel the seller to make compensation for all damages resulting from excess, and by stringent laws against *Abortion*, *Seduction*, and the traffic in *Vicious Literature* and merchandise, made punishable some causes of demoralization which our forefathers considered must be exempt from punishment because the victim was a willing one.

These topics might well receive extended explanation; and if space could be allowed, the writer would gladly add some descriptive sketches of *Celebrities*—of our eminent judges, brilliant advocates, and judicious legislators; some narratives of the *Great Trials* of the century, with explanations of their influence upon the tone of judicial thought; and perhaps some revelations of the methods and achievements of American *Detectives*.

"SHE HATH DONE WHAT SHE COULD."

These achievements of Jurisprudence, when compared with the works of her sisters in other fields of labor, appear moderate, plain, and plodding, rather than rapid, brilliant, or extensive. But then, for many, many centuries, Jurisprudence has had no gift of new powers. Sudden and wonderful progress in either of the various fields of human effort is generally observable within a few centuries after some new power or means has been bestowed. Not three centuries have passed since the *Novum Organon* of Bacon gave to practical science a new method of research, which has substituted astronomy for astrology, chemistry for alchemy, and has rendered attainments in science rapid and easy which upon old methods would have remained impossible. The steam-engine was a new gift to Commerce and Manufactures; so was the printing-press to Literature; so has been the telegraph to Journalism. The enunciation and application of the principle that "governments derive their just powers from the consent of the governed," as a substitute for the idea of a divinely given, hereditarily transmitted right, was a gift of a new power to Government. These were not improvements in old methods; they involved the total subversion of old methods and substitution of new ones. They are comparatively modern; some of them are very recent, and one need not wonder that brilliant results are flowing from them within our century. But how long it is since Anglo-Saxon Jurisprudence has received any new endowment! We have only the ancient methods. When a controversy arises we employ a lawyer—a species of agent which flourished in the times of Demosthenes and Cicero; he brings the cause before a judge—an officer suggested by Jethro to relieve the labors of Moses; who summons a jury—as ordained by Alfred. We have statutes—so had the Medes and Persians; and codes—so had Justinian; and a common law—so had the Saxons. What is older than our courts, our trials, our prisons? Trial by jury—a device ten centuries old—is the most modern of all the important means and instruments with which Jurisprudence does her work. All we can say for her in the century now closing is that, with her antique tools, "she hath done what she could."

XVI.

HUMANITARIAN PROGRESS.

THE spirit of humanity belongs to all races, and has been stimulated by many of the religions of mankind.

It has attained its highest development and greatest power under Christianity; and so imbued is modern society with its silent influences, that even those who deny the supernatural origin of the Christian religion, and who reject its doctrines, are often filled with the spirit which it has especially cultivated in the world. The history of this republic has been no exception to this silent and powerful working of the Christian faith. Both through its organized forms, and even as effectively through external agencies inspired by its spirit, through literature and law and associations for reform and charity, this divine impulse has been slowly overcoming in our history the instinct of selfishness, the indifference to human ills, the ignorant pride of race, and the hardness and cruelty which have come down from ages of barbarism. In no nation has this spirit, which has been spread abroad in the world by Christ, had such power as in this; and yet we seem to be but just touched by its civilizing influences, and scarcely yet to have emerged from the savagery and inhumanity of barbarous times.

Many dreadful abuses and cruel evils yet exist. Still the whole opinion and feeling of the day are against them; much ability and labor are expended to diminish these ills or remove their sources; and the path of true progress and reform has been steadily entered upon. Another centennial will probably see Christianity enthroned in this country, in custom and law and institution, as it has never yet been in modern days; and the spirit of humanity, guided by reason and culture, governing more human beings, in their relations to the great evils of mankind, than were ever witnessed before.

This sketch being necessarily brief, the writer has been obliged to choose certain distinct fields where the progress in the spirit of humanity can be clearly tested; such as the treatment of prisoners; the penalties and enactments against crime; the punishment of debtors, and the legislation in regard to them; the treatment of criminal and neglected youth, and the care of the insane poor. Great departments of the subject, such as the emancipation of the slaves, together with the sanitary labors of the civil war, could only be alluded to.

THE PRISONS.

One of the tests of the progress of the race in humanity and civilization is its treatment of criminals and the large and varied class of unfortunates. The infliction of severe and bloody punishment for comparatively slight offenses, the use of degrading and brutalizing penalties, the treatment of offenders against the law as if they were an irreclaimable and distinct class of the community, and the neglect of the elements of hope and reform in the management of criminals, are all being gradually left behind, as relics of barbarism, by Christian nations in their onward progress. The true indications of advance in the spirit of humanity are not in any false and sentimental views of punishment and its object. The criminal has violated human law, and, in the interest of social security, must be deterred himself from committing the offense again, and through his punishment must deter others. But it is equally for the interest of society, and a duty of humanity and religion, that he should not finish his period of penalty worse than he began it. It is quite possible that he may not be worse, morally, than many whose offenses have not been detected or whose temptations have not been so great. But human law can not regard this: it must treat his violation of it as an offense, and inflict a "deterrent" penalty. But here humanity and sound policy can suggest modes and modifications of punishment which may bring with them improvement on the part of the prisoner, and which will at least prevent him from becoming worse, and thus injuring society more in the future than he has done in the past.

Wisdom in this matter of punishment will naturally suggest that offenses which are caused by pure misfortune, or which are technical in their nature, should not be punished as are immoral actions. The debtor should not suffer the same penalty as the thief, and certainly should not share the same cell. The smuggler or the unintentional violator of revenue laws is not to be treated as the robber or the forger.

Classification of prisoners is one of the first elements in true progress in the science of punishment. The innocent—such as witnesses or persons arrested on suspicion—should not be imprisoned with the guilty; the young should be separated from the old, the recent offender from the experienced and hardened convict, woman from man, and each similar grade of prisoners as much as possible be kept together. It is of vital importance that the young criminal should not learn in the jails new lessons of crime; and that the old should not grow worse by vile associations.

The weakness at the foundation of criminal life is the want of habit of continuous labor. It becomes, then, of the utmost consequence that the convict should be trained to constant and steady industry. Occupation in the prison will fit him for a better life outside, and, at the same time, will pay the expenses of his support. No offender of civil law ought to be a burden on his fellow-citizens.

But the prison life has the same principles at its basis as life outside. There can be no reform without the element of hope. The convict needs, in order to elevate him, the same forces which work upon society generally: the prospect of reward, the approval of the worthy, and a certain liberty of action bringing either penalty or profit, according to his self-control, or feebleness of principle. There must be, then, in a real advance in the treatment of offenders against the law, a system which would first show the prisoner the magnitude of his offense, and give him time and cause for sober reflection, which would have the severe and deterrent effects of punishment; he must have terms of solitude and idleness. Then he must gradually be admitted to a higher stage of prison life, where work is offered him as a relief from idleness. Here he begins to see a reward from labor and good conduct, both in the proportion of his wages allowed him, and in the commutation of his punishment which they will bring. He has all the time, to a large degree, his future in his hands; he can cause his own penalty to be light or severe. A failure of self-control, a neglect of industry, will lengthen his imprisonment, and diminish the wages he would carry forth at his release.

Finally, strengthened thus by years of hard labor and virtuous conduct, he is admitted, in his final term, to a greater freedom of action, which will prepare him for his life in the world; in which a failure of principle will cause him to serve the full term of years to which he had been sentenced.

Under such an improved prison-system, there will be both solitary and cellular imprisonment and congregated labor; there will be the influences of secular-school and Sunday religious teaching, of lessons and libraries. The cells will be clean and healthy; no brutalizing punishments of tread-mill and cat will be permitted; penalties will be the deprivation of what has been gained, or, at the worst, solitary confinement. The convict will come forth, not imbittered against society, nor depraved by bad association, nor weak through long dependence on others. He starts on a vantage-ground as he leaves the prison; he has learned habits of industry and self-control, he has been approved by the prison authorities, and has perhaps regained his rights of citizenship; he has saved money, and has felt the power of religion, and his mind has been awakened by instruction and knowledge. He will not easily fall again.

This ideal prison-system, set forth in so remarkable a manner by Edward Livingston,[1] fifty years since, is the high-water mark in the tide of human thought thus far on this subject. How far has this nation approached it in a hundred years, and from what beginnings in the management of criminals has it advanced?

---

[1] Livingston's *Code of Criminal Reform* (published in 1833) contains, fifty years before their adoption, the best ideas of this generation on prison reform. The Crofton system is there in its essential features.

OVERCROWDING OF FORMER PRISONS.

The accounts of the crowding of convicts in the various prisons and jails of the country during the first fifty years of our history as a republic are distressing in the extreme. It is stated on the best authority[1] that the average number of prisoners, from 1776 to 1826, confined in each cell at night in the penitentiaries of New Hampshire and Vermont was from 2 to 6; in those of Massachusetts, 4 to 6; of Connecticut, 15 to 32; in New York City, 12; in New Jersey, 10 to 12; in Maryland, 7 to 10; and in Pennsylvania, worst of all, from 29 to 31. In the Philadelphia prison the cells only measured 18 feet by 20, so that each convict at night "had only a space as large as a coffin," or about 6 feet by 2. In the Massachusetts prisons the cells were so narrow, that the prisoners were often lodged by swinging hammocks, one over the other; and in one Connecticut prison it is related that during the hot weather of July, 1825, 32 convicts were confined in a basement under 7 feet in height and only 21 feet by 10, the only ventilation being one small window and an orifice over the door.

During more than fifty years (from 1773 to 1827) the enlightened State of Connecticut had an under-ground prison in an old mining-pit on the hills near Simsbury, which surpassed in horrors all that is known of European or American prisons.

The passage to the "New-gate Prison," as it was called, was down a shaft by means of a ladder, to some caverns in the sides of the hill. Here rooms were built of boards for the convicts, and heaps of straw formed their beds. "The horrid gloom of these dungeons can be realized only by those who pass among its solitary windings. The impenetrable vastness supporting the awful mass above, impending as if ready to crush one to atoms; the dripping waters, trickling like tears from its sides; the unearthly echoes—all conspire to strike the beholders aghast with amazement and horror."[2]

Here from thirty to one hundred prisoners were crowded together at night, their feet fastened to bars of iron, and chains about their necks attached to beams above. The caves reeked with filth, occasioning incessant contagious fevers. The prison was the scene of constant outbreaks, and the most cruel and degrading punishments failed to reform the convicts. "The system," says the writer quoted above, "was very well suited to make men into devils, but could never make devils into men." The prisoners educated one another in crime. "Their midnight revels were often like the howling in a pandemonium of tigers, banishing sleep and forbidding rest!"

Nearly all the county jails had what were called "dungeons," or cells not fit for human beings, in which convicts were confined.

At Northampton, Massachusetts, a dungeon is described, only four feet high, without window or chimney, the only ventilation being through the privy-vault and two orifices in the wall. In Worcester, a similar cell was only three feet high and eleven feet square, without window or orifice, the air entering through the vault and through the cracks in the door. This was connected with a similar room for lunatics. At Concord was a cell of like construction; and in Schenectady, New York, it is related that three men confined a few hours in such a dungeon were found lifeless, though afterward they were revived.

Worse even than the overcrowding was the indiscriminate association, in the American prisons, of all ages, classes, and sexes. Of the Philadelphia Walnut-street Prison it was said, "Its crowded night-rooms, undisciplined throng, enormous expense, dreadful mortality; its issues of highway robbers, incendiaries, and thieves, as proved by its recommitments, are believed not to be surpassed in the United States."[1]

Of the old Market-street Prison in the same city, Mr. Vaux says, "All ages and sexes are mingled: the trembling novice in crime, the debtor, the disgusting object of popular contempt besmeared with filth from the pillory, the unhappy victim of the lash streaming with blood from the whipping-post, the half-naked vagrant, the loathsome drunkard, the sick and the condemned criminal."

An old report says of the New York Bride-

[1] Report of Boston Prison Discipline Society for 1826.

[2] *A History of the New-gate Prison*, by R. H. Phelps, East Granby, Conn., 1844.

[1] Report of Boston Prison Discipline Society for 1826, p. 77.

well, "More to be lamented than its fever and mortality is the indiscriminate mingling of over two thousand persons annually of all ages and degrees of guilt." The French commissioners who visited the prisons of this country, MM. Beaumont and De Tocqueville, state that in 1834 they saw more than fifty untried persons in the same room with old offenders, there being no bed, chair, or plank in the cell, and no means of obtaining pure air. A common custom in the prison was what was called "blanketing a stranger;" that is, the new-comer was tossed in a blanket by the older ruffians until he parted with all his superfluous clothing, to be used in exchange for liquor.

Of the Leverett-street Jail, Boston, it is stated, in 1831, that over one thousand debtors were confined in the same crowded night-rooms with over a thousand criminals and vagrants. Men and women, old men and black boys, idiots, lunatics, and drunkards, all mingled together in two buildings. No restraint was used to prevent gambling, lascivious conversation, or quarreling.

It is said in regard to the old prison in Connecticut, that if the prisoners themselves had been permitted to build the prison with the greatest facilities for the concealment of crime and the least possibility of detection, they could not have succeeded better.

Of the State-prison in New York City, the French commissioners report that the prisoners, when the cells were unlocked in the morning, flocked confusedly into the yard, and, at the sound of the bell for meals, they moved like an undisciplined mob to the mess-room.

The New York Society for the "Prevention of Pauperism" states in its second report, 1820, that "in Bellevue Prison, New York, more than three hundred wretches of all ages, and graduating in crime, are placed in a community by themselves, often without employment, without instruction, without admonition or advice, to become the subjects of reformation." Girls from ten to eighteen years of age were confined here in the same cell with old prostitutes. "Why," says the report, "this melancholy spectacle of female wretchedness has claimed no more attention and excited no more sympathy in a city like ours, we can not say. Why no female messengers have entered this gloomy abode of guilt and despair like angels of mercy, is a matter of deep reflection and regret!"

In 1828, it is stated that the convicts in Bellevue Penitentiary were so crowded in the night-rooms that they could not lie down on the floor without mingling their limbs in one solid mass. The natural results were repeated attacks of terrible jail-fevers.

In the old prisons of Philadelphia, particularly in the one on the corner of High and Third streets, it is stated that, in 1837, women caused their own imprisonment for fictitious debts, in order to join in the orgies of the jail. Intoxicating liquors were bought and sold at the bar kept by one of the prison officials; acquitted prisoners were kept there for jail fees; the custom of "garnish" prevailed, whereby a new prisoner was stripped of his clothing, which was held by the other convicts till the man redeemed it by "drink-money." No instruction or religious teaching was known there. It is related that the first clergyman, the Rev. Dr. Rogers, who was admitted there to preach, obtained entrance with the greatest difficulty. There was supposed to be danger of a riot and a combined escape of the prisoners. He was, however, finally admitted to a platform at the top of steps leading to the prison-yard, where a man stood with a cannon and a lighted match during the preaching of the first sermon in that prison.

Mr. Edward Livingston, the great penal reformer of this country, mentions, in 1822, that from fifteen hundred to two thousand persons of both sexes were committed to prison in each year in New York City, all being presumed to be innocent, and the large proportion really so, and were forced into association with old criminals, eating, drinking, and sleeping in the same rooms with them; then, after having learned the lesson of crime, they are turned out to practice it.

"The innocent stranger, unable to find security, is joint tenant to the same chamber with three-times-convicted convicts; vagabonds sunk in vice and brutified by intoxication, perpetrators of every infamous crime, and even with the murderers taken in the fact."

"Women of innocence and virtue are sometimes forced, by this unhallowed administration of justice, into an association with all that is disgusting in female vice, with vulgarity and intemperance."

With regard to Western and Southern prisoners, the French commissioners report that in 1832 they found in the Cincinnati prison one-half the prisoners loaded with irons, and the rest plunged into infected dungeons.

In the prison of New Orleans they found men together with hogs, in the midst of all odors and nuisances.

A natural effect of these wretched and overcrowded prisons was that they became schools of crime. Here were learned the arts of making false keys, of counterfeiting coin and bank-paper; here youth received their first lessons in petty thieveries and the practice of picking pockets; here, also, extensive combinations for crime were made among the prisoners.

As a natural result, too, the proportion of recommitments was enormously large. In the New York Penitentiary they reached the proportion of 50 out of 100; in the New York City State-prison, 25 out of 100 convicts; in the Philadelphia Penitentiary in 1817, and in the Massachusetts Penitentiary, there were 33 in 100; in the Charlestown Prison, Massachusetts, there were 30 out of 100; in the Maryland prison, the recommitments are given about 14 in 100; in the Walnut-street Prison, Philadelphia, $16\frac{1}{6}$; in the Connecticut Prison, 25; in the Boston Jail, $16\frac{1}{6}$. The present proportion is given as 10 per cent. in the Pennsylvania prisons; 13.44 in those of Massachusetts; in Wisconsin, $5\frac{1}{10}$; in Ohio, $6\frac{1}{3}$; and in New Hampshire, 5 per cent.

All these figures, however, are to be received with hesitation, on account of the loose way in which statistics are made up in our prisons.

Another frightful effect of these overcrowded prisons was their extreme mortality. The death rate of the old State-prison in New York City from 1805 to 1823 reached 60 in 1000; in the Richmond Prison, Virginia, it was 70; and in the Philadelphia Old County Prison it attained the extreme point in one year of 130, and in six years it averaged 60. When it is remembered that during the last forty-two years the death rate in the Philadelphia prisons has been only $17\frac{65}{100}$, and in Massachusetts, during four years, $19\frac{35}{100}$, while Auburn has even attained (1874) 13, and the Alleghany County Prison $2\frac{1}{2}$ per cent. to 1000, we can judge of the sanitary progress made during the last one hundred years.

IMPRISONMENT OF DEBTORS.

One of the frightful abuses of the past was the mode of imprisonment and treatment of debtors. It is not, necessarily, an evidence of low degree of progress, that persons who have incurred a money obligation, and have been unable or unwilling to discharge it, should be by legal enactment punished; still, experience has shown that imprisonment of debtors does not in itself tend to make the community more honest, and seldom aids the creditor in recovering his debt. It is a great hardship, moreover, to persons who have been unfortunate in business through no fault of their own; and as it was executed in this country, it degraded the debtor to a level with the criminal and pauper. Even as late as 1829, it was estimated that there were as many as 3000 of these unfortunate persons confined in the prisons of Massachusetts; 10,000 in New York; 7000 in Pennsylvania; 3000 in Maryland, and a like proportion in other States. In the Philadelphia prisons of that year, there were imprisoned for debts of less than one dollar 32 persons; and in thirty prisons of the State, 595 persons were imprisoned for debts of between one and five dollars. Many of these were honest debtors, who had been unable to pay solely through misfortune. The proportion of debtors to other prisoners was as 5 to 1.

The Report of the Boston Prison Discipline Society, page 388, says: "We have known of a respectable mechanic imprisoned for a debt of five dollars, contracted by his family at a grocer's while he was very ill; he was sent to jail, and he was not only without a shilling, but his family was without bread, because he was not able to work." The keeper of the debtors' department of the Philadelphia Prison reported, in 1828, 1085 debtors imprisoned; their debts amounting to $25,409, their expense to the community $362,076; the amount of the debt recovered in jail was $295. In 1831, the *Gazette* of that city reported forty debtors imprisoned for debts amounting to twenty-three dollars and forty cents. One man was confined thirty days for a debt of seventy-two cents; another, two days for two cents; another, thirty-two days for two cents; seven were confined one hundred and seventy-two days for two dollars and eighty-four cents, and the only debt recovered was one of twenty-five cents. During fifteen months, five hundred and eighty-four persons were confined for debts of less than five dollars. In the Arch-street Prison, one hundred debtors per month were received. No attendants were provided for the sick, no medicines, no additional nourishment; none of the prisoners received bedding or a supply of clothing. The poorest class slept on the floor. A bed, says the same report quoted above, is seldom seen in this prison. No provision is made by law for either sex, though some 4500 debtors are sentenced here annually. It is a common receptacle for all untried prisoners. Highway robbers, murderers, burglars, vagrants, together with those arrested for most petty offenses, are here confined with debtors.

In New Jersey, food, bedding, and fuel were provided for criminals, but "for debtors, only walls, bars, and bolts." Their prisons were fearfully filthy and neglected. Many of these debts were what were called "rum debts;" that is, they had been incurred for alcoholic liquors with those who had tempted them to drink, and had perhaps ruined their families.

In all the States, these unfortunate persons were thrust into the same prisons with the most abandoned offenders against society. The voice of humanity was raised incessantly against these abuses, and by none more than by the members of the Prison Discipline Societies of the country. Imprisonment for debt was gradually abolished throughout the country.

In New York State, it was abolished in 1831, except in certain cases where fraud was supposed, or in cases of torts, or wrongs to the public interest. This arrest was permitted where the debtor had been a non-resident, or where his debts were for moneys collected as a public officer, or in any professional employment, or in a fiduciary capacity; also if the debtor seemed about to remove his property, with intent to defraud. He could avoid his imprisonment by paying his debt; by giving security that the debt should be paid within sixty days; by giving an inventory of his property, and making an assignment of it for the payment of his debts; or by giving a bond that he would not remove his property or defraud his creditors. If imprisoned, he could petition the judge for an assignment of his property, and thus secure the benefit of the act. No arrest was allowed for debts under fifty dollars. The same principles in the treatment of debtors were adopted in the New York Code of 1849. Arrest was forbidden in civil cases, except in actions for injury to person or character, etc.; or where personal property was concealed or kept out of the reach of the sheriff; and also where the defendant was guilty of fraud in contracting the debt, or avoiding the payment of it, or in concealing the property. Females were exempted from arrest, except in an action for willful injury to person or character. The law was still further amended in 1875, with the intent to embrace cases of embezzlement by public officials, and where they seemed about to remove property from the State, or were concealing property which they had illegally acquired. In other respects the principles of the law of 1831 were re-affirmed; and these are substantially the features of the laws against debtors throughout the Union. The present law in regard to imprisonment for debt in Massachusetts dates from 1857.

Any person can be arrested upon "mesne" processes or execution, upon a claim of not less than twenty dollars, exclusive of costs, and committed to jail, unless the debtor gives bail, or pays the debt. The writ or execution must have affidavit of plaintiff or his attorney attached, signed by a commissioner, setting forth, in case of an original writ, that the debtor is about to leave the State, and, in case of execution, that the debtor has property he does not intend to apply toward payment of the debt. The commissioner will always grant the affidavit on payment of one dollar, and either plaintiff or attorney signing it; the debtor is then arrested, and he must go to jail or give bail. If he gives bail, which is for thirty days, he must take the "poor debtor's oath," or the bail is liable. He can cite the plaintiff or attorney if he has money, and if he has not, he must go to jail. If he does cite, he can have a hearing within twenty-four hours. It will be observed that the presumption or suspicion of fraud is the ground for action against the person of the debtor. No innocent debtor can remain, under this law, long in jail.

In Kentucky, imprisonment for debt was abolished in 1821; in Ohio, in 1828; in Maryland, in 1830, for debts under thirty dollars; in Connecticut, in 1837. In Alabama, in 1848, arrest was permitted, but no imprisonment, except on conditions similar to those of New York. In Louisiana, it was abolished in 1840; in Missouri, in 1845. In fact, the law in all the States seemed substantially the same: that imprisonment is permitted where fraud is reasonably suspected, or in cases of torts.

Under United States law, this punishment was finally abolished in 1839, or made to conform to State laws. In 1840, the provision against non-resident debtors was struck out.

SEVERITY OF PENALTIES.

One of the barbarities of the past was the extreme severity of the penalties. Progress in humanity is not necessarily shown by abolishing the death penalty, but this should be reserved alone for the extreme offense of murder in the first degree.

In Massachusetts, under the early legislation succeeding the Declaration of Independence, ten different crimes were punished by death—among them being rape and burglary. Fornication was punished with fine, and if this was not paid in twenty-four hours, the offender was punished with ten stripes of the whip. Blasphemy was punished with the pillory and stripes, even till the year 1829. Persons recommitted to prison were branded on the arm, at the end of their imprisonment, with the words "Massachusetts State-prison."

In Rhode Island and Connecticut, the death penalty was also inflicted for ten different crimes. In Rhode Island, the sentence for forgery was exposure in the pillory, a piece of the offender's ear to be cut off, and branding with the letter C.

In Delaware, the penalty for pretended magical arts was twenty-one stripes. In Pennsylvania, in 1718, twelve crimes received the death penalty, and several others on the second conviction. These, with two or three others, remained capital offenses till after the Revolution. In 1776 twenty crimes were liable to the death penalty; among them, high and petit treason, murder, robbery, burglary, rape, sodomy, malicious maiming, manslaughter by stabbing, witchcraft, arson, and the second conviction for any crime except larceny; and besides these, the counterfeiting or passing of counterfeit money, whether bills of credit, gold or silver.

In Virginia and Kentucky, twenty-seven offenses were punished by death or maiming; among them perjury, the destroying or concealing of a will, the obtaining of money or goods on false pretenses, horse-stealing, the stealing of any record or writ of court, and the breaking out of jail where the offender was imprisoned for crimes punishable with death. The "benefit of clergy" was denied to certain criminals; as, for instance, all principals in murder, burglary, or arson, to all those convicted of a willful burglary of a court-house or public institution; to those sentenced for stealing goods from a church, for robbing on the highway or in a dwelling-house, and for *horse-stealing.* In Indiana, even in 1807, horse-stealing, treason, murder, and arson were punished with death. Burglary, robbery, larceny, hog-stealing, the striking of parent or master, received the penalty of whipping.

In New York, in 1712, a negro convicted of being engaged in the negro plot was burned in that city; another was broken upon the wheel; and another hanged alive. Negroes were sometimes burned with green wood, to prolong their agony; at other times they were hanged in iron frames, to die of starvation, their bodies being devoured by birds of prey. In 1733 several negroes were burned in that city. In 1741 an instance of this punishment is recorded. Even in 1822 the degrading punishment of the tread-mill still continued in this State.

For a long period, one of the well-known sights at the head of Broad Street were the public whipping-post, pillory, and stocks. In almost every village of this country, the stocks, whipping-post, and pillory were to be seen.

Whipping with the "cat," burning, branding, and cropping of ears were common punishments. The objection to this description of penalties is, it should be remembered, not that they give pain, but that they tend to degrade and brutalize, not merely the criminal, but the community who witness them, and thus form a soil, as it were, on which the same kind of offenses will grow luxuriantly.

Thus the experience of all civilized countries is that the punishment of the "cat" for brutal offenses against women tends to keep up the class of brutalities. Continental countries and the United States are mainly free from the horrible brutalities inflicted in England by ignorant husbands on wives; it is these countries which have mainly abolished corporal punishments.

COUNTY PRISONS.

The most crying abuse during our colonial history, and in this first century of the nation's growth, has been the condition of the county prisons. In Boston the Leverett-street Jail, even in 1835, is described as a horrible den of filth and iniquity. The old and young were mingled here; the idle and industrious; the hardened convicts and persons arrested merely on suspicion, or as witnesses. There was no ventilation in the prison and no cleanliness; the prisoners were under no proper discipline, and moral or religious instruction was unknown.

In Providence, Rhode Island, the prison is described as having broken windows stuffed with rags; the wainscoting dark and filthy, with the doors open between the different cells, so that there was free communication between the prisoners. Gambling prevailed, and liquors were bought and sold in the jail.

In Middlebury, Vermont, the jail contained one dungeon ten feet by twelve in dimensions, without window or orifice, except the stove-pipe hole, where the old and young, those sentenced and those arrested, were confined for months.

In Ohio, in 1840, says the secretary of the Prison Discipline Society, "I have seen in the prison of the principal town a respectable stranger, a debtor, confined in the same cell with an insane black woman." He speaks even of a prisoner's feet being frozen by the want of proper warmth in the jail. The Hamilton County Jail he describes as having no window or fire-place in the cells, light, heat, and air entering by the grated doors. There were no beds in the jail, and slops were emptied only once a week. The building was exceedingly unhealthy and filled with vermin. No religious instruction was known there.

In Hartford, Connecticut, in 1838, the county jail is said to have contained from six to ten persons in each cell. Drink was freely supplied to the prisoners, and a tavern communicated with the prison. The New Haven County Jail was one of similar character. The prisoners had free access to liquor, and both jails became schools of vice where many combinations of crime were formed. Very few of the county jails of this country were superior to these.

REFORM OF THE PRISON SYSTEM OF THE UNITED STATES.

The great reforms in the prison systems of the United States began where the abuses were the greatest—in the State of Pennsylvania. In 1786 the first alleviation of the severity of punishment was made through the Society of Friends, and the efforts of the Philadelphia Society for the Alleviating the Miseries of Public Prisons. Three of the former offenses punishable by death were now punished by the forfeiture of the real and personal estate of the offender, and by confinement at hard labor. By the same act all barbarous punishments were abrogated. Under the former system, the convicts of Philadelphia were obliged to perform labor in the public streets under degrading circumstances. These prisoners were called "the wheel-barrow men," and were often exposed to insult and ill-treatment by the mob. This practice was now done away with. In 1788, the Philadelphia Prison Society addressed the Legislature, recommending more private and solitary labor in the prisons. In 1790 all the previous penal laws were repealed, and a revised system adopted, which provided for a better union of punishment and labor. Separate cells were authorized for hardened offenders. Criminals were henceforth to be employed in the jail; the introduction of intoxicating liquors into the prisons was forbidden. Already, ten years previous, in 1780, the law had passed authorizing the erection of the Walnut-street Prison in Philadelphia with the principle of seclusion—a great advance in the prison system, beyond any thing which had been known in Europe or America. Unfortunately this prison was subsequently so much crowded as somewhat to defeat the purposes of the law.

By the reforms of 1790, labor was to become a necessary part of the system of punishment; the sexes among the criminals were to be separated; the untried prisoners and debtors were to be kept in different compartments from those convicted; suitable food and clothing were to be supplied, jail fees abolished, and secular and religious instruction to be provided. The custom of "garnish" was forbidden. In 1794, an act was passed abolishing the punishment of death except for murder in the first degree. In the same year an effort was made to introduce separate confinement into the prisons of the State. In 1795 further provision was made for the classification of prisoners and their employment at hard labor; the punishment of whipping was abolished, and confinement in cell, with bread and water, for not more than fifteen days, substituted.

In 1803, the erection of the Arch-street Prison was ordered, which was finished in 1818; a prison constructed on the improved principles of prison reform.

In 1814 an allowance was made to debtors by law of fourteen cents a day for clothing, bedding, fuel, and food. In 1818, an act was passed authorizing the erection of the Western State Penitentiary, and another, in 1821, authorizing the Eastern State Penitentiary, both on the principle of solitary confinement of convicts. The latter prison was finished in 1829.

The system of solitary confinement, though now generally held by the prison reformers as too severe for the reformation of convicts, was a great advance on the promiscuous herding of prisoners which prevailed before, and was a fitting introduction to the reforms of the present day. In other States, similar reforms were carried out; in New Hampshire, the old and bloody code of 1791 was improved in 1812, and revised in 1829; by this, burglary, robbery, rape, and arson, which had been punished by death, were now punished by solitary confinement for not more than six months, and hard labor for life. The punishment of death except for murder was finally abolished in 1837.

In New York, in 1796, capital punishment was abolished for fourteen offenses, and only retained for treason and homicide. Whipping for minor crimes was forbidden. The same Legislature forbade the use of the lash in the prisons; but, unfortunately, in 1819, this punishment, so easily abused, was re-authorized in our State-prisons. No conviction in that State (except of treason) can work forfeiture of goods, chattels, or lands. As far back as in 1822, the punishment of the tread-mill had been given up in New York State as barbarous.

In 1847, a law was passed attempting to reform county prisons. Sufficient room was required to keep the witnesses from criminals separate; and an entire separation was endeavored to be effected between those arrested and those convicted, and between males and females. Hard labor was also prescribed upon the public works for the constant offenders. Each keeper was required to have a Bible in every cell. No whipping of female prisoners was permitted. In 1851, an act passed the Pennsylvania Legislature designed to effect sanitary reform in the construction of county prisons. In Connecticut, in 1790, the punishment of death for burglary, arson, horse-stealing, rape, and forgery was replaced by confinement in Newgate. Cropping and branding of criminals were abolished. In Rhode Island, in 1838, a mild code, like that of Pennsylvania, was introduced in place of a cruel one.

In Massachusetts, the first improved penitentiary of the country was probably erected—that at Charlestown—in 1805.

In nearly all the modern prisons of our different States the reforms of combined labor in the day, and separation in the cell at night, have been introduced. Strict classification so far as possible is the rule. The abuses of the old prisons have passed away; discipline, sobriety, industry, and cleanliness prevail. The former brutalizing punishments within the prison have been mostly done away with. The penalties now inflicted by the keepers are solitary confinement in a dark cell, bread and water, the withholding of letters, and the loss of commutation. In many of the States the lash is no longer employed, and in all, except Kentucky, the power of punishment by under-officials is taken away.

In the New York prisons alone certain severe punishments are still permitted. In very many of the States the greatest reform of the modern prison system has been introduced—that of "the commutation" of sentences; that is, the convict, by good conduct and industry while in the prison, can reduce the term of his sentence by a specified amount, and can earn wages to support himself or his family after he is discharged. In 1867, in nine States of the Union the convict could earn five days per month by good conduct. In New York he could diminish his sentence from seven and a half to ten days per month; so that if the prisoner were sentenced for ten years he could shorten his sentence by two years and one month; if for twenty years, by five years and five months. All the States testify to the remarkably good results of this reform.

In Connecticut, more than 80 per cent. of the prisoners had a perfect record of conduct for the year. In Michigan, for 1864, more than 90 per cent. presented such a record. In all except Maine the commutation can be forfeited by bad conduct. In Ohio, Wisconsin, or Illinois, the gaining of a certain number of marks by the convict in his prison will enable him to recover his rights of citizenship.

As an instance of the highest point which our prison system has reached, the Ohio Penitentiary of Columbus may be taken. In this prison the convict may, by good behavior and diligence, diminish his sentence by a period of five days per month, and he is permitted to receive an allowance not exceeding one-tenth of his earnings. Should he violate the rules, he may lose not only all the time he has gained in the month and his earnings, but also a portion gained in previous months. If his labor is diminished by sickness or other causes beyond his control, two and a half days commutation are allowed him in each month. The names, penalties, and commutations of the prisoners are read publicly in the prison. At the end of his time of sentence, if he has gained his full commutation, the convict is restored by the governor of the State to his rights of citizenship. No cruel or degrading punishments are employed in this prison; even prison clothing is done away with as degrading. Flannel under-clothing is supplied, and good corn-husk mattresses are provided in each cell. The library of the prison is much used; the Sabbath-school and prayer-meeting are constantly attended; while there are two hundred well-conducted members of the prison church. A chapel is now in process of building.

Without having accurate returns as yet of the number reformed, it is believed that in no prison in the United States are there so few recommitments. Financially, it is by far the most successful one. The convicts on their discharge have received the following amounts as wages: in 1868, $1872; in 1869, $2890; in 1871, $5598; in 1873, $6271. Besides earning this extra money for the support of their families, the convicts have been able to pay not only all the current expenses of the prison, but the cost of the permanent improvements, and to turn in a large sum of money to the treasury of the State. For instance, from 1869 to 1873 the prison paid all its own expenses; paid for permanent improvements $58,145, and turned into the State treasury $38,818. In 1873, the ordinary expenses were $152,163, while the receipts from the labor of the convicts were $174,450.

RELIGIOUS INSTRUCTION.

In the prisons of the country immediately after the Revolution there was no religious instruction. As we have seen, the first pastor who preached in the Philadelphia Penitentiary had to be supported with a cannon, with a lighted match at the side. Even fifty years since there was no regular chaplain in any State-prison of the United States, and very little religious instruction was given. In 1828, more provision was made for religious teaching in the prisons of New England and the Middle States. In 1833, every prison was supplied with Bibles, and a Sabbath-school was established in ten of the whole number, while fifteen hundred convicts received religious instruction. In 1867, there were regular chaplains in ten State-prisons, and stated preaching in five others. Ten also enjoyed the benefit of Sabbath-schools, wherein about two thousand convicts were taught by two hundred teachers. In some of the prisons there was daily religious service.

SECULAR TEACHING.

In New York, schools were first established in the State-prisons in 1822; Sunday-schools were opened in the Auburn Prison in 1826. In 1829, an act was passed by the New York Legislature ordering convicts to be taught. In 1841, there was secular teaching in several of our State-prisons. In 1847, the law was passed in New York to provide teachers for all the State-prisons; other States followed this enlightened example. In 1848, a society was formed in the Massachusetts State-prison by the convicts themselves for mutual improvement and debate.

LIBRARIES.

The first notice we have of these is in 1802, in the regulation of the Kentucky State-prison in regard to donations of books. One of the first prison libraries was formed in Sing Sing in 1840. In 1867, there were libraries in most of the State-prisons, one in Ohio containing 3000 volumes, another in Sing Sing with 4000. Thirteen prison libraries contained in that year 20,413 volumes. A fixed sum was appropriated by the Legislatures of many States for the purchase of prison libraries.

THE TREATMENT OF CRIMINAL AND UNFORTUNATE CHILDREN.

Nothing is more characteristic of the barbarous period of society than its utter neglect of children; while, on the other hand, the highest attainment of social wisdom and the realization of Christianity are shown in the most watchful care for the young, and especially for the children of the unfortunate and the criminal. The culture of the young guards the future of society, and the prevention of misery and crime among children is a duty at once of economy and humanity.

In no way can society save the vast losses it now sustains through pauperism and criminal offenses so well as by the care and education of the children of the most destitute classes. The extent and wisdom of this care are the measure of the civilization of a people. The records of our early criminal administration show that children who had committed offenses against the law were treated precisely like any other criminals; and what that treatment was we have sufficiently indicated in the description of the wretched prisons in Philadelphia, New York, and Boston during the first fifty years of our existence as a nation. Old and young, criminals and accused, witnesses and hardened offenders, persons of all ages and both sexes, were often crowded together in the day, and confined so as to communicate with one another at night. The young took lessons in crime, and the prisons became a nursery of criminals. A child once condemned to one of these schools of vice came forth, if confined a sufficient time, a skilled and hardened young offender. The prison was never under this system a place of reform. The offenses of children became a crying evil. New convicts were being constantly trained. And this young country, with all its boundless possibilities for the laboring classes, became cursed with some of the worst evils of old communities, in the increase of the criminal classes among the young.

Edward Livingston, in his celebrated essay on *A Code of Criminal Reform*, speaks of an infant of nine years of age being tried and executed for murder. And in another passage he describes a boy of eleven in the Philadelphia Arch-street Prison awaiting trial for felony who had been a year in a New Jersey prison for horse-stealing, and during this period the only lessons he received were the histories related by his fellow-convicts of their exploits. A boy is also mentioned who was first committed to a New York prison at ten years of age, and, under various sentences, was twenty-eight years a convict.

Livingston also gives this testimony to the character of previous legislation in regard to the young. "The provisions of law have heretofore pronounced the same punishment against the first offense of a child that they awarded to the veteran in guilt. The seducer to crime and the artless victim of his corruption were confounded in the same penalty; and that penalty, until lately, was here, and in the land from whence we derived our jurisprudence still is, death. We have substituted imprisonment. * * * For the minor offenses affecting property indictments against children are frequent; and humanity is equally shocked whether they are convicted, or, by the lenity of the jury, discharged to complete their education of infamy" (*A Code of Criminal Reform*, p. 60). In one of his annual messages, Mayor Colden, of New York, reports that he had sentenced youth between twelve and sixteen years several times to the penitentiary, from which they invariably came out worse than they entered. Innumerable facts of this kind can be gathered in the early reports of the prison associations of New York, Boston, and Philadelphia. The first institution founded in the country for youth charged with crime was the New York House of Refuge, in 1824. Its influence, especially in its earlier years, when but few children were inmates, was remarkably reformatory, and great numbers of youth were saved then, and many others have been since, from lives of crime, by its excellent teachings and the effect of regular industry. This reformatory was soon followed by others in various parts of the country.

How immensely these useful institutions have increased may be gathered from the following statistics: There were, in 1874, in twenty States and one Territory, thirty-four of these reformatories for youthful criminals; they owned in the aggregate 6153 acres of land; the total estimated value of buildings and lands, with the personal property, was $7,826,480; the average number of inmates was 8924, and the whole number received since their opening was 91,402, of whom 77,678 were boys and 13,724 girls; the whole number of persons engaged in this work was 771, and the total annual cost for maintenance was $1,358,885, or $152 for each inmate. Three-fourths of the inmates, or nearly seventy thousand, are reported as permanently reformed. These figures, however are to be received with great caution, as there is no accurate tabulating of the results; and in a country like this, the fortunes of boys in after-life can not be easily traced out.

These useful institutions are an immense advance on the prisons which preceded them. The youth is no longer confined in company with mature criminals; the young alone are placed in the reformatory; the sexes also are separated; and at night, as a general practice, there is but one child in each cell, or, if in a large dormitory, the children are carefully watched, to prevent evil communications. They are all taught useful trades, and have regular day instruction in schools, besides religious teaching on the Sunday. After their term of sentence has expired, or previously, if their good conduct permit, they are indentured with worthy and respectable farmers and mechanics. Great numbers are, no doubt, thus saved to society. Still there is a radical defect in the constitution of most of the houses of refuge and reformatories throughout the country. They are managed, with the exception of the Ohio State Reform School and a few others, on the "congregated system," and whatever influence is exerted is on the children *en masse* rather than individually. There is too much machinery, and too little personal influence. No criminal child can be thoroughly reformed without a direct and personal influence. These large reformatories should be broken up, their land and buildings, if possible, sold, and farms purchased where small groups of children could be placed in separate cottages, under individual teachers or superintendents. Then each child may be reached by personal example, with a much greater probability of thorough reform. The present system of the houses of refuge in the United States can not be regarded as the highest point to which reform among youthful criminals is able to reach in this country; and viewed as an indication of humanitarian progress, the prevention of misery and crime among children is more important even than their reform.

PREVENTION OF CHILDREN'S CRIMES.

Owing to the enormous emigration of destitute laboring people from Europe to the United States, New York, the port of entry, became crowded with masses of exceedingly poor, ignorant people. As the children of these persons grew up, without care or instruction, and often without homes, they formed a singularly miserable and dangerous element in the New York community. Hundreds and thousands were known to be roving about the streets of the city without any lawful occupation, and without any settled home. They were growing up, naturally, as vagrants, beggars, petty thieves, and prostitutes; the prisons became full of them; the House of Refuge was crowded, and the whole public began to feel the dangers which might arise from these miserable youths, and to consider what could be done for their elevation and improvement. The first distinct note of alarm was sounded in 1848, by Captain Matsell, then Chief of Police, in a public report, wherein it was stated that over ten thousand of these wretched and half-criminal children were wandering vagrant through the streets of New York. This report was accompanied, or followed, by a number of preventive or reformatory movements in various parts of the city, among which should be noted especially the foundation of the two missions in the Five Points (1850 and 1852) and the forming of the Juvenile Asylum in 1851; but more important than any or all of these was the foundation, in 1853, of one of the most remarkable associations for the prevention of children's crime and misery that have been known in modern times—the Children's Aid Society of New York.

So wide-spread, however, were the crime and misfortune among children, that for several years but little effect was produced upon them by the labors of this association. Thus, even in 1859, the number of female vagrants committed to prison was 5778, and in 1860, 5880; and even in 1863, 1133 young girls were committed for thieving or petit larceny; in 1863, 403 little girls under fifteen were committed for various offenses. Among boys, in 1859, 2829 were committed for vagrancy, and 2626 for petit larceny. In 1853, the Children's Aid Society began its labors, with the formation of one industrial school, and the sending-out to homes in the country of 207 boys and girls, the expenses for this first year being $4191. In 1854, the first Newsboys' Lodging-house was founded, at an expense of about $700. This association has now been in existence twenty-three years. The plan and methods of the society were peculiar: its great object was to save the vagrant, homeless, and semi-criminal children of the city by drawing them into places of instruction and shelter, and then by transferring them to carefully selected homes in the rural districts. It was seen that the condition of this country was peculiar, in an economical point of view, there being an almost unlimited demand here for children's labor, and no necessity existed for placing homeless and vagrant children in asylums or institutions. The best of all institutions for a poor child is the farmer's home. Here he would be elevated and reformed sooner than any where else, and with very little expense to the community.

The effort of the society was, accordingly, to draw the poor and vagrant children of the city into industrial schools or lodging-houses, to instruct and train them there for a brief period, and then to forward those who were willing to go, or who were without friends or parents, to places in the country.

The "industrial schools" were also designed for that large class of children who, though having friends and home, are too poor and ragged to attend the public schools, and are obliged to be on the streets a part of the day engaged in street occupations. To these children a simple meal is given; clothing and shoes are distributed to the needy; and industrial branches taught, besides the common-school branches. The "lodging-houses" were contrived with special reference to the wants of the street children. Each child paid a certain small sum for his maintenance, and received in return simple and substantial meals, a comfortable bed, a pleasant play-room, means of cleanliness with hot and cold water, a place to deposit his savings and to store his little property, while the only obligations in return were neatness and good order, and obedience to the rules of the house. A night-school was opened in each lodging-house to teach common-school branches, and simple religious teaching was given on the Sunday evening.

The growth and success of this association have been truly remarkable. In 1876, the society counts twenty-one day industrial schools and thirteen night-schools as founded by it, where over ten thousand children annually are partly fed, clothed, and instructed. It had founded six lodging-houses for boys and one for girls, where in the course of the year some 13,000 different homeless children were sheltered; the average each night being about 600. A single lodging-house, the Newsboys', has contained, since it was founded, over 100,000 different boys. The society sent forth to country homes over 3000 children during 1875, and in all the twenty-three years it had provided over 30,000 homeless children with homes and work in the country. Besides these works of education and charity, it had supported a Sea-side Summer Home, where some 2000 children during the summer had enjoyed a week of recreation and country air. Several hundred sick children had also been tended and supplied with food and medicine through its benevolent agency. The total outlay, during twenty-three years, for these various benevolent enterprises has reached the large sum of $1,877,569, and the receipts during 1874 alone amounted to $230,604. A single one of its lodging-houses had been erected at a cost of $200,000.

The effect upon the increase of crime in New York City of these benevolent labors for children has been remarkable.

The commitments of females for "vagrancy," a term which includes many of the peculiar offenses of girls and women, have fallen from 5880 in 1860 to 548 in 1871—the latest year to whose reports we have access, as no public reports are now issued by the Commissioners of Charities and Correction. If this class of offenders had increased with the population, the number would have been, in 1871, over 6700.

The arrests of female vagrants fell from 2161 in 1861 to 914 in 1871. The commitments of young girls for petty thieving fell from 1133 in 1860 to 572 in 1871; "juvenile delinquency," from 240 females in 1860 to 59 in 1870: the commitments of female young children from 403 in 1863 to 212 in 1871. Among males, the commitments for vagrancy diminished from 2829 in 1859 to 934 in 1871: the natural increase would have been 3225; for petty larceny the decrease is from 2626 in 1859 to 1978 in 1871: by natural increase, the number would have been 2861. The classification of commitments of lads under fifteen years only begins in 1864; but the decrease is from 1965 in that year to 1017 in 1871. The arrests of pickpockets have diminished from 466 in 1861 to 313 in 1871. This comparison might be followed farther, but enough has been shown to prove the distinct effect produced upon the growth of juvenile crime by the labors of the Children's Aid Society and similar organizations.

When it is remembered that during the period covered by its operations there have been the disasters of two business panics and a gigantic civil war, with all the demoralization naturally arising from them, besides an immense influx into New York of poor foreign laboring people, the profound influence of such preventive and educational labors upon the criminal classes may be partially estimated. In fact, these labors may be considered as one of the historical landmarks to indicate the gradual but sure elevation of the spirit of humanity among our people since our century opened.

While even fifty years since, according to Livingston, the practice of this and all civilized nations was to punish the criminal or vagrant children, as the old offender and tramp were punished, by confining them, without moral influence, among older convicts and rogues, and punishing them with extreme severity, at the same time society permitting the children of the street to grow up half-starved and neglected, to inevitably become criminals; now not only does each State open reformatories for youthful law-breakers, but a large part of the best of the community set themselves to work to prevent crime and misery among children. The Children's Aid Society illustrates the higher Christian estimate of the duties of society: that the fortunate classes can and ought to prevent the growth of the pauper and criminal classes, and that it is the wisest economy, as well as the highest humanity, to educate and rescue the outcast children and youth of large cities.

Another remarkable instance of the working of the spirit of humanity among our intelligent classes is the formation of committees of leading ladies and gentlemen throughout this State to inspect and improve public charities. These "State Charities Aid" associations have already, in New York State, thrown a new spirit of kindness and order and improvement into those worst of all institutions in modern days, county almshouses. The county jails, however, throughout the Union unfortunately remain yet untouched by the spirit of the age, and are as bad as they were at the time our independence was declared. Those useful organizations also, State Boards of Charities, have in our most populous States brought about much-needed reforms. In New York State they have gradually succeeded in transferring all the pauper children in alms-houses to orphan asylums or to private families. In several States they have removed the pauper lunatics, the blind, the deaf and dumb, and other unfortunates, from the poor-houses each to their appropriate asylums. This grand reform is one of the most encouraging evidences of human progress which the country offers.

TREATMENT OF LUNATICS.

One of the incomprehensible things to the student of humanity, and its progress in the spirit of brotherly kindness, is the treatment, in all ages and countries, of those unhappy persons who are bereft of reason. These unfortunate beings could not usually suffer more from society if they had committed the greatest crimes. The history of this nation is no exception to this inhuman and stupid practice of dealing with lunatics. Fifty years since it was customary to confine these sufferers in jails, a custom which still prevails in many parts of this country. In 1826, a young clergyman, rendered insane by overwork, was found in the Bridewell Prison of New York, herded with ruffians and murderers. At that time there were in the prisons of Massachusetts thirty lunatics. Of one who had been in his cell nine years, the report of the Boston Prison Association says: "He had a wreath of rags around his body, and another around his neck. This was all his clothing. He had no bed, chair, or bench; a heap of filthy straw, like the nest of swine, was in the corner. He had built a bird's-nest of mud in the iron grate of his den." Others were confined with thieves and murderers. Of one prison the report says: "It was difficult after the door was open, to see them [the lunatics] distinctly. The ventilation was so incomplete that more than one person, on entering, vomited. The old straw and filthy garments made their insanity more hopeless."

In the Boston House of Correction, it is said, were ten insane persons. Two, nearly seventy years of age, were in one cell. The woman had been there *twenty-one years*. She lay on a heap of straw under a broken window. "The snow, in a severe storm, was beating through the windows, and lay upon the straw round her withered body, partly covered by a few filthy and tattered garments." The man had been there six years, and lay in a similar condition. Another is described who had never left his cell but twice in eight years, the door of which was not opened for eighteen months, his food being furnished by a small orifice in the door. There was no fire, and the poor creature did not look like a human being.

In 1834, the message of the Governor of New Hampshire stated that in 141 towns of the State there were 189 lunatics, of whom 76 were kept in prison, 25 in private houses, and 34 in alms-houses. Seven were reported as kept in cells or cages, and six in irons. "Many of these forsaken beings, during the dreadful period of dungeon life, had been systematically subject to almost every form of privation and suffering." It not unfrequently happened that in the cold and exposed cells where they were confined, these unfortunate creatures were frozen. The fate of one who was thus treated in the New York prison in 1826, and died from cold and nakedness, aroused a profound feeling among the humane. In a New Hampshire prison an insane woman was so housed that her feet froze, and they had to be amputated, and she was restored thus to her friends. Another is described as imprisoned so long in a low cell that he lost the use of his legs, and was obliged to walk on his feet and hands; still another, who had been in easy circumstances, was now "fastened in a kennel like a wild beast." It was estimated that, in 1833, there were 2400 lunatics thus confined in jails and prisons in the United States. They were, however, no worse off than the crazed in the county poor-houses, or sometimes those under the care of private families. Within thirty years, under the writer's knowledge, in a Connecticut town, was a lunatic woman who lived habitually in a hole in the ground under a hay-stack, and was fed as an animal would be fed.

The deepest feeling was aroused among the humane by these enormities and sufferings, and at length asylums for the insane were opened in various States. The first of these was, undoubtedly, the one at Williamsburg, Virginia, in 1773. The present Bloomingdale Asylum, New York, dates its care of the insane from the close of the last century, or about 1797. All of these, so far as we have record, began their management under the modern reform, or the "non-restraint" system, never having employed chains and cells, and blows and torture, as had so often been done in Europe; yet none of them now carry out the non-restraint method so far as do the English asylums.

These asylums were an unmingled blessing to the unfortunates taken from the prisons. The report of the Worcester Asylum (1834) says: "Many who, in their paroxysms, used formerly to lacerate and wound their own bodies to a degree that threatened life itself, now habitually exercise an ordinary degree of prudence in avoiding the common causes of annoyance or accident. Not less than one hundred of those brought to the hospital seemed to regard human beings as enemies, and their first impulse was to assail them with open or disguised force. Now, there are not more than twelve who offer violence. Of forty persons who formerly divested themselves of clothing, even in the most inclement season of the year, only eight do it now......." "The wailings of the desponding and the ravings of the frantic are dispelled. The wide-circling and heart-sickening variety of horrors exhibited by the inmates when first brought together have been greatly reduced in extent and mitigated in quality."

Great as was the reform in removing these diseased creatures from the prison to the hospital, there still remained a fearful crowd of unfortunates in the county poor-houses. These institutions have usually no facilities for the proper treatment of lunatics. They must be imprisoned with the other inmates, old and young, criminal and innocent, or be confined in dungeons. The officials are ignorant of the only proper method of dealing with the malady, and are often hard and cruel in their habits toward the paupers; and if they chance to be humane, they have no means, or a proper number of assistants, to manage these persons suitably. They can not watch and regulate the habits of the insane (which are often very disgusting), nor keep their bodies clean, nor furnish the simple comforts which at once mitigate the violence of the disease, or in any way minister to the mind as well as the body. They neglect all this, and usually are almost forced to treat the crazed as if he were a dangerous and filthy brute. The consequence is that the acme of human suffering and of horrors is reached in those relics of barbarism—the lunatic wards of the county poor-houses.

There, are innocent but diseased human beings treated worse than the most abandoned criminals. They are whipped, scourged, chained, ironed, fastened in cages, and shut in close cells, left for years in their filth, naked, hungry, exposed to bitter cold, taunted and jeered at by villainous ruffians, disregarded in their every feeling and wish, half fed, their feet often frozen, wallowing in dirt and straw, surrounded by a pandemonium of paupers and criminals. If women, it often happens that they are suffered to be tempted and ruined by the ruffians of the poor-house, and a hideous progeny begins, the offspring of the pauper and the lunatic, of the epileptic and the criminal. It is not strange that in such places the disease only becomes more intense, and there are very few cases of recovery.

Miss Dix's reports in 1844, and Dr. Willard's report in 1865, together with the reports of the State Board of Charity, reveal the horrors of these "dark places of the earth" in New York State. In 1868, the New York State Board of Charity found that out of 1528 insane in the county poor-house, 213 were locked in cells, or chained habitually. Dr. Willard reports that in 1865, in many alms-houses, the insane were never washed, and that their bodies were in an especially filthy and disgusting condition; their clothing was torn and scattered about their cells, and that they often lay naked on straw, which was wet and unchanged for days. The cells had no ventilation, and sometimes no means of access to pure air. In many towns they were kept in dark dungeons or in cages, without shoes or stockings, under intense cold, sleeping on heaps of filthy straw. There was no place for exercise, none for amusement; the diseased mind was left to itself. There was no classification; old and young, virtuous and vicious, male and female, were crowded together. Frequently insane females were employed to take care of the quarters of male paupers or vagabonds, with consequences which might have been expected. Out of the 1345 insane in one year in the county houses, it was estimated that 345 were able, in part or in whole, to support themselves.

We need not add to the evidence as to the condition of the insane in the alms-houses of New York State. The same terrible picture could be drawn of these unhappy beings in all the county houses of the other States. But in New York a great reform has begun. By an act of Legislature (1865), the insane of the county poor-houses were to be transferred to State asylums, and supported there at the expense of the counties. Probably no one legislative measure (except the national act of emancipation) ever diffused within a limited space so much happiness, and lessened so much suffering.

As a landmark, showing the point to which the tide of human feeling and practice in this matter has reached in the United States, we would speak somewhat in detail of the great "Willard Asylum" for the chronic insane poor of New York, at Ovid, on Seneca Lake. Here are gathered a thousand lunatics, taken from the alms-houses of the rural districts of the State, nearly all chronic and incurable cases. The first patient who was brought was a delicate woman, heavily ironed, led by three strong "supervisors." She had been kept in a cell in a state of nudity for some ten years, tearing her clothes from her body, very violent, and disgustingly dirty. The first step in the new treatment was to take off her irons, then to give her a warm bath and clothe her in decent garments; next she was fed in a Christian manner. She had a long, light, warm corridor to walk in, if it was winter, and pleasant grounds in summer. At night she was placed in a comfortable bed, and treated as a mother watches her babe. Soon a little work was given to her. The nervous irritation of the disease was soothed, the mind was somewhat occupied, the body was well cared for. If, after an interval, a paroxysm returned and she would tear her clothes, a leather muff was the only restraint, or a cloth camisole; or, if very violent, she might be fastened to her chair by a strap. When we saw this particular patient, she was a quiet, decent, industrious lunatic, and needed no restraint.

We saw another bright, active young girl in a neat attire, who in the county alms-house had been kept for years in chains, scourged and beaten, having the marks on her body of this treatment. The only thing which ever quieted her there, she confessed, was when "they tied her up by the thumbs and flogged her!" In this asylum she was one of the best patients.

A man was shown us who looked calm and quite rational, who had been ten years in an alms-house, naked and in chains. A Spaniard from Dutchess County was pointed out who had been kept *nineteen years* in chains. Another, from St. Lawrence County, was eight years in a cage, his garments not removed for weeks, fed like a wild beast, flogged, jeered, and gazed at, and finally in such a condition that to his diseased mind it seemed to him "the people threw in lice at me." He was in this confinement many years. Here he was like any other patient. We spoke with another man who had been shut up for fifteen years in an outhouse (in Richmond County) in so narrow a place that he had lost the use of his flexor muscles, in the midst of indescribable filth. Now, though crippled, he could sit at table, and was a quiet, inoffensive lunatic.

Some had lost their toes or feet through the exposure to which they had been subject. Many were marked with blows; and hundreds had been ironed, or chained, or caged before they were brought to this asylum. Several women were pointed out to me who had been *mothers* in the alms-house. We saw but two or three out of the thousand with the restraint even of the "muff," and two or three were fastened to a chair. They all sit at table, and have healthful fare. The bedrooms are clean and well-aired, the corridors warm and pleasant, their dress neat and well kept; they have plays and amusements in their public room, and attend worship on Sunday. Though peculiarly weakened and diseased, they perform considerable industrial work. The disgusting and fearful habits of insanity are to a large degree broken up. So far as such people can do so, they enjoy life, and the pains and evils of their disease are lessened.

The Willard Asylum is one of the milestones of human progress in this country.

There are questions, however, connected

with the congregating so many human beings in one institution and the reserving one asylum for the incurables, as well as the degree to which restraint can be dispensed with, and labor usefully performed by the insane, which we need not here consider. The wonderful advance is from the county poor-house to the State asylum.

In reconsidering the various topics in which we have endeavored to show the steady progress of the American spirit of humanity during the century past, we are struck with one field where the advance has been little or nothing: we mean in the county institutions of the various States for the relief of the unfortunate and the punishment of the criminal. Great reforms, it is true, have begun in some of the States, in the removal of pauper children, and of the insane and idiotic, in alms-houses, to their appropriate State asylums. But, on the whole, taking the country through, the condition of the rural jails and of the county poor-houses is not essentially changed since 1800. The greatest abuses and the worst instances of inhumanity in the country are found in these "institutions."

The explanation of this singular obstruction to humane progress in one field is that, in our rural administration, we have followed the old English system of decentralization in the public care of the poor, unfortunate, and criminal, to an excessive degree. No small rural community, like a county, for instance, can do justice and observe the spirit of humanity in its management of those persons who are thrown on its public charge.

The first condition of reform and of humane treatment in regard to the "defectives," the poor and the offenders against law, is classification. But no county has the means and appliances for classifying public dependents and criminals. No such small division can afford to employ the kind of officials needed, nor can it carry out any method of improvement requiring expense, nor are its places of charity and penalty under much public observation. The consequences are what we have seen, that the county alms-houses and jails become abodes of unspeakable misery and degradation. The advantages of local administration are not to be foregone in many important particulars; but these can be retained, while the greater benefits from larger management of the pauper and criminal subjects may be secured.

The erection of State work-houses, State lunatic and idiotic asylums, State "intermediate or reformatory" prisons, would at once drain from the county houses and jails all the subjects who are now herded together in these places, and who are there degraded or injured. With the erection of these State institutions should be passed strict laws, requiring every pauper child of sound mind and body to be removed from the alms-houses, and placed in private families or orphan asylums, and the transference of the other inmates as far as practicable to their appropriate State institutions. When this is accomplished throughout the Union, a new century of improvement will begin for some of the most unfortunate and neglected members of modern society.

In reviewing the management of the prisons and penitentiaries of the country, we have beheld a marked advance during the century; and an approach, at least in the State of Ohio, to Livingston's great ideal, since realized in the Irish, or Crofton, prison system. Yet it is but justice to say that, on the whole, the progress in this matter in the American Union has not been equal to that of Europe. The great evil here has been the connection of prison management with political and party interests, and the consequent appointment of unworthy and ignorant men to have charge of these difficult places of administration.

The great prison reform of the century, the Crofton system, has scarcely as yet been introduced into a single prison of the country—the State-prison at Columbus, Ohio, being the nearest approach to it. The introduction of "commutation," however, shows a great advance.

One great step in improvement has been made by the formation of a National Prison Association," whereby the methods adopted in different States can be compared and unity of plan can be introduced. Under the influence of the conventions meeting at the call of this association many great reforms will undoubtedly be carried out during the coming century in our prison management.

The barbarities of the past; the imprisonment of debtors with felons; the use of cruel and brutalizing punishments; the herding of young and old, male and female, innocent and guilty, in common prisons, we have mainly abandoned, and we have introduced every where the influences of education, industry, and religion to work upon the characters of the convicts. There remains much, however, to be done in this field.

An immense progress has also been made in the treatment of the insane, the blind, the deaf and dumb, and idiotic. These unfortunate beings, if not belonging to the pauper class, are all now comfortably treated, and often much improved, in their appropriate asylums. A considerable number of the insane (though not so large as might be expected) are cured and restored to society; the idiotic are much advanced in self-control and the use of their faculties; the blind, if not taught to see, are at least so instructed that they join steadily in labors for production, and obtain much enjoyment from life; the deaf and dumb are taught to articulate, so as apparently to be able to join in the business of the community, or they are so highly instructed in sign-language that they can form a social community of their own of culture, and capable of much social enjoyment.

The greatest practical advance in humane methods during the century has undoubtedly been in the care of the neglected, exposed, and criminal youth, as seen in the foundation of so many reformatories for youth in the various States, in the opening of innumerable mission-schools for poor and ignorant children through every part of the Union, and in such extended, original, and successful labors for the prevention of childish misery and crime as those of the Children's Aid Society of New York. Nothing surpassing these efforts, in their spirit, their organization, and their success, can be found in any part of the world.

Did space permit, much should also be said of the astonishing labors in behalf of the sick and wounded during the civil war of the various State Soldiers' Aid Associations, and of the National Sanitary Association — efforts on a prodigious scale, and introducing into modern warfare a new element of individual care and watchfulness over the health of the soldier, and of individual supply of the wants of the wounded and sick in the armies and hospitals, in combination with official and government care and management.

These remarkable labors have, however, been sufficiently described elsewhere. They are a striking evidence of the humanitarian progress of the country, and are destined to affect the practice and feeling of all nations in future wars, and to bring a new influence of humanity to soften the passions, and lessen the sufferings of these bitter struggles.

The great event of this century in the United States, the emancipation of the slaves, is undoubtedly, in large part, a result of the spirit of humanity, which, under the silent influence of Christianity, has gradually permeated all nations. But this event is so connected with political complications, and was so hastened finally by military necessities, that it must be regarded as a part of the political history of this country, and be treated of in that connection.

This, however, can be said, that but for the profound sense of human rights and of the brotherhood of humanity which has penetrated our people, they would never have carried their hostility to slavery and its extension so far as to risk civil war. It does not lessen our respect for their humanity, that their wise instinct and foresight saw that the future of the republic and the success of this political experiment depended on its freedom from this great organized injustice. Patriotism and humanity impelled together; and being in the struggle, humane feeling, as well as sound policy, bid them go to the extreme point of entire and forcible and immediate emancipation.

The freedom of four millions of human beings from slavery, after enormous cost of blood and treasure, is the crowning fruit of humanitarian development in the United States during the past century.

XVII.

RELIGIOUS DEVELOPMENT.

OF the many forces which have entered into the development of the United States, religion must be regarded as one of the first in time, the steadiest in mode, and the most potent in quality. If it were possible in imagination to eliminate this factor from our growth, we should find not only that the colonization of the Atlantic and Gulf belt would have been delayed many decades, but that the entire complexion of that colonization would have been different, the final protest in speech and deed against foreign rule would have been later and otherwise made, and our civilization have resulted in a poor copy of that of the Western tier of European states, and our government in a servile imitation of either the British monarchy or of the Bourbon rule in France. "Let processions be made," wrote Columbus to the treasurer of Spain, on returning from the New World, to lay a new continent at the feet of his sovereign; "let festivals be celebrated; let temples be adorned with branches and flowers! For Christ rejoices on earth as in heaven, in view of the future redemption of souls. Let us rejoice, also, for the temporal benefit which will result from the discovery, not merely to Spain, but to all Christendom." Chains and darkness and hunger were the ironical reward which crowned these pious aspirations; while, so far as his own part of "all Christendom" was concerned, Spain's chief care was far less to enlarge the household of heaven than to replenish her treasury from mines in her new continent, and yet to sanctify her lust by presenting to Pope Alexander VI., as the firstlings of her far-off El Dorado, enough gold to furnish a solid plating of that metal for the entire ceiling of the Roman basilica, Santa Maria Maggiore. It is most interesting to observe, in our whole colonial development, the unfailing presence of the religious instinct, which, for the first time freed from its European shackles, could choose at will its own fields, mark out for itself a new mission, and proceed upon a higher destiny than its previous vision had ever ventured to picture as a reasonable possibility for what Bunsen calls "the Church of the Future."

In order to appreciate fully the religious element in our first century of national life, it will be necessary to take careful note of its existence in our colonial life. There is no such thing as isolation in history, and particularly in American history.[1] Our colonial and national history are two departments of the same organism. They are related as foundation and superstructure. The Revolution of 1776, far from being an anomaly in the current of American history, or an unexpected turn in the affairs of the colonies, was the natural consummation of the colonial planting and training, and long foreseen by the best statesmen of Europe. The tedious ordeal, lasting from Lexington to Yorktown, was the natural product of the genius and daring of the James River and Plymouth colonies. Nothing but a narrow oppression could have been expected from the house of Hanover, whose sixty-one years on the English throne—whither a happy accident had translated it from the obscurity of the humble palace and trim little garden of Herrenhausen—had not proved long and punitive enough to reveal to it the spirit of the colonists, while only the most stubborn and successful resistance could have been anticipated from those who suffered most from the oppressive policy. The Colonial, the Revolutionary, and the National eras were cast in the same mold, and together constitute a beautifully rounded unity. They all prove the same great fact of the world's readiness for the free conscience and free citizenship. When independence finally came, there was the opportunity for monarchy; but it was rejected as an unworthy prize. It is the lesson which Talfourd puts on the lips of Ctesiphon:

---

[1] Shedd, *Philosophy of History*, p. 14.

"Go teach the eagle when in azure heaven
He upward darts to seize his maddened prey,
Shivering through the death-circle of its fear,
To pause and let it 'scape, and thou mayst win
Man to forego the sparkling round of power,
When it floats airily within his grasp!"[1]

If we would learn the true character of the religious life of the colonies, we must inquire, first of all, into its *European antecedents.*

The period of the settlement of this country was singularly identical with that of the breaking-up of the old religious life of Europe. Indeed, since the Crusades the Old World had passed through no such convulsions as shook her whole religious, political, intellectual, and social frame-work at the time when every nation was sending forth her sons—albeit many exiles in the number—to establish themselves on the Atlantic coast of this continent. It was not from any stagnant nation that immigrants came to our wooded shores, but from stirred and aroused peoples. The political questions that arose as a necessary consequence of the great Reformation were not adjusted until the close of the Thirty Years' War, in 1648, or only twenty-eight years after the landing of Plymouth colony. Europe's best blood was hot with new aspirations — we might better call them inspirations — at the very moment when this new field was opened for the greatest fulfillment in modern history. The Pilgrims who stepped ashore at Plymouth Rock were men who had been bearing no small share of Britain's burdens; and while they still retained vivid recollection of the disabilities and sufferings consequent upon the enforcement of the Act of Uniformity, theirs was not the regret of idleness and despair, but of great unattained privileges. And hence those who survived the first winter, with the new colonists who re-enforced their strength, addressed themselves to the work before them with all the vigor and aggressive spirit which have ever since characterized the sons of New England. They possessed the true Roman power of adaptation to every circumstance without complaint, as expressed by Cicero: "Edi quæ potui, non ut volui, sed ut me temporis angustiæ coëgerunt." The Dutch brought with them both the discipline and the indignation that grew naturally from the cold hate of Philip II., the barbarous cruelty of Alva, and the final triumph of the national spirit over both. The Huguenots, whose land had been any thing to them but "Fair France," came with the great fresh sorrow over friends and co-believers who had gone to their coronation by way of the fagot-pile and the executioner's block.

Is it surprising that these fugitives from the dragonnades of swift-footed persecution should form an important element in this new life? "Such an element," says Storrs, "of population was powerful here, beyond its numbers. Its trained vitality made it efficient. It is a familiar fact that of the seven presidents of the Continental Congress, three were of this Huguenot lineage—Boudinot, Laurens, and John Jay. Of the four commissioners who signed the provisional treaty at Paris which assured our independence, two were of the same number—Laurens and Jay. Faneuil, whose hall in Boston has been for more than a hundred years the rallying-place of patriotic enthusiasm, was the son of a Huguenot. Marion, the swamp-fox of Carolina, was another; Horry, another; Huger, another. It was a Huguenot voice — that of Duché — which opened with prayer the Continental Congress. It was a Huguenot hand—that of John Laurens—which drew the articles of capitulation at Yorktown. Between these two terminal acts, the brilliant and faithful bravery of the soldier had found wider imitation among those of his lineage than had the cowardly weakness of the preacher; and two of those who, thirty years after (in 1814), signed the treaty of peace at Ghent were still of this remarkable stock—James Bayard and Albert Gallatin."[1]

The Germans who came hither had set out from the hearth-stone of the Reformation, and knew as well all the distinctions between Augsburg and Geneva as the differences between Wittenberg and Rome. The Swedish colony started from a land fervid enough and just ready to send its king, Gustavus Adolphus, to take charge of the Protestant forces in their long conflict with the troops of Wallenstein and Tilly. Indeed, of the eighteen languages spoken by

[1] *Ion*, p. 58.

[1] *The Early American Spirit*, p. 52, 53.

the colonists, representing at least ten different nationalities in the Old World, there was not one which had not of late been used beyond the Atlantic as the vehicle for the discussion of religious and theological questions, for scientific investigation, for the highest fields of literature, and for national and international jurisprudence. The century which produced the colonists of our country could count among its sons Richard Hooker, Chillingworth, Usher, Laud, and Whitgift; Arminius, Episcopius, Grotius, and Vossius; Hutterus, Gerhard, Osiander, and Calixtus; Buxtorf and Casaubon; Lord Bacon, Descartes, and Jacob Böhme; Rubens, Rembrandt, and Murillo; Galileo, Kepler, and Tycho Brahe; and those two greatest names in the British literary pantheon—Shakspeare and Milton.[1] It was a century of prodigies, and not least among them were those cosmopolitan and heroic bands of colonists which it sent to people and develop the Western hemisphere. There was an element of high moral purpose in them for which we search in vain in the colonial plantings of Phœnicia, Carthage, and Rome. In fact, the nations themselves, which in the seventeenth century furnished scions for the new life here, were never, either before or since, permitted to produce for distant lands men of equally elevated motives, fine intellect, and far-reaching destiny.

What Green says of the great character of the eight hundred emigrants under John Winthrop might really be said of the colonists as a body: "They were not 'broken men,' adventurers, bankrupts, criminals; or simply poor men and artisans. They were in great part men of the professional and middle classes; some of them men of large landed estate; some zealous clergymen, like Cotton, Hooker, and Roger Williams; some shrewd London lawyers, or young scholars from Oxford.......They desired, in fact, 'only the best' as sharers in their enterprise; were driven forth from their fatherland, not by earthly want, or by the greed of gold, or by the lust of adventure, but by the fear of God, and the zeal for a godly worship."[2]

Of Hooker, Stone, and Cotton, and their reception by the Massachusetts Colony, Palfrey says: "They were men of eminent capacity and sterling character, fit to be concerned in the founding a state. In all its generations of worth and refinement, Boston has never seen an assembly more illustrious for generous qualities, or for manly culture, than when the magistrates of the young colony welcomed Cotton and his fellow-voyagers at Winthrop's table." The most of the clergymen who came to New England had gained celebrity at home, and a large number had studied at Cambridge, and particularly in Emanuel College.[1]

[1] Cf. Storrs, *The Early American Spirit*, p. 42 ff.

[2] *Short History of the English People*, Am. ed., p. 498.

But while the element of religion was dominant in the initial idea and impulse, it was not less mighty and pervasive through the whole colonial period of one hundred and seventy years. The colonial territory fell into three distinct sections: 1. The New England, or Northern District; 2. The New York, or Central District; and 3. The Virginia, or Southern District. In each of these, though there was difference in the time and source of the colony, there was the same general recognition of religion. The charter of the James River Colony established religion according to the doctrines and usages of the Church of England. The religious fermentation was very decided, and even our present multiplicity is a legacy from the mother country. It provokes a smile to read an act of the Maryland Assembly, passed in 1664, against blasphemy and profanity, which pronounces against the following "motley brood," as Waylen calls them with a degree of relish: "Schismatic, Idolater, Puritan, Lutheran, Calvinist, Anabaptist, Brownist, Antinomian, Barrowist, Roundhead,"[2] etc.

With all our national religious development, we have not yet reached the great altitude of the humane spirit of one of the provisions of the first charter of the Virginia Colony toward the Indians: "All persons shall kindly treat the savage and heathen people in those parts, and use all proper means to draw them to the true service and knowledge of God."[3] As late as 1705 the Virginia Assembly decreed three years' imprisonment and many political disabilities

[1] *Bibliotheca Sacra*, vol. xviii., p. 191.

[2] *Ecclesiastical Reminiscences of the United States*, p. 414.

[3] Stith, *History of Virginia*, bk. i., p. 40.

upon any one who should a second time assert disbelief in the Trinity and the Scriptures. The West India Company, which in 1640 controlled the settlement of New Amsterdam, was required "to provide good and suitable preachers, school-masters, and comforters of the sick;" and later, after 1664, when the English became masters, they enacted that "no person shall be molested, fined, or imprisoned, for differing in judgment in matters of religion who professes Christianity."[1] Of the Dutch, who furnished the basis of the settlement, Storrs says: "An energetic Christian faith came with them, with its Bibles, its ministers, its interpreting books."[2] The New England Colony was grounded in religion, and the administration partook largely of that character. The people who established it remembered too keenly the fires through which they had passed to run any unnecessary risks. Hence they enacted that no man should have the freedom of the colony who was not a member of some church within its limits; and the New Haven Colony said plainly: "Church members only should be free burgesses."[3] The "Blue Laws of Connecticut," however, are a wretched imposture. The time has come when not a child in the land ought to be without the information that there never did exist such a code. It is a fabrication of one Peters, author of a *History of Connecticut*, who fled to London at the beginning of the Revolution, and employed his time in aspersing the character of the struggling colonists.[4]

The colonization of the Southern territory partook of the same general religious character with the Central and Northern. This may be seen, for example, in the establishment of Carolina. In 1662 certain noblemen applied to Charles II. for a grant on the express ground of "zeal for the propagation of the Christian faith in a country not yet cultivated or planted, and only inhabited by some barbarous people, who have no knowledge of God." And in 1665, when there was a new charter, and the former guarantees were confirmed, the religious element was brought out still more into the foreground. It declared that "no man shall be permitted to be a freeman of Carolina, or to have any estate or habitation within it, who doth not acknowledge God." Still, freedom was granted all faiths: "Jews, heathens, and other dissenters from the purity of Christian religion may not be scared and kept at a distance from it, but by having an opportunity of acquainting themselves with the truth and reasonableness of its doctrines, and the peaceableness and inoffensiveness of its professors, may, by good usage and persuasion, and all those convincing methods of gentleness and meekness suitable to the rules and design of the Gospel, be won over to embrace and unfeignedly receive the truth; therefore, any seven or more persons agreeing in any religion shall constitute a church or profession, to which they shall give some name to distinguish it from others."[1]

As the Revolutionary struggle approached there was a quickening of the free religious impulses of the people. The fear that the Church of England would be supported by the crown in its effort to absorb the New England churches, and establish a Protestant episcopate over all the colonies, "contributed as much as any other cause," says John Adams, "to arouse the attention, not only of the inquiring mind, but of the common people, and urge them to close thinking on the constitutional authority of Parliament over the colonies."[2] How keenly the colonists felt on this subject may be seen in the special instruction of the Assembly of Massachusetts to its agent in London, in 1768: "The establishment of a Protestant episcopate in America is very zealously contended for" (*i. e.*, by the arbitrary party in the British Parliament); "and it is very alarming to a people whose fathers, from the hardships they suffered under such an establishment, were obliged to fly their native country into a wilderness in order

[1] Thompson, *Church and State in the United States*, p. 32–40; *Documents of Colonial History* (Holland), vol. i., p. 123; *Historical Society's Collection*, vol. i., p. 332.

[2] *Early American Spirit*, p. 47.

[3] Thompson, *Church and State in the United States*, p. 57, 58.

[4] Compare Kingsley, *Historical Discourse*, and Hall, *Puritans and their Principles*, p. 17 and note.

[1] Dalcho, *Historical Account of the Protestant Episcopal Church of South Carolina*, p. 5. In Appendix I. to Dalcho, see "The Church Act for Establishment of Religious Worship in the Province of Carolina."

[2] *Works*, vol. x., p. 185.

peaceably to enjoy their privileges—civil and religious. We hope in God that such an establishment will never take place in America; and we desire you would strenuously oppose it."[1]

It is not without significance that the troops of Great Britain were first fired upon by the colonists from a church just forsaken of its royalist rector, on the shore of Massachusetts Bay. "Paul Revere," says Loring, "filled with patriotic daring, proposed to use a church, just abandoned by a loyal rector, as a beacon-light for the patriots just about to strike their first blow for freedom. How sudden and complete the change! As the representative of royal power in church and state steps down, in obedience to the dictates of his conscience, the representative of a struggling people takes his place, and at once, as by a decree of Providence, the destiny of this church is changed, and its history is immortal. For more than half a century it had stood, the emblem of a great religious faith; in an instant it rose to a still higher duty, and became the signal of an heroic effort to preserve a free conscience to the believers, and free citizenship, with all its opportunities, to the masses of mankind."

It was natural that the clergy of the Church of England should be mostly partisans of the royal cause; and yet many of them distinguished themselves for fidelity to the defense of the Colonies. Of this number were Bishop Madison, and Bracken, Belmaine, Buchanan, Jarratt, Griffith, Davis, and many others; while Muhlenburg, of Virginia, relinquished his rectorate, became colonel in the American army, raised a regiment from among his own parishioners, and served through the whole war, retiring at its close as brigadier-general.[2] What was done by the clergy of the Church of England, in spite of their special and natural attachments to the mother country, was performed by the clergy of other churches on a grander scale, and with more magnificent results.

For ten years previously to the outbreak of hostilities, the preachers in a great number of the churches spoke from the pulpit and the platform, in the most positive language, concerning the necessity of defense. Some of the fast-day and thanksgiving discourses of the New England clergy, during the whole struggle, have passed into literature as among the strongest specimens known to men of how thoroughly the clerical mind can be identified with a national cause. Some of the favorite psalms of those days were no poor paraphrases of David's metrical imprecations on his foes, while the prayers might well be placed in the same category with that of the Suabian chief who prayed that the God of battles, if he did not see that it would be for his glory to grant victory to his forces, would at least remain neutral for one day.

The religious condition of the country at the beginning of the national era was one of great prostration. What with the want of pastoral care, decay, and destruction of the church edifices, the separation of families, and the absorbing character of the political issues, the spiritual interests were neglected to a degree without approach in the history of the country from 1735 to the present time. The sufferings of the Church of England may be regarded as an index of those of all professions. In Virginia, where this body was strongest, it was almost obliterated. At the beginning of the war there were ninety-five parishes, one hundred and sixty-four churches and chapels, ninety-one clergymen; but at the close of the war a large number of the churches had been destroyed; twenty-three parishes were extinct or forsaken, thirty-four were destitute of ministerial supply; and only twenty-eight of the clergy were found at their post.[1]

The Presbyterians, Baptists, and Congregationalists, almost without exception supporters of the cause of the colonies, were treated without compassion by the British troops. The Methodists, who had been in the country only since 1766, were treated inhumanly by petty colonial officers, on the alleged ground that Bishop Asbury and his coadjutors were disloyal; until the Maryland Assembly, convinced of the loyalty of the itinerants, permitted them "to exercise their functions without taking the oath of allegiance." Many churches were burned;

[1] Thompson, *Church and State in the United States*, p. 42, 43.

[2] Thatcher, *Military Journal*, p. 152.

[1] Hawks, *Contributions to the Ecclesiastical History of Virginia*, p. 153, 154.

seats of others were torn up for fuel. A large number of the churches, such as those at Elizabethtown and Morristown, were used for hospitals. During the British occupation of New York many of the churches were used as stables. The schools were discontinued in most parts of the colonies. Many of the colleges, like that of New Jersey, closed their doors for a time. "Religious institutions," says Gillett, "were paralyzed in their influence, even where they were still sustained. Sabbath-desecration prevailed to an alarming extent. Infidelity, in many quarters, soon acquired a foot-hold. The civil character of the war, especially in the Southern States, gave it a peculiar ferocity, and produced a licentiousness of morals of which there is scarce a parallel at the present day. Municipal laws could not be enforced. Civil government was prostrated, and society was well-nigh resolved to its original elements.[1]

Intemperance increased to an alarming degree in consequence of the war. During the colonial period the country had been comparatively free from it. In the account which Belknap gives of an early expedition against the Indians, in New Hampshire, he says the American forces had only one pint of "strong waters" among them; a statement which could hardly be made of any subsequent expedition of equal size in American history. From 1750, the West-India trade had introduced increasing quantities of rum, which was supposed to furnish special strength in the French and Indian wars in the North; but after the war the use of intoxicating liquors steadily increased far beyond the ratio of population. In 1792, there were 2579 distilleries in the United States, and by 1810 these had multiplied to 14,141, or an increase of sixfold, while the population had increased less than twofold. From September, 1791, to the same month, 1792, there were consumed 11,008,447 gallons of wines and distilled spirits, which would be two and a half gallons for every human being in the young republic.[2]

To all the moral and material decadence of domestic origin must be added the influence of the French spirit, which was very great, and threatened to overspread the country. To France the colonies had been indebted for nearly all the European sympathy which came to their aid. Some of her best sons came over to help them fight their battles. Paris, where the Encyclopedist school was powerful, was the first place whither young Americans of culture resorted after the declaration of peace, and they were cordially welcomed to the *salons* of the leaders of society and advanced thought. The newspaper press and the higher schools in America were the first to exhibit traces of the incoming of this new element. The effect, however, was transient. The urgent demand for evangelization and education in the West; the excitement of the political campaigns; the unsettled relations with Great Britain which culminated in the war of 1812; and especially the great revival at the close of the eighteenth century, with the whole train of benevolent movements which came from it, so diverted public attention from the French skepticism, that not even the conspicuous example of Franklin and Jefferson, who had represented the Government at the French court, had any enduring force.

How thoroughly religion entered into the new national life, and re-asserted its divine prerogatives at every stage of our history, may be seen primarily in the religious-civil relations. As the colonial period had been marked so distinctly, from its beginning to its close, by the presence of religious motives; and as the provincial government constantly legislated, sometimes even to pettiness, on the relations of religion to the civil life, it followed as a necessity that one of the problems for the country to solve would be the attitude of the state toward the church. Here was a realm where America was without teachers. In education, government, literature, nay, in every thing else, the Old World furnished abundant lessons; but when the question of religion in relation to the civil law confronted the people, they looked in vain for example and instruction. Was not "the history of the colonization of the country," as Bancroft says, "the history of the crimes of Europe?"[1] The state churches of the Old

[1] *History of the Presbyterian Church*, vol. i., p. 196.

[2] Dorchester, in *Zion's Herald*, vol. liii., No. 5.

[1] *History of the United States*, vol. ii., p. 251.

World had been the growth of over fourteen centuries, and not since the reign of Constantine had the history of civilized nations furnished a positive example of how a great people can have religion without making it the foster-child, if not the bondmaid, of the government. But the lessons learned by the colonists in the lands of their nativity had struck too deeply to be without avail when their children should begin the sublime work of rearing a government for themselves.

To these memories, frequently rehearsed and still fresh, must be attributed the avoidance of all mention of religious preference in the Constitution of the United States: "Congress shall make no law respecting an establishment of religion, or prohibiting the free exercise thereof." There must be nothing—so said the great framers of our written law—which shall remind us of the pit whence we were dug, or make it possible that another be dug into which any portion of our posterity shall be thrown. Hence, in the national legislation there was left large liberty for the conscience and faith of the private citizen. But the traces of the rigid colonial legislation remained a long time, and in some cases still continue, on the statute-books of the individual States. While the government recognized no union of church and state, the State constitutions had to submit to a gradual process of independence in the relations of the church to the state. Virginia, the stronghold of the Established Church, was the first State to declare absolute religious freedom. The Legislature of 1784 considered two important measures: one to "incorporate all societies of the Christian religion which may apply for the same," and the other to make a general assessment for the support of religion. Although warmly defended by Patrick Henry, both projects failed in the end, and not through the influence of Thomas Jefferson, but because of the unwearied protests and petitions of the Presbyterians, Baptists, and Quakers.[1]

In 1785 the Legislature of Virginia adopted an act drawn up by Jefferson "for establishing religious freedom." The triumph of this measure was most gratifying to its author, not so much because of the liberty of growth to Christianity, but because of its total indifference to any faith; or, in Jefferson's own words, it comprehended "within the mantle of protection the Jew and the Gentile, the Christian and the Mohammedan, the Hindoo and the infidel of every denomination."[1] Virginia taking the lead in the severance of church and state, other States followed in prompt succession. Maryland, New York, South Carolina, and the New England and other States, erased the provisions for the support of the clergy from their constitutions.

With the total abandonment of all civil provision for the salary of the clergy began the real or positive development of the religious life of the people; and the whole subsequent history has shown that however much of a prophet Cotton Mather may have been in some respects, he was a very poor one in his vaticination of the straits to which preachers would be reduced who might have to depend upon voluntary support. "Ministers of the Gospel would have a poor time of it if they must rely on a *free contribution of the people* for their maintenance." But while there is not state provision for the support of churches or their pastors, the religious element is nevertheless positively recognized. The constitution of Massachusetts still says, "It is the right as well as the duty of all men in society publicly and at stated seasons to worship the Supreme Being, the great Creator and Preserver of the universe.......All the people of the commonwealth have also a right to, and do, invest their Legislature with authority to enjoin upon all the subjects an attendance upon the instructions of the public teachers, as aforesaid, at stated times and seasons, if there be any whose instructions they can conscientiously and conveniently attend;" that of New Hampshire, "The people of this State have a right to empower, and do hereby fully empower, the Legislature to authorize from time to time the several towns, parishes, bodies corporate, or religious societies within this State to make adequate provision, at their own expense, for the support and maintenance of public Protestant teachers of piety, religion, and morality;" that of

[1] Baird, *Religion in America*, p. 221–223.

[1] Cf. Baird, *Religion in America*, p. 224, 225.

Vermont, "Every sect or denomination of Christians ought to observe the Sabbath or Lord's day, and keep some sort of religious worship which to them shall seem most agreeable to the revealed will of God;" that of Delaware, "It is the duty of all men frequently to assemble together for the public worship of the Author of the universe, and piety and morality, on which the prosperity of communities depends, are thereby promoted;" and that of Ohio, "Religion, morality, and knowledge being essential to good government, it shall be the duty of the General Assembly to pass suitable laws to protect every religious denomination in the peaceable enjoyment of its own mode of public worship and encouraging schools and the means of instruction." The constitution of Mississippi declares, "No person who denies the being of a God or a future state of rewards and punishments shall hold any office in the civil department of this State....... Religion, morality, and knowledge being necessary to good government, the preservation of liberty, and the happiness of mankind, schools, and the means of education shall forever be encouraged in this State;" that of Maryland, "No religious test ought ever to be regarded as a qualification for any office of profit or trust in this State other than a declaration of belief in the existence of God; nor shall the Legislature prescribe any other oath of office than the oath prescribed by this constitution;" and that of Tennessee, "No person who denies the being of a God or a future state of rewards and punishments shall hold any office in the civil department of this State."[1] Similar expressions can be found in the constitutions of the several States. With time, whatever is objectionable in such language will be rescinded. Thus far in our national history, however, such civil sanctions of the obligations of religion upon the citizen have wrought no evil.

Our denominational life is almost as much outside the ordinary confessional examples of the Old World as the relation of the American Church to the State. In all countries where a state church exists there can be no such thing as a perfect independence of the denominations. One is supreme, while the rest must constantly suffer disabilities and annoyances. One is called "the church," while the rest are "dissenters," or "sects." "The 'sects' of the Old World," says Dr. H. B. Smith, "are the leading churches of the New World. Most of our sects came to us from Europe, to get rid of state coercion, and they have here had free scope. Our Christian history is not that of the conversion of a new and civilized nation to the Gospel; but of the transplanting of the Christianity of Europe, freed from its local restrictions, to a new theatre. It is Europe itself developed on a new continent. Our leading denominations still stand on the substantial basis of the confessions of the Protestant Reformation, many of them adhering to the old symbols with a tenacity which is now rare in the lands from which they came."[1] The variety of healthy and vigorous religious life in the United States is greater than anywhere else in the world. It has grown with the nation, and is to-day one of the most beautiful and hopeful features of our national development.

We may take seven of the great American Protestant bodies, and the Roman Catholic Church, the foundations of all of which were laid in the colonial era, as indicative of the variety and power of the religious life in the United States. The Protestant Episcopal Church dates from the founding of the Virginia Colony, in 1607, on James River, by Captain John Smith and other members of the Church of England. One of the petitioners of the charter granted the London Company, on April 10, 1606, was the Rev. John Hunt, a clergyman of the establishment; and this man became a member of the colony, and most probably the one who saved it from threatening ruin.[2] By the year 1619 there had grown up eleven parishes. This church extended in the South and throughout the Middle colonies, and became by far the most important religious body south of New England. It was governed during the colonial period by the Bishop of London, and its clergy received orders only by crossing to London.

The first step toward the union of the churches was taken at a meeting of a few

[1] Bierbower, "Religion in the State Constitutions," *New York Independent*, January 6, 1876.

[1] *Theological Review*, vol. v. (new series), p. 572.

[2] Hawks, *Contributions to the Ecclesiastical History of Virginia*, p. 17, 18.

clergymen at New Brunswick, New Jersey, in May, 1784. Though the immediate object was to revive a society which had formerly existed in the colonies for the support of the widows and orphans of deceased clergymen, provision was made for a later meeting, looking toward union of the churches.[1] In 1785 the first general convention assembled. The first American bishops ordained were Seabury, in Scotland, in 1784, and White and Provoost, in Lambeth Palace, London, in 1787.[2] The Thirty-nine Articles were ratified in 1832. The Reformed Episcopal Church is a secession from the Protestant Episcopal in 1873, under the leadership of Bishop Cummins.

The Congregationalists are the direct ecclesiastical posterity of the Puritan Church. The original colony came over from England, after a stay of some time in Holland, in 1620—"a church without a bishop, and a state without a king." Their spiritual guide in Holland, and even in England before leaving for Holland, was John Robinson. He gained great renown in Leyden among his co-believers by publicly contending against the Arminian Episcopius. Robinson failed, because of death, to carry out his purpose of joining the Pilgrims in America.[3] Though the Plymouth colonists were reduced to one-half their original number during the first winter, they were soon reenforced by men of similar spirit and motive, and the church grew rapidly throughout the New England colonies. This Puritan element has been the most aggressive in our American national life, and has exerted the chief influence in the settlement and building-up of the Great West. The chief conventions have been those of Cambridge (1648), Saybrook (1708), Albany (1852), Boston (1865), and Oberlin (1871). At this last a permanent organization was formed, to meet triennially, under the name of "The National Council of the Congregational Churches of the United States."

The Reformed Church in America, formerly the Reformed Protestant Dutch Church, was planted in the colony of the New Netherlands by the first Dutch immigrants in 1623. Five years later a permanent organization was effected, and the Rev. Jonas Michaelius became the first pastor of the church on Manhattan Island. In the latter half of the eighteenth century great embarrassment arose from the use of the Dutch language instead of the English, and the connection of the American with the home church; but an independent organization was brought about in 1771, through the labors of the Rev. Dr. J. H. Livingston. The convention held in that year established the new church on a firm basis. In 1822 a feeble secession (the True Reformed Dutch Church), through Froeligh, took place, on the ground of a return to the original life and doctrines of the church.

The Baptists were among the earliest and worthiest settlers in this country. Their first church was founded by Roger Williams at Providence, Rhode Island, in 1639. No sect was treated with more bitterness during the colonial period than the Baptists.[1] They were persecuted in nearly all the States, and enjoyed no freedom except in Rhode Island, Pennsylvania, and Delaware. They were among the foremost supporters

[1] Butler, *Ecclesiastical History*, vol. ii., p. 584. The Society for the Relief of the Widows and Children of the Clergy of the Church of England was first formed in South Carolina in 1762, and later had auxiliaries in each province. Compare Dalcho, *Historical Account of the Protestant Episcopal Church in South Carolina*, p. 190 ff.

[2] For interesting details of the visit and ordination of White and Provoost, compare White, *Memoirs of the Protestant Episcopal Church in the United States of America*, Philadelphia, 1820. This is a singularly prepared book, the work proper comprising only forty-five pages, while the appendix (additional statements and remarks) consists of four hundred and twenty-nine pages. But it is in just this appendix that the rare value of the work consists, for it embraces matters relating to the early history of the Protestant Episcopal Church, and its relations to the Church of England to be found nowhere else.

[3] While in Leyden, Robinson connected himself with the university, where, as an evidence of the public favor he enjoyed, he was so far exempted from taxation that he might have, free of town and state duties, half a tun of beer every month, and about ten gallons of wine every three months.—Bacon, *Genesis of the New England Churches*, p. 242, and note; Sumner, *Memoirs of the Pilgrims at Leyden*, p. 18, 19.

[1] Bailey, in *Trials and Victories of Religious Liberty in America*, gives some notable instances, p. 14–52. Anderson, in his *Baptists in the United States*, traces with great candor and care the remarkable development of the denomination. Curry pays minute attention to the early struggles of the Virginia Baptists; see his *Struggles and Triumphs of Virginia Baptists*, Philadelphia, 1873. One of the best denominational histories published in this country is Backus, *Church History of New England from 1620 to 1804*. It is of broader scope than its title would indicate.

of the Revolution, and after the national independence, the church commenced a career of remarkable progress and honor. They are fully entitled to Judge Story's high encomium: "The Baptists were early distinguished for their advocacy of freedom of conscience. In the code of laws established by them in Rhode Island we read, for the first time since Christianity ascended the throne of the Cæsars, the declaration that conscience should be free, and men should not be punished for worshiping God in the way they were persuaded he requires." They are not only numerous, but worthy alike of their numbers and influence. They have been distinguished for their evangelistic and missionary zeal, and are among the foremost advocates of education.[1]

The first Lutherans in this country were in New York, and their first pastor was the Rev. Jacob Fabricius, in 1669. In 1671 their first church, a log-hut, was built. A second settlement was in Delaware in 1676. The first synod was held in 1748. The Lutherans are a vigorous and aggressive religious body. They derive their models chiefly from the great historical Lutheran Church of Germany. Unfortunately, the American Lutherans have great diversity in worship. They early abandoned some of the distinctive features of the maternal church in Germany, such as exorcism, private confession and clerical absolution, consubstantiation, baptismal regeneration, and the imputation of Adam's transgression.[2] Of their diversities here, Krauth says: "In the United States wider extremes in the mode of worship in the Lutheran Church sometimes existed in a single locality than could be found in her whole communion in other parts of the world. This diversity has been deeply lamented, and earnest efforts are making, with marked success, to introduce greater uniformity of usage."

The Presbyterians owe their origin in this country to the persecutions in Scotland. From 1660 to 1685 three thousand persons of Presbyterian faith were transported as slaves to the colonies. In 1688 there were many immigrants, especially in Eastern Pennsylvania. The first General Assembly, with John Rodgers as moderator, was in 1789. There was a division of the Presbyterian Church in 1838. In 1866 an attempt was made to initiate the reunion of the church (Old and New schools). The reunion, which was finally consummated in 1870, was regarded as a victory of the New School, but the prevalent theological tendency of the church is that of the Old School. With the reverend and revered Dr. Hodge, our great theological Nestor, at Princeton, and the polished and learned Dr. Shedd in New York, no immediate fears need be entertained for the crystalline purity of the Calvinistic fountains in the United States.[1] The history of the Presbyterian Church is a fair reflex of the progress, the stability, and the culture of the nation itself. Efforts are now being made to unite the Presbyterians of all countries into more intimate relations.

The Reformed Church in the United States, formerly the German Reformed Church, arose from a body of four hundred German emigrants from the Palatinate, who came to Pennsylvania in 1727. The first synod was held in Philadelphia in 1747, and consisted of thirty-one members, representing a population of thirty thousand. Its growth has been greatly retarded because of the internal conflict between the conservative and progressive, or High and Low Church, parties of the church. An attempt to unite this church and the Reformed (Dutch) Church in 1872 failed, because the former does not regard the Belgic confession and the decrees of Dort as standards of faith.

The first Methodist society in this country was formed in New York, in 1766, and the first edifice erected in 1768. The period of development began with the national independence, through the labors of Bishop Asbury, who had been sent out from England by John Wesley in 1771. The first conference was held in 1773, at which time there were ten preachers and eleven hundred and sixty members in the whole country. In 1844 the church divided on the question

[1] The proceedings of the National Baptist Educational Convention (New York, 1870 and 1872) present the best discussions on educational topics furnished by any denomination in the present century.

[2] Schmucker, *American Lutheran Church*, p. 168 ff.; 237 ff.

[1] On the relation of the Old and New schools, previously to reunion, see article on Presbyterian Reunion, in *American Presbyterian and Theological Review*, p. 624–665. Probably written by Prof. H. B. Smith, D.D.

of slavery, the Northern portion bearing the original name (the Methodist Episcopal Church); and the Southern, the Methodist Episcopal Church, South. In 1866 the centenary of the church was celebrated, when contributions amounting to about $8,000,000 were made, chiefly for educational purposes.

Of the minor Methodist bodies there are two classes: Episcopal and Non-Episcopal. 1. Episcopal—Colored Methodist Episcopal, African Methodist Episcopal, African Methodist Episcopal Zion, and Evangelical Association. 2. Non-Episcopal—the Methodist Church, Methodist Protestant, American Wesleyan, Free Methodist, and Primitive Methodist.

The first Roman Catholic settlement in this country was the colony of Maryland, which had been guaranteed by special charter to Lord Baltimore (Cæcilius Calvert). The first emigration was in 1632, and in 1634 two hundred emigrants settled at St. Mary's. In Louisiana and other Southern States, there were important accessions through emigration from France. The Jesuit missions along the St. Lawrence and up the Mississippi were very important in attracting people of the same faith. The episcopal see of Baltimore was founded in 1789. The Roman Catholic opposition to the Bible in the public schools began in 1840. Since the war of the Union there has been a careful and extensive system of proselytism in force throughout the South. The first American cardinal (M'Closkey) was consecrated in 1875.

The chief concern of the Roman Catholics in America has been to provide for the prevention of their members from lapsing into Protestantism, to indoctrinate the young and neglected into their faith, and to preserve the balance of political power. The spirit of the leaders is in sympathy with the extreme decrees of the Vatican Council. This church has made no important impression on the literature or thought of the nation, and produced no great public benefactors in educational or humanitarian life. The following jeremiad, which has just appeared from a Roman Catholic source, can hardly be read without sympathy; though as to the causes of the fearful failures of this body, there will be no difference of opinion among Protestants:

"The Catholic influence on the country at large, then, and even now, is slight. The tactics of parties exclude Catholics almost entirely from all higher offices in the country. We have had one Catholic among the chief-justices of the Supreme Court of the United States; a few, very few, members of the United States Senate; scarcely a single Cabinet officer; here and there a Catholic reaches the position of governor of a State, but too rarely to be noted. The army and the navy show many Catholic officers, whose record is of the noblest. In literature, science, and the arts we have made little mark, and are behind even the modest position of the country at large. At the earliest period, Mathew Carey and Robert Walsh occupied a higher position in general literature than any Catholic does at the present day. Even the wonderful ability and depth of Dr. Brownson in his *Review*, in his "American Republic," that should be a classic, and in his minor works, have failed to take their place among far inferior works, and are seldom noticed in writing or speech in such a way as to show their influence.

"Archbishop Hughes left no great work to take its place in the literature of the country, great as was his influence in life; and the same may be said of Bishop England. Archbishop Kenrick, in his varied learning, enriched our Catholic rather than the national literature by his *Theology*, his essay on the *Primacy of the Apostolic See*, and his version of the Bible. Archbishop Spalding took a more popular tone; and in lighter paths for Catholic readers there are names of merit, but few that will make an enduring reputation. In the field of history, O'Callaghan, M'Sherry, Meline, and others have indeed won a place by critical research, sound judgment, and eloquent narration. In poetry, Shea and M'Gee will be remembered by some of their minor poems which found their way to collections; but we have no poet to rank with Longfellow, Bryant, and Whittier. Thebaud, in his *Irish Race*, and still more in his *Gentilism*, lays claim to a higher position in the more serious school of general literature. Still it must be confessed that, on the whole, we are behindhand. Our college course is, perhaps, too elementary; and Catholics even more than their neighbors, perhaps, underrate literary culture, and, in their anxiety to throw their sons into the world of business and care, deprive some of that learned leisure that is needed for great and enduring work. Among the clergy the science, learning, and ability that might add laurels to the body are often kept unused by the severe toils of missionary life or by modest diffidence; and an occasional article in some magazine unnoticed, and hence unappreciated, alone reveals what might be.

"It must be admitted, too, that although industry, talent, and probity have brought to many Catholics, in professional and mercantile life, great earthly rewards in wealth and means, these successful men have produced few men of such public spirit as we behold in the various Protestant denominations. While every college under Protestant influence shows its scholarships, professorships, special schools, and libraries established and endowed by individuals, there is scarcely a case to be met with of similar Catholic liberality. It is still more rare to find a church or institution of any kind among us built or endowed by a wealthy Catholic. What has been accomplished hitherto has been mainly the work of the poor; but the wealthy Catholics seem sadly lacking in public spirit. Yet the noblest monument a man could erect would be a church or an institution. There are monuments in our cemeteries, mere ornamental structures, evidences of family pride, which have cost more than would have built a beautiful church to stand for a century, where mass would be said constantly for the founder. Better a hospital for the sick or afflicted than a palace for the dead; better something Christian than any thing so essentially pagan."

The following table presents an approximate view of the ecclesiastical strength of the country at the time of the Revolution:

Denominations.	Ministers.	Churches.
Episcopalians	250	300
Baptists	350	380
Congregationalists	575	700
Presbyterians	140	300
Lutherans	25	60
German Reformed	25	60
Reformed Dutch	25	60
Associate	13	20
Moravians	12	8
Roman Catholics	26	52
Methodists	20	11[1]
Total	1461	1951

[1] Circuits.

With a total population of the country at the time of the Revolution of 3,000,000, of which one-sixth consisted of slaves, and 1461 ministers and 1951 church organizations, there was one minister of the Gospel for every 2053 souls, and one church for every 1538 souls. With our present population of 38,558,371, we have one church for every 535 souls, and one minister for every 757 souls. The rapid increase of church property can be seen by a comparison of the years 1850 and 1870. In 1850 it amounted to $87,328,801; but in 1870 it had increased to $354,483,581, or an increase in twenty years of $267,154,780.

The order of growth of the denominations was not anticipated by any of the seers, of whom the number was large, at the beginning of our national history. Dr. Stiles, President of Yale College, grandly prophesied in 1783 as follows: "When we look forward and see this country increased to forty or fifty millions, while we see all the religious sects increased into respectable bodies, we shall doubtless find the united body of the Congregational and Presbyterian churches making an equal figure with any two of them." The Methodists were not enumerated in any of the religious statistics as worthy of note, and even Baird does not include them in his table. But the presaging Dr. Stiles knew of them, though not enough to escape two blunders in his orthography, and says, "There are Westleians, Mennonists, and others, all of which will make a very inconsiderable amount in comparison with those who will give the religious complexion to America." The numerical order was as follows, at the beginning of the nation's first century: "Congregational, Baptist, Church of England, Presbyterian, Lutheran, German Reformed, Dutch Reformed, Roman Catholic." At present it is, "Methodist, Baptist, Presbyterian, Roman Catholic, Christian, Lutheran, Congregational, Protestant Episcopal."[1] According to sittings, the order is: Methodist, 6,428,209; Baptist, 3,997,116; Presbyterian, 2,198,900; Roman Catholic, 1,990,514; Congregational, 1,117,212; Protestant Episcopal, 991,051; Lutheran, 977,332; Christian, 865,602. The order in church property is: Methodist, Ro-

[1] Diman, *North American Review*, January, 1876, p. 22, 23.

man Catholic, Presbyterian, Baptist, Protestant Episcopal, Congregational, Lutheran, and Reformed Church in America.

The following is a table of the respective denominations, according to the census of 1870:

Denominations.	Organizations.	Edifices.	Sittings.	Property.
Baptist (regular)	14,474	12,857	3,997,116	$39,229,221
Baptist (other)	1,355	1,105	363,019	2,378,977
Christian	3,578	2,822	865,602	6,425,137
Congregational	2,887	2,715	1,117,212	25 069,698
Episcopal (Protestant)	2,835	2,601	991,051	36,514,549
Evangelical Association	815	641	193,796	2,301,650
Friends	692	662	224,664	3,939,560
Jewish	189	152	73,265	5,155,234
Lutheran	3,032	2,776	977,332	14,917,747
Methodist	25,278	21,337	6,528,209	69,854,121
Miscellaneous	27	17	6,935	135,650
Moravian (Unitas Fratrum)	72	67	25,700	709,100
Mormon	189	171	87,838	656,750
New Jerusalem (Swedenborgian)	90	61	18,755	869.700
Presbyterian (regular)	6,262	5,683	2,198,900	47,828,732
Presbyterian (other)	1,562	1,388	499,344	5,436,524
Reformed Church in America (late Dutch Reformed)	471	468	227,228	10,359,255
Reformed Church in the United States (late German Reformed)	1,256	1,145	431,700	5,775,215
Roman Catholic	4,127	3,806	1,990,514	60,985,566
Second Advent	225	140	34,555	306,240
Shaker	18	18	8,850	86,900
Spiritualist	95	22	6,970	100,150
Unitarian	331	310	155,471	6.282,675
United Brethren in Christ	1,445	937	265,025	1,819,810
Universalist	719	602	210,884	5,692,325
Unknown (Local Missions)	26	27	11,925	687,800
Unknown (Union)	409	552	153,202	965,295
Total	72,459	63,082	21,665,062	$354,483,581

Among the causes of the remarkable outward growth of the American Church, we must give evangelization the first rank. The country being new and unsettled, except along the Atlantic coast, and the population drifting westward constantly, the religious demands of the people seemed never to admit of satisfaction. As fast as a new region invited the settler, a great spiritual need was perceived by the strong churches in the East, and every effort was made to relieve it.

The zeal of the pioneer preachers in this country in dealing with the elements of nature and hostilities of the aborigines has not been surpassed in the history of evangelization, and takes equal rank with that of Boniface, Columban, Gallus, and Ansgar in supplanting Teutonic and Scandinavian idolatry with the Gospel of Christ.

The strain which the emigration from the Old World has made upon the New has been nowhere felt as in the religious sphere. How to assimilate a foreign and varied adult population, with its foreign training and tastes, was a problem which might well tax the energies of the strongest and most powerful church in Christendom. This emigrant tide has never ceased. The uniform annual rate from 1784 to 1794 was small—only about 4000. In 1794 it suddenly increased to 10,000; but declined again, and never recovered until 1817, when the European wars were over.[1] From 1820 to 1874 Great Britain and Ireland alone have sent to this country 4,319,048 emigrants, or nearly a million and a half more than the entire population of the country at the beginning of the national century. The aggregate of immigrants from 1783 to 1874 was 9,058,141, and at the last census (1870) one-sixth of our entire population was of foreign birth. To provide religious instruction and schools for this vast number of new citizens has been a burden of great magnitude. Yet it has been borne with calmness and resolution; and while there has been some restiveness on the part of certain fractions of the foreign population against the Sunday laws and other traditional regulations, it has never been strong enough to change a single important feature of the religious life of the United States.

The mining regions in the Far West and on the Pacific coast have been visited by the missionaries of the leading churches, and organizations have been established wherever secular interests have drawn people together. The most neglected portions of the population of the great cities, both in

[1] Draper, *Civil Policy of America*, p. 101–103.

the East and West, have attracted attention, and every care is bestowed upon the erring and the young among the lowest poor. The colored population of the South, declared free by the proclamation of President Lincoln, January 1, 1863, were destitute of all material and spiritual care at the close of the civil war.

An act of Congress of March 3, 1865, established the Freedmen's Bureau, which provided for the wants of the emancipated negroes, and continued in operation until 1869, when the educational department alone remained. This latter continued in force until 1870. The total amount contributed for the education and support of freedmen, down to 1871, was $14,996,480. The Indians have likewise come in for their share of attention from the churches. They number about 350,000. They occupy ninety reservations, in eight States and eleven Territories, and compose one hundred and thirty tribes, speaking as many as fifty different languages. They have been so far placed by President Grant under the supervision of the leading churches as to leave to the latter the nomination of agents for the tribes. All the chief denominations, with the Friends and Moravians, have missions among the Indians.

A difference must be observed between the case of the freedmen and Indians and the remaining needy portions of our population. In those two cases there have been material wants of an aggravated character, and the government has taken upon itself the burden of their provision; but in strictly spiritual need it has never expended one dollar on any class, from the beginning of our national era until the present day. And it can not do it. Should a single dime be taken out of the United States Treasury to aid in payment of the salary of the humblest missionary in the land, it would provoke a protest from one side of the continent to the other.

The revivals that have at various times visited the American Church have been attended by such phenomena, and have produced such lasting results, that they must be regarded a leading factor in the religious life of the people. There has been no period of long duration during the entire history of the church, whether Christian or pre-Christian, which has not been marked by an occasional return to spiritual vitality and power. No two seasons of quickening have been distinguished by the same features, or brought to pass through precisely similar agencies. The use of the mendicant orders; the preaching of Peter the Hermit in behalf of the first Crusade; the eloquence of Tauler and his brother Mystics in Germany; the denunciations of Savonarola in Florence; the sermons of Wycliffe in England, Huss in Bohemia, and Luther in Saxony; the meditations of the Quietists in France, and the restless labors of the Wesleyan itinerants in Britain—were all diverse manifestations of the same spirit. No year of darkness, even in the depth of the Middle Ages, was without its bold voice here and there, demanding a return to Pentecost and the warm, new life of the first disciples in Jerusalem and Antioch.

The absence of wealth and social comforts, and the inability to lean on the civil treasury for support, early accustomed the American Church to look to its religious life as the great basis of its strength. Outpourings of the Divine Spirit were expected and experienced even in the early colonial time, and many of the churches multiplied through success in revivals.

There have been four periods of revival in the history of the American Church. The *first* was in the colonial era, and began in New Jersey in 1731. Even as early as 1630, and continuing down to 1660, there had been an active and steady religious life in New England, which was quickened still more by special visitations. In 1680 there was a revival in Massachusetts, and one in Connecticut in 1721. But the revival which began in 1731 was the first in American history which assumed a general character. By the year 1734 it had reached Northampton, Massachusetts, and continued down to 1742, overspreading all New England, and reaching through the Middle States down to Southern Virginia. The year of its climax was 1740. Hence, in religious history, that revival is called the "Great Awakening of 1740." Jonathan Edwards, then pastor in Northampton, preached a series of sermons on Justification by Faith, and the immediate result was a powerful spiritual awakening. Many of the members of the church over which Edwards was pastor did not profess regeneration of heart; for by this time the doctrine of "the venerable Stoddard," who had been pastor in Northampton, had not only affected that single church, but many others throughout Massachusetts and other New England States. In 1707 Stoddard published a sermon in which he held that "sanctification is not a necessary qualification to partaking the Lord's-supper;" and that "the Lord's-supper is a converting ordinance."[1] This view had brought into the church many persons who led irreligious lives and were destructive of its best interests. Hence Edwards, seeing this, laid stress on justification by faith—the one great cure for all spiritual decline. His preaching had the immediate effect of a revival within the pale of the church; but the influence soon extended to the more indifferent circles. Whitefield arrived in this country in 1740, and immediately preached to vast audiences. He became a powerful promoter of the revival, and made a tour through New England and the central colonies.

While there was a certain degree of liberty in the evangelistic labors of certain preachers, the practice of ministers traveling from one parish to another, as evangelists for the promotion of revivals, aroused very bitter opposition in some sections. In 1741 the Consociation of Guilford, Connecticut, declared against it, and in 1742 the Legislature of the same State enacted laws against it, with heavy penalties in case of violation. No less a character than Samuel Finley, afterward President of Princeton College, was dealt with as a vagrant, and sent from one constable to another, out of the bounds of the colony.[2] With Edwards and Whitefield, as leading agents in the revival, must be mentioned the Tennents (Gilbert and William), Bellamy, Griswold, Croswell, Parsons, Wheelock, Robinson, Blair, and Roan.[3] As results of the revival, from twenty-five thousand to thirty thousand converts were added to the New England churches; twenty ministers, near Boston alone, ascribed their conversion to Whitefield; and from 1740 to 1760 not less than one hundred and fifty new churches were organized.[1] After the year 1750 there was a gradual disappearance of revival influences, and the churches returned to their wonted condition. It was not long before there appeared proofs of spiritual declension owing to many causes, but chiefly to the churches that arose in opposition to the revival tendencies, to the civil troubles occasioned by the old French wars from 1756 to 1763, to the threatening Revolution, then to the long conflict itself with England, and, last, to the absorbing political questions incidental to the establishment of independence and our relations to foreign powers.[2]

There now began the *second* revival period, 1792–1808. New England was the principal scene. All classes of people were pervaded by it. Dr. Griffin, of Connecticut, says: "From that date [1792] I saw a continued succession of heavenly sprinklings, until I could stand at my door in New Hartford, and number fifty or sixty congregations laid down in one field of divine wonders." This revival, like that in which Edwards and his coadjutors were the principal agents, resulted from the vigorous preaching of the great doctrines of Christianity, such as repentance, faith, the judgment-day, and eternal rewards and punishments. The day of

[1] Tracy, *The Great Awakening*, p. 4, 5.

[2] Uhden, *New England Theocracy*, p. 275.

[3] The literature of this first great religious awakening in American history is abundant. The best source is Prince, *The Christian History; containing Accounts of the Revival and Propagation in Great Britain and America.* This work first appeared as a weekly serial, in small octavo, eight pages, the first number being issued March 5, 1743. It continued two years. Thomas Prince, Jun., who conducted it, was the son of one of the pastors of the Old South Church, Boston, and his facilities for information were very abundant. Gillies, *Historical Collections* (Bonar's edition, Kelso, 1845, is the best), furnishes, besides copious extracts from Prince, very valuable details. The work of Gillies is the finest in theological literature on revivals of religion in all periods. Edwards wrote a book on the revival in which he took part: *Thoughts on the Revival of Religion in New England.* It was the latter part of this work that suggested to Prince his now invaluable *Christian History.* Tracy, *The Great Awakening*, (Boston, 1842), gives a very full and impartial account of the whole movement. The effect of this revival on the Presbyterian Church is given by many authors. Hodge, *Constitutional History of the Presbyterian Church*, and Hall, *History of the Presbyterian Church in Trenton, New Jersey*, may be consulted to advantage. Marvin, *Three Eras of Revival in the United States* (*Bibliotheca Sacra*, vol. xvi., p. 279 ff.) is disappointing.

[1] Smith, *Chronological Tables of Church History*, p. 71.

[2] *Contributions to the Ecclesiastical History of Connecticut*, p. 198, 199.

evangelists had not arrived. Even Nettleton had not as yet begun his zealous and loving labors. But the sermons of such clear and honest preachers as Backus, Smalley, Hooker, Griffin, Hallock, Mills, and Gillett produced a powerful effect, and many thousands were aroused from their spiritual lethargy. Subsequently to this revival there were seasons of unusual life in the church, and now and then great awakenings in isolated sections. For example, in 1813, 1821, 1826–27, and 1831, there were very many awakenings, but there was no general revival of religion in any of these years.

In 1858, however, there occurred the *third* general revival in the history of the country. This visitation was very different from the two which had preceded it. In the preaching there was no new stress on the leading doctrines of revelation. There were no prominent evangelists who seemed to be the chief agents in bringing about the extraordinary displays of divine power. But there was a singular union, never before approached in the history of American Christianity, of the principal religious bodies in prayer and conference.

The daily prayer-meeting in Fulton Street, New York, was a new feature in the religious life of the people; but such was the interest in it that it has not yet been abandoned, and the anniversaries of its inauguration are seasons of special religious exercises. Daily prayer-meetings were established in many cities and larger towns. Christian conversation, singing, and the distribution of practical religious literature were powerful agencies in promoting the movement. The revival extended to Great Britain, and when it began to subside here it increased in interest throughout the British Islands.

The permanent effect of the revival of 1858 has been chiefly in the increased fraternity of the great religious bodies. Clergymen and Christian laymen who had always stood aloof were brought together, for the first time, as participants in a great work of common interest and enjoyment. These beautiful relations have never been interrupted, and the fraternity and cordiality of the evangelical churches of America during the last eighteen years have brought in a new era in modern ecclesiastical history.

The *fourth* national revival began in the winter of 1875–76. There had been during the preceding year more than the ordinary evidences of popular religious interest. Messrs. Moody and Sankey went to England during 1873, and labored with remarkable success. Their success, in Scotland especially, was such as to silence all objections. They continued their work southward, and in London were heard by people of every class. They returned to this country in the summer of 1875, and began their evangelistic work in New England, but early transferred the scene of their labors to Brooklyn, thence to Philadelphia, and then to New York. The directness, simplicity, and strictly Biblical character of Mr. Moody's sermons, and the manly pathos of Mr. Sankey's singing, have reached every stratum of society, and, besides leading thousands to the profession of faith, have quickened many churches in all the chief denominations.

The fraternity, which assumed a positive and aggressive character for the first time, through the unifying power of the revival of 1858, has exhibited itself in various practical and decisive forms even in the brief time which has since elapsed. When the civil war began, in 1861, there was suddenly thrown upon the religious life of the people a burden hardly less important than that which was placed upon the government. No American war has ever been without the great advantage which comes from an aroused religious sentiment; and when the last strife came, the clergy and the laity united in special services, apart from the days of thanksgiving, fasting, and prayer appointed by the civil authorities, for the divine blessing on the national arms. Clergymen of established position willingly gave up their parishes to become chaplains, and others to become officers in the army; while those who remained at home united with the government in sustaining the popular enthusiasm.

The Christian Commission was an organization which arose directly from the religious impulse of the people to provide spiritual and temporal care for the soldiers in camp, on the march, and in hospital. It was an important arm of the government, and furnished such voluntary and unpaid aid as would have been impossible for the government to secure in any other way. The total receipts of the Christian Commission, in money and other directions, were $6,264,607; its delegates numbered 4859; it distributed $3,700,000 in stores, and over one million of dollars' worth of Bibles, Testaments, books, religious journals, and other publications.

The Sanitary Commission, which in nowise dealt with the spiritual interests of the soldiers, had at its head a clergyman, the Rev. H. W. Bellows, D.D.

Another evidence of the developing fraternal spirit of the Church may be seen in the session in New York, in the autumn of 1873, of the Evangelical Alliance. The Alliance was organized in London in the year 1846, and important sessions were held in London, Paris, Berlin, Geneva, and Amsterdam; but the one held in New York far excelled in interest any previous session. Delegates from all parts of the Protestant field of Europe were in attendance, and, besides the important service which they rendered in furnishing reports of the condition of the countries which they represented, they enjoyed the experience of finding in this country what they never saw before—a church which had grown great through no nurture from the fatness of a civil support, but through the spontaneous aid of its own members. The scenes which they here beheld produced a lasting impression upon them, and books are still appearing from their hands, in the Continental languages, recounting the new experiences through which they here passed. Never has an ecclesiastical body been so characterized by unity of feeling, scope of investigation, and universality of representation, and no single event in American ecclesiastical deliberation has, even in this brief interval, been followed by such salutary results.

The theology of American Protestantism has grown out of the active religious life of the people. It is singularly devoid of the contemplative element. For the development of that, the day has not yet arrived. The great material problems to be solved by the people, and the immediate spiritual necessities of a new population and a vast unoccupied territory, have left no leisure for speculation. What to be Done was more a question than What to be Thought. The robust theology of England at the time of the most rapid emigration gave tone to the entire religious life of the colonial time. The fundamentals of faith, such as they are construed and maintained by people with the gibbet and stake and block in sight, were brought over to New England during the Stuart persecution, and became the controlling theology of the colonies, and even of the United States. The Cambridge Synod of 1648, the Boston Synod of 1680, and the Saybrook Platform of 1708, substantially moulded the religious thought of the New World. The preachers and house-fathers of the time drew their opinions from such theology as was furnished by Ames's *Medulla*, Wolleb's *Compendium*, and Willard's *Body of Divinity*. At the time of the great revival under Edwards and his coadjutors, there was a strong party in the New England Church which opposed the special measures, though more by reserve than by active antagonism:

> "Those gentle theologues of calmer kind,
> Whose constitution dictates to their pens;
> Who, cold themselves, think ardor comes from hell."

President Clap and Drs. Stiles and Chauncey did not sympathize with the earnest preaching and numerous awakenings. The great body of the Calvinistic clergy were divided into formal and revival, or Old Lights and New Lights. Even the Connecticut Legislature went so far as, in 1742, to inflict penalties on enthusiasts.[1] Hopkinsianism, which makes all virtue a disinterested benevolence, and infers man's readiness to be damned for the glory of God, had gained such favor by the close of the eighteenth century that in New England not less than one hundred preachers had accepted it. The protest against the prevalence of this bold type of Calvinistic theology had been for some time gathering strength before its culmination in 1805. In that year two events took place which, however small in themselves, had a profound influence upon the religious thought of New England, if not of the entire country. We refer to the election of the Unitarian, Dr. Ware, to the Hollis professorship in Harvard University, and to the publication of the essential inferiority of Christ, by Hosea Ballou, in his work

[1] Smith, *Chronological Tables of Church History*, p. 73.

on *The Atonement.* The gauntlet was thus thrown down to the orthodox Church of New England, and a period of controversy began which, in spite of the occasionally excessive ardor of the contestants, has been one of the most productive periods in modern theological thought. Channing was leader of the protesting party, while Stuart and Woods took the most active part on the evangelical side. The contest was well sustained, and the literary fertility of the time was very great; some works being published which have found a permanent place in the theology of the country.

Among the names which appeared during the crisis for the first time, may be mentioned Worcester, Sparks, Miller, Ripley, Norton, Dewey, Ellis, and Brownson. The chasm between the Unitarians and the Evangelical Church constantly widened. Unitarian churches increased with great rapidity, and the defection from the old standards threatened to be very serious. By the year 1843 there existed no less than one hundred and thirty Unitarian congregations in Massachusetts alone—"hardly twenty of which," says the late Bishop Burgess, "were Unitarian in their origin."[1] The extreme of the protest may be seen in Ralph Waldo Emerson and Theodore Parker. For a time Emerson was connected with the Unitarians, and in 1826 was "approbated to preach." In 1829 he became colleague of Henry Ware, pastor of the Second Unitarian Church of Boston. He preached but three years, having asked for his dismission on account of differences with the members on the Lord's-supper. His entire subsequent life has been occupied in arduous literary labors. There is no department of our higher general literature which has not been enriched by his careful and chaste pen; but his poetry and essays every where give abundant evidence of his early theological tastes, and, after a careful reading of him, it occasions no surprise when informed that for six successive generations his family had not been without a preacher, on the paternal or maternal side. He has never constructed a system. Perhaps Professor H. B. Smith's definition of his views is as near an approach as can be expected: "He apparently adopts a pantheistic idealism."

Parker never forsook the ministry, but, having left the Unitarians, he became pastor of the Twenty-eighth Congregational Society in Boston. He denied miracle and the supernatural, and preached with great eloquence the gospel of humanity and nature. Parker espoused the cause of the slave when slavery was popular, and had its apologists in every part of the country. His great sympathies were so aroused that the wrongs of the negro occupied an important place in his sermons, lectures, and writings. He struggled heroically against disease, and finally died in Florence, Italy, while on a tour for the restoration of his health. He left no school. His humane spirit, however, which possessed the courage of the real reformer, served immensely to mature the sentiment which culminated in the downfall of slavery and the assertion of equal rights for all inhabitants of the land. His glowing style was a distinguishing feature of his authorship, and his warmth of diction never left him. Such periods as the following, from his last monograph, distinguish all stages of his career: "History shows that the Hercules' Pillars of one age are sailed through in the next, and a wide ocean entered on, which in due time is found rich with islands of its own, and washing a vast continent not dreamed of by such as slept within their temples old, while it sent to their very coasts its curious joints of unwonted cane, its seeds of many an unknown tree, and even elaborate boats, wherein lay the starved bodies of strange-featured men, with golden jewels in their ears."[1] It is but just to say that he never lost his distaste for the evangelical doctrines. We have Miss Cobbe's authority for saying that when, on his last Sunday morning in Florence, and on earth, he was told, "It is Sunday; a blessed day, is it not, dear friend?" the dying consumptive replied, "Yes, when one has got over the superstition of it, a *most* blessed day."[2]

Another form of conflict in religious ideas, though in a very different department, is to

[1] *Pages from the Ecclesiastical History of New England*, p. 121, 122.

[1] *Experience as a Minister*, p. 89.

[2] *Religious Demands of the Age*, p. 60. This little volume (American edition) is a reprint of the Preface to the London edition of Parker's *Collected Works.*

be found in the relation of Roman Catholicism to Protestantism on the subject of the use of the Bible in the public schools. In 1840 the Roman Catholics of New York made their first attempt in this country to prevent the use of the Bible in the common schools. From that time to the present, the controversy has been uninterrupted, though changing form with the revolutions and relations of the political parties. The policy of the Roman Catholic Church has been to control alike the parties and the education of the entire land. With what interest it watches the training of the young, and how desirous it is of taking the rudimentary instruction in its own hand, may be seen in the following bold language of *The Catholic World* of September last: "The superintendence and direction of the public schools, as well as those wherein the mass of the people are instructed in the rudiments of human knowledge, as of those where secondary and higher instruction are given, belong of right to the Catholic Church. She alone has the right of watching over the moral character of those schools; of appointing the masters who instruct the youth therein; of controlling their teaching; and dismissing, without appeal to any other authority, those whose doctrines or manners should be contrary to the purity of Christian doctrine."

Where this Church can not prevent the use of the Bible in the public schools, it withdraws the children of its fold, and then demands special appropriations from the public treasury for the support of its institutions. From the city treasury of New York alone, in the year 1869, the Roman Catholics obtained the sum of $651,191; in 1870, $711,436; in 1871, $552,818—an aggregate, in three years, of $1,915,445. There was a just interruption, after 1872, to these receipts, owing to the loss of sympathy in consequence of the overthrow of Tweed and the other thieves who had fattened on the public treasure. But two institutions alone (the Roman Catholic Protectory and the Foundling Asylum of the Sisters of Charity) received from the treasury of the city, in 1872, the sum of $276,836; in 1873, $290,000; in 1874, $370,410; in 1875, $398,355, with $47,000 yet to be paid—making in all, for 1875, $445,355. The amount proposed in the tax levy of 1876 for these two Romanist institutions is $428,050.

The Roman Catholics do not care so much that religion is taught in the common schools. But it is not their religion which they can hope to see taught in them. "Had this controversy," says Diman, "turned simply on the reading of a few verses of King James's version at the opening of the daily exercises, it need have caused no intelligent Protestant embarrassment. Simple justice would have dictated a concession involving neither disrespect to the Almighty nor peril to the spiritual welfare of the child. But the difficulty lay deeper; the real grievance of the Catholic was, not that too much, but that too little, religious instruction was given in the schools; he dreaded an education from which all positive religious influence had been eliminated; he rejected, in other words, the whole theory on which the public-school system had been based."[1]

In looking at the aggregate of the religious life and opinions of the American people during the first century, we find a progress fully equal to the expectation of those seers who stood at the threshold of our national history and looked into the future with hopeful anticipations. With obstacles such as no modern nation has had to contend with, the people have been supplied with a religious literature that has been at once quickening and elevating. The religious journals, theological quarterlies, popular religious works, and theological treatises deserve to stand beside those of the British and Prussian nations. The schools for the education of the clergy have grown with the religious wants of the people. The religious life has been earnest and evangelistic, and yet not without aspirations and efforts for the highest culture. The churches have come out of the dim twilight of mutual misapprehension, and have seen the great American fulfillment of the diversity of gifts and the sameness of the Spirit. The great bodies have developed from feeble beginnings to vast organizations, whose operations are felt from the Atlantic to the Pacific, and in many heathen countries. The American churches are now making gigantic attempts, not merely to preach the Gospel in pagan

[1] *Religion in America*, 1776–1876, *North American Review*, January, 1876, p. 39.

lands, but in those European nations where Romanism and skepticism have long held sway.

It is one of the ironies of history that American missionaries are to-day preaching in Berlin, old Upsala, Frankfort, and Rome, while the capital of Constantine, and Beirut, the seat of the celebrated school of Roman law, are powerful centres for the distribution of religious knowledge to the people of many languages. The religious care of childhood has grown in this country to such proportions as have led the leading denominations to adopt uniform subjects of study in Sunday-schools, and some of the best minds of the country have made it a chosen task to provide an elevated juvenile literature for the country. The Sabbath, notwithstanding the strong Continental prejudices of some of the people, has had among its warm defenders even organized associations.[1]

The great temperance reform, which has frequently leaned for support on the political arm, has learned at last to take high moral grounds, and look to the conscience as its strongest stay. The American pulpit has been, and will still be, one of the most powerful agencies for the promotion of the great vital interests of American civilization. Thompson's words are amply justified by the facts of the century, "The pulpit in the United States," says he, "has ever been among the foremost of social forces, stimulating the people to intellectual life, encouraging culture and science, and creating a public sentiment outside of the church itself for all that is true and noble and good."[2]

While our theology has been largely derived from Continental and British sources, there has grown up of late a disposition for original theological investigation which could not have appeared at an earlier period in our history. The absence of great libraries has been severely felt, but this inconvenience is now in process of removal—first, by the judicious purchase of libraries in Europe; and, second, by the now frequent completion of professional studies in the German universities, and in contact with foreign masters in every science. There is less dependence now than ever before on foreign sources, and yet a more healthful and appreciative utilization of every aid that can come from any quarter.

The discriminating spirit with which the American mind and conscience have selected the better fruits of European culture and religion, and rejected the unworthy and ill-grown, has been too great to be appreciated at this early date. But this virtue will still be exercised, and the future American Christian will accept and discard as right requires, and will say:

> "The leaves, wherewith embowered is all the garden
> Of the Eternal Gardener, do I love
> As much as He has granted them of good."

The interchange of evangelistic efforts is constantly increasing. Pearsall Smith went from Philadelphia, and made the tour of France and Germany; Varley came from London, and made the tour of the United States and Canadas; and Moody and Sankey, Americans, were not familiar to American ears until they achieved their wonderful success in Great Britain. To the religious bond between America and England we must look as an important agent for the preservation of fraternal relations. Alston's glowing tribute to Anglo-Saxon unity is more a fact in religious than political life:

> "While the manners, while the arts,
> That mould a nation's soul
> Still cling around our hearts,
> Between let ocean roll,
> One joint communion breaking with the sun:
> Yet still from either beach
> The voice of blood shall reach,
> More audible than speech,
> 'We are one!'"

Good Bishop Howley said, many years ago, in plain prose: "The surest pledge of perpetual peace between the two countries is to be found in their community of faith, and in the closeness of their ecclesiastical intercourse." Have not all the events of the first American national century proved the truth of these wise words?

---

[1] Probably the first attempt made to protect the sanctity of the Sabbath was in the forms of popular protests against the Congressional act of 1810, which required the carrying of mails on that day.—Davis, *Half-century*, p. 184, 185.

[2] *Church and State in the United States*, p. 123, 124.

INDEX.

The subjects in this Index indicated by an asterisk (*) are illustrated.

D.

N.

T.

U.

V.

THE END.

STANDARD HISTORICAL WORKS,

PUBLISHED BY HARPER & BROTHERS, NEW YORK.

ALISON'S HISTORY OF EUROPE. History of Europe. FIRST SERIES: from the Commencement of the French Revolution, in 1789, to the Restoration of the Bourbons in 1815. In addition to the Notes on Chapter LXXVI., which correct the errors of the original work concerning the United States, a copious Analytical Index has been appended to this American Edition. SECOND SERIES: from the Fall of Napoleon, in 1815, to the Accession of Louis Napoleon, in 1852. By Sir ARCHIBALD ALISON. 8 vols., 8vo, Cloth, $16 00; Sheep, $20 00; Half Calf, $34 00.

ALISON'S LIFE OF MARLBOROUGH. Military Life of John, Duke of Marlborough. With Maps. By Sir ARCHIBALD ALISON. 12mo, Cloth, $1 75.

ABBOTT'S FREDERICK THE GREAT. The History of Frederick the Second, called Frederick the Great. By JOHN S. C. ABBOTT. Elegantly Illustrated. 8vo, Cloth, $5 00; Half Calf, $7 25.

ABBOTT'S FRENCH REVOLUTION. The French Revolution of 1789, as viewed in the Light of Republican Institutions. By JOHN S. C. ABBOTT. 100 Illustrations. 8vo, Cloth, $5 00; Sheep, $5 50; Half Calf, $7 25.

ABBOTT'S NAPOLEON BONAPARTE. The History of Napoleon Bonaparte. By JOHN S. C. ABBOTT. With Maps, Illustrations, and Portraits on Steel. 2 vols., 8vo, Cloth, $10 00; Sheep, $11 00; Half Calf, $14 50.

ABBOTT'S NAPOLEON AT ST. HELENA. Napoleon at St. Helena; or, Interesting Anecdotes and Remarkable Conversations of the Emperor during the Five and a Half Years of his Captivity. Collected from the Memorials of Las Casas, O'Meara, Montholon, Antommarchi, and others. By JOHN S. C. ABBOTT. Illustrations. 8vo, Cloth, $5 00; Sheep, $5 50; Half Calf, $7 25.

BACON'S GENESIS OF THE NEW ENGLAND CHURCHES. The Genesis of the New England Churches. By the Rev. LEONARD BACON, D.D. With Illustrations. Crown 8vo, Cloth, $2 50.

BRODHEAD'S HISTORY OF NEW YORK. History of the State of New York. By JOHN ROMEYN BRODHEAD. 2 vols. published. Vol. I., 1609–1664; Vol. II., 1664–1691. 8vo, Cloth, $3 00 each.

CARLYLE'S OLIVER CROMWELL. Letters and Speeches of Oliver Cromwell, including the Supplement to the First Edition. With Elucidations. By THOMAS CARLYLE. 2 vols., 12mo, Cloth, $3 50; Sheep, $4 30; Half Calf, $7 00.

CARLYLE'S FREDERICK THE GREAT. History of Friedrich II., called Frederick the Great. By THOMAS CARLYLE. Portraits, Maps, Plans, &c. 6 vols., 12mo, Cloth, $12 00; Sheep, $14 40; Half Calf, $22 50.

CARLYLE'S FRENCH REVOLUTION. History of the French Revolution. By THOMAS CARLYLE. 2 vols., 12mo, Cloth, $3 50; Sheep, $4 30; Half Calf, $7 00.

DRAPER'S INTELLECTUAL DEVELOPMENT OF EUROPE. A History of the Intellectual Development of Europe. By JOHN W. DRAPER, M.D., LL.D. 2 vols., 12mo, Cloth, $3 00; Half Calf, $6 50.

DRAPER'S AMERICAN CIVIL WAR. History of the American Civil War. By JOHN W. DRAPER, M.D., LL.D. In Three Vols. Cloth, Beveled Edges, $10 50; Sheep, $12 00; Half Calf, $17 25.

GIBBON'S ROME. History of the Decline and Fall of the Roman Empire. By EDWARD GIBBON. With Notes, by Rev. H. H. MILMAN and M. GUIZOT. To which is added a complete Index of the whole Work. 6 vols., 12mo, Cloth, $6 00; Sheep, $8 40; Half Calf, $16 50.

GIESELER'S ECCLESIASTICAL HISTORY. A Text-Book of Church History. By Dr. JOHN C. L. GIESELER. Translated from the Fourth Revised German Edition. By SAMUEL DAVIDSON, LL.D., and Rev. JOHN WINSTANLEY HULL, M.A. A new American Edition, Revised and Edited by Rev. HENRY B. SMITH, D.D., Professor in the Union Theological Seminary, New York. Four Volumes, 8vo, Ready. (Vol. V. *in Preparation.*) Price per volume, Cloth, $2 25; Sheep, $2 75; Half Calf, $4 50.

GREEN'S SHORT HISTORY OF THE ENGLISH PEOPLE. A Short History of the English People. By J. R. GREEN, M.A., Examiner in the School of Modern History, Oxford. With Tables and Colored Maps. 8vo, Cloth, $1 75.

GROTE'S HISTORY OF GREECE. A History of Greece, from the Earliest Period to the Close of the Generation Contemporary with Alexander the Great. By GEORGE GROTE. 12 vols., 12mo, Cloth, $18 00; Sheep, $22 80; Half Calf, $39 00.

HALLAM'S WORKS:

THE MIDDLE AGES. View of the State of Europe during the Middle Ages. By HENRY HALLAM, LL.D., F.R.A.S. 8vo, Cloth, $2 00; Sheep, $2 50.

CONSTITUTIONAL HISTORY OF ENGLAND. The Constitutional History of England, from the Accession of Henry VII. to the Death of George II. By HENRY HALLAM, LL.D., F.R.A.S. 8vo, Cloth, $2 00; Sheep, $2 50.

LITERATURE OF EUROPE. Introduction to the Literature of Europe, in the Fifteenth, Sixteenth, and Seventeenth Centuries. By HENRY HALLAM, LL.D., F.R.A.S. 2 vols., 8vo, Cloth, $4 00; Sheep, $5 00.

STUDENT'S MIDDLE AGES. View of the State of Europe during the Middle Ages. By HENRY HALLAM, LL.D., F.R.A.S. Incorporating in the Text the Author's Latest Researches, with Additions from Recent Writers, and Adapted to the Use of Students. Edited by WILLIAM SMITH, D.C.L., LL.D. 12mo, Cloth, $2 00.

STUDENT'S CONSTITUTIONAL HISTORY. The Constitutional History of England, from the Accession of Henry VII. to the Death of George II. By HENRY HALLAM, LL.D., F.R.A.S. Incorporating the Author's Latest Additions and Corrections, and Adapted to the Use of Students. Edited by WILLIAM SMITH, D.C.L., LL.D. 12mo, Cloth, $2 00.

HAYDN'S DICTIONARY OF DATES. Haydn's Dictionary of Dates, relating to all Ages and Nations. For Universal Reference. Edited by BENJAMIN VINCENT, Assistant Secretary and Keeper of the Library of the Royal Institution of Great Britain; and Revised for the Use of American Readers. 8vo, Cloth, $5 00; Sheep, $6 00; Half Calf, $7 25.

HELPS'S SPANISH CONQUEST. The Spanish Conquest in America, and its Relation to the History of Slavery, and to the Government of Colonies. By ARTHUR HELPS. 4 vols., large 12mo, Cloth, $1 50 each; Half Calf, $3 25 each.

HILDRETH'S HISTORY OF THE UNITED STATES. The History of the United States. FIRST SERIES: From the First Settlement of the Country to the Adoption of the Federal Constitution. SECOND SERIES: From the Adoption of the Federal Constitution to the End of the Sixteenth Congress. By RICHARD HILDRETH. 6 vols., 8vo, Cloth, $18 00; Sheep, $21 00; Half Calf, $31 50.

HUME'S HISTORY OF ENGLAND. History of England, from the Invasion of Julius Cæsar to the Abdication of James II., 1688. By DAVID HUME. With the Author's Last Corrections and Improvements. To which is prefixed a short Account of his Life, written by himself. 6 vols., 12mo, Cloth, $6 00; Sheep, $8 40; Half Calf, $16 50.

KINGLAKE'S CRIMEAN WAR. The Invasion of the Crimea: its Origin, and an Account of its Progress down to the Death of Lord Raglan. By ALEXANDER WILLIAM KINGLAKE. With Maps and Plans. Three Volumes now ready. 12mo, Cloth, $2 00 per vol.; Half Calf, $3 75 per vol.

LEWIS'S HISTORY OF GERMANY. A History of Germany, from the Earliest Times. Founded on Dr. DAVID MÜLLER'S "History of the German People." By CHARLTON T. LEWIS. With Illustrations. Crown 8vo, Cloth, $2 50.

MACAULAY'S HISTORY OF ENGLAND. The History of England from the Accession of James II. By Lord MACAULAY. In Five Volumes.—A handsome Octavo Library Edition, complete. With elaborate Index, of indispensable value to a Library Edition. Cloth, $10 00; Sheep, $12 50; Half Calf, $21 25.—A popular Duodecimo Edition, complete. With elaborate Index. Cloth, $5 00; Sheep, $7 00; Half Calf, $13 75.

LOSSING'S FIELD-BOOK OF THE REVOLUTION. Pictorial Field-Book of the Revolution; or, Illustrations by Pen and Pencil of the History, Biography, Scenery, Relics, and Traditions of the War for Independence. By BENSON J. LOSSING. 2 vols., 8vo, Cloth, $14 00; Sheep, $15 00; Half Calf, $18 00.

LOSSING'S FIELD-BOOK OF THE WAR OF 1812. Pictorial Field-Book of the War of 1812; or, Illustrations by Pen and Pencil of the History, Biography, Scenery, Relics, and Traditions of the last War for American Independence. By BENSON J. LOSSING. With 882 Illustrations, engraved on Wood by Lossing & Barritt, chiefly from Original Sketches by the Author. Complete in One Volume, 1084 pages, large 8vo. Price, in Cloth, $7 00; Sheep, $8 50; Full Roan, $9 00; Half Calf or Half Morocco extra, $10 00.

MACKINTOSH'S HISTORY OF ENGLAND. A History of England to the Seventeenth Century. By Sir JAMES MACKINTOSH. 3 vols., 12mo, Cloth, $3 00.

MOSHEIM'S ECCLESIASTICAL HISTORY. Ancient and Modern Ecclesiastical History, in which the Rise, Progress, and Variation of Church Power are considered in their Connection with the State of Learning and Philosophy, and the Political History of Europe during that Period. Translated, with Notes, &c., by A. MACLAINE, D.D. A new Edition, continued to 1826, by C. COOTE, LL.D. 2 vols., 8vo, Cloth, $4 00; Sheep, $5 00.

MOTLEY'S DUTCH REPUBLIC. The Rise of the Dutch Republic. A History. By JOHN LOTHROP MOTLEY, LL.D., D.C.L. With a Portrait of William of Orange. 3 vols., 8vo, Cloth, $10 50; Sheep, $12 00; Half Calf, Extra, $17 25.

MOTLEY'S UNITED NETHERLANDS. History of the United Netherlands: from the Death of William the Silent to the Twelve Years' Truce. With a full View of the English-Dutch Struggle against Spain, and of the Origin and Destruction of the Spanish Armada. By JOHN LOTHROP MOTLEY, LL.D., D.C.L. Portraits. 4 vols., 8vo, Cloth, $14 00; Sheep, $16 00; Half Calf, Extra, $23 00.

MOTLEY'S LIFE AND DEATH OF JOHN OF BARNEVELD. Life and Death of John of Barneveld, Advocate of Holland. With a View of the Primary Causes and Movements of "The Thirty-Years' War." By JOHN LOTHROP MOTLEY, D.C.L. With Illustrations. 2 vols., 8vo, Cloth, $7 00; Sheep, $8 00; Half Calf, $11 50.

NEAL'S HISTORY OF THE PURITANS. History of the Puritans, or Protestant Non-conformists; from the Reformation in 1518 to the Revolution in 1688; comprising an Account of their Principles, Sufferings, and the Lives and Characters of their most considerable Divines. By DANIEL NEAL, M.A. With Notes by J. O. CHOULES, D.D. 2 vols., 8vo, Cloth, $4 00; Sheep, $5 00; Half Calf, $8 25.

RAWLINSON'S MANUAL OF ANCIENT HISTORY. A Manual of Ancient History, from the Earliest Times to the Fall of the Western Empire. Comprising the History of Chaldæa, Assyria, Media, Babylonia, Lydia, Phœnicia, Syria, Judæa, Egypt, Carthage, Persia, Greece, Macedonia, Parthia, and Rome. By GEORGE RAWLINSON, M.A., Camden Professor of Ancient History in the University of Oxford. 12mo, Cloth, $2 50.

ROBERTSON'S WORKS:

AMERICA. History of the Discovery of America. By WILLIAM ROBERTSON, LL.D. With an Account of his Life and Writings. With Questions for the Examination of Students, by JOHN FROST, A.M. Illustrations. 8vo, Cloth, $2 25; Sheep, $2 75; Half Calf, $4 50.

CHARLES V. History of the Emperor Charles V.; with a View of the Progress of Society in Europe to the Beginning of the Sixteenth Century. By WILLIAM ROBERTSON, LL.D. With Questions for the Examination of Students, by JOHN FROST, A.M. Illustrations. 8vo, Cloth, $2 25; Sheep, $2 75; Half Calf, $4 50.

SCOTLAND AND ANCIENT INDIA. A History of Scotland during the Reigns of Queen Mary and James VI., till his Accession to the Crown of England. With a Review of the Scottish History previous to that Period. Included in the same Volume is a Dissertation concerning Ancient India. By WILLIAM ROBERTSON, LL.D. 8vo, Cloth, $2 25; Sheep, $2 75; Half Calf, $4 50.

SMILES'S HISTORY OF THE HUGUENOTS. The Huguenots; their Settlements, Churches, and Industries in England and Ireland. By SAMUEL SMILES, Author of "Self-Help," "Character," "Thrift," "Life of the Stephensons," &c. With an Appendix relating to the Huguenots in America. Crown 8vo, Cloth, $2 00.

SMILES'S HUGUENOTS AFTER THE REVOCATION. The Huguenots in France after the Revocation of the Edict of Nantes: with a Visit to the Country of the Vaudois. By SAMUEL SMILES. Crown 8vo, Cloth, $2 00.

STEPHEN'S HISTORY OF FRANCE. Lectures on the History of France. By Sir JAMES STEPHEN, K.C.B. 8vo, Cloth, $3 00; Half Calf, $5 25.

STRICKLAND'S QUEENS OF SCOTLAND. Lives of the Queens of Scotland and English Princesses connected with the Regal Succession of Great Britain. By AGNES STRICKLAND. Complete in 8 vols., 12mo, Cloth, $12 00; Half Calf, $26 00.

THE STUDENT'S SERIES. With Maps and Woodcuts.

THE STUDENT'S OLD TESTAMENT HISTORY; from the Creation to the Return of the Jews from Captivity. Edited by WILLIAM SMITH, LL.D. 12mo, 715 pages, Cloth, $2 00.

THE STUDENT'S NEW TESTAMENT HISTORY. With an Introduction, connecting the History of the Old and New Testaments. Edited by WILLIAM SMITH, LL.D. 12mo, 780 pages, Cloth, $2 00.

THE STUDENT'S ANCIENT HISTORY OF THE EAST; from the Earliest Times to the Conquest of Alexander the Great. Including Egypt, Assyria, Babylonia, Media, Persia, Asia Minor, and Phœnicia. By PHILIP SMITH, B.A., Author of the "History of the World." 12mo, 649 pages, Cloth, $2 00.

THE STUDENT'S GREECE. A History of Greece, from the Earliest Times to the Roman Conquest. With Supplementary Chapters on the History of Literature and Art. By WILLIAM SMITH, LL.D. Revised, with an Appendix, by GEORGE W. GREENE, A.M. 12mo, 738 pages, Cloth, $2 00.

THE STUDENT'S COX'S GREECE. A General History of Greece, from the Earliest Period to the Death of Alexander the Great. With a Sketch of the Subsequent History to the Present Time. By GEORGE W. COX, M.A. 12mo, 737 pages, Cloth, $2 00.

THE STUDENT'S ROME. A History of Rome, from the Earliest Times to the Establishment of the Empire. With Chapters on the History of Literature and Art. By H. G. LIDDELL, D.D., Dean of Christ Church, Oxford. 12mo, 778 pages, Cloth, $2 00.

THE STUDENT'S MERIVALE'S ROME. A General History of Rome, from the Foundation of the City to the Fall of Augustulus. B.C. 753—A.D. 476. By CHARLES MERIVALE, D.D., Dean of Ely. 12mo, 700 pages, Cloth, $2 00.

THE STUDENT'S GIBBON. The History of the Decline and Fall of the Roman Empire. By EDWARD GIBBON. Abridged. Incorporating the Researches of Recent Commentators. By WILLIAM SMITH, LL.D. 12mo, 705 pages, Cloth, $2 00.

THE STUDENT'S FRANCE. A History of France, from the Earliest Times to the Establishment of the Second Empire in 1852. By Rev. W. H. JERVIS, M.A. 12mo, 742 pages, Cloth, $2 00.

THE STUDENT'S HUME. A History of England, from the Earliest Times to the Revolution in 1688. By DAVID HUME. Abridged. Incorporating the Corrections and Researches of Recent Historians, and continued down to the Year 1858. 12mo, 805 pages, Cloth, $2 00.

THE STUDENT'S STRICKLAND. Lives of the Queens of England, from the Norman Conquest. By AGNES STRICKLAND. Author of "Lives of the Queens of Scotland." Abridged by the Author. Revised and Edited by CAROLINE G. PARKER. 12mo, 681 pages, Cloth, $2 00.

THE STUDENT'S HALLAM'S CONSTITUTIONAL HISTORY OF ENGLAND. The Constitutional History of England, from the Accession of Henry VII. to the Death of George II. By HENRY HALLAM, LL.D., F.R.A.S. Incorporating the Author's Latest Additions and Corrections, and adapted to the Use of Students. By WILLIAM SMITH, D.C.L., LL.D. 12mo, 747 pages, Cloth, $2 00.

THE STUDENT'S HALLAM'S MIDDLE AGES. View of the State of Europe during the Middle Ages. By HENRY HALLAM, LL.D., F.R.A.S. Incorporating in the Text the Author's Latest Researches, with Additions from Recent Writers, and adapted to the Use of Students. Edited by WILLIAM SMITH, D.C.L., LL.D. 12mo, 708 pages, Cloth, $2 00.

THIRLWALL'S GREECE. History of Greece. By Rev. CONNOP THIRLWALL, D.D. 2 vols., 8vo, Cloth, $4 00; Sheep, $5 00; Half Calf, $8 50.

TICKNOR'S HISTORY OF SPANISH LITERATURE. History of Spanish Literature. With Criticisms on the particular Works, and Biographical Notices of Prominent Writers. By GEORGE TICKNOR. 3 vols., 8vo, Cloth, $5 00; Half Calf, $11 75.

WHITE'S MASSACRE OF ST. BARTHOLOMEW. The Massacre of St. Bartholomew: Preceded by a History of the Religious Wars in the Reign of Charles IX. By HENRY WHITE, M.A. With Illustrations. 8vo, Cloth, $1 75.

www.ingramcontent.com/pod-product-compliance
Lightning Source LLC
LaVergne TN
LVHW021319110826
845150LV00003B/615